Williamson County 1836-1973

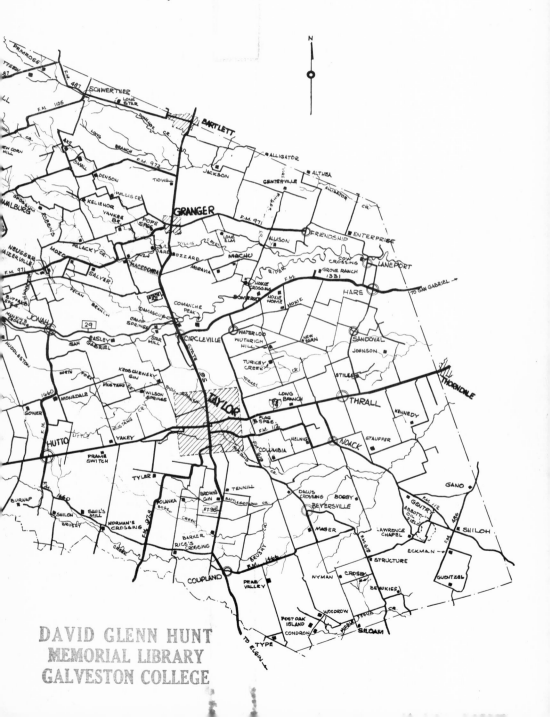

Land of Good Water

Takachue Pouetsu

A Williamson County, Texas, History

LAND OF

Special design by Donna Scarbrough

Chapters by Don and Linda Scarbrough

GOOD WATER

Takachue Pouetsu

A Williamson County, Texas, History

Clara Stearns Scarbrough

Illustrated by J. U. Salvant

WILLIAMSON COUNTY SUN PUBLISHERS • Georgetown, Texas

Printed in the United States of America.

Library of Congress Catalog Card number 73-89552

J. U. Salvant, illustrator, furnished the county map as well as the sketches of buildings.

Donna Scarbrough provided portraits of the Tonkawan Brave, of Chief Placido, and the symbol on the title page. The stylized design consists of Indian symbols representing a tree, the land, and water courses.

Dust jacket designed by the author.

The title subhead, *Takachue Pouetsu* (tah'-kah-choo-ee pooh-ate'soo), is Tonkawan for "Land of Good Water."

The quotation in introduction is from Ralph Waldo Emerson.

Acknowledgments

Grateful thanks for generous assistance are due the long list of individuals named in the bibliography under "interviews" and "letters"; for the facilities of the archives and libraries at The University of Texas in Austin, the Texas State Library, the Austin Public Library and its Travis County Collection, the Georgetown Public Library, the Taylor Public Library, the Southwestern University Cody Memorial Library, and the National Archives.

Many of the photographs were made by the author, by her daughter, Donna, and by Don Scarbrough. Others were furnished through the courtesy of the Taylor Public Library, the Nevada Historical Society (photograph of Governor Sparks), the Travis County Collection of Austin Public Library, the Williamson County School Superintendent's Office, the National Cowboy Hall of Fame, the *Williamson County Sun*, the *Granger News*; other photographs were loaned by many individuals interviewed and noted in bibliography; also by Miss Myreta Matthews and Mr. and Mrs. Marshall Richardson of Liberty Hill, Mr. and Mrs. Arnold H. Bean of Fort Worth; Mrs. Julia Friedsam, Miss Lulu Ames and Mrs. Mary Starnes of Austin; Mr. and Mrs. A. C. Stearns and Thomas McDonald of Taylor, John P. Trlica of Granger, Mrs. Roscoe Craven of Leander, Mrs. C. A. Forbes of Thorndale, Mrs. Jean J. Baldwin of Houston, Mrs. Betty Foy of Corpus Christi, and the following from Georgetown: S. A. Keeling, Mrs. Ora Miles Rowlett, Mrs. John Fredrickson, Mrs. Sam Harris, Mrs. Alfred Mueller, Homer Caswell, Mrs. Ed Behrens, Mrs. Bertie McDaniel, Robert Hausenfluck, and Emil Ischy. The author also thanks Robert E. Davis of Texian Press, Waco, for permission to reproduce a river scene showing Tonkawan Indians, which appears in *Indian Tribes of Texas*, published by his firm; also Congressman J. J. "Jake" Pickle for the photograph of attorneys who tried the famous Ku Klux Klan case.

Graphics arts credits are due John King and Patsy Blackwell Raby. Proofreaders were Donna Scarbrough, Mrs. Vella Evans, and Mrs. Doris Clifford.

Introduction

This county history has been long a-borning. A rich heritage of traditions, stories, and old records came to the author from grandparents and their families who arrived in the county in 1847, 1853, 1870, and 1880, and from parents, Auburn Clare Stearns and Margaret Tegge Stearns, born in the county in 1878 and in the 1890s, both of them living.

Three homes in diverse sections of the county gave the author valuable insights. The locale began with Circleville, a pioneer village by 1854, situated on the San Gabriel River, which has sustained man for thousands of years. Cotton's grand half century was closing during my childhood there, but on our farm I saw it planted and growing, picked it, and watched wagon after wagon of the white fluff waiting for processing in my father's gin yard. The next home—my school years—was Taylor, a vital, ambitious offspring of railroads. This trade center teems with a number of richly varied ethnic groups who came to the surrounding flat prairies where tenacious blackland soil yields such abundant harvests. My marriage to newspaperman Don Scarbrough and my association in his businesses furnished new vantage points for studying and understanding our fascinating county, first in Taylor and then in Georgetown. Our county seat home has been a good perspective. A university town, Georgetown was founded simultaneously with the county in 1848, is steeped in history. It is located between the farmlands and hill country ranchlands and is edged on the west by a craggy, hypnotic scenic splendor.

About a dozen years of public school and university teaching helped the author develop the tough self discipline needed for completing this voluminous research and writing. The author did not stint on research nor in diligence for accuracy. Original sources were consulted when possible, otherwise, the most reliable ones available. I do regret that lack of time and stamina prevented polishing some of the writing. The spelling and grammatical forms in all quoted passages are retained in their original forms unless changes are noted in brackets.

One event took this history into unexpected directions. Late in 1968 an invitation from President and Mrs. Johnson came to us for dinner in the White House. It was a treasured and unforgettable evening in a place which dazzles with history. The trip also permitted me a full day in the awesome National Archives to study postal records of Williamson County. These included an uncatalogued folder of crudely-drawn old maps, some torn from brown wrapping paper, and letters from early applicants for post offices, seeking names acceptable to Washington, or plaintively admitting that no maps of their area had ever been made. By day's end at the Archives, I had thirty-two names of early county post offices which were unknown to me. These villages must be found and, finally, all were. Only two living persons remembered the post office called Small, and only through archival records was Ponton located. Other difficult places were Draco (early Indian name for Rock House community), Neusser (for a German family who anglicized the name to Naizer), and Leubner (for another German family). About seventy-five unmapped rural schools were similarly located, one by one.

Correspondence with three Leubner sisters, who signed their letters "the Leubner girls," reveals a charm and a concern which was typical of nearly everyone I interviewed or corresponded with in my years of research. In response to my questioning, the Leubner correspondent replied, "Honestly I have squeeze my head, trying to remember things that my father told us about the early days. . . . It's a nice and beautiful and sad story—the hard times the people had in the early days, and had to suffer. God must [have] taken care of all." The author is deeply indebted to every single person who has contributed a part of this book—and there are several hundred of them. Each is named in the bibliography under "interviews" and "letters."

One overwhelming sadness haunts me. Several of those warm, generous, dear people, who helped and encouraged me, and who were so eager to see this book, left this life before my task was done. I shall always feel somehow that I failed them.

My own family has helped me in countless ways, particularly my parents, husband, and two daughters, Linda and Donna. Don and Linda have written chapters which I'm extremely proud to include. Donna sketched the Indian portraits and designed the cover symbol, translated from Spanish into English a 1750 description of this county, and offered much valuable editorial advice and proof reading.

Time brings births and deaths. In 1973 historic sites and buildings are dying. Trees which took a hundred years to grow are ripped up in minutes, sometimes needlessly, always to make way for new births. Sometime in the future, lakes will cover a natural environment of rare scenic beauty and about a hundred archeological sites of Archaic, Neo-American and possibly Paleo civilizations. The San Gabriel River, crystal clear to depths of twenty feet a century ago, is filled now with muck and trash. Garbage and commercial signs are epidemics along our roadsides to mar the landscape. Only after rains can one still see almost all the way across the county from high places like East View. To a few, land is only a thing to exploit.

But "always, always something sings." Many people in 1973 are awake to the present and future. Life proceeds. A few men struggle for power, but most struggle for survival and for serenity within themselves. They try to nourish this land which sustains us all. Young people are looking hard at themselves and at the land—their home. Their creative minds seek ways to hold what is good, change the bad. They have the brains to do it. I believe they will.

Clara Stearns Scarbrough
Georgetown, Texas
August 31, 1973

Contents

ACKNOWLEDGMENTS vii

INTRODUCTION ix

I. ". . . AND BEHOLD, IT WAS VERY GOOD" . . 3
The Land. Animal Life. Plant Life. Scientists.

II. THE INDIANS 21
Prehistoric Man. Tonkawas. Lipan Apaches. Comanches.
Tawakonis. Other Tribes. Indian Economy and Relations
with Immigrants. Cultural Contributions.

III. THE SPANISH AND FRENCH 51
Early Exploration. Missions on the San Gabriel River. Later
Exploration and End of Spanish Rule. Heritage from the
Spanish.

IV. ANGLO-AMERICAN SETTLERS AND
THE INDIANS: THREE DECADES 71
New People. New Pathways. Tumlinson Block House; the
Texas Revolution. Kenney Fort. Adam Lawrence and G. W.
Glasscock. Battle of Brushy. Flores-Córdova Affair. The
Webster Massacre. Skirmishes. Santa Fe Expedition. Raids.
The Archives War. Settler-Mexican-Indian Relations. An-
nexation.

V. 1848: A NEW COUNTY 113
Clear Water, San Gabriel, or Williamson. How the First
Settlers Lived.

VI. THE PIONEERS DIG IN: 1850–1860 141
Population. A Trip across the County. Schools, Lodges,
Churches. Post Offices, Boundaries, Roads and Stage Lines.
County Business. Earning a Living. Early County Seat. Early
Swedish Immigration. Early County Historians. U.S. Census
1850.

VII. THE CIVIL WAR 183
Prelude. Sam Houston, the War, and Williamson County.
The Bandera Hangings; Going to Mexico. Wofford Johnson
Family, Last Victims of Indian Attack. The War at Home;
Reconstruction.

VIII.   CATTLE EMPIRES   195

IX.   FIFTY YEARS: 1860–1910   217
Towns and Population. Ethnic Groups. Churches and
Lodges. County Business. Agriculture, Business, Industry.
Education: Public and Private Schools. Georgetown College,
Southwestern University. Round Rock Academy, Round
Rock College. Corn Hill Academy, Corn Hill College.
Liberty Normal and Business College (L. N. & B. C.).
Florence College. Trinity Lutheran College, Round Rock.
The Medical and Legal Professions. Communications. Life
Style in the Victorian Decades. Violence in Williamson
County.

X.   THE RAILROAD ERA   301
1876: Stiles Switch—Thrall. 1876: Taylorsville—Taylor.
1876: Hutto Station—Hutto. 1876: Palm Valley. 1876:
New Round Rock. 1878: Georgetown Tap Line. 1881–
1882: The Narrow Gauge Line: Rattan, Cummings, Rut-
ledge (Pond Spring), Running Brushy (Brueggerhoff-Cedar
Park), White Stone, Walkerton, Block House, Bagdad-
Leander, Liberty Hill, Grover. 1882: Bartlett, Granger,
Circleville, Taylor. 1887: Coupland. 1890: Georgetown and
Granger Line Creates Weir. 1909: The Four Gospels Line:
Bartlett, Schwertner, Jarrell, Florence.

XI.   THE TWENTIETH CENTURY   345
Population. Transportation and Communications. Agricul-
ture and Business. County Medicine; Accidents. Floods and
Dams. Public Life: Three Governors, a President, a Presi-
dential Advisor, a Moon Explorer, a Woman Leader,
Others. Educators, Writers, Artists, Others. Entertainment,
Sports.

XII.   THE PASSING GLANCE by Don Scarbrough . .   403

XIII.   THOUGHTS OF A COUNTY EXPATRIATE
by Linda Scarbrough   411

NOTES ON THE PLACES
OF WILLIAMSON COUNTY   414

NOTES   468

BIBLIOGRAPHY   490

INDEX   512

I

"... And Behold, It Was Very Good"

Genesis I, 31

THE LAND

Split almost down the center by a scarring fault line, Williamson County straddles the Balcones Escarpment and from the time man first saw this land it has shown a kind of double-faced profile. The county is a crossroads in several respects, encompassing hill country brushland called the Western Plains or Grand Prairie, and the Gulf Coast Plains which include the blackland prairies and a small bit of post oak section. The rocky western section averages an elevation of 850 feet, the prairies to the east, 600 feet.

Each geologic era left its aesthetic and economic contribution to the county. Billion-year-old granite just west of present Williamson County flaunted its spectacular outcropping and was noted by early scientists who visited the area. The rock chugged across Williamson County in the 1880s* to furnish material for the state capitol. The eastern half of the county's face lies just below the Balcones Fault, whose formation fed the present prairies and rolling hills with clay soils. These flat areas, treeless except along streams, grew rich and fertile and, by the time settlers arrived, nourished buffalo and scores of other animals with prairieland grass several feet high. For the immigrants, the blackland soil proved unbelievably fertile, so bountiful that many of them who arrived as penniless indentured workmen within a few years owned their own small farms. Across the

---

* The date should read "1880's" according to strict grammarians. The author strikes a small blow for simplicity by omitting the apostrophe in such instances, invoking a liberal version of open punctuation.

county most of the scenery is limestone, formed seventy million years and more ago when the last great seas covered the land. During these Cretaceous times, valuable sediments were deposited, later to harden into the commercially important limestone layers—some of them as much as three thousand feet thick in the western half of the county. A younger scenery from the Eocene epoch, beginning fifty million years ago, can be found in the southeast corner of the county.[1] Much of the limestone adapts well to the manufacture of lime and cement. A considerable amount is quarried for construction uses. Some of it is sufficiently uniform and white to be ground smooth for ornamental building, such as the Old Library Building built in 1911 at the University of Texas,[2] renamed Battle Hall in 1973. In the 1970s, large quantities of limestone were mined in the county for the calcium carbonates used in manufacturing steel, glass, neutralizing acids and for limestone itself, and for construction purposes including road materials, railroad ballast, agricultural limestone, black top hot mix for highways, concrete and riprap.[3]

The San Gabriel River, with its long North and South forks and a short Middle Fork, is the only river in the county. It runs west to east, joining the Brazos River system a short distance east of the county. Brushy Creek,

San Gabriel River west of Water Valley (Jonah).

which winds across the southern part of the county, and Berry's, Willis, Turkey, Mustang and Cottonwood creeks are other prominent streams, all feeding the Gabriel. Brushy's confluence with the Gabriel is a few miles east of the county line where the early Spanish San Xavier missions were located. Salado and Donahoe creeks in the northern part of the county run into Lampasas and Little rivers north of Williamson County. Along these streams rich river bottoms and alluvial plains grew heavy stands of timber, much prized by settlers for building and for firewood.

Recovery of sand and gravel from river beds and nearby areas has proved commercially valuable. In the fault zone serpentine rocks act as reservoirs for petroleum where small oil and gas deposits from 250 million-year-old Paleozoic systems have been tapped.[4] Southwest of Florence calcium carbonate is produced at the Carbotex plant for use in stock and poultry feeds and in the preparation of rice for the market.[5]

The presence of springs to feed the streams and artesian water flow in Williamson County exerts considerable economic significance. Streams and springs furnish ample water supply, recreational possibilities, and mineral springs have been commercially developed from time to time.[6] Erosion by water is responsible for the numerous caves enjoyed by spelunkers, some of which have been promoted for sightseers. Other souvenirs of ancient geologic times are igneous masses in the fault zone; flint pebbles and boulders in abundance at the foot of the escarpment; drifts of flint on land surfaces, both west and east of Georgetown and between Georgetown and Hutto; flint fragments and foreign stone along the north bank of the San Gabriel from Circleville to Jonah; oyster beds, noted by eighteenth- and nineteenth-century visitors, along the Gabriel between Jonah and Circleville; numerous

Gabriel Peak, locally called Pilot Knob.

fossils; celestite and walnut marl found near Leander; limestone stained by oxide of iron found in 1883 twenty miles north of Georgetown. Meteorites were discovered at Florence sometime prior to 1927.[7]

Early assessments of the escarpment area took special note of the ancient volcanic disturbance of Pilot Knob[8] (shown on state highway maps as Gabriel Mountain southwest of Andice), the richness of mineral fertilizers, the great variety and abundance of building materials, and the diverse soils suitable for agriculture. Among the building materials listed in the nineteenth century were building stone, paving stone, road material, cement stone, Portland cement material, hydraulic cement material, firebrick and tile clays, gypsum for plaster of Paris, sands, flint for glassmaking and sandpaper, occasional lumps of limonite iron ore, and gold "in small and unprofitable quantities in the chalky regions of Williamson County." By 1889 Caprina limestone had been found near Brueggerhoff (Cedar Park) and was shipped as far as New Orleans and San Francisco. This material was used as structural stone and for macadamizing roads, including an early highway at Waco. On the Washita limestone was found "the small unique *Exogyra arietina* or ram's horn oyster, which occurs [near Round Rock] in no other known horizon in the world."[9]

The Balcones* Escarpment and Fault bisects the county approximately at Round Rock, Georgetown, and Jarrell, and is a part of a three hundred-mile long landmark, prominent in nearly every early description of Texas. The fault was created about seventy million years ago by an uplifting of the earth which was followed by rapid erosion. The dissolving clays provided the eastern half of the county with some of the nation's most fertile blackland soil where the flat, plowed fields produced record cotton crops prior to the 1930s. The fracture varies in height from one hundred to two hundred feet and is visually one of the most interesting places in the county. Porous rocks in the fault are underlain by non-porous rocks, resulting in the numerous springs, two hundred of them counted within a seven-mile radius of Georgetown in 1960. The early movement of ground water dissolved out softer limestones, leaving canyons of scenic beauty and several hundred caves in the areas west of Round Rock, Georgetown, and Jarrell. The springs that feed the streams of the county emerge from breaks in the rock and insured both timber and good water so necessary to early settlers. Mexican cedar and oaks dominate vegetation west of the fault, contrasting with the treeless prairie to the east.

---

* *Balcones*, Spanish for "balcony." So the line of hills appeared to early explorers.

Among the many caves two have been commercially developed, Cobb Cavern northwest of Georgetown and Inner Space Cavern (earlier designated Unnamed Cave and Laubach Cave) just south of Georgetown. Scientists believe that Inner Space may be "slightly older than most of the caves" in the area. Although many animal fossils have been found there, no date pattern has emerged suggesting it was used as an abode, but rather it is believed to have been a rock shelter. The skull of a Pleistocene peccary (Platygonus compressus) found there could be a million years old. Fossils of jaguars, the enormous extinct mammoth, extinct miniature horse and camel, prehistoric elephant, bat, giant sloth, dire wolf, sabre-toothed tiger, and glyptodont (armadillo) have been recovered from the large cave.[10] Many of these rock shelters may have been suitable for human occupancy in the late Quaternary ten to twenty-five thousand years ago, but evidence to date points to man's use of the caves only since late Archaic times.[11]

Among other interesting examples are Breathing Cave, Tin Can Cave, Sewer Cave, and Bat Well Cave, near Round Rock. Raccoons and a skunk were found in the last room of the Breathing Cave and reported by Richard Finch (son of Dr. William C. Finch, former president of Southwestern University) and J. R. Reddell in 1963.[12] In the Georgetown area the Bat and Steam caves near Inner Space, Ballroom Cave under State Highway 29, Four Mile Cave and Ku Klux Klan Cave have been explored. Several bat caves in the county have been commercially developed for the bat guano which could be gathered in large quantities and sold as fertilizer. The steam cave, which emits a steam as the cool air from the cave and warm air outside meet, was entered early in the century by exploring youngsters who carried candles and were let down in a bucket. Since then the ceiling near one opening caved in and a chinaberry tree grew up from the fifteen foot drop, reaching out above ground level and giving the cave another name, Chinaberry Cave. Two caves about which both legend and fact are told are the Ku Klux Klan Cave southwest of Georgetown, where secret meetings were said to be held, and the Gold Mine Cave west of Georgetown where speculators operated.[13] Several caves have been used for parties and dances, including the Ballroom Cave under Highway 29 west of Georgetown, now filled in.

> Caves also served the drinking citizens of Williamson and Travis County well. . . . In the 1920's, anyone wishing to beat Prohibition in Williamson County had only to visit Four Mile Cave conveniently stockpiled with liquor. In this delightful hole in the ground the younger population of Georgetown and Jarrell held dances and drinking parties. [Officials tried to close off the

entrance to the cave, but] this make-shift speakeasy . . . was used until the repeal of Prohibition and it remained open until the highway department filled it after using it to store dynamite in 1963.[14]

Seven or eight miles up Berry's Creek from Georgetown there is a cave in the creek bed for which a heavy lid with hinges was made by L. P. Imhoff, so that he could keep water from filling the cave, or lower the stream at that point by removing the lid and allowing the water to enter the cavity. The lid was still on the cave in 1973 after many years' use. Near Cobb Cavern on Cobb Ranch southeast of Florence is the Blow Cave in which openings are so arranged that a strong draft "blows all the time." Another cave on Salado Creek west of Jarrell has been involved in numerous fruitless searches for buried gold treasure, believed by some to have been buried there by Steinheimer. The last search was in the winter and spring of 1964-65 when, like all the others, it was unsuccessful. That project ended when the Texas State Securities Commissioner ordered the promoters to stop selling shares in the enterprise.[15]

The first modern geographer to travel extensively, Alexander von Humboldt, mapped the Balcones Fault in 1812, although he did not name it. By 1847 Roemer's map indicated the escarpment by its Spanish name and described the distinct line of hills or cliffs at the edge of the lowlands from Del Rio to the Williamson County area. The escarpment disappears as a conspicuous topographic feature about at the San Gabriel River, continuing northward as a structural feature in several irregular parallel lines through the county and on toward the Red River. The faulting runs near Round Rock and Georgetown, with another line several miles west of Georgetown.[16]

Indian residents of this area found the escarpment useful. Their middens were located near the springs; high bluffs of tilted limestone beds were scenes of stampedes when hunters forced buffalo over the cliffs to their deaths; and natural amphitheatres formed by the terrain provided the Indians with sports arenas. One legendary race track of the county appears to have had a small balcony knoll for the spectators.[17] The bluffs were also legendary settings for the demise of romantically disappointed Indian lovers who plunged to their deaths there.*

Curious sights to pioneers were the numerous hog wallows reported in the area east of Thrall[18] and over almost all Central Texas prairies.**[19]

---

* Such a story is quite persistent about Comanche Peak at Circleville.

** The best preserved hog wallows found in 1973 were one mile due north of Campground Springs northwest of Circleville.

Seeping springs and fern-laden banks dot county streams. View at Camp Spring.

Hog wallows after a rain near Circleville, 1973.

Cultivation had obliterated most of them by the twentieth century. Buffalo wallows, larger in size, are identified with the western end of the county. These depressions, said Dodge, were caused by cracks in the soil into which rain tightly packed additional soil. Firmer soil retained water longer, and finally a depression was formed three to five feet broad, five to ten feet long, and six inches to two feet deep. The hog wallow

> is an admirable reservoir for the preservation of water. . . . Often when marching in unknown regions, across hot and dusty plain, with men and animals suffering for water, I have hailed with delight the appearance of these natural tanks, and many a pleasant camp have I made beside one, the fuel for cooking being the ample store of dried buffalo droppings . . . scattered in profusion over the prairie.[20]

ANIMAL LIFE

After the great sea subsided for the last time from Williamson County areas, the land assumed generally its present topography. Plant life developed, then changed, adapting first to the moist climate and finally to subsequent dryer conditions. Animal life appeared on the scene, and likewise underwent gradual changes as climate varied. During the last great glacial period man is believed to have arrived in North America as he hunted some of the huge woolly beasts which were already here.

The tiny dawn horse Eohippus, about a foot high, and an equally small camel migrated to America from Asia about fifty million years ago. Their descendants left fossilized bones in the Inner Space Cavern at Georgetown. By a million years ago, the dog-sized horse had evolved into donkey size; then, during the great ice ages, it and the camel roved in Asia but became extinct in America. The horse was returned to America by early Spanish explorers, this time to start a new breed—the wild horse of the plains. The mustang, as it was called (Spanish: *mesteño*, wild horse), multiplied, moving north from Mexico, and was discovered in great numbers all over Williamson county by settlers of the 1800s. Mustang Creek and Mustang Springs are namesakes; the wild mustang grape is another. Another extinct animal—the camel—was reimported to Central Texas in the nineteenth century, but failed to thrive.

Williamson County farmers and construction workers occasionally uncover fossilized bones of prehistoric beasts. Others discovered in caves have been identified as the peccary or javelina, the only pig native to the United States; the elephant; the giant bison, mammoth and mastodon, which looked much like hairy elephants and inhabited the plains before becoming extinct; the dire wolf and the sabre-toothed cat, both extinct. Dinosaur tracks are plainly visible in what was originally western Williamson County (lopped off and placed in Burnet County when it was formed), about five miles south of Bertram. They are about one hundred yards off the farm-to-market road near Oatmeal Creek.[21] A food enjoyed by this prehistoric beast survived him by millions of years. In 1972 equisetum was found growing south of Georgetown at the rest stop just off Interstate Highway 35 on the southbound road. The plant, once believed extinct, is a jointed stalked perennial with creeping rhizomes.[22]

If animal aristocracy is dated according to the length of time the family has lived in a land, the genealogically elite of Williamson County include the turtle, frog, toad and lizard, belonging to the most ancient order of all, 200 million years on this continent; snakes, 135 million years; the opossum, 70 million; the bat, hare, rabbit, wolf, coyote, vulture, turkey buzzard and owl, 55 million; armadillo, 40 million; deer, badger, skunk, quail, pigeon, dove and woodpecker, 36 million; bear and the gopher or prairie dog, 26 million; the cat family, including mountain lion (panther, cougar, puma) and bobcat, 12 million. Two of the younger families, around only about a million years, are the Texas horned toad and the hummingbird. A few of these animals have given way to the clearing of land and denser population and are no longer seen wild in the county; most, however, still inhabit it. The opossum, bat and armadillo, often called living fossils since they have changed so little in millions of years, remain.[23] The solemn opossum* roamed the continent with dinosaurs and the same kind of fellow was seen in great numbers when pioneers came to the county 150 years ago. Opossum creek, Opossum School and Opossum Church (frequently shortened to 'possum) are its namesakes. As this is written in 1973, one little opossum, whether courageous or foolhardy, has been living near the writer's home in a busy part of Georgetown for several years. One of the best actors in the business, she plays dead in emergencies and her babies can feign convulsions or death like a true star's offspring. Bats frequent the caves of the county where they have deposited large quantities of guano. Used as a fertilizer for many years, its commercial value was noted in 1890.[24] The third of the "living fossils" still frequently seen in Williamson County is the armadillo (Spanish for "little fellow in armor"). The descendant of an ancient order, his fossilized ancestor has been found along with that of the

---

* Captain John Smith first used "opossum" from the Algonquin *opassom*.

bat in Inner Space Cavern. The glyptodont or turtle armadillo, sometimes called the most bizarre of all mammals, probably did not arrive in this area until about 12 million years ago, although his American ancestors are much more ancient. He was an armored soldier with a spike-like ball at the end of his tail. Nicknamed the poor man's pig, the latter-day armadillo and the opossum were hunted for their tasty flesh by Indians and early settlers.

The American bison, erroneously but popularly called buffalo, is a descendant of the much larger, woolly bison of the ice ages. When county pioneers saw buffalo watering at springs near the confluence of Weir and Stone creeks, they named the spot Buffalo Springs. Buffalo School and Church were nearby. The shaggy-haired, timid American bison, henceforth in this book called buffalo, meant essential food and provisions to the Indian and to the pioneer settler in Williamson County. Before 1850 the prairie was covered with countless buffalo trails,

crossing in all directions, reminding one of a European grazing ground, [and great numbers were seen grazing along Willis Creek. On the prairies, they separated into small groups and on the distant horizon they appeared as black specks.] When several hundred of them, disturbed by our presence, bolted, the ground resounded as at a charge of a regiment cavalry. In their fright the herd came directly toward us and we had to hurry to get out of their reach, as they do not change the course of their flight, but trample under foot any object confronting them. [The great buffalo slaughter is generally placed after the Civil War, but Roemer predicted it in 1846, estimating that more than 100,000 buffalo skins were being traded from the western prairies each year.] The number of animals killed for sport or just for their meat is no doubt much larger for hardly half of the year is suited for the treating of skins. Diminished annually in such considerable numbers brings home the thought that their extermination is not far distant.[25]

The German visitor to Williamson County and central Texas accurately predicted one of the early ecological disasters of that century.

Nearly all early historians from de Vaca on described the buffalo.

His enormous bulk, shaggy mane, vicious eye, and sullen demeanour give him an appearance of ferocity very foreign to his true nature. Dangerous as he looks, he is in truth a very mild, inoffensive beast, timid and fearful, and rarely attacking but in the last hopeless effort of self-defence.[26]

The domestic cattle of Texas, miscalled tame, are fifty times more dangerous to footmen than the fiercest buffalo. He is the most unwieldy, sluggish, and stupid of all plains animals. Endowed with the smallest possible amount of instinct, the little he has seems adapted rather for getting him into difficulties than out of them.[27]

If not alarmed at sight or smell of a foe, he will stand stupidly gazing at

his companions in their death throes until the whole herd is shot down. He
will walk unconcernedly into a quicksand or quagmire already choked with
struggling, dying victims. Having made up his mind to go a certain way it is
almost impossible to divert him from his purpose. He is as timid about his
flanks and rear as a new recruit. When travelling, nothing in his front stops
him, but an unusual object in his rear will send him to the right-about at the
top of his speed.[28]

Although not all authorities agree about the poor mentality of buffalo,
they do appear to agree that the animal was extremely clumsy.

Bear furnished meat for the pioneer, but exited with colonization of the
county. Bear Creek in west Williamson County bears its name.

Deer, highly prized for food and hides both by Indians and settlers, were
plentiful when Dodge was in the state, but they disappeared from the
county as man turned predator. After conservation measures had been in
effect many years, the deer reappeared in Williamson County. By mid-
twentieth century, they were present in sufficient numbers to permit re-
stricted hunting. A ranch* just west of Georgetown, spanning the Middle
and North Gabriels, was stocked with twenty-five fawns in 1939. Only six
to ten of them survived. The next year, six grown deer were added and, in
1941, six more. From this stock and from a growing and spreading population over the state, Williamson County regained its wild deer. In 1971, the
same ranch was estimated to have four hundred to five hundred deer. The
total deer population, according to state wildlife officials, was 35,000 in the
county in 1971.[29] As new residential subdivisions and increased population
came to the county in 1972, a marked decline in deer numbers was noted.[30]

Until about 1850 Williamson County had a plentiful supply of small
game, including wild turkey, prairie chicken, squirrel, coyote, fox, prairie
dog, gopher, rabbit, and the raccoon, which naturalist John Burroughs
called "clear grit." In 1779 "along the banks of the streams and the outskirts of the woods the droves of wild turkeys [were] so numerous that
they disturb[ed] the traveler with their clucking. The number of magpies,
quails of all kinds, and wild hens, [was] incalculable."[31] A hundred years
later, wild turkeys, in addition to being hunted with guns, were also killed
with a stick from horseback. The hunter shooed the birds toward open prairie, the first flight lasting about four hundred to six hundred yards. A second flight of two hundred to three hundred yards and a third one of one
hundred to two hundred yards usually left the turkey so weary that he could
only run and dodge. Then the hunter carrying a four-foot stick could kill it

* D. B. Wood ranch, Joseph Fish survey.

with a smart blow to the head. Dodge found quail plentiful in Texas. Each animal must be hunted differently, Dodge advised, but one rule applies to all of them: "When within shot, do not show yourself until perfectly cool; never fire when panting or blown with exertion, unless it is a desperate case."[32]

The cat family was represented by mountain lion and bobcat, and although a few cats were seen in the twentieth century, they were scarce. A mountain lion was shot near Bartlett about the middle of the twentieth century and a bobcat was killed near Taylor in 1970.[33] Skunks (polecats) furnished many an early settler with colorful experiences and stories. The fifty-five-million-year-old vulture family was ever present, known by the popular name of buzzard. This clumsy-looking bird provided an early-day garbage disposal system as well as the name of an early village and saloon, Dare Buzzard. Located on the north bank of Willis Creek, Dare Buzzard was on a mail route which was proposed in 1856 for residents along Willis Creek. This route was from Bryant's Station (near Cameron) to Georgetown, via Dare Buzzard.[34] Turkey Creek, Rabbit Hill and the town of Hare are among other county places named for its small creatures.

The once pristine streams of the county were filled with a tremendous number and variety of fish. In the eighteenth century de Mezieres wrote:

There is not, in the entire province, a river, creek, brook, lake, or pool, no matter how small, in which trout, pullon (yellow cat), catfish, sardines, carp, eels, barbel, sea fish, robalo (pike), turtles, alligators, and other kinds of fish are not found in incredible numbers. . . . Otter and beaver are also found in all the rivers and streams.[35]

So plentiful were alligators in the early 1800s, they provided sport for some of the lighter-hearted members of the Santa Fe Expedition when it encamped at Double File Crossing on the San Gabriel River in June 1841. The 'gator holes, numerous along the banks of the streams, during dry seasons often provided the only water for beasts or birds. Soon after the white settlers came, the alligators rapidly disappeared and their shallow pools quickly filled with silt and brush, no longer serving as water reservoirs up and down the creeks and rivers. On rare occasions after about 1860, a single alligator was seen and shot, but by the twentieth century the only remnant of this animal was Alligator Creek, its namesake in the northeastern part of the county.

The most ancient order of all, the turtle, and members of the frog family including the Texas horned toad, sometimes adorned a pioneer family meal, or provided fun for the children or a chorus of music in the evenings. Flat

Rock School near Jarrell was nicknamed Frog Hollow and the Bartlett Western Railroad was often called the "Bullfrog Line." Snakes were less entertaining to the settlers. Rattlesnake Inn, located near Terrapin Ridge northwest of Georgetown, honors that reptile in the 1970s. An early scientist reported that he had never heard of anyone dying from rattlesnake bite. However, for any poisonous snakebite he recommended pouring spirits of ammonia into the enlarged wound and taking a few drops internally with a little water. He noted that old rattlesnakes have large quantities of fat, very useful as a lubricant, especially for locks of guns.[36] Dodge saw many rattlesnakes and reported they were especially fond of tents.

Thousands of years before the conquistadores brought horses back to the continent, Indians learned to tame native wolves and coyotes and to use them as beasts of burden. After the west was settled, the federal government encouraged and practiced systematic killing of the wolf and coyote, resulting in a present-day ecological imbalance.

Nearly all early chroniclers of this area described the sounds of their time. These were the sounds of nature. In 1846, Roemer said the voice of the bull frog resembled distant bellow of cattle, and at twilight, the hollow gobble of turkeys could be heard competing with the whippoorwill.[37]

PLANT LIFE

From the Balcones Fault to the western boundary of Williamson County, the land lies in the western or Great Plains of the Grand Prairie, part of which is in the Edwards Plateau and part in the Lampasas cut plain. Growing in these limestone formations are native short grasses, mesquite, juniper, live oak, Spanish (Texas red) oak, shin oak, post oak, hackberry, cedar, elm chittamwood, sumac, agrito* and yucca. The eastern half of the county lies in the Gulf Coastal plain, the larger and central section encompassing blackland prairies, and a tiny triangle at the southeastern end reaching into the east Texas timber belt. The large eastern half of the county is generally smooth, rolling and treeless. Its vegetation is native mixed grasses, including buffalo or curly mesquite and grama grass, and tall bunch grasses such as bluestem which covered the land before it was cultivated. In about 1800 the open, brushless, undulating plain was interrupted by seams of woods only along the river courses, although one mile east of Barker School south of Taylor was a well-known cedar elm flat. Along river and creek bottoms grow several species of elm and oak trees, pecan, hickory, walnut, cottonwood and ash; and undergrowth of redbud, wild china, box elder,

* Also frequently agarita.

buckbrush, smilax and grapevines. Timber in the eastern tip is mostly hickory, post oak and blackjack oak. The county has an elevation of 1250 feet in the northwestern corner, which drops to 1050 feet at Liberty Hill, 750 feet at Georgetown, 580 feet at Taylor, and 450 feet at San Gabriel just east of the eastern county line. Average annual rainfall is usually judged to be about 32 inches, but this varies, decreasing as much as three inches from the east end of the county to the west. Mean annual temperature is 67 degrees. Frost-free season is from March 4 to November 27.[38]

Visitors to central Texas in the nineteenth century found an "immense territory . . . watered by . . . rivers and numberless creeks that assure the permanent fertility of this beautiful land," woods along the streams to supply building materials,[39] and grama grass two or three feet high.[40] It was "a highly favored land with its unsurpassed fertile soil and its mild climate," its beautiful spots along little streams such as Brushy Creek, San Gabriel River, and the alternating prairies and forests which made the region especially charming.[41]

The Indian practice of burning the prairies kept cedar from growing except along streams in the western part of the county and kept down mesquite which quickly spread into the eastern blacklands after the Indians departed. The settlers in the mid-nineteenth century found the prairies still free of vegetation except for the tall, lush grasses, but by the time farmers began settling in the eastern half of the county in 1880, the mesquite cover had developed all across the county.[42]

The Indians and early settlers were naturalists, one and all. They knew or quickly learned the best plant or animal materials to use for shelter, tools, fuel, food, medicine, and household articles. In addition to timber required for shelter and fuel, myriads of other uses were found for the plant life in Williamson County, many of them first discovered by the Indians.[43]

The mesquite tree, scorned by ranchmen in the twentieth century, was highly regarded by Indians and early farmers. Since its roots descended sixty feet, the tree could withstand drouth and it lived in the poorest of soils. Mesquites provided food for men and animals: the foliage and bean were fed to livestock, and Indians ground the seed pods in metates or holes in rocks to make flour or meal. A gum used by Tonkawa Indians came from the bark. A cough syrup tea was made by boiling the inner bark with sheep sorrel leaves, roots, and a little honey.[44] Settlers used mesquite bean pods to make jelly or wine. They cut fence posts, railroad ties and fuel of the rot resistant hard wood, and since the wood takes an excellent polish, it was desirable for cabinetry.[45] One writer wryly observed, however, that for shade, mesquite was like dipping water with a sieve.[46]

Another central Texas tree, the bois d'arc, meaning bowwood, is also generally considered a pest but once was almost as versatile as the mesquite. Also known as the Osage orange, it was prized by Indians because of its fine wood for bows, arrows, and war clubs. The bark contained tannin for dressing leather, the milky sap was used to treat ringworm, and the large apple-like fruit was put into hen's nests to keep out mites. A deep yellow-orange dye was made from the roots.

Huisache (sweet acacia) furnished nectar for excellent honey and for perfume. Its fruit and bark produced tannin from which ink, dye and tanning substances were made. Its leaves were used as forage, and almost every part of the tree furnished some kind of medicinal product. Since the flowering dogwood's bark and roots contain a substitute for quinine, early settlers chewed the twigs to prevent malaria. The hard wood made fine tools and a scarlet dye was obtained from the bark. The agrito (meaning "little sour") yields nectar for honeybees, acid berries for jelly and wine, tanning extract, ink, and both Indians and pioneers made a yellow dye from its wood and roots. The desert willow was used for fence posts, its branches were made into baskets, and a tea brewed from the flowers. Wild plum, wild grape, prickly pear, ground cherry, dewberry and Mexican apple all had fruit or berries which were edible or could be made into jelly. The nuts of pecan and walnut trees were nourishing and tasty.

Tender greens of pokeberry were considered a delicacy by early settlers, although the older plant and root were avoided as they contained a poisonous substance. Young leaves of the prickly pear were cooked as greens and stems of the plant were fed to cattle after the spines had been burned off. The prickly pear fruit (also called Indian fig, or *tuna*) was as important a food to many Indians as a beefsteak is to a Texan. Early settlers made prickly pear dressing, fruit sauce, jelly and marmalade. The housewife cooked dandelion greens, fried or pickled spring blossoms of the redbud, and cooked or pickled unicorn pods (devil's claws), a dish much like okra.

Herb seasonings and flavorings were available from many native plants: wild dill, sour dock, sheep sorrel, peppergrass, red careless, lamb's quarter, watercress, bird pepper, wild onion, mints and sages. Leaves of the small rabbit tobacco were chewed as gum. Bird pepper was beaten to a pulp and rubbed over jerked meat to keep it free of flies.

Tea brewed from many native plants had numerous uses among Indians and pioneers. Soothing medicinal teas were furnished by lemon mint, mullein, prickly ash, frostweed, bark of slippery elm, elder, queen's delight, croton, the yellow-flowered dog's chamomile, huisache, tansy mustard and senna. Tea from mesquite treated coughs, from gumwood alleviated colds, asthma and rheumatism, and from dried horehound leaves and stems relieved coughs and colds. Candy was made from horehound or mint. For influenza, a tea of sheep sorrel tops, tamarind and wild sage seeds was recommended.[47] To relieve fever, teas were brewed from the dried flowers of Joe Pye weed and its relatives, or from feverfew, green pecan nuts or mountain pink. Plants of the madder family were boiled for coffee or quinine, and quinine was made from bark or roots of the dogwood. Oils of medicinal value came from American pennyroyal and purple horsemint, the latter also used for perfume, or the dried plants were placed in hen's nests to discourage fleas and mites. Pale wild bergamot of the horsemint family furnished a flavoring for tea, a stimulant, and a tea for colic pains. Cassina tea was made of yaupon leaves, although it was bitter and contained much caffeine and tannin. Desert willow flowers furnished a brew for heart and lung disease. Retama branches were steeped in a tea for diabetes and the seeds were eaten by humans and fed to cattle. False foxglove leaves provided a laxative tea. Snakebite was treated with a tea which caused profuse perspiration, made from prairie blazing star (gay feather), or the bite wound was dressed with the beaten pulp of cocklebur leaves, or with infusions from the roots of wild carrot, Texas milkweed or rattlesnake master. Catnip tea was said to be good for teething. All parts of the versatile little mullein plant were boiled into medicinal teas. In addition, the leaves were smoked as tobacco or used as lamp wicks, and the stalks made torches for hunters. Asthma was alleviated by smoking Jimson weed leaves. The Comanches burned locoweed, letting the smoke drift into their eyes in order to improve their night vision. It was their custom to observe this rite on nights prior to raids. Yarrow leaves were chewed to relieve the toothache. Hallucinatory brews used in certain Indian rites were made from plant products as were, later, alcohol and drugs.

Broomweed was handy around the house for kindling fires and to make brooms. A soap substitute was concocted by crushing gourd roots in water. The common sunflower, a present-day pest to farmers, was one of the most versatile of all the wild flowers. People found the seed tasty, either raw or toasted, and they fed the seed to poultry, the dried leaves to livestock. Sunflower oil was used in making soap, candles and salad dressing, and the fibers were made into thread.

Indians loved bright colors and showed considerable creativeness in their use of dyes obtained from plants. Agrito wood and roots produced yellow; dogwood bark, scarlet; Mexican persimmon, black. The large pokeberry, also called ink berry, furnished ink and a purplish dye from the shoe-button-like berries. Red dye was made from the berry of the small pokeberry, especially profuse in Williamson County, and also from madder plants. Bloodroot produced a deep red color, black walnuts a green-brown, elderberry a green, and elderberry leaves a golden brown dye. Roots of bois d'arc gave a burnt orange dye, lichens and onionskins a golden color, French mulberry roots a buff shade, sunflower petals yellow, and red oak bark a rosy-tan dye.

Wildflowers, luxuriously profuse in early days, are still abundant in some rural areas of Williamson County, although present day mowing practices along county roadsides are eliminating many of the less hardy or prolific varieties.

The bluebonnet, so-called because its shape resembled the bonnets worn by early Texas women, was also named buffalo clover because settlers thought the buffalo ate it, or the wolf flower (*Lupine*) because it was, mistakenly, thought to rob the soil of fertility. As a matter of fact, the bluebonnet gathers nitrogen from the air and enriches the soil. This flower, later adopted as the state flower of Texas, was also called *el conejo* (the rabbit) for the white-tipped buds of the flower, which reminded the Spaniards of a disappearing cottontail rabbit. Numerous legends grew up about the bluebonnet. During a period of long, terrible drouth, the Comanches were told to burn a sacrifice in order to obtain rain. A small girl, who had a doll made of animal skin and trimmed with the feathers of a bluejay, offered the doll as the sacrifice. Its ashes were scattered, rain came, and the next day the ashes had changed into the bright blue flowers of the bluebonnet.

Other well known flowers and plants of Williamson County include anemone, violet, Indian paintbrush, cone flower, blackeyed Susan, evening buttercup, various daisies, blue curls, wild mustard, Queen Anne's lace, sensitive briar, white prickly poppy, thistles, standing cypress, wild morning glory, goldenrod, rain lilies, mistletoe and cactus.

SCIENTISTS

A number of distinguished scientists explored and studied the Central Texas region and recorded their findings. Witty and observing Dr. Ferdinand Roemer, geologist from the Berlin Academy of Sciences, was in the area from late 1845 until mid-1847. He gathered geologic and natural history material, visiting from Torrey's Trading Post (near present Waco) to New Braunfels. The good doctor Roemer bought himself a mule to ride on his expeditions. Friends dubbed it "the scientific mule." He camped on the San Gabriel River and on August 27, 1846, had breakfast with a Yankee farmer who had been living for about ten years on Brushy Creek, near present Round Rock. Dr. Roemer was joined in part of his studies by Ferdinand Jacob Lindheimer, well-known botanist.[48]

Professor Charles Wright, another botanist, was in Texas from 1837 to 1852, holding teaching and administrative posts at Rutersville College and in Austin. He contributed greatly to cataloging the botany of Texas. Another natural scientist, Scottish Thomas Drummond, spent more than a year working from Austin's colony north as far as Tenoxtitlan (on the Brazos, near present Caldwell), gathering 750 species of plants. Collecting insect specimens over a period of fifteen years, Swedish nobleman-naturalist Gustaf Wilhelm Belfrage apparently worked intensively in the Round Rock area as well as elsewhere, and furnished at least eight museums in this country and Europe with valuable collections.[49] Dr. Gideon Lincecum acquired collections in central Texas in 1867 for the Smithsonian. A German medical doctor-scientist, Benno Matthes, came to Texas in 1853 and spent some time gathering natural history specimens at Round Rock. He returned to Germany, but was back in Round Rock in 1856.[50] Eighteen or more other early scientists explored central Texas land, plant and animal life.[51]

II

The Indians

PREHISTORIC MAN

Primitive man was probably hunting when he first stepped onto this continent during the fourth ice age 15,000 to 38,000 years ago. He reached Texas in Paleo times about 10,000 years ago[1] and could have come to the Williamson County area by then.[2] There is ample proof that middens along the San Gabriel River were occupied by about 4500 B.C.[3] If, indeed, man was in this county 10,000 years ago when the ice sheet was beginning to melt and recede, he was unquestionably hunting the now extinct mammals of that earlier cold, moist climate, fossils of which have frequently been found in Williamson County. The case for some Paleo activity there is supported by discovery of a few dart points which appear to be from that ancient time. No Paleo Age skeletons of human beings have been located in this area but primitive men were few in number and since they may not have practiced burial rites evidence of them is extremely scarce over the entire country. "The chronological and cultural developments [in Williamson County] remain vague and poorly defined." Considerable archeological research, some of which is projected, is needed to complete the story of primitive and prehistoric Indians. Tentatively indentified Paleo evidence includes a point discovered on the San Gabriel River four miles northeast of Circleville, another found on the South San Gabriel near the site of a proposed dam, and additional findings reported by Schuetz.[4]

Although the question of Paleo inhabitants in the county is not fully resolved, the Archaic period hunting-gathering people who descended from those first Paleo men did hunt and live there. They invented darts for small game, traps for rodents and birds, fish spears, stones to grind seeds, and baskets for gathering roots, and hunted meat such as bison and deer whenever it was plentiful.[5] Large mounds of shells along Williamson County streams noted by early explorers revealed that local Indians often lived on shellfish. This was a practice of the Archaic period which continued for thousands of years and was typical of the earliest-known Tonkawas.[6] Many of these hunters and gatherers lived along streams like the San Gabriel and Brushy, camping on or near burned rock middens of previous cultures, in semi-permanent settlements or villages, probably at certain times of the year. The use of round milling stones (*manos*) and shallow bowls or hollow-shaped stones (*metates*) for grinding plant food increased greatly

Indian metate and mano; and ladder designs, possibly depicting water courses, on rock found in the county.

during Archaic times. Other tools and weapons of that period were darts, atlatls (spear throwers), light spears, drills made of flint and awls of bone. Ornaments were made of shell and worked stone.[7] A midden campsite* located on the north bank of the North Gabriel was investigated by archeologists in the late 1960s. Excavations revealed layers of materials denoting three distinct periods of occupancy: from about 4500 B. C. to 3500 B. C., from 3500 B. C. to 1000 B. C., and from 1000 B. C. to A. D. 1. More than 1200 artifacts were found and classified. Although the midden was occupied "by a stable tradition of hunters and gathers [*sic*] over a relatively long period of time," alluvial modification of the terrace from time to time suggests that people lived there in certain seasons.[8]

Whether the middens served as cooking, dumping or living areas, or a combination of these, is still debated. Sorrow believes that the Indians re-

---

* On the John Ischy place three miles west of the Court House, Georgetown.

sided near the fringes of middens and that additional evidence must be gathered to determine whether the midden itself was a cooking or dumping site, or both. Burned rock middens abruptly went out of general use about 1000 to 500 B. C. for reasons not yet ascertained. They could have been abandoned suddenly because of shifts in economic patterns resulting from population displacement, environmental changes, or technological advances. Plentiful numbers and many kinds of Archaic stone weapons and tools were found on the Ischy Site, including dart points, arrows, burins, drills, awls, knives, choppers, hammerstones, scrapers, and manos. One specimen each of a gouge, milling stone, grooved stone, bone awl and an abrader, was uncovered. The chipped stone artifacts are of gray or gray-brown cryptocrystalline quartz, available on the site; of ledge flint, probably from an outcrop or valley wall; and of quartzite and granite, available twenty miles to the southwest from Colorado River gravels or from the Llano area fifty-five miles to the west. Both quartzite and granite were used for manos.[9] Burned rock middens are numerous along the San Gabriels and Brushy Creek. In three relatively small areas expected to be flooded by dams on the North and South forks of the San Gabriel, and at Laneport, more than a hundred archeological sites have been designated as worth investigation, many of them midden oriented.[10]

Other archeological explorations in the county have been recorded. The Merrell* Site on the J. E. Merrell place, one-fourth mile northeast of Round Rock and north of Brushy Creek, was discovered in 1934 by Dr. J. E. Pearce of the University of Texas and A. M. Wilson of Austin. Two burned rock middens, each two feet and nine inches thick, plus a third site revealed ash, charcoal, bones of deer and bison, and artifacts—knives of two types, side scrapers, projectile points, blades, graver, gouge, handstone fragment, drills, pitted stones, hearthstone fragments, flint flakes, picks, fist or hand axes, choppers, abrading stone, pigment on hematite, and a pendant of freshwater mussel shells. These were found in a terrace from the ground surface to a depth of eighteen feet. Artifacts from the lower terrace level are estimated to be three thousand to five thousand years old, and those from the upper strata no later than 1500 A. D.[11]

The Cedar Park Mound on the former S. C. McClure farm, four hundred yards south of the highway intersections at Cedar Park, was excavated by Dr. J. E. Pearce and Erich Pohl in 1937-38. Located on the south side of Brushy Creek, the mound originally covered more than an acre and was seven feet high.[12] A bone awl was found among the tools.[13] This site is

* Frequently spelled Merrill. Captain Nelson Merrell and his descendants write *Merrell*; apparently this is the correct form.

believed by some scientists to have been one of the most interesting in the county, but little scientific data was documented from it. An enormous amount of material was recovered after the mound was bulldozed, some of it sold at a World's Fair, and some kept in private collections. Contrary to several published reports that the materials were being placed in the Smithsonian, that institution never received them nor any communication about them.[14]

The San Gabriel Mound, three miles northwest of Leander on the South San Gabriel River, was discovered near where the stream flows under the railroad.[15]

The Hughes Mound on the South San Gabriel, one-fourth mile from the site of the Webster Massacre, disclosed ash pits containing bones, but no burials, and a large quantity of material including a three-inch bead conch shell, a slate ceremonial piece, two effigy arrows, a rare corner tang artifact, bone awls, and the bones of buffalo, deer, javelina, fox, coon and wild turkey.[16]

Lake Locke Mound near Jarrell contained numerous points, implements, knives and blades.[17]

At Cobb's Spring Mound, near Cobb Cavern northwest of Georgetown, a large piece of pottery was found among the artifacts.[18]

Schuetz also notes a "solid copper hammer" from a mound near Leander.[19]

Pendants have been found at three different levels on midden sites of Williamson County. At one large Cedar Park midden, eight were found at a depth of from one inch to eighteen inches and five from a depth of twenty-five to forty-eight inches. The perforated pendants were found on the chests of skeletons and were apparently made to be worn around the neck.[20]

Jackson mentions fist axes and bone awls from Williamson County middens and thinks that potsherds found there lend credence to the belief that the Tonkawas or their ancestors used some pottery, probably making a little themselves and obtaining some from neighboring tribes.[21] Krieger and Suhm concur with that view. They identify central Texas pottery types as Leon plain, made by coiling a very fine clay-grit and pulverized bone, the bone often showing on the surface. The finished product was brown, gray or gray-brown. Most pieces were bowl shaped, with two loop handles and a knob, and were not decorated. The type is scarce on central Texas sites. Trade pottery is found on the same sites, some from the Caddoan Indians and occasional Doss Red potsherds nearly identical with those of the

Huastecan area on the east coast of Mexico, dating about 1000 and 1100 A. D.[22]

Indians left occasional art work or picture writing in Williamson County. "A trace of an orange colored rayed sun-disc" was discovered on a boulder near a spring in the southern part of the county. A flat piece of limestone, carved by a fine-pointed instrument in what appears to be an abstract arrangement of numerous ladder-like designs, came from the central area. From a midden in the west end of the county a small stone roughly carved on one side with a figure of an animal and, on the other side, with two square shouldered human figures, was found in an open campsite. Several additional ladder-like designs have also been discovered.[23]

Indian burial grounds are occasionally uncovered in Williamson County, usually by construction workers who, by the nature of their profession, must be concerned more with expediency than with the tedious and time-consuming task of archeological investigation. Information has been lost in this way. Other loss occurs in casual or large-scale relic-hunting by amateurs, whose natural curiosity or commercial ambition is not always tempered by care in locating, identifying, cataloging and reporting materials which are uncovered.

Known Indian burial sites in Williamson County include one near Interstate Highway 35 between Georgetown and Round Rock; the area between North and South San Gabriel rivers west of Highway 81 at Georgetown, where excavation for a swimming pool revealed the site; another, possibly a continuation of the one near the pool, at the site of the Highway 81 bridge—also uncovered during construction; and Comanche Peak (McFadin) Cemetery at Circleville, where legend tells of Indian burials. The latter site continued in use as a cemetery for early settlers.

TONKAWAS

The flint-working Tonkawas were the natives of central Texas, calling their country *takatchue pouetsu*, meaning "land of good water." Their villages dotted all the areas where the Balcones Fault disgorges many hundreds of permanent springs and streams.[24] Ancestors of the Tonkawas are believed to have lived on Williamson County lands as long as 10,000 years ago. In early historic times they were a proud and powerful people of many independent tribes, related to more than 200 groups linguistically affiliated with the Coahuiltecans of the western Mexico Gulf coast.[25] The prehorse tribes were not nearly so isolated from one another as is often believed. The early Tonkawas moved by foot quickly and easily over great distances. Advanced cultures of Middle America sent products across the Gulf of Mexico in dugout canoes, diffusing their ideas and goods to the north. Agriculture, religious and political forms, architecture, and the arts and crafts radiated north in this way. But it was no one-way highway. The primitive people north of the Rio Grande introduced important ideas of their own to tribes in Mexico, including the bow and arrow. The Tonkawas, in historic times, were famous for their superior bows and arrows, possibly were the first to present them to Middle America. Cabeza de Vaca told of Indians travelling north into Texas for the single purpose of obtaining the weapon. Travelling afoot, Indians traded a great deal, learning in the process and leaving criss-crossed trails over the country.[26] They were primarily after buffalo which provided food, clothing, shelter, and other essentials. When the herds migrated north in the summer because of their heavy fur or to leave the parched fields in search of better grazing, Indians followed along the plainly marked trails left by buffalo. The animals led primitive people to water, to good crossings over streams, and to protected valleys.[27]. The same paths guided Spanish and French explorers, and later, Anglo settlers across the country. In varying degrees, these same trails became, in turn, military roads, stagecoach or horseback routes, cattle trails, some railroad right-of-ways and, finally, modern highways.

Even when hunting afoot, Indians knew how to take advantage of the clumsy and obstinate nature of the buffalo. They drove converging lines of the huge animals over the edge of cliffs, as at Tonkawa Bluff east of Georgetown and at Comanche Peak east of Circleville, or drove them into corral-like valleys along the upper Gabriels. Buffalo blindly follow their leader, and an entire herd could be led over a bluff by turning a single animal, the rest unable or unwilling to halt or turn quickly to avoid death at the bottom of the precipice.[28]. Indians also killed buffalo in the "surround," luring them into a group by the artful use of fire, then encircling them, and shooting them as they dully remained fixed targets.[29] The wasteful practices of the stampede and the surround began in very ancient times. Plainview points found in Texas reveal a mass slaughter of buffalo between 7500 and 10,000 years ago.

> The Plainview people effectively dispel the romantic illusion that early man was innately a conservationist who killed only as much as he needed for food. His very method of hunting . . . necessitated the slaughter of many animals to obtain only a few for food.[30]

De Vaca saw inland Indians using firebrands,

setting fire to the plains and timber so as to drive off the mosquitoes, and also to get lizards and similar things which they eat, to come out of the soil. In the same manner they kill deer, and they do it also to deprive the animals of pasture, compelling them to go for food where the Indians want.[31]

Vast portions of the prairie were burned every fall, leaving a good section of grass where the braves planned to hunt. "The buffalo, finding nothing to eat on the burnt ground collect on that unburnt—reducing greatly the labor of the hunt."[32] The kill was extremely high, even with bows and arrows. No speculation has been found suggesting that burning of the prairie grasses might have had another purpose. Nevertheless, Indians probably knew that the hard-coated seed of the buffalo grass, which furnished much food for the buffalo, could only be prepared for germination by subjecting it to extremely high heat. Whether deliberate or not, the apparent promiscuous firing of the prairie paved the way for next year's crop of grass.

For thousands of years, buffalo meat was the Indians' basic diet, but the usefulness of the animal did not stop there. Buffalo brains softened buffalo skins, which, in turn, furnished clothing and shelter; horns were made into spoons and drinking cups; shoulder blades formed tools for digging and clearing the ground; tendons made thread and bow strings; hooves produced glue to feather arrows. Hair of the tail was woven into ropes and girths and the wool made into belts and ornaments. Hides were used for tents, shields, helmets, containers and cooking pots. After horses were reintroduced on the continent, hides made saddles, bridles and tether ropes. The tail furnished whips or fly swatters, and the beard decorated bows and lances.[33] After buffalo became scarce, deer were similarly utilized—meat for food, hides for fine leather, fat for grease and candles, antlers for tools, utensils, weapons, glue, sizing, ornaments, and tendons for ropes.[34]

The first European definitely to meet and describe the Tonkawas was Alonso de Leon, who found them hauling buffalo hides on dog-drawn travois in 1690. They were living in 150 villages between the Colorado and Brazos rivers, "following the buffalo for a living."[35]

Bison or other meat was eaten fresh, roasted, smoked, or boiled by means of hot stones placed in rawhide containers or dried and mixed with other ingredients to make pemmican. It was also made into jerky by slicing into thin strips and placing on a rack of sticks to dry in the sun. Jerked meat was stored in rawhide bags known as *parfleches*.[36] To make pemmican, Indians dried the meat, pounded it into a powder, then mixed it with dried, crushed berries, pecan meal, fat, or other ingredients. This mixture was stuffed into a bag of animal membrane and sealed with a coating of melted fat and marrow.[37] Tonkawas sometimes ate rabbit, bear, skunk, rat, rattle-

The Tonkawas built villages on upper banks of streams in scenery like this.
Courtesy of Texian Press.

snake, land turtle, dog, horse, fish, oyster, and wild turkey meat as necessity demanded. Their diet also included wild plants, herbs, roots, fruit and seeds such as acorns and pecans, and *tuna*, the fruit of prickly pear.[38]

Williamson County was an extremely fine deer range in historic times, and when the Tonkawas could not hunt on the plains for bison, they sought deer and other small game. One trader, about in 1807, reported that he sometimes obtained five thousand deerskins from the Tonkawas in one season.[39]

An oven, dug in the center of the tepee (*tipi*, from *ti*, to dwell, and *pi*, to use for) served as a hearth, fireplace and cookstove. In the more comfortable tents smoke was carried out an opening at the top where ventilation was controlled by two adjustable flaps fastened onto poles. In 1828 however, the Tonkawan dwellings were cruder, without windows, very small, and smoke went out the door opening. By this time, the Tonkawas grew no crops, were nomadic, "horse-poor," and afraid to hunt buffalo because of the Comanches, newly arrived on the scene.[40] The nineteenth-century Tonkawan males lay around the fireplace in complete inaction, while the women [were] in constant motion either curing the meat or the game, or tanning the skins, or preparing the food, which consist[ed] chiefly of roast meat, or perhaps making arms for their indolent husbands. The elder women work[ed] the hardest because the younger ones [had] a few moments of rest at the expense of the wretched elders.[41]

The Indians ate with their fingers or used wooden or shell spoons. Tobacco smoking was a universal habit among them. They made fire by twirling a drill through a hole in wood, producing both sawdust and friction, or by using flint and stone with iron pyrites which gave off sparks when struck together. When wood was scarce for fuel, they substituted dried buffalo dung. Early Anglo Americans adopted this practice, calling the material buffalo chips.[42]

Although not known for their agriculture, the Tonkawas appear to have done a little gardening in the late 1700s, possibly after being taught the principles in missions, such as those on the San Xavier (San Gabriel) where corn, beans and squash were grown.[43] But agriculture did not become a strong habit with them. After Stephen F. Austin came to Texas in 1821, he importuned Tonkawan Chief Carita to plant some corn, giving him a supply of seed and supplying him with hoes and other implements. The project was a failure. The Chief made bread of the corn and when it was all eaten, reported to Austin that the Great Spirit told him he must not raise corn, but should continue to hunt, and that his tribe could look to their friends for bread. "Carita was a very shrewd Indian and sharp at driving a bargain."[44]

Roaming from the Rio Grande to the Trinity River and from the Gulf of Mexico to the Staked Plains, the Tonkawas, like other tribes, "knew nothing of a country. They believed that they had a right to the land the same as to the air and water throughout the universe as known to them." They shared provisions of food, or fasted together when supplies were short. Kenney thought Tonkawas improvident and careless of the future. They hunted in parties and he noted that when each inevitably claimed a share of the day's take, it was often grudgingly given.[45] They often suffered "greatly from hunger."[46] The wife of one of the well-known Burleson family of central Texas decided to teach Tonkawa women in her community a pioneer form of canning. In order to impress the Indians sufficiently for them to carry out her instructions, she knew she must dramatize the procedures. Adding rituals to basic canning practices, she provided the recipe: clean and dry a pottery bowl, then heat it and cover it with wax; heat fresh fruit and sweet-en with honey, pour into the bowl and seal with hot beeswax; bury the container in a plum thicket for one year, less one week; at the end of the time, dig up the jar. The Indian ladies who tried the recipe found the preserved fruit in perfect condition at the end of the designated time. They previously dried their fruit in the sun and covered it with grease to preserve it.[47] They obtained grease, as well as a mosquito repellent, from alligators, which were plentiful in Williamson County streams.[48] Oil from bear fat was used for "hernia, rheumatism, gout, cold humors" and in a pomade for the hair.[49]

A few Indian sign trees remain in 1973, as these at Rowe Valley two miles west of Circleville.

Like other tribes over the entire country, the Tonkawas used an ingenious but delightfully simple device to show direction—the bent sapling. Now large trees, quite a number of these horizontally growing sign trees remain in the county located near good springs and water—growing highway signs pointing out sites of native villages. In addition the Tonkawa Indians had another sign which was theirs alone consisting of

three feathers tied together and placed on a tree limb or yucca plant. The feathers were meant to attract attention, and the limb or stem of the yucca plant showed direction. If a hunting party was going on, a hawk feather was used, or a heron or crane feather if it was an organized hunt. An eagle feather indicated a war party; a crow or buzzard feather indicated an attack with no quarter given.[50]

Like many other tribes the Tonkawas wore little or no clothing in early historic times, except for protection from the weather or for special ceremonies. The mode of dress in 1828 was an elongated loin cloth in front and back for the men, and a miniskirt and possibly a simple shirt for the women. Women also tattooed themselves, with

one, two, or three black lines . . . beginning on the forehead and running across the nostrils down to the chin. The breasts [were] painted with numerous concentric circles around the nipples. [Additional lines decorated the abdomen and the back. Ornaments for the men were iron or copper bracelets] and earrings and necklaces often made of pearls which they fish for in the streams, but they used to make them of the claws of fierce animals.[51]

More elaborate coverings included leggings, moccasins and leather jacket for the men.

Tonkawas were excellent craftsmen and were sought especially for their superb arrow points and bows of bois d'arc (Osage orange) by tribes far to the south across the Gulf. Scientists and amateurs have collections of these fine points which were gathered from along Brushy Creek and San Gabriel River. Tonkawas also made excellent spearheads, sliver knives, awls, skin scrapers, and other flint tools which are still found along the Balcones Escarpment.

De Vaca heard on the coast of constant warfare between tribes, and some of the natives along the Gulf persuaded him to go forty or fifty leagues inland to trade for them. In exchange for shells, they wanted arrow points, glue, hard canes, flint, tassels of deer hair, hides, and red ochre for a dye.[52] Newcomb believes these inland tribes referred to may have been Tonkawas.

Horses and guns, which proved both asset and liability to the Indians, were introduced into America almost simultaneously. Spaniards brought horses and cattle into Mexico in the sixteenth century,[53] trying at first to keep them out of the hands of the natives. Nevertheless, a few Indians somehow learned to ride, then occasionally stole an animal with which to teach nearby bands to ride and manage a horse. The spread of horses was slow for about a hundred years but, by mid-seventeeth century, the first "horse" Indians were on the scene. Wild horses reached central Texas before 1700 and multiplied rapidly. Guns came to the Indians in the 1600s through the British and French fur traders.[54]

When La Salle was in Texas in 1686, he saw only a few Indians with horses. They galloped toward the French party "booted and spurred and seated on saddles."[55] Just three years later when Henri de Tonti was searching for the lost La Salle, he noted that the Indians had many horses.[56] Most historians believe that La Salle travelled somewhat east of present Williamson County, but whatever his route, he met a number of tribes whose names strikingly resemble names of Tonkawan tribes: the Maghai (Mayeye of historic times), Enepiahos (Ervipiame), or Hebabame (Hierbipiame). He also mentioned the Konkone, believed to have been the Tonkawas.[57] La Salle heard of the Maghai at Bocherete Village, north of La Maligne River (the Mischievous River), believed to be the present Colorado. It was so named "because in Monsieur de La Sale's [sic] former journey, an Alligator devour'd one of his Servants, who was swimming over [the river]."[58] Each early explorer named the Texas rivers as he wished until finally it was almost impossible to identify a stream by a specific name—which had probably already been applied to several other streams. For example, present Colorado River was known for many years as the San Marcos River and the present Brazos was often called the Colorado.

One of La Salle's chroniclers, Father Douay, described their crossing of the Hiens River on rafts, about four leagues beyond Bocherete Village.[59] Pichardo identifies Rio de Hiens as Rio de San Xavier (San Gabriel), although other historians disagree.[60] Pichardo's map, Provincia de Texas, shows "Rio de San Xavier o de Hiens," "Presidio de San Xavier," "Arroyo de las Animas" (Brushy Creek), and a Tuacana (Tawakoni) tribe living along the north bank of the San Xavier. If one wishes to justify the possibility of La Salle's coming through present Williamson County, it should be noted that he began his journey from the coast to the interior of Texas on January 12, 1687, and was plagued by heavy rains all along the way, of which he made frequent mention. In later years, travellers found that during the wet, flooding seasons, the rivers of Texas could not be forded even as far upstream as El Camino Real, which passes through Bastrop and just east of Williamson County. When this highway was not passable, an upper highway, Camino de Arriba, which crossed the San Xavier in Williamson County, was taken to east Texas.

Alonso de Leon most assuredly did meet the Tonkawas and found them the most impressive of the tribes he saw. "Famous warriors all, the Tancaoye were the most renowned and their chiefs bore many battle scars." At that time they were enemies of the Hasinai and friendly with the French.[61] "The Tonkawa at an early date secured a goodly supply of French arms and ammunition."[62]

Prior to using guns, Tonkawas believed that they were poisoning their arrow tips with juice from the mistletoe, and when they acquired guns, they put the juice into their gun barrels. After metal was available, they tipped their flint arrow points with the metal. An Irish priest, Father Morfi (Murphy) said that the Tonkawas were a "terrible and bellicose nation . . . divided into *rancherias*, or bands, each with its own captain . . ., roaming people, who do the bidding of their leaders."[63] Tonkawas fought at times for the Tejas, at other times, against them.[64] During the eighteenth century, they became skilled horsemen and had good animals, as did other Plains tribes. By this time, they also learned to use firearms well.[65] Even after the single-shot musket was available, however, many still preferred the bow and arrow when they hunted horseback, for they could discharge a dozen arrows while a man loaded a gun.[66] Their "defensive arms were the leather jacket (*cuera*), shield, and cap or helmet, on which they often wore horns and gaudy plumage."[67]

The horse provided the Tonkawas and other tribes with new mobility, efficiency, and much greater range. Tribes continued to hunt collectively, practicing the stampede and the surround with more devastating effect than ever. They could now rapidly encircle buffalos on horseback, choosing either bows and arrows or guns for weapons. They adapted the horse to pull the travois. As a result, greater quantities of meat could be brought from the hunt. Tepees, also moved by travois, could now be much larger—up to twenty-five feet in diameter.[68]

The Lipan Apaches became neighbors of the Tonkawas after 1300 A. D. and relations between the two tribes were good until the arrival of the Comanches in the early 1700s. When the Comanches began pushing the Lipans from their accustomed hunting grounds and allying themselves with the Tonkawas, goodwill between the Lipans and Tonkawas was sorely strained. By the nineteenth century, the Tonkawas became hostile to the Comanches, Wacos and Tawakonis, and usually befriended the Lipan Apaches. The Tonkawas proved to be among the easiest for the Anglo-American settlers to make their allies and were most likely to consolidate with other Indian tribes, an arrangement which occurred numerous times. The Tonkawas fought against warlike Indian groups on behalf of the Anglo colonists, against both the Spanish and Mexican governments, and acted as scouts for the new settlers from the United States. Their adaptability was no doubt partially the result of an inborn, peace-loving nature, but, in addition, it was likely a trait born of necessity, for the Tonkawan tribe was not, by the nineteenth century, one of the largest nor the strongest militarily, having been considerably depleted by disease brought in by the Spaniards.[69]

Tonkawan tribal government took the form of a pure democracy. The tribe was divided into two bands equal in class, each class with secondary divisions. Each of the latter was designated by the name of a bird or animal, and headed by a chief.[70] The grandmother was, in practice, the head of the family.[71] The family unit was a clanship, all the children belonging to the mother's clan. The mother's sister was also ranked as mother, and children of both mothers were brothers and sisters, instead of cousins. On the male side, however, the mother's brother was an uncle, and his children were cousins to the mother's offspring. The father's brother was also counted a father, and both fathers' children were brothers and sisters instead of cousins. The father's sister, on the other hand, was an aunt, and her children were cousins to the father's progeny. In this way, the equality of tribe members was preserved and the Tonkawan nation was able to maintain its democratic system.[72]

At tribal council, men of both bands sat on each side of the council fire, listened to the chiefs' speeches, determined policies, and elected successors to chiefs who had died. "Their sessions were long, and discussion very earnest." Occasionally, delegations of Lipans, with whom the Tonkawas were allied, attended in an advisory capacity.[73] The totemic clans traced their antecedents through one parental line to a remote and mythical ancestor, employing clan names such as "buffalo," "wolf," "acorn," "a kind of short snake," "mouth open," "blinking with the eyelids," "Meyei" (meaning dizziness; note resemblance to "Mayeye"), "long genitals," "Sanux," and "the real Tonkaways."[74]

Each band had definite responsibilities, especially toward its own families.[75] Members could not marry within their own band; the married couple lived with the wife's clan;[76] and a widowed man married the wife's sister. A widow became the wife of her dead husband's brother. Thus, by assuming the responsibility of protecting a family, a man might have several wives. Orphans were cared for by the mother's clan.[77] In the maternal clan, any property not buried with the man, who usually owned only a few utensils and horses, was inherited by the children of his brother or sister. Property was not left to his own offspring for it would thus leave his own clan.[78]

Auxiliary huts were built for women in childbirth. Here, the mother clung to a rope during labor. Within a day after birth, she bathed in a stream, and she and the father refrained from smoking or using firearms for four days afterwards to prevent the smoke from weakening the child's eyes.[79] After Anglo settlers arrived, a Tonkawan child was given an English name in addition to his private Indian one, which was not revealed to others. Neither could the private name be called after death, as this would disturb the repose of the deceased. During the Tonkawas' alliance with the Comanches, each child received a Comanche name, in addition to his others.[80]

For military dress, Tonkawan warriors painted themselves and their horses red, yellow, green and black, and wore elaborate headdresses of feathers and horns. The brave's "facial designs were his personal posses-

DMNS

sions and, like those of clowns, were not copied by others without permission"—possibly the first copyright in this country.[81]

The annual Wolf Dance and festival was held under a great brush arbor of cedar boughs. Wearing skins of timber wolves, the men assembled under the arbor and, when night came, bayed the moon. Simultaneously they rhythmically mimicked motions of a wolf. The dancers circled the lodge, then moved around a leader who rose from the ground, pantomiming his fear that he would starve. The wolf men presented their bows and arrows to the leader, advising him to fight and kill for his needs. At the end of the dance, the participants threw off their robes to become men once again.[82]

The Fresh Fruit Ceremony was a ritualistic purging of the body, followed by eating of the fresh fruit. "Every kind of seed the Tonkawas could get their hands on was used in this ceremony, but they were not interested in planting. They might plant a plum seed, but not anything that had to be tended."[83] This festival is also called Feast of New Fruits or First Fruits.[84]

Tonkawas believed in reincarnation and as a part of this conviction, observed the ceremonial cannibalism of the Plains cultures. This symbolic act—the ritualistic eating of human flesh—was to prevent the good qualities of an enemy from dying by transferring the spirit and bravery of the deceased to the offspring of the partaker.[85]

The role of tribal priest and doctor was combined in the Tonkawan shaman. For healing ceremonies, special tepees were erected facing east and a fire was built in a small hole in the center of the tent. The patient entered from the east side, walked around the fire to the south, where he sat down on a blanket. The shaman rubbed the ailing parts with special medicines and called upon the supernatural to cure the ill person, who then left through the east door. The entire ceremony avoided the connotation of the west exit, for that was the way to death.[86]

For religious rites and visions, Tonkawas drank *frixolillo*, a narcotic made from the bright orange-red bean of mountain laurel. The beans were also made into necklaces. Drilled by a stone awl, they were strung into ornaments or sold in strings, two yards of which were worth as much as a pony.[87] *Frixolillo* was sometimes mixed with mescal or agave brandy to make it more intoxicating. Tonkawas chewed or drank *peyote*, both as an opiate and an intoxicant.[88]

Tonkawas recognized an all-powerful god, or gods, but emphasized the spirit of a man's other self, which left him during sleep and wandered in dreams, returning when the man awoke. They thought the other self could be recalled and carried this belief into the realm of the dead, calling the deceased's name and begging him to return and inhabit the body. In cases of trance, some returns may have been verified after periods of apparent death. For this reason, the Tonkawas buried a person's most treasured possessions with him and burned the others.[89] As a person lay dying, the clan gathered, formed a circle around him while they swayed, chanted, and kept watch. For burial the face was usually painted yellow, the hair cut, the body wrapped in bisonskin robes. The family fasted until after burial. Mourning continued for three days afterwards, with loud wailing at sunrise and sunset. When this period ended, the Chief spoke to the relations, after which the name of the deceased was never again to be used. Friends and relatives brought gifts to the bereaved family, especially replacing items buried or burned, and after a four-day smoking ceremony normal activities resumed. The spirit of the dead went to a home in the west, so Tonkawas were buried with their heads placed toward the west. The living slept with their feet to the west to prevent their spirit's beginning the journey prematurely. The soul of a person not properly buried could take the form of an owl or wolf, haunting those who were careless in the burial ceremony. The owl was also believed to bring messages to and from the dead. Under normal circumstances, the Tonkawas refused to kill these two creatures[90] although it was permissible to obtain robes for the Wolf Dance from a wolf mortally injured by another animal. Buffalo frequently trampled wolves almost to death.[91] The buzzard was highly thought of, even more respected than the eagle.[92] The songs of birds and animal cries had special meanings for Indians, often were connected with evil spirits.[93]

The Tonkawas improvised music for their ceremonies but in 1971 Tonkawan descendants could not remember their native songs. Instruments were improvised according to materials available. Two favorites were drums and a simple but challenging stringed piece which may have been borrowed from the Wacos. It was made from a gourd onto which two strings were fastened. The gourd was placed against the chest, the loose ends of the strings held in the teeth, and a bow played across the taut strings. One of the Tonkawan drums was hollowed out of maguey (agave), a kind of century plant. A more elaborate drum had dog skin and buffalo cow hide on the drum heads. Around the edges, brightly painted spines of devil's head cactus were fastened. The performer scraped across the spines, giving off a strange, weird and distinctive sound. For the Rain Dance, musicians imitated the roars of bulls.[94] One visitor in the early nineteeth century reported that the Tonkawas were the only singers, among half a dozen nations, who used words. "I have written them down but I do not know what they mean."*

Tonkawas called themselves *Titskan wátitch*,[96] or *Tickanwatic*, "the most human of people."[97] The Lipan Apaches, old neighbors to the Tonkawas, called them *Yané*, and the Comanches called them *Caricoë*.[98] The name Tonkawa was not used until after the eighteenth century when the Wacos first appeared in Texas, for Tonkawa is a Waco name (*tonkawéya*) meaning "they all stay together." The Waco name was well chosen to describe the many bands who formed the Tonkawan nation. "The land of good water," *takatchue pouetsu*, was what the Tonkawas named the land between present Brazos and Colorado rivers, including Williamson County.[99]

A valuable source book on the Tonkawan language was written in 1760 by a Spanish priest as a manual for missionaries. Instructions in the manual were in both the Coahuiltecan and Spanish languages. In addition to the record of the Indian vocabulary, the book contains useful information about

---

* This tantalizing statement was made by J. M. Sanchez y Tapia, a member of the Berlandier party who visited the Tonkawas in 1828. Although much scientific material from this expedition is extant, the notations about the music have not been found.[95]

the customs, beliefs, superstitions and rituals of the natives. Tonkawan has twenty-five distinctive sounds as compared with about forty-six in English, and ten vowel sounds, whereas most English dialects contain only nine.[100]

Words originating in the unwritten Indian languages have many variations resulting from the Spanish, French and English versions, and the name Tonkawa is no exception. Konkone, Tonquaay, Tanquaay, Tancaoye, Toncahua, Toncahue, Toncagués, Tancaguas, Tonkawega, Tonkaweya, Ton-ka-way. Tonkawe and Tonkewa were among the many spellings. Related tribes with similar names, each with variable spellings, included the Tohaha (Toaa, Toao, Teao, Toaja, Tuxaxa), and the Toho (Tojo, Tou, Tuu, Toxo).[101]

The name Tonkawa is used in two contexts. Sometimes it refers to the large group of many small bands of different names, who spoke the same language. It also refers to one special band which lived in the Williamson County area, and who later joined or was joined by other bands, and all of whom, after consolidation, usually were referred to as Tonkawas. The combined Tonkawan tribes formed one of the larger nations in Texas in the eighteenth century.[102] The four larger groups were the Tonkawa proper, the Yojuane (Diujuan), Mayeye (also Meghy, Meghey, Maghai, Malleyes), and the Ervipiame (also Enepiahos, Hebabame, Hierbipiame, Yerbipiame, Hyerbipiame). Each of these four was independent and roving, but all spoke the same basic language. The Ervipiame and other smaller tribes comprised the *Ranchería Grande* in the eighteenth century, and about the same time, the Yojuane and Mayeye were partially absorbed into the Tonkawan tribe.[103] Other Tonkawan satellite groups who roamed between central Texas and Coahuiltecan territory south of the Rio Grande included the Emet, Cava, Sana, Toho and Tohaha. These small bands were greatly reduced in the seventeenth and eighteenth centuries and, after 1750, also united with the Tonkawas.[104] Numerous other bands have been tentatively identified with the Tonkawas. In a few instances, tribes of other language groups intermingled with the Tonkawas or became close associates, including the Deadose and Bidai.[105]

Before Europeans brought in new diseases, the Tonkawan population was about 1500 in 1691. Disease and the Comanche invasion accounted for a heavy loss in population.[106] A *junta* at Bexar estimated they had 300 warriors in 1778. A smallpox epidemic infested the tribe in 1779, after which the warriors numbered only about 150—a loss of fifty percent in a single year.[107] A Tonkawan Indian-historian, Roger Stallings, said of his rapidly disappearing tribe:

Bad luck comes in clusters like grapes. Smallpox was introduced deliberately through contaminated blankets and dolls brought in by Europeans. Tonkawas contracted cholera from an immigrant wagon train. [In addition, the Comanches took a heavy toll.] In 1838 and 1839, a large number of Tonkawan women were captured by Comanches and many Tonkawan men were destroyed by Cherokees.[108]

Population estimates in the early 1800s range from 200 to 600 men, 80 families or a total population of about 500.[109]

From time to time, Texas Rangers hired Tonkawas as mercenaries.[110] The Tonkawan tribe remained in central Texas until 1855 when 171 of them were settled on the Brazos Reservation.[111] A few others joined the Lipans, who by now were south of the Rio Grande.[112] The Tonkawas were moved to a second reservation in Indian Territory (Oklahoma) and 167 of them, about half of those living there, were massacred on October 24, 1862. The tribes responsible for the decimation were the Delaware, Shawnee, Wichita and Caddo.[113] Remnants of the Tonkawas returned to central Texas and served as guides and scouts for the U. S. Army during the Civil War and during the Indian Wars. Others were resettled near Fort Griffin, Texas by 1870, and in 1884, they were again moved to Oklahoma.[114]

Eighteen Tonkawas trained in leatherwork and saddlemaking were apprenticed to a group of Mormons in central Texas in the mid-nineteenth century and eventually moved with the Mormons to the northwest, where they were absorbed into the population.[115] Tonkawas and Lipans intermarried in the Oklahoma territory and in northern Mexico. In the latter place, they were absorbed by Mescalero bands.[116] In 1944, the Oakland Agency of Oklahoma reported fifty-six Tonkawas there[117] and in the 1960s, their total was fifty-five.[118]

Prior to 1770, the Spaniards regarded the Tonkawas as enemies, but Colonel Athanase de Mézières was assigned the task of pacifying the Texas tribes and, after holding several councils, relations with the Tonkawas improved.[119] Stephen F. Austin treated with Tonkawas, Wacos and Tawakoni in 1824.[120]

An early Tonkawan chief, Tosque or El Mocho of the late eighteenth century, was born an Apache, was captured by the Tonkawas and through his cunning and the loss of other chiefs by epidemics, he became a powerful leader. Indeed he was so powerful and so devious, the Spaniards plotted several times to assassinate him, finally doing so in 1784.[121]

In the nineteenth century Chief Carita frequently dealt with Stephen F. Austin. Chiefs Ouchcala, Gosata and Harshokena signed a peace treaty with President Sam Houston at Bexar on November 22, 1837,[122] and

another treaty was concluded at Houston on April 10, 1838.[123] Captain
Jim, another Tonkawan leader, led a fight against the Comanches. Living
to be 110 years old, Chief Campos was involved in a number of treaties
signed between Anglo settlers and Indian tribes. Jim Pockmark, an Indian
scout, was known as a special friend to white settlers. He was active during
the 1850s when the Tonkawas moved to the Clear Fork of the Brazos and
later into Oklahoma. Chief Johnson, son of Campos, was at Fort Griffin in
1876. Possibly the best known and most admired of all Tonkawan chiefs
was Placido, whose name was given him by Mexicans because of his placid
nature. Smithwick called him friend, and he was considered by some to be

Tonkawan Chief Placido was popular among settlers.

the greatest Indian ally the new Texans had. Placido assisted Texans against
the Comanches about the time of the Civil War. Once, when visiting in
the home of General Burleson in San Marcos, he recognized the hoot of
an owl as a Comanche fake and prevented trouble with that tribe. He was
killed with three hundred Indians when the Delawares, Shawnees and Caddoes attacked the Tonkawas.[124] Two other Tonkawan leaders were called
Burnt Rock and Chunk of Coal, the latter name evolving into Coleman.[125]

The crossroads character of central Texas, the Tonkawan homeland, had
a considerable effect on Tonkawan culture. Newcomb, noting the Tonkawan
language affiliation with the Coahuiltecans of southern Texas and Mexico,
connects early Tonkawan culture with that southern area. After the Tonka-

wan bands united in the latter half of the eighteenth century, Webb, New-comb and others agree that their culture resembled that of the plains In-dians. The Tonkawas, Lipan Apaches, Tawakonis, Wacos, and Wichitas— all of them at times associated with Williamson County—were "transi-tional tribes," says Webb, "half plains and half forest." Some of them had a little agriculture, but all were nomadic and all depended upon the buffalo for a livelihood.[126]

LIPAN APACHES

Three other tribes besides the Tonkawas were at times closely associated with the territory of Williamson County: the Lipan Apaches, Comanches and Tawakonis.

The Lipan Apaches came down from the north between 1100 and 1300 A. D. and ranged along the foot of the mountains from the Rio Grande to the Brazos. They often travelled through present Williamson County and lived at times in the western hills fringing it.[127] Coronado called them proud and successful warriors in the sixteenth century. They also maintained a semi-agricultural life, combining it with hunting and gathering. Their permanent *rancherías*, in 1598, contained fifty tents of beautifully tanned hides, colored red and white, the shape of bells and as beautifully con-structed as the leatherwork of Italy. Even the smallest tent accommodated four beds. Very large ones were lightweight, weighing about fifty pounds.[128]

When the Comanches invaded their villages in the early eighteenth cen-tury, the Lipans' agriculture was destroyed, their buffalo hunting curtailed, and they reverted to hunting and raiding for survival. They made quick forays on the Spanish missions of Texas for horses to use in the hunt. Among their targets were the three missions on the San Xavier (San Gabriel) River, which suffered Lipan Apache raids a number of times. As the Comanches pushed the Lipans from the north, the Spanish pushed from the south and east, wedging them from their lands and leaving them pov-erty-stricken, "skulking, beggarly" remnants of their early majestic culture. They abandoned their last attempt at agriculture—the Lipans' Field (*Labor de los Lipanes*)—in 1822, and when F. M. Buckelew was their captive in 1866, he reported that they asked him how to grow corn. In less than half a century, the art was forgotten.[129]

Even during their bad times, as when Berlandier met them in 1828, they were handsome, clean and well-dressed. The men were tall, the women short, and their skin a copper shade. The hair was generally worn long.

Like men of other tribes, the Lipans disliked facial hair and plucked out their beards and eyebrows. Well-worked deerskin was used for clothing, including the man's loincloth, cloak and leggings, the lady's skirt, poncho-like jacket, stockings and shoes. The mantle was ornamented with painted designs and fur, and the jackets were beaded and fringed. Both men and women wore earrings and other jewelry in profusion.[130]

As pressures mounted on the Lipans from Comanches and others, they finally moved into Mexico where their identity was meshed with that of the Mescalero Apaches. Eleven thousand Lipans were living on the Mescalero Reservation of New Mexico in the 1960s.[131] For years they crossed Williamson County, travelling along the San Gabriel River and fording it just east of present San Gabriel (town) so that the crossing came to be called Apache Pass. It was near this pass that the Spaniards located their presidio de San Francisco Xavier de Gigedo in 1751.[132] The Lipans had been en route to the missions in East Texas, where they also raided for horses, and traded with the Caddo Indians.

Chief Cuelgas de Castro, most prominent leader of his tribe in the early nineteenth century, scouted for the Texas Rangers from 1836 until his death.[133] He and his son, Juan Castro, along with Juan Seis and Flacco the Younger, led a Lipan company in 1839 to aid the colonists in the Battle of Brushy. Both Flacco the Elder and his son were chiefs who also served as scouts and guides for the Rangers against Comanches and Mexicans. Castro visited Stephen F. Austin in February 1842 and was instructed to camp between Brushy Creek and Little River until he was needed.[134] An 1850 description of the Chief pictures him in heavily beaded shirt, wearing brass earrings and a red mark painted across his face. In Roman style, he wore a wreath of fresh oak leaves on his head.[135]

COMANCHES

The Comanches lived a rags-to-riches story, leaving a bleak homeland in Wyoming as impoverished and miserable people and sweeping into Texas in search of horses early in the eighteenth century. With dazzling speed they adapted to a new environment and became leaders of a Plains culture centering around the horse and the buffalo. The culture reached its peak by the early 1800s and involved many, many tribes speaking hundreds of different languages, all of whom clustered into this new Plains frontier.[136] The Penateka or Honey Eaters of the Comanches were especially familiar to western Williamson County.[137]

The communication problem between the many tribes was solved by sign languages. Messages were sent long distances by smoke signals or by drum beats. Tribes could telegraph their arrival time the distance of two days' travel. News of victories, meetings, or the route of an approaching enemy was accurately and quickly transmitted.[138]

The Comanche (also Komantcia, Camanche, Cumanche) were designated in the Plains sign language by a forward, wriggling motion of the hand or forefinger, signifying a snake, and thus the Indians themselves indicated the stealthiness of some of their fellowmen. The French named them Serpens (Snakes). "The palm for stealing" was awarded to the Comanches by other tribesmen, and "for crawling into a camp, cutting hobbles and lariat ropes, and getting off with animals undiscovered, they are unsurpassed and unsurpassable."[139]

The Comanches were fairly short, often heavyset, and appeared to be slow and awkward, but they quickly became masters of horsemanship, "the most expert and daring riders in the world." The women likewise were "daring riders and hunters, lassoing antelope and shooting buffalo."[140] Boys were strapped to the back of a horse at the age of one or two to be oriented to their second home. By the time they were four or five, children had their own ponies and took part in riding contests.[141] The poorest Comanche owned six or eight horses; wealthy tribesmen had thirty or forty plus about ten mules.[142] The war chiefs owned great herds. To attain this property, Comanches made raiding a way of life. They were also the only tribe which bred horses extensively. When Anglo settlers arrived in Williamson County, they soon learned Comanche raiding tactics.[143] Aggressive and lightning quick, Comanche ways made mortal enemies of the Lipan Apaches, struck fear into frontier settlements, and blocked westward expansion of the Texas frontier for about half a century. Their savage raids netted them horses, cattle, and slaves. Although some visitors reported that Comanches treated captives humanely, in 1828 they held five or six hundred Spanish prisoners and many more slaves who had been frontier settlers.[144]

Older prisoners were usually killed, enemies tortured, but younger captives were generally "allowed" to become members of the tribe. This practice enabled the Comanche nation to increase its population. Each Comanche man might have several slaves waiting upon him and a Comanche woman had one or two to serve her.[145] Rosita Rodriges wrote in exquisite penmanship to her father in 1846, poignantly telling of her one year as a slave of the Comanches, of her purchase by the trading post owners, and of her longing to have her little son, Incarnacion, released from the Comanches.[146]

Comanche women were in charge of all duties except those directly dealing with hunting and warfare. They waited on the men, brought in animals from the hunt, dressed and processed them, cooked, sewed, ornamented the clothing of the men (but not their own), saddled and unsaddled horses of "their lords," dressed skins, and moved and erected villages. In the latter task, the women must have been extremely efficient, for the tribe was admired and feared for its ability to remove large villages hundreds of miles— silently, quickly, and without notice. An entire *Comancheria* could vanish in thirty minutes. The women pitched the tent lodges methodically, with regularly spaced streets and village squares. The inferior position of a Comanche woman was always evident.[147]

Noah Smithwick, who lived in Williamson County, knew the Comanches well and visited them from time to time. They rarely killed an animal solely for sport, although they did shoot many arrows into the hump of an old buffalo bull for entertainment. When the animal charged the Indians, a young man ran beside him, pulling out arrows until the bull was too weary to fight. Then the Indians killed him to recover their arrows. They lassoed turkeys after chasing them on horseback "until they fell to the ground from exhaustion," and lassoed deer or mustangs which had become thirsty and had run long distances to drink water. Comanches could slip up on a band of buffalo, "crowding them so closely that the calves could not keep up, and, falling behind, were cut off and lassoed." Warriors generally needed only a single arrow to hit a buffalo. They pursued wounded animals to see that they did not suffer. "One of the Indian's principal grievances against the white man was the wholesale slaughter of the buffalo," killed "in wanton sport."[148]

In the early 1800s, the Comanche population was estimated at 20,000.[149] A map used by Stephen F. Austin in the 1820s showed them living throughout the Williamson County area, and "immense herds of Buffalos, large droves of wild cattle and horses" are also indicated in the same territory.[150] At Tumlinson Fort (1836), the Comanches left samples of their art upon the walls of the block house. Exceptionally skilled as artists, they painted with charcoal or colored chalk upon smooth bark of trees, flat stones or boards. "The subject was always the same—Indians chasing buffalo."[151] Comanches still occupied parts of Williamson County as late as 1838 and continued to raid the area occasionally about twenty years longer.[152] Chief Yellow Wolf and his band lived about two miles above Gabriel Mills as late as 1851 when Yellow Wolf brought some silver ore to Samual Mather to be made into jewelry. Comanche Chief Muguara, a friend of Noah

Smithwick, explained his tribe's feelings toward the incoming settlers:

> We have set up our lodges in these groves and swung our children from these boughs from time immemorial. When game beats away from us we pull down our lodges and move away, leaving no trace to frighten it, and in a little while it comes back. But the white man comes and cuts down the trees, building houses and fences, and the buffalos get frightened and leave and never come back, and the Indians are left to starve, or, if we follow the game, we trespass on the hunting ground of other tribes and war ensues.[153]

While Smithwick was visiting in Muguara's camp, some of his warriors were accused of taking horses from surveyors encamped on Brushy Creek.[154] Chief Muguara once negotiated a treaty with Sam Houston. Besides Muguara and Yellow Wolf, other well-known Comanche chiefs were Pah-hah-yo-ko or Old Owl who had a small, cunning face, Buffalo Hump said never to have accepted any American ways, and Santa Anna, a fine looking, affable chief. The last massacre attributed to the Comanches in Williamson County was in 1863 when Wofford Johnson and his family were ambushed near Hopewell. The Comanches were marked for extinction and these brilliant, superb horsemen and savage raiders were finally erased from the scene.[155]

TAWAKONIS

Although the Tawakonis generally lived near the Brazos River along with the Wacos, Williamson County had a Tawakoni village prior to 1834.[156] Other forms of their name were Tuacana, Tuacano, Touacana, Tahuacano, and Tehuacano or Tehuacana. They were of Caddoan stock, were closely related to the Waco. Note that *waco* is a part of the word, "Tawakoni."[157] The powerful, warlike Tawakonis were semi-agricultural, and also hunted and gathered for food. Although they robbed and murdered in Williamson County, unlike the Comanches they usually raided afoot.[158]

The Tawakonis hunted buffalo and bear and raised crops of corn, beans, melons and pumpkins. When winter came, they hid their crops in the ground and joined other tribes in the hunt. Buffalo hides figured in the deaths of Dr. Thomas Kenney and his companions in 1844. As they loaded buffalo hides for Captain Nelson Merrell, the three men were murdered by Tawakonis near Bone Hollow in north Williamson County.[159]

Like other agricultural tribes, Tawakonis celebrated the Feast of New Fruits. They loved sleight of hand games and music, were extremely superstitious, and were fine dancers.[160]

The Tawakoni village in Williamson County, located at present Rock House, was called Draco, a Caddoan word meaning "Preferred Camp." The settlement was on the North Gabriel River a few miles east of Liberty Hill. How early Draco was inhabited by Tawakonis has not been determined, but about in 1834 the Texas Rangers contrived to have them removed. Rangers furnished the Tonkawas with guns and ammunition with the understanding that they were to drive out the Tawakonis. The Tawakonis moved to the Baby Head (Llano) area, where they are believed to have practiced the burial rite of removing a boulder, placing the deceased in a crevice underneath, and replacing the boulder.[161]

Pioneer settlers in Draco continued to use the name for many years. A U. S. post office was assigned to Draco from 1890 to 1892.[162]

OTHER TRIBES

Henri Joutel reported that the Mayeyes lived along the San Gabriel River in 1687. The Yojuanes were for a time in the hill country and acted as professional hunters for the Anglo American settlers, bringing meat and tanned hides to frontier posts. A few Kiowas were said to have lived in Williamson County in about 1838.[163]

Choctaw Corners, Williamson County, tied another tribal name to the area. After a handful of settlers came to that section, a Choctaw named Fred Hardy operated a trading business along Brushy Creek and the San Gabriel. He sold seeds and was especially well known for his superior strain of peach trees, developed by crossing two kinds of peaches. The trader's presence was frowned upon by some of the settlers and he was forced to leave. He established a business near present Kerrville, where many fine peach orchards are said to have been planted from his trees.*[164]

INDIAN ECONOMY AND RELATIONS
WITH IMMIGRANTS

The horse had a tremendous economic impact upon Texas Indians, whose livelihood had depended on buffalo for thousands of years. The horse per-

* A large Indian burial ground was found at Georgetown between the North and South San Gabriels in the 1920s and 1930s during excavation for a swimming pool and for a bridge. This author has found no judgment by reputable scientists as to the identity of the tribe. A story of questionable documentation was circulated at the time that the burials were a Cheyenne group, massacred by Comanches. The pseudo-scientist who made this assertion unscrupulously gathered enormous amounts of Indian artifacts from the county, departed the state with them and sold them as souvenirs. His action would today violate state laws. That a burial ground was discovered is certain. Other evidence is needed before tribal identification is considered reliable.

mitted better hunting, quicker raids, more dangerous warfare, and led to a more nomadic, less agricultural kind of life.[165] Increased food stocks, made possible by use of the horse, allowed Indians to abandon gardening and their permanent villages and "with them went the elaborate customs and crafts, their rules for marriage and residence."[166]

Trade in buffalo hides became a big business in which the Indians participated to some extent. More important, however, the business depleted the buffalo population and thereby the Indians' bread of life. While buffalo were still plentiful, a single hunter could kill seventy to a hundred in an hour. In 1857, 75,000 buffalo hides were sent along the Santa Fe Trail. In 1870, properly tanned hides sold for about two or three dollars each in St. Louis and Kansas City. Indians had a market for all they could get.[167] Many hides were shipped out of the railroad terminal at Round Rock after that line opened in 1876.[168] The negative aspects of the buffalo slaughter were foreseen by many Indians and settlers, but it was not stopped before grave damage was done.

The cattle business was a lucrative enterprise for Indians, early Spaniards, Mexicans, and later for Anglos. Wild horses (mustangs) and wild cattle (longhorns) sprang from stock brought to the continent by Spaniards in the sixteenth century. They multiplied and spread northward from Mexico until they numbered six million in 1825. Cattle drives began on the North American continent by 1650 and some cattle trading took place in Texas before the Civil War.[169] This business was a part of the Plains culture which lasted less than two hundred years and which was more flamboyant and richer than most of the Plains Indian tribes had ever known previously.[170]

Encroachment of white settlers on lands which the Indians always assumed were as free as the air brought inevitable friction. Frauds perpetrated by Indian agents and nonfulfillment of treaties by state and national governments compounded the problems caused by Anglo Americans. Sharp attacks by Indians upon the settlements or upon isolated hunters and surveyors, raids for horses, murder, and lack of communication between nations further chipped away at good relations.[171] Disease, war, murder and starvation led to an almost unbelievable reduction in the Indian population after the white man came.[172] Stephen F. Austin and Sam Houston treated successfully with Indians but Mirabeau Lamar elected a harsh attitude toward the tribes and the Mexican government sought an alliance with them against the Texas Republic. Under the Republic, frontier Ranger stations were established and boundaries set which the Indians were forbidden to cross. Whites had free access to the entire area, however, and the double standard increased bad will. About the time Texas joined the United States in 1845, smallpox and cholera hit some of the tribes. Settlers were pushing fast into William-son County territory. Time was running out. The remnants of central Texas tribes were moved to government reservations and the Indians no longer claimed their "land of beauty."[173]

CULTURAL CONTRIBUTIONS

How much of a genetic contribution [Tonkawas] and other Texas aborigi-nes made to the white and Negro population of Texas . . . is enigmatic. That it was made is certain; that it was greater than is generally believed seems likely.[174]

Other Indian contributions are almost countless. Their mastery of nature's lore was superb. They located the easiest trails, knew well the streams and springs, including those in Williamson County, understood "the movement of wild animals, the flight of birds, the bent twig, and the tracks by the water holes."[175] Pioneers learned from them the art of sign cutting—how to de-tect and interpret marks left by something which had passed. "Facts about rain, wind, dew, disturbance of plants or vegetation, misplaced rocks, hair of an animal," tracks—all might tell Indians, hunters or pioneers something useful. The same methods were later used to find cattle rustlers, train rob-bers or other criminals.[176] The Indians had an appropriate and effective system of highway signs—bent, horizontal trees which had been fastened to the ground as saplings to grow in an abnormal position. Such markers located the better campsites along streams. A number of these bent trees grew near the San Gabriel River banks and at springs of several creeks in Williamson County in 1973.

The first settlers, often unable to obtain food, clothing, shelter and tools such as they were familiar with, adapted the Indian practices of using animal skins for clothing, linens, canoes, moccasins, and ate Indian pemmican and other foods. Indians introduced fifty foods, unknown to Europeans in 1492, to pioneers, and taught frontier women how to make grits or hominy, roast corn, cook succotash and popcorn, and brew tea and medicines from native plants. They introduced the native crops such as corn (maize), squash, pumpkins, potatoes, peppers, beans and many others. The tribes taught settlers the principles of fertilizing with ashes and dead fish, methods of ir-rigation, and used drugs to paralyze fish temporarily so they could be caught easily.

Place names and other words from the 350 Indian languages are common in Texas. Texas is derived from a Caddoan word for their confederacy, meaning friends or allies. This name also appeared as Tejas, Tayshas, Teisas, Texias, Techas, Cenis, Asinais, Asenais, Assonis and Asenay.[177] Tonkawa Bluff and Comanche Peak in Williamson County have been mentioned, as was Apache Pass just east of the county line. Yegua Creek in southeastern Williamson County came from an Indian word via the Spanish *yegua*, meaning "wild mare." Draco and Choctaw Corners, villages in the county, have also been mentioned.

About 1700 words in American English come from the Indian, the largest number of which are plant and animal names. Among these are raccoon, opossum, coyote, muskrat, skunk, woodchuck, chipmunk, moose, terrapin, maize, potato, tomato, chili, chicle, vanilla, pecan, mesquite, persimmon, hickory, hominy, succotash, squash and pone. Words describing Indian life have been retained, such as tepee(also tipi), squaw, sachem, powwow, papoose, wigwam, wampum, tomahawk, pemmican, tobacco, caucus, mackinaw, moccasin, canoe, hammack and hoochino (shortened to hooch). Chautauqua was an Indian word for "someone took out a fish there."[178]

Clothing styles, leathercraft, beadwork, music, literature and folklore, nature lore, forms of government and medical practices have been adapted from the Indian into Anglo-American usage.

Athletic contests were popular among many Indian tribes. Legend persists that such events took place in Williamson County. Makemson wrote about a mile-long race track near Kenney Fort.[179] Indian braves were said to have run races along a five hundred-yard track northwest of Georgetown. A level area in the shape of a horseshoe encircles a knoll now dotted with shrubs. Early settlers said that the flat, smooth track was always free of rocks and vegetation and was of a uniform width. Since growth of shrubs and trees was characteristic over all the remainder of the large area, the cleared path was the more obvious. An unusually large number of arrow points and relics have been gathered on the knoll or elevation inside the horseshoe. Such a concentration of them was found only on that spot. The mound is about half a mile from a water source, too far from water to have been a campsite. The story told by pioneers who hunted in the area is that the place was a kind of natural amphitheatre of about fifty acres. When tribal athletes held their contests, the older men, women and children watched from the knoll in the center. From there they could follow the course of the entire race. The place is about one-half mile south of the North Gabriel River, four miles northwest of the County Court House, on land out of the Joseph Fish survey. In 1972, the ranch belonged to Judge D. B. Wood.[180]

A late-twentieth century look at contributions of the American Indian to civilization reveals a growing list. The stunning spectre of industrialized society's disastrous waste of natural resources dawned on the world with great clarity in the 1960s. In this light, the Indian's knowledge of nature and his respect for its role in the survival of man took on a new significance.

III

The Spanish and French

EARLY EXPLORATION

The first white man ever in Texas, Spanish Cabeza de Vaca, and the first Frenchman to visit the state, la Salle, both reached central Texas and de Vaca is believed by some historians to have crossed present Williamson County. Their exact routes are unknown and a matter of considerable controversy. It is certain, however, that both explorers were in contact with Indians whose names and customs were similiar to those of Tonkawan tribes seen by eighteenth and nineteenth century travelers. Two Spaniards crossed what became Williamson County at least once each around 1690. In the early 1700s the San Xavier (San Gabriel) River became a familiar landmark on a new highway, Camino de Arriba, which crossed both Brushy Creek and San Gabriel River above the Camino Real.[1]

Cortes' entry into Mexico in 1519 quickly touched off other Spanish expeditions including that of Narváez, who went with a crew of six hundred to "the Florida" in 1527. After suffering heavy losses of men there, he headed by barges for the Texas coast where severe storms hit them and all except four of the original crew were killed. Among the survivors was Alvar Nuñez Cabeza de Vaca, originally the treasurer of the big expedition—a many-talented, well-educated man who turned author and wrote the first book ever about Texas. Adapting easily to a strange, new and primitive land and its people, for eight years de Vaca was variously traveler, explorer, diplomat, naturalist, geographer, geologist, linguist, physician and a keen observer of human nature and of the natural scene. He and his three companions, Andrés Dorantes, Estévanico and Alonso del Castillo Maldonado, the son of a doctor, journeyed afoot across Texas, spending eight years living among the various Indian tribes. They learned and participated in their customs, acquired speaking knowledge of six different Indian languages, probably including the Coahuiltecan (Tonkawan).[2] De Vaca's wandering route was determined by necessity and changing fortunes and by the Indian tribes he encountered. He and his party got along remarkably well with the natives, having the good sense to adopt many of the Indian ways. Although almost as many different routes are ascribed to de Vaca as different historians have considered the matter,[3] a number of reputable authorities recognize the possibility that he reached the Williamson County area. R. E. McDonald, botanist-entymologist, advances an intriguing interpretation of de Vaca's route based on the explorer's descriptions of the foods and plant life and on natural landmarks he described in detail. The scientist concludes that de Vaca crossed the Colorado River near Austin and Williamson County near present Georgetown.[4] De Vaca spent eight months with the Avavares Indians, whose excellent bow making, habit of trading with coastal tribes, and knowledge of the Mareames' language suggested strong resemblance to the Tonkawas. From de Vaca's calculations of the distance the Avavares traveled to reach the tuna fields, the scientist concludes that the Avavares' home "would not miss Georgetown much." On their way to the prickly pears, the Avavares camped near honey locust trees, gathering the beans for food. "That tells us that the river is the Brazos, because honey locusts do not grow west of the Brazos River bottoms, and not far from the mouth of the Little River and on very poor land from an Indian point of view." Guiding de Vaca along the Indian trails and river courses, the Avavares took the party up one of the tributaries "of the Brazos, most probably the San Gabriel, because the crossing place given of the Colorado makes this more likely."[5]

Robert Cavalier Sieur de la Salle, the French governor of Texas, also explored Texas by accident. Journals kept by Father Anastase Douay and Henri Joutel describe la Salle's trips into central Texas in 1686 and 1687 and mention several Indian tribes whose names are similar to known Tonkawan groups. La Salle met the Maghai (note similarity to the Mayeye who were in the same area 1716-44 and were associated with the San Xavier). He heard about the nearby Tohaka, Tohan, Hebabamo and others. The entourage saw many Indian villages, and took special note of the buffalo or "bullocks," the fine trees, prairies and springs, "curious shady Groves," a "delightful Landskip" and a "fine, curious country diversified with several little woods, hills, and small brooks, affording a delightful prospect." La

Salle crossed the deep Maligne River, so-named because one of his party was devoured there by a crocodile. At a populous village on la Maligne (the Mischievous), la Salle obtained horses "cheap" and the Indians took them across the river in oxhide canoes. Four leagues farther on, they crossed the Hiens River on rafts. Pichardo concluded that the Rio de Hiens was the San Gabriel River, but other historians do not concur. "It is doubtful if La Salle explored as far into Central Texas as the San Gabriel River."[6] Monsieur de la Salle was murdered en route to east Texas. His aborted interest in the area led other Frenchmen to the state and, more significantly, scared the Spanish into stepping up their exploration and colonization projects via the missions.[7]

In 1690 Spanish missions were established in east Texas to protect the Spanish frontier from the French. Captain Alonso de León made six separate journeys to the mission area after 1688, traveling from Mexico through San Antonio and to east Texas. Needing a highway to the missions, the Spanish government established El Camino Real, The King's Highway, from San Antonio through present Bastrop, skirting just to the east of present Williamson County, leading to east Texas. In dry weather this direct route was preferred, but when streams were swollen, this road became impassable. An upper route, Camino de Arriba, was designated through Williamson County land, crossing present Brushy Creek, San Gabriel River and the Brazos River just above where Little River enters it. De León took the Upper Highway at least once during his six trips. He is also credited on one journey with leaving "a bull, a cow, a stallion, and a mare at each river he crossed," thus significantly contributing to the mustang and longhorn population of Texas.[8] De León's chaplain, Father Damián Manzanet (Massanet), described meeting the Emet and Lavas (Cavas) tribes, both Tonkawan. Apparently frightened by de León's retinue, one group of natives ran into the woods, abandoning their dog packs. Guides reassured the villagers, however, and some of them came out, embracing the visitors and saying in Caddoan, " 'Thechas! thechas!' which means 'friends! friends!' (y nos decian thechas; thechas)."[9] Morfi has a slightly different version:

> The misinterpretation of a native phrase . . . gave to this province the name of Texas, by which it has been known since 1688, when the Indians greeted the Spaniards with the word *Texia*, the ordinary salutation with which they welcome their friends, meaning 'friend.'[10]

The first Spanish governor of Provincia de Tejas (la Salle had claimed the honor as a Frenchman a few years earlier), Domingo Terán de los

Rios, was appointed January 23, 1691. The same year, he left Mexico with fifty soldiers, ten missionaries and three lay brothers to take herds of domestic cattle to the missions. Going by way of the Colorado River (at that time called the San Marcos), they crossed present southeastern Williamson County and continued northeast across the Brazos, which was then called the Colorado River![11]

On another expedition, a Spanish priest, Fray Isidro Felix Espinosa, bestowed religious names upon Brushy Creek and San Gabriel River when the 1716 Saint Denis-Ramon company encamped on each of these streams. Fray Espinosa chose Arroyo de las Bendítas Ánimas (Creek of the Blessed Souls) for Brushy Creek and Rio de San Xavier (Saint Xavier River) for the San Gabriel, names which were used throughout the remainder of that century. Juchereau de Saint Denis was a dashing, aggressive, resourceful French trader who was accused of being involved in giant smuggling operations.[12] He left Louisiana in 1713 to buy cattle and horses for the French and to arrange for French trade with the Indians and the Spaniards. His activities met with something less than wholehearted approval, for he landed in a Spanish jail on the Rio Grande. Expediently, he solved his dilemma by marrying the commandant's granddaughter, who was also the niece of one Captain Domingo Ramón. Ramón was scheduled to lead the aforementioned expedition to the east Texas missions. Quickly converting his affiliations from the French to the Spanish, St. Denis got himself appointed to guide Ramón. Both Fray Espinosa and Ramón kept diaries of their journey, recording visits with a number of central Texas nations, including the Viday (Bidais), Sana, Toho (Thoó), Tiyupan (Choyopan or Tohóyopan) and Yrbipian (Ervipiame), the latter without a fixed abode.[13]

The Ramón-Denis expedition left Saltillo on February 17, 1716, with 75 men, 64 oxen, 490 horses and mules, more than 1,000 sheep and goats, equipment, supplies and gifts for the Indians.[14] Reaching the Colorado River a short distance below present Austin on May 23, 1716, they required two days to cross the river, plus another day to get the sheep and goats up the other bank. Three soldiers were sent to reconnoiter the road "which was not well known from this point on" and which took them almost immediately into present Williamson County.[15] The company resumed its march on May 27 and that day the men killed their first buffalo, whose flavorsome meat delighted them. The following night, May 28, they camped on the creek which Father Espinosa named Arroyo de las Bendítas Ánimas.[16] From las Ánimas, explorations were made to determine the best route ahead and on this scouting five Ervipiame and Mescal Indians were encountered. The natives said that their rancherías were near and they offered to guide the travelers. Castaneda's map of the route shows the expedition went approximately through Rice's Crossing and crossed the San Gabriel somewhere between Circleville and Laneport. The encampment on las Ánimas (Brushy Creek) fell on a religious holiday and would normally have remained there for a period of observance. But Ramón decided they must move on because the campsite was unsuitable. He did so "with keen regret since this was the Feast of Pentecost." They moved ahead on May 31, but with great effort, for it rained all night and continued next morning. With still more difficulty, four masses were said imploring favorable weather. At about nine o'clock the next morning the rain stopped, so on June 1, they advanced to another stream which they named Rio de San Xavier (present San Gabriel River). The name honored Saint Francis Xavier (1506-1552), born Francisco de Xavier, in Spain. He studied in Paris, met Ignatius Loyola and together they founded the Society of Jesus. Xavier served as a missionary to Italy, India and Japan and was declared a saint in 1622. Although he denied it, he was credited with the gift of tongues. At the San Xavier campsite, Ramón's men remained an extra day to celebrate the third day of the octave of the Feast of Pentecost, June 2. A solemn Mass and the *Veni Creator* were sung by all the missionaries, a military salute was fired, and Communion was received by many persons. This was the first Christian rite to be solemnized in the county. The festival was held on the banks of the river not far from where three missions were later built to Christianize Indians, and where many years still later, Protestant baptismal rites were performed in the river and brush arbor camp meetings held by pioneer worshipers.[17] From June 3 to June 12 the company had to change its course from northeast to southeast because of thick woods and streams in their path. They met another delegation of Indians who took them to their ranchería of about two thousand population, possibly near present Cameron.[18]

The most spectacular delegation to cross present Williamson County was the famous Aguayo expedition of 1721 which followed in a general way the route of Interstate Highway 35.[19] During the fall of 1720 el Marqués de Aguayo in Mexico gathered at his own expense an enormous expedition: 500 men in eight companies, a battalion of mounted infantry, 600 *cargas* (loads) of supplies, 4000 horses, 600 head of cattle, 900 sheep, and nearly 800 mules. His goal was to restore the missions which had been allowed to deteriorate in east Texas. "The most formidable attempt ever made to establish the king's dominion over the Province of Texas," the thousand-mile journey began in Mexico. Father Juan Antonio de la Peña (or, Bachiller "loquacious" Peña, according to Hackett) kept a detailed diary of the expedition which reached the Colorado River on May 23, 1721.[20] Excerpts from the priest's description of the county follow:

> Tuesday, the 27th [May 1721]. We proceeded toward the northeast, to an arroyo which they call Las Ánimas. . . . The whole country is of low hills, without thickets or trees, as far as the said arroyo, which is heavily timbered on both sides. A quarter of a league [one league equals 2.63 miles] beyond, another small arroyo is passed [probably Chandler Branch]. It is likewise wooded, and appears to rise nearby. From there the route descends to the northeast, to the Río de San Xavier, where a halt was made, that day's journey having been five leagues. Another copious arroyo, also with timber, was left half a league behind [probably Smith Branch]. The Río de San Xavier is much larger than the preceding rivers; it has the same sort of trees and grapevines, and, although it is not very wide, it has a uniform depth of about a half vara of water.[21]
>
> Wednesday, the 28th. Two equal branches of the said river were crossed [North and South San Gabriels], and, about a gunshot away, a creek with much water. [Berry's Creek is four and a half miles north; Bolton translates Morfi's phrase, "a large lake with much water," but "creek" appears to be correct in this case.] Since there was much undergrowth between, it required some time and no little labor to get the [mule] trains and cattle across. For this reason a day's journey of only four leagues was made. We halted on an arroyo, which, because of not having a name and because it was near the San Xavier the Señor governor called San Ygnacio. [Probably Willis Creek; the named honored Ignatius of Loyola, close friend and colleague of Xavier, also sainted by their church.] After crossing the river the whole route lay among high and low hills, with many obstacles, another arroyo, with its timber, being left behind.

The entourage then turned toward the north-northeast. The large company probably crossed Salado Creek, Lampasas and Little rivers (Rio San Andres) and finally el Rio de Los Brazos de Dios (also Brassos—River of the Arms of God). They had moved from Austin to Waco in twenty-eight days.[22]

El Cuilón, otherwise called Juan Rodriguez, chief of the Ranchería Grande tribes,* had selected the route through central Texas. Chief Rodriguez had previously met Aguayo in San Antonio when the Indians petitioned for a mission. Engaged to guide the expedition, Rodriguez maintained that El Camino Real was impracticable because the creeks were impassable, the ground marshy and the woods very thick. He urged them to follow El Camino de Arriba, the upper route, which he admitted crossed more streams and would come closer to the Apaches. He pointed out, how-

---

* El Cuilón's Ranchería Grande tribes included three Tonkawan groups, Ervipiame, Yojuane and Mayeye, and also the Deadose.[23]

ever, that the country was open and he was certain the Apaches would not dare to attack. The council agreed on the Chief's judgment, marching the route previously described. They reached the abandoned missions in east Texas that summer. The undertaking was a success but was the last of its magnitude in Texas.[24]

When the missions were in order and Aguayo was ready to return to Mexico, his trip was delayed by a terrific snow and sleet storm on November 11, 1721. Huge trees were uprooted and branches broken by heavy ice. "In twenty-four hours more than two hundred trees fell down within the camp and more than a thousand in the surrounding country, killing many mules and horses as they fell." After the weather moderated, the march back to the Rio Grande began, but about five thousand horses and livestock had been lost because of the severe cold and lack of fodder, so that nearly all the soldiers were obliged to walk the entire way. They arrived in San Antonio on January 23, 1722. "For the time [Aguayo] saved Texas for Spain."[25]

The San Xavier River was mentioned in 1723 in reports of a series of campaigns against the Lipan Apaches who were marauding Texas missions. A Franciscan lay brother named Pita was murdered near the San Xavier River during these engagements.[26]

A military officer described Brushy Creek (las Ánimas) in 1727: On August 24

> I travelled . . . over a level country without any timber. I saw more than two hundred head of buffaloes. I stopped on the south bank of the arroyo which they call the upper Las Ánimas. . . . The day of the 26th, I travelled eight leagues toward the east, a quarter to the northeast, through the same kind of country. At nightfall we were on the uninhabited lower Las Ánimas.[27]

The San Xavier and las Ánimas had become so familiar to the Spanish by 1730 that the Zacatecan missionaries asked permission to remove their east Texas mission to the San Xavier, since the threat from the French had dissipated.[28]

A small army of 157 Spanish soldiers, sixty mission Indians and nine hundred horses and mules traveled by way of the San Xavier in 1732 on a campaign against the Apaches, led by the then Governor of Texas, Juan Antonio Bustillo y Zevallos (Ceballos). Three additional expeditions followed this campaign, moving along the edge of the prairie just east of the Balcones fault line and from the San Xavier to Apache headquarters on the San Sabá River. About this time the Lipan Apaches became much more friendly toward the Spaniards, for suddenly they had been besieged by Comanches pushing south in search of horses and committing ravages against the Lipan Apaches.[29]

In 1744 the San Xavier was suggested as a good place to transfer one of two quarrelling groups at Bexar (San Antonio)—colonists from the Canary Islands versus other Bexar residents. San Xavier was described as a well-known buffalo hunting ground in 1746 by Father Francisco Xavier Ortiz.[30]

MISSIONS ON THE SAN GABRIEL RIVER

The idea of a permanent colony somewhere on the San Xavier River was discussed a number of times both by Spaniards and Indians prior to the 1740s. Missions San Antonio de Valera at Bexar, better known as the Alamo, was founded in 1718. After 1733 it was the home of Father Francisco Mariano de los Dolores y Viana. The Indian tribes in the mission were greatly diminished in 1739 by an epidemic. Father Mariano, who had often visited central Texas to recover fugitives and to seek new mission Indians, after the epidemic made even more frequent trips to replenish his mission. Each trip took three to ten days. Writing to the Governor of Texas he reported that prior to 1745 he had visited the Ranchería Grande (with a population of about 1,228 in 1745) nearly every year and that the Indians had in turn often visited him in Bexar. On June 2, 1745, four chiefs and thirteen tribesmen from Ranchería Grande arrived in San Antonio specifically to request that Fray Mariano select a site and establish a mission in their country. Officials invited the Indians to join a mission which they promised to establish in Bexar exclusively for them, but they declined, saying Bexar was too far from their friends and relations, from their lands, and from the Tejas from whom they obtained weapons. The petitioners were then questioned seriously about their willingness to plant and work crops, to attend school and religious services, and to fight against enemies of the Spanish. The visitors agreed to the required provisions and urged Father Mariano to return with them to their home to talk with their people. He sent some of his own mission Indians to the applicants' village for conferences. Shortly afterwards another delegation came to San Antonio with news that many other Indian nations including the Tonkawas and about twenty-two tribes, would like to join the proposed mission. This time Father Mariano took some mission Indians and soldiers and accompanied the visitors inland to locate a suitable place. He found one on Rio de San Xavier which was reported satisfactory. *Autos* (petitions) were drawn up recommending the site, the first of many, many hundreds of documents which accumulated

in a veritable flood of correspondence during the decade the San Xavier
missions existed. Since the site chosen was on the San Gabriel River, nearly
all of which is in present Williamson County, the missions were believed
to have been in this county until early in the twentieth century, when further
investigation revealed them just east of the Williamson County line. The
missions in numerous ways involved present Williamson County and the
Indians who resided there. So their story is relevant.[31]

Although Father Mariano's personal interest was the welfare of the Indians themselves, the fate of the proposed mission was determined more
on political considerations than anything else. The formal requests pointed
out that all the Indian petitioners had French guns, powder, glass beads and
vermillion, indicating possible French attempts at colonization and, at the
very least, considerable contact with the Indians. The English were also
believed to be doing some trading in the area. These were the most compelling of arguments to high officials of Spain. The proposed San Xavier
missions would serve as buffers to hold back the Apaches on the west and
discourage French or English encroachment from the east. The plan had
much support from the beginning, although many letters, much persuasion
and numerous delays intervened before the desired permission was granted,
and even longer before funds and supplies were received. Father Mariano
was impatient and in January 1746 took soldiers and mission Indians to the
San Xavier River and sometime before April 13, 1746, a mission had been
founded. By June, five Indians had been killed by Apaches and some of the
new residents had eaten the pumpkin crop before the fruit matured. But the
mission continued to function until official approval was finally granted on
December 23, 1747. A formal founding was held in February 1748, more
than two years after it was unofficially established, and it was named
Misión San Francisco Xavier de Horcasitas (Saint Francis Xavier of
Horcasitas), but generally called San Xavier for short. Writing about it on
May 7, 1748, Father Mariano called it Nuestra Señora de los Dolores del
Rio de San Xavier. It stood about three miles west of the Junction of Brushy
Creek and the San Gabriel, on the south bank of the San Gabriel, near San
Andres (Little River) Crossing. The place was near the highway the
Apaches traveled from their hill country homes to secure guns from the
French in east Texas. Apaches had many homes at a village on Brushy
Creek, Parage de las Ánimas, which were seen by mission Indians in 1747.[32]

The mission site had spacious fields of "most fertile" soil, "watered with
good and plentiful water." During its first year the mission planted potatoes, maize and other grains, received forty cargoes of supplies from San
Antonio by mule train and had spent $5,083.50 on the entire project. The

supplies included food, clothing, seed, gifts for Indians and religious ornaments. Huts were built to house the tribes already there—Tonkawa, Mayeye,
Deadose, Bidai, Orcoquiza, Hierbipiame, Yojuane and Coco, with others
coming daily. By March Father Mariano was forced to instruct his neophytes
not to solicit any new tribes. Asking tribes not already members of the
mission to remain at a "convenient distance," he had to refuse food to all
except those already helping in the fields at the missions. Twenty-eight
soldiers lived at the mission to supervise the Indians with the stock, assist
with labor in the fields, guard the horses, protect the missions and families
there, and escort supply trains of maize and other produce from San Antonio. They had also built a wooden stockade pen for stock and oxen.[33]

When the royal approval for the first mission arrived in December 1747,
it also authorized two additional missions on the San Xavier, to be built
within eight months, and sent appropriations for supplies, ornaments, and
a year's salary for six missionaries.[34]

Troubles besieged all Texas missions, but the San Xavier complex was
especially ill-fated—far inland, isolated, near the warlike Apaches, unfortunate in the character of some of the personnel, particularly the soldiers,
and almost continuously a subject of political controversy. On May 4, 1748,
more than sixty Apaches attacked San Xavier, ransacking the houses and
attempting to stampede the horses. The soldiers and two hundred Indians
living there drove them off, but two mission Indians returning with buffalo
meat were killed. The mission Indians became frightened and wanted to
move to the woods for safety. By the end of the year, the Apaches struck
with three more raids, each time running off horses belonging to the
Spaniards and Indians. They also killed three soldiers and four Indian con-
verts. Even more apprehensive, the Indians did flee to the woods but Father
Mariano persuaded them to return.[35]

The second mission, San Ildefonso, also Yldefonso (Saint Adolphus),
was ready by February 1749 a short distance down river from San Xavier,
near the junction of las Ánimas and San Xavier. Nine missionaries were
in charge of the Coco, placed there until the third mission, Candelaria, was
completed. They deserted soon for their old haunts between the Colorado
and Brazos. While away they contracted smallpox and measles but those
well enough were persuaded to return. Misión Nuestra Señora de la Candelaria (Our Lady of Candlemas) was ready by April 14, 1749, near the
other two, and like them, on the south bank of the river. Indians were assigned to the three missions according to their linguistic affiliations, with
Tonkawa, Mayeye, Hierbipiame and Yojuane, all related, at San Xavier,

totalling 213. Ildefonso had sixty-five families numbering 202, and the Coco and kinsmen were at Candelaria.[36]

During an illness of Fray Mariano's, Father Benito Fernández de Santa Ana took charge of the missions. He found the water supply plentiful, irrigation on the San Xavier easier than at San Antonio, and the soil fertile enough to support the three missions and all the Indians of the entire Texas province, plus many Spaniards, too. The climate was good and the natural fruits of the area both bountiful and useful. But he also noted that the soldiers did not have their families with them, so were lonely and unhappy; there were only two women at the post; a presidio was badly needed; the missions were almost continuously short of supplies, and a number of the soldiers were guilty of bad conduct. In the summer of 1750 Ildefonso was so short of supplies that some of the Indian residents camped in the woods about a league away. An epidemic of smallpox hit them, killing forty. That June, Lieutenant Jose Joaquín de Eca y Músquiz was delegated to survey the missions and investigate other possible sites which might be better. He went up the San Xavier seven leagues to Santa María de la Visitación crossing, about at present Hoxie Crossing. His report contained detailed statistics on the missions and detailed descriptions of the river and adjacent land up the San Gabriel and Brushy Creek (las Ánimas). The three missions had 480 Indians living there in July 1750, of whom 266 had been baptised. The report described Apache Crossing (Paso de los Apaches) five miles above the junction of San Xavier River and las Ánimas and just east of present San Gabriel community. In present Williamson County, it described the Santa Rosa de Viterbo Crossing two leagues up river from the missions and Santa María. Musquiz believed the best places for irrigation were at Santa María and Santa Rosa, recommending the missions be moved to one of them. He also reported that San Ildefonso was successfuly growing maize, beans and chili although the season was dry.[37]

At the same time Musquiz visited the area around Hoxie (Santa María de la Visitación) he found level plains, sand banks and places to obtain water on the high south bank of the San Xavier River. Near the river was a lake (*lago*) about 940 feet by 97 feet in size and containing an abundance of fish and alligators. Encircled by trees, the lake emptied into the river near a wooded arroyo which formed a semicircle. In this cove was a level pasture, abundantly wooded, about 3,400 by 1,600 feet in size. The land was rich and fertile, free of washes or gullies from overflow. Adjacent to the site were three or four sizeable low plains, separated from each other by a small, low hill and arroyos. Stone was plentiful on a place measuring about 19,500 by 5,500 feet. Musquiz suggested building a dam on a lower level of rock or clay where animals would not become stuck. Wagons could be constructed from timber nearby and used to haul the stone and tools to build missions. One huge tree measured "about thirteen feet," presumably in girth ("tan gruesos que se midio uno, y tuvo sinco varas de gruezo"). On the north was wooded land

> which rises up in a slope because of floods, but is very thickly grown up with big trees, to a height of twelve varas [about thirty-three feet] and about one-eighth of a league long, forming a large forest in which were many kinds of oak, ash, walnut, cottonwood, ayagil, hackberry [palo blanco] and live oak, all of which can be used as timber for building; and, thickly growing on the ground, plum, mesquite, buckthorn, grape, and other wild fruits.[38]

The proposed new sites were ignored, however, and long-projected irrigation ditches and a dam were finally started October 12, 1750, near the old missions. Extra rations of hominy, salt, tobacco and bulls for slaughter were issued to those working on the project. When buffalo appeared nearby, soldiers were sent out with Indians to hunt them to supplement their diet. Work on the irrigation project was intermittent. The missionaries and other officials had long urged the addition of a presidio for protection and one was finally authorized on March 30, 1751. It was placed a short distance up the river from the missions, "two gun shots" from San Xavier Misión and called Presidio San Francisco Xavier de Gigedo.[39]

If Father Mariano's plans for his missions were carried out, the San Xavier church was about twenty-eight feet long, with cell offices about twenty-two feet long close by, built around a square enclosed by palisades. Corn cane and the bark of a tree in the area were available for brush huts, apparently used until more substantial stone-adobe-timber structures could be erected of nearby materials. The master brick mason, who served also as architect, and a carpenter were in charge of the work, laying out the barracks, plazas, and other sections of the buildings.[40]

Mission life was so regulated that every morning and afternoon the Indians attended prayer services at which time the missionaries issued to each one, old or young, a gourdful of maize. This staple food was usually boiled or toasted. About every other week, a bull was killed and the meat distributed among the residents. Supplementing the diet, wild fruit, berries, prickly pear, buffalo, deer, fish and wild turkey were added when available. Christianized Indians from the San Antonio missions assisted the priests as teachers-interpreters. Neophytes learned something of agriculture, construction and crafts, as well as the tenets of Christianity.[41]

Until the end of 1751 the missions thrived about as well as others throughout Texas, but when a new captain, Don Felipe de Rábago, was assigned to take charge of the presidio it "sounded the deathknell of the San Xavier missions." Captain Rábago was accused of bad conduct in every city he passed through, from Mexico to central Texas. In San Antonio, he had formed a liaison with the wife of one of his soldiers. When they reached the missions, the captain had the soldier thrown in jail and tortured, then Rábago scorned penitence and was unable or unwilling to work with the missionaries. Fray José Ganzábal and Fray Miguel Pinilla first expressed grave concern over the rapidly deteriorating morale of the missions, then declared the captain and several soldiers who had been misbehaving excommunicate and sent a petition to Rábago on March 2, 1752. The captain disdained to reply. A Coco Indian was beaten for infraction of a rule, whereupon the entire tribe fled the mission. On the evening of May 11, Fathers Ganzábal and Pinilla stood in the door of Mission Candelaria with Juan Joseph Zevallos, husband of the woman who had an affair with Rábago. As they conversed, Zevallos was killed by a blunderbuss shot and Fray Ganzábal by an arrow through his heart. All other missionaries except one hastily left the mission. An Indian resident of San Xavier confessed that he and four soldiers had committed the murders, but at Rábago's instigation.[42]

The spring of 1752 was very dry. Shallow pools with weeds and slime appeared in the San Gabriel. The following winter and spring continued dry and dead fish were being seen in the water. By August 1753 illnesses and deaths reached epidemic proportions. The river ceased to run, leaving stagnant pools which became intolerably foul. "The phenomenon was mysterious because there was plentiful rainfall and other streams in the vicinity were full."[43] Although the missions had been Father Mariano's brain-child and special pride, he wrote afterwards of the tragedies:

The sacrilegious homicides having been perpetrated, the elements at once conspired, declaring divine justice provoked; for in the sky appeared a ball of fire so horrible that all were terrified, and with so notable a circumstance that it circled from the presidio to the mission of the Occisos [Orcoquiza], and returned to the same presidio, when it exploded with a noise as loud as could be made by a heavily loaded cannon. The river ceased to run, and its waters became so corrupt that they were extremely noxious and intolerable to the smell. The air became so infected that all who went to the place, even though merely passing, became infected by the pest, which became so malicious that many of the inhabitants died, and we all found ourselves in the last extremes of life. Finally, the land became so accursed that what had been a beautiful plain became converted into a thicket, in which opened horrible crevices that caused terror. And the inhabitants became so put to it, in order to escape the complete extermination which threatened them, that they moved more than thirty leagues away.[44]

For several years the matter of moving the San Xavier missions was hotly debated. Finally in February 1756 the *junta general* of Mexico ordered them transferred. In May the viceroy approved establishing them on the San Sabá River, where the wealthy Don Pedro de Terreros was interested in some silver mines. He had offered the Church a munificent gift if the missions were placed there, for he felt they would aid in his promotion of the mines and protect against raiding Indians. On both counts the missions failed, for disaster struck them faster than at San Xavier. After failing to attract the Lipan Apaches to the missions, suffering an attack by two thousand Comanches, the murder of two priests and six others, and repeated other raids and attacks, the San Sabá missions were abandoned. The religious ornaments which had been moved there from San Xavier were burned in one of the raids. The old mission buildings on the San Gabriel were abandoned to time. Well-known historian Herbert Bolton, who visited the San Xavier sites in 1907, still believed them to be in Williamson County. He found remnants of the dam, piles of rubble where the main buildings had stood, and identified stone used in the school at San Gabriel and in chimneys of homes in the vicinity as having come from the missions.[45]

In spite of the many disasters suffered at San Xavier, accounts of that period compared those missions in a favorable light with others in Texas, the latter said to have had fewer baptisms, less cooperation and interest among the natives, and no attendance at prayer and other services. The devotion and diligence of the San Xavier missionaries seems to have been unsurpassed anywhere. When the mission opened, more Indians sought admittance than the friars could handle. Many of the high officials who visited the missions praised the setting and the work done "in the royal place of San Xavier in the Province of Texas."[46]

LATER EXPLORATION
AND END OF SPANISH RULE

During the time he was stationed at the San Xavier missions, Rábago y Terán explored the surrounding countryside and in 1761, he returned to the Williamson County area, entering the county from Llano, following the south bank of the South San Gabriel eastward to about present Georgetown, thence traveling along the north bank. When he reached the area of Circle-ville or Hoxie, he recrossed to the south side.[47]

The brilliant, cultured Frenchman, Athanase de Mézières, son-in-law of St. Denis, also did service for Spain. Talented in dealing with Indians, he became lieutenant governor of Natchitoches presidio, a captain in the infantry and was to be named governor of Texas, but died in November 1779 shortly before his confirmation arrived. De Mézières explored San Gabriel country about sixty years after St. Denis' expedition had crossed it. Holding councils with the Indians and giving them presents along the way, de Mézières described his trip along the San Gabriel in August and September 1779:

> The San Xavier rises in the hills which extend westward. . . . It receives the waters of the San Andres, and other smaller tributaries, and joins the Brazos. There is an abundance of oyster shells, some broken, some whole, others scattered, but the greater part of them so closely and firmly amalgamated that they appear to be of the remotest antiquity.
>
> Few rivers can compare with the San Xavier in the clearness of its waters or in abundance of fish. The surrounding country could be irrigated to avoid the uncertainty of the weather, and mills could be erected. The number of wild horses and cattle that graze here and which could be utilized as beasts of burden or as food is incredible. The buffalo is not lacking, for variety; while with thyme, lavender, sage, winter savory, and other aromatic plants, the goats and sheep would thrive. The fragrant flowers that abound in the fields offer splendid facilities for the culture of bees. Hogs could be fattened freely with acorns, without the costly expense of grain. Prime oil could be obtained from the nuts, and the bears will furnish a not inferior quality of lard. In the woods will be found, in addition to abundant game, lumber, and in the quarries, all kinds of stone for building.[48]
>
> The proximity of Béxar, of the Tuacanas [Tawakoni], the Indians of San Theodoro, the Panis-Mahas, and other friends, will result in frequent visits, trade, assistance, confidences, and reconciliations. The settlement of this river will bring about the quieting or punishment of the Comanches; will furnish the shortest and safest communication with the adjoining Louisiana; and, finally, will arouse in the subject greater desire to traverse, visit, and settle this extensive territory, at sight of which I have been unable to refrain from rapture and ecstasy, which, indeed, would be occasioned in the most stupid and indifferent.[49]

Most of the Spanish and French activity in central Texas took place during the eighteenth century. French influence was intermittent and brief, but important, for it was the catalyst which spurred the Spanish to more concentrated efforts. Spanish domination of central Texas was almost complete. The King of Spain approved the founding of each of the San Xavier missions along San Gabriel River, approved the large expeditions which crossed the future Williamson County, and his government vied with that of the Indians for control of this "land of clear water." After the San Xavier missions were removed the almost constant traffic across the county greatly diminshed, but the several highways crossing it remained in use. Continuing their trade with either the French or the Spanish and with the Indians of east Texas, the Lipan Apaches, Tonkawas and Comanches followed the San Gabriel River eastward and back. Another trail from Mexico and Bexar (San Antonio) came north through the county, crossing Arroyo de las Ánimas (Brushy Creek) about at Blue Hill (Rice's Crossing) and the San Gabriel near Circleville or Hoxie, to Tenoxtitlan or Nashville on the Brazos River. This was sometimes called the Comanche Trail.[50] Spain granted some land titles in Texas for ecclesiastical purposes and to some individuals for important services to the kingdom, but most so-called Spanish land grants in Williamson County were in reality grants from the Republic of Mexico. By 1765 only approximately 750 Europeans lived in all of Texas.[51]

Early in the nineteenth century Spain was in deep trouble at home and the people of Mexico were restive about foreign domination.[52] The United States' purchase of Louisiana in 1803 accelerated the frontier movement toward Spanish Texas and soon a few daring men from the states were entering Texas to catch wild horses, to trade, or to spy.[53] By 1805 Texas was exciting much attention in the United States.[54] Almost simultaneously with Moses Austin's negotiations for a colony in Texas (1820), Mexico became an independent monarchy (1821) and the rule, but not the influence, of Spain was at an end.

HERITAGE FROM THE SPANISH

The legacies from three hundred years of Spanish rule are vast in Texas. In 1551, the University of Mexico was founded, almost a century before the colonies which became the United States were established. Until nearly 1800, Mexico City was the metropolis for all or most of the western hemisphere.[55] Certainly until the early 1800s, central Texas was in closer touch with the ancient land to the south than with the fledgling United States of America.

The Spanish considered the Indian "worth civilizing and his soul worth saving." They also held a strong mercantilistic view which favored their own people over the Indians and they projected a feudalistic government for Texas. To control revolting Indians or to keep out the French, they established missions and when Louis Juchereau de Saint Denis entered Texas in 1714, the Spanish set about seriously to colonize strategic parts of the state. Relatively few Spaniards lived in Texas, however. In 1744, the non-Indian population was estimated at 1,500. Twenty years later, the same figure was repeated, but this time, half the 1,500 were actually domesticated Indians. The politically motivated missions also provided Christian seminaries for the Indians and trained them in agricultural and industrial pursuits. Missions were planned for a life of ten years only, after which the government would return the communal lands of the mission farms, ranches and gardens to the Indians who had been trained there. Mission workshops contributed to the economic and social life, training natives to use looms, make fabrics, build irrigation systems, learn stock-raising and agricultural methods. While priests were attempting to teach new religious concepts to the Indians, they also introduced them to almost every plant and animal of Europe, taught language, law and tradition to the native people.[56]

In the more remote frontier posts, missionary-priests were usually paid $450 annually. In turn, they explored the country, negotiated peace with hostile tribes, informed the government concerning foreign intrusion and political affairs, and devotedly taught and led the Indians into Christianity and an economically more self-sufficient way of life. Father Ganzábal, who was martyred at Misión San Xavier, was only one of several priests to lose their lives in mission work. Priests held mass at sunrise and sunset for the Indians, all unmarried persons and children being required to attend. On Sundays and daily during Lent, everyone attended services and special processions were held at Eastertime.[57]

The land grants of the 1700s created the first land barons of Texas. Most of the so-called Spanish grants, however, were actually made during the Mexican regime.[58] The laws in presentday Texas concerning property rights of women, water rights on streams, and the basic principles regarding mines—all these laws were contributions from the Spanish. When the conquistadores brought horses, cattle and sheep into Texas, opening a livestock business as early as 1650, they founded one of the most important trades the state has ever known. Spaniards were driving cattle to market in 1650; the first cattle drive in New England took place in 1665, fifteen years later.[59] Mustangs were said to have been rounded up in present Williamson County and sold in about 1770. Mares in droves brought one peso or less, wild mules up to eight pesos and a broken horse, six pesos.[60] The first cowhands were Spanish. They created the first rodeos and the practice of cattle branding was introduced into Texas in the Spanish missions.[61]

Spanish architectural styles have been absorbed into the traditional and contemporary designs of Texas homes and public buildings. The folklore, literature, music and art have been greatly influenced by Spanish culture. Even today, Spanish quarters exist in many Texas towns and cities, and "from belfries . . . still sound bells that were cast in Old Spain."[62]

Although most early Texas trade was in cattle, horses and sheep, during the 1700s precious metals from Chihuahua, Coahuila, Nuevo Leon and New Mexico passed through Texas en route to New Orleans for shipment to Spain. Some of these loads of silver or gold passed through the central Texas region and led to a great store of legends about treasure buried for safe keeping, or hidden in a cave near the Balcones Fault line. Sporadically, treasure seekers have probed the many caves of the county and dug assiduously for the hidden cargo. Writer J. Frank Dobie who attended Southwestern University and others have recorded many of these legends.[63] The Texas bee industry obtained its original stock from the Spanish missions. Honey and wax were important to the pioneer as food and candles.[64]

If mailing addresses were listed for Williamson County from the time Europeans first entered Mexico in 1517, they would include:

Takatchue pouetsu, "land of good water," as the Tonkawas called the county.[65]

Nueva España (New Spain), vaguely applied from 1518 for about three hundred years to the unknown lands north of Mexico including Texas.

Nouvelle Espagne, French version of Nueva España, which appeared on French maps after la Salle and other Frenchmen visited and claimed parts of Texas in the seventeenth and eighteenth centuries.

Nuevas Felipinas (also spelled Philipinas), or the New Philippines, which designated Texas in the mid-seventeenth century. The name was borrowed from the Philippine Islands which were christened in 1543 in honor of Prince Philip of Spain, later King Philip II. A map dated 1767 designated the territory "Texas o Philipinas."[66]

Kingdom of the Tejas, well known by 1676.[67]

Texas and Coahuila, a political division of which Don Domingo Terán de los Rios was named the first Spanish governor in 1691, a post he held until 1718.[68]

"The royal place of San Xavier in the Province of Texas," mentioned December 27, 1751.[69]

Comandancia general de las Provincias Internas, a governmental territory created by the King of Spain on August 22, 1776, just six weeks after the American colonies' Declaration of Independence. The Internal Provinces included Texas, New Mexico, states of northern Mexico and the Californias. The capital was Chihuahua.

Words of Spanish derivation are common in American English, particularly the language of the southwest. Among place names in Williamson County which originated during the Spanish regime are San Gabriel, Salado Creek (meaning "salty"), Yegua Creek ("wild mare"), Sandoval and Balcones. Originally the name for San Gabriel was San Xavier.* On occasion that form was altered, appearing in early Spanish, French and English records variously as *Xavier, Xabier, Javier* and *Javriel*.[70] When settlers of the future Williamson County petitioned for a new county in 1848, they suggested calling it San Gabriel County. The State Legislature vetoed that idea but the name lived on as geographic and other titles. Gabriel designates the three main branches of the San Gabriel River, the north, south and middle forks; San Gabriel Mountain; the towns of Gabriel Mills and South San Gabriel in the western end of the county. Just east of the county line, the town of San Gabriel still exists, a place long thought to be in Williamson County and so listed on early postal records. (The San Gabriel River was shown on some Spanish maps as Rio Claro, or Arroyo Claro.) The name of Salado Creek is believed by some to have switched with that of Lampasas River to the north, for Lampasas means "channel with water plants" but is salty and cannot grow them. On the other hand, Salado means "salty," is not salty, but does grow water plants. Yegua Creek in southeastern Williamson County was so-named for the droves of wild horses found there by the early settlers. *Yegua* was an Indian word which came into English via Spanish. The community of Sandoval was probably named for Captain Manuel de Sandoval, Spanish governor of Texas 1734-1736. Balcones, Spanish for "balcony," described the long shelf of cliffs and sharp hills explorers saw along the fault line.[71]

Non-geographic words of Spanish origins are abundant. Spaniards referred to Indians as *Indios (Yndios) bravos* before they were educated in the missions. After conversion, they were *Indios reducidos*. Thus the expression "Indian brave" derived directly from Spanish. *Rancho* designated a laborer's house and *rancheria* a group of these houses. If the cluster of homes also included a church, it became a *pueblo*. Sometimes a pueblo contained "only the church and the curate's house."[72] Adobe, patio, plaza,

---

* San Xavier is not the Spanish equivalent of San Gabriel but the corrupted forms of San Xavier looked and sounded enough like San Gabriel possibly to have suggested that name to Anglo-American settlers.

mesa and sierra came into the English laguage without change. The word "canyon" added only the "y" to approximate the sound of the Spanish form. Tuna, tornado, alfalfa and cockroach are directly from the Spanish. The word "prairie" has both French and Spanish connections, but strictly French is the name "gopher" (*gaufre,* meaning "honeycomb") describing that small animal's home.[73]

The cattle business, itself a gift of the Spanish, could hardly be described without liberal use of Mexican or Spanish words. Ranch came from *ranchero,* for "headquarters"; mustang from *mesteño* (strayed cattle); lariat (from *la reata*); bronco, meaning "rough" or "wild"; vaquero (from *vaca,* "cow"); stampede, lasso, corral, cinch, burro, pinto, buckaroo and rodeo (roundup) are examples. Other such words are the outgrowth of the hard, wild life of nineteeth century cattle commerce—words like vamoose (from *vamos,* "let's go"), desperado, calaboose (*calabozo,* for "jail") and hoosegow (from *juzgado* meaning "court of justice").[74]

IV

Anglo-American Settlers
And The Indians: Three Decades

NEW PEOPLE

About the time Mexico was shaking off the authority of Spain, Anglo-Americans in large numbers were becoming interested in Texas for the first time. Moses Austin negotiated in 1820 for an Anglo-American colony in Texas and the next year his son, Stephen F. Austin, arrived with the settlers. Mexico became an independent monarchy in 1821, an empire in 1822, a Republic in 1824, and from this point began a decade as the father-land of Texas. Hoping to strengthen her frontiers and develop Texas' resources, in 1825 Mexico passed a colonization law encouraging "foreign emigration."[1] President Guadalupe Victoria was confident that the new-comers to Texas would erect mills, develop the cattle industry, and "recruit the exhausted treasury" of Mexico. The Junta (Mexican Congress) organized an empresario system, offering about 67,000 acres of land to promoters who brought two hundred families into the state.[2] All colonists were required to adhere to Catholicism, the state religion, although "the Anglo-American settlers' brand of Catholicism was relaxed."[3]

Mexico issued grants of enormous land tracts to its own people. In present Williamson County, Miguel Davila, Pedro Zarza and Joe Justo Liendo received large grants in 1833. Ten leagues on the "San Jarviel" (San Gabriel River) were transferred by the State of Coahuila and Texas on October 22, 1833, to Rafael de Aguirre, who resold some of it in 1838. In 1857 his heirs sold eleven leagues for $22,000. The Zarza property went to a daughter, Dolores de Zarza of Goliad County, who sold eleven leagues for $11,000 in 1851. These sales brought less than twenty-five cents an acre. Other tracts smaller in size, owned by Mexicans or by Anglos, sometimes brought even less. In 1861 and 1863, land sold at public auction for delinquent taxes was purchased for a total of $1.30 for 796 acres, and $4.85 acquired 2,952 acres.[4] Mexican owners apparently never occupied these early grants. Only three persons with Spanish or Mexican names, Hosea and Pritty Maria, and Francisco Maria, were listed in the 1850 census of Williamson County. They were not land owners at that time.[5]

Immigration from the United States was sporadic at first, but not for long. Texas' total population in 1821 was 7,000, but by 1836 it was variously estimated at from 30,000 to 50,000.[6] The 30,000 figure included 400 Wacos, 200 Tawakonis, 800 Tonkawas, 350 Coushattas, 250 Alabamas, 2,000 Comanches, 500 Caddoes, 900 Lipans, 800 other Indians in many small bands, 8,000 of the "civilized tribes," 5,000 Negroes, 3,470 Mexicans, and about 15,800 Anglos from the United States.[7] These new colonists were called Texians at first and through the years of the Republic of Texas, but after annexation the form, Texan, gradually took precedence.[8]

Entry of settlers and capital into Texas and use of the boundless natural resources at hand speeded the surge of national growth and unification over the entire continent, but also led to much of the turmoil of the nineteenth century: problems of slavery, tariffs, sectional strife, war, building of railroads, reconstruction and industrial expansion. A depression in the states after the War of 1812 and the financial panic of 1819 gave men an additional motive to keep moving with the frontier.[9] The flow slowed somewhat in 1822 and 1823 due to a severe drouth in Texas, to discouraging accounts from early immigrants, and because of delays in Mexico and Stephen F. Austin's prolonged stay there. But Austin was persistent and persuasive, a good organizer who looked for people of good character to bring to Texas, so his colonization plan came off. The north end of his colony was the southern ridge of what became Williamson County, the line being the watershed between the Colorado and Brazos Rivers. His colonists, handpicked because they were searching for permanent homes, soon became familiar with Williamson County lands and a number of them drifted over from the Austin Colony to settle in the valleys of Brushy Creek and San Gabriel River. These highly-regarded men from Austin's group lent an early stability to the little settlements on Brushy and San Gabriel in times when this was not always so. Austin was credited with meticulously living up to his empresario agreements. He declared that "the colonization busi-

ness is the last on earth that any man ought to undertake for the sole purpose of making money."[10] Numerous land companies speculated on Texas
land, sold fraudulent scrip, and one promoter described in "glowing terms"
the advantages of emigration, "well calculated to further his scheme. Of
the hardships and privations . . . he was discreetly silent."[11]

The Robert Leftwich-Sterling Clack Robertson empresario contract of
1825 encompassed Williamson County territory, but actual settlement was
long delayed and when Robertson finally in 1835 brought families to Texas,
he took them to the Salado (Bell County) area. A small number of them
moved into Williamson County, but most of the Williamson County settlers who did not migrate directly from the United States came from Bastrop, Hornsby's Bend and Webber's Prairie to the south, and from Nashville and Port Sullivan on the Brazos to the east.[12]

Mexico's invitation for colonization had been enthusiastically accepted,
indeed, so much so that the Republic revoked it in 1830, but not in time
to halt the whirlpool of events and emotions which led to the Texas Revolution in 1835. The new Texas nation was established in April 1836, remaining a sovereign country for a decade prior to annexation to the United
States.

NEW PATHWAYS

Before 1830, probably one or two years earlier, Indians laid out the
Double File Trail across Williamson County. This trail was especially well
known in the nineteenth century, crossing Brushy Creek at Kenney's Fort
and San Gabriel River at Towns Mill. Jim Shaw, a Delaware Indian who
acted as an interpreter and scout for the Texas army in the 1840s and 1850s,
told the story of the trail. Delawares moved into "the Redlands" of east
Texas after being pushed westward. When Anglo-Americans occupied "the
Redlands" about 1828 or 1829, many of the Delawares moved on into
Mexico near the Rio Grande. They rode in two lines or "double files," and
for many years afterwards they periodically traveled this trail to visit their
earlier home in east Texas. Texas Rangers rode over the Double File Trail
and it was well remembered by the pioneers of Williamson County.[13]

The Double File Trail crossed the Colorado River near Webberville east
of Austin, entered Williamson County south of what in 1838 became Kenney Fort, crossing Brushy Creek about 250 yards below the present Katy
railroad bridge there. Here the trail turned west, passed west of the old

Freeman Smalley graveyard,* established in 1851, continued over the hill in Merrell's field past where Frank Smalley lived in the valley south of Chandler's Branch, went by the place settled by Bony Ferguson, later owned by J. M. Jester. At this point, the trail went up the branch past the widow Chandler's place (afterwards the home of Thomas Thaxton), crossed the branch and turned eastward by the west end of Mesquite Flat, near the east line of Henry Tisdale's field. Near there, it ascended the high point where a clump of live oak trees grew, passed east of the Joseph Barnhart place (later the William and Henry Palm, the John Caldwell, and the John Nash place). The trail led near where J. J. Johnson later had a two story home, turned east and crossed Mankin's Branch not far from where Richard Sansom settled (later the La Rue place). From there it ran in an almost direct line to the San Gabriel, crossing it seventy-five or eighty yards below where Towns Mill dam was constructed. W. C. Dalrymple built a log cabin near this crossing and John C. Compton, who later resided in Williamson County, was with a Ranger company stationed there. From this point, the trail went across a branch near the Elias Queen residence on Queen Hill, over Opossum Creek on the Dick Robbins place east of Walburg, forded Donahoe Creek and headed toward Bryant's Station on Little River, between Davilla and Buckholts. The trail crossed Little River between the three forks and Bryant's Station, and crossed the Brazos River near the falls at Sarahville de Viesca (later the town of Milam) near present Marlin.[14]

Double File Trail was both an important highway and a landmark. The ambitious, ill-fated Santa Fe Expedition of 1841 intersected the trail between Brushy Creek and Chandler Branch, and followed it north through the county. The expedition had come into the county from camps near Austin via the Military Road which crossed Brushy Creek a short distance above Kenney Fort and joined the Double File Trail north of the creek. Commissary and quartermaster supply wagons also traveled the military route, especially in 1846 when Captain Ross's Rangers were stationed at the Double File Crossing on the San Gabriel. The old Military Road led to many of the earliest settlements near Brushy Creek including those of Nelson Merrell, Joseph Barnhart, Captain Ladd and Davis Chandler.[15] Deep ruts were cut by wagon traffic into solid rock at the river crossings of

* The very old Freeman Smalley cemetery is located thus: from Highway 79 east of Round Rock, turn north on FM 1460, go .7 of a mile and turn to gravel road on the right. The cemetery is several hundred feet to the right of the gravel road, along an old fence line lined with trees. (The earlier road, a part of the Double File Trail, ran along where the fence now is. The old road made a sharp turn at the corner of the cemetery, coming to that point almost directly from where Palm Valley Church is now located.) The cemetery site was owned in 1973 by John Nash.

those days. Tracks of this kind were plainly visible in 1973 along the flat
north bank of Brushy Creek, just west of Interstate Highway 35 bridge at
Round Rock.

During the 1830s, what became Williamson County was a part of a vast
area known as the Municipality of District of Viesca, named for Augustín
Viesca, governor of Coahuila and Texas. In November 1835, the name was
changed to Municipality of Milam. This district lay north of el Camino
Real and extended beyond the valley of Rio Brazos de Dios. Mexico established a fort at Tenoxtitlan, about fourteen miles northeast of present
Caldwell on the Brazos, which it abandoned as an army post in 1832. Francis
Smith turned it into a busy trading post, penning a note on March 11, 1832,
"I know not what I have wrote for I have always been in a hurry and full
of business." Smith noted that French traders sold buffalo robes at $5.25
apiece and that "those prunella shoes would never sell here they have two
faults no heels & square toes. Please never send me any square toes." The
Indians and frontiersmen exchanged buffalo, deer, beaver, leopard, bear,
otter, badger and wild cattle hides for goods. These included sweet wine,
whiskey, cheap tobacco, coffee, sugar, flour, aniseed, raisins, rice, molasses,
almonds; "tolerable good broadcloth," calico, white domestic, strong thread,
thimbles; sox, black silk handkerchiefs; candles, soap; plates, bowls, tin
pans, tin cups, pitchers decorated with red flowers; blankets, ox wagons, fire
steels, pocket knives, bullets, axes, tomahawks; spurs; fish hooks and lines,
gimlets, awls; iron, brass and Jews harps. Smith wrote his factory for brass
kettles, beaver traps and rifles.[16] The large trading post was a long distance
from Williamson County for those days, and even farther away was the seat
of the Viesca District government. First it was located at Sarahville de
Viesca, then changed to Nashville on the Brazos on present Highway 79
between Gauze and Hearne. Legal business for the few settlers in the Williamson County area had to be transacted at these villages and a large number of Williamson County abstracts were executed in Viesca District.[17]

These were years of revolution. Bartlett Sims, later of Williamson
County, was appointed to the 1832 Convention Committee attempting to
solve problems between Texas and Mexico at San Felipe de Austin. He was
a delegate in 1833 to the Convention declaring Texas separate from Coahuila and a representative at a similar November 3, 1833 meeting.[18] Sam
Houston made his debut in Texas politics in 1833, declaring that the people
of Texas were determined to separate from Coahuila and to form their own
government. Since the new settlers were children of American Revolutionary soldiers, talk of freedom was in the air and in the blood. Moreover,
these pioneers had no ties with Mexico.

A few extremely isolated settlements* appeared in the San Gabriel and Brushy valleys during the 1830s. Another depression in the United States in 1837 gave impetus to the westward movement. Exploratory sorties from Austin's burgeoning colony to the south, visits by land speculators and their surveying crews, and hunting excursions from nearby villages also increased the activity in Williamson County territory.[20] Arriving newcomers were regarded by many of the Indians as a matter of life and death to them. The frightened natives took either a warlike stance or sought protection by alliance with the pioneers. Generally, the Tonkawas and Lipan Apaches preferred to join ranks with the Anglos against their mutual enemy, the Comanches. The settlers learned very quickly that the Comanches could be particularly dangerous neighbors. As surveyors, hunters, or settlers came, Indians saw their hunting grounds threatened and organized raids against them. The Mexican government encouraged such forays and furnished the Indians with arms and ammunition.[21] The question of Indian relations became a paramount issue. In November 1835, the Texas Consultation composed a declaration guaranteeing the Indians "peaceable enjoyment of their rights to their lands as we do our own. . . . The Texans were the first violators of the pledge. . . . The ink was scarcely dry on the paper, when locators were seen in their forests."[22]

The stakes were high for surveyors—sickness or attacks by Indians were always a possibility and the workmen were usually a long way from help. On the other hand, surveyors were paid handsome acreage for their services and many of them considered the prize worth the serious risks. Early surveying practices were picturesque, if often inaccurate. Measurements might be "a cigarette's length" or "half a day's walk." Spanish law had required surveyors to indicate each corner of property to a new owner "in a loud voice." The grantee acknowledged his understanding by throwing rocks, firing guns, shouting aloud, or making other and sundry noises.[23]

Thomas A. Graves and his surveying crew were ambushed by Indians while working along the San Gabriel River in the fall of 1835 and two of the men were killed. Soon after, two men named Riley were caught as they crossed the same river. One was killed but the other managed to escape with the help of his rifle.[24] A surveyor named Lang was murdered in a fight with Indians sometime in 1836 while working near the headwaters of Brushy Creek and San Gabriel River under Captain George B. Erath.[25]

---

* Captain Cal Putnam built a block house near present Liberty Hill long before Austin was established and when his nearest white neighbor was at Hornsby's Bend, probably in the early 1830s. He had moved to Llano County by 1850.[19]

Neil McLennan, Sr. (also written McLellan) and his family moved to the Gabriel valley in the fall of 1835 or early 1836. The nearest habitation was said to be seventy-five miles away.[26] Margaret McLennan and her husband had two small sons and an infant. After unloading their wagon at their new home, Mr. McLennan and the older boy left to hunt in the woods to replenish their meat supply, while his wife and the other two children remained at camp. He returned late in the day to find the camp plundered and his family missing. Indians had tied up the woman and children, had taken their clothing and searched the camp. In a trunk they found a mirror which proved such a new and fascinating toy to the Indians, Mrs. McLennan was able to untie herself and the children and crawl with them into the brush out of sight. She located a kind of cave under a sheltering rock in the San Gabriel bottom. Searching for them, the Indians almost touched her, but darkness prevented the would-be captors from finding them. After spending the night in the cave, Mrs. McLennan and the children returned to their desolate camp the following morning. The husband had already gone to the nearest settlements for help. For several days Mrs. McLennan and the two children subsisted on "a little shattered corn" which she found in the dust by the wagon where the Indians had spilled it. When her husband and a company of men returned to camp, she thought they were Indians and ran away, but they caught her. "It is said that the meeting between Mr. McLellan [sic] and his wife was quite an affecting scene."[27]

TUMLINSON BLOCK HOUSE;
THE TEXAS REVOLUTION

One of the three first Ranger companies organized in Texas was assigned the task late in 1835 of building and occupying Tumlinson Block House Fort. This fort, four miles south of the heart of present Leander, was south of Block House Creek and about one-fourth mile east of present Highway 183. At the fort site were a spring and a large pecan tree where in 1973 a windmill stood at the A. S. Walker home. The fort consisted of a cedar blockhouse and stockade built by the spring a few steps east of a huge live oak "lookout" tree (now in front of the Walker home), where the Rangers cut steps in the trunk to climb and view the countryside. Scars on the tree trunk were still plain in 1973. In the mid-twentieth century Dr. James Edwin Pearce of the University of Texas estimated the tree to be at least five hundred years old.[28] From the lookout, early in 1836, the Rangers had a good view of the horizon since the only timber grew along the banks of the creeks. A cloud of dust in the distance warned pioneers to protect their families, cattle and other possessions from possible Indian raids. Judge Alexander Stuart Walker, who acquired the old Tumlinson Fort property soon after the Civil War as a law fee, was the first of three generations carrying the same name associated with the ranch. In 1972, the fourth A. S.

Tumlinson Fort lookout tree, and closeup showing scars where Rangers cut steps in the tree in 1836.

Walker still owned the rock ranch house built by his ancestors near the lookout tree.[29]

Rangers had appeared unofficially in Texas prior to 1835. Stephen F. Austin hired ten "rangers" in 1823 to protect his colony from the Tawakonis and Wacos who were warring against the Tonkawas. The Ranger corps was formally created by the Texas Provisional Government in October-November 1835. Three companies, under the command of one major, were to be formed, each company to consist of fifty-six men, who would elect their own captain, first lieutenant and second lieutenant. On November 28, 1835, Robert M. Williamson (for whom Williamson County was later named) was elected major in command of the three companies. An Indian fighter, Captain John J. Tumlinson, was chosen to lead the company assigned to build the fort near the headwaters of Brushy Creek.[30] The place came to be called by several names, Block House Fort, Block House Spring, or Tumlinson Fort.[31]

Captain Tumlinson and sixty mounted men, including Noah Smithwick who later recorded the story, met in January 1836 at Hornsby's Station on the Colorado River a little below where Austin (City) would be located, and from that place went to their appointed station on Block House Creek. Conrad Rohrer hauled the supplies. "We built the old Tumlinson block-house, making it our headquarters till the invasion of Santa Anna necessitated our recall, after which it was burned by the Indians and never rebuilt." The place was occupied by the Rangers for only about two months. During that time, a Mrs. Hibbons came to the fort after escaping from Indians and sought aid in rescuing her child from the natives.[32] When Tumlinson's company was recalled to Bastrop about March 1, 1836, because an advancing Mexican army threatened the ill-protected Texas frontier, the Tumlinson Rangers were ordered to cover the retreat of frightened families to safer positions—a flight known as the Runaway Scrape. The Rangers were then ordered to join General Sam Houston.[33] At Bastrop, Captain Tumlinson and his first lieutenant, Jo (Joseph) Rodgers, turned their command over to Major Williamson and went to move their own families out of danger.[34]

Noah Smithwick returned to Tumlinson Fort on a scouting mission before it was burned sometime in the summer of 1836. "We found the walls covered with . . . Indian drawings; every loose board being similarly ornamented." The pictures all showed Indians chasing buffalo. Smithwick considered the Comanches, whose art work he recognized on the Block House walls, to be remarkably skilled at drawing.[35]

> The old Tumlinson rangers were made up of citizens of Bastrop county, among them being Joseph Rodgers, who was first lieutenant, James Edmunston, Jimmie Curtice, Hugh M. Childers [sic], John Williams, Joe Berry, Jim Hamilton, Oliver Buckman, orderly sergeant; Calvin Barker, Felix W. Goff, Ganey Crosby, familiarly known as 'Choctaw Tom'; Joe Weeks and many others whose names I do not now recall.[36]

Joe Berry's family, Calvin Barker and John Williams later lived in the county, Joseph Rodgers was closely associated with it, and Hugh M. Childress received title to a league of land in the county-to-be on October 31, 1832. Besides being a hunter and an Indian fighter, Childress was a proficient fiddler and dancer and was in demand to play for dances in central Texas.[37] Joe Weeks lived for a time at Kenney Fort.

George Campbell Childress and Sterling Clack Robertson were delegates from Milam Municipality at the writing of the Texas Declaration of Inde-

pendence in March 1836 and at a meeting of the first Congress of the Re-
public on December 19 and 20, the same year.[38] A number of men who
later lived in Williamson County fought at San Jacinto when Texas won its
independence on April 21, 1836: Washington "Wash" Anderson, Willis.
Avery, Andrew Jackson Berry, John Chenoweth,* Sampson Connell,
Preston Conolee, Calvin Gage, A. M. Highsmith, Joseph Hyland, David
Hall Love, David Hutcheson McFadin, Reverend J. W. McHorse, Mc-
Dougald McLean, William Harrison Magill, Thomas H. Mays, Matthew
Mark Moss, J. L. Standefer,** William Bailey Standefer and Logan Vande-
veer. Others who did not participate in the battle but were stationed in the
camp opposite Harrisburg at the time, guarding baggage and supplies, in

*Huddle's painting of San Jacinto soldiers depicts Washington Anderson and
David H. McFadin.*

the rear guard, or sick, included John Bate Berry, Greenleaf Fisk, John A.
Gravis, Robert McNutt, Elisha Prewitt and M. J. Wells, the latter attached
to Deaf Smith's Spy Company. Closely associated with the county and in
the Battle of San Jacinto were John Angel, Micah Andrews, Jesse Billings-

---

* Thus spelled in Kemp. Variations are Chinneth (1850 census), Chenneyworth and
Chenneworth,[39] Chinneworth and Chinaworth.[40] Correct spelling not determined.
** James L. Standefer used that spelling of his surname; other branches of the family
sometimes used Standifer.

ley and Ganey Crosby. Others at the guard camp, also not residents of the county but closely connected with it in some way were Dr. Thomas Anderson and John D. Anderson (father and brother of Washington Anderson), John James Tumlinson and Robert McAlpin Williamson.[41] David H. Mc-Fadin and Washington Anderson are depicted in W. H. Huddle's well known painting,* "Santa Anna Before General Houston," also called "Surrender of Santa Anna." Other men from the county who served in the Texas Revolutionary forces included Benjamin Allen, Isaac Bunker, William A. Clopton, William C. Dalrymple, Samuel Damon, J. W. Darlington, Daniel Harrison, Francis White Johnson, William Johnson, Dr. Thomas Kenney, Adam Lawrence, James W. McSpaddin, J. P. Magill, James O. Rice, Bartlett Sims,** Henderson Upchurch and John Webster.[43]

The new Texas nation was wobbly, even stricken in many respects, but the people were resourceful and determined. Milam District, one of the twenty-three counties formed by the Republic, was huge—containing all of the future Williamson County and so many others that it has been dubbed "Mother of Counties." Milam was sparsely settled in 1836 but from that time on new families came to settle in ever larger numbers.

In its brief life as a Republic (1836-1845), Texas made several specific, unique and important contributions to western law: the union of common and civil law which produced the doctrines of community property and homestead exemption, the abolition of special pleading, and the blending of law and equity in a single court.

The Republic of Texas offered four classes of headright grants and titles. Free land went to men living in Texas before the Declaration of Independence, to soldiers or their heirs for military service, to westward moving families bent on making stable, new homes, and to land promoters with an eye to personal wealth and power. Prior to March 2, 1836, the head of a family received a league (for grazing) and a labor (for cultivation), or 4,428 plus 177 acres of land. Between March 2, 1836, and October 1, 1837, the head of a family could be granted 1,280 acres or a single man 640 acres. After that time the amounts were cut in half. Additional revisions were made in the early 1840s and in 1845, 320 acres were allotted settlers in vacant public lands under certain limited conditions.[44]

A paralyzing crop failure, depression and panic in the United States in

* Near the left of the painting, locate man with back facing viewer. Man on his right wearing a hat and standing in rear is Washington Anderson. The second person to viewer's right of Anderson, face partially hidden, is McFadin. The painting hangs near the entrance on the ground floor of the Texas State Capitol. Artist Huddle wrote Anderson to ask how he was dressed in the battle.[42]
** Also spelled Bartlett Simms.

1837 increased the flow of Anglo-Americans into Texas. The tide continued to the impoverished, struggling new nation in spite of Texas' poor crops in 1835, 1837 and 1838. Swedish immigrants began arriving from Europe in 1836, among them August Anderson, who came to Williamson County in the late 1830s.[45] With increased immigration came a rush in business transactions, and hasty surveying resulted in much confusion, duplication and overlapping of land titles.[46]

To prevent Indian depredations, the 1836 Texas Congress provided for blockhouses, forts and trading houses to be constructed along the frontier. Among President Sam Houston's strong supporters for friendship with the Indians was Noah Smithwick, who was well acquainted with central Texas tribes. Smithwick wrote:

> We finally fixed up a treaty. . . . One article of the treaty stiplated that a trading post should be established on Brushy at the site of the old Tumlinson block house, where the Indians could come and get supplies. They were fast becoming civilized in that respect, bartering buffalo robes and buckskins for blankets and clothing. V. R. Palmer agreed to take charge of the post. . . . Then, when the time in which the trading post was to have been established passed, and they came in with their skins to trade and found no trading house, they came to call on me to know why the treaty had not been complied with. As there was no plausible excuse for the failure, they held me responsible.[47]

In the summer of 1836, Captain William Hill and his company of Rangers found an Indian trail while on a scout along the San Gabriel River. Since the trail led toward the settlements, the men followed it for a day and found the Indians in a dense thicket. The fifty Rangers charged the camp of about seventy natives and drove them from that location.[48] Three Tonkawa chiefs, Ouchcala, Gosata and Harshokena, signed a treaty with the Texans on November 22, 1837.[49] About 1838, Taylor Smith, who settled near present Liberty Hill, and others in a small party of men were out hunting buffalo when they were fired upon by Indians. Smith had his arm broken, but none of the group was killed.[50]

Mirabeau Buonaparte Lamar succeeded President Houston in December 1838. His policy toward the native tribes was for merciless pursuit and their removal.[51] Lamar "favored war, hated Indians, and hated Houston."[52] To compound these problems in the fledgling nation, the currency was still weak and credit waned. Officials discovered in 1839 that some county commissioners had manufactured land certificates and circulated them so widely that it was impossible to distinguish between the genuine and the fraudulent.[53]

KENNEY FORT*

Brushy Cove, where Dyer Branch flows from the south into Brushy Creek, was the spot selected in 1838** by Dr. Thomas Kenney of Bastrop for his home and a fort. The doctor, along with Joseph Barnhart and others, built the fort on an elevated coveland on the south bluff of Brushy Creek and just west of its confluence with Dyer Branch. Down the hill from the fort was a spring which furnished drinking water for residents. Several log cabins fronting north (two to four are mentioned in various accounts) were erected, one of them described as "a double log house with a hall between the rooms" and with portholes on the exposed sides of the house.[54] To protect the houses, a picket stockade fence of upright logs eight to ten feet high enclosed about one-half acre of land. The fort overlooked the cove and occupied a commanding view of the countryside. Some of the original buildings remained in fairly good condition in the 1860s. When the Missouri-Kansas & Texas railroad bridge was built across Brushy Creek, it was located about two hundred yards west of Kenney Fort, south of Palm Valley. In the mid-twentieth century, foundations of the cabins, cedar posts and a portion of the flag pole remained.[55]

About fifteen people lived at Kenney Fort those first years, including Joseph Weeks and his family, Major Chenneyworth, James O. Rice, Henry A. Castleberry (or Castlebury), John Courtney, Jack Angel, Joseph Barnhart and Dr. Thomas Kenney. By the fall of 1838, Dr. Kenney was ready to move his family from Bastrop to the fort and in October he brought his wife, Mary Jane, and their daughters, Mary Jane, Clarissa and Anna (Ann) to their new home. On the evening of their arrival, smoke was seen to the north of the fort, so next morning Dr. Kenney, Major Chenneyworth, Mr. Weeks and Mr. Angel set out to investigate. Indians attacked them on the south bluff of Gunn's Branch where it runs into Chandler Branch, about four miles from the fort. Dr. Kenney was shot through the leg, the ball passing into his horse; Mr. Weeks' left arm was shattered from shoulder to elbow, and Major Chenneyworth was wounded in the nose by an arrow. The men fled toward the fort on horseback, but Dr. Kenney had to abandon his wounded horse after about a mile. The doctor then rode Mr. Angel's horse while Angel ran along afoot, carrying Dr. Kenney's saddle. They reached home without further mishap.[56]

---

* Also written Kenney's Fort.
** Both 1838 and 1839 are cited in various records, but overwhelming evidence supports 1838, including Smithwick, Jenkins, Wilbarger and official government papers. Makemson once cited 1839, but later changed it to 1838. Mrs. Blanch Stark Summers, great granddaughter of Dr. Kenney, also gave 1838.

Shortly after Kenney Fort was built, Davis Chandler settled north of Brushy Creek at a place later called Wadkins (or Watkins)* Crossing. Captain Ladd, who had escaped from an Indian attack by jumping a bluff while hunting on the San Gabriel River in the late 1830s, lived near the junction of Brushy Creek and Chandler Branch, and Captain Nelson Merrell,** well-known as a buffalo and bear hunter and frontiersman, established his home about one-half mile above Barnhart. Chandler sold his land to Sam Wadkins and moved farther up the branch.[57]

Jacob Harrell, who built the first house at Waterloo (later Austin City) and a blacksmith shop next door, near the foot of Congress Avenue, came over to Kenney Fort and planted a small patch of corn there in 1838. He had been prospecting on Brushy Creek when he decided to plant the corn. That fall, Harrell sent his son, John, and Major Chenneyworth and one or two others from Austin to harvest the corn. On their return trip, they were attacked by Indians near the present site of Austin State Hospital, and several members of the party were killed. The wagon, oxen and corn were recovered at Shoal Creek.[58] Corn crops were particularly good over the state in 1838 and 1839.[59] A man named Rogers or Rodgers planted corn at Kenney Fort in 1839 and although he may have lived on the Colorado River, he seems to have remained at the fort for a time, perhaps while tending his crop. He was killed in the fall of 1841 between Chandler Branch and the San Gabriel River and was buried near the Barnhart place (later belonging to William and Henry Palm).[60] There were several Rogers or Rodgers in central Texas at the time: Joseph Rogers had been killed in 1837[61] near Hornsby's Bend; James, J. B. and Joe Rogers are also mentioned. William Lawson, who was born in 1855 in the W. T. Dyer home at Kenney Fort, recalled that "only small patches of corn were cultivated" there when he was a small boy.[62]

An Indian attack on Kenney Fort was repelled in August 1840. Joseph Weeks correctly interpreted the hooting of owls as Indian signals. Admitting that they sounded real, he explained his conclusion: "Owls don't cough."[63] Dr. Kenney and his family were hospitable people, befriending passersby and the settlers of the area. In 1841, a surveyor named Force became ill and stopped at the fort for treatment. He improved, but, unknown

* Samuel Wadkins was so listed in the 1850 census, but his name was clearly written Samuel Watkins on the 1848 petition to form the country. According to the census, he could not read nor write, so possibly someone wrote his name for him. Early records use both forms of the name with about equal frequency.
** Nelson Merrell wrote his name thus, but the family name has very frequently been written "Merrill." Descendants corroborate that *Merrell* is correct. The town in north Travis County named for him, Merrell Town, was originally spelled thus, later corrupted to Merrilltown.

to Dr. Kenney, he ate some rich bear meat brought in by Captain Merrell and died shortly after. He was buried on the hillside across Dyer Branch, east of the fort.[64] Force is likely the same person referred to in the following letter:

M. Reuben Hornsby will please deliver to Jas. O. Rice all papers and property in his possession belonging to the estate of Wm. A. Force died
　　　Austin 11 Aug. 1841
　　　Wm. Farley
　　　Admst.[65]

Dr. Kenney, a native of Kentucky, had lived in Quincy, Illinois, and served in the Black Hawk War prior to emigrating to Texas in 1833. His brother, Reverend J. W. Kenney, was one of Texas' early Methodist ministers. Dr. Kenney moved to Texas for his wife's health, for she was consumptive. They settled first in Bastrop where he practiced medicine until 1836. Then he joined the Texas Army, serving as surgeon in Coleman's Company, and was at the Battle of San Jacinto. After the war, he engaged in the mercantile business at Bastrop until he moved to the fort. Mrs. Kenney's health remained precarious in Texas. She died at Kenney Fort on December 12, 1841, in the presence of her husband and three small daughters, Captain and Mrs. Nelson Merrell and Mr. and Mrs. Davis Chandler. With a whipsaw, Captain Merrell cut planks from a walnut tree to make a coffin. Mrs. Kenney was buried across Dyer Branch from the fort near a small cedar tree which served as a headstone, and adjacent to Mr. Force's grave. The two older Kenney girls, Mary Jane and Clarissa, were enrolled in a private school in Austin and the baby, Anna (Ann), remained at the fort with her father and the other families living there.[66]

ADAM LAWRENCE AND G. W. GLASSCOCK

Adam "Ad" Lawrence* and his family moved to the southeast section of what became Williamson County in 1838 about the same time Dr. Thomas Kenney was establishing his settlement east of present Round Rock. Adam Lawrence, a member of Austin's Second Colony in 1822, married Sarah Lucinda Miller, whose parents, Mr. and Mrs. Simon Miller, Sr., also lived in the Austin Colony. From his brother-in-law, Simon Miller, Jr., Lawrence purchased three thousand acres of Williamson County land and moved there in 1838, building a crude log hut at present Lawrence Chapel.

---

* The name was originally spelled Laurence, but Adam changed it to avoid confusion with another early family—no relation—by the same name in the community.[67]

Within a short time he replaced the temporary residence with a story and a half double log house of huge hand-hewn timbers. Each side of the house had two rooms separated by an open corridor, or "dog trot." In 1972, the

Huge timbers at corner of dog run, Adam Lawrence log home, used as barn in 1973.

farm was owned by a descendant, G. Carl Lawrence, Sr., and the second old log home was being used as a barn. The first crude log hut had burned.

Ad Lawrence was an Indian fighter, a Texas Revolutionary soldier, a farmer, stockman, and was known as one of the most expert mustang ropers in Texas. Before moving to central Texas, he lived on the Trinity River. From there he and two companions went mustanging. When a long way from home they were suddenly attacked by Indians who had been hiding in the tall prairie grass. "About fifty arrows were whizzing about my ears," Adam said. One hit his horse in the neck and another lodged in his heavy jacket. Both his companions were killed, but Lawrence and his wounded horse made a determined and exhausting run for safety. Finally reaching the banks of the Trinity and all the time wondering if his horse would take the jump, Adam urged him over the lowest bluff in the vicinity—fifteen feet high—and into the water. The horse made it and they were soon in safer territory. Lawrence commented afterwards about the daring jump: "I tell you I fairly loved that animal at that moment."[68]

Adam Lawrence established what became Lawrence Chapel Cemetery in 1838 and donated the land to the community about 1840. He also gave land adjacent to the cemetery where a Methodist Church was built, a church still active in 1973. After the Civil War, Ad Lawrence could see smoke rising from five chimneys as he sat on the porch of his home and he and his wife decided to move to California. A series of bad fortunes plagued him there, including the loss of his wife and financial difficulties, so he returned to Texas. He died October 2, 1878, and is buried at Lawrence Chapel Cemetery.[69]

About the same time that Ad Lawrence came to the county and Kenney Fort was being built, George Washington Glasscock visited at some length in San Gabriel country. He described his impressions of the land and its potentials in a letter to his brother, which was delivered by hand from Bastrop to Zavala, Texas, by a Mr. Baird. The brother was Joseph Millegan Glasscock. The letter follows:

Bastrop 30 June 1838

Dear brother

I send you a few lines to inform you that the Indians has not killd me yet I Just Returned from the woods a trip of four weeks I was very mutch pleasd with my trip I was on the head of the sant gabrels up about the head of it at the foot of the mountains there is the finest waterd part of Texas that I have seen fine springs limestone water and rock and soil as good as any in Texas and tolerable timber I have 4 Leagues on that stream I am holding a peace for your headwrigh by a third of my own till the 6 months is out it is a splendid piece of land as I ever saw if I can succeed in getting it for you it is worth 5 dollars per acre to you I have made arrangement for you for a hous to keep Tavern in here board is $30 per month here now 3$ per day for man & hors I have bot 3 lots here property is very high and rising there was some small lots on main street sold for 10$ per foot mine are back lots one lot to live on my self 3 acres other smaller I shall live in this place till the Sant Gabrels is settled then I shall go out there tell Sanders that this is the place for him he can get 4 dollars for shoeing a hors tell Jack he can get 6 dollars per day to haul with his teem here this place is improveing very fast business is brisk of all kinds money is tolerable plenty star money is plenty I think I shall be home about the last of July if I have no bad luck if Britton had of come in as expected I should of been reddy to of went home with Baird my respect to all Your Brother till death

G W Glasscock[70]

BATTLE OF BRUSHY (ALSO BATTLEGROUND)

Comanches were reported encamped on the San Gabriel River about fifty miles from Austin City early in 1839 and, on January 25, three companies of volunteers under Captain John H. Moore were organized at the Colorado River settlements to march on them. Noah Smithwick was in charge of a company from Bastrop, and the Lipans formed another group led by Chief Castro, his son, Juan Castro, and young Flacco and Juan Seis assisting the Chief.[71] When the volunteers arrived at the San Gabriel, they found the Comanches had moved upstream. The Rangers trailed them to the head of the Gabriel but were delayed by a sleet and snowstorm and had to seek shelter in a post oak grove on the divide between the Colorado and San Gabriel rivers. When they could move on, they located the Comanches on the San Saba River and met them in battle February 14, 1839.[72]

Retaliating for this invasion, a large number of Comanches a few days later raided the settlements near Will's Prairie and Webber's Prairie a short distance south of Williamson County, killing Mrs. Robert Coleman and her son, Albert, and taking a five-year-old boy, Tommy, prisoner. Captain Robert Coleman had succeeded Captain John J. Tumlinson, had built Coleman Fort, and the family lived there.[73] Two little Coleman girls were brought to Kenney's Fort where Mrs. Kenney cared for them. Word of the raid spread quickly. Twenty-five citizens formed a company, electing Jacob "Jake" Burleson captain; another twenty-seven men under Captain James Rogers joined the first group. A Mr. Adkisson (possibly A. J. Adkisson who was in the Flores Battle a few months earlier) described their encounter with the Indians in southeastern Williamson County, about ten o'clock one morning. "We descended a long prairie slope leading down to a dry run, a little above and opposite Post Oak Island, and when about three miles north of Brushy, we came in sight of the enemy." In front of the volunteers, on the north, was a channel covered with a thicket, and when the Indians were spotted they were about a half mile above and to the west of the thicket and heading toward it. The volunteers were on horses, however, and got to the thicket before the Indians, most of whom were on foot. There was considerable hesitation on the part of the volunteers for they had had no time to organize or reconnoiter. Some of the men dismounted several times, expecting to join battle, but others held back. "One of the boys, only about fourteen years of age, in his excitement mounted his horse while yet hitched to the tree. The Captain [Jacob Burleson] saw the condition of the boy, dismounted from his horse, cut the rope, but as he was again mounting was shot dead. The Indians cut off his right hand and foot, and took out his heart, thinking all the while that he was General Edward Burleson," who was a brother to Jacob. The men were ordered to fall back to Brushy Creek in a mile-long line. "The main body of us [was] mortified at the result of the morning's conflict, unwilling and ashamed to return to the settlements without a fight, and being loath to leave the dead body of the gallant Captain upon the field, we halted at Brushy."[74]

Meanwhile, General Edward Burleson had heard of the raid at the Coleman home and had raised thirty-two men, with Captain Jesse Billingsley of

San Jacinto distinction, as his assistant. These reinforcements arrived and by early afternoon the settlers were ready to attack. They found the Indians in a horseshoe-shaped hollow, in a high position at the bend of the shoe. The volunteers decided to divide into two parties, Captain Billingsley to take the run below the Indians, and the others to take a ravine just above. But both groups discovered that a broad, open plot spread between the ravines and the Indians, making an attack on the Indians extremely hazardous. The pioneers took safe positions until sundown, hoping that the Indians would show themselves, but they did not and during the night they withdrew. Next morning, the settlers made litters to carry the wounded and dead back home. Jacob Burleson, Edward Blakey and John Walters were killed. Reverend James Gilleland was severely wounded and died ten days later.[75] The Indians, believed to have numbered about one hundred, lost twenty or thirty warriors.[76] After General Edward Burleson joined the two companies of volunteers, the Rangers totalled about eighty-four.[77] John G. Matthews, who later moved to the county, was one of them.[78] Another small group of men under William Handcock [sic], of which John H. Jenkins, Sr., was a member, approached Burleson's force about sundown, was suddenly charged by a band of Indians and had to seek cover in some timber. Unable then to locate Burleson, they returned to the settlement.[79]

The Indians had the advantage in this battle because of the rapid fire of their primitive weapons, compared with the old single barrel, muzzle-loading rifle, "an advantage which told heavily in a charge. An Indian could discharge a dozen arrows while a man was loading a gun, and if they could manage to draw our fire all at once they had us at their mercy unless we had a safe retreat."[80]

At the time of the battle early in 1839, Brushy Creek was often called Boggy Creek. Present-day terminology applies "Boggy" to a branch leading into Brushy Creek. Boggy Creek, Battleground Creek and Brushy Creek form a three-forked pattern to the south of Taylor. Since the battle ranged in the area of all three streams, the event is variously referred to by any one of the names—Battle of Boggy, Battle of Brushy, or Battle of Battleground.

FLORES-CÓRDOVA AFFAIR

The capture of Mexican documents outlining a plot to incite Indian tribes to make war against the Texas nation took place in Williamson County territory and is regarded by many historians as one of the most significant battles ever fought in Texas, second only to the Battle of San Jacinto. The three-mile long attack and capture occurred between the north and south forks of the San Gabriel River on May 18, 1839, after a prolonged chase. Lieutenant James O. Rice was in command of the seventeen men who cornered Manuel Flores, Juan Bautista Soto, thirteen other Mexicans and eleven Indians on a steep bluff of the North San Gabriel.[81] This confrontation culminated a series of events which began a year earlier.[82]

Manuel Flores, a Mexican agent to the Indians, received a letter written in July 1838 saying that the commander at Matamoros wished Flores and Vicente Córdova of Nacogdoches to raise troops which would serve as auxiliaries of the Mexican army. These soldiers were to excite the frontier Indians to make war on Texas, especially while Mexico was having difficulties at home.

> [The Indians] must not trust to flying invasions, but to operations having a more permanent effect—causing, if not daily injury, at least perpetual alarm and inquietude to the enemy, and depriving them of their commerce, the spoils of which were to go to the Indians. . . . They were not to cease to harass the Texans for a single day, to burn their habitations, to lay waste their fields . . . and if the Texans should assemble in considerable bodies, the Indians were directed to hang about them in small parties. . . , endeavoring at every cost to cut off their horses.[83]

In the spring of 1839, Córdova and Flores came into Texas from Mexico. George Davis and Reuben Hornsby saw their trail near the Colorado River, and, mistaking them for Indians, spread an alarm and gathered a volunteer force. Among the company were James O. Rice, Colonel Edward Burleson, Jesse Billingsley and Micah "Mike" Andrews. They followed the enemy toward Seguin, fought and skirmished March 28 through 30, took some prisoners, but Córdova fled to Mexico, and Flores and some of his men managed to escape.[84] Another ranging group headed by Captain Mike Andrews and Lieutenant James O. Rice was organized to protect families living along the Colorado. Lieutenant Rice and B. B. Castleberry, while scouting on Onion Creek south of Austin on about May 16, 1839, discovered Flores and his party traveling north. The Rangers followed the trail but could not determine the size of the Mexican force. A civilian in the group, Wayne Barton, warned Captain Andrews that they might all be slaughtered, after which the Captain ordered a retreat. As the Mexicans moved into a cedar brake, A. J. "Ad" (Uncle Jack) Adkisson, a Cumberland Presbyterian minister, asked permission to pursue the enemy. The Captain agreed, saying that he, too, would join in search of the Mexicans. Dismissing any who did not wish to join them, the Captain led nineteen Texans in the direction of Flores, following his trail into the mountains at a rapid gait, all that day. (What Williamson Countians now call *hills* were referred to as *mountains* by early writers. The steep cliffs and hills made rough riding, in any case.) [85]

A hard rain fell in the night, making the trail more difficult to follow the next morning. Captain Andrews' horse became crippled, and since the Captain weighed about two hundred pounds, he and two other men whose horses were also quite lame returned home. This left seventeen men, with Lieutenant Rice in command. Some of their horses were also lame from traveling through the rough country the day before but they continued to follow Flores' trail. It led out of the mountains at Huddleston's place two miles north of Bagdad, went east onto the prairie and to the South San Gabriel River where the men from Mexico had camped the previous night. (The site was where the Leander-Liberty Hill road crossed the river.) The Texans reached the place about two o'clock on the afternoon of May 18, stopping at a "celebrated spring" near the future residence of "Uncle" Billy Johnson. There the Rangers saw that the Mexicans had "nooned and cut down a bee tree." The bees had not yet settled. Only four camp fires were evident, indicating that the Mexican force was small. The Rangers renewed the pursuit with more vigor, and about a mile farther along, Felix McClusky and B. B. Castleberry, who were scouting in advance, signaled for the men to dismount and cut switches. They advanced and were told that the enemy was just over the hill. Flores was sighted a quarter of a mile away. Apparently stalling for time, he began maneuvering, but the Texans charged ahead "until they had driven the enemy on to a steep bluff on the [south] banks of the North San Gabriel, which was so steep that it was impossible for the enemy to descend." Flores charged toward the Texans "who had just dismounted, did not have their horses hitched, and were, therefore, not prepared to properly receive the enemy; but William Wallace . . . who happened to be a little quicker than the balance, had gotten in position ready for action, and just as Flores was in the act of wheeling his horse to retreat, Wallace took good aim, fired, and at the crack of his gun, Flores rolled off of his horse upon the ground, shot through the heart." The small party with Flores immediately fled, "leaving behind them all their horses, mules, baggage, munitions of war, etc. The last seen of the enemy, they were making their way as rapidly as possible to the mountains beyond the Gabriel. The Texans then gathered up the horses and mules, numbering one hundred and fifty-six or seven,* several hundred pounds of powder and lead, seventeen dollars in Mexican silver dollars, besides a good

* Webb, *Rangers*, says one hundred fourteen, page 48.

deal of Mexican luggage, all of which had been abandoned by the enemy in their flight."** Also captured was printing material, including hand set type.[86]

The weary Rangers returned to the South San Gabriel, camping where Flores had stayed the night before, then continued on to Hornsby's Bend, meeting on the way two other relief groups who meant to assist in the fight. At Hornsby's, they investigated the leather sacks which had been abandoned by the Mexicans and found they contained several official communications detailing the plot against Texas and involving both Flores and Córdova. The Rangers relayed the information to the Texas government. President Lamar and his cabinet found the activities described in the captured documents to be treasonable, and Lamar's severe policy toward the Indians as well as toward Mexico stiffened.[87]

Legend tells of one member of the Flores party who escaped. He was Karl Steinheimer, a German, who had been associated with the pirate, Luis Aury. Steinheimer mined gold in Mexico for twenty years and en route to visit a lady friend in St. Louis had decided to join Flores for a time. He was taking along ten burros carrying heavy loads of gold. When the Ranger force intercepted Flores and company at the North Gabriel, Steinheimer escaped with his treasure, burying it nearby because he feared unfriendly Indians were close. He was said to have written the St. Louis lady describing the hiding place—where three creeks met, sixty feet from an oak tree into which he drove a brass spike.[88] The legend has not netted the ten loads of gold but has initiated many a search, considerable digging, various "authentic" maps, multiple interpretations of Steinheimer's directions, and high hopes—all as elusive as the treasure itself.

THE WEBSTER MASSACRE

The Webster Massacre took the lives of fourteen men one June morning in 1839 near Leander, including the life of John Webster who was leading a group of settlers from Hornsby's Bend to their prospective new home in present Burnet County. Mrs. Webster and her two children, three-year-old Martha Virginia and thirteen-year-old Booker, were taken captive by the Comanches.

John Webster, distantly related to Daniel Webster, came to Texas from his plantation in Virginia in 1835 (or 1838, according to one source).[89] A lawyer, banker and businessman, John Webster, like many others of his

** Wilbarger's excellent narrative is followed. He placed the date of battle on May 17; Webb, Brown and government documents indicate May 18 is correct.

time, sought new opportunities and challenges. He brought forty-four picked men with him to Texas, including John W. Darlington, who later related the story. By the spring of 1839 he planted a corn crop on rented land at Hornsby's Bend, about ten miles below Austin on the Colorado River. After the harvest, Webster planned to move northward to his head-right, just west of the present western boundary of Williamson County. He purchased three hundred head of cattle, beef and milch cows and set out on June 13, 1839, with his wife and two children and thirteen men, includ-ing surveyors, guards and a Negro man—a total of seventeen in the party. Webster planned to select a site and build a fort, after which he would be joined by Colonel Burleson and one hundred men. When all the survey-ing and other work was completed, Webster and his family were to own one-half the land, the others in the party the remainder, with Webster bear-ing all expenses. The seventeen in the advance party were to be joined shortly by other members of the Webster group. They had been detained because some of their cattle had stampeded and had to be rounded up again before they could rejoin Webster.[90]

John Webster's wagons were very heavily loaded with supplies, guns and ammunition. His daughter's later account mentions six wagons at one point; at another place in the same narrative she mentions four. Drawn by four yoke of oxen, each wagon moved slowly and with some difficulty, but the small caravan had crossed west Williamson territory and was on the ridge between the North and South San Gabriels within about six miles of the site of the proposed fort when the company spotted Comanches nearby—too many for their small party to engage. They turned back on June 19, hoping to meet the remainder of their men with the cattle. Traveling until late in the day, they broke the axle on one of the wagons as they crossed the South San Gabriel River. They worked most of the night mending it and at about three o'clock in the morning, June 20, resumed the laborious journey southward. They reached Brushy Creek at sunup, but the Indians were wait-ing for them.[91]

After a hurried conference, the group chose to defend themselves from inside a barricade of their wagons which were quickly placed in a hollow square. The Comanches had the advantages of timber for cover and of overwhelmingly superior numbers. The fight of the settlers was brave, desperate and hopeless. It started about sunrise, was all over by about ten o'clock that morning. All fourteen of the men were killed. Mrs. Webster and her young son and daughter were to be spared but taken captive. The three Comanche chiefs who were "in absolute possession of this region" at the time—Yellow Wolf, Guadalupe and Buffalo Hump—cut the hilt of

John Webster's sword in three pieces as mementos for themselves. Other tribesmen divided what was left of the sword and Mrs. Webster's silverware into small pieces to make into trinkets. The daughter especially recalled in later years seeing her father's sword broken into bits. The Comanches spent the remainder of the day dividing their battle prizes. What they did not want, they destroyed, breaking Mrs. Webster's fine china, pouring sacks of coffee on the ground, and turning over and burning the wagons. They left with the three prisoners after dark that evening, traveling a number of days to their villages.[92]

The bloody scene was discovered by one of Webster's surveyors, John Harvey, who had been delayed at Hornsby's Bend. He found a weird and awful sight—skeletons lying within a thirty-foot circle around the remnants of the wagons. No one was identifiable except Milton Hicks, whose leg had been broken in the Battle of Anahuac. Guns lay broken and had apparently been used as clubs in the last moments of the struggle. Spokes of the wagon wheels and wagon tongues were riddled with bullet holes and arrow spikes. Harvey hurried back to the settlement, finding that General Burleson and about fifty or sixty men could return with him to the scene. "A strange, unreal sight of horror met our eyes. Only fleshless bones scattered around remained of a brave and courageous band of men. In the absence of coffin, box, or even plank, we collected them into an old crate, which was found near and buried them." The victims' common grave is located in the Davis Cemetery on FM Road 2243 nearly two miles east of the center of Leander. Henderson Upchurch and M. J. Wells, who later lived in the county, helped bury the remains.[93] The inscription on the tomb gives the date of the deaths as August 27, 1839, but Martha Webster Simmons' positive statement declares that incorrect, and the correct date to be June 20, 1839.[94]

Martha Webster remembered with horror the days and months she and her mother spent as captives. The boy was taken by a different tribe, and Mrs. Webster and Martha Virginia did not see him during their eight months' captivity. When a peace treaty between the State of Texas and the Comanches was signed in 1840, stipulating that all white prisoners were to be returned to San Antonio, Mrs. Webster learned about it. She had acquired some knowledge of the Indian language by that time. Although she had previously tried twice to escape with her daughter and failed, she felt the signing of the treaty made it a good time to try another escape. She took Martha Virginia and followed the trail of some Comanches who were on their way to San Antonio. They traveled at night only, hiding in brambly thickets during the daytime. Starved, their bare feet and legs bruised and cut from walking through brush and thorns, they finally reached the outskirts

of San Antonio, exhausted and extremely weak. There they found friendly
hands who took them into town, and both mother and daughter recovered
from their long ordeal. About six days after their return, young Booker
Webster was brought back. In 1846, he enlisted in the army in the war
against Mexico and died at Monterrey.[95]

When Martha Virginia Webster-Strickland/Strickling-Simmons wrote
about the family tragedy in later years, she prefaced it with the statement,
"This story is what was told me by my mother, my uncles and aunts, and from
my own recollections. . . . My father was murdered June 20, 1839. The
date on the tomb is wrong."[96] At the age of seventeen, in January 1853,
Martha Webster married Marmaduke D. Strickling (as he wrote his name.
Other early historians also spelled it Strickling, although Martha wrote it, in
later years, "Strickland.") They lived in Burnet County on the headright
along the North Gabriel where John Webster had intended to establish his
home. The community came to be known as Strickling/Strickland (spelled
both ways). Some years after the death of Mr. Strickling/Strickland, his
widow married Martin V. Simmons and moved with him to the west
coast.*[97]

Apparently no complete and infallible list of those killed was written and
preserved soon after the massacre. A composite from available early
sources shows the following lost their lives: John Webster, John Stillwell,
Washington Perry Reese, William Parker Reese, Milton Hicks, Nelson
Fletcher or Wilson Flesher (both forms are given; Flesher may be correct
since Martha Virginia Webster mentions Paul Flesher, her uncle), Albert
Silsby, Martin Watson, James Martin, Nicholas Baylor, a Negro man named
Nelson, a Mexican named Antonio, a Mr. Bazeley or Bazley, and a Mr.
Lensher.[98]

A decade of violence had passed in the future Williamson County, and,
although it was not over, rarely if ever again was it experienced with such
large-scale intensity.

SKIRMISHES

During the decade of the 1840s, which culminated in the formation of
Williamson County, Anglo-American settlers continued to trickle into San
Gabriel and the Brushy Creek country. The land looked much as it had for

---

* Martha Webster-Simmons' manuscript is the basis for most of the above story of the
massacre. John W. Darlington, who came to Texas with the Webster family, gave a slightly
different version in J. H. Griffith's account. Many others have told the story, but none so
closely involved as Mrs. Simmons and Darlington.

centuries. The newcomers found the mountain tops along the San Gabriel River covered with "oyster, mussel, conque, and clam. My host shewed me a large specimen of ammonite from the San Gabriel." Writers of that period agreed that the area deserved its Indian name, translated "Land of Beauty."[99]

> The bottoms on the streams are extremely rich and beautiful, the water pure, and the uplands of the highest order of fertility. Its prairies enjoy an almost perennial bloom of flowers, and even the wild Indian hunters have been so captivated by its attractions, that they have named it the 'Land of Beauty.'*[100]

Some of the Comanche nation and remnants of the Tonkawas and Tawakonis remained in or near Williamson County, but gave little trouble to the colonists in the 1840s. The Wacos were usually blamed for "small-scale theft and murder."[101]

Much-used trails such as the Double File Trail and the Upper Highway continued to be used. In 1840, the Republic of Texas under Colonel William G. Cooke, commander, and William J. Hunt, engineer, laid out the Military Road from Austin City to the Red River, crossing Brushy Creek due north of Austin (at Round Rock), the two forks of the San Gabriel at present Georgetown, and Opossum Creek near the headwaters of its three forks. There were no villages on the Military Road at that time. It led to Preston, located on the Red River, and was often referred to as Preston Road as well as the Military Highway.[102]

Captain George T. Howard skirmished with a number of Indians on October 24, 1839 between the San Gabriel and Little rivers," in which he succeeded in killing three or four."[103] Now promoted, Major Howard and his Ranger company were greatly outnumbered when they met the Comanches on Opossum Creek just east of present Weir in 1840 and found it necessary to resort

> to a stratagem. Secreting his men in a thick grove of timber, he started off alone, well mounted, in the direction of the enemy. The moment the Indians saw him they considered the possession of his scalp as certain as though it was already hanging at their saddle skirts, and, with frightful yells, gave chase. The gallant officer trusted to his steed at a time when a stumble would have been inevitable destruction to both. . . . [He led] the savages directly within range of his own men. . . . A well directed volley tumbled seven of

---

* Tonkawan Indian, Roger Stallings, translates it "Land of Good Water," from which this book's title has been chosen.

the Comanches dead from their horses. So sudden and unexpected was this reception that the Indians turned their horses and made a precipitate retreat.

The brother of one of the slain Indians heroically attempted to recover the body of his brother, but was shot through the heart just as he reached him, and both were fallen on the ground together.[104] George T. Howard became a general and the aide-de-camp to General Hugh McLeod on the Santa Fe Expedition shortly thereafter.[105] When the Santa Fe Expedition passed the site of Major Howard's encounter the following year, Major Bird described the event. Bird said his group had thirty or forty Rangers, the Indians three or four times that number, and that the fight took place not far from the hill on which later stood Elias Queen's residence, known as Queen Hill.[106]

Frontiersmen from settlements a short distance from Williamson County, like Bastrop, Webber's Prairie and Hornsby's Bend, frequently came up to Brushy Creek on hunting trips. Eighteen-year-old Claiborne Osborn and his brother, Lee, and James Alec Hamilton of Bastrop were on such a hunt in 1840 near Rice's Crossing.[107] While the others went to hunt for game, Osborn, on his horse tending the pack animals, was shot at by Indians. His horse stumbled as he fell; Claiborne was caught by the natives and stabbed. One Indian had partially removed his scalp when the other hunters, alerted by the shots, returned to the scene, firing as they came. The Indians fled. According to Smithwick's version of the story, the Indians hesitated a few moments during the scalping episode, disputing about the possession of Osborn's scalp and his double brown curl which they considered a special prize. When Alec Hamilton arrived, the Indians disappeared. "They've cut my head; have they scalped me?" asked Osborn. His companions covered his head with a wet cloth and took him to the Noah Smithwick home on Brushy, where Mrs. Smithwick dressed the wound. It was a small one and healed over within a few months, the patient recovering to rear a large family.[108]

SANTA FE EXPEDITION

The ponderous and ambitious undertaking officially designated the Santa Fe Pioneers, but better known as the Texan Santa Fe Expedition of 1841, assembled at three camps near Kenney Fort and Austin to head for New Mexico. After the more than three hundred personnel arrived, all the men and material were transported to headquarters of General Hugh McLeod, inspector general of the Texan army, who was encamped near Ken-

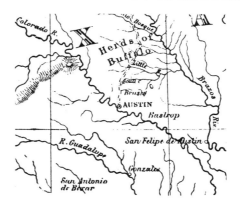

Route of Santa Fe Expedition through central Texas showing "herds of buffalo" and "Scull" Creek instead of San Gabriel River.

ney Fort at the rendezvous site, Camp Cazneau.* It was also called Brushy Creek Camp.[109]

Texas' President Lamar sponsored the expedition. His plan was to open a trade route between Mexico and Santa Fe. He promised to furnish wagons to any merchants joining the expedition who would take merchandise to Santa Fe to sell. Some historians believe that Lamar had in mind the acquisition of New Mexican territory by Texas.[110] At any rate his blustery administration was both applauded and condemned, and the Santa Fe Expedition was no exception. It has been called everything from "ill-advised,"[111] "a piece of folly,"[112] a "wild-goose campaign,"[113] to a project comparable to the Lewis and Clark Expedition in concept.[114] In Lamar's defense, one could point out that the viceroyalty of New Spain had legalized trade between Santa Fe and towns on the Missouri River and that the first caravan left Missouri in 1821. Trade over the Santa Fe Trail, thus established, grew from $15,000 in 1822 to $450,000 in 1843.[115] Lamar no doubt had a canny eye on the Texas economy which needed bolstering. Regardless of his intentions, history proved the venture to have been abominably planned, ill-equipped and very badly directed.

About 320 men and boys from all over Texas—soldiers, merchants, adventurers, or pleasure seekers—met General McLeod at Camp Cazneau in June. Official communications designated June 20, 1841, as takeoff day, and this date is corroborated by the *Austin City Gazette* of June 23, 1841. Other dates were given by diarists on the trip, but all diaries except one were

---

* Cazneau was located on what was once known as the old Freeman Smalley place, just south of the two-story home built in 1870 by Captain Nelson Merrell near Palm Valley. It was named for William L. Cazneau, member of Congress of the Texas Republic.

confiscated in Mexico when the men were taken prisoners, and their diaries were rewritten later from memory. The single diary not confiscated was kept in a journal for the previous year (1840) and Gallagher's "Sunday, June 19, 1841" should read "Sunday, June 20, 1841."[116]

More than twenty wagons, large quantities of supplies and food, beef cattle, draft oxen and horses were also gathered along Brushy Creek. President Lamar rode over from Austin to bestow his personal blessings on the project. The President unsaddled and staked his own horse—"a specimen of Republican simplicity—the chief magistrate of a nation cooking his own dinner and grooming his own horse." Lamar roughed it that night, sleeping on a single blanket on the ground.[117] George Wilkins Kendall, founder of the *New Orleans Picayune*, a member of the expedition, wrote a vivid, dramatic description of the entire journey. Another prominent member of the company was a man Donahoe, a Santa Fe merchant, for whom Donahoe Creek was named.[118]

As the volunteers traveled on the old military road from Austin to Camp Cazneau, they passed "over rolling and beautiful prairies, occasionally relieved by the silent skirting of timber which fringes the margins of the small streams, or by a small grove of timber so regularly planted by nature that it would almost seem the hand of man had assisted in the production." Camp Cazneau was in a beautiful and romantic situation, located near several large springs of cool, delicious water.[119]

Most of the pioneers were under thirty years old, many less than twenty. A large number of them had been waiting at the Brushy Camp three or four weeks and they were more than ready to go. They spent two days loading the wagons for the long journey which they believed would be five hundred miles. The distance was, in fact, a thousand miles. In addition, the company was to travel another three hundred miles out of the way. The wagon train was very heavily loaded, moving off with considerable difficulty in double file formation, especially since some of the young oxen had never before been yoked. "The consequence was that a number of the wagons were upset," delaying the progress that first day, Sunday, June 20. But the company was exuberant, beginning the journey with hearty optimism and anticipating a great adventure. It was an "animating spectacle." A band consisting of fifes and drum plus "two or three clarionets [sic], a horn and bugle" played a rousing march as the companies swung into their double files. "The road this day was over beautiful rolling prairies, the land rich, and susceptible of cultivation." The military road intersected the Double File Trail between Brushy Creek and Chandler's Branch, and, at the intersection, the entourage took the Double File route northward.[120] This route was approximately from Palm Valley north to Towns Mill, west of Weir. It was nearly night when the caravan reached "our camping ground on the San Gabriel."[121]

Kendall reported that the San Gabriel was picturesque, that one or two families had tried to make a settlement a few miles above the camping place at Double File Crossing, but they had been attacked by Indians and those who were not killed had been driven off. The river abounded with trout, perch and catfish, and some of the party spent their time fishing and shooting alligators in the Gabriel. At the encampment just below where Towns Mill was later built, some of the badly overloaded wagons were lightened by dumping one or two loads of lead into a large hole in the stream just below the crossing.[122]

On the second day, it was found necessary to send for more supplies, and men of the party killed two buffaloes, the first they had seen. Some of the company familiar with the area between the San Gabriel and Opossum Creek recalled in passing the scene of Major George T. Howard's famous encounter with Comanches. He had ridden his men in a thick grove on Queen's Hill east of Weir. Major Howard acted as a decoy, leading the Indians close to the trees where they were attacked and routed.[123]

The Santa Fe-bound pioneers spent the second night at Opossum Creek, having swung somewhat northeastward. A thunderstorm that night blew Kendall's tent from its moorings and "the rest of the night . . . we 'took plain without kiver,' " he quoted one of his tentmates. As they crossed rolling prairies the next morning, they began to see small gangs of buffaloes. The third night was spent on Deer Creek, probably present-day Donahoe Creek, said to be named for a member of the expedition. There they found fossils of oysters and other shellfish in abundance "and in good preservation."[124] The next encampment was at Little River. The trip across Williamson County was light hearted, often boisterous. No such imposing procession had crossed that land since more than a century before, when el Señor Marquéz de San Miguel de Aguayo took his enormous expedition along almost the same route.[125] The non-military impromptu activities which included shooting alligators in the San Gabriel, fishing, and an unrestrained buffalo hunt were perhaps subtle portents of hard days to come. Problems multiplied as the march continued toward New Mexico—there was unknown terrain, drouth, lack of grass for cattle and of water for both man and beast, insufficient food, too few oxen and wagons to transport the merchants' goods. To these were added bickering, intrigue, thievery, traitorous activity, court martials, harassment by Indians, massacres, smallpox, yellow fever and diarrhea. By the time it reached New Mexico in September, the company had broken up into small groups, arriving separately. The governor in New Mexico was antagonistic and found it easy to arrest the ragtag groups. Not a shot was fired. But all the men were made prisoners—prisoners who walked the entire two thousand miles from Santa Fe to Mexico City, unless they died first. The walking horror ended early in February 1842 when they reached their destination and prison. The men who survived were finally released, but the loss was extremely heavy.[126]

Sam Houston had opposed the expedition; Andrew Jackson and John Quincy Adams were critical of it. De Shields, however, credited it with the ten million dollars which Texas received for its claim to New Mexico in 1850. "The evidence seems to support the idea . . . that the attempt to establish a trade route across Texas was a good, hard-headed business venture that might have meant a great deal to Texas."[127]

RAIDS

A Dr.* Miller settled on the south side of Brushy Creek, about three-fourths of a mile below Wadkins Crossing, in 1841 but abandoned his place two or three years later.[128] In the fall of 1842, two buffalo hunters, Joseph Barnhart and a man named Newcomb, were resting on a log near Brushy Creek after dressing buffalo meat to take home when they saw an Indian approaching. Barnhart hailed him and when the Indian ran away yelling, they realized he would return with companions. As they mounted their horses to leave, Indians arrived, gave chase for about four miles, but the hunters managed to escape.[129] Indian troubles increased so much that year that three trusted Tonkawas and eight settlers from Bastrop went up Brushy Creek to investigate.[130] Comanches also raided that year, venturing on moonlight nights into the settlements on foot to capture horses and ride away on them. The settlers avoided traveling by moonlight if possible; if not, they took care to enter a timbered area at a different point from that expected after they had crossed a broad prairie. Approaching the woods "nearly within gunshot," then they galloped full speed parallel to the timber for a distance and suddenly entered it to prevent an ambush.[131]

THE ARCHIVES WAR

Lamar's administration ended in 1841. He had moved the capital to the village of Waterloo, renamed Austin City, in 1839. During his presidency,

* Dr. J. B. Miller was in San Felipe District in 1834, according to Robinson's biography of Judge Robert McAlpin Williamson.

relations with the Indians and with Mexico had greatly deteriorated and the Santa Fe expedition had been a disaster. But he had laid the groundwork for Texas' free public school system, granting each county four leagues of land to support the schools. Houston began his second administration a short time before Mexico invaded Texas in 1842. By September, he advised the settlers to fall back east of the Brazos where they could be protected from Mexican and Indian attacks. All the Brushy Creek settlements near Kenney Fort were abandoned except for the fort itself, in the second "Runaway Scrape."[132]

Houston was not happy with the removal of the capital from his namesake city of Houston. Shortly after he was reelected to the presidency late in 1841, he moved his government back to Houston and called a session of Congress to meet there the following June, citing the threat of Mexican invasion as justification for the move. He felt too, that the Republic's archives should be transferred to a safer place, but action on that matter was delayed. Meanwhile, the subject was much-discussed and became an extremely controversial one. One outspoken gentleman wrote to President Houston:

> Sir Old Sam
>   We did heare that you was goin [to] move the seat of government and the publick papers ant that you swore you would do it. . . .
>   You Dam old drunk Cherokee. . . .
>   You shall hear more from me when I am ready.
>   John Welsh[133]

Necessary accommodations for the seat of government were not available in Houston, however, so in the fall of 1842 Sam Houston moved to Washington-on-the-Brazos. News came in September that the Mexicans had advanced to San Antonio, and that Indians had attacked five Austinites on Brushy Road, two miles from the city. Colonel T. W. Ward, land commissioner, closed the Land Office by proclamation on September 28, 1842, and proposed moving essential records eastward to Brushy Creek. Local wagoners refused to do so, however, and the records remained in Austin. At a session of Congress in Washington-on-the-Brazos on December 1, Houston reviewed the problems in regard to the archives and then ordered the Land Office transferred to the temporary capitol.[134] Despite the adamant position of some of the Republic's high officials, Houston cited the need for guarding essential records without dividing the armed forces between Austin and the temporary capitol, the dangers from Indians and from the Mexican army and the confusion which would result with the loss of the land records. Rumors of attempts to burn the records were rife and Houston's friends admonished him that his life was being threatened if he moved the archives from Austin. The Select Committee to which the matter of removal of records was referred met and reported its conclusions: since the seat of government was moved to Austin by law, the heads of departments should establish themselves there "which will obviate the necessity of moving the archives, save an unnecessary expenditure of the people's money and have a salutary effect in restoring confidence and tranquility to the frontier settlements."[135]

Houston felt strongly about the matter and on December 10, 1842, ordered Major Thomas I. Smith and Captain Eli Chandler to load the records quietly and to move them to Washington. On December 30, the two officers and a company of eighteen men "placed into three waggons the boxes containing the most important land papers furnished them by the commissioner of the General Land Office."[136] Attempting to halt the removal, an Austin lady, Mrs. Angelina Belle Peyton Eberly, fired a cannon but, in spite of her threat, the three ox-drawn wagons and the company of twenty left Austin for Kenney Fort on Brushy Creek, traveling over the same road the Santa Fe Expedition went the previous June.[137] Thus began what might have been a tragic episode known as the Archives War, which was partially enacted in the plaza of Kenney Fort. It turned out to be more comedy than tragedy.

Kenney Fort had a strong blockade fence around its half acre of ground and was known throughout central Texas as a good place to come for protection. When the public archives arrived at the fort, the two officers asked permission of Dr. Kenney to bring in the wagons and to camp inside the stockade, which was large enough to take care of their precious cargo. Dr. Kenney agreed. Meanwhile, the citizenry of Austin had been busy. Alarmed that the removal of the records might presage a permanent arrangement, Mark Lewis gathered a company of men and the home guard and followed the wagons to Kenney Fort. The next morning, they forced Major Smith at cannon point to surrender and to return the documents to Austin. No shot was fired.[138] Among the home guard men was eighteen-year-old John G. Matthews, who later resided near Liberty Hill where he established the community of Matthews.[139]

SETTLER-MEXICAN-INDIAN RELATIONS

Whitfield Chalk and Joseph Berry, son of pioneer John Berry, were among members of the ill-fated Mier Expedition late in 1842 in Mexico. Chalk managed to escape the evening the Texan force capitulated and reported the death of Joseph Berry to his father, John Berry, who moved to Williamson County in 1846. Chalk became Williamson County's first sheriff.[140]

Soon after the second Runaway Scrape, Captain Nelson Merrell returned to his old place on Chandler's Branch, remaining there until about 1846, when he moved to Merrelltown, across the line in Travis County. After the Civil War, he was to return to Williamson County, purchasing the Freeman Smalley place below Round Rock, and there in 1870 built the two story stone home with Indian lookout on top which still stood in 1973.[141]

In an effort to pacify the Indians and to accommodate both them and the colonists, the Republic of Texas in January 1843 authorized the establishment of frontier trading posts. The Torrey Trading Houses were the result: one each at Austin, New Braunfels, San Antonio, and on Tehuacana Creek eight miles below Waco. Stocking up with goods from Boston and New York and collecting tremendous numbers of skins which they sold to New York furriers,[142] these posts were the nearest sources of supplies for the handful of settlers along Brushy Creek and San Gabriel River.

James O. Rice accompanied the expedition commanded by Jacob Snively as guide, early in 1843, attempting unsuccessfully to capture a caravan of Mexican goods north of the Red River.[143]

A skirmish, which began on the Colorado River southeast of Austin in the spring of 1843, ended at Brushy Creek. About twenty Indians, thought to be Caddoes, were raiding for horses when they were discovered, and W. C. Reager, William S. Hotchkiss, Nathaniel Gilleland, Joseph Hornsby and Dow Puckett chased them off. The men continued the chase, but each time they came near the Indians, six of the natives "dropped upon their knees and began to rub their arrows across their bow strings in such a way as to produce a sound that seemed to be a sort of hybrid between caterwauling of half a dozen tom cats and the yelping of many cayotes." The settlers' horses were frightened by the sound and wheeled away at full speed. Again the settlers neared the Indians and again the Indians fiddled while the Texans vainly attempted to restrain their horses from stampeding. The chase continued to Brushy Creek, where the Indians found cover in timber. Hotchkiss received an arrow under the left shoulder.[144]

Corn crops near Kenney Fort were tended by a number of Austin citizens. In the autumn of 1843, Captain Pyron, Mr. Donovan, John Gravis, Jim Berry and one of the Harrell men went out to Brushy Creek to get a load of corn from their field near the fort. On their way back to Austin they were attacked by fifty Lipans. Pyron and Donovan were killed; the others escaped.[145]

Black-haired, fair skinned Washington Anderson was nineteen when he fought with distinction at San Jacinto. One pioneer said that "Wash Anderson was the true hero of San Jacinto. . . . Wash was never known to shout 'Go on' in battle but was always known to say 'come on' instead." In 1843 Anderson came to his headright on Brushy Creek and on the north bank at what became known as Anderson's Spring he put up the sixth log house in Milam District. He also erected a saw and grist mill which washed away in 1845, believed to be the first mill in the county. After the flood, Anderson moved to Webber's Prairie to recover from his losses, then in 1847 returned to Anderson's Spring where in 1859 he started the stone home which still exists in 1973 in excellent condition. He lived there until his death in 1894. Washington Anderson married his cousin, Mary Ann Glascock, daughter of George John Glascock and Ann Payne Coleman Glascock, in 1838. Washington Anderson's father, Dr. Thomas Anderson, lived at Bastrop but practiced surgery and medicine over all central Texas. The doctor and another son, John D. Anderson, were also at San Jacinto, the father guarding a camp opposite the battleground and John D. guarding baggage on April 21, 1836.[146]

Shortly after 1840, "the Mercer brothers settled on the Gabriel with a man named Orr, and of that party Peter Mercer, Captain Orr and a Negro servant were killed by the Indians in 1843.[147] Probably another version of the same story says that a group of Indians "went to Mr. Mercer's house on the San Gabriel" asking for food. Mercer gave them a beef which they proceeded to butcher about two hundred yards from the house. Meanwhile, Mr. and Mrs. Mercer and two other men who were living there, and the three or four small children of the family, went to the creek to launch a large canoe they had built. Indians attacked them, killed the men and took Mrs. Mercer and the children captive. A Negro man who was nearby seized one of the children and ran toward the woods, but was hit by six arrows. "Being closely pressed he was compelled to drop the child and flee." He reached the home of Mr. Thompson and reported the tragedy.[148]

Buffalo still ranged in Williamson County in the fall and winter of 1843-44 and buffalo hides figured in the deaths of Dr. Thomas Kenney, Henry Castleberry and John Courtney, all residents of Kenney Fort. Captain Nelson Merrell, also of that community, received an order for a flatboat load of buffalo skins from Michael Ziller of Austin. To improve his hunting capability, Merrell asked the gunsmith, Noah Smithwick, to increase the bore of his gun. After Smithwick worked on the gun, he commented that "the tremendous charge [caused] a rebound that almost dislocated his shoulder." When Merrell was satisfied with the gun, he hired Henry

Castleberry and John Courtney to help him take care of the hides. On the hunt, he shot "hundreds of the animals." The men left the hides in north central Williamson County near Salado Creek, planning to return in the spring and pick them up in Dr. Kenney's wagon. Merrell and his two helpers returned to Kenney Fort.[165]

Meanwhile, Dr. Kenney's two older daughters, Mary Jane, 12, and Clarissa, had been attending school in Austin. On April 5, 1844, Dr. Kenney brought them to the fort from school, expecting next day to take them to Rutersville College, where he had arranged to enroll them. That same evening, Castleberry and Courtney came in to tell Dr. Kenney that the weather was getting quite warm, and they felt they should go for the hides. They requested the use of the wagon and two yoke of oxen for about a week. The doctor agreed to delay taking the girls off to college and joined his friends—Castleberry, Courtney and Merrell—on the trip to the Salado, leaving early April 6. The Kenney girls, Mrs. Courtney and a man remained at the fort.[166]

A few days after the men left their homes, they were intercepted by Indians who "took revenge on them, just as white men would have done had they caught Indians killing their stock." (According to Smithwick's version of the story, Captain Merrell was with Dr. Kenney, Castleberry and Courtney, and "narrowly escaped by having a good horse." Makemson's version omits mention of Merrell until after the massacre.) After the men left Kenney Fort, word of depredations along the Colorado River had reached and alarmed those at the fort. According to Makemson, Captain Merrell, a Mr. Stephens, John Brothers, an Englishman, and a Negro man searched for the three men and found their bodies near Salado Creek. Indians, identified as Tawakoni, had taken Dr. Kenney's flintlock holster pistols, hack knife and horse, and Courtney's gun. One yoke of oxen had been killed and the meat taken, but the wagon was left, loaded with the skins and camping equipment. The two other oxen made their way back to the fort a few days later.[167] Wilbarger reported that the three men were scalped.[168]

The searching party returned to Kenney Fort with the sad news. Several days later, Captain Merrell, Brothers, Judge Joseph Lee, John Wooldridge, John G. Matthews, and several others returned to the scene of the ambush, where they buried the bodies in a pen they built on the ground out of large stones. From that time, the place was called Bone Hollow. Matthews, one of the Rangers on this assignment and later a resident of Williamson County, described the scene. "It was during a severe cold spell when the bodies of the slain were found and the ground was frozen so hard that, with the means at hand, they could not dig graves so the bodies were piled together and a mound of stones built over them."[169]

The elder daughter, Mary Jane, later married John Lee, whose brother, Judge Joseph Lee, established the first law office in Austin. The couple occupied the fort from 1848 until 1852. She died October 30, 1910. The second Kenney daughter, Clarissa, married a Mr. Click and lived on the Colorado above Bastrop, later moved to San Angelo. Anna (Ann) was married to W. R. Mason of Georgetown. She died there in 1865 and is buried in the Old Georgetown Cemetery.[170] Mary Jane Kenney Lee sold the fort property to S. M. Swenson, who passed it to his sister and her husband, Mr. and Mrs. William T. Dyer.[171] It later belonged to the Otto Stolley estate and then to Mrs. Jennie Davis. In 1973, a portion of the old flag pole and bits of broken china occasionally found on the grounds were the only remnants of the pioneer village.

Efforts to work matters out with the Indians continued as long as Sam Houston was in power. A council was held May 13, 1844, at Tehuacana Creek. The Comissioners informed Chief Ke-chi-ka-roqua, a Tawakoni, that white men had been killed twelve days before between the Gabriel River and Brushy Creek, about twenty miles east of Austin. Ke-chi-ka-roqua declared that he knew nothing of it. "I do not think any of my people did it." At another council held the same place on July 22, Red Bear reported that Comanches, one Waco and two Wichitas had killed the men on the Gabriel. The Indian Commission reported to Houston on May 23, 1844, the news of the murder of Dr. Thomas Kenney and his two companions. Several hunting parties were seen on the waters of Brushy Creek early in 1845 and officials wrote "it is rumored that Some Delaware who were hunting on Brushy, Saw the Austin children in possession of the Waco." On December 12, 1845, it was reported that "the Lipan have been removed from the San Antonio River to the San Gabriel."[149]

Friendly relations with Indians were sometimes maintained. A notable example was Jim Shaw of the Delaware tribe, who was well known in central Texas as a scout and who served as a mediator between various tribes and the colonists. One Comanche chief demonstrated his confidence in Shaw when he informed Sam Houston in a council that "any time you send to them Jim Shaw or John Conner, the Comanche will be ready to come in" to another meeting. When the Superintendent of Indian Affairs wrote to two of his Indian agents about difficulties between the Delawares and the Comanches, he asked, "Where is Jim Shaw?" and in May, Shaw went on a tour with Captain Sloat to the Comanche to work toward a reconciliation.

In later correspondence, officials noted that Shaw and his tribe left in October 1845 for their fall and winter hunt "on the waters of Brushy and therebouts." Shaw promised to be in Austin in about ten days for instructions.[150]

The same year, Shaw and Jack Harry, another Delaware interpreter, attended the November 13 Council meeting at Trading Post 2, and Shaw certified a list of presents which he had given to Indians. They included 21 silk handkerchiefs, 3 cotton handkerchiefs, 4 cotton shawls, 8 pieces blue prints, 41½ yards blue and red strouding, 7½ pieces blue drills, 75 lbs. brass wire, 4 3/12 dozen tin pans, 13 tin buckets, 12 lbs. vermilion, 10 doz. 6 inch butcher knives, 1½ doz. cocoa handles, 5 doz. horn combs, 2 8/12 doz. ivory combs, 2 4/12 doz. files, 7½ M brass tacks, 2 lb. linen thread, 1 1/12 doz. fire steels, 1½ M needles, 1½ doz. looking glasses, 4½ lbs. Indigo and Verdigris, "2½ doz. Squaw Hatchets," 4 doz. tin cups, 1½ pr. [sic] blankets, 42 small bars lead, 19 large bars lead, 2 pc. unbleached domestic, 35 lbs. powder.[151]

The "services of this Indian [Shaw] I regard as extremely important to us," one official wrote. "His intimate acquaintance with the country, and the various Indian tribes, enables him to obtain and give information." Because the Indians had confidence in him, Governor J. Pinckney Henderson declared, "I think it quite important to secure his services in future."[152] A citizen of Williamson County wrote that Shaw was

> prominent in his tribe, and was a man of considerable intelligence, spoke English very plainly and was of a much more communicative disposition than the average Indian. He was always a true friend to Texas and her people and was recognized by the old settlers as a faithful, trustworthy scout and guide.[153]

ANNEXATION

Talk of annexation began in the early 1840s and in 1845 after ten years as the Lone Star Republic, Texas became the Lone Star State.[154] Among the legislators who voted favoring annexation were R. M. Williamson, for whom Williamson County would be named, and Camp Cazneau's namesake, General William Leslie Cazneau.

A stage line came near the county, serving Austin via Webber's Prairie, Bastrop, Brenham and Houston, by 1845. When weather was favorable, the trip took two or three days and nights. A line from San Antonio to Waco was established soon after annexation, the first to cross Williamson County.

For the most part, however, people still traveled short distances on foot or long distances on horseback.[155]

The frontier bulged past the ninety-ninth meridian by 1846 "to the western edge of the well-watered, partially wooded area which was to become a great cotton empire."[156] This meant that surveyors were busier than ever in Williamson County territory. That year, Captain Bartlett Sims lost one of his two-man surveying crew, killed by Indians.[157] Surveying meant camping out for months, often far from any settlements and in areas threatened by Indians. When someone acquired land from the government, the owner requested a survey. The district surveyor of the state commissioned deputies to do the work, with mounted armed men to protect them. Expenses were defrayed by a tax based on the number of acres involved, and payment was often made in land transfers to the surveyors. Many of the large landholders of central Texas acquired their land in this way.[158]

A Ranger Company was stationed on the San Gabriel River just below the Double File Trail during the fall and winter of 1846, with Captain Shapley Prince Ross, later the father of Governor Sul Ross, in command. John C. Compton, one of the Rangers who made his home in Williamson County, said the camp was on the southwest bank of the river, "about three or four miles below the Junction [of the North and South San Gabriels] and just below the old 'Double File Trail' crossing" seventy-five yards below Towns Mill dam. While they camped on the San Gabriel, two rangers, Perry Neal and Tom Roberts, died of winter fever (pneumonia). A man named Fleming,* who had moved to the camp for protection from Indians, made two coffins of lumber from a wagon and the men were buried in a live oak grove just south of the river bank, in what later was the A. C. Beaver pasture. Guns were fired across the graves for a military service, but no monument was erected. While Fleming lived at the camp, he had given hats full of pecans to the rangers to use as stakes in games they played. A romance and marriage took place between Fleming's daughter, Mary, and one of the Rangers, Whitfield Chalk, later first sheriff of Williamson County. In the fall of 1846, Colonel W. C. Dalrymple settled on the northeast bank of the river across from the Ranger station, and Captain Ross's men helped him raise his log cabin near the Double File Trail.[159] When Captain Ross completed his assignment on the Gabriel, he was sent to a station on nearby Berry's Creek.[160]

Texas' annexation brought another surge of settlers to the state, and

---

* Probably William W. Fleming, who first settled northwest of Georgetown on the place later known as the John Ischy place.

since Williamson County was at that time on the frontier and sparsely settled, newcomers arrived there at a fast pace. David H. McFadin and Josiah Dyches located on the San Gabriel at Circleville in the summer of 1846, and about the same time, Greenleaf Fisk came to the South San Gabriel bringing wagon loads of building materials, tools and slaves.[161] That fall, Dr. W. I. Anderson, Levi Asher, and his son-in-law, Reverend Freeman Smalley, settled with their families on Brushy Creek about a mile below Wadkins Crossing, and Calvin and E. B. Barker, Willis Avery and William McCutcheon established places below them on the same creek. Thomas Hornsby moved to the place later occupied by James H. Faubion near Leander, and James Standefer located below him on Brushy Creek in what was called Live Oak Prairie.[162] During the winter of 1846, John Berry moved to his headright near some good springs where Indians frequently camped, on what was to be called Berry's Creek. He built a small water mill to grind corn, one of the first in the county. "They came from far and near to see my mill spring, to see this great fountain of water boiling up out of the earth—pure and cold," he wrote.[163] Indians were on good terms with John Berry and often returned to the springs to have their corn ground. They knew the art of weaving baskets and other articles from the rattan forest along Berry's Creek. Berry's Mill was enlarged and was operated continuously for about seventy years, known in later years as Gann's Mill.[164]

Matthew Moss, James G. Harrell, Dr. D. F. Knight and several others settled on Brushy Creek in the summer of 1847 about two miles above the site of Old Round Rock.[172]

A man named Enoch Oxley of Vermilion County, Illinois, visited Brushy Creek country in the mid-1840s and went back home with glowing descriptions of the land and its opportunities. Several families previously mentioned had come from Vermilion County in 1846—the Smalleys, the Ashers, and Dr. W. I. Anderson, whose son Edwin R., was born soon after they came to Texas and was said to be the first white baby born in the county. Within two years, one of the largest delegations of settlers from a single place had arrived from Vermilion County, Illinois. Among them came in 1847 Dr. William and Mary A. Knight and their family, including their son James Knight; Zara and Mary (Smalley) Stearns and their son, Zara Stearns, and a nephew, Harvey Trueman Stearns; Samuel and Martha (Knight) Makemson and their family including a son, W. K. Makemson, all locating along Brushy Creek from the Stearns place south of present Hutto to a little above Old Round Rock. They were among the petitioners who sought the formation of Williamson County. Most of these families were Republican in their politics and, coming from Abraham Lincoln country, were generally strong Union advocates, opposing secession ten years later when the Civil War loomed over the nation.[173]

Still more Vermilion County people came to Williamson County in 1848: James and Nancy A. Juvenal and their son, William Juvenal, and Luther Stearns, Sr., brother of Zara Stearns, Sr., who brought those of his fifteen children who were not yet married, and joining his son, Harvey T., who had come the previous year with his uncle Zara. Luther planted one crop at the Stearns farm south of present Hutto, near Wilbarger Crossing and Shiloh community (owned in 1973 by Dr. J. J. Johns of Taylor). The crop was ruined by a flood, and Stearns bought a farm two miles east of Water Valley (Jonah) in 1850. There he built a log home on the north

Log home built 1851 between Water Valley and Circleville by Luther Stearns.

side of the San Gabriel. The house burned at an early date, leaving the native stone chimney standing, but the log home was rebuilt in an almost identical structure. It still stands in 1973.[174] Records do not reveal whether the Juvenal and Stearns families came together, but it seems likely that they did, as they arrived about the same time and settled as neighbors. The Juvenal trip was long, weary

> and fraught with accidents and filled with privations. Near Rock Island, Illinois, the Sny bridge fell, precipitating three teams into the stream; there were many tedious waits for swollen streams to fall, and finally sickness and

death invaded the company. [James Juvenal's wife died on the trip and was buried at Ashley, Missouri.] They finally reached their destination; the country was new, thinly settled and wild game abounded from the jack rabbit to the buffalo.[175]

On the Luther Stearns wagon train, one of the women died on the trip. After she was buried in the countryside which was Indian territory, the wagon train made numerous circles over her grave to obliterate it to prevent desecration by Indians.[176] "In the spring of 1849, Mr. Juvenal constructed a breaking plow, and using his ox teams with this implement prepared much of the land . . . for cultivation." He also engaged in freighting goods from Houston to the "upper country," remarried and reared a large family.[177]

In addition to many early settlers listed in the 1850 census, a few others not on that list were in Williamson County at an early date, some of them moving away before the census was made. August Anderson arrived in the late 1830s and promoted the movement of Swedish people to Texas. David Wright, who settled in the Robertson Colony prior to November 15, 1830, received title to a league of land in present Williamson County June 1, 1835, although when he moved there has not been determined. John Pettijohn erected a log cabin near Freeman Smalley's about 1847 and Ebenezer Hanna lived in the county from 1847 until 1850. William Jenkins came to the county in 1849 but soon moved on to Hamilton County, and W. C. and Mary J. May Beard and their fifteen children came about 1850. They had six neighbors, drove their ox team to Houston for supplies. Francis White Johnson went into the land business after the Texas Revolution and made his home both in Round Rock and Austin. He authored a five-volume *History of Texas*.[178]

V

1848: A New County

CLEAR WATER, SAN GABRIEL, OR WILLIAMSON

Jacob M. Harrell, the first blacksmith in Austin, moved his shop and home to the north bank of Brushy Creek in the spring of 1848, becoming one of the first settlers at Round Rock. The Harrell home stood in a grove

Jacob Harrell's log home at Round Rock was moved a short distance to Harrell Memorial Park to serve as headquarters for Old Settlers Association.

of trees near the creek, where later L. M. Mays and John Ledbetter established their residences. In the summer of 1848, a log cabin school, believed the first in the county, was built at Moss's Spring, located on Lake Creek about two miles southwest of the center of present Round Rock. Soon after, another log cabin school was built north of Brushy Creek near Round Rock by Samuel L. Makemson and Dr. D. F. Knight, with George W. Laymon serving as teacher.[1]

Nelson Morey is said to have opened the first general merchandise store in the county in 1848, located on the north bank of Brushy Creek near Wilbarger Crossing and Shiloh (south of present Hutto and south of the onetime residence of William Juvenal). In the fall of that year, Josiah Taylor settled on Brushy Creek near where Shiloh School later stood south of Hutto, and sold goods there until he moved to Georgetown in 1850.[2] "About all the stores had was a barrel of whiskey, a few boxes of axle grease and some sulphur matches." The stores are believed to have been in the rooms of dwellings and two or three customers a day were about average. The store opened when a customer arrived.[3]

After holding the first protestant service in Freeman Smalley's home [4] in 1847, Reverend R. H. Taliaferro in 1848 organized the first Baptist church of the county. The log church, built about one mile north of Old Round Rock, was called Missionary Baptist Church. It had ten or twelve members, with George Glascock* serving as clerk. The church disbanded about 1852 "as the congregation was so scattered."[6] The indefatigable Robert Hay Taliaferro "preached as often as possible in all the destitute places such as Georgetown, Webberville, Bastrop and San Marcos. . . . Brother Taliaferro organized the first church in Williamson County when there was not a glass window nor plank in the county."[7] Reverend Taliaferro married the only daughter of Washington Anderson of Round Rock.

It was a long way in the 1840s from the Brushy Creek and San Gabriel River settlements to the seat of government at Nashville-on-the-Brazos in Milam District, where legal matters were transacted. The valley settlements were growing and by 1848 some of the settlers decided it was time to form a new county. Early in 1848, two copies of a hand-written petition were circulated in the western part of Milam District asking the legislature to create a new county. One was in the distinctive writing of Washington Anderson and was circulated by Anderson and James O. Rice. Both copies of the petition suggested the name San Gabriel County, but on one, "San Gabriel" was scratched out and the name "Clear Water" written in its place. The petitions may not have reached everyone living in what would become Williamson County, particularly those in isolated areas, for a few

* George D. Glascock [sic] signed the petition to form Williamson County,[5] was probably the same man as the clerk of the first church. Connection with the land developer, George Washington Glasscock, Sr., has not been established.

names of known residents at that time are not on the petition. Since many of the men and most of the women of those times could not write, some signatures may have been lacking for that reason. Legend says that in order to obtain a sufficient number of signatures, women and children were also asked to sign. This may have been so in a very few instances, but most of the signatures are known to be those of adult males. W. K. Makemson, who was eleven years old at the time, wrote fifty-six years later: "I remember distinctly when Washington Anderson and James O. Rice brought the petition to my father's house for his signature. After he had signed it, they insisted that my mother sign it also, and I, a boy of but eleven years, signed it at their request."[8] The original manuscript pages of signatures in the Texas State Archives do not corroborate his statement, however. Samuel Makemson, W. K.'s father, did indeed sign the petition, but none of the other signatures bears that surname. Some such measure may have been discussed and either ruled out or found to be unnecessary. Several signatures do appear twice—once on each of the petition lists. Few, if any, of the 107 signatures were apparently of children or of women. Historian W. K. Makemson's estimate that 250 persons lived in Williamson County in 1848 may be somewhat modest. It is known that 120 ballots were cast by eligible voters of the area in the November 7, 1848, presidential election.[9]

The two petitions to form the county were almost identical. On both, the name originally written for the county was San Gabriel, and on both this name was crossed out. The copy in Washington Anderson's hand substituted the name Clear Water. No name was inserted in the other petition. The other minor variation is indicated in brackets in the exact copy of Anderson's petition, which follows:

> *Petition of the citizens of the western portion of Milam County; Febr. 2, '48*
> To the Honorable Legislature of the State of Texas
> Your Petitioners citizens of the western portion of Milam County would most respectfully ask your Honorable body, as an act of convenience and justice to themselves, to grant unto them a new County to be known and
> "Clear Water"
> Styled the County of ~~San Gabriel~~ with the following limits and boundaries to wit: Beginning on the dividing waters of Colorado and Brazos rivers at the S. W. corner of a Survey of 19 ¾ labors in the name of Thomas A. Graves. Thence N. 19° w. to the Salado, known as one of the Three forks of Little River. Thence S. 71° W. to the dividing waters of Colorado and Brazos. Thence down said divide with the meanders of the same to the beginning.
> Your petitioners would further represent to your Hon. body that in their present situation it is very inconvenient for them to attend the courts of Milam County, most of them having to go from 40 to 50 miles. Your pe-

To the Honorable Legislature of
the State of Texas
        Your Petitioners citizens of
the western portion of Milam County
would most respectfully ask your
Honorable body, as an act of convenience
and justice to themselves, to grant unto
them a new County to be known and
Styled the County of "Clearwater" with
the following limits and boundaries to wit:
Beginning on the dividing waters of Colorado
and Brazos rivers at the S.W. corner of a
Survey of 19¼ labors in the name of Thomas
a Graves. Thence N19°w to the Salado, known
as one of the Three forks of Little River
Thence S75°w to the dividing waters of Colorado
and Brazos, Thence down said divide with
the meanders of the same to the beginning
        Your petitioners would further represent to
Your Hon body that in their present Situation
it is very inconvenient for them to attend the
Courts of Milam County, most of them having
to go from 40 to 50 miles. Your petitioners
earnestly hope Your Hon. body will take their
Case into consideration, and grant to them
what they ask, and they will Ever pray &c
David Lee
James M. Burris

titioners earnestly hope your Hon. body will take their case [claim] into consideration, and grant to them what they ask, and they will ever pray it.

[signed] *

DAVID LOVE		
JAMES M. BURRIS	1	
IRA E. CHALK	2	
WHITFIELD CHALK	3	
JOHN FLEMING	4	
WASHINGTON FLEMING	5	
MOSES HUGHES	6	
D. C. COWAN	7	
GIDEON P. COWAN	8	
JAMES E. WILLIAMS	9	
BELA COLLINS	10	
JACOB CASNER	11	
H. A. CHADWICK	12	[Henry A.]
W. C. DALRYMPLE	13	
REUBEN QUEEN	14	
ELIAS QUEEN	15	
WM. CLIFTON	16	
JOHN C. ROBEY	17	[*Deed Book* I, 238]
D. W. WILLIAMS	18	
EVAN WILLIAMS	19	
ALLEN STROUD	20	
IRA STROUD	21	
SAMUEL A. STROUD	22	
WM. Y. CANNON	23	[name appears twice]
G. T. WILLIAMS	24	[name appears twice]
JOSIAH DYCHES	25	
THOMAS Seaton	26	
ANDREW MAKAY	27	[in 1850 Census, Andrew J. McKay; often appears in other records as Andrew Jackson Mackay, Mackey, or Makay, which appears to be his signature. *Deed Book* I, 363; II, 230, and others.]
G. Bomine [?]	28	
JOSEPH BISHOP	29	
SAMUEL W. HART	30	
JOSIAH HART	31	

* Names printed in upper case letters are unmistakeably and plainly written, or have been corroborated by other records. Those in lower case indicate some difficulty in deciphering. David Love's name was the first one on the Anderson petition; James M. Burris was first on the other copy. Numbers beside names are as they appear on the original pages. Given names in brackets were frequently-used forms found elsewhere in records.

Ira E. Chalk — 2

Whitfield Chalk 3

John Fleming 4

Jo Washington Fleming 5

Moss Hughes 6

D. C. Cowan 7

Gideon P. Cowan 8

James E. Williams 9

Bela Collins 10

Jacob Garner 11

W. T. Chadwick 12

W. Dalrymple 13

Reuben Queen 14

Elias Queen 15

Jno. Clifton 16

John C. Baley 17

P. W. Williams 18

Evan Williams 19

Allen Stroud 20

Ira Stroud 21

Samuel A. Stroud 22

Wm. Y. Cannon 23

G. W. Williams 24

Josiah Dycha 25

Thomas Grates 26

Andrew Bralery 27

C. K. Minor 28

Joseph Bishop 29

Samuel Wheat 30

Josiah Hart 31

John Miller 32

Abel Cook 33

C. C. Cook 34

Real H. Cook 35

Washington Anderson 36

Charles Harris 37

John Berry 38

William Berry 39

D. J. Walling 40

D. Perkins 41

J. P. Perkins 42

J. L. Perkins 43

Jared Keagans 44

R. M. Webber 45

J. H. Anderson 46

Sam Safford 47

John Halse 48

David Harris

Danl. Hamblen

John Marshall

L. M. Baker

Isro D Glascock

Washington Anderson

Levi Asher

Jno. A. Harrell

Edward one

Archabell McDowload

J. M. Harrell

J. G. Harrell

J. J. Harrell

P. J. K. Baban

Matthew Hoss

Joseph H. Thurstone

Benjamin Thurstone

J. H. Hornsby

J. H. Hornsby

A. J. unis

JOHN MILLER	32	
OBED. COOK	33	
C. C. COOK	34	
RIAL A. COOK	35	
WASHINGTON ANDERSON	36	[name appears twice]
CHARLES HARRIS	37	
JOHN BERRY	38	
WILLIAM BERRY	39	
D. J. DOBBINS	40	
D. PERKINS	41	
I. P. PERKINS	42	
J. D. PERKINS	43	
ZARA STEARNS	44	
R. M. WEBBER	45	
T. H. ANDERSON	46	
JOHN Lansford [?]	47	
JOHN Harris	48	[1850 Census]
DAVID HARRIS		
DAN'L. KIMBRO		[scratched out; name appears again]
LEWIS CHANDLER		
JOHN MARSHALL		[name appears twice]
D. M. BAKER		
GEO. D. GLASCOCK		[*sic,* see *Deed Book I,* 226]
WASHINGTON ANDERSON		[repetition]
LEVI ASHER		
JOAB. B. HARRELL		
EDWARD ORE		[*Deed Book I,* 39]
Archabel McDonload		
J. M. HARRELL		
J. G. HARRELL		[James G.]
J. J. HARRELL		[John J.]
T. H. BACON		[Thomas]
MATTHEW MOSS		
JOSEPH H. FREESTONE		
BENJAMIN S. FREESTONE		
T. M. HORNSBY		[scratched out]
T. M. HORNSBY		[Thomas M.]
A. Rice		[note A. P. Rice, *Deed Book* V, 326; R. A. Renick, *Deed Book* VII, 602]
THOMAS PRICE	49	
JASON CASNER	50	
SAMUEL WATKINS	51	[*sic*; see 1850 Census, Samuel Wadkins]
JAMES O. RICE	52	
BENJAMIN ALLEN	53	

Thomas Price
Jason Casnen
Samuel Watkins
Larry O Price 52
Benjamin Allen 53
W. J. Anderson 54

John S Knight 55
Samuel Makenson 56
William Knight Jr 57
William Patterson 58
William Knight 59
John R Smith 60
Freeman Smalley 61
Richa'd Saukersby 62
napoleon graham 63
G. J. Williams 64
John Marshall
W J Cannon 66
J. Wm Roby 67
James R McSmith 68
Lewis H. Tankersley 69
Francis J Robey 70
Tobias B Allen
L D Marshall 71
Elias G marshall
Lewis Shafoller 73

Greenleaf Fisk
Wm H Fisk
Jesse Graham
Isaac W. Graham
John B Smalley
William S Smalley
Dan'l Kimbro 98
Phil A Barton 99
G. W. Franklin
James B Allen
Wm Blankenship
John Roby

We the under signed
partition to have our
County named
Clearwatter county

W. I. ANDERSON	54	
JOHN S. KNIGHT	55	
SAMUEL MAKEMSON	56	
WILLIAM KNIGHT JR.	57	
WILLIAM PATTERSON	58	
WILLIAM KNIGHT	59	
JOHN SMITH	60	
FREEMAN SMALLEY	61	
RICHARD TANKERSLEY	62	
Napoleon GRAHAM	63	
G. T. WILLIAMS	64	[repetition]
JOHN MARSHALL	65	[repetition]
W. Y. CANNON	66	[repetition]
WM. ROBEY	67	
JAMES A. SMITH	68	
JAMES H. TANKERSLEY	69	
FRANCIS A. ROBEY	70	
TOBIAS B. ASHER		[not numbered]
L. D. MARSHALL	71	
ELIAS G. MARSHALL	72	
GREENLEAF FISK		
WM. A. FISK		
JESSE GRAHAM		
ISAAC W. GRAHAM		
JOHN R. SMALLEY		
WILLIAM A. SMALLEY		
DAN'L KIMBRO		[repetition]
R. A. BARTON	99	
G. H. P. Franklin [?]		
JAMES B. ALLEN		
WM. BLANKENSHIP		
JOHN ROBEY		[possibly repetition of John C. Robey]

We the under signed partition to have our County named clear watter county[10]

Acceding that the petitioners did have to travel forty to fifty miles to attend court and transact other business, the State Legislature promptly approved the creation of a new county on March 13, 1848.[11] The names suggested by the petitioners, Clear Water County and San Gabriel County, were ignored. Double names were frowned upon in some governmental circles, and besides, the legislature was in the habit of honoring one of its own most distinguished or best-liked members when selecting county names. Handsome, personable Judge Robert McAlpin Williamson, affectionately called "Three-Legged Willie," met the qualifications and may have gently prodded his colleagues to remember him. When the bill to create the "county of San Gabriel" came before the Senate, "three legged Willie arose, being somewhat excited in spirit, and protested against having any more saints in Texas, whereupon San Gabriel was changed for Williamson."[12]

Establishing county boundaries, the Act also stated that

John Berry, Senr., William C. Dalrymple, David C. Cowen,* Washington Anderson, J. M. Harrell, and J. O. Rice, are hereby appointed Commissioners, who shall proceed, (paying due regard to donations of land that may be offered,) to select two eligible sites, neither of which shall be more than five miles from the center of said county; and shall submit the same to the legal voters residing within the aforementioned limits, at public election, to be held on the first Monday in May next.

The Act further provided that if no land was donated, the commissioners were to purchase up to 320 acres, selling a part or all of it to obtain money for necessary public buildings, and "reserving to themselves one dollar per day for each and every day they may be required to serve." The balance of the funds were to be under the supervision of the Commissioners. Civil suits would be transferred from Milam to Williamson County. After placing the county in the second Judicial District and ordering the election on the first Monday in May, the Act concluded, "Be it further enacted, That the Chief Justice of Milam county shall organize said new county in the conformity to law; and that this act take effect from and after its passage.

"Approved, March 13, 1848."[13]

Judge Robert McAlpin Williamson never resided in the county named for him but was well known in the area. Outgoing and energetic, he traveled over the state in his various roles as a country school teacher, preacher, newspaper editor, lawyer, judge, soldier, patriot, and successful political figure. He encouraged Texas' fight for independence, supported its joining the Union, and named a son, born in 1845, Annexus. When the Republic of Texas established the Texas Rangers, Major Williamson directed the organization of the first three ranging companies, one of which, Captain John J. Tumlinson's, erected the block house near present Leander early in 1836. As judge of the Republic's Third Judicial District, R. M. Williamson rode circuit of six counties to hold court—the counties including Milam District which encompassed the future Williamson County. He served in the Congress of the Republic and in the Texas State Senate.[14]

As a young man of fifteen, Robert Williamson had a serious two-year illness, then diagnosed as white leg. His right leg was left crippled and

* Misspelled; should be David C. Cowan.

Judge Robert McAlpin "Three-Legged Willie" Williamson.

shriveled. For the rest of his life, he kept it drawn back at the knee, fastening to it a wooden leg and acquiring for himself a nickname, Three-Legged Willie. During his long illness, the youth read prolifically. He was admitted to the bar before his nineteenth birthday. A broad-shouldered handsome man with wavy black hair and deep blue eyes, he was known in Texas as a powerful orator, a colorful story-teller with a flair for the dramatic, an effective campaigner. He played the banjo, sang, and often patted the juba "for some nimble footed scapegrace to dance" and was called a "nimrod of no mean order." Noah Smithwick, a blacksmith who lived in Williamson-Burnet counties, was a friend of Williamson's and once had the assignment of repairing the famous wooden leg.[15] Legend tells of an early visit Three-Legged Willie made to Williamson County which led to the naming of a stream. He was riding his horse toward a creek bank with several other men when the horse unexpectedly stopped, throwing Williamson off. His peg leg stuck firmly in the mud and his friends had to help extract him. From that time, the stream was known as "Willie's" or "Williamson" Creek. There may be truth in the legend, for in 1856 the editor of the county's first newspaper, the *Georgetown Independent*, editorialized in favor of a new mail route between Georgetown and Cameron for residents "upon Williamson's or Willey's creek."[16] At any rate, the source of the stream in question is called Williamson Creek from its headwaters until it converges with Opossum Creek, whereupon it becomes Willis Creek, possibly a corruption of Willie's Creek.

The men entrusted with the task of locating a county seat met in May 1848 under a large live oak tree a few blocks south of the two forks of the San Gabriel. This spot became the corner of Locust* (present Ninth) and Church* streets in Georgetown. As the Commissioners deliberated, George Washington Glasscock, Sr., member of a land development firm which had extensive land holdings in the area, arrived on horseback. He had a proposition: if the Commissioners would select *this* site and name the town Georgetown in his honor, Glasscock would donate a tract of land for the county seat. He delineated the tract—all land within a line from the live oak tree where they stood, due north to the South San Gabriel River, and within another line from the same tree due west to the same river. This pie-shaped area contained about 173 acres. "Paying due regard to donations of land" offered, the Commissioners accepted the proposition and quickly had a county seat, a new town,* and a name.[17] A variation of this story was told to historian, W. L. Mann by his great grandfather, Washington Anderson:

> The five commissioners were looking at the various sites to establish a county seat and were resting one day under the large oak tree (destroyed by lightning in 1887) near John M. Cluck's present [1941] residence in Georgetown. George Glasscock, Sr., came riding along on a mule and ran into his cousin Washington Anderson and the other four commissioners. Washington Anderson spoke up and said, "George, if you will give us all the land, pointing north, between here and the San Gabriel River, we will make this the county seat and name the prospective city after you, calling it Georgetown." Mr. George Glasscock agreed to the proposition.[18]

The land was actually owned jointly by Glasscock and his partner in the real estate business, Thomas B. Huling, but since Huling was a member of the Texas Legislature he preferred for political reasons not to be di-

---

* For a short time, Locust was "Blue Street," and Church was "Red Street."
* Although there was no Georgetown before May 1848, the community did boast a post office, called Brushy, the fourth one assigned to Milam District. It was designated on November 2, 1847, with Richard Tankersley as postmaster. Since Tankersley owned the property and is believed to have had his home near the west bank of present Smith Branch (on the 1973 site of Southwestern University's golf course), the post office is thought to have been in his home there. "Brushy" was applied to numerous localities at that period, for it was an apt description of them. Even in 1973, the banks of Smith Branch in that vicinity remain brushy. Brushy Post Office was changed to read "Georgetown" on July 27, 1848, and the office was presumably moved "uptown" where Francis M. Nash, the new postmaster, had just put up a new building at present Eighth and Austin Avenue. Frank Nash, as he was called, erected an eighteen-foot square cabin of cedar logs, one and a half stories high, with shed room kitchen in the rear and a lean-to on the north, used as a dining room. It became the first hotel in Georgetown.[23] The records prior to 1848 for Williamson County were a part of the Milam County collection which unfortunately burned in a Courthouse fire in Cameron in 1874, explaining a scarcity of data about these earliest post offices and other matters probably recorded in Milam County, but destroyed.

rectly involved in such transactions and had authorized Glasscock to act for him. The deed drawn transferring the land to the county lists both Huling and Glasscock as owners.[19]

Two surveyors, Matthias Wilbarger and D. C. Cowan, marked the tract into lots and on July 4, 1848, a public sale of the lots was held, the proceeds going to the new county.[20] An election was called for August 7[21] at which time the following officials were chosen:

Greenleaf Fisk, Chief Justice. (The office was later called County Judge.)
Whitfield Chalk, Sheriff.
George T. Williams, County Clerk.
Ira E. Chalk, District Clerk.
John Gooch, County Treasurer
Jacob M. Harrell, W. I. Anderson, D. H. McFadin, Richard Tankersley, County Commissioners.[22]

When buildings were scarce in the tiny new town, the live oak tree at the southeast edge of the city lots was a popular meeting place. On October 10, 1848, the grand jury held the first district court under the tree. Washington Anderson was foreman, and jurymen were D. C. Cowan, William Berry, John Berry, Sr., James G. Harrell, Jackson Berry, Calvin Barker, James Standefer, Peter Banta, Thomas Hornsby, Elias Marshall, Abner Gray and Daniel Kimbro. The court found "no presentments to make, and no bills to return." One civil case was called for, "Cause No. 1, M. C. Hamilton vs. James O. Rice, trespass to try title." The case was continued until the next term, set for March 22, 1849.[24] The historic live oak tree blew down in a storm on June 15, 1886, according to W. K. Makemson.

For a Courthouse, county officials built a small log cabin "about sixteen feet square" on Main Street, facing west toward the center of the town square.

At one time they were holding court in the log court house when several buffaloes, which were being chased by dogs and horsemen, ran through the town, and they were killed about a quarter of a mile below Georgetown. Mrs. [James] Knight in those early days saved the life of his [James'] cousin twice in one day, first by killing a large American lion, and next a large wild male hog.[25]

One of the earliest known photographs made in the county is of the log Courthouse, apparently built late in 1848 or early in 1849.[26]

The first time a jail was needed in Georgetown, a makeshift one was improvised by turning a wagon bed upside down near the live oak tree

First Courthouse, a log cabin, 1849 to May 1851.

meeting place. The culprit was confined underneath the wagon bed while the constable slept on top of the wagon to prevent his escape.[27]

Like Williamson County's patron, R. M. Williamson, the donor of land for the county "site" was a colorful man. George Washington Glasscock, Sr., came to Texas in 1834, fought in the Texas Revolution, and for about twenty years dealt in land certificates in partnership with Thomas B. Huling and Henry Mallard. Between 1838 and 1845, he surveyed more than 200,000 acres of land in central Texas, locating his own league of land in Williamson County in 1838. He moved to Bastrop County in 1840 and on to Williamson County in 1848, settling on a farm about one mile east of the junction of the North and South San Gabriels, remaining in the county five years. That first fall of 1848, he put up his water-powered mill on the farm.[28]

For some years during the Glasscock-Huling partnership, Glasscock was the contact man for land deals. Huling served for a period in the State Legislature and he cautioned Glasscock never to sell lands in Huling's name. Huling handled most of the firm's correspondence, which was voluminous and included many communications with Williamson County men like W. C. Dalrymple, Benjamin Gooch, Joel A. Houghton, John J. Stubblefield and Neal McGaffey. Huling was apparently in a position to know of the formation of Williamson County and Glasscock was ready to make the right offer to the Commissioners. The legal agreement for the donated land reads:

> . . . We, George W. Glasscock and Thomas B. Huling for and in considera-
> tion of the location of the County Site of Williamson County, being lo-

cated thereon and the sum of one dollar to us in hand paid . . . convey
unto the County . . . [the tract] out of the locations of the head right
of Clement Stubblefield, Nicholas Porter and William Addison . . . containing one hundred and seventy two acres and one thousand and forty three
square varas of land . . . with all the rights and privaledges . . . the twentieth
day of November 1849.[29]

Glasscock ventured into a number of businesses, in 1853 moved to
Travis County and during the tenth and eleventh sessions was the representative from Travis and Williamson counties in the State Legislature.
He died in 1868 as the result of injuries received when he fell from a
mule he was riding at his Webberville farm. He had ten children, a number of whom made their homes in Williamson County.[30]

George W. Glasscock, Jr., came to Georgetown in 1879 to practice
law, held several public offices, built an imposing Victorian-style home on
the north bank of the North Gabriel River (a short distance west of present
Highway 81, standing in 1973). He painted the large home white, using
bright red around windows and for decorative trim. Others of the children
who lived in the county were Albert Horton, Andrew J. and Elizabeth
Jane Glasscock.[31]

HOW THE FIRST SETTLERS LIVED

The frills of life were almost unknown to the handful of pioneers who
came to Williamson County in the 1830s and 1840s.

Shelter from the elements and from Indian raiders was of prime concern to newcomers. A small, simple log cabin of one or two rooms was

Early log home in western section of county.

usually raised as quickly as possible when a family arrived. The men built a scaffold seven or eight feet high, rolled a log on top of the scaffold, and one man there and another beneath pulled a saw up and down until the log was cut. Floors were puncheon (split logs) or, more likely, dirt, the latter wet down and beaten with a maul to harden it. Mud, clay, or adobe filled cracks in the walls between logs. Many cabins had no windows and none at first had glass. If there were windows, they were hung on hinges, to open for air and light, and were usually covered with buffalo hide. When the first glass came into the county in the 1850s, it was a rare luxury. Wooden doors were held together with wooden pegs, were hung on wooden hinges and fastened with wooden latches. A two-room log cabin was the first "manor" house of a farm. Homes of this size were adequate since the mild climate permitted much work to be done outdoors.[32] After 1850 some few homes were built of hand hewn stone or of lumber cut by hand with whip saws, although most postdate the Civil War. The early cabin contained one fireplace to provide warmth and to serve as a cook stove. These homes, said Noah Smithwick, who lived in them, "were absolutely devoid of comfort."[33] Fire making followed the Indian custom of splitting a stick filled with pith. With the pith side turned up, a sharp stick was placed in the pith and turned rapidly until the pith caught fire. In similar manner, flint and steel were used with spunk or punk found growing in post oak trees.

A few hardy souls lived in tents for a few years. Daniel Kimbro, who lived north of Brushy Creek and who signed the petition to form the county, hunted vension for his food, dressed the skins to make his clothing and harnesses, and sold the surplus to traders in Austin. "His home was built just in the edge of the bottom and prairie land and was made by setting posts in the ground and covering the sides and top with deer skins, trophies of the chase which he loved so well."[34] Another man was said to have lived in a·tent for several years on the peninsula between the North and South San Gabriels, just above their confluence.[35]

Home furnishings were often extremely crude and scanty, including only the necessities, but sometimes they were finer, depending upon the means of the settler and also how he got to Texas. Those who came on horseback brought nothing. Those arriving by wagon train often brought family treasures. Others went to Galveston by steamer or schooner, or down a navigable river such as the Ohio by keelboat to the Mississippi, the Red River, then completed the trip overland. If there was space, the immigrants brought along furniture, farm tools, cooking utensils, provisions, and clothing. Those arriving empty handed made their own tools, furniture, deerskin clothes, and improvised with whatever materials were at hand to provide the essentials of life. Even the simplest home, however, usually contained bedsteads and feather mattresses.[36] In 1846 Roemer found most houses furnished with a bed, table, and a few chairs with calfskin seats tightly stretched. Over a huge fireplace was hung a long barrel rifle, a shot gun, and possibly a tall cabinet containing books.[37]

> In order to be convenient to wood and water, the first settlers built their log cabins and made their homes near the creeks. At the time the county was organized, with few exceptions, the settlements were confined to Brushy Creek and San Gabriel River. Comparatively few settlements were made far out in the prairies until the era of barbed wire and the advent of railroads.[38]

Several families usually clustered near each other for security in these valley settlements.[39] However, some wanted isolation and complete privacy and a few hardy souls were so much disturbed at having neighbors a few miles away, or at seeing smoke from someone else's chimney, they indignantly moved beyond the frontiers. But they were exceptions. "Our common danger was a strong tie to bind us together. . . . The sound of galloping hoofs, in the middle of the night . . . heralded a tale of blood," of a neighbor who had been killed and his family taken captive or murdered.[40]

The settlers and their ancestors had lived in the wooded eastern states for as much as two centuries. Now migration onto the plains required a new way of life. The riverboat used in the east was not practical in Texas and was replaced by the horse. A horse and a gun were the most needed tools.

Money was scarce. Pelts were the standard medium of exchange; buffalo tallow and wild honey could also be traded for provisions. Bastrop was the closest trading center in the 1840s. Ox teams could be sent there for supplies, but there was always danger of meeting unfriendly Indians. If the ground was wet, the trip was slow, indeed. Powder and lead were priority items; then came coffee, sugar, calico and possibly some castor oil and rhubarb—medicine for the children.[41]

First arrivals lived without bread for a while, eating buffalo and other wild meats, but as soon as a family could grow a crop, corn became the staff of life for both man and beast. Logs with hollowed out basins often served as mills where shelled corn was mauled with a "hominy pestle." Or, the Indian-type mortar and pestle or the small hand-run Armstrong steel home mill slowly ground the corn. To operate any one of these primitive mills was tedious and extremely tiring. Housewives not only baked cornbread; they scalded the kernels of corn, peeled off the skin and cooked them into hominy or mush.[42]

Captain Jake Harrell said that after a man had hauled water and ground his bread on a steel mill or beat it in a mortar for a year he was unfitted for any business requiring energy and perseverance. "I got so that I knew to a grain how much corn it would take for a meal and I couldn't turn another lick till driven to it by the necessity of bread for the next meal."[43] [Nevertheless, the slow, laborious process yielded a bread which] was sweet, nutritious and palatable, and far superior in quality to that made from meal turned out by grist mills in later times.[44]

But those old mills and mortars were a kind of connecting link; a touchstone as it were, to test a man's willingness to earn his bread. When you rode up to a cabin and heard the old mill grinding away or the pounding of the mortar, if you were willing to earn the welcome that was sure to be extended to you, you recognized your opportunity. [After preliminary greetings were exchanged,] let me spell you awhile [was] an offer which was gratefully accepted. Then if you were ambitious to still further ingratiate yourself, you would be up betimes in the morning and bag a wild turkey or perhaps a deer to replenish the stock of provisions you were helping to diminish. Corn was generally plenty, and so long as you were willing to assist in converting it into bread you were welcome to remain. Thus every family had its retinue of retainers if it could boast of no other evidence of aristocracy, and, in fact, it was necessary to keep up the retinue to guard against the Indians. And, by the way, those same Indians were an important factor in the solution of the social problem. But for the ever present danger which kept the white people "rounded up," herded together as it were, love of dominion would, like with the patriarchs of old, have isolated the families, precluding the possibility of schools or any other social organization.[45]

After crops were grown, wild game, wild honey and edible wild plants supplemented the diet, and many of the unfortunate encounters with Indians occurred when men of the family were out hunting buffalo, deer, bear, and smaller game. Domestic animals were so scarce that anyone owning them was likely to be nicknamed to indicate a special status.[46] Roemer found settlers raising hogs in 1846, and said their chief meat was pork. Beef, hogs and chickens were gradually acquired and the more industrious farmer or his wife planted vegetable gardens both spring and fall.[47] Farmers raised corn, cotton, sugar, tobacco and, in the vegetable garden, beans, peas, sweet potatoes, watermelons, pumpkins, peaches and figs. Oxen pulled homemade plows made of forked limbs, one limb serving as a plow, the other branch as a beam to which handles were attached. This plow was sharpened with a knife. Cattle thrived and multiplied "in a remarkable degree" in the prairies which offered "the most natural luxuriant pasturage." Pecans were gathered from the river bottoms in the fall and "whole wagon loads" were taken to Houston from where they were shipped to the northern states. "The wealth of flowers in the extensive prairies" made bee culture a recommended industry and "the natural fertility of the soil assures excellent crops for years to come," wrote Roemer.[48] The luxury of bread came when a crop of wheat was grown. Then the housewife made her own yeast and kept a small piece always as her "start."

Buckskin clothing was accepted dress for men and children, and it was not uncommon in early years for the women. But the ladies soon managed what must have seemed to them the luxuries of civilization by turning their homes into miniature textile factories, with carding, spinning, weaving, fulling, dyeing, and tailoring equipment. The men often assumed the responsibility of growing a small patch of cotton near the house, but usually the ladies and children gathered it, picked out the seeds by hand, carded the cotton, spun the thread, and wove the cloth. When wool became available, it was used, but for a long time hides continued to provide blankets and some clothing. Dyes were made from native berries and juices of plants and trees. One early "receipt" for dyeing ten yards of handwoven cloth read: mix four pounds logwood, two pounds madder and boil well. Dissolve two ounces bluestone in earthen vessel, pour this into the dye and stir well. Add the cloth, boil one hour, stirring all the time. Hang out to dry. Repeat the entire process until cloth is black.[49] After fabric was woven and dyed, the housewife cut and sewed it into garments, creating her own patterns according to her talents. A rare treat was the arrival in the settlements of a strolling peddler with a piece of calico or domestic or linsey, or the infrequent opportunity to purchase such goods from the nearest trading post. If a family had managed to collect an extra supply of pelts, honey, or other barterable items, it might mean a length of "bought" fabric for the housewife. "Bought" cloth in those days was as rare an extravagance as a length of hand woven fabric of the finest quality to the middle class seamstress of the 1970s. Pioneer women and children worked even at night by firelight at their textile chores, and when the ladies were not otherwise occupied, their knitting needles were apt to be clicking away at warm socks for the family.[50]

"Beholding the loveliest natural scenery . . . and taking part in the stirring adventures of the chase" were the only luxuries afforded the frontiersmen.[51] However, the tasks of survival, of building, of improvisation and innovation, and of hoarding toward a better future were ever-present adventures and challenges. Never had the man and his lady a better opportunity to be creative—to design home and tools, to establish churches and schools, to build mills and dams, to study the weather and experiment with crops, to learn the meaning of nature and read the signs it had for man. Families planned, built, were wiped out by disaster, then revised, re-planned, and rebuilt. Pioneers learned by *doing* a century before the same procedure became a fashionable method in public education. The house-wife improvised in the kitchen, invented recipes to fit her commodities, and traded her best ones with her neighbors. She created color in dyes, designs in quilts, bedspreads, and clothing. She knew the art of weaving, sewed and pieced quilts by hand, patiently making dainty, deliberate, accurate stitches. Her handiwork graces many a museum collection.

Noah Smithwick said that the Tonkawas of central Texas always re-mained friendly toward the whites and that the only point of dissension he knew was in conservation theories. The Indians derived a substantial revenue from the pecan crops of the county, "but with reckless prodigality they persisted in killing the goose that laid the golden egg, in chopping off the limbs of the trees to faciliate the gathering. This the owners of the land on which the trees grew objected to." The Tonkawas sold wild game, mainly venison, to pioneer families until feeding grounds were in-vaded and deer became scarce. One lady customer asked a Tonkawa why he did not bring wild turkey, as it was still plentiful. He replied, "Turkey too hard to kill. Injun crawl along in the grass, deer; he say 'Maybe so, Injun; maybe so, stump.' and then he go on eat. Injun crawl a little close and shoot him. Turkey look, 'Injun, by God,' and he duck his head and run."[52]

"The Texan Indians, unlike their eastern brethren, scorned to till the soil, and the few Mexicans scattered through the country did so only to the extent of supplying their own wants; so when the colonists used up the breadstuff they brought with them they had to do without until they raised it."[53]

Floods, drouths and epidemics sometimes swept the frontier settle-ments. The Great Overflow and Asiatic cholera hit Texas in 1833, mainly in the southern part. Smallpox epidemics struck in 1830, 1835, 1840 and 1844. Yellow fever was rampant in 1839 and 1844 and malarial fevers in the summer and fall of 1843, especially in the river areas from the Brazos to the Colorado. Dysentery was an almost ever present ailment.[54] Williamson County had all these diseases, but the availability of pure drinking water and the absence of mosquito-infested swamps minimized them most of the time. In fact, the area had the reputation of being one of the healthier places in the state—a factor in the choice of Georgetown for the relocation of what became Southwestern University, where the school would be free from the devastating yellow fever prevalent in the lowlands. Typhoid or smallpox at times swept through an entire family, killing all or most of its victims. Nearly every early settler established a small family cemetery on his farm. In some of these graveyards, every burial is said to be a person who died of smallpox.

Doctors came as early as other settlers. A few were trained in medical schools but many had acquired their knowledge much as young would-be attorneys who "read" law. Forty-six-year-old Dr. Edward H. Scruggs was probably the second medical man to live in the county, after Dr. Thomas Kenney (1838). Dr. Scruggs lived in the household of Josiah Dyches, who arrived in the summer of 1846 and built his home on the San Gabriel just east of where the Katy depot later stood at Circleville. Dr. William I. Anderson, 41, brought his wife, Nancy P. Knight Anderson, and daughter, Hellen, from Illinois in the fall of 1846, settling on Brushy Creek one mile below Wadkins Crossing. Dr. William M. Owen and his wife, Sarah, came to the county before Georgetown was established, arriving in 1847. He lived between the two forks of the San Gabriel near Blue Hole and was Georgetown's first doctor. Two other physicians arrived in 1847, William Knight and David F. Knight, from Danville, Illinois, living for a time on Brushy Creek near Round Rock. Dr. William Knight moved to Georgetown in 1848 and Dr. David Knight moved there in 1850. A medical doctor and historian of the county described one of the first county doctors as a " 'yarb' and goose grease" practitioner who had considerable success regardless of his lack of training.[55]

In spite of the pioneers' fierce pursuit of privacy and independence, there was much loneliness, especially for the women. Often they had left far behind all their close relations and friends to come to a strange country. Many a letter went to the Carolinas or Tennessee or Illinois, or wherever home had been, containing glowing reports of this inviting and beautiful new land. On occasion, the reports were somewhat over optimistic in an attempt to persuade loved ones to join their families in Texas. Other letters poignantly told of heartache, fear, isolation, danger, sickness, or sorrow. Dr. Roemer generally praised central Texas, but admitted he found much malaria, ague, and dysentery, the latter occurring in the fall "in a very malignant form." He noted that the Comanches were the most dangerous Indians of the area, but the Wacos were also depredating on white settlers. Although life was simple and often crude, many well-educated men were enduring it with resignation "if they could only secure for themselves a station in life."[56]

Unfamiliar night sounds could be frightening in this new, remote home.

Smithwick visited Williamson County when there were many alligators in the streams and in shallow pools alongside them. The alligator's

> bellow was just such a hideous sound as might be expected to issue from the throat of such a hideous creature. . . . The tuneful mosquito, whose song, like the opera singer's, has a business ring to it [and] wolves and owls added their voices to the dismal serenade. . . . The whippoorwill's silvery notes filled in the interludes, but they seemed strangely out of tune.[57]

The first church services and school classes were held in log homes. When separate structures were possible, both church and school usually shared the same building. Often the Masonic Lodge put up the school-church and became a third partner in sharing the physical plant.

> In a log house of Mr. Freeman Smalley just below Watkins Crossing on Brushy Creek the first sermon was preached in Williamson County, Texas by R. H. Taliaferro on December 1847. [Fannie Taliaferro, the daughter of Reverend Taliaferro, described the scene in the Smalley log cabin.] We see in memory the great enormous fireplace, with the crane to the side of the chimney with large iron pot containing the turnip greens, and good old cornmeal dumplings, the Dutch oven containing the yellow yams. The mantle board is festooned with a string of red pepper across to dry for the winter use. When the preaching service closed it was the custom to invite all to partake of the frugal meal.*[58]

In the summer of 1848, James G. Harrell and "one or two others" erected a log cabin at Moss's Spring on Lake Creek to be used as a school, west of present Round Rock. The builders employed a Mr. Allen, probably Hudson Allen, (1850 census) as teacher, and among the first students were Henry Bratton, F. M. Harrell, Azalee Harrell, and several of the Moss children. Makemson says it was the first school building in the county.[60] The early log schools had dirt floors, no windows, and were not yet state supported. Families who were ambitious for their children provided facilities, a teacher, and administered school affairs. Teachers were expected to be strict disciplinarians. Students sat on log benches, studied the "three Rs" and learned to write with goose quills, carefully sharpened and frequently mended.[61] A few mastered the art of using this difficult pen, writing in beautiful script with graceful flourish, but many deeds, letters, and records from that period are evidence that others found the goose

---

* Dr. Wm. L. Mann, an avid collector of Williamson County history, was a grandson of Taliaferro. Reverend Taliaferro organized a church in Austin in July 1847, with eight members, had close ties with Williamson County, having married the daughter of Washing Anderson.[59]

quill too difficult to conquer. School was in session when weather and work on the farm permitted.

The ancestor of Southwestern University at Georgetown, the first college in Texas, officially opened on February 1, 1840. It was located at Rutersville, near present La Grange, named for Reverend Martin Ruter, a Methodist missionary who came to Texas in 1837. The college had about a hundred students within a few years, of whom more than half were girls. Three to five faculty members taught Latin, Greek, German, French, Italian, Spanish, calculus, logic, philosophy, surveying, geology, botany, and piano. Actually, most of the students were not sufficiently advanced for college work, and Prince Solms of New Braunfels disdainfully called the college "an American elementary school." It was said, too, that the boys who enrolled at Rutersville did little but hunt Indians prior to 1842.[62] The college's early trials did not lessen the dedication of those who believed in higher education nor their determination to keep the school operating. It was then the custom to place the school building in an isolated position on a hill, and Roemer noted that Rutersville College "presents a stately appearance from the distance."[63] Dr. Thomas Kenney of Kenney Fort postponed enrolling his daughters in Rutersville a few days to help Nelson Merrell gather his buffalo hides, and lost his life as a result.

Various Baptist, Presbyterian, Methodist and Episcopal groups came to Texas in the 1820s and 1830s, but denominational activity began only after Texas' independence and its release from the state religion, Catholicism. These denominations had representatives in Williamson County at early dates.[64]

From religious services held in homes with resident farmers often acting as ministers, the growing communities progressed to formal church houses and travelling ministers or circuit riders. The Methodist Church organized early camp meetings and other denominations joined in this popular custom, especially after Texas joined the Union. Brush arbors were built in shady groves near good drinking water. The annual summer meeting lasted four to ten days, with families arriving from as far away as forty or fifty miles. They brought camping equipment, slept in tents or in wagons on the grounds, and cooked in the open. Preachers spoke several times a day. Singing was an important part of the services, unaccompanied at first. In later years, a piano or reed organ provided accompaniment.[65] When song books were not available, and they usually were not, a layman or the minister "lined out" the hymns, reading or singing a phrase, which the congregation then repeated. Baptists and Methodists were especially known for their vigorous singing. Anticipated as social events as well as serious religious experiences, camp meetings supplied the setting for developing lifetime friendships and romances. Presbyterian, Baptist and Methodist churches admitted Negro members to their congregations and sometimes helped them organize their own Negro churches, usually under the leadership of a white minister. Circuit riders endured loneliness, poverty, life in the wilderness, and danger of Indian ambush to carry out their work. They were "not afraid to die or sleep in the woods."[66]

As the frontier crossed Williamson County, buffalo became scarcer, but were hunted as long as a few remained. John Holland Jenkins wrote about his experiences with buffalo in central Texas. The hunter must aim at the head of the animal, for their matted manes made them hard to kill. In rough country, one could not catch buffalo on horseback, but on smooth, firm ground, it was another story.

> Headlong the great body plunges forward, without turn or pause no matter what obstruction or difficulty presents itself—over bluffs, hollows, saplings, caloes—everything! And there is no earthly chance to break down a buffalo which is in medium order and fresh at starting. It is wonderful how long and how fast they can run.

Jenkins found the meat delicious, the wool good for knitting thread, and recommended the mop for ropes, girths, bridle reins, and the hide for lariats and moccasin soles.[67]

Trading three hundred acres of his land for a derringer pistol, Jenkins traveled with an Indian named Phillip, learning bee hunting and wood-craft. On camping expeditions, they hunted bee trees. Jenkins could follow a bee half a mile. He carried an axe to cut the tree, but never brought a vessel for the honey. Instead, he killed a deer, removed the hide from neck to heels, and closed off all bullet holes with buckskin ties secured by small wooden pegs to prevent the strings from slipping off. The hide, turned wrong side out, was blown up to check it for tightness, then was laid out in the sun to dry. It was then ready to hold fifteen or twenty gallons of honey, and filled, weighed almost two hundred pounds. This treasure was hung on the limb of a tree and when honey was needed a leg was untied to serve as a spigot.[68] Wild bees were plentiful in central Texas and furnished the sweetening in many pioneer kitchens. Scientist Gustaf Wilhelm Belfrage, on a collecting expedition, was told that people standing on the hills near Round Rock periodically saw what appeared to be a spiral of smoke rising from the ground. Intrigued, he investigated and discovered that the "smoke" was actually a great swarm of bees emerging from a small slit in a ridge. The edges of the adjacent rock had been worn slick by this movement of the bees.[69]

One of the most astute and prolific observers of central Texas was scientist Dr. Ferdinand Roemer, who wrote with insight and humor of scientific matters and of social customs and conditions in the Williamson County area in 1846. The sudden northers, typical from November to May, were indicated only by a few signs—a peculiar cloud formation or flight of birds southward.

> The stranger is not aware of their coming until he hears their doleful whistle and feels their icy blast. . . . Convalescents have particular reason to guard against this influence of the wind, for exposure to it may cause a chill and a recurrence of malaria fever. . . . Uprooted, decaying trees were strewn about everywhere. If a tree happened to fall across the path, it was not removed but the course of the road was changed, according to an American custom. [The level, unbroken, grassy plain] extended for miles before us on which a few islands of trees and shrubs were scattered in irregular order. The oft-made comparison with an English park on a grand scale appeared very appropriate to me. . . . All of us, including the ladies, rode . . . on horseback, as oxcarts were the only other conveyances used in this region. The women of Texas . . . learn to ride in early youth.[70]

Four yoke of oxen were hitched to each wagon and urged on by Roemer's encouraging shouts. Thus all commerce in the entire state of Texas was carried on. During the winter months, many farmers hauled goods while the fields did not require their presence, thus supplementing the family income with what was usually a profitable business. The oxen lived on grass along the way. Their hoofs were broader than those of horses and mules and did not sink into the mud as easily. A yoke of oxen could be purchased for $40 or $50, whereas a pair of good draft horses cost $150 to $200. The pace was slow, however. Oxen averaged about ten or fifteen miles a day, and it took skill to drive the beasts. Roemer's wagon was stuck in the mud twenty times in one day. If all the horses or oxen were hitched to one wagon, sometimes it could be pulled out of a mud hole, but often even this did not work, and all the freight had to be removed from the wagon. "This was done at least five times in the course of the day. When complete exhaustion of man and beast compelled us to halt at night, we had gone only six miles and were still a mile from the river." When rain fell in torrents, the travelers sought shelter under their wagons. Farm homes served as inns, where the washing facilities were a tin basin, gourd dipper and bucket of water. Supper might include tea or coffee, fried bacon and warm cornbread. A more elaborate menu added biscuits, eggs, butter, honey and canned fruits.[71]

Dr. Roemer reported there was no rock on the prairies, but plenty of suitable materials north of Austin for road building. "Road building was confined chiefly to indicating the directions between important points, [felling] trees along the river banks where necessary, [lowering] the inclines at the fords, and [installing] ferries at the larger rivers." There were many hog wallows. Camping on the Yegua, which crosses the southeastern tip of Williamson County, he recorded: "Nowhere was I molested more by mosquitoes than there. No sooner had I lain down under a liveoak tree tired and worn from the long trip, when I heard their ominous humming." After a sleepless night of being stung mercilessly, the men were advised at their next stop to sleep on the roof of an outhouse. There they were high enough off the ground not to attract the insects.[72]

The party of scientists saw two prairie fires. One, occurring at night, was

like a sparkling diamond necklace [in which the mile-long strip of flame] raced along over hill and dale, now moving slowly, now faster, now flickering brightly, now growing dim. . . . My companion was of the opinion that Indians had without doubt started the fire, since they do this often to drive the game in a certain direction, and also to expedite the growth of the grass by burning off the dry grass.

Possibly also Indians knew that intense heat was required to germinate the hard-coated buffalo grass seed. The travelers burned the grass off near their camp to assure their safety when they saw a second fire.

An especially beautiful view was afforded by a group of live oaks, on which magical illuminations were cast by the burning grass. . . . As a general rule the fire does not advance so quickly that one cannot escape with ease. Furthermore, the burning strip is usually so narrow that one could easily jump over it. Only when fanned by heavy winds and when the grass is exceptionally long, do the flames move rapidly and the heat become intense. As a rule the fire is not fierce enough to consume shrubs of the thickness of a finger which lie in its path, but it merely destroys the leaves. However, in such an event a mounted man would have little difficulty to escape from the approaching fire or to find a place where the grass is short. These fires often cause severe losses near the settlements, since they destroy the fences enclosing the fields. When the settlers sight a prairie fire nearing their farms, especially during a strong wind, all the inhabitants hurry to the threatened place, and an effort is made to extinguish the flames by beating them with wet sacks, or a ditch is drawn to halt their advance.[73]

Roemer visited a Lipan Apache camp where he was reminded of the oriental lifestyle, with men in domineering positions and the women doing

much of the hard work. He found the women of good humor and all the
Lipans friendly. He watched the squaws pack all their movable possessions, mainly dried meat and hides, into large buffalo skins. The Indians carried them to the river, set "a pair of blackeyed papooses" on
each bundle, and then propelled them over the swift streams "with the
greatest dexterity. Two squaws always swam near a bundle." At the new
campsite, the women cut branches as framework for the tents and covered
them with skins. "The men did not participate in this work, but primped
and decorated themselves during this time. After everything had been
prepared for their reception, they swam across the stream on their horses.
Later the squaws drove the rest of their many horses across the stream,
and in a short time the transfer of the camp was accomplished." At Torrey's Trading Post on the Brazos, Roemer saw a long caravan of Indians
arrive, riding single file on their horses, bringing pack horses loaded with
skins and household goods. On arriving, the women immediately got busy
cutting branches to set up their tents; skins were traded and goods chosen,
the whole visit lasting several days. It all reminded Roemer of a country
fair. When the scientist and his party headed back toward Austin, they
crossed the Brazos at the falls (near present Marlin), then "took a direct
road to Austin" through the heart of Williamson County.[74]

On the first day's trip from Little River, the scientist saw only three
human habitations, one of them belonging to a Mr. Bryant, a farmer on
Little River, who complained that the Comanches had taken most of his
half-ripe corn several days earlier.

On leaving the bottom [of Little River] we had an immeasurable prairie,
covered with mesquite trees, before us. After a ride of several hours we came
to a little brook called Willes Creek where buffaloes in great numbers were
grazing. After a ride of forty miles we camped under the sky on the banks
of the St. Gabriel River. This river is as clear and beautiful as the Guadalupe
at New Braunfels, but of less volume. Despite the great natural advantages
there were no settlements found here. Several years ago a German by the
name of Schubert, who later was employed by the Verein, established a settlement a little lower on the river, but he had to abandon it on account of
sickness and for other reasons.[75]
On the following morning we rode fifteen miles before breakfast. This we
ate at the isolated home of a Yankee on Brushy Creek who had lived here
for two years. During breakfast our host informed us that he had in mind to
abandon his farm and to move farther up the river. When my companion,
who on a previous trip found this man well satisfied with his present home,
asked in astonishment what induced him to make such a resolve, he answered
in a tone of voice which sounded as though he were suffering from an intolerable condition: "The country is getting too crowded, I cannot live here

any longer." This reason seemed peculiar to me since I had seen no houses far and near and I therefore asked him how close the nearest neighbor lived. "Well, the next fellow lives but ten miles from here," he answered. I expressed my deep regrets to the man for being so hemmed in and at the same time thought to myself, that it was indeed fortunate that everyone in old Europe did not require so much of the earth's surface as did this old backwoodsman. From here it was only twenty miles to Austin, which place we reached at noon.[76]

VI

The Pioneers Dig In: 1850-1860

POPULATION

Kenney Fort, other tiny settlements up and down Brushy Creek, and Georgetown were the most densely populated places in the county in 1850. The U. S. Census of that year listed 1,379 whites and there were 155 Negro slaves in the hands of 41 families. John Williams owned 18, T. Allen and William Ake, 15 each. The census showed 230 dwellings in the entire county. Georgetown had about a dozen houses.[1] By 1858 the population had about doubled (3,779), of whom 667 were qualified voters. It was a youth culture, for 988 of the population were school-age children between six and eighteen; 805 males were under eighteen, 558 between eighteen and forty-five, and only 156 men were over forty-five years old. County tax rolls for 1858 showed 249,528 acres of land valued at $545,520, with only 22,618 acres in cultivation; 11,100 were planted in corn, 9,350 in wheat, 1,378 in cotton. The county listed 4,000 horses, 25,000 cattle, 21 money lenders, and aggregate taxable property of $1,419,648.[2]

Indians were still much in evidence in and near the county and, although the new residents generally found them friendly, there were occasional troubles. An officer reported in January 1850 that "the Indians came in on Willeys Creek and drove of [sic] forty head of horses," and that between Spice Wood Springs and Georgetown "Indians are sean by some person every day." A large number of Comanches appeared near Georgetown in May 1850. Four years later, Governor Elisha M. Pease addressed a letter to A. J. Strickland, A. S. Walker and Dr. W. M. Owen of Williamson County regarding a petition for Rangers to protect the frontier.[3]

A TRIP ACROSS THE COUNTY

J. H. Kuykendall, prolific diarist and note keeper of Austin's Colony just south of Williamson County, often traveled into Williamson County territory. In 1853 he visited this "Northern Frontier of Texas" along with five other men, starting from the West Yegua and traveling through sandy, post oak country on May 10, 1853, toward Brushy Creek.

> Upon reaching the waters of Brushy the aspect of the country greatly improves. . . . There is a sparse settlement here but no houses in sight of our camp. After encamping, one of our party killed a deer—coffee, biscuit, "corn dodgers," "Old Ned" and roast venison constituted our bill of fare. . . . Distance travelled, 28 miles. [The next morning the party saw many hog wallows in the rich but "tenacious" soil. Riding over the prairies to the San Gabriel River in the eastern part of the county, they saw] a beautiful stream affording a considerable volume of water. The current is swift and the water looks as blue as the sky above it. . . . The chimneys of a house near the road are built of limestone, hence, I infer, there is a quarry in the neighborhood, though we have seen no outcrop of rocks. The bed of the Gabriel is, however, covered with pebbles. [North of Donahoe Creek they saw a bois d'arc hedge belonging to a man named Pennington.] This hedge we are told is four years old and seems likely to succeed very well. It enclosed a farm of six or seven acres. [Kuykendall and his friends went to the headwaters of the North Gabriel. Descending along this stream, they found] far and near . . . innumerable extensive groves of postoak and liveoak. . . . Cool, gushing springs and brawling brooks intersect your course at every furlong. Indeed there are some localities where, without poetic exageration [sic] one may, at the same moment "List to the music of a hundred streams." This is an admirable section and must soon attract attention. There are but two or three settlements hereabout, where there is room for a hundred.[4]

The times were not limited to poetry and pleasure, as even the indefatigable Noah Smithwick admitted, for life was rugged and survival often in jeopardy. A lady of the area wrote in 1857 to a relative who lived far away, "Times is hard. . . . their is prosspect of them being better." Her letter was filled with messages to various members of the family and her main theme was that she wanted all of them to visit Texas in the summer, "for she wants to see her so bad. . . . I will quit and take a dip of snuff."[5]

SCHOOLS, LODGES, CHURCHES

The first community schools were organized by ambitious pioneers who could afford to hire a teacher, and were primarily for their own children. When a minister was available, religious services were held in the homes. Moss's Spring and Knight's schools, organized in 1848, were the earliest and have been previously described. "To promote the progress of education," a place for an academy was reserved in Georgetown by the Police Court* at their February 1850 meeting. The school was to be located on the south bluff of the South San Gabriel in the second block west of present Austin Avenue, between First and Second streets. The school obviously was established, for in 1867 the county sold the block "whereon the old School house" was situated to the Georgetown Male & Female Academy trustees.[6]

Common School laws enacted by the State in 1854 and 1856 had little local effect because only sixty-two cents per student for an entire year was made available. The county officials, on March 20, 1854, ordered fourteen school districts organized in the county and appointed presiding officers to hold school elections. Like the early schools themselves, these districts were not named, but were referred to by the name of the person on whose property the school stood or the person responsible for operation of the school, usually the same man. The fourteen men and their approximate districts were:

1. Isaac Garner—west and north of Granger, including Dare Buzzard, Macedonia, Denson, Ake, Bartlett and Granger communities.

2. Nathaniel Burden—Water Valley (Jonah), Towns Mill (Weir) and surrounding areas.

3. Columbus Gillett—Circleville and areas south to Brushy Creek and east to Mustang Creek.

4. Wilaby Ethridge—northeast Williamson County to the area of Thrall.

5. Adam Lawrence—Cross Roads (Lawrence Chapel), Post Oak Island and the southeastern section of the county.

6. James E. Robinson—areas between Taylor and Hutto, including Blue Hill (Rice's Crossing).

7. Zara Stearns—from Shiloh (on Brushy Creek south of Hutto) to the Round Rock area.

---

* Police Court included the Chief Justice and four Commissioners. A few decades later, it was called County Court; the presiding officer was County Judge and the entire body known as the County Court or Commissioners Court.

8. James Boyce—Round Rock and area.

9. James Standefer—from Running Brushy south to county line and area.

10. James Branch—Bagdad and area.

11. G. S. C. Harper—Georgetown and surrounding area.

12. John Caskey—Brooksville (Florence) and vicinity.

13. M. S. Skaggs—Gabriel Mills and surrounding area.

14. Greenleaf Fisk—Liberty Hill and area between North and South San Gabriels to within about three miles of Georgetown.[7]

A Williamson County Board of School Examiners was appointed in 1858 to consider qualifications of prospective teachers and to issue certificates to those approved.[8] Georgetown's "male and female school" and fifteen other schools were reported by M. W. Northington, tax assessor-collector, in 1858. Most of the buildings at that time were log.[9]

Masonic lodges sometimes brought the first school and church facilities to a community. The first lodge in the county was San Gabriel No. 89, established at Georgetown in 1851, followed soon by Mount Horeb Lodge No. 137 in Gabriel Mills in 1853, and by Post Oak Island No. 181 in 1855. To avoid trouble with Indians, meeting times were often set for the first Saturday after the full moon.[10] One of the early schools in the county, Mount Horeb School, was founded in 1856 and sponsored by the local Gabriel Mills lodge. Round Rock Lodge No. 227 was established in 1858, Mountain Lodge No. 277 at Burleson Springs (Hopewell) in 1863, and another lodge-sponsored school, Greenwood Masonic Institute, was founded in Round Rock in 1867.[11]

Churches, like schools, were started by a handful of people, usually in a home. Reverend Freeman Smalley, hosting the first protestant sermon in his home near Kenney Fort late in 1847, has already been mentioned. Baptists, Cumberland Presbyterians, Methodists and Christians were the denominations mentioned in existing early records, but not many pre-Civil War church records have been preserved. The *1850 Census* lists five ministers, John T. Cox, Methodist, of Round Rock; Noah McChristian and James W. Lloyd, both Methodists of Georgetown; Stephen Strickland, Christian of Georgetown; and John H. Russell, Baptist of Liberty Hill.

Circleville Church and Opossum Creek Church were organized in October 1855, with Dr. Isaac Newton Hodgen, minister. Between that time and 1862, James Eubank and a Dr. Kendrick also preached at the two churches and held baptismal services.[12] Most of the early churches occupied the same building as the community school and most were "Union" churches. That is, various demoninations alternated holding Sunday services and nearly everyone in the community attended all Sundays that meetings were held. Since most ministers of that time rode the circuits, church met only when a preacher was available or when local men served as lay ministers.

POST OFFICES, BOUNDARIES, ROADS
AND STAGE LINES

The Texas Republic organized a postal system on the U. S. plan but funds were short and service was poor. After Texas joined the Union, mail went to populated areas by hack or coach service and to remote settlements as someone happened to pass. Since envelopes were unknown, letters were simply folded and secured with sealing wax, addressed, then sent with a passerby to whatever post office he saw on his travels.

Before Williamson County was organized, that area had one post office, at "Brushy" (Georgetown), established November 2, 1847, the fourth office in Milam District. Soon after the Williamson County seat was selected, the name "Brushy" was changed on postal records to Georgetown, July 27, 1848. Blue Hill (Rice's Crossing) post office was authorized November 12, 1849, receiving its mail from Austin via horseback. "Brushy Creek" post office was approved May 27, 1851, and three years later, August 24, 1854, the name of the office was changed to Round Rock. In 1852 a line of two horse hacks was established from San Antonio through Austin, Round Rock, Georgetown, Waco, Dallas and Memphis, Tennessee. Contracting with the government to carry the mail, private companies made the two trips a week over this line, later increasing to three a week.

Another stage line left Austin, turning northwest over the "mountain road," otherwise called the Central National Road, which passed through

Remnants of rock fence which lined stagecoach route through Pond Spring.

Stagecoach Inn, Bagdad

Jollyville, Pond Spring, Running Brushy (Cedar Park), Bagdad, Liberty Hill, South Gabriel and Lampasas. Liberty Hill got its post office on December 2, 1853; Pond Spring on March 16, 1854, and Bagdad on May 8, 1855. The stage dropped mail at these towns for nearby communities. Until Florence was granted a post office November 25, 1857, Mahomet, just over the line in Burnet County, received mail for both Florence and Gabriel Mills, sending it there once a week by horseback and saddlebags. Gabriel Mills post office was approved June 29, 1858.[13]

A horse mail came weekly from Brenham via Lexington, Post Oak Island and Circleville to Georgetown. Post Oak Island's post office was assigned August 1; 1855, and Circleville's on March 13, 1857.[14] Cross Roads (Lawrence Chapel) had a post office November 1, 1858.

The famed Indian fighter, Big Foot Wallace, drove an early stagecoach on the Austin-Gatesville road via Georgetown. Colonel W. C. Dalrymple of Georgetown contracted with that line to deliver corn to the soldiers at Fort Gates and the road was frequently referred to as the Old Corn Road for this reason. Corn Hill, north of Georgetown, through which the line passed, was named by Judge John E. King for his home on a hill and his nearby cornfields. He was proud of the fine corn he grew, hanging several especially large ears on his porch for stagecoach travelers to see. Thus the community was named when the post office was assigned July 9, 1855.

Corn Hill stage stop-post office-residence of Judge John E. King.

During its first ten years of existence, the county had an even dozen post offices.[15]

Relay stations, also called stage stands, were located about eighteen miles apart, and were where the coaches changed their teams of four or six horses. Williamson County's western stage line stopped to rest under a

John T. Bryson home, Liberty Hill, where stagecoach stopped, had rock fence and stile.

giant live oak tree at Thomas Rutledge's home in Jollyville. Short routes had stopping places for meals and lodging—the stagecoach inns. The place where the line changed horses was usually thought of as the official "stop," but a stage often made several stops, even in small communities— at the stable, the inn and the post office, or sometimes the tavern. John T. Bryson at Liberty Hill decided his home should be a stage stop, so he put up a sign, and the coach honored it, although it stopped elsewhere in the village. Stagecoaches on long routes traveled night and day and in all weather. Passengers carried their own food as there were few opportunities for them to get it elsewhere. Passenger fees were about ten cents a mile. Each person could carry thirty pounds of personal luggage, plus a blanket and guns, which might be needed along the way.[16]

Williamson County had a thirteenth post office in its first decade— chronologically the third in the county—San Gabriel, assigned on August 13, 1850. Boundary lines of the county were not clearly defined even at the end of the century, and this uncertainty led to mistaken county affiliations for several post offices, towns and schools. The town of San Gabriel was actually in Milam County and the correction was made by the postal department in 1856.[17]

As settlements spread to the west and northwest, the need for another county arose and on February 5, 1852, Burnet was formed from parts of Williamson, Travis and Bell Counties. Originally, Williamson County included the headwaters of the South San Gabriel in a wedge-shaped piece fastened onto the present southwestern border. That area was lost to Burnet County and included South Gabriel, later Bertram. Compensating somewhat for this loss, a wide, shallow gable-shaped piece was added north of Florence on February 7, 1853 from Bell County. Until then, Williamson's northwest boundary line ran just at the north edge of Florence.[18]

County roads were little more than beaten pathways across the prairies or hills and at the fordable places in streams. The blacklands of eastern Williamson County became tenacious mudholes in wet weather, slowing, stopping or preventing normal travel. A favorite story of the times tells of a horseman who saw a large hat lying on the mud of a road. Slogging to it, he found there was a man underneath. The stranger declined his help, saying, "Don't move me. I'm on a good horse, and it has just found solid bottom."

After the government in 1851 established a string of frontier forts, including Fort Croghan (present Burnet), the Austin-Bagdad-Liberty Hill highway, previously referred to as the "mountain" or Central National Road, was popularly called the "military" road because of the military traffic over it between Austin and the forts. The grove where Bagdad was soon to be built was about halfway between Austin and Fort Croghan so it was a favorite camp ground for the army stationed at the fort. Charles Babcock kept a "wayside inn" at Bagdad and many officers, including the popular and distinguished Robert E. Lee, frequently stayed there. Lee had been sent to command Fort Mason shortly after the forts were established and had the additional assignment of hearing court martial proceedings at forts all over the state. Since he enjoyed seeing as much of the state as he could, Lee made it a practice to travel as many different routes as possible. His was a familiar figure in Williamson County, particularly in the western section.[19]

Texas Land Office maps for the 1850s show two towns, Georgetown and Post Oak Island in 1851; Florence, Liberty Hill and Round Rock added to the first two in 1856, and a Colton map for 1857 includes Blue Hill.[20]

William E. Bouchelle in the mid-1850s described his trip to Austin from Georgetown "down Brushy Road," which had numerous forks branching off toward the settlements up and down Brushy Creek.

> The whole wide prairie was unsettled. None of these roads were worked . . . and of course there were no sign boards, but settlers on Brushy Creek coming to Georgetown would take certain objects and ride or drive to them, so that what at first were mere trails soon came to be plain roads. If a person started out alone to ride over a prairie where he had never been before, it was necessary for him to notice closely everything within the range of his vision, unless he wanted to be wandering over the prairie like a lost lunatic not knowing north from south.[21]

Soon after leaving Georgetown down Brushy Road, Bouchelle came to Double File Trail. He looked back and could see where this trail would cross the San Gabriel, just below Towns Mill. "On looking south I could see that it would strike Brushy higher up than I thought Ben Allen crossing ought to be, so after riding along the old trail some distance I took a left-hand road which brought me straight to Ben Allen's." Allen offered Bouchelle some peaches from his orchard, remarking, "I reckon you don't get many peaches in Georgetown." His guest agreed, adding that John Shell had begun experimenting in fruit raising at Georgetown. Bouchelle asked about the road to Austin. Allen told him that it was "as straight as an arrow and nothing to put you out. It was run with a compass . . . by the government of the Republic of Texas . . . and put through during Lamar's administration." The traveler crossed the creek, turned west to where Dyer had built a mill, rode up the incline until he could see across the prairie and found that the road was, indeed, plain and straight. "I did not see a single human habitation until I came in sight of the timber on Walnut Creek. Judge Fisk's farm was the first settlement that I came to." At this place (Fiskville), the most traveled road left the straight compass route which was the line set out from Coleman's Fort a little below Austin. The newer road, not quite on the compass line, led directly to the new capital, Austin City.[22]

At nearly every meeting of the Police Court or Commissioners Court held during the nineteenth century, officials heard reports from overseers and road committees appointed to "examine and mark" or "lay out" the most "direct and elegible rout" from one village to another. Overseers were "authorized and required to call out all the hands," meaning every able-bodied male in that area. "Marking" consisted of placing near the roads large, flat native stones on which were carved "G. T. 8 m" (Georgetown, eight miles), or similar directions.[23]

Five roads designated in the summer of 1850 indicate the most traveled routes at that time: from Georgetown to Brushy Creek, from Georgetown toward Bastrop, from Alligator Creek toward Austin, from the main divide between the San Gabriel River and Brushy Creek to the county line in the direction of Austin, and from Georgetown to Austin via Jacob M. Harrell's place. Since Bastrop pre-dated Williamson County towns and had a saw mill and other needed facilities, that road was in considerable demand. Personnel lists on road committees lengthened as the population of the county increased. The early lists apparently were hurriedly prepared, with incomplete names and misspellings, but also indicate a real effort to get the road work done.[24]

The men to lay out a road from Georgetown to Bastrop were John Lee, Thomas Price, Harrison Hynaman, Samuel Wadkins, Robins at prices, Kyzer, James Forbis, J. N. Wright, B. Allen and negro, William West, Mr. Faris, J. Casner, Luther Stearns, David Stearns, William Blankenship, Abram Wright, Loren Oxley, George Ellis, J. S. Allen, John Stearns, William Dantz, Jesse Smalley and Mr. Rains.[25]

Brushy Road, which led south on what was then Brushy Street in Georgetown (now Austin Avenue) was the way traveled "by the widow Knight and John Knight." The workers were J. Ake, James, Robert and S. Alexander, Dr. Allen, Payton Allen, D. and H. Baker, Bate and J. Berry, Baylor Black, George Blackman, Birkett Bowmer, James M. Burris, Aza O., J. E. and Jesse Chism, D. C. and Gideon Cowan, Wm. C. Dalrymple, Fleming, G. W. Glasscock, Hanna, James G. Harrell, Charles Harris, Highland (probably Hyland), Moses Hughes, Hudson, Jennings, Kelsey, John

Knight, Bery Levett, Love, A. McEntire, A. J. Mackay, Samuel Mankins, D., Elias and Baker Lewis Marshall, Mekker, J. Mercer, Moses, O. Bryeans, Dr. Ogle, Jerry and Reuben Queen, Eldridge Rains, Robbins, Roberts, John D. Rowland, F. Schwab, Shadreck, Shell, Smilser, James A. Smith, Samuel Stroud, James Tankersley, Rice and John Ben Thomas, Thornbery, Utz, David Williams, Evan Williams, George T. Williams, Thomas Windsor, Yarberry, Ake, Hughes, Smith and Williams.[26]

To plan the road from Alligator toward Austin were J. Armstrong, J. Bingham, A. and O. Cook, Wm. Covington, J. Crow, James, John and Riley Dawson, Preston Dyches, James Ellmon and two sons, Elias Gardner, Isaac Garner, Gorman, Wm. Harris, J. Jones, D. H. McFadin, G., H. and J. Robbins, L. West, J. Wilkinson and J. R. —earth.[27]

From the Brushy-San Gabriel divide toward Austin, road hands were Willis Avery, Richard Bain, C. Barker and brother, Elihu Casner, Josiah Clifton, Benjamin and James Freestone, R. W. Hornsby, Daniel Kimbro, D. F. Knight, J. Kuykendall, Samuel Makemson, John Payne, Robert Parsons, Bartlett Sims, Wm. Taylor, Wm. Walters, M. Wilbarger and Wm. Young.[28]

Those assigned to work Georgetown to Austin road via Brushy—"hands" to view and mark the way—included A. and S. Acres, W. Anderson, M. and T. Asher, T. Bacon, Wm. Bratton, Crain, G. D. Glascock, Graham, H. Hanes, A. J., Jacob M. and John Harrell, John and J. Lewis, G. and J. Ratliff, A. and J. Robey, F. and S. Smalley, Stevens, Walsh, and several names undecipherable.[29]

Within a short time, additional roads were required in the direction of Hamilton Valley (later Burnet), Mather's Mill, Glasscock Mill, Berry's Mill, Ft. Gates, Bryant's Station, Nolanville and Cameron. In August 1850, a committee was appointed to work out a road from Georgetown toward the home of Adam Lawrence: Adam Lawrence, John P. Payen, James Olive, Nelson Morey and Henry A. Sample.[30]

Besides marking the best route, the committee might remove obstructions from the paths, such as fallen trees. Sometimes on impassable and difficult muddy places, timber was cut and logs laid side to side, creating the ill-famed corduroy road.

COUNTY BUSINESS

The first seven pages of Williamson County Police Court records for 1848 and most of 1849 have been lost. Some sources suggest that the Court rented the first "log cabin" Courthouse, but minutes for the 1852 May session mention "a certain logg cabin originally built by said Court for a County Clerk's office."[31] At any rate, the sixteen-foot square house proved extremely cramped quarters. In March 1850 the Commissioners planned a stone Courthouse fifty feet square, two stories high, with walls two feet thick, to be erected on the Public Square. Each floor would have two fireplaces. Lots not already sold in Georgetown were to be auctioned and the money used to pay for the new building. Dr. William Knight, William C. Dalrymple and John Williams were appointed to supervise the construction.[32]

Meanwhile there were other pressing matters such as the need for a jail. In December 1850, the Court ordered a two story double log building, twelve feet square, built in the rear of the log Courthouse. It was to be five feet below ground level and seven feet above, have two openings two feet square and a trap door leading to a stairway. The double walls of oak timbers were to be filled with flint rock. John Rowland, contractor, agreed to build it for $399.75. It was completed March 26, 1851. A year later, the trap door was found "deficient." Someone bored a hole through it so that prisoners could escape. The Commissioners ordered that the door "be so amended as to stop the said breach."[33]

Before the projected stone Courthouse was finished, the Court, in a called session in May 1851, bought the one story frame home of William

Second Courthouse, 1851–1857, formerly a frame residence.

Patterson and the south half of the lot on which it stood for $390. It was located on the southeast corner of the block due east of the Square, and on the same block with the original log Courthouse and the new jail. (The

Federal Post Office stood in 1973 about where the Patterson home had been.) The house was about fourteen by thirty feet in size and was "weatherboarded but not ceiled inside."[34] Floor space was about double that of the log house. Repairs on the second Courthouse were ordered in February 1852: "make and hang two window shutters . . . & furnish the said windows with sash & glass & place railing across the house in a suitable manner for a barr, also procure seats, chairs, tables, & c."[35] Whether the "barr" was to preserve the privacy and the dignity of the Court (most likely) or to provide a refreshment place was not indicated by the minutes.

Lacking suitable offices for the district and county clerks, the Court decided to sell the log Courthouse "and 60 feet square of the front part of the lot on which said house stands" in May 1852. Money from the sale would be used to add a ten-foot shed on the east side of the frame Courthouse for offices. The sale had been made by November but the Court rescinded plans to add the shed, ordering instead that the Patterson house be partitioned and the rooms lined with "suitable domestic" at a cost of thirty dollars. At the same November 1852 meeting, the Commissioners considered the "unsafe situation of our County Jail," and employed Robert Alexander to repair the trap door which had already caused a great deal of trouble. The officials rented from Evan Williams "both rooms in his large new building" for a district court session, paying $2.50 per day, at their May 1853 session. Similar arrangements for extra space were made periodically, but rental was for a brief time and such rooms were never called nor considered the official Courthouse.[36]

After four years of planning for the new stone House, in March 1854 the Court paid Joseph S. Williams five dollars for a plan he drew, and a contract was let to John Dunlop, with W. I. Anderson as superintendent. Erecting the building took almost as long as the planning. In August 1854, specifications were altered to include a hipped roof, upper walls of rock as in the lower story, and outside walls were to be plastered. Dunlop or "his attourney Samuel Mather" was allowed $850 on the job in November 1854. Difficulties regarding the contract had developed by the next August. The County Court agreed to arbitrate with Mather. He was awarded $51 and was requested to make a contract to complete the Courthouse, the cost not to exceed $5,000. Ed H. Vontress and E. B. Turner acted as attorneys for the county during the arbitration. Apparently these plans collapsed, for Evan Williams contracted to complete the building. In February 1856, his request to use oak in place of pine lentils over the doors was granted. More problems arose. By August 1856 it was noted that plans for the stairs were "not rightly laid out." The two rooms in the upper story were deemed unnecessary and were eliminated from the specifications. C. A. D. Clamp was engaged to construct a proper stairway for $30. Separate contracts were let for plastering both the inside and outer walls. When the job neared completion in February 1857, the Commissioners Court ordered window

Artist's conception of third Courthouse, used 1857-1877, the first to be built on the Public Square. Drawing is based on meager specifications in Police Court minutes.

blinds for the House equal in quality to those of the Josiah Taylor residence, at $9.25 a window.[37]

The new stone Courthouse was examined by the Chief Justice and Commissioners and was accepted during a called meeting March 30, 1857. Evan Williams collected the remainder of his money and the county at last had a building on the Square. The project had taken exactly seven years from the planning stage to its completion. About six weeks later and without illuminating comment, the Court ordered four braces for the "support of the roof of the Court House," the braces to be made of pine or cedar, each six inches square. Also at this time the officials agreed to rent one of the Courthouse rooms to Attorney A. S. Walker.[38]

"Order for Stopping Martins out of Court House" was the heading for action taken in May 1858 when the Commissioners paid William Fitzgerald fifteen dollars to close openings in the upper story "to prevent Martins & other Birds from Entering in Said Room."[39]

The Court authorized Stephen Strickland to sell and dispose of the frame Courthouse (Patterson home) for $150 on the condition that the house be moved from the lot, during their February 1859 meeting. There

was no immediate sale. W. A. Miller rented it in May 1860 at three dollars
a month for his tin shop. Meanwhile, still more repairs were needed on
the "new" stone Courthouse, in June 1860. Early in 1861 Patrick O'Conner
was engaged to lay three hearths on the upper floor.[40]

Another duty of the County Court was issuing liquor licenses "to sell
spirituous liquors" in quantities of less than a quart. The first such permit
went to Ezra Cartledge of Georgetown in May 1856. His saloon was located in a stone grocery store on the northwest corner of the block south
of the Square. At that time, the Masonic Lodge Hall was the upstairs of
the same building.[41]

Random purchases by the county during the 1850s included a lock,
three padlocks, a chain and screws for the jail from J. H. Shaffer of Georgetown for $4.96; a county seal made by James B. Eubank of Circleville, $5;
a broom, a fire shovel, 1¼ pounds sixteen-inch candles, 2½ pounds
twenty-one-inch candles and two candlesticks from E. W. Talbot, Georgetown, totalling $2.95; two loads of wood used to heat district court, hauled
by Sheriff E. Thomason, $2; twelve barrels of water hauled by saloon-
keeper James A. Smith for the county at twenty-five cents a barrel. The
Court received a bill from Dr. C. W. Lewis in 1853 for attending Henry
Miller, who died of confluent smallpox. John Bryson of Liberty Hill sent
the Court a statement totalling $3.80 to reimburse him for a plank to make
a coffin, his labor, and for burying John Sanders.[42]

After an early tax assessor-collector for the county defected, the Commissioners decided "there is conclusive reasons for believing that he has
absconded thereby causing said office to be vacant." They appointed a successor and planned to sue the defector for "several hundred dollars," but
apparently nothing further was done. Funds were always low—in May
1852 the county treasury has a total of $55.91, of which $28.50 were
proceeds from estray sales. Several times county-owned land was sold to
replenish county funds or to pay off debts. Matthias Wilbarger, who
marked off the original town lots in the county seat, was still due $76 for
this service. His heirs were finally paid the debt with Georgetown lots.[43]

EARNING A LIVING

Unsettled conditions in Europe—unsuccessful revolutions, overpopula-
tion, persecution of Jews—all led to migration, as did expansion of railroads in the United States, the cattle boom in Texas, prospecting for mining and the simple urge to own land. Land was the key in Williamson
County. Three-fourths of the male adults living there in 1850 were listed

as farmers and most of the men in other professions or occupations combined their special work with farming.[44]

The frontier man worked extremely hard to "put a roof on the house, corn in the crib, potatoes in the hill, apples and cider in the cellar, and [to extend] the limits of the farm." His main instruments in conquering the country were the axe, rifle, and horse. Not only were the first homes made from the forests, but almost everything else the pioneer needed— cradles, feed troughs, well casings, gate hinges, wagons, wheels, plow beams, bee hives, keg staves, barrel staves, nails, pegs, furniture, mash for hogs, forage for livestock, and ashes which were utilized in tanning hides, making hominy and soap—all were from wood.[45]

Unimproved land, which sold for as little as twenty-three cents an acre in 1848, brought three to five dollars an acre by the late 1850s, and by then little vacant land was left. County farmers produced 25,000 bushels of wheat in 1856 plus modest amounts of cotton, corn and fruit, principally peaches. Cattle and hogs supplied meat to eat; bread was made from corn or wheat grown on the farm; and sweetening was syrup made from sorghum also raised at home. Sheep flourished and stock raising was already recognized in the county as a major source of revenue. Deer were the only wild animal still abundant—"the others have fled"—but turkey and quail were plentiful.[46]

Two young Kentucky attorneys, Thomas Proctor Hughes and Ed Vontress, cousins, decided to come to Texas when they were ready to start practicing law. They reached Georgetown early in 1851. Hughes, who was to build his home on his farm "away out on the prairie" not far south of the present Wesleyan Home, wrote his mother shortly after settling in the county seat:

Georgetown, Texas March 31, 1851

My dear Mother

I was caused to leap for joy this morning when sentrys handed me your long looked for letter, for I had concluded that owing to the defectiveness of our mails, I should never, or rarely ever receive a letter from Ky., as I have personal knowledge of some of its defects as regards tardiness & uncertainty. So I have determined to answer letters promptly & request my correspondents to do so likewise, and thus doing, we will to some degree counteract said defects. I have writen a number of letters directing them back to Ky. and several to different points in this State and yours is the first that I have received. So Ma be punctual, remembering that I am far from my native land and from those whom I hold very dear and that consequently my sources for information are few. When I wrote from New Orleans I designed settling in Washington town, thinking it was the county seat of Washington Co. but learning that the Seat of justice had been moved from there to a more central point, Brenham which was off of the river I advised with several lawyers to whom I had letters of introduction and with those whose acquaintance I made and they refered me to Brazoria & Richmond as good points to locate, so Ed & I turned our direction, took passage on the Gen. Hamer and steered for those places, not liking Brazoria we went to Richmond, and still not liking, we determined to go to Austin, and arriving there we found the place litterly filled with law offices, not having much means we thought it best to retreat for awhile where we could get the county business which would sustain us, at the same time, we would be becoming thoroughly acquainted with the statute law of the State and the mode of practice which is entirely different from that heretofore used in Ky.; So we retreated to a respectable distance, a very prospering, healthy little village, the location of which is extremely sitely, intersperced with live oaks, and surrounded on one side with the a creek that is the clearest water I ever expect to see, why it is perfectly transparent and seems to offer no impediment to the vision, I walk down every morning and look at fish floating about in water from fifteen to twenty feet deep, the fish measuring from a foot and a half to two feet the only way we have of ketching them now is by giging them; I shall procure a net shortly. I when fishing see the little perch taking hold of my hook in fifteen feet water, the large ones rarely bite. I see no local cause for sickness and a flattering prospect for this county' becoming densely populated by stock raisers, we being rather to far off for raising cotton, untill there is no doubt about the navigation of the Colorado, it being twenty five miles to its nearest point, Austin. We have citizens religiously disposed, & some who are disipated, and we have parties here other than democrat & whig. there are a great many indictments found by the Grand juries and most of the land in the county is in dispute which will not be finally settled for years. We have been engaged in several cases, our clients having been indicted by the Grand juries, and several land suits will likely be brought by us. We have made some $30.00 and have enough money to sustain us for several years; we will study together this summer; and will follow the circuit next fall and one will likely settle at some point on a different side of Austin, where we will manufacture popularity by strict attention to business and when we think it advisable we will meet at Austin, holding on to our practice at the former places and in the mean time acquire as much practice as possible in Austin. We had the district court in session in our place last week, at which 17 lawyers were present, and at least 10 of them had Judge prefixed to their names, so you see that we will have to contend with experience; some of them having been judges [remainder of letter missing].[47]

Samuel Dinsmore Carothers, who lived at Ponton a short distance east of present Seward Junction, wrote vividly of life and hardships on a west Williamson County farm in the 1850s.

We moved on the 14th Nov., [1856] family and everything from Austin prairie and I have been at work all the time putting up houses, fences, etc. [His letter is dated January 10, 1857.] I have built three stone chimneys and have three yet to build next spring and summer. [Money was scarce. Carothers had grown two successive short crops and pork was thin.] Too late for me I had sold my corn and could not buy any nearer than 30 or 40 miles and that at $1 per bu. and my hogs very poor, so that I had my pork to buy—go fifty miles for it—drive it myself and pay 5 cts. It takes $40.00 or more to do us. All my neighbors have to buy this year and they all sell pork every year but we may all be glad if we can save our hogs. They are poor now and winter just set in very fierce and we may expect it to last until the 15th or last of Feb. and probably later. We have had a fine fall dry and mild. We had but little cold weather some piercing northers and some ice until this week. . . . This is the fifth day that we have been housed up with raining and freezing ground and everything loaded with ice and timber breaking all the time for we are in the timber, but the sun is shining today and a strong norther blowing and still freezing. . . .[48]

In this country we are all stranger (as it were) to each other and not much credit or indulgence given. A man owes a debt it must come when due or be sued. There's little chance to borrow money and if you should be able to borrow it, it must be paid to the time, and short time at from ten to fifty per cent and often at five and ten per cent per month. Them are extreme cases to save property. . . . You must pay or be sued and probably whipped besides. . . .[49]

My hands sore and cold for I have just finished killing 22 hogs and eat too freely of the pork and had a through of caleromobis [cholera morbus: acute gastroenteritis] but well enough now. My hands are in a bad fix from the effect of lime mortar in stone & brick building. I write bad at best, but worse now than usual. . . .[50]

Grasshoppers, or migratory locusts, hit central Texas in the fall of 1848, in October 1856, and again in 1858. Sam Carothers wrote his brother, Thomas, in June 1858, describing the weather and crops: Spring was wet and just as wheat began to head out, grasshoppers came

and trimmed every blade off it and cut down all the small tender roots, which made it thin but it headed out right away and looks well but the rust struck it and injured nearly all the wheat in the country. . . . Mine was hurt some. . . . It will probably make ten bushels per acre grasshoppers, rust and all. That will leave me four hundred bu. after paying rent and I have 40 acres at home, new land sowed in Feb. (too late). The grasshoppers cut it to the ground but it put up and will probably make 100 Bu. We are stacking now for the thrashers.[51]

We are rather low in spirits now—it is five weeks tonight since we had rain to wet the ground one inch and corn is now shooting and some in roasting ears and beginning to suffer. If we get rain in a week or two we will make thousands of corn.[52]

They elected old Sam [Houston] Governor. . . . I am personally acquainted with A. J. Hamilton (Rep.). I lived two years one miles from him . . . but old Sam, I never seen. . . .[53]

There is a very heavy emigration to our state this fall, I suppose thousands. . . . The grasshoppers come up from the south near the Gulf where they hatch. They come upon us on 7th May from the south & southeast in swarms about 11 o'clock, then air and sun darkened passing over and dropping down as thick as flakes of snow all over the face of the county and went to work and in a few hours every blade of wheat and corn and everything that they could eat was devoured. The ground and timber was covered and some places piled two & three deep. They rest in the night and next day was cloudy—they lay still but Saturday evening was clear they all rase in a cloud and we have heard nothing of them since. All went north. A few stayed a few days. Thos. it is not in my power to describe them and my feelings, I can't do it. It looked like one of Pharos Plagues as I have imagined it. We saved our garden by staying in it all hands with bushes part of three days.[54]

[After farming his land for two years, Carothers in 1859 wrote his brother, John, that the land] is not so good [for] cotton too dry generally but this is the best for wheat . . . but for stock raising the grass is the best & first thing with us which is the cause of farming to be neglected for no one cares much if they dont raise much crop for the stock that every man has here is his principal study. Cropping is a secondary business . . . farming is a good business here if it were not for the grass.[55]

On August 17, 1860, Samuel D. Carothers became postmaster at Ponton, which was, in fact, his home. He reported to his brother in the fall that there had been no recent Indian depredations "but once in a while they come in & take off a bunch of horses & kill a man or two." Carothers also mentioned abolitionists who came from Kansas to burn dwellings, mills and property, prior to the elections. After the furor of elections was over, there was a general settling down. The winter started mild, beef was plenty and hogs were fat. Carothers had corn and wheat to spare, would gather about 150 bushels of "pease" which would bring two dollars a bushel.

After all the threatened hard times we will get along if the Indians and Republicans will let us alone. . . . You have seen by this time how Texas voted in Nov. about four to one for cesession and mass meetings being held in nearly all the country. . . . Old Sam is a perfect blank and a pest to this state for he has had some influence and has his friends yet and always opposes everything that the masses and good men attempts and tries to crush every good and prominent man in the state and even in the union. I think him a grand old villian.*[56]

* Carothers came to Texas from Tennessee, held the southern point of view, disagreeing with Sam Houston who strongly opposed secession.

At the same time Sam Carothers was describing his west Williamson County farm, twenty-year-old Ann Lee Eubank Hayslip was writing her cousin about her new home in Circleville in east Williamson County. Mrs. Hayslip was the daughter of James Eubank, tinner, cabinet maker and silversmith, who brought his family to Circleville late in 1853. Mrs. Hayslip's husband was DeWitt Clinton Hayslip, the first blacksmith in that village. This was blackland farming country where three Eubank brothers and their families settled and built homes in a semi-circle, giving the community its name. The two other brothers, Joseph Jr. and William Eubank, knew the crafts of blacksmith, wheelwright, gunsmith, watchmaker, gold and silversmith, carpentry, wool and cotton grading, milling and ginning. Living a short way to the east were the McFadin and Dyches families, and not far to the west were the David McCurdy Sloan and Sam A. Easley farms. J. P. Smith and Charles G. Wilcox would arrive in the same area in a few years.[57]

Young Mrs. Hayslip wrote from Circleville on May 31, 1855:

Our house is a log cabin, 18 feet square, with stick and mud chimney . . . which often endangers the house by catching on fire and blazing nearly to the roof. . . . Our house is built of small, crooked hewed logs and serves as kitchen, family and sitting room, parlor, dining-room, and also lodging apartments, besides holding a great deal of plunder, such as table, cupboard, boxes, trunks, and Mother's and Frances'** beds. There is a shed-room adjoining the house, in which Mr. Hayslip and I sleep. It, however, is more crowded then the other room, for Pa does all his carpentering, cabinet making, and tinning there, and has a perfect museum of tools crammed all around the room, besides all the sheet-iron and tinware which is piled up and strung up from floor to ceiling and all overhead.[58]

Mother* also has her storeroom and dairy there. So you may imagine how it looks. Even the Texans open their eyes with wonder when they come in to buy tinware. Beverly and Virgil sleep in one of the wagons and Louisa and Jerry occupy one of the tents.[59]

Pa and the boys have been busy tending the corn and have not had time to do anything in the way of building, more than the fence around the field, the shed-room and corn-crib. Pa is working on his farm some and does a little tinning between times. He rented a field ten miles from home, and when they work it they have to camp out a week at a time. We have had a very dry spring, and everything is very backward. No vegetables and only half a crop of wheat will be made. Corn will do tolerably well, if we can have one or two good rains. Pa and Mr. Hayslip [her husband] intend to raise stock. Pa already has thirty head of cattle, twenty-seven head of hogs,

** Frances Eubank was Ann Lee's younger sister. Frances "Fannie" married H. T. Stearns and was the author's paternal grandmother.
* Mary Jane Bransford (Mrs. James Eubank).

and eight head of sheep. But we do not intend to sell hogs, as it costs too
much to feed them. The cattle and sheep live all the year on prairie grass.
We milk about twelve cows and have as much milk and butter as we can
use. Mother churns every day, and has to shorten bread with butter. We
have also made some cheese. We have two pens, one for the cows and one
for the calves, and manage it in this way—turn in the cows after they have
grazed all day, turn out the calves at night, and in the morning put them
up again and turn out the cows. We take about one-fourth of the milk from
the cows or the strippings. Mother and I are raising fowls. We have over
two hundred chickens, a few wild turkeys and two ducks.[60]

I suppose you heard that Tom died before we had been here three weeks.
We had very good health for a while, and ate more than we ever did before, but since the warm weather set in we have been more inclined to in-
dolence and want of energy. This unfortunate desire is peculiar to those
who are acclimating, and, it is said, only a few ever get over it. . . . We have
plain clever neighbors, some of which are always more ready to befriend us
than some of those whose society we used to like better.[61]

I will now give you an idea of the enormous insects we have. I have seen
such spiders as these: [here she draws an excellent picture of the tarantula
and the tarantula wasp, each about $3\frac{1}{2}$ inches across. She says the tarantula
has been known to catch baby chickens, but they are not numerous, are
seldom seen—only when out fighting each other.] Snakes and insects are as
rare here as they were in Kentucky. We have killed only one snake in the
yard and have not seen a mosquito.[62]

During the decade before the Civil War and a for a few years after,
"all articles of clothing and furniture were made by hand from material
produced at home" with all the family participating in the business of
growing, carding, spinning, weaving, sewing or knitting the wool or cotton. Cooking was done in the fireplace or in the yard.[63]

Just as farming was by far the most important occupation in the county,
milling was the primary industry until well after the Civil War. The
early water-run burr mill was gradually replaced by steam roller mills,
which processed both corn and wheat. Some millers added saws to cut
the timber growing along county streams for use in buildings. Occasionally, mills were washed away by floods or severely damaged by high waters
or by fire. More often than not, they were rebuilt.

Washington Anderson's gristmill built on the north bank of Brushy
Creek in 1843 at present Round Rock was the first in the county. A flood
in 1845 washed it away, but others replaced it in the Round Rock area,
including a large one on the south bank of Brushy Creek just west of
Old Round Rock and near the present dam.[64]

John Berry's widely-known gristmill on Berry's Creek northeast of
Georgetown was erected in December 1846 and was operated for nearly

seventy years. It was known in later years as Gann's Mill. A grinding stone from the mill now stands on the Courthouse lawn.[65]

John Gooch is said to have built a corn mill in 1849 at Mill Hollow or Mustang Springs, later called Wilson Springs for John S. Wilson (also Willson), who bought the property in 1854 from Ben Gooch.[66]

Several of the Gooch family were millers. Benjamin Gooch, in partnership with George Washington Glasscock, Sr., built a mill about three-fourths of a mile from the junction of the North and South San Gabriels in 1850. Before the enterprise was well established, it was damaged by flood, but was soon repaired.[67]

Samuel Mather began operating his water mill at Gabriel Mills at least by 1852, serving a large area and converting to steam power in 1860.[68]

About 1853, Ira Chalk ran a small horse-powered corn mill at Brooksville/Florence, and in 1855 Enoch D. John and Sidney Seymour built their mill there. John McNiel or McNeil owned land at Brooksville, was listed as a millwright in the 1850 census.[69]

Sometime between 1852 and 1855, Benjamin Gooch and John W. Owen built a flour mill on the North Gabriel at what came to be known as Knight's Springs, west of Georgetown.[70]

Knight's Springs or Crockett Gardens, about 1900.

T. C. Thompson had a wheat mill in full operation in the fall of 1856, in Round Rock, according to the *Georgetown Independent* of October 29 of that year.

Two new mills were erected in 1857. Less than a mile to the west of Circleville, Christopher Columbus Gillett, a Methodist minister, and David H. McFadin, cattleman-farmer, put up a flour mill valued at

$1,000 on the south bank of the Gabriel, just west of Logan Crossing.*
Nine years later, Gillett sold his interest in the mill, a flat boat, "colting
cloth," his entire stock of "hoggs" and some land to C. T. Dalton, H. D.
Miller and T. W. Miller for $5,000. After Gillett and McFadin sold it,
the mill became known as Star Mill.[71]

A wheat and corn mill was projected for Water Valley, later known as
Jonah, in 1857. James P. Warnock agreed to furnish the land and Joseph
T. Mileham $3,000 for the dam and equipment for the mill, in which
they were to have a partnership. Their agreement was signed March 3,
1857, and the project was to "proceed immediately." The mill was known
as Eureka Mills or by names of subsequent owners.[72]

Only when sawmills were later built in central Texas could houses be
built of sawed lumber instead of logs. Gristmills and cotton gins eliminated much difficult hand work in grinding flour or preparing cotton for
cloth. Building materials of the decade were still mostly log, although a
few stone buildings predated the Civil War. Split rails or stone were used
for fences until after 1873, when barbed wire was invented.

Surveying along the frontier continued in the mid-nineteenth century.
Young men of Williamson County joined these crews to earn a little
money, carrying the surveyor's chain and a gun to protect themselves from
Indians. "Another occupation that attracted a good many men was freighting. [Men went from Central Texas to the] head of navigation where
the boats unloaded their cargo" and transported goods by ox team back
home. Surplus commodities such as wheat, corn and hides could be ex-
ported from the county and such needed items as flour, molasses, whiskey,
salt, dry goods and shoes were brought back for sale. It took several weeks
to make the trip, often delayed by Indians, bad weather or muddy roads.
Sometimes freighters traveled in a trail in order to help protect each
other. "An ox team consisted of from one yoke to eight or ten yokes."
John G. Matthews drove one team, his Negro slave, Plum, another. At
night, the oxen grazed while the freighters ate supper and rested, and in
bad weather Matthews and Plum occupied the same wagon bed.[73]

Lively community newspapers appeared in many of the small towns of
Williamson County, the first in 1856. Most of the papers were four
pages, were issued weekly, and were in handset type run hand operated
presses. National and international news and features and advertising
were carried on page one, whereas local news items were relegated to the

* For G. W. Logan who owned the land where the crossing was located.

inside pages. As a general rule, long editorials dealt with national or state politics. Headlines were extremely modest in size, twelve and fourteen point generally the largest, and were rarely more than one column in width.

The *Georgetown Independent* was the county's first and only newspaper before the Civil War, its first issue appearing September 6, 1856. It was published by Andrew Marschalk, Jr., who also became Georgetown's postmaster on that same day. Andrew Marschalk, Sr., was editor, with offices on Brushy Street (Austin Avenue). "Independent in all things, neutral in nothing," was the motto in the masthead. The Marschalks moved their publishing ventures to Belton between February and April, 1857.[74]

Men other than farmers whose professions or occupations are listed in the 1850 census are as follows:

Eleven blacksmiths—Samuel, Robert and James Alexander, Daniel M. Baker, Levi Bright, all of Georgetown; John Berry, Berry's Creek; James G. and Jacob M. Harrell, Micajah Johnston and Thomas Crow, of Round Rock or nearby areas; Noah Smithwick, near Hopewell.

Five Wheelwrights—Daniel Kimbro, Rice's Crossing; John C. Lee and Caspian Seay, Round Rock; James Crow and Aaron Robbins, Georgetown area.

One millwright—John McNiel, Georgetown area.

One cooper—Hariman Lewis, Circleville (William Dyches home).

One gunsmith—John Gooch, Georgetown.

Nine carpenters—Seth G. Kimson and John H. Wells, near Liberty Hill; Josiah Clifton, John Rowland, John Shell, Eleazer Tucker and Andrew Utz, Georgetown; James H. Lewis, west of Round Rock; William R. Standefer, Jollyville area.

One turner—Greenbury W. Dorsey, home not determined.

Three stone masons—John Chinneth, Round Rock; George B. Hudon, Georgetown, and John Harness, home undetermined.

One tanner—Cyrus Gooch, Georgetown.

Four surveyors—William Armstrong, Circleville; Matthias Wilbarger and George W. Sanon, Georgetown; Bartlett Sims, Rice's Crossing area.

Six Merchants—Newton D. Johnson, William E. Stuart and Josiah Taylor, Georgetown; Norton Moses, near Gabriel Mills; Thomas C. Oatts, Round Rock; T. Henry Allen, east of Circleville.

One trader—Andrew J. McKay (Mackay), Georgetown.

One grocer—Howard J. Dewitt, Georgetown.

Two clerks—Benjamin Gooch and John C. Gooch, Georgetown.

Two lawyers—Neal McGaffey, Georgetown, and James Armstrong, Circleville.

Seven doctors—Edward H. Scruggs, James S. German, Lewis A. Ogle, William M. Owen, William Knight, William I. Anderson, David F. Knight. (Dr. Thomas Kenney, believed the first doctor in the county, had lost his life to Indians before the first census was taken.)

One hotel keeper—John J. Ake, Georgetown.

One teacher—Hudson Allen, Round Rock.

One artist—George R. Allen, east of Circleville.

Five ministers—John H. Russell (Baptist), near Liberty Hill; James W. Lloyd (Methodist), Noah McChristian (Methodist) and Stephen Strickland (Christian), Georgetown; John T. Cox (Methodist), Round Rock.[75]

Dr. Lewis A. Ogle and his young wife lived in Georgtown; Dr. James S. German probably in the Elm Grove-Circleville area. Dr. M. Jennings came to Georgetown shortly after the census was taken and operated a drug store for five years. Although he was not trained in medicine, he studied it and eventually built up a large medical practice. In 1851 Dr. George Rumsey came to Corn Hill where he was the pioneer doctor. Dr. G. S. C. Harper of Georgetown attended a State Medical Association meeting in Austin in 1853 and was named to the Counselors Committee and selected as a delegate to the American Medical Association meeting.[76]

Besides minor age children of families in the 1850 census, three young men were listed as students—Richard Owen, 16, son of Dr. William M. Owen of Georgetown; Isaac Williams, 18, son of John Williams, a farmer of Georgetown; and Oakhurst Hogemann, 22, born in Prussia, who lived with the Joseph Rubarth family at Circleville.[77]

The census showed that the county in 1850 had 230 dwellings, 242 families, 274 farmers, 33 laborers, and 11 women who were the head of the household.[78]

EARLY COUNTY SEAT

The county "site," as Georgetown was frequently called in the early 1850s, looked much like a pioneer farm of that time, with no streets except on surveyors maps, a few rutted lanes, scattered log cabins which doubled as homes, Courthouse, store, post office, stage stop, hotel, or whatever needed. Comanches approached town occasionally from the west; Tonkawas sometimes camped as near town as the present San Gabriel

Park, using the bountiful Tonkawa Springs which were later converted into Georgetown's water system. Buffalo, bear, deer, wild turkey and other wild things roamed near or even down the lanes of the tiny village. George and Rebecca Matsler spent Christmas Day 1852 with George Glasscock, Sr., at his log house in town. Tonkawas came from their camp, wanting to touch little Emily Matsler's bright red hair because they admired the color. From that time on, Mrs. Matsler plaited combings of the child's hair into tiny braids to give the Indians when she saw them. The Matslers found the village clustered into a few blocks which were enclosed by railings to pen up cows, horses or other domestic animals.[79]

One pre-1848 resident of Georgetown was said to have lived in a tent of animal hides between the forks of the San Gabriel—a trader who hauled his oxcart filled with hides and furs to Galveston periodically. Dr. William Mitchell Owen and his wife and their seven children lived in a log house between the North and South San Gabriels facing Blue Hole by 1847. John J. "Jack" Ake was said by some to have built the first log house in Georgetown proper. Others believed that Francis M. "Frank" Nash was first, for he finished a story and a half log cabin, eighteen feet square in time to become postmaster there on July 27, 1848. His cabin of cedar logs had an extra shed room in the rear for a kitchen, a leanto on the north used for a dining room. Thus the little building was Nash's home, the town's first hotel, stagecoach stop, inn and its second post office. It was on the west side of Brushy (Austin Avenue) at the south corner of Oak (Eighth) Street. Across the street to the east was a natural spring which furnished a watering place for horses when the stages passed. Hurriedly providing himself a temporary residence while he surveyed the townsite, David C. Cowan lived in a tent facing present Jail Hill. Cowan worked with Matthias Wilbarger to mark out the town lots sold during the summer of 1848. Dr. William Knight moved up to Georgetown that year from Round Rock.[80]

A young twenty-year-old trader, Andrew J. Mackay, built the first small log store in town on the southwest corner of the block north of the square. He had about $250 worth of goods, became postmaster at his store October 1, 1849. Late that year, Josiah Taylor arrived in town, bought out Mackay's merchandise and set up a store of his own, was appointed postmaster August 9, 1850. A year later, Taylor put up a two story building where the present First National Bank stands. Neal McGaffey, a lawyer, also came to the county seat in 1849.[81]

James Alexander, a young blacksmith, was in business by 1850, the same year John Shell and family and laborers arrived in Georgetown to establish a home. They built a residence on Jail Hill about at present 414 South Austin Avenue of native oak lumber, later used it as a stage-coach stop and hotel. San Gabriel Lodge No. 89, the first Masonic order in the county, was organized May 14, 1851, held meetings in early years in the upstairs of a building on the northwest corner of the block south of the square, the lower floor on which was a saloon and ten pin alley. Two lawyer cousins, Thomas Proctor Hughes and Ed H. Vontress, made their home in town that year, participating in the political, social and civic life of the community for many years. Christian Augustus Daniel (C. A. D.) Clamp, a skilled carpenter of German descent, also arrived in town in 1851 to discover there were less than a dozen houses, one blacksmith shop, one church, two stores and two saloons, and decided it was a good place to open a cabinet shop. He made furniture, built spinning wheels, looms, doors, sashes and blinds; was responsible for many early buildings. He often saw wild turkeys roosting in the trees near his home. Joe Cluck was another early carpenter whose handiwork was seen in the area for many years.[82]

Frank Nash sold his hotel to Jack Ake in 1853. Ake added a two story structure next to it, operated it as Ake Hotel for many years. Among his many distinguished patrons were Judge R. M. "Three Legged Willie" Williamson for whom the county was named, Judge R. E. Baylor, J. W. Throckmorton, and Judge Jones Rivers, the latter making the hotel both famous and infamous. The hurriedly-built structure could hardly have provided much more than the bare necessities to the traveler. Still on the frontier, Georgetown received its religion and its justice by circuit. The popular, capable and well-known Judge Robert Jones Rivers held court for his district in each county seat from Columbus to Georgetown and stayed at the Ake Hotel during sessions of Williamson County court. While holding such a session in Georgetown in December 1854, he

fell violently ill with pneumonia. Two days later his condition appeared hopeless and it was suggested that a minister be sent for. Parson [Stephen] Strickland, "a respected and estimable" Christian gentleman was accordingly summoned to the bedside and told Rivers of the seriousness of his condition and informed him that his life was nearing its end.[83] [Rivers asked someone to raise the curtain which was over the window.] The curtain of cheap calico was raised. The window frame was small, and the window lights only about eight or ten inches in size. The sash rattled in the frame as the intermittent blasts of a norther struck the house. Georgetown . . . was then a mere hamlet on a hill, with almost limitless prairies stretching away on every side. There was a thin sheet of sleet on the ground, and the brown and sere grass could be seen through it. Altogether it was a desolate and depressing scene.[84]

Turning to Parson Strickland, he said, "Parson, I have always been a firm believer in the fitness of things and I have never been more forcibly impressed with this doctrine than I am at the present moment. I have been a great traveller in my day and time—have visited Europe, spent some time in the principal colleges, stopped at magnificent hotels, lodged in inns and taverns, and I tell you now, Parson, with all these experiences flashing before me, I know of no place that I can quit with fewer regrets than the new city of Georgetown and particularly this Ake Hotel." And it is said that upon delivering himself of these last words, he turned his face to the wall "and was no more."[85]

Jones Rivers' tombstone marks his burial place in the Old San Gabriel or Old Georgetown Cemetery. His daughter, Jennie Rivers, married William Byrd, Sr., who had moved to Texas in 1853 to practice law. Their first child was Richard Evelyn Byrd, Sr., father of Admiral Richard E. Byrd, Jr.,* the famous explorer, and of Senator Harry F. Byrd of Virginia. Temple Houston, son of Sam Houston, who also lived for a time in Georgetown, described Jones Rivers as a man "whose keen flashing of wit, startling brilliancy of thought, and impassioned eloquence have given him immortality in the memories of the people of Texas."[87]

Elias Talbot opened another store in Georgetown in 1853. The same year, Dr. W. I. Anderson purchased a drug store run by Dr. Owen and Dr. G. S. C. Harper. A few years later, he formed a partnership with Cyrus Eubank in the drug business. Others in business soon after this time were Jim Smith, meat market; Napier Brothers and Jim Makemson, saloons; J. L. Brittain and Sam Gans, stores; M. E. Steele, David Love and Morrow & Price stores; M. D. Miller, bank; George Harris and son, bank, all by the 1870s. Other doctors of the period were Dr. Charles W. Lewis (1854-1869), Dr. John E. Walker, 1857, and Dr. Henry North Graves, who rode his buggy with a heated brick at his feet and a buffalo robe around him to keep warm.[88]

EARLY SWEDISH IMMIGRATION

Swedish immigrants in substantial numbers began arriving in Williamson County from 1853 throughout the remainder of the century. The

* During Texas' Centennial celebration in 1936, Admiral Richard E. Byrd planned, while on a lecture tour, to participate in the dedication of a marker honoring Jones Rivers in Georgetown. Weak from long illness resulting from his Antarctic expedition, he was struggling to carry out his tour obligations and found he could not make the trip to Georgetown.[86]

business and immigration partnership of Svante Palm* and his nephew, Svante Magnus Swenson,** could boast a number of successful enterprises in Texas after Swenson came to the state in 1838 and his uncle joined him in 1844. Operating first in south Texas, then in Austin and elsewhere, they encouraged and arranged for Swedish families to come to Texas, at the same time buying land in central Texas including acreage along Brushy Creek. Mrs. Anna (Andres) Palm, the widowed sister-in-law of Svante Palm, and her six sons*** came in 1853, settling on the land now known as Palm Valley (so named for her and for her late husband, Gustaf). Swenson's sister, Anna Catherine, married William Thomas Dyer, an overseer on a Swenson ranch. Swenson purchased the 400-acre farm of John C. and Mary Jane Kenney Lee, which included the Kenney Fort site, and deeded the property to his sister and her children on December 27, 1853. The Dyer family lived there for many years. Swen Lawson, a carpenter-farmer, and his wife came by boat from Sweden in 1854, arriving after a three-month voyage to live on the Dyer farm. Swen William Lawson, their son, was born there July 18, 1855. A. (Arvid) Nelson and his wife, Anna Lena, their two sons, Andrew John and August, and two daughters, Matilda and Lena, made the long trip from Sweden and reached their Palm Valley farm on April 10, 1855. Andrew John Nelson married Hedvig Nelson, daughter of John Nelson. August Nelson married Augusta Palm. He was killed, shot in the back, in 1866 after he witnessed against a horse thief. Matilda married A. Newlin; Lena wed A. J. Palm, all of the Palm Valley community. In 1861 A. J. Nelson built a log church in Palm Valley, the forerunner of the church formally organized in 1870. John Anderson and John Israelson immigrated from Sweden about 1859 to live in Palm Valley, John Israelson working for John Palm.[89]

The flow continued. In the summer of 1867, the *Georgetown Watchman* reported that seventy-five Swedes arrived on May 31.[90] Of the seven thousand Swedish immigrants who came to Texas between 1838 and 1890, more of them came to Williamson and Travis counties than to any other part of the state. Many of these thrifty, ambitious and hard-

---

* Svante Palm, appointed first Swedish consul in Texas in 1866, was well educated, a civic leader, was knighted by the King of Sweden in 1884 while he was on a visit to Sweden. Sir Svante Palm presented a ten thousand volume library to the University of Texas, plus numerous other materials including newspapers. Also correctly written Swante Palm.

** Svante Magnus Swenson became owner of the famous SMS ranches, was an eastern capitalist.

*** The Palm sons: Johannes (John), August B., Karl, Andrew J., Wilhelm (William) Sven, and Henning.

working people came without much more than the clothes on their backs; others had some money to invest. Many young women obtained employment as household help; young men worked someone else's farm, and within a few years most were able to start buying their own farms. The Palm family was well-known for assisting newcomers to obtain employment, either on the Palm land for a percentage of the profits, with the understanding that they could buy some of the land in the future, or on other farms of the area. The Swedish people strongly supported elementary education and their church, holding services almost as soon as they arrived in the county and formally founding in 1870 Palm Valley Lutheran Church (first called Brushy), the first of its conference in the state.[91]

Johannes Swenson wrote about his voyage to Texas in 1867. His ship landed at Galveston in July; he traveled from Houston to Brenham by train, and by wagon on to Brushy in Williamson County. "Finally at eleven o'clock on July 31, our party came to a halt at John Palm's house on Brushy, the present Palm Valley. We had reached our destination and many Swedes who lived in the neighborhood came to extend a welcome."[92]

Svante Palm wrote on July 27, 1869 to N. Nelson in Paxton, Illinois, about what Williamson County had to offer to Swedish settlers:

Green things are growing all around, flowers are budding, but the leaves are falling. Here in the highlands winter is seldom but for a few days. The roads are not well constructed as yet but man can drive almost where he wishes because they are so hard. It has been quite rainy here this year. . . . The streams have overflown but have not done much damage. . . . Of wild fruits, several kinds are found. Especially of wild vines of which the good wine is made. There are many plums, black and dew-berries, etc. Almost all the greenery of Sweden is here. In regards to churches we really have no church now. We have written to the Erke Bishop in Sweden of this but have not received an answer. We intend to build a Swedish-Lutheran church here in Austin and one in Brushy, 18 miles from here. All the Swedes here are in good health and are increasing their wealth annually. They who have been here for five years now own land. They are better liked here than other nationalities; consequently, better work and better pay. That the climate is better all the year around, and that the cattle can feed themselves all the time and gain weight faster here, I suppose is not necessary to say. The summers may be longer but the heat is at times much drier than in the northwestern states. Good land at very low prices can be found in abundance. The people are straight-forward and are perhaps more friendly than in the north, formerly called the U. S. Money means more here and the poor can soon become rich down here if they manage well and work. We have toleration in politics, religions, etc. Those who are here and have obtained homes are thriving well. The disturbers of peace are found here as well as elsewhere. . . .[93]

When William S. Palm married Miss Mary Caldwell in 1870 and purchased the T. J. Caldwell home (built by slave labor about 1850-1860) at Caldwell Heights, the place had a big two story house, two other houses, a cotton gin and a school on it. About this time, Palm had a trusted young Negro man living on the place who also carried the Palm surname, Will Palm. Orphaned at a young age, the boy was educated and trained with children of the Palm home and learned to speak the Swedish language fluently. Sometimes when immigrants from Sweden were due in the area, W. S. Palm sent the Negro youth to meet and welcome them, and assist them to their destinations, as he communicated with them in their native language. The curiosity of one fair-skinned group of Scandinavians was too much for them when they saw the dark-skinned Negro, and they asked him about it. Still speaking in Swedish, the youth jokingly explained that this was a natural result of the hot Texas sun—it simply turned a person's skin dark. Taking him seriously, the newcomers were impressed, if not entirely delighted, with the strange power of the Texas sun.[94] Will Palm worked as a butcher in Joe Ischy's market and in a bakery shop in Georgetown for many years and was always credited with being "quite a comedian."[95]

EARLY COUNTY HISTORIANS

Noah Smithwick turned historian of central Texas and Williamson County late in life, after a career as blacksmith, gunsmith, naturalist, Indian diplomat, adventurer, miner, soldier, miller, armorer, postmaster, justice of peace, and attorney. He smuggled tobacco with John F. Webber, learned to speak the Spanish and Comanche languages, lived for a time with the Comanches and gained their confidence along with the trust of other central Texas tribes. Soon after Texas' statehood, Smithwick felt people "had begun to 'crowd' me in Webber's prairie [near present Austin]. I moved out on Brushy creek, where I could get elbow room and went into the stock business." His home was three miles above that of Jimmie Standefer of the Cedar Park area, and only a mile from the timber of the Colorado River. Smithwick was listed in the 1850 census of Williamson County, but his residence was located so far to the west, it was in Burnet County after its formation in 1852. Survey lines were not drawn until about 1855 or 1856.[96]

Smithwick wrote lucidly and vividly of the mid-nineteenth century in

Williamson and nearby counties. As a participant, he described the Ranger force which built Tumlinson Fort. Occasionally he outfitted wagons for prospectors' trips to California, once made a special gun bore for Captain Nelson Merrell, the buffalo hunter. He braced the wooden leg of R. M. "Three-Legged Willie" Williamson, the namesake of Williamson County, who broke it while fending off a buffalo calf on a hunt. Smithwick assisted pioneer doctors and learned many of their techniques, searched for gold, fought against Mexicans and Indians, and frequently interceded in behalf of Indians. He knew nature's lore by following a "bee line" and could course a bee in flight to its hive. Born in 1808, his memory spanned the birth of a new state and many decades after. At the age of eighty-nine with the help of a secretary, he wrote *The Evolution of a State*.[97]

Francis White Johnson, another early and prolific historian who lived for a time at Round Rock, has been mentioned previously.

John Wesley Wilbarger, author of *Indian Depredations in Texas*, spent twenty years collecting the pioneer stories which he published in 1889. He lived on Brushy Creek at Wilbarger Crossing, near present Hutto and his name frequently crops up in the early records of Williamson County. Numerous relatives also lived in the county, including a brother, Matthias, who helped mark off the first lots in Georgetown. Two sisters, Mrs. W. C. Dalrymple, the former Elizabeth Wilbarger, and Sallie Wilbarger, also lived in Georgetown for many years. A married daughter of John Wesley and Lucy (Anderson) Wilbarger was living in Georgetown in 1889 when her father's book was published. A large Wilbarger family plot lies in the Old Georgetown Cemetery. Wilbarger Point was a familiar bluff on the river east of Georgetown. The Wilbarger book was based primarily on stories "from the lips of those who knew most of the facts stated."[98] The writer assembled a more complete set of stories dealing with early Williamson County than any other author, and, according to Raines, they were compiled "from authentic sources [and] may be considered in the main reliable."[99]

William K. Makemson came to the county with his parents when he was about eleven, arriving November 25, 1847, and settled on Brushy Creek near the Smalley, Knight, Stearns, Oxley, Asher and W. I. Anderson families, all of them moving from Vermilion County, Illinois, between 1846 and 1848. The father died when William K. Makemson was fourteen and the young man began farming, then freighted and learned the shoemaker's trade, operating a shoe shop for several years in Georgetown, where he lived the rest of his life. He began reading law, but was interrupted by the Civil War, after which he resumed that study. He was admitted to the bar before Judge A. S. Walker on May 20, 1865. From this time on, he was active in politics, publishing, and civic matters and became the only early historian who wrote exclusively about Williamson County.[100]

Makemson was elected sheriff of the county in November 1863 while he was away in the war; was appointed district attorney by Governor A. J. Hamilton and reappointed for several terms. In 1892 he was the Republican nominee for lieutenant governor of Texas, and in 1894 the candidate for governor on the same ticket. He edited the *Georgetown Watchman* which started publication soon after the Civil War, was a director in the Georgetown and Granger Railroad Company, president of the Old Settlers Association, active in the Masonic Lodge. In his law practice he made a specialty of criminal cases. He died in Georgetown June 17, 1919.[101]

This busy man in 1904 published *Historical Sketch of the First Settlement and Organization of Williamson County, Texas.* It is the most prolifically-quoted single source of the county's history. Judge Makemson gathered his data with care and in the few instances when corrections were in order he made them in subsequent newspaper articles, the most notable being the date when Dr. Thomas Kenney built his fort on Brushy Creek. The correct year is 1838.[102] On page twelve of Makemson's *Sketch*, the narrative about the capture of secret agent Manuel Flores in west Williamson County should read that Lieutenant James O. Rice and his Rangers followed Flores and his party "through the mountains two or three days, finally overtaking them on the *North* Gabriel at a bluff on the south side of the creek."

Along with Noah Smithwick and John Wesley Wilbarger, William K. Makemson did an invaluable service by preserving county records of the nineteenth century.

U.S. CENSUS 1850[103]

The 242 families who lived in 230 dwellings, according to the Williamson County U. S. Census of 1850, totaled 1,379 free persons. They are listed below in this manner: heads of household are in upper case letters; ages are in numerals following names; the monetary figure represents amount of taxable property; names followed by asterisk* are listed alphabetically with more complete information. Spelling as shown in census is adhered to except in a very few instances when positively proved to be incorrect in which case correct form is used. There were two census takers, one of whom appears to have been partial to the unusual "Catharine" form of that name. One of the men apparently was Washington Anderson, whose handwriting is clear and easily read. The other man's is not so legible and is difficult at times to interpret.

A survey of birthplaces listed in the 1850 census shows that most citizens in the county were natives of Tennessee; next largest numbers were from Kentucky, North Carolina, Arkansas, Illinois, Missouri, Alabama, Ohio, South Carolina and Indiana, in that order. From foreign countries, the birthplaces were Germany, 5; Hanover, 4; Mexico, 3; Prussia, Wales and England, 2 each; France, 1.

ACRES, DELILAH, 46; Smith Acres, 24, farmer; Harvey Acres, 22, farmer, $200; Anderson Acres, 19, farmer; 7 minor children; Henry Chambers,* Thomas Wilcox.*

AKE, JOHN J., 35, & Jane, 28; hotel keeper; $600; Panelope, 10.

AKE, WILLIAM, 59, farmer, $300; Joseph Ake, 27, farmer; Castletown ["Cash"] Ake, 24, farmer; Panelope Ake, 15.

ALDRICH, JONATHAN, 39, & Mary, 27; farmer; $300; 6 children.

ALEXANDER, SAMUEL, 46, & Thirza, 42; blacksmith, $500; Robert Alexander, 22, and James Alexander, 20, both blacksmiths; 9 other children; George W. Wilson.*

ALLEN, BENJAMIN, 28, & Martha, 26; farmer, $3200; 3 children; Benjamin Freestone.*

ALLEN, HUDSON, 57, & Deborah, 54; school teacher, $420; Joseph Allen, 25, & Mary, 18; farmer; Thomas P. Allen.*

ALLEN, JAMES B., 39, & Nancy, 29; farmer, $6000; 6 children; John Stearns*; Joseph H. Freestone*; Eliza E. Morey, 1.

ALLEN, THOMAS J., 44, & Matilda, 41; farmer, $25,000; T. Henry Allen, 21, merchant; George R. Allen, 19, artist; 2 other children; John H. Connell.*

Allen, Thomas P., 26, & Eliza, 21; farmer, $350. Resided with Hudson Allens.

ALLISON, Elihu, 42, & Margaret M., 41; farmer, $4000; 8 children.

ALLISON, JAMES, 40, & Delila, 38; farmer, $100, 10 children.

ANDERSON, HENRY, 40, & Sally, 36; farmer; James Anderson, 21, farmer; 8 children.

ANDERSON, URIAH H., 38, & Elizabeth E., 26; farmer, $1500; 2 children.

ANDERSON, WASHINGTON, 32, & Mary [Ann Glascock], 27; farmer; $5000; Chloe, 11, [later married R. H. Taliaferro].

ANDERSON, WILLIAM I., 41, & Nancy P. [Knight], 32; physician; $1200; 2 children.

ARMSTRONG, JAMES, 38, & Caroline, 27; lawyer; $8000; five children; William Armstrong, 28, surveyor, $10,000.

ASHER, LEVI, 50, & Mary, 47; farmer; $2000; Marion J. Asher, 18, farmer; Bartlett Asher, 16; farmer; Mary C., 11.

ASHER, TOBIAS, 22, & Maria, 20; farmer [nicknamed "Bi"]; Harriet J., 8 months.

ASHER, WILLIAM K., 42, & Catharine, 20; farmer; Sarah, 12; lived in Tobias Asher home.

Aubery, Henry, 17, laborer, lived in James A. Smith household.

AVERY, WILLIS, 40, & Elzina, 37; farmer, $5300; Vincent Avery, 16, farmer, and 7 other children.

BACON, THOMAS, 23, & Martha, 21; farmer, $550; 2 children.

Baker, Daniel M., 29, blacksmith, $500, lived in G. W. Glasscock home.

BAKER, SHEPARD, 40, & Lina, 22; farmer, $400; 5 children.

Ballard, James C., 17, laborer in Levi Bright home.

BARKER, CALVIN, 26, & Nancy, 25; farmer, $4000; Eliazer, 15, Margaret A,. 11, and Jesse, 9, each in school and each with $400 taxable property; 3 other children one of them with $400; Willam Gage*; Ira Luffinwell.*

BARR, JOHN, 36, & Thennie, 20; farmer, $320.

BARTON, JOHN, 32, & Melissa A., 22; farmer, $1640; 2 children.

BARTON, JOHN, 28, & Mary, 27; farmer, $150; 3 children.

Barton, Nancy, 63, in household of Isaac Kelly.

Beardin, Hannah, 75, in household of Frances Harris.

Berns, John, 17, laborer in David C. Cowan household.

BERRY, ANDREW JACKSON, 34, & Rhoda, 24; farmer, $2000; two children.

BERRY, JOHN, 64, & Hannah, 38; blacksmith; $5750; William Berry, 24, farmer; 8 other children at home.

BERRY, JOHN BATE, 36, & Martha E., 20; farmer, $2000.

Bingham, James, 21, & Lavica, 18; in William Dyches household.

BLACK, WILLIAM, 33, & China, 31; farmer, $600; 6 children.

BLANKENSHIP, WILLIAM, 32, & Almeda, 29; farmer, $300; 4 children; Abram Wright.*

BLANKSTON, ABNER, 34, & Susan, 38; farmer; Joshua H., 16, and 7 other children.

BLYTHE, ANTHONY W., 28, farmer; William Cox, 28, farmer; Pernelia Cox, 26; 3 children.

BOLTINGHOUSE, DANIEL, 21, & Mary J., 22; farmer, $200; 1 child.

BOWMER, BIRKETT D., 58, & Ruth C., 54; farmer, $130; Peter E. Bowmer, 20, farmer, and 3 other children.

BOYD, JOHN, 68, & Elizabeth, 67; farmer.

BRADBURY, JAMES, 48, & Elizabeth, 30; farmer, $1200; 5 children.

BRANCH, JAMES, 33, & Nancy, 32; farmer, $600; 4 children; Nicholas Branch, 37, farmer, $600.

BREEN, CARLTON M., 26, farmer; Charles, 1; William Hanavan.*

BREEN, CHARLES, 63, & Martha, 55; farmer, $5000.

BRIGHT, LEVI, 66, & Mary, 64; blacksmith, $300; Samuel T. Bright, 22, farmer; Noah McChristian* and James C. Ballard.*

BROOKS, ELISHA, 25, & Sarah, 24; farmer, 4 children.

BROWN, JOHN H., 33, & Jane A., 29; farmer, $200; 5 children.

BURRIS, JAMES M., 34, & Nancy C. [Tankersley], 25; farmer, $5000, 5 children; William Lackey.*

BUTLER, NICHOLAS C., 42, & Mary, 36; farmer, $700; 3 children; Jackson McFarland.*

CAMPBELL, NATHANIEL, 35, & Amelia, 22; farmer, 2 children.

CASNER, JACOB, 58, & Jane, 52; farmer, $5000; 1 child.

CASNER, MARY A., 50; Elihu B. Casner, 22, farmer, $700; Jason Casner, 30, $1000; 3 other children.

HENRY A. CHADWICK, 28, & Margaret, 24; farmer, $150; 2 children.

Chambers, Henry, 23, laborer, in household of Delilah Acres.

Champion, James, 30, farmer, in household of James S. Standefer.

Champion, John, 32, farmer, and Naomi, 16, in James S. Standefer home.

CHANDLER, LEWIS, 25, & Mary, 17; farmer, $200; James, 3 months.

CHANDLER, MARY, 65; William Chandler, 40, farmer; Caroline, 22, and Almeida, 18; Francis Lewis.*

Chandler, Priscilla, 45, $240, and 4 children, in John Marshall household.

CHANDLER, SAMUEL G., 36, & Martha, 21; farmer, 2 children; William Ourin.*

CHAPMAN, JAMES, 33, & Celinda, 29; 6 children.

CHINNETH, JOHN, 49, & Elizabeth, 33; stone mason, $5000; 6 children.

Chism, John E., 28, farmer, $600; Alexander B. Chism, 22, farmer, $160; Jesse B. Chism, 21, farmer, $160; Aza O. Chism, 20, farmer, $150; Angeline A. Chism, 16; all resided in Benjamin Gooch household.

CLANTON, CATHARINE, 36; William H. Clanton, 18, farmer; 5 other children.

Clifton, Josiah, 25, carpenter, $400, in Matthias Wilbarger household.

Clifton, William, 18, laborer, in William C. Dalrymple home.

Connell, John H., 17, farmer, lived in Thomas J. Allen home.

Conner, Alfred, 25, & Lucinda, 24, farmer; $300; 3 children; in John S. Reed home.

CONNER, ANTHONY B., 38, & Rachel, 25; farmer, $200; 4 children.

CONNER, JOHN, 23, & Mary, 22; farmer, $260; Daniel Conner, 65.

COOK, CHARLES C., 45, & Mary, 44; farmer, $2240; 6 children.

COOK, OBED., 26, & Eliza, 26; farmer, $600; 4 children.

COVINGTON, JOSIAH, 41, & Unity, 39; farmer; William B. Covington, 21, & Linruda, 21; 2 children.

COWAN, DAVID C., 44, & Elizabeth, 39; farmer, $1000; Gideon P. Cowan, 28, farmer, $200; 4 children; Ruth Cowan, 65; John Berns,* and Margaret Thorp, 8, and Ella Thorp, 3.

COX, JOHN T., 47, & Mary, 46; Methodist clergyman, $1700; 6 children; Nancy T. Muchison* and five children and Alexander Mackintire.*

CROW, JAMES, 26, & Rachel J., 25; wheelwright; 2 children.

Crow, Thomas, 19, blacksmith; in Thomas F. Windsor household.

DALRYMPLE, WILLIAM CORNELIUS, 35, & Elisabeth [Wilbarger], 39; farmer, $3000; 4 children; Sally Wilbarger,* William Clifton,* Andrew J. McKay.*

Davis, Huldah, 23, 2 children; in household of Reuben Queen.

DAVIS, JOHN, 35, & Rebecca, 21; farmer, $150; 2 children; John, Jane and Mary Graham (children); Joseph Davis, 70, farmer.

DAVIS, JOSIAH B., 46, & Priscilla, 26; farmer, $100; 5 children.

DAWSON, FIELDING, 25, & Nancy, 22; farmer, $250; 2 children.

DAWSON, JAMES, 39, & Temperance, 29; farmer, 3 children.

DAWSON, JOHN, 38, & Temperance, 35; farmer, $200; 5 children; John H. Wells.*

DAWSON, SAMUEL, 66, & Anna, 63; farmer.

DAWSON, SAMUEL R., 25, & Margaret, 20; farmer; 2 children.

DENNIS, LOUISA, 39; Hugh Dennis, 16, farmer, and 5 other children.

DENNIS, OSRO, 23, & Rebecca T., 22.

DEWITT, HOWARD J., 36, & Rhoda, 33; grocer, $700; 1 child.

DORSEY, GREENBURY W., 30, & Nancy, 30; turner, $500; 5 children; Melchiger Dorsey, 23, farmer.

DYCHES, JOSIAH, 50, & Elizabeth, 31; farmer, $1800; 6 children; Edward H. Scruggs* and Phebe J. Jewel, 13.

Dyches, Lucinda, 75, Lydia C. Dyches, 12, in David H. McFadin household.

DYCHES, WILLIAM, 37, & Jane, 48; farmer, $960; 4 children; James Bingham*; Hariman Lewis.*

EASTHUP, ELIJAH, 21, & Abagail, 24; farmer, $400; 2 children; John C. Montgomery.*

ELLIOTT, GEORGE, 23, & Susan C., 21; farmer, $300; 1 child.

FARBER, JOSEPH, 33, & Lanissa, 33; farmer; 4 children; William West.*

FARRIS, SOLOMON, 27, & Laurinda, 27; farmer; 4 children; Margery A. Hinds.*

FISK, GREENLEAF, 39, & Mary A., 39; farmer, $20,000; 6 children.

FLEMING, WILLIAM W., 50, & Elizabeth, 40; farmer; John W. Fleming, 20, farmer; and 8 other children.

Freestone, Benjamin, 21, laborer in Benjamin Allen household.

Freestone, Isaac, 16, laborer, in household of William Knight.

Freestone, Joseph H., 25, laborer, in James B. Allen household.

Gage, William, 21; farmer, in Calvin Barker household.

GARDNER, THOMAS, 49, & Ellena, 33; farmer, $640; 9 children.

GARNER, ISAAC, 39, & Mary, 28; farmer, $1000, 4 children.

Garner, John, 21, farmer, member of Johnston Micajah household.

Garner, Leroy, 22, farmer, in Johnston Micajah household.

GERMAN, JAMES S., 37, & Margaret, 28; physician; 6 children.

Gilbert, Cynthia P., 54, resided in Daniel Kimbro household.

Gilreath, Nathan D., 25, farmer, in James S. Standefer household.

GLASSCOCK, GEORGE WASHINGTON, 40, & Cynthia C. [Knight], 35; farmer, $53,000; 4 children; Daniel M. Baker,* Eleazer Tucker,* Andrew Utz,* John Sherman,* Guy Morris,* and Joseph Glasscock, 15.

Goff, Ambrose, 36; farmer; in John Gooch household.

GOOCH, BENJAMIN, 56, & Elizabeth R., 49; county clerk; $5000; John E. Chism,* Alexander B., Jesse B., Aza O. and Angeline A. Chism; Angeline E., Vermilla M. and Nancy A. Mathews, ages 10, 6 and 4.

GOOCH, JOHN, 56, gunsmith, $500; Cyrus Gooch, 21, tanner; James W. Lloyd* and Ambrose Goff.*

GOOCH, JOHN C., 22, clerk; Jemima E., 18, Martha E., 16, Matilda R., 14; Delinda A., 10, Roseann E., 8, and Benjamin Gooch, 12; Thomas Gooch, 23, laborer; Cyrus Gooch, 21, laborer.

GREGG, ABNER, 53, farmer, $4000; 4 children.

GUEST, JOSEPH, 25, farmer; 1 child; Phyllis Guest, 74; George B. Hudon.*

GUTHRIE, JAMES M., 48, & Belinda, 34; farmer, $1000; 7 children.

Hanavan, William, 21, laborer, in household of Carlton M. Breen.

HANNA, SAMUEL, 23, & Havanna, 23; farmer, 2 children; John Hanna, Sarah J., 19; farmer.

HARNESS, JOHN, 41, & Sophia, 36; stone mason, $1000; 7 children.

HARRELL, ANDERSON J., 27, & Darthulia, 22; farmer, $1000.

HARRELL, JACOB M., 45, & Mary, 47; blacksmith, $4800; Emma, 7; Richmond Hill, 12.

HARRELL, JAMES G., 43, & Catharine, 40; blacksmith, $1900; 4 children.

HARRELL, JOAB, 36, & Arretta, 38; farmer, $350; 5 children.

HARRELL, JOHN, 25, & Elizabeth, 21; farmer; $1000; John, 6 months.

HARRIS, CHARLES, 23, & Susan J., 19; farmer, $300.

HARRIS, FRANCES, 44, (female) and 7 children; Hannah Beardin.*

HARRIS, JAMES, 29, & Martha, 28; farmer, 6 children.

HARRIS, JOHN, 49, & Elizabeth, 52; farmer; William Harris, 21, farmer, and Benjamin Harris, 17, farmer.

HARRISON, DANIEL, 33, & Nancy, 32; farmer, 4 children.

HILL, JAMES, 23, & Sarah A., 17; farmer, $100.

HINAMAN, HENRY, 52, & Elisabeth, 48, laborer.

HINDS, BENJAMIN J., 32, & Mary J., 23; farmer, $1500; John Walters* and John Castlebury, 15.

Hinds, Margery A., 22, in Solomon Farris household.

Hogemann, Oakust, 22, student, in household of Joseph Rubarth.

Hornsby, Reuben, 25, farmer, $5300; member of Jonathan Wilkins household.

HORNSBY, THOMAS M., 45, farmer, $900; 3 children.

Hudon, George B., 25, stone mason, $200; in household of Joseph Guest.

HUGHES, REBECCA, 48; Nimrod Hughes, 20, farmer; William Hughes, 18, farmer; James, 15.

HYLAND, JOSEPH, 37, & Sarah E., 35; farmer, $6000; 3 children; also three Campbell children and Elizabeth Mullens, 13.

JACKSON, WILLIAM R., 25, & Martha J., 27; farmer; 2 children; Mark Stewart.*

JOHNSON, NEWTON D., 25, & Susannah, 23; merchant, $1000; Susannah Johnson, 55; Samuel R. Johnson, 19, farmer; 3 other children.

JONES, JAMES, 30, & Rebecca, 26; farmer, $400; 5 children; Richard Robbins.*

JOPLIN, JAMES, 26, & Julia, 24; farmer, 1 child.

JOY, GEORGE, 69, & Martha, 46; farmer, $150; 2 children.

JOY, JAMES A., 22, & Elizabeth, 19; farmer.

JUVENAL, JAMES, 43, & Nancy [Ann Smalley], 26; farmer, $1080 for James and $600 for Nancy; 5 children; Nancy E., Sabra C. and Freeman J. Smalley, ages 5, 3 and 1.

KELLY, ISAAC, 30, & Nancy J., 18; farmer, $160; Nancy Barton.*

Key, Jesse, 18, laborer, in household of John R. Payne.

KIMBRO, DANIEL, 40, & Mary, 34; wheelwright, $300; Euclid Kimbro, 16, farmer, 4 other children; Cynthia P. Gilbert.*

KIMSON, SETH G., 32, & Sarah, 32, carpenter, $400.

King, John W., 28, farmer; 2 children; in household of Luther Stearns.

KIRKPATRICK, WESLEY, 25, & Prudey, 19; farmer, $125.

KISER, JACOB A., 25, & Nancy J., 17; farmer; George W., 2.

KISER, WILLIAM, 52, & Frances, 49; farmer; John Kiser, 17, farmer; 5 other children.

KNIGHT, DAVID F., 41, & Susanna, 36; physician, $2500; 4 children.

KNIGHT, JOHN, 46, & Hannah, 44; farmer, $2400; William Knight, 20; farmer; 3 other children; John Smith.*

KNIGHT, WILLIAM, 51, & Mary A. [Baugh], 37; physician, $5660; 4 children; Isaac Freestone,* Ferdinand Schwab,* Anthony Smith.*

KUYKENDALL, JOSIAH A., 35, & Malissa, 27; farmer, $3000; 4 children; Caroline Canetch, 14; Robert R. Parsons.*

Lackey, William, 25, farmer, resided in James M. Burris household.

LAREMON, JOHN, 37, & Elizabeth, 33; farmer, $250; 4 children; John Scott,* William Scott.*

LAWRENCE, ADAM, 48, & Sarah [Miller], 37; farmer, $2500; Edmund Lawrence, 17, farmer; 5 other children; Adam Lawrence, 21, laborer; Joseph Lawrence, 78, farmer.

LEAVITT, BENJAMIN, 36, & Lucinda, 21; farmer, $300.

LEE, JOHN C., 35, & Mary J. [Kenney], 21; wheelwright, $10,000; 1 child; Clarissa Kenney, 13, student; Ann Kenney, 11, student; Middleton W. Rains,* James Rust.* (Mrs. Lee was elder sister to the two Kenney girls, daughters of pioneer Dr. Thomas Kenney, massacred by Indians.)

Lewis, Francis, 33, farmer, $200; 3 children; in household of Mary Chandler.

Lewis, Hariman, 40, cooper; in household of William Dyches.

LEWIS, JAMES H., 37, & Malvina, 28; carpenter; 4 children.

Lloyd, James W., 36, Methodist clergyman; in household of John Gooch, the gunsmith.

LOVE, DAVID, 28, & Mary J., 20; farmer, $800; 2 children.

Luffinwell, Ira, 32, farmer, in Calvin Barker household.

Mackintire, Alexander, 25, laborer, $100, in John T. Cox household.

McChristian, Noah, 28, Methodist clergyman, $1200, in Levi Bright household.

McFADIN, DAVID H., 34, & Jerusha [Dyches], 38; farmer, $3000; 3 children; Lucinda Dyches, 75; Lydia C. Dyches, 12; Duncan St. Clair and 2 children.

McFarland, Jackson, 23, & Cordelia, 17; farmer; in Nicholas C. Butler home.

McFARLAND, SAMUEL, 49, & Jane, 46; farmer, $300; James G. McFarland, 19, farmer, and 4 other children.

McGAFFEY, NEAL, 54, & Hannah, 49; lawyer, $6000.

McKay, Andrew J. (also written Mackay, Makay), 22, trader; in William C. Dalrymple household.

McNIEL, JOHN (possibly McNeil), 34, & Elizabeth, 20; millwright; 2 children.

MAKEMSON, MARTHA, 35, $600; 5 children. Her husband, Samuel Makemson, died June 9, 1850, in the county.

MANKIN, SAMUEL, 35, & Dotia, 34, $1000, 10 children; William Sherwood.*

MARIA, HOSEA, 35, & Pritty, 30; laborer; Francisco Maria, 25, laborer.

MARSHALL, JOHN, 67, farmer, $450; Priscilla Chandler* and 4 children.

MARTIN, DANIEL, 40, & Rebecca, 30; farmer, $200; 3 children.

MERCER, JESSE, 40, & Alice, 20; farmer, $4570; 5 children.

MICAJAH, JOHNSTON, 38, & Susanna, 31; blacksmith; 5 children; Leroy Garner* and John Garner.*

MILLER, JOHN, 31, & Telitha C., 23; farmer, $300; 3 children.

Montgomery, John C., 22, & Emily, 16; farmer, in home of Elijah Easthup.

Morris, Guy, 21, farmer; in G. W. Glasscock household.

MOSES, NORTON, 27, & Nancy A., 20; merchant, $300.

MOSS, MATTHEW, 48, & Mary A., 26; farmer, $2000; 6 children.

Muchison, Nancy T., 23, $3000, 5 children; resided in household of John T. Cox.

NORTHINGTON, MARSHAL W., 36, & Jane M., 26; farmer; 5 children.

OATTS, THOMAS C., 28, & Elizabeth, 24; merchant; 3 children.

OGLE, LEWIS A., 27, & Sarah, 18; physician, $200.

OLIVE, JAMES, 43, & Julia A., 30; farmer, $100; 6 children.

Ourin, William, 16, member of Samuel G. Chandler household.

OWEN, WILLIAM M., 43, & Sarah, 38; physician, $1500; 7 children including Richard, 16, student.

OXLEY, ENOCH, 50, & Elizabeth, 42; farmer, $1200; Lawson Oxley, 17, farmer, and 3 other chidlren.

Parsons, Robert R., 21, laborer in Josiah A. Kuykendall household.

PAYNE, JOHN R., 34, & Hannah, 34; farmer, $200; Cornelia C. Woodruff, 6; Jesse Key* and William West.*

PREWITT, ELISHA, 30, & Frances, 29; farmer, $900; Byrum Jenkins, 12, and Eliazer Jenkins, 10.

PRICE, THOMAS, 44, farmer, $4000; Thiadori J. Smith.*

PUTNAM, MADISON, 37, & Olivia C., 31; farmer, $150; 5 children.

QUEEN, REUBEN, 64, & Mary, 61; farmer, $1000; Huldah Davis* and 2 children; William Queen, 57, farmer.

Rains, Middleton W., 35, laborer, in John C. Lee household.

RALSTON, MATHEW, 26, & Sarah A., 28; farmer; 3 children; Margaret A. Clark, 7.

RATLIFF, GUILFORD, 41, & Mahaley, 43; farmer; $1500; Archillus Ratliff, 21, farmer; James C. Ratliff, 18, farmer, and 5 other children; Winslow Turner.*

RATLIFF, JAMES B., 45, & Catharine, 44; farmer; Guilford Ratliff, 21, farmer; Mary Ratliff, 18; Jobi Ratliff, 16, farmer; 5 more children.

REED, HARRISON, 36, & Adaline, 28; farmer.

REED, JOHN S., 19, & Susan A., 20; farmer, $500; Alfred Conner* and family; William D. Reed* and family.

Reed, William D., 25, farmer; 3 children; Mary Trent,* Nancy J. Miller, 13; Mary Reed, 56. All lived in John S. Reed household.

RHODES, ELISHA, 55, & Rachel, 56; farmer, $1900; Vina Rhodes, 20; Henry Rhodes, 18; farmer; Margaret, 16; Henry Rhodes, 74, farmer, $100; Elisha Jenkins, 8.

RICE, ALPHEUS, 27, & Julia A., 19; farmer, $250; 3 children.

RICE, JAMES O., 35, & Nancy D., 25; farmer, $15,000; Elizabeth, 2; Mary E. Fox, 13.

RICKETTS, JAMES M., 33, & Elizabeth, 29; farmer; 6 children.

RICKETTS, REUBEN W., 39, & Sarah, 33; farmer; 6 children.

ROBBINS, AARON, 46, & Elizabeth, 46; farmer; Richard D. Robbins, 14.

ROBBINS, AARON, 23, & Susannah, 20; wheelwright, $150.

ROBBINS, GEORGE M., 58, & Orry, 55; farmer, $2000; Henry Robbins, 32, farmer; Joseph Robbins, 28, farmer; George S. Robbins, 20, farmer; Lemuel Robbins, 17, farmer; two daughters, Jane, 22 and Sally, 8; Fleman Skein.*

Robbins, Richard, 20, farmer; member of James Jones household.

ROBBINS, ROBERT R., 32, & Sarah, 25; farmer; 4 children.

ROBERTS, WILLIAM, 24, & Rachel, 23; farmer, $500; 2 children.

ROWLAND, JOHN, 39, & Nancy, 27; carpenter, $500; 5 children.

ROYAL, JESSE, 38, & Sarah, 32; farmer; 3 children.

RUBARTH, JOSEPH, 52, & Martha, 42; farmer, $4000; 6 children; David E. Stanton* and Oakust Hogemann.*

RUSSELL, DANIEL W., 24, & Mahaley, 19; farmer, $200; 1 child.

RUSSELL, JOHN H., 47, & Sarah S., 42; Baptist clergyman, $1100; Cornelius A. Russell, 19, farmer; 2 children.

Rust, James, 21, laborer, in John C. Lee household.

Sanon, George W., 31, surveyor, $750; in Matthias Wilbarger household.

SAXSON [sic], JAMES, 35, & Rachel, 25; farmer, 2 children.

Schwab, Ferdinand, 29, laborer, in William Knight household.

Scott, John, 24, farmer, in John Laremon household.

SCOTT, JOHN W., 27, & Charlotte, 20; farmer; $2000; James F., 1; John Wilkenson.*

Scott, William, 21, farmer; in John Laremon household.

Scruggs, Edward H., 50, physician; in Josiah Dyches household.

SEAY, CASPIAN, 39, & Nancy, 30; Wheelwright, $250; John Willson.*

SHELL, JOHN, 33, & Auzeline, 20; carpenter, $250; Albert C., 1.

Sherman, John, 26, farmer, in G. W. Glasscock household.

Sherwood, William, 23, laborer, in Samuel Mankin household.

SIMS, BARTLETT, 57, & Sarah, 43; surveyor, $5000; James C. Sims, 22, farmer; 5 other children.

Skein, Fleman, 22, farmer, in George M. Robbins household.

SLAUGHTER, JOHN, 40, & Matilda, 45; farmer, $1000; Elijah M., 22, Simeon, 20, Elias, 18, Eliazer, 17, and Samuel Slaughter, 15, all farmers; 6 more children.

SMALLEY, BENJAMIN F., 24, & Angelina, 23; farmer, $400; Irene, 3.

SMALLEY, FREEMAN, 60, & Catharine, 58; farmer, $2500; Moses Smalley, 21, farmer; Elizabeth, 19, and William Smalley, 12; Mary C. Tennihill, 2.

SMALLEY, JAMES K., 31, & Mary, 25; farmer, $400; 2 children.

SMALLEY, JESSE J., 21, & Hannah [Stearns], 17; farmer; Olive Smalley, 27.

SMILSER, HARMON, 52, & Elizabeth, 44; farmer, $700; 5 children.

Smith, Anthony, 23, & Amanda, 22; farmer; in Taylor Smith household.
Smith, Anthony, 21, laborer, in household of Dr. William Knight.
Smith, Charles, 38, farmer, in George West household.
SMITH, JAMES A., 27, & Clarissa W., 23; farmer, $300; 2 children; Henry Aubery.*
Smith, John, 37, farmer in John Knight household.
SMITH, TAYLOR, 40, & Sarah, 35; farmer, $2000; 3 children.
Smith, Thiadori J., 17, laborer, in Thomas Price household.
SMITHWICK, NOAH, 42, & Therza, 42; blacksmith, $1000; 4 children.
SOMERVILLE, SAMUEL E., 26, & Mary M., 30; farmer, $300; John M. S. Chrisman, 13; Angeline Smalley, 16.
STANDEFER, JAMES S., 43, & Caroline, 43; farmer, $1500; 8 children; John Champion,* Naomi Champion, Nathan D. Gilreath,* William R. Standefer,* James Champion,* Mary A. Stillman.*
Standefer, William R., 22, carpenter, in James S. Standefer household.
Stanton, David E., 22, farmer, in Joseph Rubarth household.
St. Clair, Duncan, 66, farmer, $2500; Stephen St. Clair, 15; Duncan St. Clair, 13; lived in David H. McFadin home.
Stearns, John, 20, laborer, in household of James B. Allen.
STEARNS, LUTHER, 65, farmer, $650; Susannah Stearns, 26; Luther Stearns, Jr., 21, farmer; David Stearns, 16; Harvey Stearns, 12; John W. King* and two young children.
STEARNS, ZARA, 56, & Mary [Smalley], 52, farmer, $1000; Zara, 10.
Stewart, Mark, 17, laborer, in household of William R. Jackson.
Stillman, Mary A., 48, member of James S. Standefer household.
STRICKLAND, STEPHEN, 49, & Eda, 46; Christian clergyman, $300; 6 children. ["Strickland was a Baptist preacher until about 1840 when he lost a debate and he and some of his flock changed to the Christian church."][104]
STRODE, THOMAS, 46, & Emeline, 35; farmer, $1000; 5 children.
STROUD, ALLEN, 52, & Arza, 43; farmer, $300; Samuel A. Stroud, 22, farmer; 5 other children.
STUART, MARY, 64; Elisabeth Stuart, 42; Farris C. Stuart, 21, farmer; Robert D. Stuart.
STUART, WILLIAM E., 47, merchant, $3500.
TANKERSLEY, JAMES, 25, & Louisa, 22; farmer, $300; Richard D., 2 months.
TANKERSLEY, RICHARD, 67, & Sarah, 50; farmer, $3000; Richard J. Tankersley, 17, farmer; and 2 other sons.
TAYLOR, JOSIAH, 37, & Catherine [Lee], 29; merchant; 5 children.
THOMAS, JOHN D., 30, farmer; Mary Thomas, 17.
THOMPSON, JOHN S., 36, farmer, $1000; William G. Thompson, 25, farmer.
TRENT, JOHN, 41, & Jane, 40; farmer, 6 children.
Trent, Mary, 17, in household of John S. Reed.
Tucker, Eleazer, 57, carpenter, $3000; in G. W. Glasscock household.
Turner, Winslow, 38, laborer, member of Guilford Ratliff household.
Utz, Andrew, 30, carpenter, $500; in G. W. Glasscock household.
WADKINS, SAMUEL, 59, & Christina, 19; farmer, $5000; Elizabeth, 1.
WALDEN, HUGH, 27, & Rachel, 19; farmer; 1 child.
WALDEN, JOHN, 27, & Nancy, 21; farmer; 2 children.
Walters, John, 26, laborer, in Benjamin J. Hinds household.
WARREN, CHARLES, 26, & Mary J., 24; farmer, 2 children.
WATTS, JOHN W., 29, & Nancy J., 26; farmer, 1 child.
Wells, John H., 23, & Mahala, 19; carpenter; in John Dawson household.

WEST, GEORGE, 30, & Rachel, 38; farmer, $80; David C. West, 17, farmer; 4 other children; Rachel Morgan, 10; Sarah West, 63; Isaac West, 21, farmer; Charles Smith.*

WEST, LEWIS, 29, & Nancy, 23; farmer, 3 children.

West, William, 23, farmer, in Joseph Farber household.

West, William, 23, laborer, in John R. Payne household.

WESTFALL, ZACHARIAH, 39, & Marinda, 29; farmer, 7 children.

WILBARGER, MATTHIAS, 42, & Sarah M., 32; surveyor, $5400; 5 children; George W. Sanon* and Josiah Clifton.*

Wilbarger, Sally, 44, in household of William C. Dalrymple.

Wilcox, Thomas, 22, laborer, in household of Delilah Acres.

WILEY, ELISHA, 24, & Eliza A., 23; farmer; 3 children.

Wilkenson, John, 23, farmer, in John W. Scott household.

WILKINS, JONATHAN, 43, & Susanna, 42; farmer; Catharine C. Wilkins, 21; Lucinda M. Wilkins, 20; George Wilkins, 18, farmer; 6 other children; Reuben Hornsby.*

WILLIAMS, DAVID W., 24, & Elizabeth, 23; farmer, $500; 3 children.

WILLIAMS, EVAN, 32, & Nancy, 31; farmer, $400; James C., 8.

WILLIAMS, GEORGE T., 26, & Jane, 23; farmer, $500; 2 children.

Williams, James, 26, & Sarah, 27; farmer, 5 children, living in household of Kelsey Williams.

WILLIAMS, JOHN, 55, farmer, $1000; Isaac Williams, 18, student.

WILLIAMS, KELSEY, 31, & Mary 24; farmer, $400; 3 children.

WILLIAMS, MARGARET, 39; Jesse Williams, 17, farmer; Mason Williams, 16, farmer; Vincent Williams, 16, farmer; 4 other children.

WILLS, JOSIAH, 25, & Sarah A., 23; farmer, 2 children; Elizabeth Brittain, 14.

Willson, John, 25, laborer, in Caspian Seay household.

Wilson, George W., 23, farmer, in Samuel Alexander household.

WINDSOR, THOMAS F., 33, & Verlinder A., 33; farmer, $200; 3 children; Thomas Crow.*

Wright, Abram, 24, farmer, in William Blankenship household.

WRIGHT, BARBERRY, 45; John Wright, 22, farmer; Mary Wright, 16; 4 younger children.

WRIGHT, ISAAC H., 22, & Mary J. 23; farmer, $200.

YARBROUGH, MATTHEW, 35, & Rhoda, 56; farmer, $600.

VII

The Civil War

PRELUDE

The Negro slave population of Williamson County remained relatively small. David H. McFadin sold a sixteen-year-old female, Marime or Marrene, plus about 150 cattle and horses, to Josiah Dyches for $2,000 on March 4, 1843. Archibald B. McMillan, on February 21, 1853, complained to county officials that a Negro belonging to him had been imprisoned and sold by the sheriff in 1852 to John J. Ake for $615.05. The Court ordered that amount paid to McMillan. James W. Allen and wife sold an eleven or twelve-year-old "negro girl of dark complexion" named Eliza for $600 to John C. Montgomery in 1856. Elias W. Talbot bought Peter, age 46, a slave "of black complexion" for $800 on June 18, 1862, from a Travis County resident. Since Talbot was known to be a Union sympathizer and was credited with running an underground station in the basement of his home for escaping Negroes, it seems likely that this purchase was in some such context.[1] Many years later when the Talbot-Whittle home* was torn down, the underground tunnel beneath the house was exposed and was in 1973 remembered by a number of Georgetown citizens.[3]

Ripples suggesting agonies to come were evident as early as 1853 when the County Court appointed a patrol "to exercise jurisdiction over the slaves of Georgetown." Captain John J. Ake and five privates, Joseph

* Located approximately 209 Church Street, Georgetown.[2]

Ake, Evan Williams, Thomas Hughes, Alfred Van Eyck and Samuel Alexander, made up the patrol for three months. Similar patrols were appointed periodically until the war broke out. One was added in Round Rock in February 1856, another on Brushy Creek "in the Orgain neighborhood" in August 1858; one in Florence and one in Sam Easley's neighborhood by November 1858. There were more than a dozen such patrols by 1861, one each at Georgetown, Round Rock, Florence, Bagdad, Crossroads, near Samuel Mankin's on the San Gabriel, Collins', Avery's, Sims', Barker's and Payne's neighborhoods on Brushy Creek, one each at "Willies" Creek, in the Sloan's and Mileham's neighborhoods near Jonah, at Pond Springs, and at Corn Hill.[4]

SAM HOUSTON, THE WAR,
AND WILLIAMSON COUNTY

As distant rumbles of civil war reached Texas, Sam Houston occasionally visited with friends and supporters in Williamson County who, like Houston, opposed secession. During his campaign for the governorship in 1859, Houston was a guest in the home of Elias W. Talbot on the south bank of the South San Gabriel near its confluence with the North Fork.[5] Houston's daughter, Nancy Elizabeth, who later lived in Georgetown, was often quoted as saying that her father frequently stayed at the Talbot home and that he met a representative of Abraham Lincoln there shortly before the war broke out "when the Yankees were attempting to buy him off." Houston also "told forth in thunderous tones his political beliefs and ideals" to audiences in San Gabriel Park.[6]

A majority of the county's citizens came from southern states and held the traditional viewpoint of the South, but a large number had come from Illinois, Massachusetts and other states which supported the Union. In 1860 a Texas Constitutional Union party was organized, meeting over the state and passing resolutions denouncing secession. One such resolution was adopted at Round Rock.[7] That fall, Thomas Proctor Hughes, a young Georgetown attorney, canvassed the county as an anti-secessionist. He and five others were elected delegates from Williamson, Milam and Travis counties to the January 1861 Secession Convention held in Austin. Elisha Thomason, a planter who came to Georgetown in 1856 from Hughes' home state of Tennessee, was a second member from Williamson County. A third delegate, C. M. Lesueur, represented both Williamson and Milam counties. In the voting for or against secession, Hughes answered roll call with a resounding "no," creating a shock wave in the legislative hall.

During successive readings of the proposed ordinance, followed each time by a vote, the tallies varied, as 152-6 or 67-7, but always overwhelmingly favoring secession. Williamson County was one of the three counties in the entire state to vote against the ordinance to withdraw from the Union. The legislative act provided for a statewide election to approve or disapprove the ordinance. After votes were cast and while they were being counted, Houston left Austin for Belton, stopping "overnight at the home of Elias Talbot in Georgetown where a stranger who introduced himself as George D. Giddings handed General Houston a letter from Abraham Lincoln."[8] The confidential messenger brought word that "Lincoln was willing to send 50,000 troops to aid in keeping Texas in the Union."[9]

Houston returned to the Governor's Mansion in Austin, called four of his closest friends and advisors to his home, and asked their advice. All agreed that they personally opposed secession, but advised Houston not to resist the decision of the Secession Convention and what they believed would be the electorate's judgment. "The Governor stepped to the fireplace and dropped the letter . . . into the flames. 'Gentlemen, I have asked your advice and will take it, but if I were ten years younger I would not.' "[10] Descendants of Colonel J. T. Coffee, another friend of Houston's, tell of the Governor's visits to the Coffee home east of Georgetown* during these same years. Family tradition has it that Houston stayed at the Coffee residence on his way to Belton that election week.[11] It is entirely possible that Sam Houston was in both the Talbot and Coffee homes at Georgetown the evening in question. He was a master politician and would hardly have missed seeing old friends nor an opportunity to press his campaign against secession.

The secession ordinance carried. Federal troops at Texas forts were permitted to leave as state troops took charge, one of the latter under the command of Colonel W. C. Dalrymple of Georgetown.[12] In forty years, Williamson County had been governed by Spain, then in rapid succession by Mexico, the Republic of Texas, the United States and now the Confederacy. It was a dizzying pace for a new county.

Overt warlike acts were comparatively limited in Texas. Soon after the war began, the State of Texas ordered the County Court to list all arms in Williamson County. A War Tax of five cents on each $100 property evaluation was levied. The Court purchased eight kegs of powder, six hundred pounds of lead and twelve thousand percussion caps to be kept

---

* The Coffee home still stood in 1973, at 1401 James Street.

under the control of the Court, and handled appropriations for military units formed in the county, including those of Captain H. M. Burrows, Captain R. H. Calhoun, Captain W. C. Dalrymple's Cavalry Company, and Captain James O. Rice's Spy Company.[13]

THE BANDERA HANGINGS; GOING TO MEXICO

One flagrant atrocity occurred in July 1863 near Bandera, Texas, when eight men from Williamson County, well equipped, well mounted, with $900, passed that way as they headed for Mexico. They were hanged without a trial by a detachment of Confederate soldiers stationed at nearby Camp Verde under the command of Major William J. Alexander. The eight men were accompanied by a young boy, about thirteen, who escaped the hanging, but whose identity and fate were apparently never determined.

At least several of the eight men had done service in the Texas Militia.* All sources do not agree on reasons for the trip to Mexico. Some claim that the men were on a forty-day furlough and, sick of the war, had decided to go to Mexico. Some of the men in Alexander's detachment thought the men were attempting to avoid conscription. Whatever their real reasons, the Williamson County men were substantial citizens who obviously felt they were violating no laws,[14] for they made no effort to conceal their leisurely movement through the country. When they stopped at Bandera, they freely discussed their destination and it was from there that news of their presence reached Camp Verde, twelve miles to the north. Major Alexander's detachment was sent to intercept them and overtook them at a place below Hondo. Being assured they would be given a fair trial, the men willingly gave up their considerable weapons and were taken back to Julien Creek two miles southwest of Bandera, where the soldiers said they would spend the night before returning to Camp Verde. Alexander's men drank heavily and, as the evening wore on, some of them became restive, suggesting that they hold a necktie party for the "deserters." One soldier wanted to hang all eight at the same time, but others wanted a longer ceremony and more "entertainment." A few of the soldiers opposed the action, but Major Alexander remained silent, thereby leading his men to believe that he gave tacit approval to the

* William M. Sawyer, whose farm was eight miles west of Georgetown on the North Gabriel, had enlisted in the Confederate Army July 8, 1862, was in Gurley's Regiment, Company D, Texas Partisans of the Texas Cavalry. His brother, Coston J. Sawyer, was also in the Texas Cavalry, Company A, Morgan's Squadron, having enlisted March 26, 1862. Another of the group, George Thayre, was a brother-in-law of W. M. Sawyer.

"gruesome proceeding." Troopers opposing the executions left camp and disappeared in the brush.[15]

Hands of each of the eight men were tied behind them, nooses of horsehair rope were prepared, and the grisly spectre began. One by one they were hanged, not by being dropped as from a scaffold, but by being hauled into the air and left dangling to strangle slowly to death. As each stopped struggling he was cut down, but the rope and knot were left around the neck. One victim "pled for a rifle shot to end his life and one of the soldiers obliged, but carelessly or deliberately left his ramrod in the rifle barrel. His shot sent the ramrod through the man, killing him and pinning him to the ground." The victims were then stripped of their clothing, their money and supplies. Their horses were also appropriated by the soldiers, who thereupon left the scene. Wearing some of the garments taken from their victims, they returned to Bandera, where for several hours they drank and bragged about the details of the spectacle.[16]

Their story was so fantastic that little heed was given to it by listeners until a local resident, Joe Poor, came to town with corroboration. The morning after the hanging, Poor was searching for strayed horses and discovered the bodies. He mistook the protruding ramrod in one corpse for an arrow and believed that Indians had massacred the men. He hurried to Bandera for help, and a number of local people, including O. B. Miles, George Hay, John Pyka, Robert Ballentyne and Amasa Clark, returned to the scene. On closer examination they realized that Indians had not been responsible for the affair. The evidence matched the eerie stories told the preceding night by the drunken soldiers. After digging a shallow grave near Julien Creek, they buried the men. The young man was not seen.[17]

Soon after the war was over, on April 24, 1866, the State of Texas indicted William J. Alexander for murder and highway robbery, but the Major had disappeared and conveniently for himself, perhaps, was never known to return.[18]

Some years later a monument was erected and carved with the names of eight men: "C. J. Sawyer, W. M. Sawyer, George Thayre [sic], William Shumake, Jack Whitmire, Jake Kyle, John Smart, and Mr. Van Winkle died July 25, 1863." An added inscription popular in that day warned, "Remember, friends, as you pass by, as you are now, so once was I; As I am now you soon will be; Prepare for death, and follow me." The grave is near a large oak tree not far from the now-peaceful grove of many live oaks including the hanging tree. The site in 1972 was on the Lazy G Ranch of the L. F. Gusman, Sr., family, two and a half miles southwest of Bandera.[19]

*Grove near Bandera where Williamson County men were **mercilessly hanged**, and detail of their gravestone.*

Quite a number of Unionists succeeded in reaching Mexico. Luther Stearns, Jr., informed in 1862 that he would have to take an oath of allegiance to the Confederate States, wrote, "This I would never do, so I made my property over to a widowed sister, and, the night before the drill, with eight or ten others, mounted my horse and started for Mexico." The men reached their destination in eight or ten days. The following spring, Stearns "crossed the Gulf of Mexico to New Orleans, in a steamer sent by the U.S. to carry Union refugees to the States. In the fall of 1863 I joined a company of scouts [attached to the 13th Corps, U. S. Army] being paid for special duty. We were discharged in Oct., 1864."[20]

Beverly Fulton Eubank began a trip to Alexandria, Louisiana, on March 21, 1862

to avoid the call for volunteers for the rebel army, returned June 18th, 1862. And still further to avoid the conscript law of the rebellion he resolved to leave the state as he would not take up arms. He prepared to go leaving all he held dear behind. On the 24th of June when the sun was just sinking from sight, Pa, Mother, Ann, Ma Hayslip, Ellen and I, with the younger children, went down to the gate to bid him goodbye (and oh how could we know it was the last on earth) in company with Luther Stearns, bade us farewell. His last "Goodbye Mother" lingers with us yet. We watched them as they passed over the western hill and he was gone from us forever. They went to Mr. King's 4 miles above here [from Circleville to Water Valley (Jonah)], thence to Willis Creek to meet those who were to accompany them on their perilous journey through western Texas to Mexico. They were John Grice, Wm. Lee, John Cavanaugh, Tom & Wm. Ake, Wm., Tom and John Gardner, Pike McFarlane [*sic*]. After the war was over Pike McFarland [*sic*] brought us his pocket book containing the following note in his own hand. "From home to Brooksville [Florence] and Burnett up Llano and by Fredericksburg to the head of Llano, then to the mouth of San Felipe on Rio Grande—to Piedras Negres then to Monteray and from there to Matamoras and to New Orleans. Beverly Eubank, Circleville, Texas." [Josiah Talbot wrote his wife from Matamoros on January 20, 1864, that Eubank died of camp fever at New Iberia, Louisiana in 1863. A Mr. Page of Georgetown saw Eubank there in October 1863 after he was ill.] He was lying in the sun—with high fever, and delerious. He removed him to shade, cooled his fever, and had him carried to the hospital intending to visit him the next day, but failed to do so as he became sick himself—but learned that Beverly died the second day after—also said that Beverly had been troubled with chronic diarhea for six months. . . . Pike McFarland was in the hospital sick, saw Beverly brought in sick, and carried out dead, that he was delerious all the time he was sick. He told the superintendent to have his grave marked. . . . He left home to avoid the army but in barbarous Mexico, among strangers whose language he could not speak, he could not well live, and enlisted in the first company made up there, Company A, Cavalry, 1st Texas Regiment.[21]

WOFFORD JOHNSON FAMILY, LAST VICTIMS OF INDIAN ATTACK

The last Indian attack which took lives in Williamson County was during the Civil War near Hopewell. The inscription on a gravestone in Hopewell Cemetery reads, "Wofford Johnson, wife and Little Dau. massacred by the Indians Aug. 15, 1863."

Several slightly different versions of the violent event have been told. When the War began, many men from east Burnet and west Williamson counties went into service. Since Comanches still ranged close by, a group of young boys, old men, ministers and others formed a company for scouting, with Captain Jeff Maltby, a Texas Ranger, in command. Wofford Johnson lived near Maltby, operated a small molasses mill at his home, and joined the patrol. A short time prior to the murders, horses had been stolen from the vicinity. On a Sunday morning, Mr. and Mrs. Johnson, their two daughters and their baby boy rode to the home of a neighbor, a Mr. Whitehead, about a mile away. Late in the day, the Johnsons started toward home, Mrs. Johnson holding the baby and the older girl riding on the horse behind her mother. Johnson took his four-year-old daughter on his horse. As they rode near a dense thicket of dogwood along Dog Branch, they were attacked by Comanches. The father and his youngest daughter were apparently killed first. The eldest girl jumped from the horse and managed to escape, running the short distance—about three hundred yards—to her home. Mrs. Johnson fell from her horse about one hundred yards farther on, but managed to slip the baby boy into a thicket before she collapsed. A Comanche Indian named Japee told Captain Maltby later that he and others of his tribe had killed the Johnsons. The Johnson daughter reported the tragedy, and John Owens, Maltby and Alex Barton spent the night gathering thirty men to investigate at daylight. As they passed the dogwood thicket, they heard a sound which led them to the baby. The boy was feverish, hungry and thirsty, and had an arrow through his arm. An uncle took him home to care for him. The Wofford Johnson's niece, Mrs. C. C. Proctor, a girlhood friend of Mrs. Johnson, was staying with them at the time of the tragedy while Mrs. Proctor's husband was away with the Confederate Army. Mrs. Proctor recounted the story, giving the names of the children as Mary Jane, who was killed along with her parents, and Elvira (who ran for help) and the baby, Georgiana. Mrs. Proctor said the baby was a girl, rather than a boy. She also said that Mr. Whitehead had the molasses mill, to which Johnson, a cattleman, and his family had gone to make molasses that fateful day. The three Wofford Johnsons were among the the early burials in Hopewell Cemetery.[22]

THE WAR AT HOME; RECONSTRUCTION

Many families found themselves in destitute circumstances because their men were in service. The County Court ordered that a list of such families be made and that they receive such assistance as the county was able to give. Since clothing for soldiers was in short supply, the county arranged for contributions to be collected, then had them delivered to Little Rock, Arkansas, in October 1862 by J. J. Stubblefield, W. H. Henderson and T. P. Hughes. Also to help alleviate the clothing shortage, in November 1863 the county received $1500 with which to obtain cotton cards from the Military Board at Austin, the cards to be sold to local citizens at $15 a pair. The County Commissioners obtained cloth for the families of soldiers from the state penitentiary and distributed medicine to such families early in 1865.[23]

Many citizens of Williamson County who were anti-secessionist, if not anti-slavery, fell into step with the majority and served either in the Confederate Army or in the Home Guard. Others preferred leaving the country to serving a cause they thought wrong. The turmoil of the times and the emotionally loaded issues involved resulted in the goading and threatening of some citizens, in the destruction of their property, or personal harm because of their views. A few were summarily disposed of, although most such incidents were recorded only by word of mouth within the family.

Industry came to Williamson County as a result of the war. Cotton was much in demand and farmers were encouraged to increase their production, or ginners to build more gins. Such requests should have fitted well in the county of fine blacklands, except that able bodied men were usually away at war and many of the slaves had departed. If the Negroes were willing to work, there was no money with which to pay them. Nevertheless, production was urged, and a cotton card factory was established at Circleville in 1862, where "cotton cards, of good quality, were manufactured." Joseph Eubank, Jr., ran the business as "Eubank & Co.," and is generally credited with establishing it. Records of the Circleville Church for 1862 contain the notation, "John White [listed as new member] moved in a card factory."[24]

Economic and labor problems, worry, heartbreak and bereavement, shortage of food and supplies—all these plagued even comparatively war-free Williamson County. A poignant communication from Samuel D. Carothers to his brothers, Franklin and Thomas, dated March 4, 1867, reveals the strain of the war years. Carothers had carried a heavy financial burden during the war—he gave away much clothing, rigging, many horses, and quantities of meat, bread, wool, cotton, and hundreds of pounds of beef. Yet, he wrote, "If I can have health I can make a good living even at my age 56." His letter conveys a rare combination of utter weariness combined with wistful optimism. Carothers' mail service was affected. He had gone to considerable effort to obtain a post office for his community, which Reverend W. O. Spencer said would be called "Tucumcary." The name approved by postal authorities, however, was Ponton, assigned August 17, 1860, with Carothers as postmaster and the office in his home. He held the position throughout the war but the office was discontinued on November 5, 1866, probably an act of Reconstruction. Carothers had never hidden his affection for the South, but among other things, this respected citizen was a manager. On December 3, 1866, Ponton post office was reactivated with Miss M. J. Faires, a relative of his, as postmistress. He told his brothers, "If we can get a R. Road to Austin it will be a great help to us all. . . . The mails are not reliable now. Write to Ponton p. o. Williamson county. It will come to Georgetown the county site we send there every week 10 miles."[25] Later, on April 27, 1867, the Ponton office was again discontinued, never again to be reinstated. Reconstruction acts continued heavy in Texas. Samuel Dinsmore Carothers lived just long enough to see this period ebb away. He died December 31, 1877, at the age of 67.[26]

The news that the war was over brought both joy and pain to families partially reunited. At Circleville, a church service was held April 16, 1865. "The church . . . met once more. Those present were a few who had remained in Circleville through the war storms."[27]

Besides the political upheavals which were a part of Reconstruction in Texas, office holders on a county level frequently found themselves without a job, including numerous Williamson County postmasters. Both black and white found Texas a difficult place to earn the necessities of life. Many ex-Confederate soldiers were unable to find assistance of any kind, and the ex-slaves were now free, but without jobs or any means of support. Those willing to hire Negroes had no money with which to pay them.

A 150-acre tract of brushy land along the southwestern Williamson County line, spilling over into Travis, was said to have been an encampment site for Civil War soldiers. Some ex-slaves who had no place to go were allowed to live in that area after the war. Nearby were farms belonging to three Negro brothers, Milas, Richard and Nelson Miller, who helped other families in need and formed a substantial community for black people along Jenks Branch south of Liberty Hill. The Millers donated land for a school, church and cemetery site and descendants were still living in the area in 1972.[28]

Another Negro settlement in the county grew out of the Civil War. Harry Bailey, a black man, traded a horse and saddle for some acreage west of Mankin's Crossing and sold lots to other Negro families looking for a place to live. Working together, those in the community managed to build a school, which was also used as a church.[29] Bailey school was on the bank of what was then known as Harry Bailey Creek.[30]

The County Court, burdened with caring for "vagrants" without home or job, in August 1865 declared that whites or blacks depending upon the county for support could be assigned to work on county roads.[31]

The daughter of a distinguished Texas family became a bride soon after the Civil War was over and she and her husband lived in Georgetown for many years. She was Nancy "Nannie" Elizabeth Houston, eldest daughter of Sam Houston. Born September 6, 1846, Nannie was considered an apt pupil all during her school years, and her father declared that at the age of six she was a genius at letter writing. She studied as a young lady at Baylor Academy and, three years after her father's death, she and Captain Joseph Clay Stiles Morrow, a successful merchant in Georgetown, were

Nancy Elizabeth Houston and Captain J. C. S. Morrow on their honeymoon, 1866.

married. Their wedding was August 1, 1866, and they immediately set up housekeeping in Georgetown. A year later, Mrs. Morrow's mother died, leaving five minor-age Houston children, Nannie's younger brothers and sisters. Four of the children were away at school, but the youngest, Temple (born in 1860 in the Governor's Mansion—the first baby to be born there), was primary school age. Mrs. Morrow took responsibility for all five children and brought Temple to Georgetown to live in her home.[32]

Temple enrolled in the Georgetown Male & Female Academy which at one time met in the basement of the Presbyterian Church (built 1872-73 and still standing in 1973).[33] When he was thirteen, Temple went on a cattle drive to Montana, later entered Baylor University at Independence and was graduated in 1878. He then read law and eventually practiced that profession, returning to Georgetown for frequent visits for many years.[34]

Dr. Samuel Houston, Jr., namesake of his distinguished father, practiced medicine in Georgetown in 1874 and, after moving to Waco, often returned there to visit. He married Miss Lucy Anderson of Georgetown in 1875.

Sam Houston's second youngest son, William Rogers Houston, read law in T. P. Hughes' office in Georgetown, moved to Belton in May 1881 to set up a practice.[35]

The Morrow family left Georgetown for a brief time in 1876 when the county's first railroad came through Round Rock, where Captain Morrow moved his mercantile business. He later traveled over Texas operating a wholesale trade. Mrs. Morrow soon brought her family back to Georgetown where her home remained. The Morrow homes were located just west of Brushy Street (Austin Avenue) at the corner of Tenth Street, later at about 704 East University Avenue, and still later at approximately 905 College, the latter home facing west toward the old Georgetown College/Southwestern University/Fitting School (Prep School) building and campus in the five hundred block of University Avenue. From this last home Mrs. Morrow walked regularly to the First Methodist Church, where she taught a Sunday School class. Regardless of the season or the weather, she invariably wore a belt or ribbon around her waist, from which a fan dangled, hitting her knees as she walked, and she always carried a black parasol. She fanned vigorously during church services. Friends and neighbors remembered Mrs. Morrow as an extremely independent lady, seeming rather reserved, aloof and strict to young people. When young girls walked past her home on their way to school, she often admonished them to wear more clothing. "She wore the neck-to-floor kind of clothes. I remember her as being peculiar but very nice. She and a relative of mine taught Sunday School classes and often argued about their beliefs and teachings. I learned Texas history from her."[36] Sometimes Mrs. Morrow invited the children of her friends to "ride" Santa Anna's saddle, which she had in her home. One of the children reported the experience at school during a Texas history class. The teacher was aghast, warning the child not to make up such stories. Insisting that the story was true, the student urged her teacher to call Mrs. Morrow, who corroborated the statement.[37]

Nancy Elizabeth Houston Morrow died May 19, 1920, and was buried in the I.O.O.F. Cemetery at Georgetown. Captain Morrow died in 1925 and is buried in the same family plot.

VIII

Cattle Empires

When the Spanish padres nurtured their missions along the frontiers of Texas, they "made every mission a horse ranch."[1] A native to the North American continent, the tiny aboriginal horse had been long extinct in the western hemisphere when the Spaniards arrived late in the fifteenth century and introduced stock from Spain. From this stock came the wild horses or mustangs (*mesteños*) which spread into Texas in large numbers by the eighteenth century, altering the life styles of Texas Indians, drawing Comanches and other tribes into the state, and providing the Anglo-American settler with one of his two most important tools for survival: his horse and his gun.

General Alonso de León crossed central Texas in 1689 on his way to the east Texas missions with 720 horses and mules. At least thirty-six of them stampeded along the route and were left behind. The next year, traveling much the same road and crossing the San Xavier (San Gabriel) River, he had 400 horses and 200 stock cattle. This time he deliberately left "a bull and a cow, a stallion and a mare" at each river crossing to populate the area.[2] Indians are said to have killed " 'unbelievable' quantities" of cattle the next century,[3] and the San Gabriel had "an incredible number" of wild horses and cattle as far back as 1779.[4] In 1807 Zebulon M. Pike described "immense herds of horses east of the Colorado River, on San Antonio-Nacogdoches road," and on the "prairies west of the Trinity River." George W. Kendall, New Orleans editor who camped on the San Gabriel with the Santa Fe Expedition in 1841, wrote about the wild horses he saw in Texas on that trip. Comanches considered the horses of any central Texan fair game, raiding for them so frequently that local residents spoke of the full moon as the "Comanche moon." This tribe knew how to come noiselessly, rousing neither man nor beast, including dogs, to carry away a man's most highly prized animals. In 1850 Comanches owned about five thousand horses. A warrior's success depended partially on the number of horses he owned, anywhere between fifty and two hundred.[5] When Noah Smithwick moved to Brushy Creek about 1850, he found many cattle which he thought were descended from those brought to the San Xavier missions a century earlier. They were "handsome . . . coal-black and clean-limbed, their white horns glistening as if polished."[6]

"The west was discovered, battled over, and won by men on horseback," James Frank Dobie once wrote. Cattle were often used as a medium of exchange, provided food, lard, tallow, and became a tremendously big and important industry. In 1866, about one hundred Comanches or Apaches drove ten thousand cattle west from the San Saba River. A year later, an Indian agent reported that fifteen thousand horses and three or four hundred mules were herded at Comanche camps in Texas. Both Spaniards and Indians rode the range to obtain food, hides, tallow, or the live, barterable animals. They pioneered the industry which later Williamson Countians pursued with great success soon after the Civil War. (J. F. Dobie, considered the ultimate authority on both mustangs and longhorns, lived in Georgetown while he attended Southwestern University, wrote numerous articles for school publications, and for a time, published a column in the *Williamson County Sun* of Georgetown.)[7]

Mustang and Yegua (wild mare) creeks in Williamson County were so-named for the large numbers of the animals explorers found along those streams.

The cattle business was tailor made for Williamson County. When pioneers arrived, droves of wild cattle drifted along Brushy Creek, San Gabriel River, and the smaller streams and springs, and herds of tough, wild horses were ready to break for the catching. Tenacious, aggressive and flexible, the early settlers had the traits to become successful cattlemen. At first, the raw material was at hand. Even after the frontier pushed north and west of the county and wild animals were no longer abundant at home, Williamson County stockmen and cattlemen from other parts of Texas continued to drive their herds through Williamson County on their way to one of several famous trails to the markets. For about twenty years after the Civil War, central Texas was very much a part of trail drives and the cattle industry. Every town in the county saw herds gathered in

large pens prior to launching a long drive and saw herds from farther
south pass through or near the town, moving about eight or ten miles
a day.

Many trails crossed Williamson County. In the large area east of the

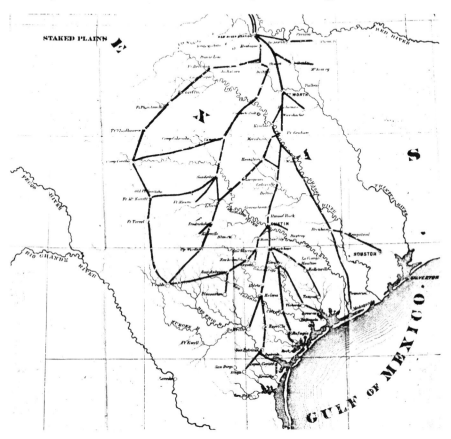

Cattle trails across central Texas.

Balcones escarpment "from Ad Lawrence's place" southeast of Taylor to
Calvin Bell's farm a few miles south-southeast of Georgetown "could be
seen thousands of head of cattle in different herds passing at one time in
the prairie." The county had many "fine open spaces" to make trail driving easy except in bad weather.[8] People in the Round Rock area watched
herds move east of their town, crossing near old Kenney's Fort, or west
of Round Rock near Bagdad, or through the town itself, later known as
Old Round Rock. Numerous drives went directly through Georgetown,

approaching it from down Rabbit Hill and by Judge Thomas P. Hughes' place south of town, along Brushy Street (Austin Avenue), down "jail hill," and across the Gabriels near the intersection of the two forks. Pioneers remembered that the river bank was worn slick by these herds just west of the present State Highway 81 bridge at Georgetown. Other river crossings short distances above and below this point were used. Some of the drives headed north from Georgetown toward Corn Hill and Belton; others fanned westward, passing through Gabriel Mills and Florence; or, to the east, the prairies offered choices limited only by adequate river crossings. One primary route came from Lexington to Beaukiss, crossed near "the Olive pens on the Taylor prairie." Another popular way was from Webberville east of Austin to Rice's Crossing to Taylor or near Taylor, then westward to intersect the central or western trail (via Georgetown-Corn Hill, or Georgetown-Gabriel Mills, which went up the North Gabriel from Georgetown).[9]

Nearly all the trails described above have been called the Chisholm Trail. Technically, this is not correct. Jesse Chisholm made wagon tracks from the Canadian River near present Yukon, Oklahoma, north to Wichita, Kansas, in 1865 so that he could freight goods up and down that trail and trade with Indians. The next year, he took a wagon train of goods and 250 head of cattle over the same tracks—Chisholm's trail. The pattern was set and in 1867, the year Williamson County's first drive was made, about 35,000 cattle were driven to Abilene, Kansas, all of them eventually traveling over Chisholm's trail in Oklahoma and Kansas part of the way. As herds from Texas moved toward that trail, the name came to be used for numerous routes which led to the comparatively short Chisholm Trail. In time, general usage made it acceptable to call the trails leading through central Texas by that name. On that basis, however, any trail which eventually led to Chisholm Trail (and most of them through Williamson County did) could claim that title.[10] Trails through Williamson County were feeder routes, leading to the primary trails to markets: Western Trail, Dodge City Trail, Shawnee Trail, and Chisholm Trail.[11]

The spectacle of the mass of long horns on a herd of cattle was unforgettable—whether "grazing in tall grass," swimming across the San Gabriel, or when "lightning [played] on a sea of wet horns."[12] The lore is well known of stockmen gathering herds, hiring cowhands, purchasing supplies for the long trip, avoiding timber and looking for good water and grass along the way, and always hoping for good weather.

Youngsters in Williamson County perched upon fences or watched from the best vantage point as the ambling cattle moved forward. The dust they created was forgotten in the excitement and glamor attached to this adventure. When they passed, residents sometimes complained that their cattle were gathered and added to the herds of the trail drivers.[13] Often the cowmen stopped to refresh themselves at local saloons while the men in charge might stock up on supplies from the general store. Joseph "Jack" Melasky, a pioneer Taylor merchant, ran a store which was frequented by cattlemen who often bought out his entire stock of goods on credit, promising to pay him when they returned from the trip months later. Melasky was never disappointed, never lost any money on these transactions.[14] T. J. Kamp's Hotel at West Main and First Street, Taylor, "was a rendezvous for all the stockmen of the state who had occasion to visit [that] prairie village."[15]

Until the cattle business burst upon the state, pork was the staple diet of the average American. Beef quickly replaced pork on the table. Hides were equally salable, and even horns found a ready market. They were made into buttons, spoons, small containers and dishes, horns to blow, racks, hangers and many decorative pieces for the home. They were used along roads as signs, and a chair made of longhorns was considered something special in many homes.[16]

Cattle multiplied tremendously in Texas during the Civil War and, for more than a decade after it, cattlemen gathered their herds with ease. "Open range ranching" and drives up the trail were doomed by the invention of barbed wire in 1873, by the coming of the railroads, and by the spread of Texas fever and the resulting quarantine against Texas cattle crossing other states. These changes did not reach or seriously affect Williamson County until in the early 1880s, when fences closed off the open prairies. By that time, hundreds of carloads of cattle were shipped by rail annually from Taylor. On a poorly engineered strip at Circleville, a carload of cattle was overturned near the river and most of the animals killed or injured. Cattle drives continued simultaneously with rail shipments for a while. During the spring of 1879, between ten and twelve thousand head of beeves and stock cattle were driven from Williamson County, and two wagonloads (more than one hundred) buffalo, deer and antelope hides went through Georgetown in April 1879.[17] Other hides were shipped by train, as bills of lading in the McNeil station west of Round Rock show.[18] William Benjamin "Uncle Billy" Denson, son of J. H. and Mary Denson, was born in 1869, grew up near Willis Creek, remembered when Granger was only cattle trails and mesquite brush, and when fences first appeared across the ranges. Soon a law had to be passed against carrying wire cutters.[19]

Although cotton farming developed more or less simultaneously with the cattle industry in the county, few early cattlemen raised much cotton. The two occupations did not mix. A cowboy from Tom Green County in 1880 decided to try his hand at picking cotton. Coming with Lee Garrett to Williamson County, he wrote, "I soon found out I coulden do thing at that Business So I went Back home and staid that winter."[20] As cattle were fenced out of their traditional natural watering places in the 1880s, the windmill came into use in Williamson County. This machine permitted breaking the land into smaller farms, since the owner was no longer forced to obtain water from a spring or stream.[21] The cattle business continued in Williamson County on a small scale, but larger operations moved far to the west. In the twentieth century, new forage crops and improved feeding methods permitted ranchers and stockmen of the county to increase their herds.[22]

If the number of cattle brands registered with the County Clerk in the 1850s and afterwards is any indication, almost every man in the county could have been classified as a stockman. Those known to have engaged in the business on a large scale are mentioned below.

Nelson Merrell was in what would become Williamson County by 1841, hunting bear and buffalo, selling hides, and frequently driving herds of mustangs into a huge log pen about three miles southwest of Georgetown on the old Bagdad road. One of these roundups netted him eight hundred mustangs. Other hunters came at this period to find bear, which were plentiful in the county then. Bear fat was used for greasing wagon axles.[23]

David H. McFadin started working in the stock business in Texas in 1831. In 1846 he and his father-in-law, Josiah Dyches, settled near Circleville to continue in the cattle business.[24]

Elias Queen moved to the county in May 1848, establishing a horse ranch at Queen's Hill east of present Weir. He brought wild horses to it from Mexico.[25]

Richard Tankersley was known for the fine horses he brought to the county from Kentucky. When the county was established, he was living on his ranch near the site chosen for Georgetown.[26]

In 1867 George C. Arnett and Captain W. J. "Jeff" Maltby went on a cow hunt on the North Gabriel. George Arnett became foreman of Thomas Snyder's ranch at Liberty Hill, in 1879 taking charge of a large herd sent by Snyder to Cheyenne. Arnett was also well-known as an Indian fighter.[27] D. W. Arnett was also one of the Snyder brothers' ranch managers.[28]

The first cattle drive to leave Williamson County was said to have been collected in 1867 by R. M. Overstreet, a Presbyterian minister, along with A. J. Hanna and a Mr. Julin. The three men gathered their herd along Brushy Creek from where they drove to market.[29]

Several drives left the county in 1868—those of the Snyder Brothers, and also John and Tom Owens.[30] W. A. Franks was engaged in the sheep business about this same time.[31] Another early stockman, Greely Weir, built a large cattle pen near the watering place of wild horses on the San Gabriel River.[32]

The Georgetown Watchman of April 23, 1870, reported that

> those crowders, the Snyders, have their large herd of 3000 head of fine cattle en route for Omaha, Nebraska. Morrow & Price's herd of 2000 has also left, together with A. J. Nelson's, and James A. Smith's will soon be on the drive. . . . Hurrah for Williamson.

Daniel Moody, who became the father of the future Governor Dan Moody of Texas, was living in Missouri in the 1870s and drove cattle from Texas to Missouri. He moved to Texas to make his home during that decade.[33]

The Wilson family raised cattle and sheep on their Wilson Springs place and were the first in the county to put up wire fences to keep their cattle in. Will Lannen, who came to Taylorsville with his father in 1877, said that Charlie B. Wilson went to Galveston for telegraph wire before barbed wire was available, possibly before it was invented, and used it for fences.[34] Since Charles B. Wilson acquired the property at Wilson Springs March 8, 1871,[35] it seems probable that this version is correct. Other Wilsons associated with the same property include John S. Wilson, who bought it in 1854, and Robert Wiggington Wilson. The latter has also been credited with erecting the first fence in the county.[36]

W. E. Laughlin of Bartlett and A. J. Durant from near there went on a drive in 1870, and made two other drives, including the Soules-Armstrong drive in 1880 to Nebraska. "We began making up this herd in February, started the drive in April, and reached our destination the following July."[37]

Greenup M. Kuykendall, Sr., who was born at Rice's Crossing in 1850, began trail driving at the age of twenty, made five trips up the Chisholm Trail, driving 3,600 head on his last trip to market in 1879. He continued in the cattle business at home for many years afterward. Kuykendall described one severe blizzard in Kansas when he had to seek protection in a dugout. All the horses in his outfit except one were frozen, and one of the cowhands froze to death.[38]

Andy Hanna, Jim Haley and Parson Bruce took a herd to the Platte River in 1870.[39]

Willis Thomas Avery of the Hutto and Taylor areas was a drover who took several herds to Kansas and Wyoming in the early 1870s. His 1872 drive suffered Indian raids, stampedes, and encountered so much rain, he stopped for a month to graze the cattle before reaching market.[40] Vincent R. C. Avery drove herds to Kansas from 1871 until 1874.

One of the most unusual drives ever to leave Williamson County was that of George W. Cluck, who lived west of Round Rock. His romance in 1860 with Miss Harriet Standefer led to a happy marriage. In 1871,

Trail lady and her husband, Harriet Standefer Cluck and George Washington Cluck of Running Brushy.

when her young husband planned a drive to Abilene, Kansas, Harriet decided to bring along their three children, Allie Annie (seven), Emmett (five) and Harriet Minnie (two), and join the drive. Mrs. Cluck was expecting her fourth child in October. The affable husband agreed, preparing a hack to serve as a carryall and adding camp outfits and a pair of strong ponies for his family. They left Round Rock in the spring of 1871, requiring four days to cross Williamson County from Round Rock to Salado. When they reached the Red River, it was flooding, so Mrs. Cluck rode with her husband on a strong pony across the swift waters. Three cowhands took one child apiece in the same way, and the hack was floated across, lashed to a log raft at each side. Negotiating with aplomb in several frightening encounters with cattle rustlers and Indians, the Clucks reached Abilene in the fall, sold the herd, and settled there for the winter. Their son, born October 17, was named Euell Standefer Cluck. The next spring, the family returned to Williamson County, purchased a ranch and made their home at Running Brushy (later Brueggerhoff/Cedar Park).[41]

Another Bartlett man, M. L. Bolding, made a drive in 1871, and was one of several Williamson Countians on the W. T. Avery crew which left Brushy Creek April 15, 1872, for Kansas.[42]

J. C. Juvenal took a successful drive to Kansas in 1872, although in 1867 he had questioned the "glib promises" of Kansas promoters seeking to establish new trail routes and broaden their markets. In an interview with the *Georgetown Watchman*, Juvenal said he was wary "of Kansas sharpers, whose soul and principle are constructed of greenbacks and who are prompted by no other motives."[43]

Albert G. Boyce, who moved with his family to the Rice's Crossing area in 1853, was also in the cattle business.[44] Some of the Boyce family later lived in Georgetown.

James Henry "Little Jim" Saul came to the county with his parents about 1850, grew up in the cattle business about twelve miles below Round Rock, on Brushy Creek. In 1872 he took a thousand head of cattle to Kansas with a crew including Buck and Jack Blanton, the Crum brothers, Summers brothers, and Charlie Saul, his own brother. He drove a 2,800-head herd to Nebraska in 1879, and 2,900 to Kansas the same year.[45]

At least four of the Palm brothers were in the cattle business. In 1872 at the age of seventeen, Swen William Lawson was a cowhand for A. B. Palm when he sent three thousand head of cattle to Ellsworth, Kansas. John, A. J. and W. S. Palm registered their cattle brands in 1869 and 1870.[46]

John B. Pumphrey, born in 1852 near Round Rock, worked as a cowhand for J. C. Juvenal. In 1872 he gathered a herd at the Morrow Ranch two miles from Taylor and drove it to Kansas along with his brother, Beal, and Taylor Penick. He spent four months on the trail up and back, earning sixty dollars a month. Later that year, he and Dave and Ike Pryor took a drive to market for Bill Arnold of Llano County. He continued on drives for several years and worked with cattle in Mexico, Texas, Oklahoma and Wyoming. Reminiscing about those years, Pumphrey wrote about the feel of the saddle at the end of a long day, the weight and pull of the six-shooter, and the blessings of a yellow slicker to cowmen. Those were days of hard work, but good health; of plain food but strong appetites; days when people expected to work for their living, with short hours and big pay unknown.[47]

R. Beal Pumphrey started working with cattle when he was about sixteen, went on a drive with his brother in 1872, and on a crew hired by W. T. Avery in 1873 headed for Kansas.[48]

J. W. Jackson and his father, Jacob, and family came to Donahoe Creek in 1851. J. W. later lived in Bartlett and took his first drove of cattle up the trail in 1872. He had gathered the herd from Brushy Creek and the Little River bottoms.[49]

Frank M. Evans, a stockman-farmer who settled near Rice's Crossing in 1870, made several trips overland with cattle destined for western Kansas.[50]

James Knight took cattle to Kansas between 1877 and 1880. Knight lived on Brushy Creek before the county was formed, but moved to Georgetown in 1848.

Andrew "Andy" Mather, born at Gabriel Mills in 1851, had a varied career as a Texas Ranger and Indian fighter. He was also a drover and mustanger and was said to ride a horse as though he was born on it.[51]

Ben Juvenal, a brother of J. C. Juvenal, herded about three thousand cattle for his brother toward Colorado in 1874. Leaving on April 1, they were near the Brazos River three days later when they suffered an intense blizzard and some of the cattle froze to death.[52]

David M. Sloan and other Circleville stockmen were reported busy with driving herds to the border or to market in April 1878.[53]

T. J. Garner was working for Dudley and John Snyder in 1878 when he took 2,700 steers through Austin, Round Rock and on up the trail.[54]

Landrum "Landy" Poole of the Liberty Hill community took a herd to Cheyenne in 1879.[55]

John P. Burns, born four miles southeast of Hutto in 1859, ran herds into the Indian and Oklahoma territory in the late 1870s and early 1880s.[56]

After the railroads were connected from Taylor to St. Louis and Chicago, R. Kennedy of Taylor shipped many loads of cattle north.[57]

The Allison family of east Williamson County were active stockmen. Francis A. Allison and a crew of eleven men drove 3,500 cattle to Nebraska in 1880 and made two other drives from Texas. Later, they shipped cattle to market.[58]

T. T. Hawkins made a trip from Taylor to Kansas in 1881 with a horse herd owned by Kuykendall, Saul and Burns, with John Burns as trail boss.[59]

John Wells of Bartlett helped gather a herd of eight thousand in 1883 in the central Texas area, including Williamson County.[60]

S. B. Brite of Taylor was on a drive in 1884.[61]

S. M. Swenson, who had extensive financial interests over the country but did not live in Williamson County, was related to people of the county and his activities often touched them and other Swedish settlers. Swenson hired a kinsman, A. E. Dyer of Kenney Fort, to superintend a fencing job on his huge SMS Ranch in west Texas.[62] Among Round Rock area cattlemen, a number announced their brands in the columns of the *Georgetown Watchman* for 1869-1870 and the *Round Rock Sentinel* of 1871: J. B. Walker, L. M. Mays, N. Merrell, John O. Rhea, D. H. Snyder, John Palm, W. L. Telford, David Love, A. J. Palm, George Cluck, R. W. Eller, T. A. Roby, H. B. Sheppard, J. W. Christian, W. E. Palm and W. M. Stinnett.[63]

Losing tremendous sums of money on the trail was not unknown. Many kinds of disasters led to losses. John S. Kritser, cattleman and businessman of Taylor, may have suffered the worst loss among stockmen of the county, a total of $21,000 on a drive from New Mexico to Chicago. Kritser undertook a number of successful drives as well.[64]

Cowmen from other counties sometimes had occasion to recall their drives through Williamson County. G. W. Mills of Lockhart reached Taylor on April 22, 1879.

> A rain, a terrible rain, came up about four o'clock in the evening, raining all evening and all night. It was very cold and we came near to freezing to death. . . . Every horse that we rode that bitter night was unfit for service the balance of the trip. . . . Cattle drifted before wind-driven rain, and by morning we were at Hutto, eight miles away; we had had no supper and no breakfast, and not until noon did we have anything to eat. When these "drifts" take place every man and the boss is in front of the herd, holding them as much as possible; there are no shifts then, but every man to his post all night long, and the nights are long, too. . . . At noon as everyone looked forward to a hearty meal, the cook was found covered with blankets in the wagon—no fire, no coffee—nothing. He was promptly fired. I can see that cook now making it over those hog-wallows, filled with water, to the nearest town.[65]

A herd of fifteen hundred went near Taylor, by Flag Springs, in 1870 on its way to California. George W. Saunders remembered a drive in 1870 which passed through Gonzales, Lockhart, Austin and Georgetown. "On the Gabriel we had a bad stampede during a thunderstorm, and the herd split up into several bunches." Ben Drake recalled riding the trail in mid-

March 1871 through Manor, across Brushy Creek, then across Boggy Creek which "lived up to its name, for it would bog a snake." A heavy rain started before the herd crossed Alligator Creek. After a hard rain and hail about March 15, 1878, a herd on the trail stampeded on the North Gabriel River, mixing with other herds being driven north. It took two days to separate them.[66]

Three of the largest cattle operations of Williamson County during the decades of the 1870s and 1880s were those of the three Snyder brothers, the Olive family, and a future governor, John Sparks.

James "Jim" and Julia Ann Brashear Olive came to Texas in 1843, settling on Brushy Creek near the West Yegua Creek at Cross Roads (Lawrence Chapel). Olive and his sons, Prentice "Print" Olive, Thomas Jefferson "Jay" Olive and Ira Webster Olive, hunted cows on the creek the year round. In 1866 Print managed a roundup for the region. There was "always plenty of whiskey in the Olive cow camps, Jim Olive ruling only that there be no drunkenness" and that the hands be "able to ride next day." When James Olive warned his sons about cattle thieves, Print Olive patted his revolver, an omen of violence to come. Ruthlessly, Print and others dealt what they believed was justice—first to apparent rustlers, then to enemies or people who disagreed with them. James Olive and his wife were considered gentle people, as were their daughters. But the rough, hard life of cattle business bred a toughness into other men of the family which erupted to the point that several of them were forced to leave the country, and most met violent deaths. The Olive pens were built north of Brushy Creek at the southeast corner of the Alva Stiles holdings at Thrall, and from these pens the Olives loaded cattle to ship by railroad after 1876.[67]

Although some Texas cattle were driven into Kansas and Missouri before the Civil War, no herds were made up by Williamson County cattlemen for drives until after the war. The Snyder brothers, Dudley Hiram,* Thomas Shelton, and John Wesley, by the time the conflict ended had cut their teeth on the art of trading, cattle raising and trailing, and were ready to launch their cattle operations with assurance and success.

Dr. Thomas Hale, grandfather of the brothers, settled near Round Rock in the early 1850s. When the Snyder boys' father died, their mother took them and a sister to Missouri to live. Dudley Snyder, the tall, black-haired eldest, rode horseback from there to Round Rock to work for his grand-

_____

* Frequent references show the name to be Dudley Hiram Snyder, as well as the word of descendants, although it is written Dudley Hale Snyder in one University of Texas Archives manuscript.

father "as collector of accounts" in 1855. On his ride to Texas, a horse trader taught him that profits were not made by selling horses, but in the buying. Young Dudley became well acquainted in central Texas. In the spring of 1856, he returned to Missouri and that fall brought his middle brother, John, back to Texas with him. They had enough money to buy twenty-five bushels of apples in Missouri, which they loaded onto their two-horse wagon, selling them along the way to Round Rock at one dollar a dozen. With the $250 in gold this venture netted them, they rented a farm in Palm Valley from S. M. Swenson. A late freeze in 1857 killed their crops, but they found work with other farmers and traded or sold Spanish horses from San Antonio. That autumn they returned to Missouri, picked up young Tom and two loads of apples, and all three of the boys returned to Texas, marketing their fruit for $500 profit. They continued farming, renting a place from Shirley Tisdale between Round Rock and Georgetown, and continued to buy Spanish horses in San Antonio. The boys bought a thresher, the first in the county, and threshed wheat for people of nearby communities. By this time, their mother had moved to the county and Dr. Hale presented her with two hundred acres of land west of Round Rock. The sons embarked in cattle raising.[68]

The Snyder brothers' trading ventures and cattle business prepared them for their next assignments. Dudley enlisted in the Confederate Army in August 1861 and was ordered to procure Texas beeves and trail them to the Army Commissary Department in Tennessee. In an unfortunate business decision, he invested his army earnings in Negro slaves. Tom entered the service, took two herds of cattle from Texas to Louisiana and was assigned to help Dudley as purchasing agent for the Trans-Mississippi Army of the Confederacy.[69]

When the war was over, the Snyders found their savings invested in slaves gone. In the fall of 1865, they borrowed $200 and purchased two hundred work oxen to haul cotton from east Texas to the ports at Brownsville and Matamoros. From their profits they reestablished their cattle business. Thomas lived at Liberty Hill and Dudley and John first in Round Rock, later in Georgetown.[70]

By 1868 the Snyders had bought enough cattle on credit to make their first drive. They had paid $1.50 to $7 a head for the stock, hired W. C. Dalrymple of Georgetown to direct the drive, and sold the yearlings to Charles Goodnight and Han Curtis near Fort Union, New Mexico, for $7 each. They disposed of the other cattle in Colorado at from $7 to $35 a head. Returning home by stage and railway, they came back to the county. The next year, the Snyders took a herd to Abilene, Kansas,

lost 140 beeves to Indians, but made a good profit on the balance. Dudley
built a home two miles north of Round Rock in 1869 and in 1870 he
and John became formal partners. Although Tom was not a partner, all
three men worked closely with each other. The size of their herds increased, in 1870 to five thousand head which they took to Schuyler,
Nebraska. The next year they went to Cheyenne, Wyoming, which they
made one of their headquarters until their last drive in 1885. The herd
was delivered to Goose Creek, Nevada in 1872, but at the end of the
1873 trail to Wyoming, they found the cattle market had dropped. Ar-
ranging for ranch space, they borrowed money at thirty-six percent and
kept their five thousand-head herd there until the next year, when the
market stabilized. They sold at $38 a head.[71]

The Snyders often rode the trains to intercept their herds along the way,
or to meet them at their destination. Sometimes the wives joined their
husbands at the end of the journey. Each year the family kept careful records of the trails, the purchase of supplies, and events along the way,
many manuscripts of which are fortunately preserved. In 1877 Dudley and
John Snyder contracted for 17,500 cattle to be delivered to J. W. Iliff of
Denver. They actually handled 28,000 head that year. The wealthy Iliff
died in February 1878 "and at the earnest request of Mrs. Iliff we took
charge of the entire cattle business of the estate." Meanwhile, in 1879
Dudley moved his home to Georgetown, living on the south side of University Avenue on the east corner of the five hundred block. His
office was west of his home. John also moved his family to Georgetown,
building on what is now Southwestern University campus. His home stood
where the Fine Arts Building is, and he and Dudley built an extremely
fine barn behind, where they kept their prize horses. The barn was sometimes called Old Dud's Folly because of the investment in it. A larger
barn was built southeast of the intersection of University Avenue and
Hutto Road. (It burned to the ground in the mid-1890s and all the fine
horses kept there were lost.) Purchasing an interest in the Iliff stock business, the brothers operated it until 1887.[72]

In the 1879 drive up the trail for Tom Snyder of Liberty Hill, cowhands listed by Baylis John Fletcher, one of the younger hands, were Jim
Andrews, guide; Albert Cochran, Joe Felder, Will Russell, Dick Russell,
Will Bower, Manuel Garcia, the cook; and Anderson Pickett, Snyder's
Negro servant. Sam Allen, John Ledbetter and Andy Marcus started with
the outfit but left it at Hutto. George Arnett was foreman. "We forded
the San Gabriel River near Jonah, a few miles east of Georgetown,"
moved on across Opossum Creek and followed the Belton road. The trip

took them to Cheyenne where they met Landrum Poole, another Liberty Hill man who had come up with a herd.[73]

The Snyders were as innovative in the cattle business as they had been at selling apples. During his drives for the Confederacy, D. H. Snyder used two work oxen which he trained especially to lead the cattle as they swam across the large rivers, including the Mississippi. His plan solved a serious problem which had plagued all cattlemen.[74] When their drives began in 1868, the Snyder brothers adopted three simple rules which they required their cowhands to follow. Dudley listed them:

"First: You can't drink whiskey and work for us.

"Second: You can't play cards and gamble and work for us.

"Third: You can't curse and swear in our camps or our presence and work for us." Snyder recalled that they kept all those rules inviolate as long as they were in the cattle business. All three brothers were religious men, all supported their churches, schools and institutions of higher learning, in Round Rock, Liberty Hill and Georgetown, and particularly Southwestern University. Their rules of the trail lent an air of respectability not always encountered on the long, difficult trips which required the endurance of rugged outdoorsmen. The brothers were also credited with abolishing the practice of slaughtering calves born on the trail. They discovered that calves could stay with the herd and arrive at their destinations in good condition.[75] These perceptive men had little difficulty with Indians up the trail. When the Snyders approached Indian villages, they sent word to the chiefs inviting them to the trail camp and inquiring about the size of the village. They then told the chief that all his tribe was invited to a barbecue at camp. In nearly every instance, the Snyder cattle were unmolested.[76]

Neely Landrum, born and reared near Georgetown, recalled a story about the Snyders and Georgetown banker Frank Carothers.

One night about two o'clock one of the Snyder brothers, and I don't know which one, drove up to Mr. Carothers' house [near the old Southwestern University mess hall in the five hundred block of east Eighth Street. Snyder] had sold a bunch of cattle and he had received twenty thousand silver dollars. He had it in tow sacks in a wagon and two cowboys guarding it for him, and he rode up and woke Mr. Carothers up and told him he wanted to deposit that twenty thousand dollars. Mr. Carothers said, "Well, the bank's closed. I can't take a deposit this time of night," and Mr. Snyder says, "All right, I'll just go on down to Taylor and take it there and put it in one of those banks there, then." So [Carothers] said, "Well, just a minute, let's see what we can do." So he dressed, Mr. Carothers did, and said, "Let's go down to the bank." They went down to the First National

Bank. They had a cistern on each side [of the bank] and they took those tow sacks full of silver dollars, got some bailing wire, and put them down in that cistern to keep them there until the vaults were open the next day.[77]

For seventeen years the Snyders took cattle up the many trails leading to market, making their last drive in 1885. John M. Sharpe, a close friend, described it. "As a boy, this writer saw the splendid herd of five thousand beef cattle in its seemingly endless column pass, as he sat on a gate-post and gazed in childish wonder and admiration at the stately herd and the gallant cowboys charged with their delivery in a distant state."[78] The panic in 1886 led the brothers to sell their Wyoming holdings and they returned to concentrate their ranching activities in five counties in Texas. Leaving a lasting imprint on the northwest and midwest, their herds became the foundation for many large cattle outfits in Colorado, Nebraska, Montana and Wyoming.[79] Frank Yearwood of Georgetown was employed as ranch boss at the Snyder Renderbrook Spade Ranch in Texas. Yearwood was an organizer and an early president of the Texas Hereford Association. The Snyder activities had reached from the Gulf and Mexico to the Pacific and north to Canada.[80]

Dudley Hiram Snyder, born in 1833, married Miss Mary Ann Oatts, daughter of the first postmaster of Round Rock, in March 1864. They had five daughters and three sons. Active in civic and religious projects, he was on the first board of directors of the Trail Drivers' Association of Texas in February 1915. He lost his sight in 1905 but kept his interest in civic matters. Writing to *Sun* editor F. T. Roche in 1909, he recalled moving to Round Rock on September 12, 1855, when Georgetown

was a small, but tough, frontier town; there were no boys or ponies here then, they were all men and race-horses. . . . The time has come when we must make a forward movement. . . . First, we must recognize the fact that the cow and the horse running at large on our streets is a nuisance. When we correct this evil, then we can give attention to the unsightly stockyard corral that cuts our old campus [Southwestern University] in two parts, take down the little two-bit "ferdigo" steps that cross the iron fence at the University and open the gates. These steps are a discomfort to our visitors, a shame during the school year and a disgrace at Commencement. . . . Just now the "old town cow" stands in the way of much of this progress.[81]

Captain Snyder, or Uncle Dudley, as he was often affectionately called, died at his Georgetown home September 12, 1921.[82]

John Wesley Snyder, second eldest of the three brothers, married Catherine Jane Coffee of Georgetown and to this union were born eight children. J. W. and D. H. Snyder, in addition to their many trail drives

*Snyder Brothers advertisement of their stock farm, June 1891, Williamson
County Sun; and John D. Hughes' cattle brand.*

to northern markets, were partners in the San Gabriel Stock Farm, Georgetown, raising and selling fine horses. Their ranch encompassed much of
the present campus of Southwestern University and eastward from there.
John moved to Austin where he spent his latter years and died April 15,
1922.[83]

The youngest of the Snyder trio, Thomas Shelton Snyder, was reddish-
haired, dark-eyed and had a ruddy complexion. He and his wife, the
former Lenora A. Bryson of Liberty Hill, had nine children. They built
a handsome two-story home in Liberty Hill. Later, he moved to New
Mexico to raise sheep and in 1925 moved to Dallas where he lived with
a daughter. He died in 1934 at the age of 95.[84]

One of the Snyders' most trusted men was Thomas C. Oatts, first postmaster at Round Rock and father of Mary Ann Oatts whom D. H. Snyder
married. Oatts' journal of life on a cattle drive, which he called "Cattle
Dairy," is one of the most delightful unpublished writings by any Williamson Countian. The account is frank, simple, solemn, humorous, vivid,
contains abominable spelling, and reveals Oatts' zest for life. Excerpts
follow:

> Left Round Rock Williamson County Texas on the 12th of April 1871
> got on safe for 5 miles whare our waggon broke dowin . . . herded the cattle
> in the Peraria [prairie]. [They camped the second night at Liberty Hill.
> There was a] fine vew all round . . . for maney miles which was veary
> Pleasant and delightfull at thes season of the year the Peraria bloming
> covered with beautiful flowers which gave a veary pleasant oder.

The drive reached "Aberlene" by May, encountering a "tolerable brisk"
rain. One cowhand drank, all the way up, "sick, too." The diarist dwelt
only briefly on their troubles, however—"all wright side up this morning
no one hurt or drounded." The cowmen "faired soumtusly" on Irish po-

tato and bean soup, coffee and pickles. Care was taken in setting up camp, the men attended church regularly on Sundays, and special consideration was given to those who were ill. Oatts was a keen observer of nature and the countryside:

> All well this morning and struck out for Skyler   and we heare as we drift
> on that the citizens wd stop us at the next creck but we have not bin stopt as
> yet   we are still hearing that we will be stopt
>   1st Comanchas
>   2 Chickasaw
>   3 Cados On Witchataw
>   4 Cheynes & Rappahoes south of Red fork, Arkansaw
>   5 Osage—North of Red Fork to Arkansaw River
>   6 Creek & T
>   7 Tonkaways
>   8 Cherakees
>   9 Chocktaws
>   90 mils from Arkansas River to Aberlene.
> [Oatts philosophized frequently in his diary and fragmentary notes]. All
> cow drovers claim to know the best way to manage cattle and tel how
> little one another know about driving.[85]

The drive reached Schuyler, Nebraska, in time for a big July 4 celebration, starting with a procession of girls dressed in white, carrying flags, and boys with badges, ribbons and flags. People arrived in

> Buges, waggons & vehickels of all kinds and shapes, and in front a
> splended Brass Band with ther Base drum and the marshel and Flag Barer
> on horse Back all dressed up in uneform and the whole presented a veary
> grand appearance. Thar was about 500 at the speacking . . . and at night
> the 4th close up with a ball . . . allso . . . a Poney Rase . . . and just
> befour dark the citizens met and put up a fire works near whare the
> publick speaking was to be . . . about dark the fire works comeanced
> firing . . . and tha got faster and faster and more of them and after a
> while it got in full blast and the Brass Band Played and the Base drum
> beat and the boyes whoped and holowed and the shots went high up in
> the sky and the sparcks of fire fell fast and thick and all was the smel of
> Powder. those crackers and rockets cast [cost] about one hunderd dollars
> fer the ocation and theare was life in every thing and all went off well and
> about 2 hours in the night thare came up a rain and it just pord down
> heavey And broke up the antisipated Ball the ladeys fled for hom in evey
> direction and all and every thing culed off.[86]

Weather was important to cattlemen, as well as to Oatts personally. "Watter spouts or turnadoes are two common in this county for me. . . . it is two storme & for me and too cold some dayes—veary hot—and some, veary cold." While at Schuyler, Oatts "herd a discourse forem a Piskipalian minister" and saw a group of Indians who had been "on a Bufalow hunt." The Snyders arrived at Schuyler by train September 11, 1871, to meet the drovers, after which the crew returned by train to New Orleans, took a steamer to Galveston, docking there on September 27. They "left on a waggen for Round Rock," reaching home October first after a rough ride.[87]

John Sparks, another wealthy cattleman of Williamson County, distinguished himself in business and in politics and was twice elected governor of Nevada. Born in Mississippi August 20, 1843, he grew up in Lampasas County, Texas, and served in the Confederate Army, attaining the rank of Captain. Between 1878 and 1883, he bought considerable acreage in Williamson County and was living in Georgetown at least by March 1879, possibly the year before. On a tract of land which he purchased from the Knight family south of Georgetown, he built a long, low ranch-style home in a pasture west of the 1900 block of South Brushy Street (present Austin Avenue). His first wife was Rachel Knight, daughter of Dr. David Knight, and after her death on February 14, 1879, he married her half sister, Nancy Elenora (Nora) Knight. The Sparks children were Maud, born 1874, who married Reverend James McKenzie, a Presbyterian minister; Rachel, born 1877 and died 1881; Deal, born 1880, died 1882; R. A., no date; Benton H., born 1882; Charles M., born 1885; Leland, born 1887.[88]

The Sparks residence was considered one of the finer homes in Georgetown, containing many excellent pieces of furniture,* art objects and curious pieces which Captain Sparks collected in his extensive travels. The skeleton of a whale** for many years was "placed so that in walking up to the house you passed through it." This distinctive decoration was of special interest to passersby and to children, who sat upon it to "ride" it, or who swung in a smaller seat-like bone. The Town and County column of a local newspaper noted that Sparks' home contained "a unique chair made of the 'long horns' of Texas bovines which graces the private room of one of our leading stockmen. The horns are highly polished and conveniently grouped together, making the seat comfortable and chair attractive." The same newspaper announced in 1885 that a large chair of elk horns had just arrived in Georgetown from Wyoming, belonging to Captain Sparks.[89]

When the Southern Presbyterian Church needed land for a cemetery,

---

* Antiques from the Sparks home were in homes of Judge and Mrs. Sam V. Stone, Mrs. Elizabeth Sanders and others in Georgetown in 1973.
** The whalebones are now stored in Southwestern University Science Building.

Captain Sparks donated two acres from his farm south of town for it, and there his first wife, Rachel, was buried, and three of his children. In 1889 the Texas Chautauqua Assembly of Georgetown was organized. Seven or eight summer homes were built on the grounds near the official buildings, all of them on the north bank of the South San Gabriel River. Among these homes and dominating the scene was a round tower-like structure of stone dubbed "Captain Sparks' Castle."[90]

The Sparks cattle and ranching interests were also developed during the 1870s and 1880s. In 1877 Ab Blocker of Austin delivered three thousand head of cattle to Sparks' ranch in Wyoming. Sparks purchased about ten thousand acres of prairieland between Taylor and Thrall, south of Noack. This land was covered with mesquite and prickly pear and abounded in deer. Longtime law officer of Taylor, Jim Dellinger, said, "We used to hunt down there all the time, a bunch of us, and the first deer I ever killed in all my life was right there in that Sparks pasture." Foreman of the place was Greenup Kuykendall, who named a son Sparks Kuykendall for Captain Sparks. Will Pickett, the famous Negro bull-dogger, learned his art on that ranch.[91] Sparks owned half interest in the Steele and Sparks bank in Georgetown, made frequent trips to the northwest to check on his ranching interests there. During the time he lived in Williamson County, John Sparks, who was of English ancestry, always wore a coonskin coat, English corduroy pants, boots, and carried a flask of whiskey and a gun.[92]

John Tinnin, another cattleman-resident of Georgetown, purchased the steamboat Gothic style home at 1220 Austin Avenue (still standing). Like John Sparks, he was a colorful man. The landmark home, built in 1879 by Clarence Dilley for his young bride, was sold to Tinnin soon afterwards by the wife when her husband died.* Tinnin owned much fine furniture and was especially well known for a parrot which he had bought from a sailor. The bird's vocabulary was limited to words which frequently shocked people walking by. In 1881 Tinnin and Sparks engaged in gold mining and founded a huge 387,000 acre ranch they called Winecup, north of Wells, Nevada. About eight years later, Tinnin sold his interest in the ranch to Barney Harrell, who continued its operation along with Sparks.[94]

---

* Clarence E. Dilley died October 31, 1881, in Shelbyville, Illinois, while visiting his wife's relatives there. He and his wife, Antonia W. Dilley, had one small child, George M. Dilley, Jr., named for the child's grandfather, George M. Dilley, an active businessman in Williamson County. The bereaved widow did not wish to return to Texas and at her request the deceased's father, George M. Dilley, settled the estate, selling the homestead to John Tinnin on July 18, 1883.[93]

Although Sparks spent more and more time in Nevada, he maintained his old home in Georgetown, completely furnished, with August and Annie Lindquist, a Swedish couple, living there as caretakers. In Nevada,

Home of Captain John Sparks, Georgetown. August and Annie Lindquist stand near Sparks' bone swing and whalebone collection.

Governor John Sparks of Nevada.
Courtesy Nevada Historical Society.

Sparks and his partners gave huge barbecues, inviting entire communities, becoming well acquainted over the state. In 1902 Sparks ran for the governorship of Nevada, was elected, then was reelected to a second term. Several years after he was elected, Governor Sparks visited in Georgetown and entertained with a huge party at his home. Among the guests were the Governor of Texas and many high state officials and almost everyone in Georgetown, including the children, whom the mothers took along. During his second term, Governor Sparks died, in 1908, was buried in Reno, Nevada. "He was a man of distinguished appearance, graceful of figure, six feet and one inch tall and very erect, easy in his manner, with a clear cut face and kindly expression." One of his nieces recalled a portrait of "rich Uncle John" which hung in their home, a full length picture of John Sparks wearing a fur coat and sitting in a chair. The Winecup ranch, owned in the mid-twentieth century by actor Jimmy Stewart, was sold in 1969 for three million dollars.[95]

The days of gathering wild cattle from the prairielands, of droving to midwest markets, of ranch operations almost wholly dependent upon nature's provisions of grass and water—all these rapidly came to a halt. The change brought considerable anguish while adjustments were being made. Gradually the emphasis shifted from capturing wild animals to breeding finer ones, from an open range watered by springs and streams to smaller, fenced areas no longer completely dependent on a cattle brand or upon a neighbor's honesty for protection of a man's cattle. When natural water was not available, a rancher drilled a well and installed a windmill. Operations were no longer, as a rule, on such a grand scale, but a rancher could work toward quality. The anguish was felt among oldtime cowmen who wanted to hold to old traditions and among the new ranchmen who fenced their property and repeatedly had their fences cut. During just one season in 1883, the *Taylorsville Times* reported that John Sparks, William Robbins, Willis Avery, General Griffith and another Robbins had their fences cut. Similiar incidents were frequently heard of in the Circleville farming community. Old ways die hard, especially those which grew along with the widespread legend of the cowboy and those tied with an economy many an old rancher believed could never be replaced.

IX

Fifty Years: 1860-1910

TOWNS AND POPULATION

County population increased ten percent from 1860 to 1870, with a total of 6,368 in 1870, 405 farms, fifteen industrial establishments, 1,116 dwellings, and sixty-six deaths reported that year. The county seat had 320 residents. Georgetown had been incorporated by special legislative act in 1866. In 1877, the county tax lists showed 450,231 acres of taxable land out of a total of 994,127 acres; 15,564 horses and mules, 33,790 cattle, 15,821 sheep and 17,672 hogs. Population soared to 15,155 in 1880, more than doubling during the decade, and taxable property jumped from nearly two million to nearly five million dollars. The railroads had arrived.[1]

Politics attracted considerable attention during the last quarter of the nineteenth century. Newspaper editorials and letters to the editor reflected the main concerns: prohibition or not, various economic philosophies, and the possibility of dividing Williamson County into two separate counties, the proposed new section on the east end generally referred to in public debate as "Willie County."

Votes on the question of local option and prohibition were cast in March 1878 at the following boxes: Georgetown, Berry's Creek, Bagdad, Dodd's Store, Pond Springs, Liberty Hill, Brizendine Mill (Gabriel Mills), Rock School House, White School House, Florence, Marrs' School House, Corn Hill, Ake's School House, Circleville, Macedonia, Gentry School House, Bennett's School House, Young & Hill's Store, Round

Berry's Creek grocery-saloon-stagecoach station.

Rock, Hutto, Taylorsville and James Allison's house. Totals were 494 for local option, 461 against. The presence of open saloons in Georgetown was a thorn to Texas Methodist officials, particularly those connected with Southwestern University. In 1884 a Precinct One option election was held for the Georgetown section, but the effort at prohibition was turned down at the polls. The issue was revived in 1893 and on May 29, another Precinct One election was held. Out of 1197 votes cast, 724 were in favor of prohibition, 473 against. Saloons in Georgetown were ordered closed and sale of liquor prohibited after July 8, 1893.[2]

When the tax collector made his rounds of the county in the 1870s, he visited the places already named as voting boxes, plus Jollyville, Hopewell, Gabriel Mills, Post Oak Island, Pleasant Hill, Running Brushy and Rice's Crossing. Political speakings were scheduled throughout the county by H. L. Bently, J. L. Mullen, J. L. Brittain, W. C. Dalrymple, Robert Hanna, Sr., and J. N. McFadin at most of the same communities, and at Olive's (Lawrence Chapel) and Tompkins' Store (Rice's Crossing). Delegates to the county convention in August 1878 were W. M. Key, Georgetown; William Hunt, Corn Hill; J. H. Faubion, Bagdad; J. G. Matthews, Liberty Hill; L. T. Lawler, Florence; J. T. Jackson, Circleville; S. M. Slaughter, Post Oak Island; J. H. Robertson, Round Rock.[3]

The hotly debated issue of a new "Willie County" filled newspapers in the county and over the state periodically for fifteen years or more. Residents in eastern Williamson County supported the division. The matter was argued, reargued, taken up by writers of papers in other sections of Texas, and reams of letters, editorials, petitions and speeches on the subject were recorded. One committee of eight was appointed in Taylor to go to Georgetown "with a view of inducing them to withdraw their opposition to the creation of Willie." The committee was composed of J. N. McFadin, R. L. Penn, John Allen Gano, John Threadgill, C. P. Vance, Dan'l. Moody, A. V. Doak and J. W. Parker. They addressed their communication about a meeting to W. Y. Penn, Emzy Taylor, T. P. Hughes, T. B. Cochran and D. S. Chessher of Georgetown.[4]

A new post office named Conel was listed from 1878 to 1880 where the Allison home near Granger was located. Other new towns were Stiles Switch (Thrall), Taylorsville, Hutto Station (1876). New post offices between 1880 and 1890 were listed at Buttercup, Beaukiss, Brueggerhoff, Bartlett, Leander, Jonah, Granger, Peyton, Walburg, Rattan, Grove Ranch, Cedar Park and Coupland; Shiloh had a new election precinct. The last decade of the century brought another rash of new post offices at Theon, Draco (Rock House), Laneport, Allison, Neusser, Beyersville, Waterloo, Gower, Sandoval, Small, Leubner, Rutledge, Gravis, Keliehor, Townsville (which became Weir in 1900) and Andice. New schools added by 1900 were Armfield Store (Rice's Crossing), Chalk Ridge, Cedar Valley, New Hope, Seymour, Mankin's Branch, Somerset, Dacus Crossing, Wilson, Tyler, Long Branch, Stiles, Sycamore, Cedar Point, Fisher and Owens.[5]

ETHNIC GROUPS

The pioneers of the county were mostly westward-moving people of English ancestry from the United States, some of them bringing with them Negro slaves. Next came the Swedish immigrants in the 1850s,* settling first in Palm Valley, named for a Swedish family there. Swedes continued to come throughout the century, fanning out to farmland around Hutto, Georgetown, Round Rock (which they continued to call Brushy for many years), Weir, Jonah, Taylor and the smaller communities of Union Hill, Bell, Berry's Creek, Caldwell Heights, Hoxie and Type. John Nelson and G. Johnson obtained their citizenship papers February 22, 1861, as did many others. Swedish churches were organized in or near all these com-

---

* August Anderson came in the late 1830s to the county, promoted Swedish immigration to Texas, but was not listed in the 1850 county census.

munities in the 1880s and 1890s, some of them offering Swedish language services until well into the twentieth century. Although most of the second generation understood Swedish well, many could not read it, for they learned only English in the public schools. At Union Hill school south of Georgetown around the turn of the century, for several summers citizens of the area organized classes to teach children to read Swedish.[6] Trinity Lutheran College was established at Round Rock in 1904 and a Swedish mutual fire insurance group in 1911.

German, Austrian, Swiss and Wendish immigrants entered Williamson County in the late 1870s and afterward, also seeking good farms. Numerous towns and communities bear their influence. The Swiss went to New Bern and to the North Gabriel northwest of Georgetown. Walburg was named for an early settler there, Henry Doering, who came from Walburg, Germany. A number of German-Wendish families gave this community a distinct character, still notable in 1973. Germans-Austrians lived east of Corn Hill, at Theon, Macedonia, Neusser (Naizerville); along Berry's, Willis and Opossum creeks; at Bartlett, Schwertner, Waterloo, Wuthrich Hill, Sandoval, Taylor, Noack, Beyersville and Thrall. A few Danish and Norwegian immigrants lived at Frame Switch and Hutto, a few French at Monadale and Sandoval. Numerous Lutheran churches bear the imprint of these pioneers, noted for their large family gatherings, elaborate wedding celebrations with dancing and bountiful meals served to hundreds of friends and relatives, their love of music, brass bands, dancing and good food.

Czechoslovakian, Moravian and other Slavic settlers came much earlier to Texas than to Williamson County. Large numbers migrated to the county in the 1880s and 1890s, especially near Taylor, Granger, Friendship, Corn Hill, Machu and Mozo. Most of the immigrant Czechs were farmers looking for a land more politically stable than their own and fiercely appreciating their own individual independence. They, too, established their own churches—Catholic and Czech Moravian primarily— and held to native customs such as the arranged wedding, the festive wedding meal, the singing of folk music, dancing, and playing of musical instruments, also often native. The embroidered, colorful native costume of the men and women was abandoned in this country for work clothes suitable on the farm, but those precious costumes were lovingly packed away, then taken out for special occasions by men, women and children. Several Czech language newspapers have been published in Texas. One of them, *The Nasinec*, official organ of the Catholic Czech Church of Texas, was printed in Taylor from 1916 until 1937 and since 1937 has

Churches Dot Farming Settlements

Sandoval Zion (built 1932) and Prince of Peace Lutheran (built at New Bern 1912, moved to Wuthrich Hill).

St. Peter Lutheran Church, Walburg, organized in 1889, and Holy Trinity Catholic Church, Theon, erected in 1913.

been published in Granger. Numerous fraternal and benevolent organizations provide cooperative insurance, support education, and provide retirement and nursing homes, among them the S. P. J. S. T. lodge and home at Taylor. Czech ladies are well-known for their unusual pastries, food fairs and barbecue dinners, usually prepared to benefit a church or other group. Between 1914 and 1924, a Hus Memorial School, *Husova Skola,* was run in Granger by Reverend Josef Barton and Reverend Josef Hegar, in an effort to teach the Czech language and prepare youngsters in the Bible and music.[7]

The Scandinavian, Germanic and Slavic immigrants to Williamson County were almost unanimously devoted to farming when they came. They worked very hard, knew useful crafts such as carpentry and, even without any finances to start with, in short order became some of the most prosperous farmers in the area. Most were insistent that their children be educated, although it was not unusual to keep them from school during seasons of heavy farm work. Religious, self-sustaining and thrifty, they could be counted as some of the county's best citizens. Second and third generation children of immigrants had more time for education and, during the twentieth century, large numbers have entered the professional and business world.

In the last three decades of the nineteenth century, architectural styles became varied, reflecting many backgrounds and tastes: the simply styled colonial or New England house, or the handsome southern plantation manor home, often with summer house and other buildings; the sharply slanted and many gabled roofs of the Swedish frame houses, many of them two story and large, but otherwise simple in style; the more ornamented but steep-roofed houses of Germans and Swiss; the gingerbread decoration of Victorian residences built by well-to-do farmers and townspeople; occasional hints of Spanish influence in stone ornament, public buildings or private homes; the Greek revival styles often preferred for public buildings. Occasionally one can find examples of less common designs, such as the "steamboat" house at 1220 Austin Avenue, Georgetown, built by former New Orleans importer Clarence Dilley; or the Kroschewsky home on the road between the old Sam Easley place and Taylor, which has unusual window treatment in truncated gables upstairs and suggests German or low countries influence.[8]

Small numbers of Dutch and Polish immigrants were absorbed into the county's population; a Chinaman established a new laundry in Georgetown in 1883 and children around the turn of the century sat on fences and caught hold of his queue, which prank he seemed to accept with

Homes of Varied Architecture, 1973

Log cabin (Gabriel Mills, 1851); Cole home (Old Round Rock); Nelson Merrell (1870, Round Rock); Dilley-Tinnin (1879, Georgetown); Julius Kroschewsky (near Wilson Springs); H. T. Stearns (Circleville, 1894); Allison and M. R. Kennedy homes, Taylor.

equanimity. Sam Lee and Sue Sing had a laundry in Taylor beginning in 1895. Several Jewish immigrants from Russia, Lebanon and other countries came quite early to the county. Joseph "Jack" Melasky peddled goods from his uncle's store in Austin to the area where Taylorsville would be established, walking at first, then using a team of mules and a wagon, arriving at the right time to spend the night with some of his friends and customers, like the Barkers on Brushy Creek. When Taylorsville was established he put up a store there in 1877. Others of Jewish origin were successful merchants in Taylor and Georgetown. Jacob "Jake" S. Melasky ran a store at Sandoval from about 1909 until 1924, selling "everything from wagons to groceries." A few Greek citizens lived in the county, including Jim Athas of Taylor who ran a confectionery for many years. The previously-mentioned Nelson family who settled early in Palm Valley were especially civic-minded and successful businessmen, establishing a number of enterprises in Round Rock during the twentieth century.[9]

Small numbers of immigrants from Mexico were in the county before 1900, but no large groups came until about 1910.

CHURCHES AND LODGES

Until after the Civil War most churches were served entirely by circuit ministers or by preachers who happened to live in a community and who followed another occupation for a living. A few of the larger churches obtained ministers of their own after the war, but rural and other small congregations continued to use circuit riders, or to alternate services with other denominations in a Union building, calling on those lay or trained preachers who were available. Also after the war, they progressed from meeting in homes or in log churches doubling as schools to frame buildings, generally put up by members of the congregation and other residents of the community. A few stone structures were erected as early as the 1870s, a particularly well preserved one, the present First Presbyterian Church, Georgetown, built 1872-1873 under Reverend John McMurray, son-in-law of skilled carpenter-craftsman C. A. D. Clamp, who apparently had a part in the project. The church was organized in 1857, held school as well as services in their earlier church, and in the basement of their new church after it was built. The first ladies admitted to Southwestern University met classes in that basement. In 1867, W. C. Dalrymple, writing for the *Texas Almanac*, said that Old School Presbyterian Churches were active at Round Rock, Georgetown, Brooksville (Florence), Bagdad and Cooke's Settlement (Mankin's Crossing).

Camp meetings continued in popularity, sometimes held in the open in a grove of trees near good water, sometimes under tabernacles for summertime services. Evangelistic services were combined with camp meetings if an evangelist was available. Major W. E. Penn* was an extremely popu-' lar lay evangelist, who held such a meeting in the Fair Grounds (now San Gabriel Park) at the five springs, Georgetown, in September 1879. There were twenty springs within a quarter of a mile, clear and cool. Town people brought suppers, spread tablecloths on a gravel bar by the river along with picnics of campers, and here many lifetime friendships were formed. A sundown prayer service was held after the meal.

> Who can ever forget them—the flaring lamps, the immense cowd, the deep bass voice of Major Penn, the campfires and the camps, the flag seats full of mourners, the choir on the rostrum flanked on either side by the good old men and women, the fervent prayers, the powerful sermon, the happy conversions.[11]

Five hundred persons affiliated with churches during the meeting, seventy-five of whom became members of the First Baptist Church of Georgetown. Assisting during the revival was a Baptist circuit minister who had preached at the Georgetown church, Reverend George W. Baines, Sr. Rev. Baines was later to become president of Baylor University (1881-1882) and was the maternal grandfather of President Lyndon Baines Johnson, with whom Williamson County became well acquainted in 1936 when he first ran for Congress.[12]

Baptists had been active in the county since 1847 when R. H. Taliaferro preached in Freeman Smalley's log home. Homer S. Thrall, a pioneer circuit riding Methodist parson, and Orceneth Fisher were popular in Round Rock and Georgetown after the 1870s, the town of Thrall being named for H. S. Thrall. Cumberland Presbyterians were on the scene at an early date but factions in the church developed during the Civil War years. The Unionists and the Southern branches were quite active in the county. Thaddeus McRae enlisted a group of Georgetown Presbyterian Unionists to join with others and form the Presbytery of Austin. According to the *Texas Almanac* for 1870, there were about twenty churches in the county at the time. There were probably more. Newspapers for 1878 mentioned new churches at Brushy Chapel (later Palm Valley), New Hope, Macedonia, Bagdad and Taylorsville. Taylorsville, before the end of the century, listed churches founded by Methodist and Presbyterian groups in 1876, a Christian Church in 1877, Episcopalian and Catholic

* W. E. Penn was also a lawyer. As a pioneer Baptist evangelist, he published a pamphlet and his preaching was judged "somewhat sensational."[10]

groups in 1878, Baptist in 1882, and the Czech Brethren Church in 1895.[13]

The complicated task—sorting out church histories from the time a handful of people met in various homes to the time a church was formally organized with charter members and places of worship built—becomes even more complex for churches which merged or altered their philosophies and their names. Examples were the pioneer Cumberland Presbyterian and the Old School Presbyterian churches, later to be called the Southern Church and the Northern Church. At Georgetown one editor despaired of the whole thing after irritating the members of *both* churches in his town by calling them names they did not care for. He wrote, "The *Sun* can't please everybody, and sometimes fails to please itself. If you can't stand what it says cut the objections out and read the hole in the paper." The same issue contained notices of preaching at First Presbyterian (Rock) Church and a meeting at Southern Presbyterian Church. The next week, the editor elaborated on his problem:

> The Presbytery of the Northern Presbyterian church has given it the name of the "First Presbyterian Church of Georgetown." The Presbytery of the Southern Presbyterian Church has also given it a name, to-wit: "The First Presbyterian Church of Georgetown." In speaking of them if we call one the Northern church its members do not like it; if we call the other the Southern church its members inform us that it is not the proper name. If we say "The First Presbyterian Church" how will our readers know which church we refer to? There is but one solution that we can see, *viz.*: To call one "The Original First Presbyterian Church" and the other "The Simon Pure First Presbyterian Church." If any of the members have any suggestions to make in regard to the matter we will take it in verbal doses every three days as the patient can stand it.[14]

When these two groups united a few years later, they solved the difficulty by choosing a name, but complicated the job of a careful historian. Multiply this single instance by several hundred and the result is a project of many years' research and what would be a thick volume about the many fine churches of Williamson County.

Masonic Lodges, closely aligned with churches, which postdated the Civil War in the county, were Norton Moses Lodge No. 336, chartered in 1871 in Bagdad and moved to Leander in 1899; Florence Lodge No. 338 chartered 1871; Liberty Hill Lodge No. 432 chartered in 1875; Macedonia Lodge No. 443 founded 1874 and chartered in 1875; Solomon Lodge No. 484 in Taylorsville, 1878; Corn Hill Lodge No. 567 chartered in 1882 and moved to Jarrell in 1912; Granger Lodge No. 677, 1889; Bartlett Lodge No. 692, 1890; and Hutto Lodge No. 801, 1896.[15]

COUNTY BUSINESS

Soon after the Civil War, official titles changed in Texas counties. The Police Court presided over by the Chief Justice became the County Court with a Presiding Justice. For a short time the Commissioners were called Precinct Justices. Within a few years, the presiding officer was known as the County Judge and the Precinct Justices again were called County Commissioners. The changes took place from about August 1866 until a decade later. Duties of the officials were much as always, although they gradually expanded as the county and its services grew. Finances, roads, court sessions, juries, schools, elections, and assistance to the "blind, paupers, indigents and idiots" continued to occupy the Commissioners. The Court decided to establish a County Farm for indigent persons, purchasing land on December 22, 1882. J. R. Bryant was the first superintendent at the Farm, succeeded by G. W. Dykes (1887), whose salary was $400 a year; John T. Bryson (1888), S. K. Brown (1891), John Sudduth (1893) and W. P. McNeill (1894).[16]

Long lists of cattle brands were registered with the county; butcher's reports were received and approved regularly; bounties were paid on wild animal scalps such as the cat and wolf. Miscellaneous expenses were for firewood, stove pipe, stationery items, nine pairs of shackles made by Aaron Williams, a Georgetown blacksmith, and for blankets, mattresses and medical attention for prisoners or paupers. F. M. Green presented the Court a bill of $1.13 "for hauling 750 shingles from Morrow's Mill about 3½ years ago," in July 1876.[17]

The County Court was vexed almost continuously with the unstable first stone Courthouse, with the first three jails, and even with the old frame former Courthouse (Patterson home) which the Court had tried unsuccessfully to sell. Once in 1863, the frame house was rented to Terrell A. Monroe as a saloon. During the war, it was offered "for Confederate Treasury notes" to the highest bidder but there was never a buyer and in August 1865 former Commissioner Joseph Mileham "removed [it] from the town of Georgetown." The Commissioners were indignant: "Said County has suffered great loss and damage by said act of removing said house," the Court declared, authorizing County Treasurer Cyrus Eubank to take legal steps to recover the value of the house and damages resulting from the move. A settlement was reached in 1866. The old William Patterson home (second Courthouse) was set by Mileham on the north bank of the San Gabriel River at Water Valley (Jonah), where a log room was added. It was used as a residence until about 1910.[18]

Special taxes were levied in 1867 to finance repairs on the jail and Courthouse, but early in 1868 county officials, despairing of fixing the old jail, set a tax to build a new one. The second jail was a three-story log and stone building, fourteen by nineteen feet in size, with hipped roof and doors at the east and west ends. It was placed where the old Patterson Courthouse had stood (approximately where the Federal Post Office stood in 1973) and was completed that summer. An unused room was rented to publishers Makemson and Foster of the *Georgetown Watchman,* who previously rented a room in the Courthouse. "The stone [jail], lined with hewn elm logs driven full of ten penny nails, and thought to be a very Gibraltar for strength and security . . . when put to the test . . . proved to be a snare and a delusion." Just a year after it was finished, the Court ordered $600 worth of repairs on the jail, along with $1200 on the Courthouse—sizeable sums at that time. J. J. Cluck was awarded the contracts. Only seven years later in 1875, the third county jail was erected on the northeast corner of the square. The two story stone building had two cells, office, cook room, privy in the corridor, was twenty-two by thirty feet in size, boasted an iron roof, and was planned so that it could be joined to the new Courthouse, soon to be built. The jail cost $7,000, was accepted by the Court on October 21, 1875. William K. Foster, proprietor of the *Georgetown Record,* rented the upper story of the jail, agreeing to do all the county's printing the following year "including county estrays" in exchange for the room rent. But there was not a complete meeting of the minds between the county fathers and the publisher, and the financial acumen of the Commissioners broke down. They noted in February 1876 that the *Record,* "the only newspaper published at this place, refuses to print the financial statement of the county" for the year 1875 for $50, the maximum allowed by law. The Court ordered three copies of the statement posted as the "law requires," requesting that B. E. Chrietzberg draw them up. The next month, Chrietzberg billed the county $120 for the job. The court paid him $60.[19]

Cryptically indicating basic structural flaws in the Courthouse, the Commissioners in 1873 ordered installation of four iron rods extending through the building "so as to make the same safe if possible." Next spring, a resolution sent to the State of Texas stated that Williamson County was "largely indebted," that warrants were of "scarcely any value," selling at thirty cents on a dollar, and asked that the county be allowed an ad valorum tax "to assist in building a new Court House, the old one being in a dilapidated condition & liable to fall down or to have to be torn down at any time." The crumbly structure that had required six years to build was used only twenty years, and was unsafe much of that time because of "a parting at the seams." At Commissioners meeting August 14, 1877, a new house was ordered. Handsome plans by Preston & Ruffin

Fourth Courthouse, built 1877-1878. For ten years the jail was on the Square northeast of the Courthouse.

were accepted, a contract was made with John Didelot for $27,400, and the job was finished in less than a year and accepted September 2, 1878.[20]

Traffic downtown centered around the Courthouse the rest of the century. An iron fence was later added around the square, the hub of considerable activity every "First Monday" when estray sales were held. This custom of a monthly auctioning of stray cattle continued for many years and drew visitors from a wide area. Hitching posts and sidewalks were installed around the square in 1881, water troughs decorated the public square lawn between 1888 and 1892, but were then ordered removed. A public well on the square was available quite early, for it was repaired in 1866 when a "good frame" was put around it, the well cleaned out, and a bucket and rope attached, for the sum of fifteen dollars. A public privy also stood on the lawn. In 1872 the Court ruled that it must not be locked, but kept open for everyone to use. "Anyone desiring exclusive priviledges" must build his own facility adjoining, at his own expense. This may or may not account for permits issued to Attorney A. S. Fisher to put up a stone room on the southwest corner of the Courthouse yard (granted November 1872) and to J. A. Turner to place a tent there in May 1879. Privies continued in use on the grounds until a sewage system was installed after February 1894. Cows on the square had "well nigh become an intolerable nuisance" in 1887, it was reported.[21]

The third jail (built 1875 on the square) had almost immediately become crowded and insecure, with almost countless escapes. It was a time when desperadoes, cattle thieves and other lawless men ranged throughout the country. As local newspapers editorially urged a new jail, the Grand Jury took note of the situation and strongly recommended that a new and stronger one be constructed. Plans for the present native limestone building styled after the French Bastille, drawn by architects Dodson & Dudley of Waco, were accepted on February 18, 1888. Thomas Lovell &

French Bastille style jail, the county's fourth, built 1888-1889.

Miller of Brownwood contracted to build the jail and a jailer's residence for $20,966. A lively argument ensued regarding the jail's location, many supporting a site adjacent to the Courthouse. Other views prevailed and it was "inconveniently situated three blocks north of the Court House," in the three hundred block between Blue (Main) and Red (Church) streets. The building was accepted January 10, 1889. Old timers recalled that when the workmen completed the job, they celebrated the occasion with a drinking party. One workman imbibed too freely and wound up being the first prisoner in the jail he had just helped to build.[22]

The strong stone jail was considered a fine building and an ornament to the town. (The previous jail on the Courthouse lawn was torn down and the material from it used "to construct the County Record Vault and County Judge's office.") The new building was still in use in 1973, after having undergone several remodelings which wisely kept the outer appearance of the heavy structure on jail hill undisturbed.[23]

After the war, the County hired a Road Overseer for the first time. In 1872 he was authorized to buy a good yoke of oxen, wagon and tools. Attorney T. P. Hughes of Georgetown in 1876 was granted his request to erect two gates across the Georgetown-Elgin road on his place south of town, provided the gates be self-shutting and "capable of being opened on horseback without alighting & ten feet wide."[24]

Highways remained hardly more than trails. When a route was occasionally changed, it was to shorten the way or to avoid difficulty with a farmer who objected to the road crossing his land. The desirable river and creek crossings were by this time well known, and all roads led to places where the banks were not too steep to climb and the bottom of the stream was rock or gravel. Such crossings determined the locations of many homes, villages and towns. For pedestrians, particularly school children, foot bridges—usually big logs spanning the streams—provided dry crossings except when someone lost his footing. When the streams rose, foot logs were somewhat dangerous over the deep, swift water. Northtown students at Georgetown walked to school south of the river over log bridges as did Circleville youngsters for most of the nineteeth century.[25]

The need for bridges was especially critical in the blackland prairies of eastern Williamson County. Scarcity of timber and of good surface water caused this section to be settled later than the western part of the county. In addition, farming on a large scale did not develop until after the railroad came in 1876. When these blackland farms were established, the streams with mud banks and mud beds were extremely difficult to ford. Farmers sometimes built small bridges at very little expense to the county, with the county and farmer splitting the cost. The $500 bridge over Dacus Crossing at present Beyersville was perhaps the first in the county. It was "received" by the County Court on November 15, 1881. A bridge was planned for Goodwin Branch on the Round Rock-Circleville road on July 11, 1882, and in December of that year, the county fathers inspected the fords on the North and South Gabriels at Georgetown with bridges in mind. Nothing came of the inspection at that time. The next year, three bridges were ordered: one for $30 on the Taylor-Hutto road, another for $50 on the Georgetown-Belton road, and a third one on Snyder Lane at Liberty Hill. The Georgetown-Belton road bridge, presumably over Berry's Creek, turned out to be narrower than the road leading to it. The Commissioners dexterously ordered the road made narrow enough to fit the bridge![26]

The first bridges were low and usually not very substantial. By 1885, Dacus Crossing had to be rebuilt. In 1886, George Irvine put up two bridges over streams between Georgetown and Granger; another was erected at Lawrence Crossing over Brushy Creek. Meanwhile, officials stipulated that the new Dacus bridge be of iron at a cost of $2500, with area citizens paying one-fourth of the cost, the county the balance. Similar structures were ordered over Opossum Creek and Yankee Branch crossings on the Granger-Belton road in 1887, and one for Mustang Creek in 1888. Pressures on the county officials mounted for bridges over the San Gabriel and they appointed a committee to investigate the feasibility of two at Georgetown and one at Circleville. Reporting November 16, 1889, the committee concluded that in view of the poor financial condition of the county, the Court was advised not to heed the demand for bridges at that time. A small bridge over Donahoe Creek needed replacing on the Granger-Bartlett road in 1890.[27]

Bridges became a political issue in the summer of 1890 when J. M. Black, candidate for County Commissioner, ran on the platform that "no two places . . . need bridging worse than the two Gabriels at Georgetown and Brushy at Round Rock." That same year, twelve iron bridges were

Iron bridges with plank floors, from 1890s, standing in 1973 near Keliehor and the Easley-Sloan community.

purchased from the Berlin Bridge Company for creek crossings. Citizens continued to insist on structures across the larger streams and by October 28, 1891 plans were underway for "stone piers for the two bridges across the South and North Gabriel at Georgetown and also for the bridge across

Brushy Creek at Round Rock." The two iron bridges from Chicago Iron Bridge Company were completed across the two San Gabriels at Georgetown and were accepted August 18, 1892.[28]

AGRICULTURE, BUSINESS, INDUSTRY

Cotton production came into full flower between 1870 and 1900 in Williamson County with the advent of machines that substituted for hand cultivators when they could be shipped in by rail. Pioneer John S. Knight whose log house was south of Georgetown on Brushy Road is credited with planting some of the first cotton in the county, by 1870. The log house was photographed around the turn of the century and is one of the few extant pictures of those very early houses. As more and more acreage was planted in cotton, gins sprang up, some communities having as many as four or five. The McFadin and McGuire gins at Circleville were reported in 1877 to be averaging about ten bales a day and "yet

Taylor's Main Street looking north, 1887, with wagons of cotton.

they [kept] far behind the demand."[29] During the 1899-1900 ginning season, 89,237 bales were processed in the county, more than any other county in the state. "Three of the largest ginneries in the United States, ginning annually over 7000 round bales each, are located at Waco, Farmersville, and Granger," it was reported. In 1900-1901, Ellis County surpassed Williamson in total number of bales, but Williamson had increased to 104,761 bales. The big cottonseed oil industry was an inevitable spin-off, with large plants established in Granger, Taylor and Georgetown.[30]

Wheat and other cash crops were grown in smaller quantities. The cattle industry reached its zenith during the last quarter of the century. Some truck gardening was practiced well before 1900. In 1884 James Knight operated a garden at Knight's Mill (later known as Crockett Gardens) west-north-west of Georgetown, and shipped strawberries to Austin. Captain Emzy Taylor had a garden and nursery at Georgetown, later converted into the City of Georgetown pecan orchard, shipping vegetables as far as Colorado. Two Swiss brothers and their families, Eugene Noel Redard and Louis Redard developed a truck garden at Camp Springs, Circleville, about 1903, and also at the Crockett Gardens site near Georgetown. Pecans were harvested in the county by Indians. By the late 1880s, the crop was recognized as valuable although the supply came exclusively from native trees at that time. A less successful venture of the 1880s was the planting of Johnson grass, felt at that time to be a fine new fodder crop—hardy, resistant to drouth, quick to mature and good for hay. It was all of that but more—a pernicious and unbelievably persistent pest. Although farm journals soon warned of its stubborn nature and advised farmers not to plant it, merchants continued to import the seed from Turkey and sold it for a number of years. In 1895, it was made a penal offense in Texas to sow Johnson grass (Russian thistle) on land belonging to another person.[31]

Central Texas farmers met at Salado in 1873 to organize the Patrons of Husbandry, better known as the Granger or the Grange, whose goals were to gain economic benefits through cooperative effort, improve rural home life and encourage social communication. The organization was very active in Williamson County and became influential in state and local politics. By the 1880s several cooperative Grange stores had opened to handle farmers' produce—one at Macedonia which soon moved to the new railroad town to the east named Granger, perhaps a namesake of this organization. The Farmers' Alliance, a similar group, was extremely active in Williamson County in the eighties and nineties.[32]

Freighting continued after the Civil War until railroads served the county. Among those engaged in this business during or after the war were R. D. Love and William Fleager of Florence, Harvey T. Stearns of Circleville, and John Israelson, John Palm and Andrew J. Nelson of the Palm Valley community.[33]

Mills remained a local industry throughout the century. An especially large and successful one was southwest of present Weir at Towns Mill, called Excelsior Mill. The Towns family were mechanical experts and operated a number of mills and gins in the county. Doddville, also known as Buttercup, had a mill run by B. F. Johnson, about a mile south of Cedar

Gann's Mill, successor to much earlier Berry's Mill.

Park. T. M. Barton ran one in the 1870s on the San Gabriel near Liberty Hill. Other mills noted previously continued to operate. Syrup mills, sometimes called syrup presses, advanced from the home variety to commercial presses of which there were several in the county. John S. McGuire ran an early one at Circleville. Paul and John Machu ran syrup mills in the Machu community near Granger. John Maresh put one up at Waterloo around the turn of the century and J. T. Simcik operated one at Beyersville.[34]

Quarrying and brick manufacturing were local industries soon after the

Pioneer quarry and limestone plant, Round Rock.

Civil War. The Walsh family built a lime plant at Austin in 1870 and burned the first commercial lime in the state. A few years later, the business was transferred to Round Rock. Other quarries, burned dolomite processing plants, and lime factories were developed along the western rim of the county from Round Rock and White Stone north through Leander, Liberty Hill and Florence. At Georgetown an early brick kiln on the south bank of the San Gabriel produced handmade bricks which were used in chimneys and buildings over town. The fine trash such as bits of grass and straw in these bricks could be seen in 1973 in the chimney at 211 East Fifth Street, Georgetown. A few flurries of gold and silver mining, where small traces of the ores occurred in the western section, periodi-

Typical blacksmith shop, built in 1880, Georgetown.

Ice wagon, Georgetown.

cally developed, but these amounted only to a speculator's dream. Small scale shop or home industry continued in the local blacksmith shops, tin and pewter shops and cabinet shops. Georgetown was proud of its ice factory which W. R. Chumley ran in the 1880s and sold to George Irvine in 1886. Soon after the factory opened, a young man from a farm came to town, saw the marvelous new factory and went home with the news. "Pa, they make ice there," he reported. But Pa thought ice was hauled into town once a week and did not believe his son. The boy insisted. "They *make* it, right in Georgetown," he emphasized. Still Pa was not a believer, saying "Well, they just do it once a week, anyhow." The son persisted, "No sir, they do it *every* day. They *make* it, great big blocks of it. I saw it and I touched it. And they make it *every day.*" Pa simply shook his head incredulously. "They'll finally do away with God Almighty," he intoned.[35]

The successful and long-lived broom factory at Round Rock has been previously mentioned. In 1887, Georgetown had two flouring mills, two planing and wood working mills, a mattress factory, a cotton gin, a candy factory, a bakery, a cigar factory, five blacksmith shops, three shoe shops, and S. T. Atkin's Flue Manufacturing Company. Atkin patented numerous inventions of which his most successful was a combination flue-damper-water cup, which he manufactured and sold. In 1890 Georgetown had J. P. Ischy's bottling works which offered lemon, orange and strawberry flavored drinks; a knitting mill run by Gideon Purl, with twenty machines and fifteen ladies producing about eight hundred pairs of socks a day; and Georgetown Chair Manufacturing Company. Timber for the chairs was cut on the Yegua; caners were needed in the fall of 1890, and the company reported shipping seventy-four dozen chairs one week and receiving orders for one hundred dozen more the same week. Carl Burkhardt ran a confectionery south of the Court House in 1890. The Georgetown Oil Mill was founded in 1891 by J. E. Cooper, J. W. Snyder and R. F. Young; Marsh F. Smith became general manager in 1903 and later the principal owner.[36]

Taylor's compress was organized by a stock company, of which Major B. Garry was first manager in 1892. The town was circled on all four sides by the best cotton-producing land in the county, so cotton was one of its main economic mainstays. The I. & G.-N. railroad yards, round houses and repair shops built in Taylor in 1890 provided a tremendous boost to the local economy, operating there until 1929. Jim Athas, of Greek ancestry, came to settle in Taylor in February 1898 and built a small candy business into a longtime enterprise. He spent fifty-six years in his confectionery, was known by friends and associates as "Mr. Candy Jim." In 1917 Athas began making a sauerkraut candy flavored with coconut, for which he became quite well known. He retired in 1954. In 1903 three brothers, David Fontaine Forwood, Amor Forwood and Jason Forwood, started the Taylor Bedding Manufacturing Company, making at first the now-famous Morning Glory Mattress and expanding into other related items. This business grew rapidly and is still a major concern in Taylor at the present time.

Every community of any size had an annual fair, large ones being held on the Fair Grounds of San Gabriel Park at Georgetown in the 1870s and at Taylor Fairgrounds on the hill south of town, now the site of the Country Club, from about 1880. Although mineral springs were known to exist near Georgetown before the 1880s, they were not commercially developed until then. Judge J. M. Page built bath houses in Oak Grove Park on a forty-acre tract at the approximate site of the present Westside School in 1888. The area was "high and as level as glass, shaded by great live oak trees, ready . . . to receive those who seek health or pleasure." The place was on the banks of the South San Gabriel River near woods which were full of deer and other game. Page had the water analyzed by two experts, Dr. R. S. Hyer of Southwestern University and Dr. Edgar Everhart of the University of Texas, who reported that the water was almost identical to that at the Carlsbad wells of Bohemia. Henry Peaslee had his well near Georgetown analyzed in 1887, and the Georgetown Mineral Water Company operated another well. Another mineral well was on the Jonas Shell nursery site and Colonel J. A. Fain's place had a white sulphur water well.[37]

A short-lived but colorful business was Dr. A. V. Doak's mule-drawn street car system in Taylor, which was planned and built in 1890, began operating in January 1891. Dr. Doak, of a pioneer medical family in the community, built the trolley line encircling most of the town, beginning at First and Porter streets, west on First to Main, north on Main Street to Seventh and west on Seventh to Sloan Street. There a Pavilion was built to serve as a kind of entertainment center on the line. From the Pavilion, the line for the return trip downtown went south on Sloan Street to Third, east on Third to Doak Street, south from there to Second, and then east to the Main Street intersection of the line. Dr. Doak purchased fifty Spanish mules to pull the trolleys of which forty were in use at one time. He built two mule barns near his home, 600 West Seventh, to house them. Each trolley car was pulled by two mules walking on boards placed parallel to the inside track. The Pavilion, said to accommodate a thousand

Dr. A. V. Doak's street car pavilion, Taylor, 1891-1900.

persons, was advertised as suitable for dances, plays, band concerts, religious meetings, baseball games, bicycle races or skating. The line was abandoned in 1900.[38]

"First Monday," a longtime, festive trading day in Georgetown, was established soon after the Civil War. On the first Monday of each month farmers brought their horses and cattle to the Courthouse Square to trade. Many came the night or day before with eight or ten mules or horses behind the wagon. Livery stables did big business. Some visitors took this as an occasion for a spree—the railway express office nearly always had on hand fifteen to twenty dozen gallon jugs of spirits addressed to "John Doe" or some other mythical person, to be picked up by First Monday celebrants. The trading included legitimate transactions and others of questionable intent such as disposing of horses with heaves, a respiratory ailment which did not appear until the horse did some work, or spavins, a weakness of the ankles, also difficult to detect on sight. Many cutting scrapes resulted from some of the less savory trades. Horses were hitched in a continuous ring around the Courthouse fence and hitching posts. The affair expanded to other kinds of trading. At times long tables were

"First Monday," horse trading day, west of Public Square, Georgetown.

Street water sprinkler at Georgetown, June 1, 1894, crossing Brushy Street at Eighth.

set up around the entire block from which barbecue was served. So many wagons and buggies arrived in town that in dry weather the gravel streets were ground ankle deep in dust, or in wet weather were cut into equally deep ruts. When Georgetown purchased a sprinkling wagon in 1894, the dust was kept under better control. Until well into the 1880s, the "terminus" of University Avenue was at College Street where the original college campus and buildings stood. To the east, in what is now Southwestern University and a residential area, were the Coffee and Snyder pastures.[39]

EDUCATION: PUBLIC AND PRIVATE SCHOOLS

Williamson County was organizing its public school system when the Civil War intervened and in 1873 it had only thirty-one public schools, with thirty-six teachers and 1,408 pupils. A few private schools left from pre-public school days were rapidly disappearing. Ten years later, the county had ninety-seven districts with at least that many separate schools and 2,990 students. From about this point, the rate of growth slowed. Total schools in 1904 were 105.[40]

Some effort was made to check teacher qualifications when J. W. Talbot was appointed to supervise county schools. In 1887 the superintendent of public instruction office was created and Professor E. M. Coleman was named to the post at $1,000 a year. D. H. LeSueur was appointed to fill his unexpired term. Elected superintendents from 1888 to 1900 were J. O. Patterson, John D. Hudson, A. Logan and B. H. Fisk.[41]

Since log cabin schooldays, frame buildings were generally in use, with blackboards and desks, but not always enough for everyone. Pot bellied stoves gave heat which reached only as far as the four benches placed in a rectangle around them. Children rotated sitting on "warming benches." Teacher requirements were far from rigid but many of those professors must have been remarkably capable under the circumstances. Among early teachers well remembered were the mother of a future governor of Texas, Nannie Robertson (Mrs. Dan'l. Moody); a relative of Miss Robertson's, Lillian Wester, who later was a distinguished college professor; a young attorney-to-be, Richard Critz, who became a Texas Supreme Court judge; Jesse Eugene Cooper, founder and longtime publisher of the *Williamson County Sun*; Lizzie Easley whose lifetime of teaching was long and successful.

Almost immediately after the Civil War, several towns attempted to provide better quality advanced education. The seriousness of one such project, the Georgetown Male & Female Academy (provided for in 1850 and in business at least by 1852), was recognized in 1866 by the State Legislature.[42] Among the earliest teachers, all in private schools, were Reverend R. M. Overstreet, W. H. Henderson, Reverend John McMurray, Miss Lucy Harper and Woodson Patrick, all of Georgetown; Mrs. Kitty Hutchins, John McMurray (late of Georgetown), A. P. Aten, Mrs. Wiggins and Professor Green, all operating private schools in Taylorsville, along with Professor and Mrs. J. V. Brown, who officiated at the Lone Star Institute there about 1884 and 1885. During the 1880s and 1890s, nearly all private schools were replaced by the county's growing public school system.

GEORGETOWN COLLEGE, SOUTHWESTERN UNIVERSITY

Two simultaneous movements with goals of improved education, both starting in 1869 and completely unrelated at first, resulted in the establishment of Southwestern University at Georgetown.

An academy was provided for in Georgetown in February 1850, located on the south bank of south San Gabriel River two blocks west of present Austin Avenue. The small school was sold to the Georgetown Male and Female Academy trustees in 1867.[43] Educator Dr. C. C. Cody said it was "nothing conspicuous." Late in 1869 a group of ambitious men in the community began to talk seriously about establishing a college. A sizeable group of "stockholders" met in the Courthouse on Saturday, January 29, 1870, elected officers, and at subsequent weekly meetings, selected a site for the college, planned a subscription campaign to raise about $10,000, and by May let a contract to Hiram Jones for a building "away out in the prairie.* There was not a house near the building except one and that was Judge Thomas P. Hughes' residence."[45] The cornerstone of Georgetown College was laid July 16, 1870, in a ceremony memorialized by a

---

* The site, which housed first Georgetown College, then "Texas University" a (name applied briefly to Southwestern University), was donated by John J. Dimmitt and G. W. Glasscock, Jr., the latter acting in the name of his late father, G. W. Glasscock, Sr., in deeds executed March 5, 1870, to the stockholders of Georgetown College.[44] The campus, in addition to Georgetown College building, later housed a chapel originally meant to be the Methodist Church but never completed, a small building used as a fitting school, several cottages, and a man's dormitory. After Southwestern's campus was moved four or five blocks to the east, the old Georgetown College-Southwestern main building became the Fitting or "Prep" School until it was sold to the City of Georgetown. The same site then housed Georgetown High School from 1923 to the present, although a new high school was on the architect's drawing board early in 1973 and projected soon after.

Georgetown College built 1870-1871, later "Texas University," then South-western University. The third story was added in 1881.

number of speakers. Afterwards, the many participants and spectators formed a procession, marching from the site in the five hundred block north of University Avenue to the fairgrounds (present San Gabriel Park). "They crossed the Gabriel on a temporary bridge made by placing planks on stationary wagons" standing in the river bed. The men who were active in organizing the college included J. J. Stubblefield, J. C. S. Morrow, M. E. Steele, Thomas P. Hughes, W. K. Makemson, W. P. Beall, W. I. Anderson, Elias W. Talbot, J. W. Montgomery, Emzy Taylor, J. J. Dimmitt and J. W. Posey.[46]

Even before the Georgetown College was completed, collections on subscriptions lagged, and the building was leased to the State Board to be used as a public school for a short time. Among the earlier teachers were a Mr. Hemphill, assisted by Miss Hemphill (later Mrs. Joe Talbot) and a Mr. Robbins.[47]

Another movement which began in 1869 was launched by the five Texas Methodist conferences, whose representatives felt the need to relocate the state's Methodist college, Soule University of Chappell Hill.* That place had been decimated by yellow fever in 1867, the facilities there were in

---

* So named for the Chappell family of that area. Also spelled Chappel and Chapel.

deplorable condition and hardly worth repairing, and, in 1869, rumors of another epidemic created panic on the campus. Dr. Francis Asbury Mood, who had come from South Carolina to become president of the ailing Soule University, agreed that relocation of the school would be in its best interests. After numerous meetings, conferences and resolutions among Methodist officials, at a meeting of trustees in Waco, Reverend William Monk, minister in charge of the Georgetown circuit and a resident of Round Rock, was asked to look for a location in his district. On his way home from Waco, he stopped in Georgetown to talk with Colonel W. C. Dalrymple "and suggested to him that Georgetown bid for the Methodist College and offer the Georgetown College building, then about finished, with its other property as a subsidy."[48] Georgetown College officials were informed of this proposition in August 1871, and on October 23 approved offering the College building and land "if the contemplated State University be permanently located in Georgetown and it be made a first class institution of learning."[49] Reverend Monk, Captain J. C. S. Morrow and Dudley H. Snyder presented Georgetown's proposal before a Methodist convention that fall and after many more meetings and conferences, the decision was reached. Agreeing "quite unanimously that Georgetown, Williamson County, possessed by far the greatest advantages presented by any of the competing points," Georgetown was selected on August 21, 1873. "When the news . . . reached Georgetown the citizens 'expressed their great satisfaction by firing a hundred anvils.' " Other places considered as a site were Austin, Belton, Salado, Waco, Kosse, Corsicana, Owensville, Fort Worth, Fairfield and Calvert.[50]

The facilities the University would occupy consisted of the Georgetown College two-story "plain, but capacious stone" structure, located north of University Avenue in the block between Ash and College streets. The sixty by seventy-five foot building contained six large classrooms and a chapel to seat about four hundred. The town itself had a population of about five hundred, a rather bad reputation, only fourteen persons who professed the Methodist faith, and no Methodist church. The nearest railroad was at Austin.[51]

As quickly as he could, Dr. Mood left Chappell Hill for Georgetown to prepare for the first session of the University on the new campus, which was to begin on Monday, October 6, 1873. This extremely well-educated and cultured gentleman had depleted his finances during the time he was president of Soule University, so arrangements were made for him and his family to live in the two lower south rooms of the College building. The inside walls had never been plastered, nor was there a well or cistern for water. The unfinished cracks in the stonework were favorite nesting places for birds.[52]

Within a short time, Mrs. Mood had packed their possessions and, boarding a train for Austin with their young children, they left south Texas to join Dr. Mood. Margaret, about two years old, was quite ill with a fever when they arrived in Austin on a hot September afternoon. Richey, the son, was about five then. A driver and team had been sent to bring them back to Georgetown. All went well until the driver stopped at Cocklebur, a saloon south of Round Rock and a short distance from the Williamson County line. When the driver did not come back after what Mrs. Mood considered adequate time for a rest stop, she put Richey up on the driver's seat, took the reins loose from the hitching post, and put them in Richey's hands, telling him to hold tightly to them but to let the horses walk and that they would find their way home to Georgetown. Meanwhile, in Georgetown the Moods were expected. In late afternoon, when all business houses were closing, arrangements had to be made for their reception. Thirteen-year-old Temple Houston, youngest son of Sam Houston, who was living then in Georgetown with his sister, Mrs. J. C. S. Morrow, had been delegated to watch out for the Moods. Since the only place in town remaining open after dark was the local saloon, Temple was told to wait there for the guests. Far into the night when Mrs. Mood and the children finally reached town, the only lights they saw were at the saloon, so there they went and there were greeted by Temple Houston.[53]

"Texas University" managed to open its doors on time that first Monday in October, with Dr. Mood serving as Regent, as well as professor of mental and moral philosophy, history, and English literature. There were two other men on the faculty, B. E. Chreitzberg who taught ancient languages and mathematics, and H. M. Reynolds, professor of modern languages. Thirty-three students matriculated, although during the first session six of them were dismissed "and four others were handed over to civil authorities and fined 'which had a very soothing effect upon the dangerous passions of themselves and others.' " An additional sixty-seven "child pupils [were] receiving impressively the instruction of teachers" in classes below college level.[54]

"Texas University" applied for its new charter under that name, which its Board of Curators had chosen, but the legislature was planning for a state school which they felt should bear that name. With the agreement that the Methodist school be titled Southwestern University,* a special act

* Often written South Western in the nineteenth century.

of the legislature approved the charter on February 6, 1875, and transferred the rights to Southwestern University which had been conveyed in the charters of Rutersville, Wesleyan and McKenzie colleges and Soule University. Rutersville, chartered January 25, 1840 under the Republic of Texas, provided Southwestern University with its birthdate and made it the oldest institution of higher learning in the State of Texas.[55]

Accepting male students only, Southwestern University allowed them to board in approved homes in town. Pressure for the school to provide facilities for women students, plus a rumor that another denomination was contemplating a school for ladies in Georgetown, led the University's Curators in June 1878 to request that a Normal and Young Ladies Department be opened in a separate building. The University rented the basement of the stone Presbyterian Church (still standing in 1973) at 701 Church Street for the fall semester, purchased a block of land* for $350, and by 1879 had built a two story frame building for the Young Ladies School. The same faculty served both schools, which were four blocks apart, "sufficiently near to be convenient for the faculty and sufficiently removed to prevent embarrassment in discipline." Separate catalogs were issued, as well.[57]

When additional classrooms were required for the growing student body, a third story was added to the original Georgetown College building in 1881. The remodeled limestone structure presented "a handsome appearance" with its "crested mansard roof surmounted by a dome" and bell tower. The third floor sheltered four new lecture rooms which gave the building ten rooms for classwork, a library, and meeting places for the "Societies." The previous year, officials and local Methodists began concentrated efforts to build a church in town. J. N. Preston, architect of Austin, presented plans and ground was broken in 1882 on the southwest corner of the campus (Ash and University) for the proposed church. When the first floor was up, funds were exhausted and construction ceased. For more than a decade, until a church was erected, the flat "half-dugout" like structure doubled as chapel for the University and as Methodist Church. Each member provided his own wooden bench. Window panes were covered with pastel paper for a stained glass effect. Another building was added on this original campus on the northwest corner, a two-story

---

* Located between Brushy (Austin Avenue) and Main, and University Avenue and Eleventh streets, later site of Annie Purl Elementary School. On December 22, 1877, the Greenwood Masonic College of Round Rock proposed that Southwestern University operate their Young Ladies Seminary, but no action was taken. The citizens of Salado proposed in 1880 that Salado College become a part of Southwestern University, but the offer was declined.[56]

structure used as the fitting school for students not yet meeting requirements to enter college. The Methodist conferences added five small cottages on the grounds.[58]

The extremely hard-working Dr. Mood assessed the first ten years of
Southwestern University, noting the financial support from within Williamson County and the lack of it from elsewhere. He wrote that he hoped
the fact might

> be burned into the memory of every Methodist in Texas, that although
> they have a University founded among them, possessing an unen-
> cumbered property of greater value than ever previously owned by the
> Church in this State—the contributions to this enterprise by the Church
> outside Williamson County, in which it is located, have not aggregated
> four thousand dollars.[59]

Among the men "who came to the University's rescue" financially were
Dudley H. Snyder, John W. Snyder, Thomas Snyder, Thomas P. Hughes,
James W. Hodges, J. L. Rucker, F. L. Price and J. C. S. Morrow.[60] In
1883 the Snyder brothers pledged $21,000 of a total of $35,000 to build
a Ladies' Annex to replace the Young Ladies School.[61]

The saloons of Georgetown were frowned upon by the faculty. After
fighting them bitterly, school officials accused these places of "enticing and
getting students drunk as revenge for faculty labor" in behalf of the local
option law. When some of the students were discovered carrying guns, it
was ruled that "all guns be checked," and when one student who felt
more comfortable with his guns on" was asked to empty it, the young
man walked to the window and fired until it was empty.[62] Regulations for
the young ladies in 1882 prohibited dramatic exhibitions involving costumes, attendance at dancing parties, balls or skating rinks. A new rule
forbade going home for the Christmas holidays. Miss F. received ten demerits for reckless driving after being warned previously and Miss G. received ten demerits for "conversing with a young man at the exhibition
of the graduating class."[63]

Dr. Mood had carried a heavy load, seeking funds, teaching an extremely demanding schedule, attending meetings, and organizing the
fledgling school in a new place. Not feeling well, he insisted that he attend a meeting in Waco. Very feeble and "leaning on his staff, [he] made
a speech on the subject of Christian education," after which he retired to
the adjoining rooms and fainted in the arms of friends. He died the following day, November 12, 1884.[64] Dr. Randolph Wood Tinsley, professor of biology and geology, was asked to serve as administrator until
a new regent (president) was named. During Regent John W. Heidt's

administration (1885-1889), a men's dormitory, Helping Hall (later Giddings Hall) was erected on the north part of the campus and was in use by June 1886.[65] Dr. C. C. Cody established a summer normal at Southwestern University in 1888 and the following year it was combined with the rather elaborate program of the Texas Chautauqua Assembly, held on the north bank of the South San Gabriel River just west of town.[66]

The long-awaited permanent Ladies Annex was opened on March 7, 1889, eight blocks east of the University Main Building, on what is the present Southwestern University campus. A building project closely related to the University was the construction from 1891 to 1893 of the First Methodist Church, diagonally across the street to the southwest of the old campus. Dr. R. S. Hyer designed the structure with a sanctuary in the shape of a Greek cross. He made a three-foot scaled model for stone cutters Waterston & Sons of Austin, who hewed the limestone blocks by hand.[67]

Under the Regency of Dr. John H. McLean (1891-1897), plans were made for a new Southwestern University Main Building, and the blueprints submitted by Layton and Raymond were accepted May 30, 1896, by the Board of Trustees. A fund raising period ensued. On April 31, 1898, the Board awarded the construction contract to Flume & Waterston of Austin, men who had helped build the State Capitol a decade earlier and who also constructed Georgetown's First Methodist Church. They were stone cutters from the British Isles who were imported especially for the Capitol job. The cornerstone for the new Main Building was laid September 8, 1898, on the new campus west of the John Snyder home and barn.[68] Dr. R. S. Hyer in May 1898 had been elected Regent of the University and in that position took a supervisory post in the construction.[68]

While the new Main Building was under construction, the old campus between College and Ash streets had grown into a little cluster of buildings, and residences had appeared on its perimeter. The three story native stone college building stood about where the Georgetown High School was built in 1923. To the northwest was the small "prep" Fitting School building which had been added to take care of pre-college classes, and on the southwest corner, the old chapel, never finished as originally planned. North of the college building was the men's dormitory and dining hall, called Helping Hall or Giddings Hall. Between the Main Building and the chapel was a fenced plot, shaded by trees, where Dr. F. A. Mood was buried. At the north entrance to the Main Building near the east side was a weeping willow tree and a hydrant where students slaked their thirst. The men's rest room was enclosed by a high wooden fence northeast of the "ad" building; the inside wall of this small shed was decorated with an alligator hide from an animal caught on Berry's Creek. The entire campus was fenced, with stiles as entryways at intervals on all sides except the north, where the dining hall stood. Regent Hyer and his family lived in a home west of the campus and a "couple of rows of small two-or-three-room cottages [were] on both sides of the three block campus." The Ladies Annex half a mile to the east, at a safe distance for the young ladies, was "the most pretentious" of all the University's structures until the new Main Building was completed.[69]

Restrictions on students were gradually eased until the classes were co-educational by 1895, although social contact between the sexes continued to be forbidden for many years. Rival literary societies, the Alamo and San Jacinto, were debating groups with some fraternal and social status. Some baseball and football were allowed around the turn of the century; boys pitched horseshoes or silver dollars, or played tennis. On Sundays, directors of the Ladies Annex, Dr. and Mrs. John R. Allen, saw that their young charges were dressed in their blue uniforms as they "marched double-file down the Avenue to Methodist church services. Neither male nor female student was allowed to speak to the other sex, but this did not prevent admiring and often goggle-eyed exchanges" nor the slipping of occasional notes into the hands of the opposite sex.[70]

In 1900 when the University moved into its new Main Building on the new campus, the classroom building on the old campus became an enlarged Fitting School. The University remained in the "prep" business until 1916 when that facility was sold to the City of Georgetown for $25,000. The smaller structures were soon removed, but the original Georgetown College-Southwestern University limestone school remained until Georgetown High School was erected in 1923. Meanwhile, at Southwestern's new campus, to the rear of the new Main Building, a men's dormitory was constructed by C. H. Page of Austin in 1906, ready for occupancy in September 1907, and named Mood Hall honoring the school's first president.[71]

Southwestern University experienced a remarkably steady growth in its physical plant, faculty, curriculum and enrollment from its opening year in Georgetown until its one hundredth anniversary in 1973, although difficult and even precarious times were occasionally felt. One which burst unexpectedly began with a letter from Hiram A. Boaz on March 7, 1910, to Regent Hyer asking that Southwestern be removed to Fort Worth. (His recommendation was later amended to Dallas.) This began a long and often bitter controversy, considerably fanned by Dr. Hyer's support of

Southwestern University's Main Building erected 1898-1900.

Boaz in the argument. Newspapers in Texas cities became involved. Church papers, Methodist officials, and others debated the matter publicly and privately and, after a thorough airing, the Southwestern University Board of Trustees restated their goals for the school as it was originally planned.[72] Dr. Hyer moved to Dallas where he was active in the establishment of Southern Methodist University. His successor at Southwestern University, Dr. Charles McTyeire Bishop, was the first administrator to be given the title, President of Southwestern University, rather than Regent. He served from 1911 to 1922.[73] Funds for a new science building were called for in 1917; a student Army Training Corps was inaugurated in 1918, and Dr. Paul Whitfield Horn became president in 1922, followed by James Samuel Barcus (1924-1928). Under Dr. Barcus, the principle of academic freedom became an integral part of the policy of the University. This school is considered a pioneer in this section of the nation in adopting that doctrine.

Two major calamities struck the campus within a decade. On Thursday morning, January 8, 1925, at four o'clock, nearly two hundred girls were sleeping in the woman's dormitory when fire was discovered. Miss Laura Kuykendall, Dean of Women, assembled them quietly on the ground floor and all left the four-story building safely. Personal articles were quickly gathered and many removed, although some were lost. The entire top floor was aflame and burning very fast as people helped remove from the ground floor articles of furniture, rugs, tapestries, pianos. The fire entirely destroyed the picturesque building which had been called the Ladies Annex when it opened in 1889, but had come generally to be called the Woman's Building. That same night, a citizens' mass meeting was held in Georgetown to promise University officials that the town would do all possible to assist Southwestern. The girls were housed at Mood Hall and lodging for the men was found in town.[74] From the ashes of this dormitory rose Laura Kuykendall Hall, a durable facility which was still in use in 1973.

The great depression during the presidencies of King Vivion, appointed 1928, and John William Bergin (1935), seemed to drain the University's resources disastrously. But through the faculty and staff's loyalty and willingness to give all possible financial relief and the husbanding of whatever meager resources were available in those difficult years, the University survived, and at the end of the depression seemed to be stronger than ever. Dr. J. N. R. Score became president in 1942 and launched a campaign for a building program which grew into full flower after his untimely death. Dr. William C. Finch was appointed to the presidency in 1950, and Dr. Durwood Fleming in 1961.

ROUND ROCK ACADEMY, ROUND ROCK COLLEGE

The Round Rock Academy was first projected in 1863, with a number of leading citizens including T. C. Oatts, G. W. Davis, L. M. Mays, T. J. Caldwell and D. H. Snyder supporting the effort. This culminated in the Masonic Lodge's establishing Greenwood Masonic Institute in 1867 and building a three-story school in Old Round Rock in a grove of live oak trees which suggested its name. It appears to have been called both Greenwood Masonic Institute and Round Rock Academy in those early years. S. G. Sanders was the first principal. After sponsoring the school for a decade, the Lodge voted in 1877 to donate the two lower floors of the building to Southwestern University of Georgetown for a female school in Round Rock, but the University did not accept the offer. Three years later, the Lodge offered to transfer it to the Cumberland Presbyterian Church. After due consideration, in January 1881 the church agreed to operate the school, from that time calling it Round Rock College.[75]

Round Rock College opened for its first semester in the fall of 1881,

Greenwood Masonic Institute, founded 1867, became Round Rock College in 1881.

with R. W. Pittman, a former vice president of Trinity College at Tehua-cana as the new president. T. W. Royston, president of the Board, H. B. Sheppard and H. A. Webb signed the charter filed April 11, 1881. I. N. Stephens was headmaster of the Academy. Special courses were offered in music "with instruments"; tuition ranged from two to five dollars a month from primary through collegiate grades, plus three dollars a week for board. The first term of the college opened September 5 at which time "a commodious boarding house" was to be ready for young ladies and gentlemen who wished "to board with the President." The preparatory school was patterned after those of the Old South, "disciplined almost to a military degree," with thorough training in the basic subjects.[76]

Enrollment increased rapidly and all went well until a cool spring morning, April 9, 1883. When a fire was lit on one of the stoves, the school caught fire and burned to the ground. About three hundred young children and advanced students were without a school. The term was finished in various buildings available in Round Rock while citizens of the community and the Cumberland Church united to rebuild, this time on a high knoll between Old and New Round Rock, between Lake and

Brushy creeks. The new two story frame building had six large rooms downstairs, three rooms and an auditorium on second floor. Although the church maintained its ties, Round Rock citizens took over the management of the school. In 1887 the Cumberland Church transferred its interest in the school to the Southern Presbyterian Church and on May 28, 1888, the State of Texas and local school officials took complete responsibility, operating it from that time as a public school. Presidents succeeding Colonel Pittman at Round Rock College were T. A. Brown, C. H. Dobbs and A. S. J. Steele.[77]

CORN HILL ACADEMY, CORN HILL COLLEGE

A graduate of the University of Edinburg, Scotland, named George G. Grant started a school at Corn Hill late in 1877 or early 1878 and by July 1878, Judge John E. King donated land where a frame school and church could be built. The first term of Professor Grant's school closed late in July, culminating with examinations and exhibitions on August 1 and 2, 1878. Such a large audience arrived on the first night that "Mr. King's new gin house was pressed into use for the occasion and was crowded to overflowing."[78]

"Corn Hill Academy, Male and Female," began its second term in September 1878, offering German, French, Spanish and music in addition to regular courses. Tuition ranged from two dollars for primary to four dollars for collegiate levels and boarding with private families cost eight to ten dollars a month. The location was advertised as healthy, accessible, quiet and pleasant, with "no grog shop within 15 or 20 miles." The next year, the academy was under the management of Professor W. M. Lee of Louisiana, who noted that the school had preaching twice a month, Sabbath school every Sunday and "prayer meeting every Sunday night, which affords the young people an opportunity to spend the small hours of each Sabbath night in a little innocent flirtation.' "[79]

The frame building became inadequate, so in 1886 a two story building with mansard roof was erected on a four acre tract just west of present Interstate Highway 35. The new Corn Hill College, as it was by this time called, had four large classrooms and a large auditorium. The flat roof was topped with a large bell tower and bell which was rung to announce all important events in the town. The impressive tower posed some problems, however, for it was said to be too heavy, causing the roof to leak, and no one ever was able to repair it satisfactorily. Church services of

Corn Hill College, built 1886, was first called Corn Hill Academy, established 1877.

various denominations in Corn Hill were held in the auditorium, as well as school programs, plays, entertainments, debating society meetings, band concerts and other affairs. After it had been in use for many years, the college building burned and was replaced by a public school.[80]

LIBERTY NORMAL AND BUSINESS COLLEGE (L. N. & B. C.)

Soon after the Austin and Northwestern Railroad was built through Liberty Hill in 1882, the two-room school held in the local church was outgrown. The railroad brought a burst of population growth. By private subscriptions and private loans enough money was raised to erect a two-story structure. At the same time, several petitions were circulated and filed with the State of Texas "praying for the establishment of a State Normal School at Liberty Hill." One petition stated that the population of the town was 450, that no intoxicating liquors had been sold there the past twenty years, that school grounds were ample and the new building had "five good school rooms, four of which are well seated with good patent desks; a good office with a small library; a good College Hall, forty by seventy feet, well seated and having good rostrum; also, a good under-ground cistern." The school grounds were "under fence, all complete, and clear of debt."[81]

The State Legislature approved the school, transferring credentials from Oak Grove college of the 1860s which had then moved for a time to Bluff Springs in Hays County. The charter to Liberty Hill was granted in 1884. The first Board of Directors were John Hudson, J. W. Potts, John Munro, J. D. Russell and F. M. Barton. Incorporators of the new school were Reverend R. F. Cates, J. G. Ward, T. J. Miles, Mrs. A. Hall, H. H. Thorpe, J. D. Russell, Landy J. Poole, S. A. Hamilton, W. E. Baker, Stafford Cole, F. M. Barton, Miss Francis Cates, J. Cole, L. G. Ford, T. P. Poole, H. D. Boswell, C. J. Simmons, H. T. Day, Mrs. R. F. Cates, C. C. Leatherwood, James White, N. F. Hickman, A. Simmons, Reverend W. O. Spencer and R. A. Magruder.[82]

Liberty Normal and Business College had its grand opening in January

Liberty Normal and Business College (L. N.& B. C.), Liberty Hill, 1885.

1885 with E. M. Coleman, president, and P. T. Coleman, secretary. The Colemans were generally spoken of as the superintendent and principal. Claiming to be the largest and most progressive Normal in the state, with beginning and advanced courses "in all common branches," the school offered seven courses, including commercial work and telegraphy. "Study is made a pleasure and not a burden." Many families moved to Liberty Hill to enroll their children in the school. In its second session the college, reported to be on a boom, arranged to convert the auditorium into classroom space. Enrollment in 1886 was up thirty percent over the previous year. In its first graduating class, the 1886-87 session, five students from outside the county were awarded degrees along with J. A. Hudson of Georgetown and W. H. White of Liberty Hill who received the Master of Accounts in commercial courses.[83]

Early in 1888 the Liberty Hill news correspondent to the *Williamson County Sun* reported some difficulty. "Our school falls to pieces next Thursday, the 19 inst., and both teachers and pupils will scatter to parts unknown. There will be no more big gatherings round about the college until the public crib is replenished and fine bloods are ordered. Our business men are no longer embarrassed, but simply busted." This was possibly an exaggeration, however, for the school continued to operate. Early that month, County Superintendent D. H. LeSueur, who rode his horse all over the county to visit each public school and wrote reports for the county newspaper, told of riding to Liberty Normal and Business College to see the three teachers there. Commenting on the condition of the road, he said, "The Georgetown and Liberty Hill road, I think, beyond controversy, might properly be called a 'caution.' "[84] By 1892 L. N. & B. C. had four teachers, L. Mawrey, J. H. Mawrey, Miss Moss Richardson and Miss Birdie Haygood, and a total of 166 students. One year, the catalog urged parents to see that their children attend morning chapel services. Faculty members in 1896-97 were Thomas P. Price, president, who taught language, history and professional work; J. N. Matthews, mathematics, science and common branches; Miss Charlie Taylor, intermediate; Miss Lelah Barton, primary; Thomas P. Price, commercial department; Mrs. T. P. Price, elocution. Music was also offered.[85]

The L. N. & B. C. building burned in 1903, but was replaced by a red brick structure built on lines similar to the original school. The new building had arched windows, a round steeple tower on top (replacing a rectangular shaped tower) and doors in the center wing. Four young ladies received their diplomas from the college in 1909, but by 1910, hard times had fallen on the institution and it was announced that it would be moved to Driftwood after the May 7, 1910 commencement. Mrs. Emma Barrington and Mrs. Fay Bryson Richardson were in the last graduating class. E. A. Pace, the last president, announced that he would run for the office of state representative. As was customary, the building and facilities were converted into a public school.[86]

FLORENCE COLLEGE

The Florence school in the 1890s was a two story frame building on the present campus of the public school just north of the present main building. Originally there were two rooms upstairs, two down, to which was added a one story wing. When W. J. Holder arrived there about 1895 or 1896, he thought it a good place to establish a college. A cupola

Florence College about 1895.

was built on top of the school and the college opened for business.[87]

The Florence Vidette carried the following advertisement: "Co-Educational, Course of instruction equal to that of any first class college. Rates of board and tuition the lowest. For other particulars and catalogue address W. J. Holder, President, Florence, Texas."[88]

For a few years Florence College was the center of much activity, but the dreams of Professor Holder were not to be realized. The College operated about eight years, after which it closed and the building was taken over as a public school.[89]

TRINITY LUTHERAN COLLEGE, ROUND ROCK

Augustana Lutheran Synod representatives in 1904 were sent over Texas to find a suitable location for a new Lutheran college. At Round Rock they were offered attractive concessions, which included a campus at the east end of town in a grove of large live oak trees, an area equivalent to fourteen city lots, a well on the property, and special freight rates on building materials shipped over the International & Great Northern Railroad. Round Rock's proposal was accepted.[90]

The cornerstone for the new Spanish-style three story main building

Trinity Lutheran College, Round Rock, 1905-1929.

was laid July 13, 1905. The structure was of native limestone, with two main front entrances through arched doorways, above which were twin bell towers. The building was finished in time for the first session which opened October 2, 1906. Forty-eight undergraduate students registered to study under the four faculty members. Dr. J. A. Stamline served as president from 1906 until 1909. Eleven additional students studied music.

By the end of the first year, enrollment totalled ninety-six. Curriculum was strengthened and broadened, and by 1920 the college had achieved state accreditation. Presidents of Trinity Lutheran during those years were Alfred Anderson, 1909 to 1914, and Theodore Seashore, 1914 to 1921.[91]

The 1920s were difficult years over the nation and most particularly in areas such as Williamson County, primarily dependent upon cotton for its economic welfare. Trinity Lutheran was hard hit, as were all colleges. Dr. Stamline and Oscar Nelson served as interim presidents between 1921 and 1923, followed by Harry A. Alden from 1923 to 1929. In 1929, the Synod found it necessary to merge Trinity Lutheran with Evangelical Lutheran College of Seguin (previously of Brenham). The move was made to Seguin and the college became Texas Lutheran.[92]

Campus buildings vacated by Trinity College were utilized by the Lutheran Welfare Society as homes for children and the aged, were later expanded into retirement and nursing homes.[93]

THE MEDICAL AND LEGAL PROFESSIONS

The same diseases plagued late nineteenth century doctors and patients as beset the earliest settlers. General immunization was unheard of even if serums were available. The fevers—particularly typhoid and malaria—were sometimes devastating. Smallpox broke out periodically. In 1882 the Georgetown City Council met to arrange a "secluded" place for patients with the disease, should any appear in town. The building, locally referred to as the "pest house," was northwest of town, west of the town's first swimming pool and about where the Shell addition was located in 1973.[94] The town of San Gabriel, just east of the eastern county line, had a severe outbreak in 1891, and Taylor and surrounding area reported a number of cases in 1895. Accident rates were high and often serious in gins, on railroads, and in dealing with horses. Although injuries involving horses could be extremely painful and even fatal, some had comic overtones. Somewhat typical was an affair in 1883 when Thomas Thoma was thrown from his delivery wagon after a wheel flew off. As he fell to the ground, he landed against his horse, which promptly kicked him in the knees. The report of the accident ended, "No harm done."[95]

The supply of doctors in the county during the nineteenth century was remarkably plentiful. There were seven physicians, previously mentioned, listed in the 1850 census, compared with two lawyers, six merchants, three stone masons, five ministers, four surveyors, five wheelwrights, eleven blacksmiths and nine carpenters. The roster of medical men grew as the county grew, some small villages boasting two to five doctors. Dr. G. S. C. Harper of Georgetown was the only physician from the county to attend the first meeting of the State Medical Association January 17-19, 1853, in Austin. Of the thirty-five doctors from over the state present at the meeting, Harper was one of the thirty admitted to the Association on November 28, 1853.[96]

The county medical profession came under county regulation in July 1873 when the Court appointed a Board of Medical Examiners. The Board was composed of Dr. W. H. Westfall, Dr. J. E. Walker, Dr. A. H. Graham and Dr. William P. Fleming.[97]

No records have been found to indicate when the Williamson County Medical Association was organized, but on January 3, 1874, Dr. P. H. Adams of Florence read a paper at the meeting of that group. The Central Texas Medical Association was mentioned in records of the State Association in 1887. Two years later, Dr. A. V. Doak of Taylor was elected second vice president of the Texas Medical Association. Dr. J. C. Anderson of Williamson County was named in 1903 to the new House of Delegates in a reorganization of the state society.[98]

Young Dr. Sam Houston, Jr., practiced medicine in Georgetown in 1874, married Miss Lucy Anderson of that town the next year.[99]

A doctor in southwest Williamson County during the late seventies and eighties was believed to be part Cherokee Indian. Although considered somewhere different in his community, he was affectionately and highly regarded. He was Dr. Benjamin Tomas Crumley (Indian name—Tecumseh) who was born June 22, 1822, and grew up in Charleston, South Carolina. Since the family was well-to-do and young Benjamin wanted to become a doctor, his father sent him first to Paris, France, and then to college to study. Against his father's wishes he also lived for a time with the Indians in order to learn their medical uses of herbs. During the Civil War he was in the Confederate service as second lieutenant, Company C, Second Regiment Cavalry, Texas State Troops (1863-64) as first assistant surgeon.[100]

"Doc" Crumley, as he was often called, was in Williamson County at least by 1879 when the following item appeared in the county newspaper:

[Dr. Crumley], who was in Georgetown some three or four weeks ago, and was considered, to some extent, an oddity because he wore his hair very long, and Miss Lou Rife of this county were married a few days ago at the residence of the bride's parents in the neighborhood of Doddville. Milt Tucker, who is always on hand when there is anything good to eat, happened in just in time for the dinner. He said the Doctor had his hair platted up and roses stuck about it. We wish the happy couple a long and prosperous union.[101]

The couple made their home at a tiny village called Buttercup on the creek of the same name, a short distance south of present Cedar Park. On October 3, 1881, B. T. Crumley was appointed postmaster at Butter-cup. He succeeded Lillie L. Dodd, who was postmistress on January 20, 1880, when the office first opened. Dr. Crumley had an extensive practice, was "often called for consultation by Austin doctors."[102] He wore his hair in two long braids and prepared many of his own medicines from herbs and roots which he collected in the countryside. Between 1884 and 1890, he and his family moved to a place in the north end of Lampasas County near Evant. He reared a large family and continued his practice until his death March 19, 1901.[103]

The first woman to practice medicine in Williamson County was Dr. Grace Danforth who was born in Granger. After receiving her degree in medicine, she began practicing in Dallas but found the city unreceptive to lady doctors. She contemplated making a change, but died unexpectedly while at Circleville on February 22, 1895.[104]

Many early doctors studied medicine with another doctor, and received most of their medical education as practicing druggists. Similarly, many early attorneys studied law by "reading" in the office of an established lawyer. The county seat was especially attractive to attorneys. In the 1870s, Georgetown had W. K. Makemson, A. S. Fisher, John T. Coffee, R. H. Price, J. W. Posey, W. C. Dalrymple, T. P. Hughes, W. M. Key, and Duncan Smith with active law offices. Sam Houston's second youngest son, W. R. Houston, read law under T. P. Hughes about this time; by May 1881 he had moved to Belton to set up a practice. His younger brother, Temple, who attended grade school in Georgetown, later became an attorney. By the early 1880s, Georgetown had twelve doctors, twenty-four lawyers.[105]

John Charles Townes, an attorney, practiced law in Georgetown from 1885 to 1888 as a partner of A. S. Fisher. Governor L. S. Ross appointed Townes as judge of the Williamson-Travis County Court. At Townes' request, he soon appointed a successor so that Townes could return to law practice, this time in partnership with S. R. Fisher. The attorney made his home in Austin, but continued his association in Georgetown until 1896 when he joined the law faculty at the University of Texas. Judge Townes was made Dean of the School of Law there in 1902. A son,

John Charles Townes, Jr., who was born in Georgetown, became a prominent attorney in Houston.[106]

Another well-known attorney, William R. Reagan, brother of the distinguished John H. Reagan, moved to Georgetown in 1879 "in order to secure for his children the educational advantages" there.[107]

W. K. Makemson of Georgetown, longtime attorney and county historian, was the nominee of the Republican Party for Governor of Texas in 1894. He lost the race but polled eleven percent of the votes.[108]

COMMUNICATIONS

Weekly newspapers blossomed in many Williamson County towns and villages during the last third of the nineteenth century. More muscle than equipment was required to print four or eight page, tabloid sized papers. A small press turned by a strong man, a printer to use handset type, some printers ink and newsprint and an editor-publisher were the essential ingredients for publishing a newspaper. Most weeklies continued to run local news on inside pages with small or no headlines. Editorials were very long, and page one carried advertisements along with world, national or state news—but nothing local. Relatively few files of earlier papers have been preserved. From available information, the following is a chronological list of newspapers as they appeared in their respective towns.* All are weekly newspapers[109] unless otherwise noted:

GEORGETOWN

Georgetown Independent, September 6, 1856 to March or April 1857. Andrew Marschalk, Jr., publisher; Andrew Marschalk, Sr., editor. Agents for paper located at Round Rock, Circleville, Brooksville.

Georgetown Watchman, January 5, 1867 at least to 1870s, a clean, newsy paper. William K. Foster, W. K. Makemson, publishers, joined briefly by R. Sansom. Some variation in title. "Corn, wheat, flour, bacon, lard, etc." accepted as payment for subscriptions.

Georgetown Sentinel, October 17, 1872, Nat Q. (dubbed Nat "Curious") Henderson, publisher, "a quaint, roving journalist of the republican party." John Shryock also associated with the business.

Williamson County Record. October 1872, William K. Foster, publisher, at least to 1879. On December 18, 1884, it was announced that Nat Q. Henderson had ceased publishing the *Record,* was working in Austin. He resumed its publication March 19, 1885, in Georgetown calling it the *Georgetown Record* and on February 14, 1886, had moved it to Austin. For a short while prior to the No-

---

* For the sake of continuity, newspapers published in the twentieth century are also listed in this section.

vember 1878 elections, a Greenback newspaper was issued by the *Georgetown Record* called the *Independent Era*. Publication was suspended after elections.

Williamson County Sun, oldest continuously published newspaper in county, founded May 19, 1877, by Jesse Eugene Cooper and Gus Ivey. Ivey was a newspaperman from Ohio, was listed as editor "with the assistance of Mr. J. E. Cooper as local editor." Young Cooper had taught one term of school at Matsler community. He remained in Georgetown throughout his life and even after formal participation in ownership and managment of the *Sun* maintained a close interest in it until his death in 1944. Ivey's association with the paper was brief. In September 1878, the *Sun* rented the third floor of the new Courthouse for $100 a year. Early key staff members with Cooper were W. H. Neill, editor 1877; R. Theodore Cooper, 1879; J. Charles Cameron, Sr., Cooper Sansom, R. T. Cooper and M. D. Sansom, on staff with J. E. Cooper, 1881. In December 1881, *Sun* announced "we have purchased the stone building on the east side of the square" built by John Shaffer in 1870 for a saddlery, immediately north of which stood the first Courthouse, a log cabin. The *Sun* was moved into the stone building by the end of December 1881, remaining in that location many years. *Sun* was hand set, printed on Washington Hand Press "turned" by Walter "Waller" Weatherby in 1883; press was also operated many years by a strong Negro man named Frank. When an outlaw threatened that he personally would take care of publisher Cooper and the printing shop on a certain day, the huge pressman Frank, bare to the waist, met the bandit at the door, stated that he always did Mr. Cooper's fighting. The startled intruder's antagonism was cooled instantly and he hurriedly departed. A bullet-scarred case of hand type remained in the shop for many years, apparently evidence of at least one shooting. J. E. Cooper, editor, and J. C. Cameron, business manager and partner, continued publication until July 30, 1891, when Cooper sold his interest to Marvin M. McLean, an attorney, a graduate of Southwestern University and son of Reverend John H. McLean who was Regent at Southwestern University from 1891 to 1897. Cooper resumed editorship June 8, 1893; in February 1894 he was joined by a stock company composed of W. E. Chapman, Jack Steele, T. B. Stone, M. B. Lockett, A. L. Sharp and T. S. Snyder, board of directors, with Cooper as editor. On March 29, 1894, it was announced that F. T. Roche had purchased an interest and would become editor, Cooper remaining as president of the company; April 12, 1894, E. I. Watson was added as business manager, succeeded by R. F. Cates (late of *Liberty Hill Index*) on September 3, 1896. Captain Roche, a former Confederate army officer who always wore a frock coat at his business, continued as editor until 1915, when he withdrew to become postmaster. At that time, George Keahey, Lowrey Foster and Howard Harrison, Sr., formed a company which purchased the *Sun* and Dr. John Robert Allen assumed duties as editor. Allen and his wife had been directors of the Ladies Annex at Southwestern University for many years previously. Allen left the firm by May 17, 1918, to return to the ministry, was succeeded by John M. Sharpe, editor, with Keahey, Foster and Harrison remaining in the company. The week of November 25, 1918, the *Sun* purchased the *Georgetown Commercial* from Lee J. Rountree and combined the two plants. On July 11, 1919, John M. Sharpe became president of the company, W. W. Jenkins the editor, George B. Keahey, secretary-treasurer; stockholders were Sharpe, controlling interest, and Foster, Keahey, Harrison and Donald Barron, stockholders. Sharpe took leave of absence 1933 to 1944 to serve as postmaster of Georgetown, during which time Robert Cooper, son of the founder, was editor. Sharpe returned to his editor's desk in 1944 and at the same time Fred Millholin joined the staff, later becoming editor. In October 1948, Don Scarbrough of Taylor purchased controlling interest in the company, later acquiring all the stock, and continued to publish the *Sun* in 1973.

Georgetown Record 1884 to 1886. See *Williamson County Record*.

Georgetown Gazette, about 1890, Will T. Hawkins, editor.

Williamson County News, possibly published as early as 1897, definitely by 1899, soon changing its name to the *Signal*.

Williamson County Signal, successor to *News*, known as *Signal* about 1900 when John M. Sharpe came to Georgetown and worked on the *Signal*.

Georgetown Commercial, absorbed the *Williamson County Signal* when Lee J. Rountree purchased the *Signal* in 1900, immediately changing its name to the *Commercial*. Rountree was well known as a newspaperman when he went to Georgetown; there he produced a successful paper for many years. In November 1918 he sold the *Commercial* to the *Williamson County Sun* which combined the two shops and absorbed the *Commercial* mailing list.

The Megaphone, weekly publication of Southwestern University since 1907.

Georgetown New Citizen, published briefly, known to have been issued July to December 1924.

Blackland Reporter, published briefly by Sam Harris, Jr., 1946 to 1949.

The Advertiser, primarily a shopper, published 1950 to 1955 by Vernon Holmquist.

ROUND ROCK

Round Rock Sentinel, December 1870, Nat Q. ("Nat Curious") Henderson, publisher, a wandering journalist who also published papers in Georgetown, Belton, Austin and other places. *Sentinel* suspended publication soon after first issued, due to financial difficulties, but was again publishing in September, 1871. *Sentinel* plant moved to Georgetown in October 1872 after which it was called *Georgetown Sentinel*.

Round Rock Reflector, mentioned once in 1877 as having merged with the

Round Rock Headlight, founded May 26, 1877, by William K. Foster, formerly publisher of *Georgetown Watchman* and *Georgetown Record*. Foster established the *Headlight* the week after the *Williamson County Sun* was founded. In March 1879, Minor H. Brown of Taylorsville purchased *Headlight*; in April, E. C. Stacy joined him in the business. For a short time, Brown and Stacy also printed the *Taylorsville Times* in the *Round Rock Headlight* plant.

The Two Round Rocks, founded in mid-August of 1881 by Judge John Lyle.

Quid Nunc (Round Rock), being published in August 1882.

Round Rock News, known to have been issued by H. G. Wood from 1886 until 1888, possibly longer.

Round Rock Leader, established at least by 1902, an apparent successor either to the *Headlight* or the *News*. A fire destroyed the files of the *Leader*, only newspaper in Round Rock for many years, thus destroying much history of the early newspapers there. In 1928 J. Louis Mohle edited it and in October 1929, John Herring Kavanaugh purchased the *Leader*, editing and publishing it until his death in 1957. He was a slight, quick, nimble-tongued speaker and writer, nicknamed "Firecracker" Kavanaugh. He continued to use handset type and a small country newspaper shop and press throughout his lifetime, as did his daughter, Mae Kavanaugh, who succeeded him as editor and publisher. The Kavanaugh family sold the *Leader* to the William K. Todd interests in December 1972.

LIBERTY HILL

Liberty Hill Observer, August 5, 1886, Reverend R. F. Cates founder. The newspaper continued publication many years.

The Church Helper (Liberty Hill), established late 1880s by Reverend S. C. Lockett, it became official organ of Cumberland Presbyterian Church, was moved to Hutto, 1890.

Liberty Hill Cyclone, established by 1890, edited successively by R. F. Cates, S. J. Matthews, Reverend J. K. Lane.

Liberty Hill Index, established by July 1890, published many years, was being edited by R. F. Cates in 1896 when Cates went to Georgetown to become business manager of the *Williamson County Sun*. *Index* was being published as late as October 1934.

Liberty Hill News was being published in 1928 by J. H. Kavanaugh, who the next year bought the *Round Rock Leader*.

Liberty Hill Leader, founded W. E. McCoy January 15, 1932, purchased September 5, 1947, by Vera Allen who continued its publication until December 30, 1948, when *Williamson County Sun* took over its subscription list and the *Leader* closed as a publication. Joe Peacock is believed to have been associated with the paper sometime prior to Mrs. Allen's regime.

BARTLETT

Bartlett Headlight, founded 1886 by M. L. Hair, later became *Bartlett Tribune*. *Tribune* purchased in 1902 by R. Frank Cates, who always wore a handlebar moustache, and J. Q. Sharpe of Liberty Hill and Georgetown, who sold to E. R. Arndt and Frank Werst in 1929; Walter W. Fox bought the paper in 1932 or 1933. Robert C. Ford purchased the *Tribune* in 1937, continues to publish it in 1973.

Bartlett Democrat was being published in 1890.

Bartlett Evening News was being published by a Mr. Baldridge in 1908.

Bartlett Tribune, successor to *Bartlett Headlight*, established 1886. See *Bartlett Headlight*.

GRANGER

Granger Banner, presumably issued before November 1887 when the *Williamson County Sun* stated "the *Granger Banner*, we learn, is to be removed to Georgetown."

Granger Advance, established April or May 1888 when a press was moved to Granger from Caldwell, first published in Granger schoolhouse.

Granger Guard, published shortly after the *Advance* by Fred Whipkey. The paper was jokingly nicknamed the *Granger Gourd*.

Granger News, established October 1892 and still in publication in 1973. The paper was printed during its early days in the back of Scott McCarty's store. In 1895, bought by Mell C. and Homer C. Cooke, then in succession by R. B. Owens, Bob Bland, Miss Maid Allen, A. D. Rucker and C. L. Tanner. For a time prior to Tanner's ownership, the *News* name was changed to the *Times* from 1899 to 1904. Under Tanner's regime, the paper was again called the *Granger News*, beginning 1904. R. A. Alford purchased it from Tanner December 19, 1912, remaining with the paper until 1946 when Henry B. Fox and Don Scarbrough purchased it. Henry Fox owned sole interest in 1947-1948. Don Scarbrough purchased the business in 1949. Linda Scarbrough has been owner from 1965 to the present time.

Granger Times. See *Granger News.*

Nasinec, Czech language newspaper which became the official organ of the Catholic
Church in Texas in 1918, was moved to Granger in 1937 from Taylor through
the efforts of I. C. Parma, Reverend John Vanicek, John Baca, Josef Maresh and
others. Sixty-five stockholders formed the Nasinec Publishing Company, Inc.,
with John Vanicek, president; Peter Nemec, vice president; I. C. Parma, secre-
tary-treasurer; Josef V. Maresh, business manager; Anton Stiborik, editor; and
Josef V. Maresh, F. J. Mikulencak, Sr., John Bohac and R. J. Bartosh, directors. The first issue printed in Granger plant was dated July 2, 1937. The
same plant also published another Czech language organ, *Texasky Rolnik.* Editors following Stiborik were Josef V. Maresh of *Rolnik* on October 10, 1947, and
Emil Triska of *Nasinec,* January 1959. Maresh resumed editorship of the *Nasinec*
January 1963, retiring July 10, 1971, when his son, Lad H. Maresh, took charge
and continues to edit and manage the paper.

FLORENCE

Florence Flower, founded 1890 by Marion Haygood; later owners: S. F. Perry,
Walter Miller, E. O. Hood, who changed the name to the *Reporter.*

Florence Reporter, successor to the *Flower.* E. O. Hood sold the *Reporter* to J. E.
Puckett, who changed its name to the *Vidette.*

Florence Vidette, J. E. Puckett's new name for the *Reporter.* He sold in 1898 to
W. W. Gardner, longtime publisher of the paper. After Gardner's death, his
widow and her brother, R. N. Watson, continued publishing the paper from 1930
until 1948, when the publication was discontinued.

Florence Post, founded by Frank Knight September 1949, leased to Vera Allen in
the fall 1951, later sold to Vernon Holmquist, discontinued by 1955.

TAYLOR (TAYLORSVILLE)

Taylorsville Reflector was being published in September 1877 by W. K. Foster,
with James Muir, "the sprightly local editor."

Taylorsville Clarion, published late in 1878. Its brief career was described in a
Williamson County Sun of January 1879:

Some five or six weeks ago, Mr. J. C. Denman, who had been living in Georgetown for the past twelve or eighteen months, left here and went to Taylorsville
for the purpose of running a newspaper. He tried it a while, but not quite long
enough to get out the first issue, and finding it would not pay, he rather mys-
teriously disappeared and so far as we know has not been heard of since. The
citizens of Taylorsville managed, however, to get out the first issue, which
was christened *The Clarion,* and circulated it. We are now informed by our
neighbor of the *Headlight* [Round Rock] that Minor H. Brown & Co. will
commence the publication at that place of a paper known as *The Taylorsville
Times,* during the present week. Taylorsville is inhabited and surrounded by
a live and energetic people, and if they enlist in the cause, we don't see why
a small paper could not be issued there successfully.

Taylorsville Times, established in March 1879 by Minor H. Brown and James Muir.
In March of that year, Brown took over the *Round Rock Headlight,* already in
publication, and for a time printed the *Taylorsville Times* in Round Rock. By
April 1879, E. C. Stacy joined Brown in issuing both papers. The *Times* was
published at least through 1898.

Taylor Phonograph, established in February 1880 by T. J. Weir and Judge George

Scott; Mr. Abbey, editor and proprietor. This was a temperance publication. On November 24, 1884, Scott sold his interest to H. H. Brooks.

Taylor Weekly Texan, founded by Minor H. Brown in 1880, who sold on September 1, 1887, to P. O. Willson and Howard E. Willson, Brown remaining with the firm as editor. Within a year the newspaper was printed on a new steam powered press and in 1890 the Willsons erected a new brick building to house it. Still active in 1909, it some time later merged with *Taylor Daily Democrat,* Taylor's first daily. Herbert Willson, son of P. O. Willson, and his widowed mother owned the paper after the merger. It closed about 1925.

Taylor Citizen, 1886-1887, Judge George Scott, prohibition editor.

Taylor Journal, from about 1890 to 1916, a hand set paper produced by Perry Hawkins.

Taylor Herald, German language newspaper published weekly from 1895 to about 1941.

Taylor Tribune, founded 1897, ran to 1900.

Taylor Daily Democrat, the town's first daily newspaper, founded 1903, published until 1925. The Willson family who had owned the *Taylor Weekly Texan* after 1887, merged that paper with the *Democrat.* The *Democrat* supported prohibition, was edited by Herbert Willson and his mother, Mrs. P. O. Willson.

Taylor Daily Press, an anti-prohibition newspaper, was founded in 1913 by a stock company of Howard Bland, H. C. Mantor, O. E. Roberts, Peter Schram. The *Press* was edited by George Tucker, assisted by his three sons, Will, Albert, and Henry. Minor H. Brown also joined the staff, remaining with the paper until his death in 1921. He had been a newspaperman for forty-five years, had at one time roomed with William Sidney Porter, better known as O. Henry, the writer. George Peeler came to work for the *Press* in 1921 and five or six years later became the sole owner, remaining until his death in 1952. His widow, Mrs. Eileen Peeler then took charge of the business, and in 1960 sold to Bell Publishing Company, owned by Frank Mayborn of Temple. That firm continues to publish the *Press* in 1973.

Taylor Times, founded March 1940 by Don Scarbrough, in no way connected with the much earlier *Times.* Scarbrough sold in 1948 to Henry B. Fox, who, in turn, sold to the *Taylor Daily Press,* which continued to issue the *Times* once each week in 1973.

CORN HILL

Corn Hill Weekly Gazette, published at least by February 14, 1880, by M. L. Hair, a four by six-inch miniature four page paper.

Corn Hill Express, apparently a new name for the *Gazette,* the *Express* being mentioned in 1881 when its publication was suspended because of Hair's health. Back in business in a short time and still called the *Express* in 1883.

Corn Hill Enterprise, mentioned in 1881.

Corn Hill Clipper, publication frequently mentioned in 1886.

Corn Hill Chronicle, mentioned 1890.

LEANDER

Leander Times, being published in 1897.

Leander Record, founded November 13, 1901 by D. A. Bower; in 1909, R. A. Alford was owner and editor.

Leander Light, owned by partnership by R. A. Alford and Robert E. Downey, published in 1925.

HUTTO

Hutto Enterprise, issued at least by 1890 and mentioned in 1904.

The Church Helper, originally published in Liberty Hill (1890). Reverend S. C. Lockett and J. W. Pearson became editor and publisher respectively when the community-church paper was moved to Hutto in 1891.

Hutto News, in publication in 1909. C. L. Fridge was editor-owner in 1910.

WEIR

Weir Reporter, believed to have been the name of a newspaper issued there briefly about 1910 or 1911.

JARRELL

Jarrell View was founded in 1911 by Robert E. Downey, published until late in 1914.

COUPLAND

Coupland Record, in publication in July 1914.

LANEPORT and HARE

Laneport and Hare News, a small weekly newspaper published by Miss Lou Ella Miller of Laneport who was an employee of the *Taylor Daily Press*. She edited the *News*, and the *Taylor Press* printed it for her about two years beginning about 1923.

The man considered Texas' Revolutionary War printer moved his home to his post oak farm between Siloam and Beaukiss, Williamson County, in 1876. He was David Ervin Lawhon, a tall, athletically built young man when he came from Tennessee in 1835, responding to calls for army volunteers. Upon reaching Nacogdoches he planned to join the Texas militia, but those plans were changed when local officials discovered that he was a trained printer. Only a few newspapers had appeared in Texas at that time, most of them briefly. When David Lawhon issued his first edition on November 28, 1835, his *Texean and Emigrant's Guide* was the only newspaper in the Nacogdoches area. Using old printing equipment which in 1829 had published a bilingual paper, *The Mexican Advocate*, Lawhon editorially supported Texas' fight for independence, printed military and unofficial proclamations, advertised for supplies for the army, sought financial help and volunteers for the Texas cause, and published lyrics to war tunes of the time. He continued to publish at least through January 2, 1836, possibly a month or two longer, became an Indian fighter after the war, married Nancy Carr in 1840, moved near Elgin about 1861, and to Williamson County fifteen years later. His last home was once the Marmaduke Gardner family home, relatives of Lawhon's, who settled in 1854 at Sam Smith Springs on the Middle Yegua, later known as Lawhon Springs. The Texas Revolutionary printer died at that home February 14, 1884, and was buried nearby.[110]

Telegraph and telephone wires were often strung alongside newly-laid railroad tracks, as was the case in Williamson County in the late seventies. A telegraph line reached Georgtown from Round Rock in August 1878, the Georgetown office advertising that it would send wires "to any point." From its offices in Rucker & Hodges store, "several dispatches were sent early Monday morning for grandeur more than anything else. Capt. [Emzy] Taylor sent a dispatch to New York in regard to our Railroad." The first wire from Round Rock was from Mays & Black to Captain Taylor. Two direct descendants of Samuel F. B. Morse, inventor of the telegraph, lived in Georgetown in the 1960s and 1970s—Leila Livingston Morse, a granddaughter, and attorney Robert F. B. Morse and his family. The attorney, like his famous great grandfather, was an artist.[111]

Telephones connected several business houses in downtown Georgetown early in June 1878, but were not used generally over town nor in residences until about the end of the century. Long distance calls could be made only from the local telephone office for many years before home telephone service was in vogue. Telephone lines were up between Taylor and Round Rock in 1883, linking these two towns and Georgetown by telephone. In 1886, Georgetown had connections with Austin, Elgin, McDade and Bastrop outside the county. At century's end, towns had two different telephone companies, one for local and one for long distance calls.[112]

When railroad service was available, the U. S. Postal Department made use of it, but continued contracting with stage lines to carry mail where trains did not run. Rural Free Delivery routes were activated in Williamson County by 1903, with Liberty Hill, Georgetown, Florence, Hutto and Corn Hill among the first to have them. Three rural routes were opened for Taylor and three more for Granger on September 15, 1903. The first official trip made by the rural postman on horseback was a festive occasion in every community. Rural schools often closed so that the children could witness the momentous event; farmers, ranchers and villagers greeted the carrier as he rode his route.[113]

Although communications were changing rapidly as the century waned, the earlier forms—horseback, or horse-drawn vehicle—remained the most used until the automobile came into use between 1906 and about 1920 and better roads were built. A popular, outgoing businessman of Georgetown, Frank Carothers, frequently traveled across the flat prairieland of central Williamson County where he owned property. Riding horseback to his

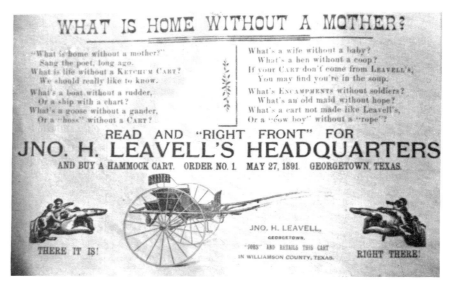

County newspaper of 1891 advertises vehicles of the day.

farms from Georgetown, then back home, he sometimes traveled after dark, when it became difficult to find the way, especially on the flat farmland with few distinguishing landmarks. Thus, it was fairly common for him to be lost in the night. Since Carothers frequented the region of Monadale and Wilson Springs (near Taylor), if anyone living there heard a shot in the middle of the night, he knew to get up and put a light on in his house, for it meant Carothers or someone else was lost on the prairie. As the lights went on in the few homes built there, the lost traveler could regain his bearings and go ahead with assurance.[114]

About 1880, Leavell's store at Georgetown advertised a new convenience for the ladies as they dismounted from their horses—large live oak logs placed in front of the store for them to step upon. Everyone rode horseback. In the 1880s and 1890s, buggies and other horse-drawn vehicles came into more general use and by the 1890s, bicycles were also the rage. Several petitions in Georgetown requested permission to ride bicycles on sidewalks "outside the fire limits." The new vehicle frightened horses and "caused one or two vehicles to be broken."[115]

LIFE STYLE IN THE VICTORIAN DECADES

The railroads and the Victorian era brought perceptible changes in the life style of the county. Precision sawed lumber for buildings, heavy machinery to work the farms, home appliances and furnishings could now be bought in the nearest town for the first time. Many large, handsome stone or frame residences ornamented with Victorian period trimmings, high-

Nearly every home in Georgetown had a picket fence in 1892.

ceilinged and tall windowed, appeared on prominent hills in the countryside and in the new residential sections of the towns. No longer must furnishings be made by the pioneers themselves or a local cabinet maker, but imported pieces from furniture makers of Europe and the United States were available, as well as furniture made of horns or antlers which was the rage in some quarters. Various combinations of horn and wood, steer and buffalo horn, or deer antlers were used, some of them inlaid with mother-of-pearl. In time for Christmas 1885, an elk horn chair arrived in Georgetown for Captain John Sparks (later Governor Sparks).[116]

Probably the housewife's greatest luxury of that day was the new wood burning cookstove which she could have shipped by rail or buy at a local store, along with newly-available grocery staples. Now she was able to abandon the heavy cook pots and long-handled utensils she had used for cooking in fireplaces. Combining foodstuffs from the markets with her own homegrown produce, she served elaborate meals, indeed. Every family had a large garden. On the farm were patches of corn and sugar cane, milk cows, hogs, chickens, geese, ducks, turkeys, pea fowl, guinea fowl, and an orchard, all providing groceries. Surplus corn, okra, peas, beans, peaches and apples were dried in large, flat boxes covered with cheesecloth and set in the sun, often on the porch. The big wood burning cook stove was fed wood, chopped and brought into the kitchen by the children. Everyday menus for a typical large family might include two gallon pots of chicken and dumplings, brown beans cooked with chunks of home cured bacon, a large pot of garden grown or wild greens, homemade hominy seasoned with butter or bacon, a pan of green grape pudding, many, many loaves of homemade bread prepared on "baking day" for the week; or homemade pork sausage, smoked ham or a large turkey; eggs; huge pans of cornbread; garden vegetables; syrup made at home from the cane grown in the field; figs, dried fruits or fresh fruit from the orchard or growing wild in the woods; other meat from the farm; milk and milk products including clabber milk, buttermilk and cottage cheese; home ground coffee, and an annual Christmas fruitcake.[117]

Such bountiful fare required much hard work but chores were divided among members of the large family, and household help if the family could afford it. The first hard norther signaled the time to butcher hogs. "Hog killing time was a community affair. Neighbors helped and shared some of the spare ribs and backbone." If a family was fortunate enough to have a spring near the house, milk was kept refrigerated by placing it in a container in the cool spring water or in a well. A milk house was frequently built over and around the spring. If there was no spring, a cooler was improvised—a long zinc pan, deep enough to hold four or five buckets of milk and some butter, was topped with a shallow trough—a lid which held water. Another long compartment under the milk held more water. "This was all covered with cloths that dangled from one trough to the other. This 'whoopie' was set on the porch in the wind and the milk was kept cool by evaporation of water in the troughs. It was really pretty good." Fresh meat could be packed in a bucket and hung in the cistern, spring water, or shallow well to keep it cool. Drinking water came either from a spring, a shallow well or cistern, where families often shared a common drinking cup, as did school children, thus sharing colds and other communicable ailments. If the cistern went dry and there was no well, the family hauled water in large wooden barrels. Windmills were installed on farms and often near town homes as well.[118]

Sweetening, provided either by honey or homemade syrup, was a luxury. Most communities had a syrup mill consisting of long rollers pulled by mule power. As sugar cane was fed into the rollers, juice was squeezed into a trough, after which it was boiled down into molasses. Youngsters of the county often found wild red haw, black haw, mulberries, grapes, hackberries, pecans, Spanish briar nuts (bull nettles), walnuts, acorns, wild onions and water cress to eat or nibble on. They chewed gum elastic, used elm bark for tobacco and smoked grape vine twigs.[119]

Family recipes were handed down from one generation to the next, the measurements usually extremely vague even in cookbooks of the period. Practice was the key to success. Since corn was the first staple food for Texas settlers, a variety of dishes had been devised from it. Grits were made by grinding corn, then washing or winnowing out the husks. To make hominy, corn was boiled in water with plenty of clean wood ashes made from burning sound, clean wood. When husks could be slipped from kernels, the corn was removed, the kernels rubbed and washed until all husks were loosened and off the corn. The first yeast was made from home ground cornmeal mixed with water to a soft consistency, allowed to ferment a day or two. More water and meal were added at intervals until the ferment was sufficient for yeast. Additional meal was then added to make a stiff dough and a final ferment obtained. Yeast was shaped into flat small patties and used as needed for bread. For yeast made of flour, the housewife mixed two cups of flour, two cups (or less) of sugar, and warm water to make a soft sponge, beating it well. This was stored in a warm place from four to seven days, until it rose, then fell. One cup of the yeast was put in a large jar with a loose top and stored in a cool place to use the next day. To the remainder was added another cup of sugar and proper proportions of flour, salt and shortening to make bread. A piece of yeast was always retained as a "starter." The efficient woman always had her starter but, if calamity fell, a neighbor was glad to oblige with a little piece from her own supply.[120]

To make soap, homemade lye and scrap grease in any form was boiled in a large washpot to the consistency of soap, allowed to cool, and was cut into blocks for use in the kitchen, bath, or for the family wash. Clothes were washed by hand over a copper rub board and tub, then boiled in a large washpot outdoors, and rinsed several times. They were wrung by hand, then hung on lines, fences or shrubs to dry all day in the sun. Most outer garments were stiffly starched, then ironed with "sad" (heavy) irons heated on wood cook stoves, over hot charcoal in a clay pot, or were ironed with a gasoline iron.[121] The section of Georgetown north and west of the Courthouse known as the Ridge was once called Blue Ridge because Negro laundresses lived there, and did so much laundering for townspeople, the ground was often covered with a foamy mixture of soap suds and bluing.[122]

JOHN H. LEAVELL, SOLE AGENT, GEORGETOWN, TEXAS.

Fashions of the 1890-1891 period in county newspaper.

Homemade lye came from ashes. A long hopper, slightly elevated at one end, made of two wide hand hewn planks plus short planks at each end, held the ashes. A half hollowed out log was placed underneath the hopper to catch the drippings as water was poured over the ashes. Water slowly drained through the seam between the planks and formed the lye. Proper strength was tested by dipping a feather into the mixture. When it felt slippery, the lye was made.[123]

Although "bought" fabrics could be purchased in town, families of modest income continued to make some of their own clothing, hand rolling or spinning wool from their sheep into thread, weaving on home looms, and making coverlets or clothing, and knitting sox or mittens. Each family owned a shoe last on which father replaced wornout shoe soles. To tan hides at home, skins were salted while fresh to prevent spoilage, and in about a week were placed in a dense soap solution for three weeks. They were removed, placed in a fresh soap solution, then hung and the hair scraped off, the hide rubbed and worked during drying. This left the skin soft and pliable. If the hide got wet, an additional soap treatment and rubbing resoftened it.[124]

Children were adept at improvising entertainment, making corn cob dolls, or dolls from young corn ears with the silks left on for hair. Planks were hewn into baseball bats and for balls "mama unraveled old stockings and wound the string into balls." For extra excitement, the ball could be soaked in coal oil, then on a dark night it was lit and a fireball game of toss ensued. "It was the fastest ball game imaginable. We were a smeared bunch when we got back home." Sling shots and bean shooters were homemade.

> At Christmas, we cut our tree from an old live oak tree in our pasture, decorated it with popcorn strings or yellow field corn, strings of colored paper ornaments and candles. Each of us had a box or pan with our name for Santa to put our gifts in. I don't suppose our Christmas ever cost more than five dollars, usually much less, but we had a million dollars worth of fun. The boys loved to hunt and fish; both game birds and fish were plentiful.[125]

Families living on farms made about one trip a month to town, an event which was planned days ahead. The eggs were gathered and packed in cotton seed to prevent them from breaking; homemade vinegar and syrup were poured into jugs; the old road wagon was put into order and the lucky child was named who could accompany the parents on the journey. An eight or ten mile trip to town and back, with time for shopping, took all day. The wagon returned home filled with sacks or a barrel of flour and sugar, crackers, pickles, molasses if not made at home, green coffee, and other produce, often exchanged for the eggs, syrup, vinegar or other homegrown produce. The green coffee was roasted at home and ground as needed. Between trips to town, a peddle wagon visited farmhouses each week. "It was a long, wide affair, with shelves and doors and drawers all around it and a place for live chickens hanging on the back." In separate drawers were home cures for both man and animals, notions, and a special place for "eggs of all ages and conditions." Also tucked into shelves or compartments were great slabs of chewing tobacco, sacks of smoking tobacco, bottles of snuff, candy, groceries and yard goods. Roads to town were often in very poor condition. In rainy weather, it was common to see wagons stuck in the main streets of any downtown section. When a trip through mud was necessary, the farmer removed everything off his wagon except a small seat, took off both the back wheels, allowing the rear of the wagon to lie on the ground. With only two front wheels to cut into the mud, the wagon was pulled by four horses with reasonable success.[126]

In 1881, Georgetown Water Works Company was established and a standpipe erected west of Main at the corner of Main and Ninth Streets by Dan Murphy and George W. Burkett. The entire system was not completed until in the fall of 1884. The same two men in 1882 began to install Taylor's first water works, erecting a big cistern or tank on North Main Street a short distance above the business section. When water which was pumped into the tank from two springs at the edge of town proved inadequate, a pipe was run in 1887 to the San Gabriel River at Circleville and water was piped into Taylor from there. The Courthouse was piped for water in 1883 and electric lights were installed in 1895.[127]

The new facilities served only a small portion of the county's population for many decades. Old habits persisted; some people were too poor to own a spigot and borrowed water from a generous neighbor. Others joined the water system but out of habit had only outdoor hydrants installed, carrying water they needed into the house in buckets. At Georgetown there were no water meters; everyone paid six dollars a year for all the water he wanted. Two Negro men employed at Southwestern University discussed the propriety of the fee, one feeling that God gave water and charges should not be made for it. The second man agreed that water should be free, but philosophically thought that God did not promise to furnish the pumps, water pipes, and standpipe free of charge.[128] There was precious little indoor plumbing in the nineteenth century, and the best method of keeping flies down around outdoor privies was sprinkling the ashes of cedar wood or commercial lime around the area.[129]

Money was not always plentiful in the county, but generally people lived very well for the times. There were many exceptions, however. The famous trainload of Coxey's Army, jobless men ready to march on Washington, D. C., had a long and troublesome journey from the far west, and rode the I. & G.-N through Round Rock, Taylor and Thrall in April 1894.[130] To provide living quarters for paupers in the county, officials established a county poor farm, located about half a mile out present Hutto Road southeast of Georgetown. The grimness of the place was indelibly marked on the memories of hundreds of people who had occasion to visit the farm, and on the somewhat fewer who called to share a little of their own goods with those trapped by an unkind fate.[131]

Between 1890 and 1900 pianos in homes of the country increased five times as fast as the population and in 1905 there were more pianos in homes than bathtubs. Most young ladies studied music. Some pianos and reed organs were manufactured in inland United States but most came from eastern manufacturers who sold "unstencilled pianos" on which a local firm could stencil its own name. Several retailers in Williamson County took advantage of this system.[132] A few pioneer families brought or shipped in heavy, beautifully carved pianos. Nearly every school offered some type of musical training; singing schools sprang up and singing conventions were held over the county in homes, schools and churches. In families of German origins, every child played some kind of instrument or sang and a family orchestra was not uncommon. Granger, Taylor and

The first Taylor City Hall housed an opera house-auditorium.

A. W. Storrs built the Granger Opera House in 1905.

Georgetown built opera houses; other communities utilized auditoriums in their colleges or schools where speakers, lecturers, evangelists, minstrels, plays, concerts and other serious programs or entertainments were presented. In addition to the theatre circuits of the last two decades of the 1800s, the Buffalo Bill, Booger Red and Gentry Brothers Dog and Pony shows were popular outdoor entertainment.[133] It was fashionable for those who could afford it to go "to the springs," and Page's Mineral Well Steam Bath of Georgetown opened in the 1880s, continued in use into the nineties. Also by this time, H. Burkhardt developed his Georgetown Mineral Wells and Sanitarium in San Gabriel Park on a "clear crystal stream," and shipped water anywhere in the state at five cents a gallon, provided the customer furnished the jug and paid express charges[134]

Despite opposition of most protestant churches to dancing, some social and folk dancing was enjoyed in homes and public halls. "Socials" and dancing parties were frequently mentioned in newspaper columns; serenaders entertained various "inmates of different dwellings" with music and song on summer evenings; croquet parties, all-day picnics were popular. Even before opera houses and early open air theatres provided a kind of mass entertainment, downtown had its share of excitement. One evening a crowd assembled in the street to watch a tight rope walker and a female artist, both of them executing their "respective parts splendidly," followed by "some first-rate manoeuvres on the ground." Even the Court-

A medicine show and a street audience near the Courthouse.

house was the setting of a social function when the court room was the scene of "another ball," guests coming from as far away as Round Rock and Austin in 1878. Camp meetings and fairs provided social as well as other benefits. Among the popular camp meeting grounds were Jenks Branch near Liberty Hill, Hopewell, Round Rock, Georgetown, Cooke's Settlement at Mankin's Crossing and Macedonia near Granger.[135]

When the chautauqua movement hit the country in the 1880s, Georgetown citizens became interested. By August, 1885, ferns were reported to be growing in the fountain on the Georgetown Chautauqua grounds. The Texas Chautauqua Assembly* was seriously launched on April 16, 1889, when the cornerstone of the Tabernacle was laid "on a high, elevated hill" immediately west of Georgetown, and on the opposite side of the South San Gabriel River "which is spanned by a magnificent suspension bridge, and is in a flourishing condition." The Assembly had a large tabernacle with roof and open sides, numerous concession stands, provisions for camping and other facilities. Well-to-do citizens built seven or eight summer homes on the high bluff, the best-remembered being the "castle"** of Captain John Sparks, later the governor of Nevada. Dr. C. C. Cody of Southwestern University assisted the Assembly in incorporating a summer normal for teachers into the Assembly's elaborate schedule. Leading educators, ministers, lecturers, entertainers and others were booked each summer in a four-week session. There were choral and vocal presentations, oratorical contests, and Professor J. B. Dunn had a museum on the grounds with about three hundred specimens of insects, reptiles, fowls and animals. Georgetown organized a Chautauqua Band to play during the Assembly and at other events throughout the year.[138]

The Chautauqua Temple or Tabernacle narrowly escaped destruction by fire one evening when the lamp under the dome was lighted, then turned too high. The rope holding the lamp caught fire, burned in two, the lamp fell to the floor and the oil which splashed out ignited. Charles Chreitzberg quickly smothered the blaze with his coat. Although his coat was ruined, he was said to have saved the building. Young men and ladies polished up their carts and rode by to look over the grounds, tabernacle, the cottages, dining hall and tents, "well floored and furnished." Supplying the Assembly's water was a pump which brought "sparkling spring water to the grounds" from nearby springs. Robert "Bob" Gaines recalled

* The Texas Chautauqua Assembly of Georgetown was chartered by the State of Texas August 27, 1888.[136]
** John Sparks and Moses Steele, partners in several business ventures in Georgetown, may have owned the "castle" jointly. The summer house was erected by Steele, who died March 17, 1889.[137]

The Steele-Sparks "castle" on Chautauqua grounds.

*"Magnificent suspension **bridge**" spanned the South San Gabriel at Georgetown leading to Chautauqua Assembly grounds atop the bluff.*

that as a youngster he sold ice cream and lemonade from the refreshment pavilions. The young Negro boy grew up to become a longtime re-spected employee at Southwestern University's Mood Hall from the time it opened in 1907, helping care for many of the students attending school there. He remembered the "magnificent suspension bridge" which not

Another view of the bridge looking toward Georgetown from Chautauqua grounds.

only provided convenient access from Georgetown to the grounds, but also a game for youngsters. By canny use of their muscles, young boys could cause the bridge to sway in a wide arc. This was great fun and whiled away much of the time when their elders were attending serious pro-grams. In addition, the swinging bridge could set off a little excitement among young ladies or staid adults as they crossed, and boys set it into motion.[139]

Tents were rented to families, furnished or unfurnished, and both lodg-ing and board could be obtained for $25 for four weeks. Some families brought their own equipment and cooked their own meals. But after a few years the Assembly began to have financial difficulties and by 1894 the program was cut to two weeks, then discontinued soon after.[140]

Taylor had an entertainment Pavilion in the 1890s at Seventh and Sloan streets located at the turn around of the mule-drawn trolley line built by

Dr. A. V. Doak. Skating, concerts, dramas, speeches, parties, and many other affairs were held there.

In the entertainment world, May Peterson Thompson became a well-known opera singer of the decades at the turn of the century. After her retirement from the stage she returned to Taylor where she made her home for many years.[141]

As late as the 1880s there was much prairieland still uncultivated and filled with three to six-foot wide depressions known as hog wallows, which are not yet fully understood by geologists. Where the tall, wild prairie grasses grew, a man on horseback could take a nasty tumble and the horse be seriously injured stepping unsuspectingly into such a hollow. Considerable mesquite grew over the prairies and had to be killed out before farmers could cultivate their fields. It had spread after Indians, who burned off the prairies, were pushed away and the firing of the grasslands was halted.

Blue northers, literally, hit Williamson County as late as the 1880s, for where land had not been broken there lay a heavy coating of peat on the soil. In the fall, warm, humid weather, abruptly altered by a cold front about in 1885 was described by Dell Tucker of Matsler community.

Suddenly, without warning blue smoke rolled over the land. Then the winds hit, frightening the animals. Moisture in the peat suddenly met the cold wind, resulting in what was a blue steamlike vapor boiling up from the ground. It was a *blue* norther, indeed.

After fields were cultivated, the phenomenon of blue smoke at the onset of a norther ended forever, but the expression remained in use.[142]

Record-making cold weather hit the county February 3, 1899. The blizzard struck on Friday afternoon with heavy sleet, increasing in intensity until first the ground, then the rivers were frozen over. By Monday and Tuesday nights "ice formed within doors" and the cold continued throughout that week. On Sunday, February 12, temperatures reached two degrees below zero at six o'clock in the morning, continuing to drop below freezing for two weeks except for two days. The winter of 1898-1899 was the coldest on record throughout Texas. Newsman Hamilton Wright described the situation in Georgetown: hydrants in the yards which ordinarily supplied water for the home and kitchen were frozen, the town had several feet of snow, and people needing water had to go to a mineral spring on the south bank of the South San Gabriel river near its mouth. "Shunting to and back once a day became really monotonous and agonizing."[143]

The alligator, along with the smoking blue norther, disappeared entirely from the county by the end of the century. When the once plentiful animal became extinct in the county's streams, its shallow lake or lagoon-like habitat which once lined the San Gabriel River banks and creek banks also disappeared, perhaps changing the water pattern of the area irrevocably. Possibly the two last alligators to be seen in the county were on the McFadin place at Circleville, where D. W. C. Hayslip and his cousins, Clyde and Auburn Stearns, saw one in the San Gabriel River and Hayslip shot it in the late 1880s, and about 1897 when another one was trapped in Blue Hole at Georgetown. Jeff Ake, a well-known Negro fisherman of that time, and a youngster, Robert "Bob" Gaines, about ten years old, knew that an alligator frequented Blue Hole. Ake had blacksmith Jeff Edmund make two hooks about a foot long, welded together back to back, which he fastened to a chain and grass rope. He then tied the rope to a willow tree on the bank, baited the hooks with a soft shelled turtle and soon the 'gator was threshing at the end of the chain. Steve Blue, who lived near, dragged the alligator from the water with his wagon and team of horses. When they loaded it, its head lay against the front of the wagon and the tail dragged the ground behind. Ake sold the animal to Iron Front Saloon in Austin. It was stuffed and placed on exhibition there. Jeff Ake let young Gaines tag along on many occasions. "I saw him catch the biggest cat I ever saw, right out of Towns Mill lake. It weighed sixty-two pounds and I was afraid of it," Gaines recalled. Ake died on the bank of the South San Gabriel of a heart attack while fishing for minnows, a very old man.[144]

Buffalo, like alligator, had disappeared rapidly during the three or four decades after the county was settled. They were rare enough in 1878 that one was displayed by its Georgetown owner in front of J. O. Charles' Drug Store during the month of July. The spectacle was said to have drawn many curious "pleasure seekers" who had not "gazed upon the outside of a live buffalo." That same summer, W. H. Muncill, a Georgetown blacksmith, had the unusual task of shoeing several oxen. An uncaptured buffalo strayed into town late in August, a Mr. Parks photographing it on the streets of Georgetown.[145]

VIOLENCE IN WILLIAMSON COUNTY

When violence between pioneers and Indians and in the Civil War finally ended, a new breed of destructive man erupted in the nation—the outlaw. He came on the scene as the nation's time clock gathered speed and an industrial empire planted its brash feet across the land. Crime seemed to grow in the shadow of the changes that swept the country. There were cattle to steal or cattle rustlers to hang, new trains to rob of spectacularly large sums, new banks to hold up, or suspected thieves to shoot. Destruction bred destruction. When farmers and ranchers put up barbed wire in the late seventies and eighties, they were harassed, threatened, sometimes were shot at and nearly all had their fences cut. The Texas Ranger no longer needed to be concerned about protection from Indians. Instead he hunted down ruthless and dangerous outlaws, who were taken seriously indeed at the time, but were romanticised and glamorized when the ugliness of their deeds was forgotten.

Williamson County met a number of the notorious gunslingers but, like all the awkward, growing and changing midwest, it had problems with its own law breakers, sometimes with its own so-called law defenders as well. Feuds over duplicate land titles or involving ownership of cattle sometimes were settled in court, but often with gunplay. One famous feud raged for years in northeastern Williamson County, involving court battles, gun-battles and several deaths. Near Georgetown, one large cattle pen was said to be the scene of many altered cattle brands. Both petty and wholesale cattle theft were common; numerous classified ads sought information about cattle "strayed or stolen." Saddles and harnesses seemed to be especially tempting to thieves.[146]

Temperance, local option and prohibition elections were much-debated from the 1870s on, partially because of open saloons in nearly every town and the carousing, brawling and shooting spawned around them. Cocklebur Saloon was in Travis County between Round Rock and Austin, but was frequented by west Williamson countians. Dr. Francis Asbury Mood's family, coming to Georgetown for the first time when he was made president of Southwestern University, lost their driver to Cocklebur, drove into Georgetown very late at night to find that the only place still open in town was another saloon where' Temple Houston awaited them. The Georgetown saloons were particular thorns to Southwestern University officials, but attempts to eliminate them failed for twenty years. The County Court issued liquor licenses by the dozens.[147]

Railroad towns like Taylorsville and Round Rock had early tent saloons frequented by large crews of workmen. A Taylorsville writer reported in 1877 that

> our town has been reasonably quiet for so large a place, except occasionally of nights when unguarded persons fire off a few pistols to the annoyance of the families living immediately in town; but when they are caught, they

own up and pay the fine.[148] W_____ M_____ who had sometime before resigned as Constable of this place (some person writing to *Galveston News*
to the contrary notwithstanding), became intoxicated, and occupied his
time for a while riding into stores and groceries, and breaking up what
came his way, and ever and anon fighting on the streets, till about an hour
by sun, when he rode for the second or third time into the store of
T_____ B_____, who fired three barrels of his pistols at him—two of
of them taking effect in his body—of which wounds he died on the
morning of the 24th. M_____ remained sober and made a good officer till
about the time of his resignation. B_____ surrendered himself, waived an
examination and gave bond for his appearance at the next term of District Court. Since this occurrence our town has been unusually quiet.[149]

Liberty Hill was one of the first dry communities in the county. When a
petition was circulated sometime between 1882 and 1884 to establish the
Liberty Normal and Business College there, the petition stated that no
liquor had been sold in Liberty Hill for twenty years. In an attempt to remove saloons and sale of liquor from Georgetown, an election was held
there in 1884, but it failed and the university town remained wet until another election May 29, 1893, reopened the issue. Supporters of the dry option won with 724 votes in favor and 473 against prohibition. The saloons
were closed July 8, 1893, and the town remains dry to the present time.[150]

Politicians, editors, preachers and others entered the big temperance debate. Presenting a colorful speech in Georgetown in 1903, the Honorable
J. H. "Cyclone" Davis, well-known state political figure, denounced liquor,
"dealing his sledgehammer blows at the saloon, occasionally rising into
flights of genuine eloquence" in his two-hour oration.[151]

Two prominent and respected men were shot and killed in the 1860s by
assailants against whom their victims had testified. Young August Nelson
of Round Rock was shot by a horse thief during the summer of 1866 soon
after his marriage to Miss Johanna August Palm. Many years afterward, the
fugitive murderer was captured and sentenced to prison for the crime.[152]
Dr. J. C. Black, 49, of Round Rock was shot and killed on June 11, 1869.
Shortly after dark on that day, two men called at his home-drug store, asking him to prepare some medicine for them. Dr. Black sent his son out with
the medicine but one man pretended to be ill. When the doctor went out to
investigate, he was shot through the chest. He, also, had denounced men of
bad repute. "Dr. McDonald hastened to the bloody scene, but Dr. Black
was past human aid. The murderers rode off yelling and firing."[153]

During one trial of a prominent citizen accused of murdering his mother
and attempting to murder his wife by means of poison, the attorneys accused each other of taking bribes, and the defendant's wife became ex-

tremely ill during the trial. The prosecution diagnosed it as poisoning. The man was acquitted.[154]

Occasionally the trains of the county were held up. A four-man robbery near McNeil in 1897 netted the bandits $165.50. Fifteen shots were fired, one of which broke Conductor Haley's arm. A passenger struggled with the men and had his cravat shot off for his trouble. The men escaped.[155]

There were lighter sides to grim days in court. In mayor's court at Georgetown

> a colored man was put on trial for allowing a hog to run at large. On entering the court room, he had placed a sack near the door. While the City Attorney was reading the ordinance defining the offense with which the defendant was charged, the latter stepped to the door, picked up the sack, walked to the table, and turned a small pig loose upon the table, remarking that this was the "hog about which so much fuss was made, and that the animal was not a hog but a pig." This unexpected exhibition and argument gave a new turn to the proceedings. The City Attorney asked for a continuance on account of the absence of a witness. In the course of two or three days more the case was dismissed.[156]

However undocumented they may be, legends of illegal hangings were no doubt often true. Gabriel Mills had a gnarled old live oak hanging tree where several cattle rustlers were said to have been hanged. The tree grew near the town church, school and Masonic Lodge building. Eight Williamson County men were hanged in a well documented and heinous episode near Bandera during the Civil War. Five legal hangings took place in the county, the first in 1886 and the last in 1906. One official hanging tree stood in the east end of San Gabriel Park at Georgetown, a short way below the present low water bridge. It held a scaffold which remained on the tree many years.[157]

The first legal hanging in the county took place in San Gabriel Park on September 11, 1886. Estimates of the crowd witnessing the event went as high as six thousand. At any rate, people were everywhere, many in trees to get a better view. The Court of Appeals had affirmed the verdict against I—— M——, a Negro man convicted of murdering his wife with an axe and razor on the night of December 10, 1885, in Taylor. The crowd arrived in various kinds of conveyances and on horseback at the square early in the morning, filling the block and pressing against the jail, then located on the northeast corner of the square. They followed the carriage with the prisoner down Oak (Eighth) Street, then north on Church to the river and the place of execution, about a mile and a quarter below the Courthouse.

Boys, youths and men on horseback! People in gigs, buggies, hacks and
wagons! Children and grown people! White and black! No thought
seeming to be given to the fact that the man was of the human species!
The terrible solemnity of the dreadful scene about to be enacted seeming
to have no effect on the minds of the crowd!

The presence of a preacher had been requested. Following a hymn which
the prisoner joined in singing, Sheriff John T. Olive, assisted by the Austin
chief of police, C. C. Palmer, took charge of the hanging. The writer described the drama, then commented that he believed Williamson County
ranked among the best counties in the state in good citizenship. "The fact
that such scenes occurred here [should] convince everyone who appreciates
the value of law and the protection of society . . . that executions should, by
all means, be private."[158]

A number of shooting incidents occurred between law enforcement officials and supposed criminals, particularly cattle thieves. A long-standing
feud of this kind involved county sheriff John Thomas Olive, no close relation to Prentice "Print" Olive and his family. While serving as deputy sheriff in 1880, John T. Olive arrested one John Armstrong on charges of horse
theft in Coleman and Williamson counties and placed him in the county
jail at Georgetown to await trial. Armstrong's brother, Neally, who was
deputy sheriff of Kimble County, journeyed to Georgetown to get John
Armstrong out on bond. Before completing his mission, however, deputy
sheriff Armstrong was arrested by Milt Tucker of Georgetown on charges
of kidnapping "a little negro" and was taken to jail in Bastrop. Neally
Armstrong made bail, returned to Georgetown, still trying to have his
brother released. While intoxicated, he threatened several officials, but secured the brother's momentary freedom and both of them headed for Taylor. There drinking and threats were reported, and the two men left "to
some business" in the post oaks (now Lawrence Chapel). Again the Armstrongs encountered Deputy Sheriff Olive, who lived out that direction on
the Lexington road. As Olive attempted to arrest the brothers, John Armstrong was shot and killed. Many years later, the place where the shootout
occurred was pointed out to Jim Dellinger, longtime Taylor law officer, by
a brother of John Olive. Two years after this episode, John T. Olive was
elected sheriff of Williamson County. In 1888, Olive offered a thousand
dollars reward for two persons "dead or alive" who had killed deputy sheriff
Stanley.[159]

Sheriff Olive had completed two six-year terms in that office and was running for a third term in the fall of 1892 when the twelve-year-old trouble

with the Armstrongs surfaced. The story was told in the *Taylor Weekly Texan* for September 16, 1892, announcing the

> untimely death of Sheriff John T. Olive at the hand of an assassin in Echo, Bell County, last Sunday morning. Sheriff Olive, in company with U. S. Marshall John T. Rankin, was returning to Taylor from the Belton fair, and was waiting at Echo for the southbound M. K. & T. train. The two had gone onto the platform of the depot and had laid down on a pallet. Mr. Olive rose from the pallet and walked to the edge of the high platform when, without warning a man arose before him in the darkness, being about 2 a.m., and fired a shotgun, the charge taking effect in the side. Mr. Olive threw his hand to the wounded place, but did not fall, and with his other hand reached for his pistol and began firing at his assailant. The murderer fled, but in his flight he stepped in a hole near the railroad and fell down, Sheriff Olive shooting at him. By this time, Mr. Rankin arose from his pallet and also opened fire. . . . Sheriff Olive emptied his pistol and was then exhausted from the effects of his wounds. Mr. Rankin pursued the assassin, who made his way across the passenger train standing on the track, and through the weeds and darkness to a horse some one hundred yards away and made his escape.[160] . . . . The wounded sheriff was brought on to Taylor and taken to the Taylor hotel.

He died the following day and was eulogized and honored by a crowd of at least a thousand who attended his services. The shooting was said to have been for revenge.[161]

The scenario for the last legal hanging in the county was almost a repetition of the first. A white man convicted of the brutal murder of a young girl, T—— Y——, was scheduled to hang on Friday, March 30, 1906. Mrs. Sam Harris recalled that as a youngster she visited the daughter of the sheriff at a time when the prisoner was in the county jail. The sheriff took Fanny "Fan" Brady (Harris) and his young daughter to see the small, wiry, rough-looking man with dark, sharp eyes. Some of the ladies of the town had visited him and he told the children he had been converted and would go to heaven. Mrs. Harris recalled hearing that ladies attended the hanging, went to the scaffold with flowers for the prisoner, and led a hymn prior to the execution. Again there was a tremendous crowd, estimated at more than five thousand. Some spectators camped in the river bottom, others stayed with friends in Georgetown. Early Friday morning teams and horsemen jammed into town as they did on "First Mondays" and on circus day. The procession, described in great detail, went past Southwestern University and the Ladies Annex, turned south along present Hutto Road, went past the Poor Farm on the hill and into an open field. "It was like a circus," with a curious, disorderly crowd. Reverend Gillette, a student at the University, delivered a scathing rebuke to the mob from the scaffold. The trap was sprung at 2:07 in the afternoon.[162]

Possibly the first of the quick-triggered outlaws in Williamson County was John Wesley Hardin, the son of a circuit riding Methodist minister, named for the founder of the Methodist Church. While still in his teens and living in Brenham, young Hardin became a horse racing enthusiast and a gambler. He moved to Round Rock in 1870 when he was eighteen and there briefly attended Greenwood Masonic Institute. "As fast with words as with the gun," he "convinced Professor Landrum of his worthiness to receive a quick diploma," presumably with the influence of his firearms. Hardin stopped occasionally in Georgetown, often enough that his face was well known and the local bankers were said to be especially wary of his visits. One of them had a balcony in the bank which gave him a view of everyone entering the door. He sat out of sight with his gun in his lap when word came that Hardin might be in for a visit. Hardin's standing was so poor in central Texas "that nobody would talk about him, the reason being Hardin's habit of killing anybody who mentioned his name."[163] Hardin moved to Georgetown sometime before 1877; then a stage was robbed near that town one night late in June 1877. It was soon reported that "a man who claimed to be John Hardin had a partial examination last Saturday for stealing a horse from Mr. Smoot." In August of that year, a Georgetown newspaper stated that "John Wesley Hardin, who at one time was a resident of this place, and is the author of twenty-seven murders, is now confined to the Austin jail, arriving there last Tuesday."[164] The next year, he was tried and sent to prison at Huntsville.[165]

A member of Butch Cassidy's outlaws, Judd Roberts, was born and brought up in the west end of Williamson County. Roberts came from a "primitive, individualistic community" where he was a friend of many "potshooting whisky-drinking wood haulers and charcoal burners."[166]

After Roberts joined Cassidy, the gang ranged over Texas and New Mexico. On occasion the ex-Williamson countian returned home to make "furtive visits to see kinfolks." For two years the depredations throughout New Mexico and Texas continued and Texas Rangers were ordered to bring in Roberts alive or dead. Once he was captured but soon escaped from the jail.[167]

In 1887, word reached the Rangers that Judd Roberts was again seen in west Williamson County. Texas Ranger Ira Aten, who lived at Round Rock and knew the country well, was assigned the job of capturing the desperado. Aten enlisted the aid of John R. Hughes, who lived in that vicinity and who had lost some horses to Roberts' raids. Hughes had just returned from a cattle drive after deciding to give up that kind of life, and had caught himself some wild horses to break. Every day he worked at mustanging, which he quickly learned was an extremely tough job, so when Roberts rustled off some of his stock he was not hard to convince that he should help Aten. For ten days they trailed Roberts, who hid near the home of Aten's friend, George Wells, at Long Hollow, almost on the county line near Hughes' ranch. The exhausted Aten stopped to rest at Wells' home for a short time. Finally Aten and Hughes were able to get a shot at Roberts as he headed for Cap Rock in west Texas. At Cap Rock they overtook the bandit, by then in bad condition from the earlier wound, and Roberts was shot and killed. When the men returned home, Hughes went to Ranger headquarters at Georgetown, informed them he wanted to join. "Been having to neglect my ranching so much to fight outlaws, I've decided I might as well get paid for it," he explained.[168]

The controversial Olive family who lived in the very heart of wild cattle country in southeastern Williamson County led enigmatic and often contradictory kinds of lives. James "Jim" and Julia Ann Brashear Olive settled on Brushy Creek near Adam and Sarah Lawrence in 1843 with their two young children, Elizabeth and Isom Prentice, built a log house, became good friends of the Lawrences and went into the business most natural to the area—cattle. Seven more children were born to the couple, the boys favoring their dark-eyed, dark-skinned and dark-haired, part Cherokee mother. They were a popular family, outgoing, party-giving, always including among their guests the neighboring cattlemen who lived up and down Brushy Creek. Jim Olive set up a small store near his home at a place first called Cross Roads, later known as Lawrence Chapel. Mrs. Olive was a religious woman, as were her daughters and daughters-in-law, but few of the men found time for church. All the Olive boys, Isom Prentice "Print," Thomas Jefferson "Jay," Ira Webster, Robert "Bob" Allen and Marion, grew up learning the cattle business and all pursued it through their tempestuous lives. The family was close, fiercely loyal and gentle to friends and relations, without an atom of mercy to enemies or suspected enemies, generous to those they loved, implacable in their quest for money, desirous of being thought law-abiding, but unwilling to seek justice through the courts.[169]

Not all the Olive men faced problems with the law except in trying to help each other. James "Jim" Olive remained to the end of his life a respected citizen of his community. His trigger-tempered eldest son, Prentice, was close to his father, but soon combined hard work with gambling, hard liquor and gunplay. He was also a manager, and as eldest of five brothers, took most of the responsibility in the family business, working closely with his father, but he nearly always was able to persuade Olive that his (Print's) way was best.[170]

The Olive story has been told a number of times with radically different interpretations—some supporting Prentice Olive and his brothers' actions as essential to survival in a terrible contest with cattle thieves, others believing the Olive family as a whole to be respectable people, but portraying Print and Bob as unbelievably cruel, ruthless and lawless. The truth may lie somewhere between. Certainly it can be said that James Olive and his other sons, Jay, Ira and Marion, never seemed to be possessed of the almost continuous and frantic paranoia Print appears to have felt—alternating moments of sobriety laced with an ever-present persecution complex, and long binges of violence. Bob was more consistent. Even by Print's standards, Bob was a carousing, trigger-fingered problem to all his family, enjoying and obsessed by violence, unable to live without it. After ten years in Williamson County, embroiled in the midst of sharp arguments, feuds, showdowns, shootouts, threats, indictments, trials and frequently whispered stories of intimidation of juries and bribery of officials, the Olive brothers moved. north to a new cattle range. In a new neighborhood with a chance for a fresh start, the story was the same all over again. Ira Webster Olive and his family had no quarrels with the law. Print and Bob were quickly caught up in a swirl of acts which finally led to their own violent deaths and to their brother Jay's death.

Prentice Olive grew up with cattle and when he finished his service with the Confederate Army he was determined to become wealthy in the business. Operating on the philosophy "men respect a gun," his years in Williamson County from 1866 to 1877 read like a court docket. Whether because his innocence was believed, or because men feared him or could be intimidated or bought by him, his worst punishments handed down by a judge or jury were one dollar fines. Robert Allen Olive's list of indictments was equally impressive. Among the court cases were Print Olive, May 1866, paid fine for assault; January 1, 1867, Print, trial for assault on Rob Murday, a cowhand working for Turk Turner—Olive shot and wounded Murday as he drove some cattle, then hired Murday to work for him—so Murday did not press charges; thirty-six other cases involving the Olives in 1867, including one for Print's gunwhipping of a cowboy at a saloon, also not pressed and later dismissed. In 1870 fourteen-year-old Bob Olive insisted on carrying his six-gun, was charged with theft of a colt from Sampson Connell of Georgetown. Connell was a friend of James Olive and charges were later dropped. Another young, ambitious cowman from Lee County

variously listed as David or Deets Phreme/Fream or D. R. Frame exchanged a few sharp words with Print in 1870. The two men drew and
Print was wounded, the other man killed. The *Georgetown Watchman* reported that the county jail was "being iron cased over-head" to prevent escapes, and three persons were confined there including a man accused of
being an acomplice "of Olive in the killing of Dr. Frame in the lower edge
of the county." Since Print had planned a cattle drive north in 1871, his attorney, W. K. Makemson, was able to have Print's trial set for March 1872
at which time evidence was presented claiming Phreme had been the member of a cattle gang. The case was dismissed. Celebrating Bob's and Print's
victories in court, the Olives gave a big community dance at the ranch.[171]

During a trail drive in 1872, one of Prentice Olive's cowhands shot another hand "for the way he talked to me" and Print was served with an
arrest warrant for abusing a hand for drunkenness. At Ellsworth, Print was
wounded in the thigh after a quarrel with a gambler. That same year, Bob's
father paid two fines for him—one for carrying a gun, the other for beating
a German farmer over the head. Other area cattlemen complained more
and more that their herds were shrinking rapidly while the Olive herds increased. There were rumors of cleverly altered brands, accusations and
counter accusations, and so many appearances in court that the bailiff commented that the Olives were in and out as often as he was. Print Olive repeatedly said that no one would convict him for shooting cattle thieves and
he was right. When he ambushed three men who he claimed were driving
some of his cattle, Print shot and wounded W. H. McDonald and killed the
other two men. The resulting indictment for intent to murder did not mention the two men killed. The original indictment disappeared, Print pled
guilty to simple assault and was fined one dollar.[172] The *Austin Statesman*
for September 1, 1876, quoted a man from Circleville who said "twenty-
one men were murdered in Williamson County last year." Print had circulated a warning that any person seen riding or driving an Olive horse or
cow would be shot on sight; several Olive horses were mutilated; Bob Olive
held one man at gunpoint for information about the cutting. Again the trial
involving McDonald's assault with intent to murder was placed on the
docket. On January 4, 1876, witnesses refused to testify against Print; Print
and Jay pled guilty to assault and battery and to simple assault, were fined
a dollar apiece.[173]

The last year Print and Bob Olive spent in Williamson County, 1876,
was so filled with frenzied fury that Print and his brother Ira talked seriously of moving their operations to Nebraska or Wyoming. Jay was not interested; he was determined to stay in Texas. Jay thought it wise for Print

and Ira to get Bob out of Texas and the Olive women were said to long for an opportunity for their men to leave the strife which seemed to follow them. In what was termed "fair" gunfights, Bob Olive killed two Negro brothers, Lawson Kelley and Dock Kelley, later shot a Negro boy who he claimed was hired to kill him. Along with a friend, Bob pistol- and fist-whipped Peter Zieschang and Ernest Poldrack who were objecting to the Olives' cattle trail crossing their land. In March 1876, James H. Crow and Turk Turner were found victims of death by strangulation, wrapped in green cowhides. The two cowmen had been waylaid and the skins of cattle they were driving sewed around them. The hides shrank as they dried in the sun, a singularly horrible torture which led to death. The Olive cattle brand was conspicuously displayed on the skins by way of explanation for the killings.[174] Early in August, the Olive brothers were at their cattle pens, apparently expecting more trouble when they were attacked one night. Jay Olive was seriously wounded, Print slightly, and two other men were wounded. Fires were set to the ranch house near the pens. Bob Olive had long been after Cal Nutt, who worked for Fred Smith, Print's closest friend outside the family. Bob produced a watch which was identified as belonging to Smith, lost at the scene of the shootout at the Olive pens. Print was convinced that Fred Smith was responsible for the raid and fire, so when Jay died three weeks after being shot, Print vowed to get Smith, so long his best friend. Bob Olive would finish Cal Nutt. The community seethed with anxiety. Smith loaded his wagon with household goods to leave that part of the country when he was met by Print, who ordered him to draw. Smith refused, saying he wanted to leave peaceably. Print insisted that he draw, later told his family that Smith did draw. Print was faster and Fred Smith died. His body was never found. Almost at the same time, Cal Nutt fell to Bob Olive's bullets. This time Bob knew he must leave quickly. Print told him to look for a good range in Wyoming or Nebraska. Bob became a fugitive, took the alias of Stevens, worked on the Carey Ranch and meanwhile was on the Texas Rangers' "fugitives wanted" list. He was killed in a shootout by Ami "Whit" Ketchum in Nebraska, November 28, 1878, and his body was returned to Lawrence Chapel Cemetery to be buried beside that of his brother Jay.[175]

Back in Texas, soon after Fred Smith's sudden disappearance, two men rode into Prentice Olive's yard. Red Banks was shot and killed and his companion, Donaldson, was wounded. Print Olive was indicted for murder and assault with intent to kill on September 22, 1876, trial date set for October 1. By this time, people knew that Print Olive's trials were attended by a kind of personal posse, made up of loyal hired men and close friends who came to see that their man received a "fair trial." Officials at Georgetown arranged a special patrol to keep the peace during the trial. Print Olive was found not guilty on both charges. Five months later, the case against him for the shooting of Fred Smith was dismissed since no corpus delecti had been found. By the time Bob Olive had hurriedly left for the north, Prentice and Ira Olive were making final arrangements to move there too, but Print had one more summons to Georgetown on March 28, 1877. The case was dismissed and he left in May to make a new home in Nebraska.[176] It was a completely new setting, but the Williamson County story began all over again. Even Ira Olive had trouble with some of his hired men which ended in a shooting. Print and Bob drank very heavily, soon alienated other settlers, including Luther Mitchell and a man on his ranch, Ami Ketchum. The adjutant general of Nebraska referred to the Olive "gang" and after Ketchum shot Bob, the finale was inevitable. A war between Olive cowmen, Mitchell and Ketchum and law enforcement officers played out the concluding drama. With Ketchum and Mitchell handcuffed together and ropes around their necks, Print Olive shot Mitchell, ordered Ketchum hanged. Depending on the narrator, the bodies were either dropped into burning brush underneath, or after Print left, some of his hands built a fire which reached the two hanged men still dangling from the tree. In either case, Isom Prentice Olive was credited, along with his foreman, with the deed, was indicted, tried and found guilty. He appealed and was released. Olive left Nebraska, moved about in Kansas and to Trail City, Colorado, where his argument with Joe Sparrow, a former employee, ended in Print's death at the hands of Sparrow and his gun on August 16, 1886. Print, too, was returned home to Texas to be buried. He had lived long enough to see his eighteen-year-old son, Billy, and his close friend, Dave Harrison, become hard-working hide skinners who occasionally cleaned up to have a good time in town. After a drinking session one evening, Billy got into an argument with the proprietor's son. Billy drew his gun and Dave intervened, trying to persuade Billy to put away the gun. Billy angrily shot his friend, who died soon afterwards. Billy rode away into "the Strip," where he wrote his mother of his swaggering escapades. Eventually brought into court, he threatened the judge, stalked away, quarreled with a saloon keeper about a woman, was later shot by the same man as he entered a local store on September 8, 1887. He had not reached his twentieth birthday.[177]

The best-remembered events of violence in Williamson County took place there in less than a week, when Sam Bass and his gang arrived in Round Rock and there ended their careers. Many of Bass's exploits took place in other states, but his death at Round Rock two days after a shootout left him tied indelibly to that town. Born in Indiana July 21, 1851, Sam moved to Denton, Texas, in 1870, to work on a farm. By 1874 he was gambling, horse racing and moving around considerably. His record of train robberies from Nebraska south to Dallas preceded him to Round Rock, where law officials were alerted that his gang might arrive in July of 1878. The tipoff had come from James W. "Jim" Murphy, also of Denton, who had become involved in one of Bass's projects but quickly lost his taste for that kind of operation. Murphy informed officials of Bass's plan to rob either the bank or a train at Round Rock. Murphy was asked to accompany the gang, which at that time included Sam Bass, Seaborn "Seab" Barnes and Frank Jackson, down from Denton. Major John B. Jones of the Texas Ranger Frontier Battalion gathered what men he could spare, but since he feared an attack on the treasury at Austin he was reluctant to deplete his force there. Rangers George Harrell, Dick Ware and Chris Connor were dispatched to Round Rock, Major Jones and Morris Moore arriving later on July 18th. They informed deputy sheriff A. W. Grimes and Henry Albert Highsmith of Round Rock of their arrangements.[178]

Meanwhile, Bass and his accomplices got to town, set up camp near the Round Rock Cemetery west of town, briefly looked around "New Round Rock" and set the date for robbing the local bank for Saturday, July 20. Doing a little sightseeing in the area, some of the men went to Georgetown, according to the *Williamson County Sun*:

> Frank Jackson and Seab Barnes, Sam Bass' pals, were in this place one day last week and one of them had his boot repaired. City Marshal, Chamberlain, thinking them rather suspicious looking fellows, went into the shop at the time they were having the boot mended, and Milt Tucker was standing in front of the shop door, but neither had any evidence, except suspicious looks, that the men were outlaws, and consequently no effort was made to arrest them.[179]

On Friday afternoon, the Bass party returned to downtown Round Rock to study it more closely. Next to the bank was a store, located at present 101 East Main Street (Main and Mays streets). When they went into the store, the trouble began. From this point about as many slightly different versions of the story have been recorded as there were people anywhere in that vicinity at the time. *The Williamson County Sun* narrated the sequence of events in three separate stories in the July 25, 1878, issue while they were still fresh in the minds of all who were involved. That newspaper was located nearer to Round Rock than any other papers preserved from that week. Although frequently quoted and referred to, the stories have not been republished in their entirety. The news about Sam

Bass was not on page one; the two main stories were on pages two and three, each with one column headline in quite small type. The first, written before news of Bass's capture, was titled "The Tragedy in Round Rock":

During the afternoon of last Friday [July 19, 1878] three strange men made their appearance on the streets of Round Rock, who attracted the attention of some civil officers—deputy sheriff Moore, of Travis county and deputy sheriff Grimes, of this county. These officers without knowing who the strangers were, but having reason to believe that one of them at least was armed, followed them into a store, and Grimes asked one of them if he did not have a pistol on, he answered in the affirmative, and before the officers had time to ask another question all three of the men drew their revolvers and commenced to fire, Grimes was pierced with five balls, without having time to fire a single shot himself. Moore received one shot, but returned the fire. The three desperadoes, who were Sam Bass, Frank Jackson and Seab Barnes, left the store and ran to their horses pursued not only by such rangers as were near but also by citizens. Every one who had a gun or pistol whether soldier or citizen (as we are informed) used it. When near their horses, Barnes fell dead, having been shot through the head. Bass received two wounds one disabling his right hand and the other through his body. He and Jackson reached their horses mounted and rode out of town, pursued by rangers and citizens as soon as horses and arms could be procured. Bass and Jackson rode by their camp, which was near the graveyard, got their guns and then struck the Georgetown road at the mouth of the lane near Mr. Oates' [should read Oatts'] house. They kept the road until they had passed Mrs. Tisdale's place, as it is called, and then turned down a lane leading to the woods, and it was not more than a thousand yards from the mouth of this lane that Bass was compelled to halt. The citizens of Round Rock, as well as the civil officers and rangers deserve credit for the promptness with which they responded to the call to vindicate the laws. We learn there is a large reward for the capture of Barnes [sic. Barnes had been killed; the reward was for Jackson.] If these rewards can be obtained we hope, that the family of deputy sheriff Grimes, and deputy sheriff Moore, one of whom lost his life, the other receiving a dangerous wound, will be remembered liberally. We hope also that Messrs. Tucker and Lane will not be forgotten and if the persons named should be overlooked, we promise to call attention to this matter again no matter who may be Governor.[180]

The second story in the same issue of the *Sun* had a one-line heading in about twelve point type, with subhead. The story follows:

THE CAPTURE OF SAM BASS

The Statement of Tucker and Lane

Not long before sundown on last Friday evening [July 19, 1878] the news of the fight with the Bass party at Round Rock reached this place; and in a short time Deputy sheriff Tucker and Constable Lane mounted their horses and started for Round Rock, arriving at that place soon after dark. They at once sought out Major Jones, informed him of who they were, of their desire to aid in the capture of Bass and his companion, and of their familiarity with the country. After consultation as to the best course to pursue, [Milt] Tucker with one ranger was sent by Maj. Jones to the Cluck spring some three miles above Round Rock, where he found Lieut. Runnels encamped with a squad of eight or ten rangers. Lane was detained in Round Rock until one or two o'clock at night, and then sent up in company with the detective Murphy* to the same place where they all remained until daylight. After getting breakfast, the rangers under Sergeant Nevils, saddled up and made ready for the pursuit, Lieut. Runnels being unwell and going on to Round Rock. The Lieut. however, before leaving camp, having learned who Tucker was, asked him to lead the rangers under Sergeant Nevils where he thought it most likely they would find Bass and his companion or get on their trail. Constable Lane with a portion of the squad went down to Bass's camp which was but a short distance above Round Rock, while Tucker with the remainder of the squad struck the Georgetown railroad about the place where Bass and Jackson struck the timber the evening before. Mr. Tucker found the trail at the mouth of the lane, and was following it on foot into the woods, and had gone about one hundred yards when Sergeant Nevils, who was in hailing distance, called him, he immediately answered the call and they proceeded about one hundred yards further when they came upon a man under a tree with his hand raised in token of surrender. The party had passed in sight of the man before but supposing him to be one of the railroad hands, of whom there were a number in the vicinity, had given him no special notice. When the squad came up to him, Tucker asked him who he was and was immediately answered, "I am Sam Bass, the man that has been wanted so long." Bass then asked "where are you going to take me?" Tucker assured him he would not be mobbed. About this time Lane came in sight with the other part of the squad, and Tucker not thinking it advisable for Bass to see Murphy who was with Lane, went out and met them and directed Murphy to keep out of sight, which he did. After a while however, Murphy came near enough to Bass, without being seen by him, to identify him thoroughly. Upon inquiry they learned from Bass that his wounds had compelled him to stop his flight on the preceding evening about seven hundred yards from where he then was; and that after dismounting from his horse he had asked his companion Jackson, to unsaddle and stake him and throw his saddle in a a thicket, and then to take care of himself as he could be of no further service to him; that he had walked during the night to where he then was; that during the morning he had walked to Mr. Sherman's house (about two hundred yards off) in order to get water for which he was suffering, but that the family was frightened at his bloody appearance and ran off; that he had then returned and tried to call to his assistance some railroad

---

* "Detective" Murphy was Jim Murphy, who informed on Bass and rather nervously agreed to accompany him to Round Rock to work with officials in apprehending him.

hands but they paid no attention to him; that he had finally attracted the attention of an old man, who brought him a cup of water and left him. Sergeant Nevils asked Bass what brought him down here and he answered "money," and went on to say "we thought we had a soft thing but it has turned out rather serious." The party intended to rob a bank in Round Rock on Saturday. When asked how many men he had, he answered "four—three who meant business and one drag." Major Jones was sent for and came with a hack and a doctor and after examining Bass privately took him to Round Rock.[181]

The third item appearing in the same issue of the county newspaper had no heading, was in a column of personal items:

The notorious Sam Bass died at Round Rock on Sunday afternoon from the wounds received in the fight at that place on Friday. We are informed that he was perfectly conscious and very often ejaculated "God have mercy on me." Perhaps there was no more desperately daring man in Texas than Sam Bass, and had he met his death suddenly in Round Rock in the fight on Friday, he would no doubt thought [sic] little of supplicating mercy even from God but after two days of reflection he quailed before the great enemy and implored Divine help. Few men would have done otherwise.[182]

The next paragraph contained the following: "This Georgetown is the poorest armed town we have ever seen. There is hardly a business man in town that has any firearms that he could use in a case of emergency."[183]

Sam Bass died on his twenty-seventh birthday, July 21, 1878, at the Round Rock Hotel run by Richard C. and Elizabeth Ann Hart. The Harts sent the State of Texas a bill for furnishing a cot, sheet and pillow for the wounded Bass after he was captured and brought there. Bass and Seaborn Barnes were buried side by side in the Round Rock Cemetery. Barnes' epitaph reads "right bower to Sam Bass." The Sam Bass story quickly became a much elaborated and glamorized folk tale. A long, biographical, sentimental ballad about him was written and sung on cattle trails by cowhands and was reputed to have a calming influence on cattle during stormy weather. Since the song has eleven stanzas, a simple melody of easy vocal range, and an equally simple two-unit beat, it may well have provided a slightly monotonous, soothing effect on the longhorns.[184] Frank Jackson escaped, was heard of no more. Jim Murphy, in constant terror of other avenging members of the Bass gang, took poison on June 7, 1879, dying in agony.[185]

The shooting and death of Sam Bass led to arguments, still occasionally heard, about who fired the shot which led to his demise. Two weeks after the gun battle, the *Sun* commented:

Between the frontier battalion and the civil officers of Williamson county a question arises as to who is entitled to the various rewards offered by the state and railroad companies for the capture of Sam Bass. The *Austin Gazette* is doubtful if any reward can be claimed. The offers, it says, were for the "arrest and conviction." The point made by the *Gazette* draws it rather too fine. What the state wanted, and what the railroads wanted, was that Sam bass [*sic*] should be stopped from levying tribute upon railroads and banks. That such operations were "stopped" by the man who killed him, hardly admits of controversy."[186]

The coroner's jury ruled that George Harrell fired the shot which led to Bass's death. Texas Ranger Lieutenant N. O. Reynolds and eight men arrived in Round Rock just ten minutes after the fight was over, and Lieutenant Reynolds' official report also credited Harrell with firing the shot in question.[187]

In addition to the folk ballad, the Sam Bass story and legends have been told in countless books and articles. Numerous businesses have taken the name of Sam Bass, particularly in Round Rock. The daring young man who robbed and was said to be generous to the poor, the former cowboy, the man who died on his own birthday and who refused to squeal on his companions—Sam Bass quickly gained an almost herolike immortality. For many, many years it was said that a mysterious lady came each year on his birthday to place fresh flowers on his grave. The town of Round Rock holds an annual frontier celebration during which the drama is reenacted at the store and in the street where Sheriff Grimes and outlaw Barnes lost their lives and where Bass was shot two days before he died.[188]

The song says, "A kinder-hearted fellow you seldom ever see,"[189] a line which has become the public's epitaph for Sam Bass. But Sam had a better one in his statement to Sergeant Nevils when Nevils was returning him to Round Rock:

"We thought we had a soft thing but it turned out rather serious."[190]

Cole Younger began his experiences in banditry with his cousins, Frank and Jesse James during the Civil War when they were trained as Confederate irregulars in guerrilla warfare. The three young men took part in a raid on Lawrence, Kansas, August 21, 1863, during which more than 150 residents were killed and a large part of the town was burned. Having cultivated a taste for violence, after the war they continued it by robbing banks and trains. In 1876 their gang of eight attempted a holdup, but were thwarted, three men being killed, three captured, and the two James brothers escaping. Cole Younger served a prison sentence and after his release organized the Cole Younger and Nichols Carnivals which traveled over the country. Georgetown was on the carnival's annual schedule and, for several years around the turn of the century, Fred and Leslie Millholin, young Georgetown messenger boys for the telephone and telegraph company, saw Cole Younger when he came to town. They were frequently called upon to deliver messages to him.[191]

From the time that the Texas Provisional Government ordered three Texas Ranger companies formed late in 1835 and assigned one of the companies to Tumlinson Fort, men from Williamson County have been associated with the Ranger organization. Robert M. Williamson, for whom the county was named, was chief officer of the three first companies. Besides John J. Tumlinson who built Tumlinson Fort, some of his sixty men were later residents of the county: Noah Smithwick, Joe Berry, James O. Rice, Calvin Barker, John N. Williams and Joseph Weeks. John G. Matthews was among the force sent to Kenney Fort during the Archives War. Nelson Merrell and Adam Lawrence were Indian fighters of the early period. Among those from the county who served in the Texas Rangers were Washington Anderson of Brushy Creek; Ira Aten and Dudley S. Barker of Round Rock; William C. Dalrymple and W. C. Shaw of Georgetown; Andrew "Andy" Mather and Thomas Williams, Jr., of Gabriel Mills; Byron Jenkins of Weir; John G. Matthews and his son, Frank W. Matthews of Matthews community near Liberty Hill, John Hughes of Liberty Hill; Benjamin Allen and Wyatt Kuykendall of Shiloh (near Hutto) on Brushy Creek; John Berry, John Bate Berry, and James B. Williams of Berry's Creek. Another Ranger, David Sparks, not of this county, while passing through in 1917 became suddenly and seriously ill and died in May, 1917, near the Berry's Creek community. He was buried in Berry's Creek Cemetery.[192] Rangers materially helped stabilize the new nation of Texas, protected the frontier settlements, sought out bandits and became as colorful in history and legend as the outlaws they pursued.

Wagon train in Jonah, 1890, near Percy Drug and McDonald—Bruce Store .

The Railroad Era

Five separate rail lines were built through or within Williamson County from 1876 until 1900, and another was begun which was not completed until 1903. The first railroad created the new towns of Stiles Switch (Thrall), Taylorsville (Taylor), Hutto Station and "New" Round Rock.

Bringing sweeping changes to the county, the rails spawned towns and villages especially in the eastern section, shifted population centers, or caused the decline into oblivion of villages the rails bypassed. Tremendous amounts of land changed hands, much of it going to the railroad companies which owned more than thirty-five million acres in Texas by 1882. Railroads were granted almost unheard of benefits and aids in Texas, by the state, counties, towns, private individuals, and through loans from various government agencies and permanent school funds. Taking advantage of the Texas prison lease system between 1868 and 1882, railroad companies built thousands of miles of track with cheap prison labor, in Williamson County as well as elsewhere. In the western part of the county, one company cut huge amounts of heavy timber for a line in the county and to ship out all over the country. Farms were arbitrarily cut by lines as it seemed expedient, and loss of cattle killed by trains sometimes was heavy in rural areas. Enormous tax benefits were granted many of the railroad companies. On the other hand, railroads increased the value of land, allowed speedier development of frontier areas, enhanced towns and their services or created new ones, opened the way for industrial development, brought comparatively cheap transportation and faster communications, provided for large-scale shipment of commodities from distant markets to the county, or, for the first time, could export produce from Williamson County with ease and efficiency. For many years the "hide room" at the depots were smelly places. Hides stored for shipping included all kinds— the early buffalo, cow, even skunk and possum.[1]

1876: STILES SWITCH—THRALL

The first tracks to touch Williamson County were in the eastern edge on the International and Great Northern lines which were to extend from Rockdale west to Austin. A station called Everett, located near the present Thorndale City Cemetery, was at the eastern border of Williamson County and this was the first section of the county reached by the rails. Convict labor under the direction of Thomas Cronin, then of Palestine, but later the owner of a railroad headquartered at Bartlett, is said to have put down the tracks in record time. They reached five miles west of the eastern county line in the spring of 1876, where Seaborn and Rebecca Fincher Stiles and their family had settled in 1849. Jim E. and Frank N. Stiles in about 1870 purchased ten thousand acres of land in the area on which they developed extensive cattle and farming interests. The railroad built a spur to the Stiles Brothers stock pens and a station stop known as Stiles Switch. At the turn of the century when a post office was contemplated for the village, the

Stiles Switch, later named Thrall, boomed with discovery of oil.

name was changed to Thrall. This was at the suggestion of the Stiles family who were great admirers of Homer S. Thrall, a well-known Methodist minister-circuit rider-historian of Texas. Although its shipping facilities were in demand, the town itself remained a small rural community until well into the twentieth century, when the discovery of oil in the area led to Thrall's spectacular growth.[2]

1876: TAYLORSVILLE—TAYLOR

Only a few scattered settlers lived on the prairies near where Taylorsville was platted in 1876. The Texas Land Company, headquartered in Palestine, purchased the townsite from an official of the I. & G. N. Railroad "and advertised a sale of town lots" for June 1876, when they thought the rails would reach that place. Although the sale did take place, the tracks were not completed to that point until about a month later. The *Galveston Daily News* for June 4, 1876, described the event.

> The sale of lots at Taylor's, the new railroad town twenty-six miles west of Rockdale, took place the 1st instant, although the streams were all up and the roads were almost impassable, preventing many from reaching the spot in time. A large number of lots were disposed of. Taylor will be one of the largest, if not the principal town between Texarkana and Austin. Parties from Georgetown, Rockdale, Belton, Bryan and other places, were among the purchasers. The place is so situated as to command without competition, the whole of the Belton and Bell county trade. Besides being in the center of one of the richest and most wealthy sections of Texas, it is directly upon the great cattle trail, and will be the principal shipping point for the cattle men for Western Texas. The Railroad company [is] putting up large and substantial stock yards. Major [Ira H.] Evans, who superintended the sale of lots, returned to Palestine yesterday. The track-layers reached the Brushy, twelve miles from here [Rockdale], this afternoon, and the iron bridge is about ready. There is plenty of iron on hand, and the road will be opened to Taylor by the 20th instant. Everything is stirring here. People are rushing in, and the new town of Taylor is all the talk.[3]

The news story above was sent by special telegram to the *Galveston News* from Rockdale.

Out of 501 acres of land from the John Winsett and James C. Eaves surveys, sixty blocks were marked for the town of Taylor. Deeds transacted on June 6, 1876, for some of this land went to Pedro Amato, Wolf Max, John E. Walker, William L. Mann, Edward Ambrose, Elias Eppstein, Henry Goldsticker and Isam P. Olive, who paid from $150 to $250 each for a lot. A short time later, other deeds were drawn to Joseph Zicaro

(Ycabo), R. M. Cooper, Mary E. Pierce, Newton Porter and Charles P. Vance.[4]

Taylorsville-Taylor was named for Moses Taylor, one of the original projectors of the International and Great Northern railroad and one of its largest owners.[5] A civil engineer of the railroad, Colonel William Elliott, auctioned the first lots. Several company officials purchased large land tracts from Mortimer R. Hoxie, general superintendent of I. & G. N., at from five to fifty cents an acre. Low prices were offered as inducements to prospective residents. Henry Dickson purchased ten acres for a total of five dollars and is said to have built the first permanent home in the new village, hauling his lumber in by wagon and soon owning the first house in town to be painted. His musically-inclined wife joined him there in November 1876, after which their residence became a popular place for social gatherings and musical events. Dickson was the first I. & G. N. Station agent in Taylorsville.[6]

Within a few months a small town had sprung up just north of the rails, with hotels run by James Sledge, Mr. and Mrs. Waggoner and T. J. Kamp, the latter's establishment also known as the International Hotel. Stores were established before the end of 1876 by R. M. Wiley and Raymond S. Porter, by James A. Simons and C. P. Vance, and by Joseph "Jack" Melasky; a lumber yard was opened by John O. Frink. The village was in a setting of "a flat, hogwallow prairie," a huge cattle range with "only a few ranch houses . . . on that vast tract." Newcomers in 1877 saw the prairie covered with sage grass, two to three feet high, with plenty of prairie chickens, quail, wolves, wild horses and longhorn cattle—dun, black and spotted and in all colors, but no short horns. There were no good roads, only dirt roads or cow trails, no bridges, and no banks. Everyone had to pay cash. Since this was cattle country, the cattle drives passed through town, right up Main Street, the animals stopping to eat fruit from the stands. A favorite corral for watering the stock and resting was at the future site of Murphy Park.[7]

"The family of S. A. Tomlinson was the first to locate in the town" [of Taylorsville] according to publications of 1893, but no additional information on the Tomlinsons has been located. Rapidly, new citizens were arriving so that by the end of 1877, the list of businesses had grown. They included Wiley & Porter, general merchandise; Napier House (John B. Napier, proprietor); M. P. Collins, grocery-hardware; Newton & Porter Saddlery; *Taylorsville Reflector*, edited by W. K. Foster; Gabe Hamilton, drilling for water; Dr. John Threadgill, Drug Store; Dr. Anderson (late of Georgetown) and Dr. G. M. Schultz Drugs; Albert Bisang, shoemaker

from Pennsylvania; Thompson and J. E. Tucker Lumber Yard; Dr. G. M.
Schultz and Dr. H. C. Morris, chemist and apothecary; C. P. Vance and
James A. Simons, general store; Jack Melasky general store; Morris and
Cook Drugs; H. Dickson Furniture; Sebastian Riley Livery Stable; Weatherford Livery Stable; Julius A. Kroschewsky Restaurant; T. J. Kamp Hotel
(International Hotel); Minor House; Cannon & Keller Saddlery and Bug-
gies; Photo Shop; Bud Saul's Saloon; Golden Rule Saloon; Jesse W.
Womack and John P. Sturgis Store; two barber shops operated by unidenti-
fied Negro men; James Meldrum rooming house. Also in 1877, it was
reported that the railroad company had solved the mud problem around
the depot grounds by macadamizing. Other very early businesses in Taylorsville included L. H. Goldstein, R. H. Talley and D. R. Meade, stores;
Mrs. McCool's bakery; William F. Gross, undertaking parlor; C. T. M.
Orr, groceries and furniture; J. W. Armstrong, livery stable; Stiles and
Long Meat Market. Dr. John Threadgill and Dr. John S. Brown were the
first two physicians there.[8]

Probably the first industrial installation in Taylorsville was a gin
erected in time for the 1877 cotton season and prophesying the importance
of that commodity to the town. Until a public school was built in 1883,
private schools served the community. A Presbyterian and a Methodist
Church were organized in 1876, as was the Volunteer Fire Department.

*Panorama of Taylor from railroads looking north on Main Street, soon after
First National Bank was founded in 1883.*

The town had no water system, however, until 1882. Meanwhile, water wagons filled their barrels from McClure Springs and Willow Springs near town, and peddled the water from house to house. The inadequacy of this system was especially vivid in the fires of 1878 and 1879.

Rapidly-growing Taylorsville continued to be called by that name, officially at least, until 1892, when the post office was designated Taylor for the first time. Taylorsville was in general usage for about a decade. Within a year after it was founded, however, a Georgetown newspaper referred to the town as "Taylor."[9]

In 1878, Taylorsville had 1,000 residents and the *Bradstreet Book* for that year listed thirty-two firms doing business. Among the new businesses were Mary and Margaret Linehan (late of New York), millinery and dressmaking shop; C. H. Booth, groceries and furniture; Boyd and Jones, groceries; M. A. Bradford, saloon; John H. Bradley, drugs; Broadnax and Hogan, saloon; G. B. Carstarphen, lumber; J. O. Frink, jeweler; S. T. Freund, general store; J. Haynie, boots and shoes; M. Holman, blacksmith; G. W. Long, groceries; Murray and Hayslip, hardware and tin; D. W. Openheimer, groceries; R. R. Pearson, blacksmith; Powell and Lydic, furniture; J. B. Simons, stationer; B. Snyder, lumber; C. W. White, hardware; McFadin & Scott, attorneys. A grand ball celebrated the opening of Martin's new Opera House on November 5, 1878.[10]

A fire late in May 1878 destroyed three business houses, but within a month two new buildings were going up, one a two-story structure with the second floor to be used for the Masonic Lodge. (The date of this fire has often been mistaken by historians for the one the following February— 1879—which destroyed most of the business section of town. Since both fires were reported in the *Williamson County Sun* for May 30, 1878, and March 6, 1879, the dates can be clearly established.) "Messrs. Schoonmaker and Powell, skilled architects," were building a new residence in west Taylor in June 1878, and about the same time, the cotton gin added a planing machine and mill.[11]

"The Great Fire at Taylorsville" was reported in the March 6, 1879, *Williamson County Sun*. It took place on February 25, 1879, starting in a wash house at the International Hotel.* The hotel owner, T. J. Kamp, discovered the blaze, but "a strong southwest wind blew and scarcity of water and the fact that the house was a small frame one and perfectly dry meant the fire was soon beyond control." First, the two-story saloon of

* At the west side of Main Street and First Street.

M. A. Bradford, then the general mercantile house of Jack Melasky to the north, two small houses on the south, the furniture store of Powell & Lydic soon caught fire. Walters & Flake was ignited from Melasky's on the north, then Vaughn's saddle and harness shop on the north. White's tin and stove house was a total loss, as were Holman's blacksmith and wood shop, his dwelling, and his smokehouse. Other complete or nearly total losses were Pat Gilden's store house, Haynie's boot and shoe shop and residence, Pearson's blacksmith shop, Shaddock's wood and wagon factory and residence. These houses burned from the flame which caught the Bradford saloon from the International Hotel and were all on the east side except the hotel.[12]

"While these were burning the post office, on the east side and north from the International Hotel, ignited and from it the store house of Womack and Sturgis," and the little house of the *Times* printing office caught, although some of the material there was saved. "Some of the mail matter was also saved" but the postmaster lost most of his stock of stationery and toilet goods. From the printing office, McFadin's hotel and law office, and a jewelry store adjoining, caught fire. The New York restaurant on the east side of Main Street caught from Womack & Sturgis store house and was burned—house, fence, out houses and all. Milbourn Wagon Company was consumed with great loss, also Drover's Exchange and ten pin alley and Sledge's saddlery and feed store. These houses burned between 2:30 p. m. and 4 p. m. "About sunset the wind suddenly reversed and a norther began blowing a perfect gale." Later that night, a fire broke out in a saloon on the southwest corner of the block, from which the family grocery of Leonard & Jones took fire, becoming a total loss. Dr. John Threadgill's L. & J. Drug Store burned to the ground; Albert Bisang lost his boot and shoe shop, Mr. Long his family grocery, and Mr. Clark his barber shop and meat market. Total loss in buildings and merchandise was estimated to be $60,000, with $25,000 of it insured. A total of twenty-nine buildings burned, leaving sixteen families homeless and thirty-four business men out of employment. Within days, Mr. Holman had put up another blacksmith shop and Mr. Kamp was operating a temporary boarding house. "Other small and temporary little shelters seem to arise as if by magic. Many talk of rebuilding with brick and stone."[13] The town did rebuild with remarkable speed, and largely with brick. The fire was credited with creating a much more substantial and imposing downtown section. Taylorsville was incorporated as Taylor in 1882 with Judge Dan'l. Moody as the first mayor.[14]

1876: HUTTO STATION—HUTTO

During the summer months of 1876, the laying of rails went quickly as far as Round Rock. A station stop was designated near Cottonwood Creek and the home and cattle ranch of James Emory Hutto. Hutto sold five acres of land for a townsite, the railroad officials designated their stop Hutto Station, and the town of Hutto was born. Hutto was a short distance due north of a much earlier village—Shiloh on Brushy Creek, where the county's two first stores, a pioneer school, church, and cemetery were established as early as 1848. In the vicinity of Hutto, besides the Hutto home, there was a log cabin home of Adam Orgain, an ex-slave said to have put up his house in 1855.[15]

The village which grew up at Hutto Station, soon to be called Hutto, was built south of the railroad tracks in the 1870s. In 1877, a depot was erected, with W. H. Farley, Sr., as railroad agent; Sam Monday opened a

Hutto Lutheran Church, founded in 1892, was built in 1900.

general store in which a Mr. Loyd owned stock; the post office opened June 27, with J. E. Hutto, postmaster; and W. H. Farley, Sr. went into the lumber business. Other businesses following soon afterwards were Hudson & John A. Blanton's store, the D. J. Davis store, Sam Monday's saloon, and another saloon run by a Mr. Scott. Dr. J. C. Flinn was the first physician in Hutto, with Dr. R. H. Eanes and Dr. J. W. Percy coming later. Dr. Joseph F. Flinn, son of the first doctor, received his medical training and returned to Hutto to practice. The first blacksmith, who also did woodworking and some dentistry, was Carl "Cap" Hansen, a Danish settler. Hansen and his family welcomed and assisted many Danish, Swedish and German immigrant families who migrated to the area during the 1880s and after.[16]

A storm in 1886 blew down the first store built at Hutto south of the tracks. Other storms damaged several other buildings in the same locality and after that time, the town began building on the north side of the railroad, where it remains today.[17]

Hutto business district, built soon after 1900.

1876: PALM VALLEY

To the west, another station stop was designated by rail officials at Palm Valley, an agricultural-church-school community a short way north

Palm Valley Church, erected in 1894, founded decades earlier.

of Kenney Fort. Palm Valley was in the heart of an industrious, prosperous Swedish settlement.[18]

1876: NEW ROUND ROCK

The railroad right-of-way near Round Rock swung to the south and east of the original town. When Round Rock was established in the early 1850s, it stood on the north bank of Brushy Creek. The first businesses were the store of Thomas C. Oatts in which he opened Brushy Creek post office on May 27, 1852; a stagecoach station with livery stable which was located on the gently sloping north bank of the creek near the northeast edge of the present low water bridge; and a tavern, about fifty yards east of the stage station. When a flood some years later destroyed the stage stop and a number of houses, plus the tavern to the east, the buildings were not replaced, but others were put up elsewhere. The name, Brushy Creek post office, proved confusing, so postal authorities in 1854 asked Mr. Oatts to supply another name. An enormous anvil-shaped boulder lay in the middle of Brushy Creek at the crossing just south of the village where Thomas Oatts and Jacob M. Harrell, a close friend, "spent many happy hours sitting on the rock & fishing." Oatts chose the new name for the town "for the loved old round rock."[19]

On October 29, 1856, the *Georgetown Independent* announced that T. C. Thompson's wheat mill at Round Rock was in full operation. Gradually, houses and other businesses appeared on the north bank, among them H. B. Sheppard's store during the winter of 1860, G. W. "Wash" Davis

Round Rock was named for this rock. To the west are low water bridge, railroad bridge and dam near which early mills stood. On adjacent flat limestone banks, heavy wagon traffic cut deep, distinct ruts in the stone.

and L. Mays stores in the early 1860s. Alex McFarland and S. H. Rutledge were granted licenses to sell small quantities of liquor at Round Rock in 1866. Dr. J. C. Black, the village physician, for whom stone mason Henry Smith had built a rock home during the sixties, was murdered at his home the evening of June 11, 1869. Two men called at his office shortly after dark, asking that he prepare some medicine for them. When the doctor mixed it, he sent his son outside to deliver it, whereupon the men pretended illness. Dr. Black stepped outdoors to investigate and was shot through the chest. "His life had been endangered for some months for his fearless denunciation & exposure of men of bad repute." A Dr. McDonald hurried to the scene, but the wounded doctor "was past human aid. The murders rode off yelling and firing."[20] Also in 1869, John T. Ricks became a partner in H. B. Sheppard's merchandising business and Henry Harris established another store. During the Civil War, John J. Harris's small home south of Brushy Creek was called Harris Tavern, which also became a stage stop. It continued as a tavern for some years after the railroad came. Several times, early mills were washed out by floods. By the 1860s or early 1870s, a gristmill, wool carding factory, and gin were said to be operating under one roof. L. M. Mays had a carding machine in 1870; B. T. Adams and A. Verse ran mills about this time. About December 1870, the peripatetic Nat Q. Henderson started the *Round Rock Sentinel*, suspended publication in 1871 because of financial difficulties, republished at least by September 1871, but in October 1872, he moved to Georgetown, where his paper became the *Georgetown Sentinel*. Other Round Rock businesses open by 1871 were J. W. Ledbetter, insurance; D. S. Cooke blacksmith and wagon shop; A. Kuykendall, blacksmith; John Kirkpatrick's Round Rock Hotel, which advertised "lime kept on hand for sale"; H. C. Maddox, books; R. B. Masterson, saddle shop; John Kirkpatrick, restaurant; and E. M. Bolen, tombstones. By 1872, G. W. Davis, J. B. Davis and H. C. Maddox were associates in a dry goods, grocery and "receiving house" business. In 1873, Mays bought out Davis and sold half interest in the business to J. M. Black. Jacob M. and James G. Harrell had very early blacksmith shops and by the early 1870s John Peterson from Norway set up his shop on West Main Street. He married Betty Olson, also Norwegian.[21]

After the December 1847 Baptist church service was held in Freeman Smalley's log home east of what became Round Rock, church activities continued. A deed was drawn January 12, 1854, to the trustees of the Anti-Slave Holding Union Baptist Church in the trusteeship of Zara Stearns, B. F. Smalley and James K. Smalley, and in 1855 the Baptists and Presbyterians built a Union Church. The two story building had an outside stairway which led to Masonic Lodge quarters upstairs. There were two doors to the church, one for men, the other for women and children. There was no segregation of races at that time, but segregation of sexes. To call people of Round Rock to church, weddings, funerals, or Masonic meetings, a triangle hanging in a tree near the church was rung. Small private schools served the community, including Mrs. Lucy (James) Harrell's, which she taught for many years in her home. In the 1860s, land was purchased for Round Rock Academy or Round Rock Seminary. This project may have led to the Masonic Lodge's establishment in 1867 of the Greenwood Masonic Institute, still later becoming Round Rock College.[22]

As the railroad in its imperturbable way bypassed this flourishing village, another Round Rock was born south of Brushy Creek. For more than a decade, both towns functioned, both were shown on maps and in official documents as "Old Round Rock" and "New Round Rock," or the latter was simply Round Rock. The two towns, separated by a creek, had a post office apiece until December 16, 1891, when the old office officially called "Old Round Rock" was discontinued. By this time, much of Old Town had been abandoned. It was largely ignored until the mid-twentieth century, when a number of the fine old buildings were restored and put back into good use.[23] The old Smothers home was renamed St. Charles Hotel, the old residence of Dr. Cole tastefully converted into the Inn at Brushy Creek, several other homes reclaimed as residences, one of them a bakery, one an antique shop, and the old John J. Harris Tavern south of Brushy Creek, considerably enlarged in later years, was a residence. What was once the old Austin to Round Rock to Georgetown highway through Old Town was renamed Chisholm Trail for the many herds of cattle which passed that way after the Civil War. The stone home, built by a Swedish stone mason who trained four Negro slaves to assist him from 1854 to 1859, was for many years the home of Washington Anderson. Then a little distance east of Round Rock, it is now a part of the residential district. In 1973 it had been restored and was in good condition.[24]

A tent city sprang up in "New" Round Rock late in July 1876 as the I. & G. N. rails arrived. Among the early newcomers was Captain J. C. S. Morrow, son-in-law of Sam Houston. Morrow had a large store in Georgetown, decided to move all his goods to the new railroad town and immediately set his two young clerks at the task. One of them, Jesse Eugene Cooper (who a year later was to establish the *Williamson County Sun*), described the move and the new place.

I was clerking for Captain Morrow at the time and was sent with the first wagon load of goods. Captain Morrow gave me an old cap and ball Remington six-shooter like this one [Mr. Cooper displayed a 45 caliber, eight-inch barrel Remington]. I was afraid to sleep much that night, and, along in the early morning hours, two rough looking fellows circled around and kept coming closer. I sat up and laid the six shooter across my knees and when they got close enough to see it, they slunk away. When we had all the goods moved, Sam W. Henderson, who was also clerking for Captain Morrow, joined me, and we slept on pallets on the floor of the store. There was a crew of Irish section hands sent in to work on the railroad terminus, and they fought for three weeks. At night, Sam and I would pile up sacks of salt around our pallets to stop any stray bullets that might whiz past. These section hands were the only men I ever saw that would knock a man down, pick him up, and knock him down again. Later, while a residence was being built in which the Morrow family, Temple Houston, son of General Sam Houston, Sam Henderson and I were to live, Sam and I occupied a tent near the store. One night a bad man from Austin rode out, rode his horse into the tent saloon under a live oak tree about where the old broom factory now stands, and shot out the light and shot holes in the whiskey barrels. With all this lawlessness going on, Sam and I had begun to get nervous, and, one night upon approaching our tent, we heard a noise inside. I stationed Sam just outside the tent flap with a heavy club and told him to mow down the intruder whom I would go in and flush. I went inside and found our visitor to be a big yearling calf which made a quick dash to the door. I began yelling to Sam, "Don't hit him, don't hit him." The reason was the yearling had run between my legs and was carrying me outside on his back. The store building in which Captain Morrow had his business in Round Rock stood next to what now is Noble Pharmacy and burned down several years ago.[25]

By the next summer (1877), New Round Rock had the following new commercial and professional places: George M. Dilley & Co. Lumber, H. B. Sheppard General Merchandise (moved from Old Town), Drs. J. J. and W. H. Tobin Drugs; J. M. Forwood & J. F. Cottingham Lumber; August Glober Hardware; Captain J. C. S. Morrow, merchant; Henry Albert Highsmith, livery stable; M. D. Miller Exchange Bank; the *Round Rock Headlight* published by W. K. Foster (late of Georgetown), Richard C. and Elizabeth Ann Hart operating a hotel called Round Rock Hotel or Hart House; E. P. Robinson Hardware and Dealer in Hides; W. S. and P. G. Peters, bankers, and James Harvey Robertson, lawyer.[26]

About the same time the railroad arrived there, the first deed involving the Round Rock Broom factory was written July 29, 1876, and a new industry was established which operated there for many decades. The Tobins sold to Robert D. Harris in 1877, and in 1879, Washington A. Taliaferro bought half interest in the business. The factory had a long succession of owners and managers, but seemed to thrive in spite of the changeover. From 1887 until 1912, it occupied the Morrow Building. Broom corn was imported from other states for the hand-sewn brooms which won many prizes for their excellence.[27]

A second industry moved to Round Rock in 1876. William Walsh had come to Texas in the middle of the century to produce lime needed by the federal government to build forts. Walsh built a kiln near Austin, the first commercial lime operation in Texas. Then, finding a better grade of limestone near Round Rock, in 1876 he moved his business there, constructing four shaft kilns. He added an office building in 1878 of limestone, lime and sand mortar, which remained in use almost a century. Lime from his initial operation at Round Rock was used in constructing the new State Capitol building in Austin in the 1880s.[28]

In 1878, Henry Koppel had added a store, Dr. Forbes practiced medicine in Round Rock but went to Memphis to care for yellow fever victims and died there, and W. D. Herrick operated a gin. The town was said to have a population of 1500, fourteen general merchandise stores, four drug stores, four lumber yards, one baker and six hotels. John Dickson Robertson was another early merchant; H. A. Christie had the Williamson

County Bank, later owned by Bradford & Rowe. R. Tatsch, blacksmith and wheelwright, put in a business in 1880.[29]

New Town, as early inhabitants called new Round Rock, had no water service and for many years water wagons brought water to sell to the residents from Washington Anderson's spring on the north side of the creek near his stone home east of town. Life was still somewhat primitive in many ways, but the railroad had arrived, and things would never be the same again.[30] Missouri-Pacific bought the I. & G.-N. lines in 1956.

1878: GEORGETOWN TAP LINE

Completion of the new line across the southern part of Williamson County offered a tantalizing spectacle to the county seat, Georgetown, which saw the development and conveniences the railroad brought nine miles to the south. The first cultivators, the first barbed wire, the first commercial flour brought regularly into the county were arriving in Round Rock's new, bustling town. Some of Georgetown's most progressive merchants had left for the railroad town. Civic leaders at Georgetown got together, pooled their finances, and built a tap line from there to Round Rock, chartering it May 16, 1878, and completing it late that year. Officials of the Georgetown Railroad Company were Emzy Taylor, M. E. Steele, J. J. Dimmitt, Thomas P. Hughes, David Love, J. L. Rucker and Duncan G. Smith. Iron for the rails was shipped by steamer but arrival was delayed, and the town waited impatiently for the line to be finished. On December 5, a headline announced "The Railroad Here at Last." The last half mile was being laid on the Georgetown end "and if a fellow wants to go to Round Rock now he can get a ride on the construction train if he will be right clever with the conductor. It will be several days, however, before the road is open for general business." Finally that great day arrived. Local businesses closed and a crowd gathered to welcome the train. When the first "locomotive reached the limits of our corporation the whistle of the engine reverberated through our hills and valleys and glad shouts rent the air throughout the town and our immediate precinct." The signal bell added its sound to the excitement, "speaking the promise of new enterprises, cheaper transportation and a forward movement in every business." Fare to Round Rock was fifty cents, to Austin, $1.30. Rucker and Hodges shipped out the first load of cotton, and M. E. Steele sent off three more cars the first week. The town had been promised two lumber dealers, a banker, a druggist, two or three mercantile stores and buyers of cotton, wool, hides and bones when the railroad was finished. For a long while, merchants frequently closed their doors when they heard the train whistle announce the approach of the engine, the "J. J. Dimmitt." New businesses and homes did appear and demand for rent houses exceeded the supply. The *Williamson County Sun* announced that its county subscribers would receive their papers on Fridays instead of Tuesdays. The new line was mentioned in the Southwestern University catalogs as a convenience and an important communications link with all of Texas.[31]

New doctors arriving in Georgetown in the 1870s were Dr. William Parke Fleming (1874), obstetrician; Dr. William G. Pettus (1877), Dr. W. K. Grayson and Dr. W. P. Beall. Dr. B. C. Crawford was a new dentist in town. Young Sam Houston, Jr., spent about a year in Georgetown practicing medicine and married Miss Lucy Anderson of that town in 1875. Hospitals were non-existent, but in June 1886 Dr. W. P. Fleming had opened a Medical Institute on Brushy Street, the second door north of the square to give "vapor, sulphur and electric baths." Dr. A. L. Hawkins, a dentist, also had something special to offer. He was described as "that genial gentleman . . . who draws painful teeth from the mouth and melodious sounds from the zither." After receiving his medical degree in 1884, Dr. Sam Harper came to Georgetown to establish his practice. Toward the end of the century, Drs. Christopher Columbus Black, J. F. Neal and E. M. Thomas were also practicing medicine in Georgetown. By the early 1880s, Georgetown had twelve doctors and twenty-four lawyers. For the convenience of Round Rock people who wished to hear the sermon at the chapel (Southwestern University), the train was scheduled to leave Round Rock at nine in the morning and return "sometime in the evening."[32]

A few problems plagued the line. Local financing was sorely strained and in 1879 the road was sold to International and Great Northern. Until a turntable was built near the depot in Georgetown in 1879, the Tap locomotive rode forward in the conventional way from Round Rock to Georgetown, but was obliged to back up all the way on the return trip. The new turntable eliminated that. People seemed never to tire of watching the locomotive being swung around headed toward Round Rock on the marvelous new turntable, as exciting as the first train was a year earlier. Reports of mechanical troubles were accepted as a matter of course. "The train due Monday at 12 (noon) did not arrive until after dark. The engine ran short of water at Round Rock and had to wait until it could be supplied." A few weeks later, Reverend G. W. Graves and Reverend W. F. Gillespie grew weary of a several-hour wait in Round Rock for the train, finally despaired and chartered a hack to bring them to the county seat, then were passed along the way by the train. The Tap line was purchased by Missouri-Pacific in the spring of 1881.[33]

By the mid-1890s, the "Old 13" ran three times a day between Round Rock and Georgetown, with "Cripple" Jack Boylen, the friendly conductor, and J. W. Daugherty, a quiet, extremely portly fellow, the engineer. Daugherty had the reputation of being a pillar in his church and a friend to runaway boys whom he allowed to sit in his cab beside him while they were gently cajoled into returning home. A small girl remembered that after a train wreck, Daugherty tried to climb to safety out a window and got stuck. Another young lady riding the Georgetown Tap recalled the train being stopped for repairs. In the big fields between Round Rock and Georgetown, bluebonnets were blooming profusely, and ten drummers riding the train disembarked, excitedly picking the flowers. When Daugherty blew the whistle as a signal to start the train, the drummers were enjoying their new experience so much they would not hurry back. The young lady and her friends were worried that they would be left behind.[34]

The Georgetown depot several blocks west of the Square was under

Half a dozen vehicles meet the train at Georgetown depot.

the direction of station agent J. M. Daniel. The ice plant was nearby, and to the north were the abandoned stock cars once used by the Snyder Brothers for shipping cattle. The showgrounds for Gentry Brothers Dog and Pony Shows of Texas and the Mollie Bailey Show (which rode the train to town) were near the old cattle cars. People still came to the depot to meet the trains, pick up Sunday newspapers, or see who was coming to town. Frank "Spike" Snyder, George W. Foster, Hamilton "Will" Wright, and Fred and Leslie Millholin were among the station clerks and Western

Union messenger boys. Accommodations were available at the "palatial" Commercial Hotel (corner of West Seventh and Rock) run by Mrs. Wright and Ella Hemphill and at Makemson Hotel on the earlier site of Ake Hotel.[35]

1881-1882: THE NARROW GAUGE LINE: RATTAN, CUMMINGS, RUTLEDGE (POND SPRING), RUNNING BRUSHY (BRUEGGERHOFF—CEDAR PARK), WHITE STONE, WALKERTON, BLOCK HOUSE, BAGDAD-LEANDER, LIBERTY HILL, GROVER

A narrow gauge railroad was the third line built in Williamson County, chartered in April 1881 by the Austin and Northwestern Railroad Company and projected to reach Abilene from Austin. As the narrow rails crept northwest, they curved to touch several established towns in west Williamson County and created several more. Although Mike Hurley, the Irish contractor, worked two- and three-hundred man crews, the rails were not completed to Burnet until April 30, 1882.[36]

A short distance north of the county's south boundary line, the railroad designated Rattan as a flag stop, near Rattan Creek. The name referred to a prolific, hardy vine growing wild in the area, sometimes used in making baskets and furniture. "Children ate the black berries from the vine and got into trouble because the berries stained their teeth." For two years, in 1887 and 1888, Rattan had a U. S. post office, but the mail was discontinued there after December 7, 1888, and left at Duval in Travis County. The flag stop never developed commercially, but did receive some notice a few years after the railroad was built when the bridge over Rattan Creek collapsed as the train went over it. The engineer had sufficient warning of trouble to jump clear of the train before it tumbled down, but broke his neck in the jump. The accident was reported in a small Merrelltown newspaper of the time. In 1973, the site of Rattan was not accessible by automobile.[37]

Cummings, a flag stop almost due west of Rattan about two miles, had a section house, but no other known development.[38]

A very early community variously called Pond Spring, Pond Springs and Rutledge, for a spring which formed a pond near the original village or for the Rutledge family who lived there, was bypassed by the railroad, which ran a mile or more to the north. There a new village, "new" Rutledge, sprang up. The Rutledge family had a home near the railroad.

Added were a section house where railroad crewmen lived, a blacksmith shop, a cedar yard, a stone quarry, a general store, and a post office.[39]

Next the Austin and Northwestern turned directly toward the early town of Running Brushy, on the Creek bearing the same name. This was the home of George Washington Cluck and his wife, Harriet Standefer Cluck, who also had the Running Brushy post office. Railroad officials insisted that Running Brushy be changed to Brueggerhoff, and for about five years, the post office was called Brueggerhoff. Emmett Cluck, eldest son of the G. W. Clucks, later suggested the name Cedar Park, which was adopted by the post office and the community after 1887.[40]

From Cedar Park the narrow gauge headed north-northwest, running parallel to present Highway 183. The railroad went through White Stone, so named because of the cluster of limestone quarries nearby. Going north, it created Walkerton station on the ranch of Judge Alexander Stuart Walker, where many of the cattle from Walker's ranch were loaded for shipment. Members of the Walker family, whose home was about half a mile from Walkerton, went there to catch the train to Austin, or young Stuart Walker rode the train to school in Leander for five cents a day the round trip. The rails north of Walkerton went just to the west of old Block House Fort, the site of the Walker family home.[41]

The flourishing old town of Bagdad, which eagerly awaited the coming of the railroad for several years, was fated to be disappointed, for the tracks were laid about a mile east of Bagdad. Long before, Tom Hornsby had put up a log cabin on Bagdad Prairie, had left, and it was in disrepair when Charles Babcock and his family came there on Christmas Day, 1851. One other early cabin stood in the area—that of Harmon Smilser and his two sons-in-law and families. The Smilsers, Babcock noted, had a puncheon floor, very unusual in those times when a dirt floor was standard. The community was named by Thomas Huddleston for his old home in Bagdad, Tennessee. Others coming there in the early 1850s were James Williamson, George Craven, Robert Marley, Eli and Andrew Hamilton, John Faubion, John F. Heinatz, Colonel C. C. Mason, William N. Carothers, John Schooley, E. A. Walker, W. R. Walker and Tom Cashion. Even earlier comers nearby were James and Nicholas Branch, Greenleaf Fisk, M. J. Wells and Henderson Upchurch.[42]

Charles Babcock surveyed the Bagdad townsite in 1854, and soon after, John H. Shaffer of Georgetown put up a box house, where coffee, sugar, tobacco, snuff and shoes were sold by James B. Knight. Soon John F. Heinatz opened his store, blacksmith shop, and obtained a post office for the village. The town grew rapidly and by the time the narrow gauge railroad was bypassing it, Bagdad had a long list of businesses: the Heinatz, John D. Speegle, John Faubion, Sr., C. C. Mason stores; J. A. Bauchman and Heinatz blacksmith shops; Tom S. Evans store and hotel; Thornberry livery; Dr. A. H. Graham drug store; Dr. T. H. Lauck and Dr. M. Jennings drug store; Colonel S. Hamilton's "city-style" meat market; two wood shops; August Nystrom's boot and shoe shop; Frederick Huster's* marble yard; two schools, one of them in the building erected by the local Masonic Lodge; a church; a new photographer in town, and a stagecoach stop. Two gins operated in the area, one of them including a flour mill, and a local literary society was sponsoring a circulating library. Several silver and lead mines, reputed to have been previously operated about three miles southwest of Bagdad in what was known as "Bloody Hollow," were reactivated, but the project was dropped after considerable fanfare when the mines proved unproductive. At one holiday party in the J. D. Mason home, several young men lost gloves, bridles, spurs and saddle bags, after which two men were arrested and some of the articles were recovered. As the Frontier Telephone Company in 1880 was putting up wire for telephone service to Bagdad, the new convenience was not universally appreciated, for a gentleman chopped down a telephone pole and used it to splice the wheel of his hack.[43]

A lively, prosperous town, Bagdad suddenly had to adjust to the railroad a mile away. By the summer of 1882, some of the Bagdad merchants moved to the new town springing up along the railroad, where the railway company sold lots on July 17, 1882. At the company's request, the new town was named Leander, for Leander "Catfish" Brown, a company official. Tom S. Evans quickly moved his home to Leander, and ran it as a hotel. John Heinatz and John Speegle moved their stores there; Magill and Evans, Emmett and Coon, and Wells and Mason put up new stores. Jesse Humble and L. Chapman erected a large new store and started the first bank in town. The Methodist Church was moved from Bagdad, and the Presbyterians erected their church at Leander. Greenleaf Fisk Cashion was one of the early railroad agents, and among the professional men were lawyers A. S. Walker and John W. Parks, and physician Dr. Sam Woolsey. Schools continued to be operated for some years both in Bagdad and Leander, but the Masonic Lodge shifted to the newly-created place. With-

---

* Huster, a talented stone mason-architect-artist, was brought from Germany by John F. Heinatz to build his residence and store, both still standing in 1973 and in excellent condition. The old stagecoach stand across the road east of the Heinatz home also remains. These three buildings are the remnants of what once was Bagdad.

Leander mill and gin were early installations in the new railroad town.

in two decades, except for some residences, Bagdad had become a ghost town.[44]

The Austin and Northwestern extended its tracks on across the Wig Jennings place on the South San Gabriel, where the train would make a station stop to fill up with water. Little Annie Jennings, born June 15, 1877, remembered that her grandfather was not happy about the rails cutting his farm in half.

> He objected, but the railroad gave him five hundred dollars and came on anyway. Oh, they had tents all up and down the creek where the hands worked—about forty-five men. They lived in the tents winter and summer. Tents were put down under a hill where they got a little protection from the weather. I used to love to stand on the hill and watch them work. They built the dump for the tracks with mules and scrapers; it was a sight to watch. . . . And then that first train—I remember when it came through and it was a sight to see. Oh, we thought it was something grand![45]

Liberty Hill was another town slightly bypassed by the railroad, but it was accustomed to moving. Twice before the town had shifted slightly to the east as a new post office, store, or stage coach stop, often in one building, was relocated. Taylor Smith and his family bought the land where Liberty Hill developed from an Englishman, Henry Field, who returned to England before 1850. A staunch anti-secessionist, Smith often said "Liberty will rule my place." John T. and Amelia Bryson came by wagon train in 1852 and Reverend William Oliver Spencer in 1853, both settling near the Smiths and erecting log cabins. Texas' U. S. Senator Thomas Jefferson Rusk, chairman of the Senate Post Office committee, stopped at the Spencer home while touring Texas to find where post offices were needed. After Rusk spent the night and had a meal with his host, he promised that a post office would be assigned to the place. Asked for a suitable name for the office, Spencer, thinking of the free and independent character of the people, said, "Call it Liberty Hill, General."* Thornton P. Poole of South Carolina came with about forty-eight settlers and fifty-two

Log post office of Liberty Hill was later moved to Thornton P. Poole farm nearby, not far from the Poole stone milk house, built over a free flowing spring.

slaves by wagon train late in 1854 to settle at Liberty Hill. About the same time, Adam C. and Henry Miller established a shop there to make wagons and furniture. Liberty Hill had a stagecoach stop, plus another at the Bryson home; a one-room store built in 1859 by George W. Barnes; schools; churches; Cox's hotel; D. V. Grant's and S. P. Stubblefield's stores established in 1870; John A. Munro's blacksmith business from 1871 until 1883; Landrum "Landy" Poole's livery stable; W. R. Bratton's dry goods store; J. P. Barrington, carpenter; the *Liberty Hill Courant* established by Mr. Denman in 1878; the Bryson Mill; Dr. William Parke Fleming who practiced medicine from 1871 until 1874.[46]

The coming of the railroad seems not to have disrupted the town very much. While that section of construction was underway, Mike Hurley, the foreman, boarded at Reverend W. O. Spencer's home, which had for many years also served the community as an Inn. Hurley fell in love with Miss Lizzie Spencer, married her in a Baptist ceremony read by Reverend John Arbuckle, then took his bride to Austin where they repeated their vows with a Catholic priest.[47]

Grover, another station stop, was located in the county but did not develop into a permanent settlement. The tracks then crossed the boundary into Burnet County and the first train ran from Austin to Burnet on April 30, 1882. The locomotive used cord wood for fuel, pulled one passenger

* Rusk was a general in the Texas Revolution.

coach and one baggage coach, making one round trip each day. When it made its first run, the train was filled with residents of the little communities it passed through. Those who did not ride stood alongside the railway to watch the train pass. It was a gala occasion.[48]

While the Austin and Northwestern line was being built, a dramatic event occurred which was soon to affect the new line. The State Capitol in Austin caught fire and burned to the ground on November 9, 1881. When new plans for another Capitol were accepted, they called for a limestone structure, the materials to be quarried southwest of Austin, but the stone proved unsatisfactory to the commission in charge of the job. The con-

Lone Star, the narrow gauge railroad engine, which pulled flat car loads of granite slabs across the county to build the State Capitol.

tractor proposed using granite from Indiana, but the commission insisted on stone from Texas. George W. Lacy and W. H. Westfall offered granite from Granite Mountain near Marble Falls free of charge to the State of Texas. When the contractor planned to use convict labor as stone cutters, a labor union of granite cutters protested, and sixty-two specialists from England, Scotland and Ireland were imported for the work. The State, as soon as an agreement for the granite was reached July 21, 1885, began building a railroad spur from Burnet the sixteen miles to Granite Mountain, finishing it December 1, 1885. The "Lone Star Engine" of the narrow gauge line pulled 15,700 flat carloads of granite from the quarry, through Grover, Liberty Hill, Leander, Walkerton, White Stone, Brueggerhoff (Cedar Park), Rutledge, Cummings and Rattan on its way to Capitol Hill. The enormously heavy loads of huge boulders impressed everyone who saw them pass, the "flatcars rocking as precariously as a little ship struck amidship by a sudden gale." Along any mile up or down the line, a boulder could be found which had skidded off, or had turned over a car and caused derailment. Occasionally an entire train went into the ditch. But the hauling job secured a railroad which had faltered financially, and the narrow gauge line continued to serve a rugged, remote area, otherwise difficult to travel.[49]

After changing hands several times, the narrow gauge line was converted to standard gauge in 1891 and 1892 at a cost of $1,300,000. Another tremendous amount of granite was hauled over the line to Galveston after the 1900 hurricane to be used in the construction of the granite seawall. The line was a part of the Southern Pacific network in 1973.[50]

1882: BARTLETT, GRANGER, CIRCLEVILLE, TAYLOR

In 1882 the Jay Gould interests, which by now encompassed Missouri Pacific, International and Great Northern and Missouri-Kansas and Texas, extended its line south from Fort Worth, "breeding towns at the end of each ten-mile section, and selling lots like hotcakes." In Williamson County the line created Bartlett; bypassed the rural village of Macedonia and in its place started Pollack, soon called Granger; went through Circleville and intersected the east-west line at Taylor, where the extension stopped until 1887. At the latter date it pushed on to Boggy Tank near Fayetteville, adding another town to the county's roster—Coupland. The flag stations, Tidwell between Bartlett and Granger, and Evans between Circleville and Taylor, were also established in 1882.[51]

Bartlett embraces two counties, Bell and Williamson. Its main street through the business section runs east and west, and the center of the street is a part of Williamson's north boundary line. Among the earliest settlers in that vicinity were Jacob Jackson and family (1851) and A. J. Durant and family and slaves (1853), both men involved in the cattle business. Arriving in the 1870s were John T. and Mary Bell Bartlett and his brother, Richard Henry Bartlett, J. E. Pietzsch and Tom McKnight. When the Missouri-Kansas & Texas Company began surveying for a railroad right-of-way, John T. Bartlett and J. E. Pietzsch donated land for a townsite, named for Bartlett, and a sale of lots began late in 1881. John Bartlett and J. P. Clark put in a small grocery store and A. Moss of Holland moved there with a general store before the rails reached town. Bartlett enlarged his store to include general merchandise soon afterwards. Other early businesses were Frank and Jack Felton's hotel, W. J. Stevens' lumber yard, E. G. Armstrong's livery stable, Hardeman Hotel, Marquadt's blacksmith shop, Mrs. Whitely's millinery and J. R. Kuler's store and cabinet shop. Dr. Tom C. Denson and Dr. Jess Denson practiced medicine in the area. The railroad reached the burgeoning village by the summer of 1882 and on October 5, 1882, a post office was approved with Thomas McKnight as postmaster. In 1886, M. L. Hair established a newspaper in town, first known as the *Bartlett Headlight,* the forerunner of the long-lived *Bartlett Tribune.* The following year, John T. Bartlett established a bank, the town built a water works and, in 1890, Bartlett was incorporated.[52]

Bartlett's earliest business district was destroyed by fire. Present buildings post-date 1900 and face the wide, brick-paved street.

From the start, the local newspaper was a staunch booster of the town. "The ring of the hammer and the buzz of the saw can now be heard in Bartlett." The local school was adding a new music room; Frank Felton's

Massive Bartlett Methodist Church is a landmark in town.

gin had processed twenty-six bales of cotton by late August, papers in 1886 reported. During the previous year, 90,000 pounds of wool valued at $18,000 were shipped out, as well as $139,000 worth of other exports and a carload of corn sent to drouth sufferers in Eastland County. Camp meetings were held on Donahoe Creek and the town had a brass band by 1887. Dr. M. O. Wright moved to town in 1887, but told newsmen that a town the size of Bartlett should have two doctors.[53]

Tidwell, a flag stop south of Bartlett, was named for the Tidwell family living nearby.

The fertile farm land attracted pioneers to the Granger area three decades before the town was established. Isaac Garner and his wife Mary and four children were there for the 1850 census; also coming in the 1850s were J. C. and Rhoda Evans Posey, who settled a mile from Granger-to-be at Posey Crossing, and W. C. Beard, who made his home a short distance below Granger. Dr. T. C. and Elizabeth Davis Denson came from Alabama in 1854 with their family, settling on Willis Creek; Jesse and Susan J. Brookshire in 1859. H. C. Ederington moved in 1867 to his place to raise horses and mules and was known for his large wheat crops. John Scott was in the cattle business by 1873; A. W. Storrs came in 1882, building a gin and mill and a general store later on in Granger. Others coming early were the Stanton, Dyches, Guthrie, Rudasill, Lindsey, Pope, Martin,

Delenaugh, Wilson, McLaughlin, McHorse, Tegge, Knauth and Molden-hour families and Colonel Joe Keliehor, whose ranching interests were west of Granger. An early tavern (1856) called Dare Buzzard and the village of Macedonia developed before railroads had appeared in the county. Macedonia had churches, a school, a Masonic Lodge, a gin and a cooperative store called the Grange.[54]

As the Katy railroad finished its lines where Granger now is, Captain A. S. Fisher and W. C. Belcher laid out some of their land for a town along the railroad "around the station of Granger" and reported early in 1884 that they had sold a number of lots. They established a lumber yard and gave the Baptist Church a lot. J. B. Wright, unofficial mayor, sold the lots for Fisher, reporting "Granger is sure to be a town." Although an early map shows the site to be Pollack, no record that the place was actually called by that name has been found. The log Grange hall and lodge was moved from Macedonia to the railroad and the place thereafter called Granger. C. M. Jones became the first Katy agent; Avent & Simmons had

Granger depot agent C. M. Jones and family in 1909.

the first general store; J. W. Wayman the second, moving from Circleville in 1884, and the Grange store came in soon afterwards. W. C. Reinhardt boarded the men who built the depot and ran a kind of hotel in his home, as well as the first butcher shop. He and station agent Jones ran the first barber shop. John Strayhorn and C. R. Faubion put in a new grocery in 1886. W. H. Camp was a druggist and later the first mayor

Handsome lion ornament adorns early building on Davilla Street, Granger's all-brick paved street.

when the town was incorporated in 1891; C. C. Echols was the blacksmith; Mrs. Beard had a hotel, and Mark Jones built the first bank in 1894. Apparently the first newspaper in the town was the *Granger Banner*, which was published in 1887. S. D. Davis opened the first hardware store. Drs. Denson and Danforth and J. W. Posey, an attorney, were among the first professional men practicing there.[55]

The fertile farm land of the Granger community was for many years tied up in litigation, unless those owning duplicate land certificates saw fit to buy up the claims. The land war over these claims, violent at times, was finally settled in the courts, Captain A. S. Fisher representing numerous clients in suits. By the 1880s and especially after 1890, the good land attracted many European immigrants, particularly Czechoslovakian and German, who became industrious, thrifty farmer-citizens. Early in 1885, the *Williamson County Sun* reported that "Granger, less than a year old, has shipped six hundred bales of cotton to date."[56]

The Katy went directly south from Granger to Circleville, where a depot was erected to serve the cattle and farming interests of that early town on the San Gabriel. In the 1850s, Circleville had the tin and pewter shops of Joseph and James Eubank, DeWitt Clinton Hayslip's blacksmith-wheelwright shop, a spinning factory, and during the Civil War a cotton card factory run by John White and Joseph Eubank, Jr. The first post office was in charge of James Eubank, opened March 13, 1857. Edward J. Brown and Company had a store, with S. D. Brown and W. D. Letting, associates, buying wool, cotton, hides and other produce in 1867. Ellis Gardner & Hamilton opened a store in 1870 and Gardner was granted a liquor license by the County Court. J. W. Wayman bought Seneca "Sim"

Brown's store in 1872, continuing to operate it until he moved to the new town of Granger in 1882. James A. Simons ran a store for Charles P. Vance beginning in 1873, moving it in October 1876 to the new town of Taylorsville. D. Hartman established a second blacksmith shop in Circleville in 1878. The community also had an early mill, gin, molasses mill and one of the earliest schools and churches in the county. David H. McFadin, who lived just east of Circleville since 1846, was in the cattle business, operated a mill and gin. His eldest son, John N. McFadin, in the summer of 1878 completed his two story stone home "on the most prominent peak near town," still in fine condition in 1973.[57] Harvey T. Stearns freighted for a number of years, traveling with ox team and wagon to the Gulf coast and back to Georgetown, Salado, or Austin and Circleville. He carried a load of surplus items from the area to the coast and returned with other produce or articles in demand, taking as much as three months for a trip.[58]

When the Circleville depot was completed, Edward Vernon Stearns served as the first agent. The stores moving to Taylorsville and Granger about this time were quickly replaced by others, Hiram Gilliam building one a short distance west of the depot, where the Circleville store has remained until 1973. Earlier stores were loacted near the James Eubank home adjacent to where the depot was later built. Dr. J. A. Denson practiced medicine in the Circleville area; Dr. John Threadgill came there in 1875, moved to Taylorsville the next year; other Circleville doctors were Dr. Jones, Dr. Rucker and Dr. R. H. Towles. In 1887 Taylor built a pump station at Circleville and obtained water from the San Gabriel until a Taylor city artesian well was dug some years later.[59]

Train wrecks all over Texas were so common during this period, one reporter dubbed a line the "Angel Maker." His description resulted in the loss of his annual railroad pass.[60] Circleville had its share of wrecks, for a curve which proved difficult to negotiate was built on the Katy near the San Gabriel. Convict labor was used to repair the lines and eventually the dangerous curve was corrected, but not before the one carload of cattle was overturned and many of the cattle killed. The sight and sounds of the injured and dead cattle left a lasting impression on Auburn Stearns, who lived there and was four years old when the railroad was built through Circleville.[61]

As the Katy lines moved southward from Circleville, flag station Evans was established. At Taylor the last spike was driven May 1, 1882, joining it with the I. & G. N. line already there. The new Katy line stopped at that point.[62]

Taylorsville, already booming since its creation in 1876, took on new life with the added shipping facilities. Within a decade, the place had many new professional men, including Dr. S. B. Williams and Dr. F. T. Cook; attorney John W. Parker. A series of water systems beginning with a local tank supplied by springs in the Murphy and Mendel pastures (1882-1883) were installed by George W. Burkett and Dan Murphy, Sr., and expanded in 1887 to include a pipe to the San Gabriel River for more ample reservoirs. The brick Murphy Hotel was built in 1882. In April 1881 Taylorsville became the feeding station between San Antonio and Palestine. Livestock was unloaded, rested and fed there, then reloaded for shipment. The first banks were private, Miller Brothers and Robertson operating them for a short time. The First National Bank, founded in 1883, was headed by railroad tycoon John R. Hoxie, president; C. H. Booth, J. L. Woodward, Howard Bland, William Keliehor, J. P. Sturgis and C. H. Welch were directors. The Taylor National Bank was founded in 1888, Joseph Spidell, president; C. H. Booth, Curran Mendel, J. M. Kuykendall, J. E. Tucker and William Keliehor, directors. The Taylor Savings and Loan Association founded in 1885 had as directors James Griffith, John Threadgill, R. E. Sherrill, A. E. Hill, Dan'l. Moody, A. H. Smith, John Lloyd, J. L. Root, L. H. Goldstein, John W. Parker, J. J. Thames, R. H. Talley, C. T. M. Orr, James A. Simons, D. R. Meade, C. R. Sherrill, Samuel Lewis, F. S. Ulmer, M. A. Belcher and J. H. Bradley. The first mayor of Taylor was Dan'l. Moody, as he always wrote his name, the father of Governor Dan Moody. The first dentist in town was Dr. C. R. Payne who came in 1887, followed soon after by another dentist, Dr. C. T. Averitt, who became known in Central Texas for Dr. Averitt's Liniment which he originated. Taylor's City National Bank was created February 10, 1900, with Dr. R. H. Eanes, president, and John H. Griffith, C. C. Hooper, S. A. Easley, J. J. Thames, C. A. Nelson, Dr. Eanes, William Pfluger, H. T. Kimbro and J. R. Hargis, Board of Directors. Robert D. Penn signed the Articles of Association at the founding, along with the directors.[63]

1887: COUPLAND

On April 26, 1886, the Bastrop and Taylor Railway Company chartered a line to extend from Taylor to Boggy Creek in south Texas, near Fayetteville. Construction began soon afterwards and the line was in use in 1887. Coupland that year became another railroad real estate venture. R. C. McLaren established his ranch north of what became Coupland about 1878. Other land along Brushy Creek was owned by Morgan Hamilton, who willed it to his deceased sister's (Karen Hamilton Coupland) five children. One of the children was Major Theodore Van Buren Coupland, Civil War officer of New Orleans, who decided to come to the county when the railroad started building near his property. Coupland joined with C. H. Welch and Henry Dickson of Taylor to plot out "Coupland City" in thirty-six blocks west of the railroad and eighteen blocks east of it, and held an auction of lots on Thursday, May 12, 1887. The original map shows also a public square, but that was never developed.[64]

John Goetz, Sr., purchased the first lot in the new town and built the first store by hauling lumber from Bastrop in an ox-drawn wagon. On December 28, 1889, he became the town's first postmaster, the post office being situated in his store. The fine farm country along Brushy Creek was attracting numerous German and Swiss settlers, who came in substantial numbers for a decade or more, and quite a busy village developed between 1890 and 1910.

Church services in German were held in the school by 1894. In 1906 a separate church building was erected from which the present St. Peter's United Church of Christ is descended. German and English services were first held during World War I. Longtime ministers were G. P. Krebs and Robert Moore. Among early school teachers were Alvin Speckles, Ernest Wolf, a Mr. Wilson and Clara Wilson. Doctors Hudson, Scharnberg and Feaster practiced there prior to 1913.

Early businesses, in addition to John Goetz, Sr.'s store, included blacksmith shops of Adolph Spiegelhauer, Max Zieger, and Adolph Kneip. The latter's shop was located at a ninety degree turn at the bottom of a hill on the highway, and was occasionally invaded by an automobile traveling too fast to negotiate the sharp turn. Other businesses included Hugo Franze, a livery stable; John Albers and the Pfluger gins; two lumber yards; several saloons; Coupland Drug Store in which Alfred Albers and Clarence White were stockholders and pharmacists, with Link Kimmons and Lee Copeland [sic], other stockholders; J. O. Ford, grocery; John Speckles, hardware and furniture; Herman Helmuth and Von Rosenberg general store; Albert Speckles, carpenter; Herman Hunziker, brick mason; Mrs. Mattie Boeneman Wernli, seamstress. The community was not incorporated, but had a small jail and bought a small fire truck which was kept in a private garage. The town developed a city water works and, in recent years, a rural water system. The Ging, Polzin, Wittliff, Boeneman, Wernli, Gaston, Preuss, Lewis and Schwarz-Buehler families were other early families in the new town.

Coupland's uniformed band performed at local social functions held at

St. Peter's United Church of Christ at Coupland was erected in 1906.

lodge halls or "Pink Hall," where barbecues, dances and other entertainments were given. From about 1918 until well into the 1920s, a Chautauqua came to town annually, performing under a big tent. Brushy Creek furnished good swimming holes and picnic grounds for the younger people. The rich cotton farms of the area drew a large Negro population, who built their own Baptist Church, and whose Saturday trip to town included being served tempting meals along the walks of Main Street by their ladies, who wore stiffly starched aprons as they performed their hostess duties.[65]

1890: GEORGETOWN AND GRANGER
LINE CREATES WEIR

The Georgetown and Granger Railroad Company chartered a link line on December 13, 1890, and put down fifteen and a half miles of track

between the two towns in 1892 and 1893. Promoted by Captain Emzy
Taylor of Georgetown, the link was to connect with other lines, including
the Trinity Cameron and Western, and to lines through Cameron into east
Texas. Financial difficulties beset the projects, as reflected in many delays
and finally in the suicide of Captain Taylor on June 29, 1895. The Missouri-Kansas & Texas system had wanted a line into Austin, purchased the
Georgetown-Granger track, chartered the Granger-Georgetown-Austin and
San Antonio Railway Company on December 5, 1902, and completed the
line from Granger to Austin in June 1904. Young Georgetown boys
George D. Whittle and others remembered working on the line east of
town as waterboys and mule skinners for the railroad crew.[66]

Once again an established community was bypassed and a new one
formed with the arrival of the railroad. Towns Mill-Townsville on the San
Gabriel River east of Georgetown was one of the county's earliest landmarks when settlers filtered in. Expeditions crossed the Gabriel at this
point, then known as the Double File Trail Crossing, including the Santa
Fe Expedition, and a Texas Ranger troop encamped at the crossing in
1846. Elias A. Queen and Calvin Weir settled there in the 1850s. When
James "Jim" Francis Towns went there in 1870 at the age of twenty,
he built a flour mill on the east bank of the river. Excelsior Mill became
one of the better known and busiest mills in the county. He and his
brother, Robert W. Towns, and their sons were gifted mechanics and engineers, building and operating a number of mills, gins, and other businesses
in the county and in Salado. Towns Mill was also called Prairie Springs
and Buffalo Springs for the buffalo which watered there when the first
settlers came. A seven-foot alligator was killed there about 1870, a three-
foot one in 1883. Others early in that neighborhood were the Cook, Mann,
Hausenfluck, King, Beaver, Burris, Dill, Anderson, Morris, Nowlin,
Wheeler, Walker, Woods, John Berry, J .W. Peace, H. Breneke, and John
Brooks families.[67]

Using the name Townsville, the community was assigned a post office
on May 6, 1895, with James F. Towns as postmaster. The railroad being
developed a short way to the northwest soon caused a transfer. The post
office was shifted, the name changed to Weir for pioneer Calvin Weir,
and the railroad town had its start. The Towns Mill-gin-blacksmith
shop remained at its old location, but the village store moved to Weir and
was run by Lucy Weir, who became postmistress in 1903. The Foster,
Brady, Emerson, Boyd, Taylor and T. A. Bergstrom families were among
the first to come there. In short order the place had four mercantile stores,
groceries, drug stores, a bank, blacksmith shop, millinery, barber shop,

Downtown Weir in the early 1900s.

livery stable, grain and seed houses, a hotel, theatre, gin, city water works, several churches, a large school, two telephone offices. Fresh bakery goods were brought in every morning by train from Granger.[68]

After Katy railroad officials saw the Towns Mill pond formed on the San Gabriel by the mill dam, they decided to develop the area into a resort. Leasing thirty acres from J. W. Gray, the company built a dance pavilion and advertised a model park for picnics, boating, fishing and camping, and the finest scenery anywhere on the railroad between St. Louis and Georgetown. S. K. Brown, a retired sea captain who owned adjacent land, built a boat concession with a dozen docks and boats for pleasure riding or excursions. Jeff Ake, a specialist in frying fish, ran a fishing camp in the vicinity. For about ten years, special excursion rates were offered from Galveston, Houston, Dallas, Fort Worth and St. Louis for vacationers to enjoy the "crystal waters of this enchanting lake." After a 1913 flood heavily damaged the facilities, the railroad ceased to promote it and visitors from long distances away quit coming. Towns Lake continued to be popular with local citizens as a camping-fishing spot throughout the twentieth century. Katy Lake railroad bridge was so damaged by the 1913 flood, a locomotive fell into the river as it attempted to cross. No one was killed when the bridge gave way, but traffic was interrupted for some time.[69]

1909: THE FOUR GOSPELS LINE: BARTLETT, SCHWERTNER, JARRELL, FLORENCE

The last and most colorful railroad built in Williamson County was the Bartlett Western. Chartered as Bartlett-Florence Railway Company on September 15, 1909, by non-county residents who believed the enormous cotton traffic of the county would make it pay, the line changed hands numerous times. The founders hoped to sell to another existing line in the county. With W. J. McDaniel as president and general manager, they built 11.2 miles from Bartlett west, turning the prosperous town of Corn Hill into a ghost town when they chose an alternate route, and producing the county's youngest town, Jarrell. This section of the railroad depleted the company's finances, and no more lines were laid for about a year.[70]

The first depot west of Bartlett was at Schwertner, a community settled in 1877 by Bernard Schwertner and his three sons, Frank, Edward and Adolf (also written Adolph). These immigrants from Austria farmed a large tract between Corn Hill and Bartlett. The town of Schwertner was established in 1903 when Adolf Schwertner erected a gin there. In 1909, on hearing of the projected railroad, he donated land for a townsite where a depot, general store, dry goods store, hardware, bank, meat market, blacksmith shops, and post office were quickly built. Gustav A. Matejowsky was the first postmaster, opening the office August 30, 1912. As the town grew, a doctor settled there; a saloon, lumber yard, and boarding house were added. The community had a school and churches nearby, boasted a brass band, and a second gin was built by Frank Schwertner near Donahoe Creek.[71]

Between Schwertner and the future town of Jarrell, a flag stop was located near the rural school called Primrose and the Fred White place. From that station stop, the train could have headed to Corn Hill. Instead, it would travel a mile or more to the north.

Corn Hill, so-named by Judge John E. King in 1855 when his home, the stagecoach stop, was designated as a post office, had been on the regular stage line since 1852. Travelers from south Texas or Austin passed it on their way to Waco or Dallas. In 1869 Major T. H. Lea built a store nearby, stocking it with "everything a farmer needed." The community already had a doctor, George Rumsey who was also a Methodist minister and politician, and who had been there since 1851. Other early-day enterprises were the Charlie Morell and Charlie Hogan store, D. W. Proctor mercantile store in 1877, R. W. Laws blacksmith, Terry livery, Dr. S. H. Weatherford drugs, Jim H. Biles and William Thomas Foster hardware, the millinery shops of May Terry, Sally Dean and Betty McCarty; the *Corn Hill Weekly Gazette*, a miniature newspaper published by M. L. Hair in 1880, and the *Corn Hill Clipper* published in 1886; A. P. Johnson and J. W. Shaver, merchants in 1883; a gin operated by Woodward and Parker about 1871, turning out three bales a day; and D. W.

Proctor, who built a large steam gin in 1878. As many as five doctors practiced at Corn Hill at one time. The medical men included Dr. George Rumsey, Dr. W. K. Grayson (1877), Dr. J. T. Huggins (1883), Dr. S. H. Weatherford who sold his practice to Dr. John Galt in 1888, Dr. McKean, Dr. Masterson, Dr. Silas McCarty, Dr. Charlie C. Foster, Dr. J. E. Wilkerson, and Dr. Armstrong. W. B. Barlow set up a blacksmith shop there and R. W. Laws sold his to R. C. Brown in 1891. C. J. Jackson and William W. Morris opened their mercantile store in 1889. About the same time, John D. Black opened a hotel in the only building of Corn Hill still standing in 1973. Built as a home soon after 1872 by John Wesley Shaver, the lumber was brought by ox teams from Grimes county. Shaver sold his home to the Black family, who combined it into their residence and the Black Hotel—the stagecoach stop and center of much social and commercial activity at Corn Hill. The Marrs and Foster families of the area raised fine horses, among them Foster's well-known race horse of the time, "Billy J," winner of many competitions and prizes at fairs. The town organized a saddle club, had several active churches, a school including Corn Hill College, a Masonic Lodge, the Odd Fellows, a school debating society and a uniformed brass band. Businesses in Corn Hill shortly before the railroad built north of it were the Drum Brothers, Johnson Smith; Alex Smith and J. E. Condra, druggists; Virgil Alonzo Harvill, Fred Harrison and J. S. Hays, ginners; J. C. Foster, cotton buyer; William H. Buchanan and James Thomas Haralson, general stores; Thomas B. Thoma, affectionately called "Old Thoma" by his neighbors, who ran a store with the post office in the back from 1906 until 1912. Other residents of the area were J. W. Rudasill, Thomas N. Dunn, Henderson Brooks, T. N. Cammach, R. Frank, V. J. Beck, S. F. Perry, J. A. Raney, J. M. Bristol, John M. Whitton, W. J. Smith, N. R. Land, A. McDonald, J. J. Richardson, J. E. Richardson, D. B. F. Belk, A. B. Bowen, Josef Mikulencak, Thom Mrazek, James Marrs, Jr, Aaron Seymour, B. H. Young, Charlie Smith, William Henry Russell, R. E. Toal, J. F. Ponder, Simon Hager, A. L. Frymire, R. H. O'Neal, R. W. Cowart, J. T. Yeargan, T. A. Grumbles, A. K. Ramsey, F. J. Burns, Henry Barber, I. M. Bridges, Polk Woodward, B. F. Griffin, E. N. Morgan, W. H. Carlisle, J. H. Monger, Jeff Strickland, Jeff Harper, J. W. Roberson, J. G. Roe, C. J. Jackson, J. Owen, John Sybert, J. R. Beardan, J. W. Cook, W. M. Wells, A. Stevenson, Captain J. A. Rumsey, Barnet Young, D. B. Traylor, "Doc" Davis, Jeff Burns, A. M. McRea, Otto Miller, Frank Yearwood, Charlie Farmer, Felix Schwertner, Sr., Lige Condra, N. P. Watkins, Julius Leschber, W. D. Lewis; the Conlee, Barlow, Craft, Vandever, Blackman, Ilse,

Neely, Robertson and Tindel families, and many relations of those named. Corn Hill's population was about five hundred in 1910.[72]

Julia Elizabeth Ross Jones, wife of Negro farmer Grant Jones of Corn Hill, was the cook at Black Hotel, for many years preparing the meals and ringing a bell in the yard to announce them. The six children of Grant and Julia Jones grew up without a school to attend at Corn Hill, so J. Conrad "Con" Foster, a teacher in the white school, came to the Jones home three nights a week to teach the children to read and write and do arithmetic. "He taught us to add and subtract by lining the grains from an ear of corn in two rows on the table. We learned our letters by taking a plain sheet of paper, rubbing it with hog lard and wiping it off to make it transparent. Then he placed the paper over letters and we traced them to learn our alphabet." Their father, Grant Jones, learned his letters and to read from handling sacks of produce marked "flour, sugar" and so on. About 1912 Claude Jones, eldest of the boys and still a youngster, built the first wireless set in his community, following instructions in *Popular Mechanics* magazine. R. S. Harvill, son of an early ginner, and a friend walked over to see Jones' set. Claude Jones became a radio and television repairman in Jarrell.[73]

Former Governor Preston Smith, who served two terms as governor of Texas from 1969 to 1973, was born near Corn Hill, the son of Mr. and Mrs. Charlie Smith, who lived on a farm about two miles south of Corn Hill. Governor Smith attended school at Mount Prospect, a rural school between Corn Hill and Georgetown. Young Preston was a member of a large family and at times lived with an aunt and uncle. Flower Smith, one of his uncles, lived on Chandler Branch, also in Williamson County.[74] The family moved away from the county when Governor Smith was still a boy.

A large number of German and Czechoslovakian immigrants settled on available farmland in the vicinity of Corn Hill, creating communities including Walburg and Theon.

The demise of Corn Hill meant the birth of Jarrell. Publisher R. E. Downey disclaims a story "that promoters demanded $10,000 bonus of Corn Hill" to bring the railroad through there. Real estate promoters O. D. Jarrell of Temple and E. C. Haeber of Bartlett purchased land along the railroad's proposed right-of-way, platted a town to be named Jarrell for the Temple man, and held a sale of lots in December 1909. The new townsite was at the intersection of the old stagecoach road and the new railroad. Almost immediately after the sale, a saloon and two small stores were built at Jarrell but business went into something of a coma when the railway appeared bogged down in financial problems. The company went into the hands of receivers. J. W. Jackson of Bartlett and others, including stockholders from Florence and Bartlett and in between, attempted to support the project, renaming the line the Bartlett Western Railway Company and building the line on to Florence. In a short time, Colonel Thomas Cronin, a career railroad man from Palestine, purchased the Bartlett Western, and operated the company until his death in 1926.[75]

Meanwhile in the spring of 1911, another sale of lots was held in Jarrell. By September, two new residences were built; Jim A. Comer organized a new bank with W. A. Wilson, president; new churches were founded and the exodus from Corn Hill began. Robert E. "Live Wire" Downey arrived in the new town to start publishing the *Jarrell View*. He described the move from Corn Hill to a mile north. "Daily [I] witnessed Jim Hawkins, with his horse-drawn equipment, move the old town to the new. I was to welcome the first train to arrive, locomotive, half a dozen box cars, and a coach in the rear. Later, a little motor car made the round trip twice daily." The homes were pulled to their new locations by means of an anchor, block and tackle and two mules, but this was a slow method, indeed. In 1915 S. A. Keeling bought a John Case steam engine to pull his thresh-

This steam engine moved much of Corn Hill to the new town of Jarrell in 1915.

er, thinking he could also use it to move the homes and business buildings still in Corn Hill awaiting transportation. Using four or six trucks, placing them and long twelve by twelve timbers underneath the house, and pulling straight ahead with the steam engine, Keeling could move the buildings in one-third the time required by mule power. It required two days to load a house on the long-axled trucks, which were about fifteen inches high. Then the engine was attached to the trucks by cables and the move was made in three hours. "I didn't count the number of houses and buildings we moved—probably twenty or twenty-five. We were too busy trying to get everyone moved over. In seven or eight months, those who wanted to go were moved. Some hesitated for a while, but after a little time, nearly everyone had left Corn Hill for Jarrell." Rufe Shaver's eight-room house was the largest to be moved in one piece. The Baptist Church was cut into two parts before moving. Most of the buildings were set on cedar blocks which were already in place in Jarrell.[76]

Located as it was on a major highway, Jarrell seemed destined to be forever moving. Several highway changes caused shifts in the town, the last when Interstate 35 was built.

The heavy drifts of Czechs and Germans into the area in the 1880s furnished Jarrell with a strong and colorful ethnic population, thrifty and industrious. Most of these settlers farmed for a number of years, but many of them or their sons and grandsons entered businesses and professions and provided Jarrell with some of its most successful leaders.

Leaving Jarrell toward Florence, the Bartlett Western embankments followed in a general way the south bank of Salado Creek. The town of Salado in Bell County is pronounced Sah-lay'-doh. Natives along the creek pronounce the stream's name differently: Sah-lah'-o, omitting the "d" sound entirely, and eliding the first two syllables almost to Slah'-o. Although the word "salado" means salty, the creek is not at all salty but has plant life suggesting that its name was accidently exchanged with that for Lampasas River, which *is* salty, but which means "water plant."[77]

Three more flag station stops were built between Jarrell and Florence, all of them for the convenience of passengers, of farmers who wished to load or unload produce to be shipped or received, and for the train itself to be repaired and filled with water. The four station stops between Bartlett and Florence were named in official railroad records: Caffrey, John Camp, Atkinson, and Armstrong. A religious lady, probably Mrs. Ida Cronin Branagan, Thomas Cronin's daughter, gave the stops other names, the "Four Gospels"—St. Matthew, St. Mark, St. Luke and St. John. At each small flag station which had a roof and benches on each side, was hung a small frame around the gospel name and appropriate verses from that gospel. Mileage between stations is shown in Railway Commission records:

STATION	MILES
Bartlett	0.0
Schwertner	5.5

St. Matthew (Caffrey)	8.2
Jarrell	11.2
St. Mark (John Camp)	13.6
St. Luke (Atkinson)	16.3
St. John (Armstrong)	18.4
Florence	23.2

At St. Mark, the first station west of Jarrell, Will Davis had a small store from about 1914 to 1935. Near the village of Peyton at St. Luke was an extra railroad siding on which stood a surplus car for the Wilson family who harvested and shipped lumber from their place. St. John, on the Salado bank, had a water storage tank where the engine refilled.[78]

Florence had been a stable community for more than fifty years when the Bartlett and Western provided it with rail connections. Located in the northwestern section of the county, scattered settlers came there in the early 1850s. Allen and Samuel A. Stroud signed the county petition in 1848 and Richard Tankersley of Georgetown, also a signer, owned land there. John W. Atkinson, James Hill Casey, Hugh Casey, J. C. Caskey, S. K. P. Jackson, A. G. Gannaway and Andrew Whittenburg and their families came by 1852 when there was considerable danger of Indian attack, when preachers kept a harquebus close to the pulpit during services, and when buffalo could often be seen on the prairie. A Mr. Brooks established a little store on the Salado in the early fifties, possibly Henry Brooks or a relative of his, and the town was founded. It was called Brooksville for a number of years, but the name was officially changed when a post office was established there November 25, 1857, with John W. Atkinson, postmaster. The name Florence was chosen either for the daughter of merchant Brooks or of Colonel King Fisher, or for the former home, Florence, Alabama, of J. W. Atkinson.[79] All three versions are casually documented and told with about equal justification.

Tom P. Redding sold land for town lots. The following businesses were among the early ones: Mrs. Murray's small store, purchased in 1856 by J. W. Atkinson, whose son, J. W., Jr., also ran a store; George C. and James Frank Atkinson, drugs; J. F. Hughes, John "Wes" Murray, Bill Ferguson, Enoch D. John, S. K. P. Jackson; J. C. Cosby blacksmith shop, J. S. Ming ten pin alley and saloon, Dr. Wales' hotel; J. C. Caskey, real estate. Ira Chalk had a horse-powered grist mill and in 1855 Enoch D. John put in a steam flour mill which Sidney Seymour ran. Other pioneers and their families of the community were Dr. Philip H. Adams, David C. Bowles, R. B. Caskey, T. P. Chapman, Henry Jordan, Levi Lawler, Henry D. Love, James Montgomery, John Montgomery, Sam Shanklin, Bryce M.

Smart, Roland Tankersley, Billy Tomlinson, Dr. B. M. Wales, William H. Long and E. Thomson.[80]

Schools and churches received special attention in the village, thriving long before the Civil War. Although many churches were integrated in the South prior to the Civil War, few remained integrated afterwards. One notable exception was at Florence, where sometime before March 25, 1873, the Church of Christ was organized. On that date, property was deeded to the church, where frequent camp meetings were held on a hill north of town with tents covering a large area between the church and parsonage. Prominent in the work of the church were Negro Jim Haynes and his wife, Sallie. During the meetings, they cooked beef and baked bread in Dutch ovens for all in attendance. Haynes farmed about three miles west of Florence, was an expert stone mason and built numerous fireplaces and chimneys in that vicinity.[81]

W. S. Houghton moved to Florence in 1863; cattle brands were registered for W. A. Smith, W. A. Fleager (who also freighted, later sold sewing machines), S. M. Strayhorn, F. F. Lynch, A. G. Suttles, P. M. McCaskill, R. Ratliff, J. C. Howell, W. R. Blevins and A. W. Wimberly soon after the war. About 1870, Columbus C. "Lum" Bauchman hauled rock from above Lawler to build a two story commercial building for Tom Benedict and John W. Atkinson, and the church occupied at the present time by Primitive Baptists was erected. Dennis Wyatt ran a leather and saddle shop in 1870; D. K. Stewart manufactured a special saddle tree in his shop; R. B. Caskey had a mill, gin and mercantile business; gins were operated between 1870 and 1900 by C. C. Jackson, Bart Wales, W. A. Wilson, and one of the Skaggs family. K. Wales managed a hotel. A local inventor, John T. Brady, built a convertible buggy plow, which could be used as a cultivator or cotton-corn planter.[82]

After 1880 stores were run by L. C. Jackson, Tom Reavis, Sr., H. B. Hoover, Bennett & Shofner, John Storey; drug stores by J. Frank Atkinson, Sr., and George Atkinson; Dr. O. B. Atkinson provided medical attention; W. C. Love and John Watson sold hardware, Dave Potts sold chili, G. A. Miller was the barber and John Reynolds had a rock quarry near Florence. By the time the Bartlett Western was constructed, John A. Brewster, W. A. Wilson, John McDowell and P. A. Wales established the town's first bank in 1906. L. G. Bobo and John Griggs ran a twentieth century store, G. E. Adams a dairy-creamery, the town had a small cheese factory, sponsored numerous fairs and had a Carbotex plant to mine calcium carbonate.[83]

Wheat was the early crop around Florence, but cotton farming was popular by the end of the century. Cattle formed an important part of the local economy, and numerous cattle drives passed through the Florence area in the 1870s. Mrs. Dell Tucker Suttles, granddaughter of pioneers George and Rebecca Matsler, recalled that a cowhand on one of the drives was struck by lightning and killed at the Matsler community. He was buried in Matsler Cemetery. *The Florence Flower* was published in 1890 by Marion Haygood, and the town continued to have a newspaper until 1952. About 1895, W. J. Holder established the Florence College which operated about eight years.[84]

When the railroad line was finally completed to Florence in 1912, the

Florence Main Street at the turn of the century.

First transfer for the new Bartlett Western at Florence.

first train was heralded with a big picnic. An excursion came from Bartlett and everyone dressed in Sunday or party clothes. A huge crowd rode the passenger and flat cars from Bartlett and other stations to Florence to enjoy the celebration at the end of the ride. Walter Kirk was the first stationmaster at Florence.[85]

The "dinky," as some in Florence called it, was converted from coal to gasoline motors to provide more efficient service. The passenger cár was styled like a trolley and could be caught almost anywhere along the line. Devising special rigs to haul freight, the engineers outfitted a Fordson tractor with flanged wheels which could pull flat cars loaded with as many as 130 bales of cotton at one time. The tracks west of Jarrell were on a difficult grade, so when heavy loads were pulled the crew carried sand along, sprinkling it on the tracks to provide enough traction for the wheels to pull up grade, or to control them when they were heavily loaded on the down grade. The Bartlett Western obtained the mail contract for its section of the county and, to handle it, bought Ford trucks supplied with railroad wheels, which operated along the line for many years. Because cars often jumped the tracks, the Bartlett Western was also called the Bullfrog line.[86]

The Bartlett Western owned six roadway machines, shop machinery, two locomotives, ten freight cars, two passenger cars, and work equipment; it leased a renovated house as a depot in Bartlett, used an $1800 depot which Schwertner furnished. Jarrell and Florence built depots. The company made good money for a number of years, its greatest income derived from hauling cotton—53,750 tons in 1912. Other commodities transported were cotton seed, flour, coke, coal, lignite, livestock, stone, merchandise, fruits, vegetables, meat and agricultural products, wool, hair, crude petroleum, salt, forest products, brick, cement, lime, chemicals and drugs, furniture, ice, iron and steel articles and other goods.[87]

After Cronin's death in 1926, his daughter, Marie Cronin, who was an internationally-recognized artist, inherited the business and, following her father's wish, succeeded him as president of the company. Cronin had often talked over business matters with Marie and with her sister, Ida (Mrs. William Branagan). Mrs. Branagan had served as the company treasurer, her husband as the general manager. Mrs. Branagan, a gifted singer-organist, was injured while getting off the train, and never fully recovered. She died the same year as her father. After Marie Cronin's many years in her beloved Paris studying painting, she appeared somewhat eccentric to casual acquaintances in Williamson County. Modishly dressed in Paris styles and with more makeup than the custom in Texas, usually wearing a large-brimmed hat, she undertook her new job earnestly.

"She was quite a dresser for that time," one acquaintance remembered. Her close friends thought her a beautiful woman, dark-haired, of medium height and size, with an exquisite wardrobe. She was about forty when her father died. Her career in the art world was at its peak. She was warm and extremely generous to her friends, was both trusting and sophisticated—but she did seem rather strange to her unsophisticated neighbors.[88]

Marie Cronin worked diligently and long at her new job, with the assistance of her popular Irish brother-in-law, William Branagan. His acquaintances remembered that he dressed in dark suits with white shirt and black bow tie. When Thomas Cronin died in 1926, the entire state was experiencing a sharp decline in cotton production and drastic reduction of cotton prices. From the $1.59 a bale the Bartlett Western had received for hauling cotton, their price fell to forty-five cents. This indicated the trend which soon reduced the company to economic disaster. Miss Cronin rode the line to give attention to detail and encouragement to others, but when she saw the job was hopeless, she requested permission of the Railroad Commission to close the line. It was finally granted October 11, 1935, after many years of financial difficulties. Miss Cronin planned to return to Paris and to painting, but failing eyesight prevented and she remained in Bartlett at the family home. She died July 24, 1951.[89]

After the Bartlett Western closed down, the rails and ties were removed—some stories say they were sold to Japan for steel which was used during World War II, others that Herman Brown of Brown & Root, Inc., purchased them. Neither version has been corroborated.[90] Except in fields which have been cultivated where the tracks once stood, the embankments can still be traced, especially between Florence and Jarrell, and just east of Jarrell.

The Bartlett Western, the "dinky," the Bullfrog line or the Four Gospels line—Matthew, Mark, Luke and John—call it what you will. This line lived a picturesque, colorful and exciting life, under the direction of a man who was an aggressive railroad magnate and under the presidency of a woman, a talented artist. The Bartlett Western truly was unique.

The Twentieth Century

POPULATION

Population shifts before 1900 were due primarily to immigration, the coming of railroads to the county, and the development of agriculture, particularly cotton farming. After 1900 the automobile, mechanized farm equipment, and the depression of the 1920s and 1930s caused other shifts. During the mid-twentieth century the trend was toward urbanization. Since Williamson County had no large cities, much of its shifting rural population drifted toward cities outside the county as well as to larger towns in the county. The population story is told most completely and concisely in the following charts:

TOTAL POPULATION OF WILLIAMSON COUNTY BY DECADES

1850—1,568	1890—25,909	1920—42,934	1950—38,833
1860—4,529	1900—38,072	1930—44,146	1960—35,044
1870—6,894	1910—42,228	1940—41,698	1970—37,305[1]
1880—15,155			

POPULATION IN TOWNS AND PRINCIPAL COMMUNITIES OF WILLIAMSON COUNTY

TOWN	1878	1890	1900	1920	1936	1960	1970
Andice					50	125	25
Bartlett		206	957	1731	1873	1650	1622
Beaukiss			114	75	75	20	20
Behrnville (Theon)					35	30	30

TOWN	1878	1890	1900	1920	1936	1960	1970
Berry's Creek						50	50
Beyersville					100	100	75
Cedar Park					200	100	125
Circleville	30	62			150	50	42
Corn Hill	17	239	239				
Coupland				150	150	250	135
Florence		263	363	650	421	600	672
Georgetown	1500	2447	2790	2871	3583	5450	6395
Granger		261	841	1944	1703	1400	1256
Hare					15	70	70
Hoxie			322			50	50
Hutto		216	563	571	538	400	545
Jarrell				200	200	410	410
Jonah					120	100	60
Laneport					10	60	60
Leander		329	283	200	200	300	300
Liberty Hill	153	309	396	500	500	300	300
Noack					20	60	60
Norman's Crossing					25	20	20
Rice's Crossing	51				25	100	100
Round Rock	1200	1438	1138	900	1173	2458	2811
Sandoval					25	50	50
Schwertner					100	150	150
Structure					10	60	60
Taylor		2584	4211	5965	7463	9500	9616
Thrall				272	422	600	619
Walburg				200	200	250	250
Waterloo					10	60	60
Weir				300	300	100	100[2]

Soon after 1900, post offices were assigned to Hoxie, Gano, Hare, Behrnville, Thrall and Noack. New schools were established in all the communities with the new post offices, and also at Flat Rock, Wales, Prairie Lea, Baker and New Bern. Voting boxes in 1908 were listed at North Georgetown, Berry's Creek, Leander, Cedar Park, Pond Springs, Liberty Hill, Gabriel Mills, Rock House, White House, Florence, Gravis, Corn Hill, Ake School House, Circleville, Granger, Gano, Beaukiss, Rice's Crossing, Old Round Rock, Hutto, East Taylor, Allison, Round Rock, Hopewell, Bartlett, Jonah, West Taylor, Pleasant Hill, South Georgetown, Walburg, Beyersville, Hare (changed in 1907 from Laneport), Coupland,

Early grocery store at Hare.

Stiles School House, Waterloo, Mager, Weir and Post Oak Osland. Within
a few decades Andice was listed instead of White House, Jarrell instead
of Corn Hill, Lawrence Chapel instead of Post Oak Island, Thrall in place
of Stiles School House or Stiles Switch, Friendship instead of Allison; and
Schwertner post office, school and voting box had been added to the roster.[3]

European immigrants continued to settle in large numbers on east Wil-
liamson County farm land until about 1910. Those of German-Austrian-
Swiss origins clustered near Coupland, Beyersville, Wuthrich Hill,
Noack, Sandoval, Walburg, Schwertner and Theon; many Czechs went to
farms around Bartlett, Granger and Taylor; the Swedish lived around
Hutto, Palm Valley, Round Rock, Georgetown, Jonah, Type, Weir and
Berry's Creek. Swiss people founded New Bern and lived in the Berry's
Creek area north of Georgetown. The 1923 school census of the county
revealed percentages of the school population by national origins: Czechoslovakian, 18.5 percent; German, 15 percent; Swedish, 14.2 percent;
English, 9 percent; Austrian, 4.6 percent; Swiss, 2.4 percent; Danish, 1
percent; Scottish, .8 percent; Irish, .5 percent; Russian, .5 percent; Canadian, .4 percent; French, .3 percent; Hungarian, .2 percent; Greek, .2
percent. The county had sixty-seven common school districts in 1923 with
seventy-six white schools, thirteen Negro schools and three Mexican
schools.[4]

Although there had been some integration of the white and black races
prior to the Civil War, there was little after Reconstruction. Negroes attended separate schools and churches, organized their own highly competi-
tive athletic events and anyone who watched them perform might easily
have predicted their great success in this field after schools were integrated

in the 1960s. That integration took place without much tension, with almost no serious confrontations. Negro leader Frank Hasty who lived on the Lewis Ranch south of Taylor in 1908 arranged an organizational meeting of the Ex Slave Union Association of Industry, with a barbecue held on the Taylor Fairgrounds October 23 and 24 of that year. In 1936 the City of Georgetown enacted an ordinance making it unlawful for a white person to live within the Negro residential zone and vice versa, "present residence excepted," with violators subject to fines from five to one hundred dollars. The law was said to promote more "efficient policing." Three years later a Negro sat on the grand jury of the county, the first to do so since Reconstruction.[5]

As European immigrants ceased to arrive in the county about 1910, large numbers of Mexican citizens began to move in from Mexico. In Georgetown, the first Mexican living quarters were adobe houses on south Austin Avenue. A large enough number lived in the area in 1908 to plan a special observance of Mexico's national independence. The gathering was held September 15 and 16, 1908 at Glasscock Springs (San Gabriel Park) with Señor Martinez in charge. Festivities opened with a morning parade of decorated wagons and buggies. At the meeting grounds, speeches were delivered in Spanish on Mexican independence, and Colonel W. K. Makemson spoke. Band music completed the formal program. In 1923 the Georgetown Mexican Mission Chapel was used as a school for Mexican children "for lack of a school building." It was pronounced a "decided success" with forty-two students enrolled in the first three grades. That fall the pastor of the church, D. W. Carter, wrote about the activities of the school, church and Sunday School and publicly requested that a school be built for children of Mexican origins. He also stressed the need for houses in the vicinity of the chapel for Mexican families to rent. Taylor built the Alamo School for Mexican and Mexican-American pupils who resided there. The annual Independence Day celebration at Georgetown is recorded as late as 1936 when Mexican-Americans met at Goodlett Park (San Gabriel) September 14-16.[6]

TRANSPORTATION AND COMMUNICATIONS

The first automobiles in the county brought no overnight transformation as did the arrival of railroads, but the impact was felt immediately and within a decade rapid changes were being made. A flurry of bicycle riding in the 1890s gave townspeople a taste of personal transportation without a horse. Bicycles with rubber tires were on the market in 1889 and the next

year citizens of Georgetown petitioned the city for permission to ride on
the sidewalks. They noted that the two-wheelers frightened horses and that
several bicycles were damaged as a result.[7]

Between 1906 and 1908 a handful of automobile owners in the county
proudly drove their machines where roads would allow. The first car in
Georgetown about 1906 was owned by an Englishman-tailor, W. H.
Crowley, who had his shop in his home on East Eighth Street. His ma-
chine was a two-cylinder Buick with chaise drive and side crank. Next,
T. J. Caswell bought a 1907 model Ford without front doors. Caswell ran
a buggy-carriage-bicycle shop in Georgetown, later ran a Ford agency.
Soon afterwards several other cars were owned by Gene Johnson and Doss
W. Stephens, local barbers, and by E. F. Booty, a merchant, who ordered
his four-cylinder, forty-eight horsepower Buick from New York in 1908.
The local newspaper reported its arrival and announced that "it has been
running smoothly ever since." Booty's chauffeur, Tom Crawford, purchased
a car of his own and opened a dealership in downtown Georgetown near
the old standpipe. In Taylor, banker-businessman C. H. Booth acquired
the first automobile there, a 1908 Mitchell. Fred B. Whipkey who was
in the newspaper business in Granger had the first car in his town. These
early cars carried only homemade licenses of which there were a wide

New delivery automobile, Georgetown.

variety including wooden ones with numbers painted on them, leather ones, or plates with porcelain letters fastened into a frame. Not until 1917 did the State of Texas begin issuing licenses of uniform design.[8]

The Crowley and Booty cars were sent from Georgetown early in December 1908 to the Block House home of Judge A. S. Walker to pick up a visiting dignitary there, William Jennings Bryan, and Mrs. Bryan. The Bryans had previously lunched with the Walker family and Bryan and men of the party went quail shooting. After coming to Georgetown, the Bryans met and greeted townspeople in the "splendid new" Mood Hall dormitory at Southwestern University. That evening Bryan addressed a large audience in the auditorium at the University. After spending the night in Georgetown, they took the Katy morning train for Galveston.[9]

When the first new cars arrived in a community and were parked, everyone—merchants, customers or anyone in town—gathered around to inspect them from every side, from top to bottom, and even underneath. The sensational machine brought new regulations. By 1906 the speed limit in Georgetown was six miles an hour or at street corners, three miles an hour. "In approaching any horse, or horses, or mule or mules" the driver must "exercise every reasonable precaution to prevent the frightening of such horse." If the animal appeared uneasy, the driver was to stop his vehicle and remain stopped until the horse had moved away or been "gotten under full control." Additional laws required "at least two lamps on the front of said automobile or other similar conveyance showing white lights, and one lamp behind showing a red light."[10]

Paved streets were non-existent in the early 1900s. Rainy weather meant boggy streets downtown, around the Courthouse, and on the highways

Scene at gin, Jonah.

all over the county, a condition which for decades caused drivers of hacks and buggies much annoyance. In such weather, the automobile was useless, but overoptimism often left them stuck in the mud. Chains for the tires to provide more traction in the tenacious soil were standard equipment on early cars. There were other trials besides mud. When J. A. "Cotton" Johnson, Swedish farmer who lived north of Hutto, drove his new car to Weir to show it to friends, he invited everyone to take a ride. He loaded his expectant passengers but the motor refused to start. After some checking and conferences, numerous suggestions but no success, the local ginner, Glenn Stearns was summoned, for he was said to understand machinery. "Mr. Glenn" walked around the car, looking carefully at it, peered underneath, made an adjustment and pronounced the trouble corrected. Johnson's drive from Hutto to Weir took him through grass and weeds on the prairie and some of the taller grass had hung in the machinery under the car. When the culprit was removed, the car started. Early manuals on how to drive an automobile rather strongly intimated that the driver should be a mechanic.[11]

But the new machine that burned gasoline instead of hay was catching on. By 1909 the county had ninety-six cars, and by the end of 1912, about seven hundred. Figures from the Texas Highway Department show totals for other years:

1922—6,299
1930—11,882
1940—12,384
1960—16,484
1970—27,232

The speed limit in 1909 was set at eighteen miles an hour on roads, and in Georgetown was increased to eight miles an hour within the city limits. Cars were still required to stop for horses, must carry lamps, and each must have a bell to ring giving notice of the vehicle's approach—a bell audible for three hundred feet. Granger Rural Free Delivery mail carrier Grover Pope was called the "most up-to-date" mailman in the county in July 1909 when he began making his route in an automobile. Road and street improvement became a priority all over the county by 1912 and late that year $400,000 had been spent on "macadam roads and the autos are run over them in wet and dry weather alike. There are fully twenty garages in the county and all are doing a thriving business. The farmers are leading now in the buying of autos," the *Granger News* for December 19, 1912, reported. In February that year, the Granger City Council voted to pave its main streets with vitrified brick, "the very best material we could use." The City of Taylor let a contract late in August 1912 to pave nine blocks of their business section with wooden bricks. The state legislature provided for road improvement in 1903, 1916 and 1921, and in 1923 levied a gasoline tax to be used for that purpose. The Texas Highway Department took over operation of state highways in 1925.[12]

Meanwhile counties slowly improved roads, but it was many years before the well-kept state and county highways and farm roads of the present day were developed. The old roads followed boundary lines through the countryside, making ninety-degree turns at property corners and double turns across railroad tracks. The secretary of the Texas Good Roads Association in 1918 released a log of the Belton to Austin "very important" road, "gravelled all the way excepting about five miles in Williamson county and just south of the Bell county line. Autoists should try this road in going to Temple or Waco. There is some beautiful scenery along the route, and the picnic grounds at Georgetown" provide a very fine place to camp. The log began at Belton, 21.6 miles from Jarrell. Continuing from there toward Austin, the mileage and directions follow:

0.0	Belton
21.6	Jarrell
21.8	Turn right
22.2	Turn left
23.5	Corn Hill
23.6	Right fork
25.1	Turn left
26.1	Straight
26.4	Turn left
27.5	Straight
28.4	School house on left
32.0	Circle left
32.8	Cross creek
36.6	Turn right
36.7	Turn left
36.9	Cross river
37.4	Georgetown, keep straight, courthouse on left
38.2	Cross railroad, turn right
46.4	Old town of Round Rock
46.5	Cross river
47.2	Round Rock. Turn right, post office and depot on left; cross railroad and turn right

52.3 Turn right
65.8 University on left
66.6 Sixth and Congress Avenue, Austin.[13]

For ten years or more, a trip from Georgetown to Austin, Taylor to Round Rock, or Hutto to Weir took the better part of a day, and it was considered remarkable if the driver arrived "without becoming unduly tired." After a journey in a Model T Ford in the 1920s from Williamson County to Colorado City, Texas, a passenger described the trip. "The weather was as hot as the 'hinges of Hades' " when the family left, and before reaching Granger, one tire had blown out. Another tire went at Bartlett, and the third at Temple. The heat was causing pressure to build in the tires, someone explained in Temple. "We crept gingerly along our way until night overcame us, at Alvarado, disgusted, busted and worn to a frazzle. We did not look for a tourist cabin, for at this time nobody had ever heard of one as far as I know, so we chose to pitch our camp under some bleachers in a ball park. . . . The trip was redeemed somewhat by a splendid camp-fire breakfast." Rain curtains were kept under the car seat in this model. "There was no man, alive or dead, who could stretch them enough so that they would button on properly. A feller got soaking wet while putting them on when caught in a rain storm and the unbuttoned parts flapped in the wind letting in the rain to the utter dismay" of the passengers in their Sunday-best.[14]

Most county bridges were washed out in the September 1921 flood and roads were badly damaged. The locally-organized Brown and Root company was low bidder on a number of bridges including two at Georgetown and two in the Circleville-Taylor area. Georgetown began a program of street paving in 1922. Road improvement was slow, however. After a downpour in September 1923 "literally hundreds of cars were stuck in the ungravelled portion of the Austin-Georgetown road." The following January, Leander car owners "on account of the miserable roads" had generally given up their cars and gone back to using wagons, buggies and horseback. New Years' fireworks "constantly discharged" the same year caused teams to run away, damaging vehicles to which they were hitched.[15]

Those first graveled or paved roads and highways were not yet lost in the anonymity of numbers—they bore impressive or elegant names as befitted a new and exciting mode of transportation. North from Taylor toward Circleville and Granger was the King's Highway, one of the first in the state to be paved. Adjoining it at Taylor a new city park was being built in 1921. The Robert E. Lee Highway, so named for the man who traveled it before the Civil War, went through Austin and north to Bagdad and Liberty Hill. Meridian Highway more or less paralleled present Highway 81 and Interstate 35 through Round Rock, Georgetown and Jarrell. In 1924 men in the Walburg community were gravelling the road from there to the Meridian Highway so that people from that section could reach Georgetown in wet weather. The county had 35.83 miles of graveled state roads and 40.26 miles of hard surfaced state highways by 1923.[16]

The popular Ford touring car sold for $295 at Detroit in the summer of 1924. A Georgetown inventor, Fitzhugh Girvin, had his Girvin Dual Piston Gas Engine patented and Eugene Towns of the Towns Mill clan was manufacturing it for Girvin. Towns himself patented an intensifying spark plug. By 1925 the horse and buggy days were almost gone. Soon afterwards the crossroads rural store and the rural school began their decline into oblivion. Automobile mishaps began to crop up frequently in news reports and a new state law was effective in June 1925 requiring mufflers on cars and motorcycles, and prohibiting muffler cutouts. During the 1930s, nearly all primary roads were topped, dangerous crossings eliminated, better bridges built, and roadways straightened.[17]

Small local telephone services of limited scope appeared before the turn of the century in the county, but general communication to most points was not available until about 1900. In 1898 F. B. Robinson of Huntsville put in an exchange at Georgetown and service at Taylor began about the same time. By 1902 Taylor had two hundred subscribers.[18]

The radio squealed in the county about two decades after the automobile. Since it appeared during the time when many men, particularly farmers, could make or repair almost any machine they owned, people often built their own crystal sets in the 1920s. Citizens of Georgetown area were invited to the Courthouse Square on September 12, 1924, to hear General John J. Pershing's farewell address as Chief of Staff of the United States Army and a brief talk by President Calvin Coolidge, both of which would "be afforded by radio." Radio broadcasting began in the county in the 1930s with unlicensed stations and home built equipment, in Taylor operated by J. J. Brewster and in Georgetown by M. L. Cates. Licensed station KTAE in Taylor opened April 1, 1948, with K. L. McConchie, Dr. R. G. Garrett and Gillis Conoley, stockholders. Georgetown's KGTN began operation December 1962, Don Scarbrough owner, and opened an FM channel in January 1972.[19]

Rural postal delivery began in the early 1900s in Williamson County, leading quickly to the closing of numerous small village post offices. Highway postal service began in 1941, a zoning system in 1943, and postal air mail in 1953. Automated equipment for handling mail was in use in the 1960s.

The State of Texas had its first commercial aviation in 1926. Four years later, a U. S. emergency landing field was established near Weir, equipped with a searchlight said to be visible for thirty miles, as a beacon for airmen flying routes between Mexico City and Chicago.[20]

County newspapers published in the twentieth century were included in the section on "Communications" in Chapter IX. Since 1910 the following places have had newspapers: Bartlett, Coupland, Florence, Georgetown, Granger, Hare, Hutto, Jarrell, Laneport, Leander, Liberty Hill, Round Rock, Taylor and Weir.

AGRICULTURE AND BUSINESS

Early in the twentieth century, the county had state or national banks, at Taylor, Georgetown, Granger, Bartlett, Florence, Hutto, Weir, Walburg, and private banks at Round Rock and Liberty Hill. Cotton seed oil mills, compresses and planing mills were located at Taylor and Georgetown. Bartlett and Granger also had cotton seed oil mills. Round Rock operated a broom factory; Georgetown, Taylor and Bartlett, ice plants; Taylor had two daily newspapers and three weekly papers; Georgetown had two weeklies, and Bartlett, Granger, Hutto, Round Rock, Florence, Leander and Liberty Hill had a weekly apiece. Three railroad systems, I. & G. N., M. K. & T. and H. & T. C., served the county. Taylor had a new City Hall and Opera House, and a "neat little theatre" had been built at Granger. Georgetown had two mineral wells two and three hundred feet deep, both of them developed for therapeutic and resort use. Flouring mills continued to do business at Jonah, Georgetown, Granger, Bartlett and Taylor. The Taylor Bedding Manufacturing Company was established in 1903.[21]

The spectacular success of cotton in Williamson County about the turn of the century led to the establishment of cooperative cotton gins and warehouses during the first several decades of the 1900s. Taylor became the largest inland cotton market in the world. All cotton was picked by hand for about forty years, providing seasonal work for labor forces, many of them transient. About 1920 the Texas Farm Bureau Federation was organized to help improve farm living conditions, distribute farm products, and to represent the farmer on political and economic questions. Gin and mill accidents continued to be frequent but as these operations improved technically, safety factors were built in and by the 1940s the gins were safer. They could also carry much larger work loads. Larger and more ef-

TAYLOR, TEXAS.   Currency of the South. (Cotton Yard No. 6.)

King Cotton's story in Taylor is told on 1906 post card.

Saturday afternoon, Second and
Main Streets, Taylor, Texas.

Saturday was a busy day in town. Taylor in early 1900s.

ficient gins replaced from three to a dozen small village gins. For another
decade or two during peak ginning seasons, long waiting lines at the gins
were not unusual and ginning season might last for several months. By the
middle of the century, diversification and restrictions on cotton production
along with better gin machinery made ginning comparatively quick and

easy. In 1972 even a bumper cotton crop was harvested mechanically in about six weeks. Once again gin yards filled with loads of cotton, now pulled to town by trucks towing an additional light trailer load behind.

Mechanical methods of farming were adopted gradually. Within a hundred year span, farmers progressed from using sticks for planting tools to hand plows, from horsedrawn plows to mechanical equipment, ever and ever more sophisticated. A demonstration of engine-powered tractors was a big event in April 1925 on the E. E. Williams farm northwest of Georgetown in Glasscock Valley. By 1940 a horsedrawn farm machine was a rarity and also by this time machine cotton pickers were beginning to

New Price-Campbell cotton picking machine in Granger, 1909.

appear. Within little more than a decade, hand picking cotton was a thing of the past. From hand cutting grains and winnowing by hand, farmers proceded to a dusty, cumbersome motor powered thresher and finally in mid-twentieth century to the combine which was air conditioned and dust-free. The combine sweeps down a number of rows at a time, cutting, threshing, separating the grain, shredding stalks and chaff to dump back onto the soil, and spreading it evenly—all in one operation. What it takes in 1973 one man and a combine to do in a few hours required many men and many days' labor with earlier machines.[22]

The boll weevil became a serious menace in Texas, spreading inexorably northward from Mexico. In Governor William P. Hobby's administration of 1917-1918 the state enacted a quarantine to attempt control of the insect which had reached eastern Texas by 1904, all the state by 1921. When it threatened Williamson County seriously in 1923 the emergency quarantine was invoked. Cotton remained the major crop of the county for a few years—the longtime commercial bread and butter of the local economy—but the spectre of the weevil, overproduction, soil depletion, and the pending economic disasters in the late 1920s were to combine to change the cotton industry radically. To combat the weevil, the cotton growing season was shortened, spraying of poison by plane was begun, the green foliage of the mature plant was destroyed to remove the pest's foodstuff, stalks were broken and plowed under deeply, and hulls were burned after the ginning process.[23]

Soil conservation programs appeared in the 1920s, encompassing crop rotation, terracing to prevent erosion, use of soil building crops, fertilization, and other scientific agricultural practices. As cotton and wheat prices fell to new lows about 1929-1930, mass meetings were held in the county to discuss problems and to endorse marketing plans for relief to farmers. By 1931 new cotton laws were designed to bring economic recovery by reducing cotton acreage. Early in 1932 the farm reconstruction office for Texas opened in Dallas with O. W. Sherrill of Georgetown as administrative officer. The Agricultural Adjustment Administration (AAA) act of 1933 set up adjusted production of cotton, wheat, corn and other crops, and dairy and hog production. The law was declared unconstitutional in 1936 but the pattern had been set. Farm loans and farm subsidies became standard practice. In July 1936, $204,000 in subsidy checks in the AAA program were sent to Williamson County for distribution. As farm programs became more highly organized, farm quotas were set and the Rural Resettlement Administration financed community projects at a low rate of interest to purchase farm machinery, establish creameries and for similar projects to help farmers. The first cheese factory in the area was started in 1925 at Round Rock and had a significant role in assisting farmers there. The plant, owned by Thomas E. Nelson and G. R. Lundelius, began with twenty patrons bringing eight hundred pounds of milk daily. By 1936 it had three hundred patrons, purchased 22,000 pounds of milk a day and was paying farmers about $3500 every week. Since it was considered a model in several respects, it was often shown to visitors from other areas of the nation who were planning similar community projects. As a continuing part of the conservation program, the San Gabriel-Little River Soil Conservation District was created at the ballot box on May 25, 1940.[24]

"The cotton gin created the economy of poor sharecroppers" in the late nineteenth and early twentieth century.[25] Installment and mail order buying about 1910, the advent of the boll weevil in central Texas about 1920 and of the automobile about the same time—all these plus the depression years of the late twenties and of the thirties—made new ways of life inevitable.[26] During the depression more emphasis was placed on the home garden, already a standard part of every farm. With the supervision of home demonstration agents, housewives could use canning equipment in community centers to preserve food for the family. The Works Progress Administration (WPA) kept sewing rooms open and busy in many communities.[27]

Seeking relief from taxes which had gradually risen over a long period of time, Williamson County citizens met, discussed, petitioned and received cuts of as much as fifteen percent in their local taxes. The county real estate taxes were reduced twenty percent in 1932. President Franklin Delano Roosevelt appointed a twenty-six-year-old Lyndon Baines Johnson of a nearby county to head the National Youth Administration (NYA) for Texas in August 1935. This was one of a number of Roosevelt's programs for recovery which provided help for the unemployed. Johnson held his post with NYA until 1937 when the death of Congressman James P. Buchanan, who represented the Tenth District, resulted in a special election to fill the vacancy. Williamson County had been in the Tenth Congressional District since it was created September 6, 1901.* Johnson resigned his NYA job to run for Congress from the Tenth District. Nine others ran for the post including Sam V. Stone of Georgetown. E. H. Lawhon of Taylor considered the race but decided against it. The election was held April 10, 1937, Johnson winning handily. He was summoned almost immediately to meet with President Roosevelt, who took him as a protege and the new Congressman began his political career as an elected official May 14, 1937. He was honored at San Gabriel Park, Georgetown, the following September with a barbecue—one of many visits he made to the county over a period of more than thirty years.[28]

Ever since the bustling decades of cattle drives, ranching remained the occupation of numerous Williamson County families, although cotton farming lured many a cattleman away from the business. Around the turn of the century, David Harrell had a large operation between Hopewell and Liberty Hill where his big stone ranch home dominated the scene. Harrell,

*To satisfy the whim of political ambition of one or more Texas politicians, Williamson County was removed from the Tenth Congressional District in 1972, shifted to the Eleventh District. In July 1973 a Supreme Court ruling appeared to place the western half of the county, including Georgetown and Jarrell (but not Round Rock) back in the Tenth District.

one of the first Shorthorn breeders in Texas, raised "Old Prince" who became a world champion Shorthorn bull at the St. Louis (Louisiana Purchase Centennial) Worlds Fair in 1904. The fine animal was greeted as a celebrity when Harrell brought him back to Liberty Hill from the fair. Crowds gathered at the depot to welcome Prince and his owner. The huge Hoxie Ranch bred and raised fine cattle on a large scale until the death of the owner, John R. Hoxie, after which its operations were somewhat curtailed. In 1910 the place was sold to be subdivided into small farms. The John Sparks Ranch south of Taylor was cut into farms and sold following the death of Governor John Sparks in 1908. The large Mumford Ranch, later known as Hoxie Flag Springs Ranch, just east of Taylor, was purchased by Francis A. Allison and Fred L. Welch of Taylor and the sizeable Gentry Ranch southeast of Taylor likewise was sold, Captain Peter Schramm dividing it into farms and reselling.[29]

From ranches which remained in existence throughout the twentieth century, considerable quatities of wool, mohair and hides were shipped. The depression brought increased interest in livestock. The county poultry industry was greatly expanded and cattle, sheep, goats and hogs were raised in increasing numbers. By 1950 Williamson County was one of the five leading counties of the state in egg and chicken production. As cotton production was reduced the cattle industry again crept eastward in the county. Farmers discovered that their rich black land would sustain many more head of cattle per acre than the less fertile and dryer soils to the west.[30] Privately-owned or community cattle auction companies were established in Georgetown and Taylor by the middle of the century and weekly sales of cattle and livestock brought buyers from long distances. A few large ranches promoted special sales once a year or so, usually appealing to buyers of a special breed, such as Charolais, and attracting purchasers from all over the world.

A native crop familiar to Williamson County as far back as prehistoric times, the pecan, was more and more highly regarded by farmers in the 1920s and 1930s after cotton production was reduced. One of the first to set out orchards of pecan trees grown from native nuts, then budded or grafted to papershell varieties, was Auburn Clare Stearns, a Circleville ginner. Soon after he planted several orchards from 1917 through the 1920s, others were set over the county and in 1939 a pecan shelling plant was established in Taylor. An even more unusual crop was commercially developed about this time—the mistletoe, normally considered a pest. W. E. Thies of Georgetown and others began harvesting the plant to ship at Christmastime. Georgetown became known as the mistletoe "kissing" capital of the world. Other central Texas counties took up the project, by mid-century shipping as much as half a million pounds of the plant in early December. A Hutto man and his son, W. L. and H. A. "Honey" Victor, developed a honey business, and shipped large quantities out from the Hutto depot.[31]

When Works Projects Administration (WPA) jobs were undertaken in Williamson County—the improving of farm roads, street paving and sanitation projects for small communities—several economic benefits accrued. Local people were hired to do the work, gravel pits and quarries were called on for materials, and local improvements resulted. In addition, quarries furnished stone for public buildings, including numerous structures on the University of Texas campus, around the state Capitol, in Fort Worth and elsewhere. A National Youth Administration shop in Georgetown in 1940 kept young people busy making tables for Georgeotwn High School, chairs for state offices, and other similar activities. The building boom of the 1960s and 1970s brought even more demand for gravel, lime, crushed stone and rock from a number of quarries over the western end of the county.

The county provides several tourist attractions. Cobb Cavern northwest of Georgetown has been visited by tourists and spelunkers for a number of years. In 1964 the Inner Space Cavern on the south edge of Georgetown was discovered during construction of Interstate Highway 35 and has become an important attraction. Bones of numerous extinct animals have been discovered there.[32]

Manufacturing and industrial plants in the county numbering about fifty in 1966 included food products, flour and grain mills, textile mills, apparel manufacturers, lumber and wood products, furniture, chemicals, printing-publishing, petroleum refining, rubber and plastics, fabricated metals, stone and clay products, machinery, instruments, and others. The major products were agricultural, with cattle and dairy products included, and stone, sand, gravel, lime, crude oil also important.[33]

Two railroads, previously discussed, were completed in the county after 1900—the Missouri-Kansas and Texas line between Granger, Georgetown and Austin, which began operation over the forty-seven mile track June 26, 1904, with two daily runs providing "direct communication with the flyer and other fast main trains" at Granger; and the Bartlett Western line from Bartlett to Florence, chartered in 1909, operated until 1935 when the line closed. The rails remained strong economic assets until well after World War 1. Presidents occasionally passed through the county by train. Theodore Roosevelt made a brief appearance on April 6, 1905. He whisked through Temple without stopping and the community was so indignant it passed an ordinance requiring all presidential trains to stop in Temple for five minutes. The train apparently did pause in Taylor where diaries of that period mention "going to Taylor to see Mr. Roosevelt." As ex-president, Roosevelt paused in Granger in 1911. "The train only stopped long enough to take water, but the gracious ex-president came out on the rear platform and shook hands with quite a number." A large crowd had gathered for a glimpse of him. President Harry Truman spoke from his whistle-stop train in Georgetown as he campaigned for election in September 1948, appearing on the rear platform for a bouncy talk to his audience there.[34] Accompanying Truman for the Georgetown appearance was Congressman Lyndon B. Johnson, who was running for the U. S. Senate that same year.

In 1921 three hundred employees worked in the Taylor railroad car shops and the roundhouse. That year the men went on a strike and the

Taylor roundhouse and railroad shops.

shops were closed for a period. After a settlement was made, twenty-five percent of the men were rehired. In 1929 the roundhouse and shop were closed at Taylor and moved to Valley Junction. Other strikes plagued the county about the same time, a week-long one interrupting service on the Georgetown and Round Rock Tap in 1922. The tap line by this time was owned by I. & G. N. During the years from the 1920s through the 1950s, railroad service was gradually curtailed in the county, as it was over the nation. Passenger service was completely abandoned. New life was fed into the county rail business in the 1960s when the Georgetown Railroad Company was reorganized, primarily to handle shipping of crushed stone from a local company to points all over the nation. The National Railroad

Passenger Corporation (Amtrak) was activated in 1971 with the goal of providing service again. By late 1972, this line was sweeping across southern Williamson County on the route the first train took in 1876— through Thrall, Taylor, Hutto and Round Rock, and on to Austin. In addition to its large shipping facilities, the Georgetown Railroad Company opened a tourist attraction in 1971, the Balcones & Hill Country Railroad (B & HC), offering eight and a half mile rides on restored vintage cars through the Georgetown-Round Rock area.[35]

A number of Williamson countians gained statewide prominence in business and finance during the twentieth century. They included John Sparks, who owned ranches near Taylor and Georgetown and lived at Georgetown for many years, who developed extensive holdings and investments in cattle and mining, and who was elected Governor of Nevada for two terms soon after the turn of the century; Colonel Edward M. House, large landowner near Taylor, financier and closest advisor to President Woodrow Wilson; Herman Brown and Dan E. Root of Taylor and Georgetown, later joined by George Rufus Brown, in internationally known Brown & Root construction company, organized in 1919; Gentry L. Rowsey, Sr., Taylor oilman who founded Taylor Refining Company and operated it and other interests for many years; Neely Landrum of Georgetown, who became a Dallas financier with national and international interests in banking, utilities, insurance and manufacturing; J. Benton Lindquist, who grew up at the Georgetown home of Governor John Sparks, where Lindquist's parents managed the home during Sparks' absence, Lindquist becoming a Dallas banker and financier; Andrew Tarkington, Taylor High School graduate of 1928, who became president of Conoco Company of New York in 1964; Louis and Billie Sue Henna of Round Rock, whose oil and business interests contributed to the establishment of Texas Baptist Children's Home in Round Rock in 1950; W. Grogan Lord of Georgetown, who developed a financial empire based on a wide range of business interests after World War II.

The internationally-known and powerful Brown & Root, Inc. began in Williamson County. In 1917 Jim Root, who ran a farm six miles from Taylor, gave his daughter Margaret in marriage to Herman Brown. Two years later Brown and his brother-in-law, Dan E. Root, founded the company. From 1920 until 1925 Herman and Margaret Brown lived in Georgetown and when the 1921 flood destroyed or devastated the roads and bridges of the county, Brown & Root successfully bid on much of the replacement and repair, including bridges at Georgetown and Circleville over the San Gabriel. Brown's younger brother, George Rufus Brown, worked for the company in Williamson County for three years during this period but did not live there permanently. Upon Root's death in 1928, George Brown bought his interest in the company, by then expanding rapidly. Brown & Root, Inc., has built dams along the Texas Colorado River, and all over the world has constructed airports, chemical plants, ordnance plants, shipbuilding yards, paper mills, tunnels, bridges, dams and freeways. Margaret Root Brown and Alice Pratt Brown (Mrs. George) are graduates of Southwestern University; Herman Brown was on that school's Board of Trustees from 1948 until his death in November 1962. George R. Brown of Houston continued to serve his company as Chairman of the Board in 1973.[37]

Texaco Inc., had its beginnings in Georgetown in 1901 when Judge R. E. Brooks of that place, along with A. A. Booty, a local merchant, and others organized the Texas Fuel Company. The same year, Spindletop oil well was brought in at Beaumont and Brooks moved there to be near the center of the oil business. In 1902 Texas Fuel Company became the Texas Company, of which Brooks was treasurer and director, serving in those offices for many years. He retired from the Texas Company in 1920. Judge Brooks graduated from Southwestern University in 1883, received his M.A. degree there in 1884, studied law in the Georgetown office of Fisher and Towns, and was admitted to the bar in 1885. He married Miss Fannie Booty in Georgetown in 1889. Brooks practiced law in the county until 1895 when he was appointed district judge of Travis and Williamson counties, was twice reelected to the post, resigning in 1901 to enter the oil business.[38]

Late in 1909 a bond election to build a new $120,000 county Courthouse in Georgetown passed 2411 to 380, and work on the new structure began March 1, 1910. The cornerstone was laid October 6, 1910. Architects were C. H. Page and Brother of Austin; W. C. Whitney of Beaumont was contractor. The building was ready for occupancy in November 1911. Major renovations in 1965 replaced the pediments and railing trim around the upper outside edge of the building, substituted unornamented vertical brickwork, much to the disappointment of the aesthete, but justified by county officials on the basis of economy.[39]

Shortly after World War II was over, the county was granted its first low cost housing project, which was located in south Taylor, completed about 1948. Twenty years later a similar project was planned for Georgetown. Through the efforts of a volunteer committee of the Georgetown Housing Authority composed of specialists in several key fields including

Fifth Courthouse, built 1910-1911.

architecture, an experimental kind of project was undertaken with the goals of combining beauty, stability, durability, economy and comfort in the units. Blending Spanish and western style architecture and utilizing native stone, the final product was pronounced successful and the units have become favorite models for state housing authorities. The first units were opened in March 1968; another group was under construction in 1973.[40]

Granger was the third community to undertake a low cost development. Both the Granger and Taylor homes were constructed of brick and both, like those in Georgetown, have provided comfortable, pleasant housing for large numbers of low income families. Granger's residences have been in use since 1970.

A Williamson County flag was designed and adopted by Commissioners Court in May 1973 through efforts of the County Historical Survey Committee. School children submitted drawings which inspired the final design. A ground of blue is centered with a map of Texas in white, on which the county map in red, and gold numerals, "1848," are laid. Thirty-three gold stars encircle the maps, the stars representing the active communities and towns of the county in 1973.

COUNTY MEDICINE; ACCIDENTS

Williamson County built its first hospitals early in the twentieth century and doctors got their first automobiles, although the horse remained essential for some years until roads were all-weather. Only after about 1920 could the country doctor reminisce about the days when he crossed all the county streams at the fords before bridges were built, sometimes when the waters were dangerously swollen; when all the roads were dirt or "soft and precipitous, beset by brush"; when he traveled in burning heat of the summer sun on the prairies or rode on sleety winter nights until his beard had icicles hanging from it. The country doctor loved horses and was skillful in the saddle—his horse knew the way home if he was too exhausted to guide the animal; and the doctor was equally a student and lover of nature.[41] Within a few decades the automobile created changes in medical practice as sensational as the coming of the railroads to the frontier.

The county Medical Association continued regular meetings in the twentieth century, in the 1930s giving up its charter and merging with Llano and Burnet counties for a year or two, after which the county society obtained a new charter in its own name. Dr. Jay J. Johns of Taylor has been a member from 1924 to the present (1973).[42]

The county's first hospitals organized after the turn of the century were housed in residential buildings. Dr. A. V. Doak arrived in Taylorsville in 1879 as surgeon for the I. & G. N. Railroad, and when his son, Edmond Doak, graduated from Medical School in 1901 he returned to Taylor to join his father in medicine. Dr. Edmond Doak established the first hospital in Taylor shortly after this time in a two story building at about Fourth and Elliott streets. An outside stairway led to the upper floor. Dr. F. C. Floeckinger and Dr. E. F. Mikeska built Floeckinger Sanitarium and School of Nursing in the 700 block of West Sixth, in 1911. Dr. Edmond Doak joined the staff in 1914 and the name was changed to City Hospital. Dr. E. W. Stromberg arrived in Taylor to practice in 1913. Dr. G. A. Wedemeyer began construction in 1914 on the Taylor Sanitarium at 800 West Seventh. In 1920 Drs. Doak, John H. Vaughan and Stromberg formed an association to build P & S Hospital at 813 North Main, later known as Doak & Stromberg, and then as Stromberg Hospital. Dr. Jay J. Johns purchased the Floeckinger Sanitarium about 1945, converting it into Johns Clinic. It was ready for use in July 1946. Meanwhile, Stromberg and Dr. W. R. Swanson bought Wedemeyer's hospital. Dr. Johns purchased the hospital built by Stromberg, combining its function as a hospital with the former Floeckinger Sanitarium which he continued to use as a clinic, adding a hospital wing there. In 1957 Johns acquired the Stromberg-Swanson Hospital (formerly Wedemeyer) and the next year leased it to the Evergreen Nursing Home.[43]

Dr. J. L. Dickey settled in Taylor in 1921, setting up a practice and providing medical care for people of the Negro race. At that time the incidence of typhoid was extremely high among black families, many of whom lived along Taylor creeks during the depression years and obtained water from the creeks because they could not afford city water. With Dr. Dickey's help, city hydrants were placed in accessible locations so that pure water was available to these families. Enlisting the aid of the State Health Department, Dr. Dickey also gave free injections to prevent typhoid. The incidence fell dramatically in a short time. The untiring young doctor had meant to stay at Taylor for only a few years but after seeing the needs there, he remained. In April 1935 he organized the Dickey Clinic which served patients both white and black, but primarily black, from the Williamson, Lee, Travis and Milam county areas. The clinic was first housed in an abandoned rooming house at 601 Bland Street, Taylor. Later, the doctor built a new clinic which also provided hospital space for his patients. Dr. Dickey was credited with alleviating many other serious health problems among his people, along with other work of social and civic nature which meant much to Negro citizens. In 1940 the first Negro park was established in the community. Dr. Dickey encouraged the organization of a Negro Chamber of Commerce and of a ladies' auxiliary, called the Welfare Workers' Club, which undertook to erect a Community Center building in 1940 at a cost of $2000. Mrs. M. P. Dickey and many others were active in this project.[44]

Bonds for a new Taylor community hospital were voted and plans were underway for this new structure in 1973.

The second hospital to be opened in the county is believed to have been in Liberty Hill. Dr. John Hershel Vaughan, a native of that community, spent his first years in the medical profession in Georgetown, practicing with Dr. E. M. Thomas. In 1912 he bought property in Liberty Hill where he built a stucco home and two years later added an upper story to his residence. The second floor was used as a hospital. In 1920 he left Liberty Hill for Taylor where he was associated with Dr. E. W. Stromberg, and moved to Amarillo in 1927. Dr. J. H. Vaughan's cousin, Dr. Thomas D. Vaughan, also practiced medicine in Taylor; from there he went to Bertram.[45]

By 1908 Georgetown had an active King's Daughters Circle, which tended to needs of ill and deprived citizens, in which Mrs. Elliott Stone and many others were active. The circle sent patients to the King's Daughters Hospital in Temple where the Georgetown organization contributed financial support for maintenance of a hospital room. The need for a local hospital was obvious. On October 22, 1917, W. M. and Louisa Allison of Georgetown agreed to sell to a committee representing the King's Daughters Sanitarium of Georgetown a house and lot—the south two-thirds of Block Eleven on the west side of Ash Street (1508-1510 Ash) for a total of $3500. Officials of the ladies organization at the time were Mrs. J. M. Daniel, president; Mrs. W. L. Coleman, secretary; Mrs. S. T. Atkin, treasurer. The residence was refurbished inside and out, an operating room and four private hospital rooms were outfitted upstairs, and downstairs were the manager's apartment, reception, dining and kitchen facilities, nurses' quarters and three ward rooms. Open house was held there on January 1, 1918. The hospital served the community several years until another hospital was built in 1923. In 1924 Dr. Reginald Platt, an osteopath, purchased the King's Daughters Sanitarium to be used as his residence, converting a room into his office for a brief time. He later opened an office downtown.[46]

Georgetown's second hospital was erected in 1923 by Dr. S. S. Martin and sons, Dr. John R. Martin and Dr. Walter Martin, and was located at 605 East University Avenue. The new two story brick building was considered extremely up-to-date, with complete facilities and forty beds for patients. In July 1947, Drs. H. R. Gaddy, Jr., Allen Barr and J. Frank Clark purchased the Martin Hospital. Barr and Clark left Georgetown after a few years and in 1957 Dr. Douglas Benold and Dr. Gaddy formed a partnership, renovating and enlarging the hospital and adding a clinic across the street to the east. The name was changed from Georgetown Hospital to Georgetown Medical and Surgical (M & S) Hospital and Clinic as new doctors were added to the staff, including Drs. James L. Shepherd, John R. Webb and Richard W. Pearce, all practicing in 1973.[47]

As communities drifted toward urbanization, smaller towns such as Florence and Round Rock found it harder and harder to keep doctors. In 1950 the community of Florence erected an eleven bed hospital and clinic which it hoped would encourage a doctor to live in Florence. For most of the time since then, the hospital has been staffed by at least one doctor.

Similarly, Round Rock, through a community effort was able to initiate work toward a clinic in the early 1960s. Louis Henna, a local businessman, put up the structure and funds were gathered by other Round Rock supporters to purchase equipment and supplies for the M. D. Clinic which was in operation in 1962. Since then several doctors have served the town and surrounding community including Dr. Thomas H. Barnett and Dr. R. L. Peters.[48]

Disease, accidents and disasters took their usual tolls. Immunization was not generally practiced until several decades of the century went by. Diphtheria was a recognized threat, especially to children, and in 1908 school was suspended for a time in Hutto because of its prevalence there. Whooping cough was often deadly and always dreaded. Smallpox remained a serious enough problem that the Georgetown city administration continued its arrangement for a house where incoming persons who were discovered to have smallpox could be placed away from other people. It was referred to locally as the "pest house." Several cases of meningitis were reported in January 1912 in Taylor and Waterloo; the Georgetown City Council placed a quarantine against train travelers stopping off at Georgetown to prevent the spread of meningitis which might be brought from other parts of the state. Persons living at Round Rock who had not been on the trains of the main lines nor in any infected places were allowed to ride the "Tap Line" to Georgetown.[49]

Railroad, gin and mill accident rates remained high during the first two decades of the century. Safety devices were unsophisticated, if used at all. Within two weeks' time in 1908, three separate railroad accidents near Georgetown claimed the life of Ed Brown, a brakeman, and injured two more men—one with two legs broken. The previous month, a brakeman was caught and crushed between two trains. A wreck on the Houston and Texas Central between Rutledge and McNeil killed the engineer and injured fifteen passengers as the train plunged into a branch after a fire had weakened the bridge which collapsed as the train crossed it. During the last week of August 1910, three separate train wrecks were reported near Taylor, Coupland and Granger. Lawsuits against the railroads became more and more common. Gin and mill accidents often resulted in maiming or crippling. Frank T. Towns, 45, was the victim of a whirling line shaft at the Salado Flour Mill which took his life. He was a member of the J. F. Towns family who operated numerous mills and gins in Williamson County. Fires were extremely devastating at the turn of the century, although by this time the larger towns had volunteer fire departments. A large section of Bartlett was wiped out by fire in September 1909. In gins and mills where combustible materials were always abundant, fires brought frequent calamities, but the gins or mills were usually rebuilt.[50.]

As automobiles became more generally used, accidents involving them accelerated. One of the most shocking tragedies of the early decades occurred at Round Rock when a Missouri Pacific train hit a bus carrying Baylor University athletes and students, killing ten of the young men on the bus including Ivey R. Foster Jr. of Taylor. The Baylor men were en route to Austin where they were to play basketball. The day was a cold, rainy one—January 22, 1927. "A slow steady drizzle was falling as the bus neared Round Rock on U. S. Highway 81." The basketball team was confident of a victory in their game, and students had accompanied the team to cheer their players. One of the students sitting up front got up, walked to the back of the bus and chatted with his friends there. Another, sitting in the back—Ivey Foster—exchanged seats, moving up to the front. "All of the windows had been closed and were badly fogged. The driver slowed down to a snail's pace as he went through Round Rock and was making only about 25 miles an hour when he reached the railroad crossing in the town. Suddenly through the mist he saw a south-bound passenger train bearing down on him. He frantically applied the brakes but not in time to prevent one of the worst grade crossing accidents in the nation's history. The train plowed into the rear end of the bus, reducing it almost to splinters. . . . The dead and injured were scattered along the right of way for several hundred yards."[51]

Dr. Dick Bolling Gregg, physician of Round Rock and the Missouri Pacific doctor there, members of the train crew, and others in the community loaded the injured men and the dead onto the train which took them to Taylor. Those needing medical aid were hospitalized. Of the ten who were killed, nine were in the rear of the bus; the lone survivor in that part of the vehicle was Ed Gooch, who had walked from the front to the back a short while before. The only man killed on the front of the bus was Ivey Foster, who had just exchanged places with Gooch.[52] The accident shook the entire state and resulted finally in two specific safety measures—the requirement that buses stop before crossing a railroad, and the building of an overpass at the crossing in Round Rock.

FLOODS AND DAMS

A rainfall which shattered U. S. records and the ensuing floods which hit every stream in Williamson County changed the pattern of thousands of lives in September 1921. Resulting from a hurricane which blew onto the Texas coast, the unprecedented rains began in Williamson County on Thursday night and Friday morning, September 8 and 9, and continued through Saturday morning. Thrall recorded the greatest amount—38.21 inches in twenty-four hours, September 9 and 10. Taylor had 23.11 inches

The 1921 flood on Taylor street and at Circleville railroad bridge.

in the same period, and a total of 23.98 in thirty-five hours, according to U. S. Weather Bureau statistics. Mr. and Mrs. J. H. W. Cobb who lived in the Yarbrough neighborhood northwest of Georgetown were swept away into flood waters of a small branch leading to Dry Berry's Creek and were drowned. Greatest loss of life occurred in the Taylor area where residences on low, flat ground along normally small branches were flooded or washed away. Many Mexican families were particularly hard hit. By the Tuesday following the deluge, twenty-five bodies had been recovered in the vicinity of Taylor. After all reports were in, the county's toll was listed at ninety-two dead or missing. Loss of life occurred in the lowlands near Georgetown, at Redville Gin, near Hogan Crossing on Brushy Creek, at other places down Brushy, on J. F. Bowers' farm on the Gabriel, near Hutto, Lawrence Chapel, Hoxie, Youngstown, on Alligator Creek, near the town of San Gabriel, and on Mustang Creek below King's farm.[53]

Observers of the storm described the fierce lightning, the garish green hue of the sky, and the water which fell—not in drops—but in great sheets hour after hour. Ten thousand square miles of farm bottom land was inundated and angry waters took out homes, bridges, railroads, roads, culverts and buildings. Where residences in the wake of the flood were not swept completely away, they were often washed from their foundations and in numerous instances the personal effects of families were either wholly lost or damaged beyond further use. Steel bridges which had stood thirty years of floods were gone and countless smaller bridges lost. Fields of corn and cotton in the low lands were stripped clean, several gins washed away, along with many bales of cotton, some of which were later recovered downstream. Schools, churches, automobiles, barns and farm buildings were damaged or destroyed. Livestock drowned everywhere—dead horses, mules, goats, sheep, pigs and cows floated down river. Sometimes an animal managed to hang in a tree for a time, or rode a log, dexterously managing to keep on top of the rotating life saver.[54]

Since Florence, Gabriel Mills, Andice, Liberty Hill, Hopewell and Leander were located near the headwaters of the streams of the county, damage in those areas was somewhat less extensive than in the eastern portion of the county, but considerable stock was lost and bridges and low water crossings were washed out there. Where bridges were not destroyed, the embankments and approaches to them were. Lee Mather near Liberty Hill lost fifty of his fifty-one sheep. Several residences at Florence were washed from their foundations and partially wrecked and other buildings damaged, but roads were not so badly damaged as farther east. At Andice, sixty bales of cotton floated away but were recovered. Dry Berry's Creek went on a rampage, drowned two people, and near its confluence with the main fork of Berry's Creek, nearly destroyed a gin. Nineteen bales of cotton from the gin also went downstream; seventeen were found. At the site of the old Berry's Mill (later Gann's) a short distance down the creek, pecan groves were destroyed. "The beautiful Jim Hogg school house" on the North Gabriel was washed away.[55]

At Georgetown, the steel bridge over the North Gabriel was torn away, but the south bridge stood. Two bridges on Berry's Creek, one on the Jarrell road, one on the road to Florence, one over Smith Branch, one over Mankin's Branch, and the causeway at Mankin's Crossing were destroyed. Professor R. F. Young, who owned the Berry's Mill property, reported 15.05 inches of rain there Friday and Saturday. Northtown (part of Georgetown) was in danger of washing away. Earl Cobb moved his grocery stock to higher ground, several Northtown homes were wrecked and others submerged, and every chicken in that section of town was said to have drowned. Present San Gabriel Park was evacuated by campers who were forced to leave hurriedly early Friday morning and the park caretakers, Mr. and Mrs. Pat Goodlett, left that night in their bathing suits. The Georgetown Water and Light power plant in the park was destroyed and the Old Settlers' grounds completely wrecked. Mail service to Georgetown was interrupted Friday night and for the next week; the nearest service was at Elgin and Smithville on the M. K. & T. On the same Friday, the last Katy train from Bartlett was forced to stop at Georgetown with two hundred passengers aboard. They spent the night but some managed to get to Austin in a day or two.[56]

A cyclone south of Georgetown damaged barns of William Palm and John Lindell. At Mankin's Crossing on the San Gabriel, water stood five feet high in the Emmett Cooke home on a high bank of the San Gabriel.

Weir. not on a stream, suffered a cyclone which damaged the walls and roof of the new brick school, damaged churches, blew away Carl Brady's "auto house" but "left his Ford car unharmed" inside where the house had stood.[57]

At the junction of Mileham Branch and the San Gabriel River at Jonah "every home in the village was inundated and nearly every family's personal effects more or less ruined." Stores and other buildings were damaged. The Christian Church was washed across Mileham Branch and was set down in reasonably good condition on the opposite bank by the flood waters. Parishioners later purchased the land where the flood had deposited the church and continued to hold services at the new site. Both the Baptist and Methodist churches at Jonah suffered considerable damage. A Jonah merchant, A. J. Rhodes, found "a three hundred pound hog in a bed in his house during the flood. Bob Hicks drifted a bale of cotton onto the Methodist church. . . . It is not known whether Bob will donate the cotton to the church, or whether Mr. Rhodes appropriated the hog."[58]

The heavy steel bridge across the San Gabriel at Circleville washed out the first night the river flooded and the Circleville School north of the river was damaged beyond repair. The A. C. Stearns gin was badly damaged. Water stood five feet inside the Stearns home nearby, although the home was several feet above ground on stilts to prevent just such an occurrence. Flood waters had risen rapidly after sundown and by nine o'clock Friday evening the Stearns family was barely able to drive away before being cut off between the river and Pecan Branch to the north, which streams soon joined to form a continuous swirling body of water. Auburn and Margaret Stearns had hastily gathered their three small children to ride through waters already engulfing the wheels of their car and crossed the San Gabriel bridge heading south. Cut off by another swollen branch, normally dry, the family spent the night at Meeks' Store, then on Saturday was able to reach the Harvey T. Stearns home high on a hill to the south. For days, water spread almost as far as the eye could see, far, far out of the river banks. It was about a week before the family was able to return to the home north of the river and measure the flood line inside the rooms. Mud on carpets was several inches thick, and all personal belongings ruined.*[59]

From Circleville on down the San Gabriel River through the remainder of the county, many families did not evacuate until very late, if they did at all, for flood waters had never been known to rise high enough to reach

* This paragraph is based largely on recollections of the author and of her parents.

them. The railroad bridge crossing at Circleville was washed away and the tracks grotesquely twisted and wrenched as if they were delicate toys; all bridges below were gone including the one at Hoxie. On the David Young place at Friendship, a Negro couple and their child too late tried to reach safety, anchoring themselves to a tree and holding to the child, but were drowned. Twenty-six Mexicans were reported drowned on the Byers place near Laneport when they were surrounded by water. A gin south of Sore Finger Creek washed away and at Friendship Hubert and Clem Blackman pushed twenty-six floating bales of cotton to a safe place when they found them bobbing in the water.[60]

Hutto reported a severe windstorm or tornado and loss along Brushy Creek to the south. The approaches to new bridges east of Round Rock on Brushy Creek were washed out, and bridges across Brushy south of Hutto and a causeway at Hutto were destroyed.[61]

The storm hit Taylor at three o'clock Friday morning. The twenty-three inch rain of the day flooded all the small streams in and near town, including Bull Branch and Mustang Creek, as well as all the low streets where many homes were wrecked. The flood reached its apex about nine o'clock Friday night when the waters rushed over the dams of the water supply basin near North Main Street and undermined the Texas Power and Light Company substation, blacking out the entire city. Bull Branch bridge washed out at that time, homes were washed against the M. K. & T. railroad a few blocks below town, and the northern approach to the Katy bridge went out as the bridge itself was bent and warped. The I. & G. N. railroad bridge across Bull Branch was also severely damaged. Bridges across North Main and near the cemetery went out, and the one on South Main Street over Mustang Creek lost much of its embankment. Paving was badly damaged. Water rose in numerous homes adding to the destruction. In the fringes of town, a bridge over Bull Branch on Beyersville road at the foot of Doak Street, and two others over an oil ditch in South Taylor were lost. Precinct 4 County Commissioner reported that ninety-eight per-cent of the wooden culverts in the precinct were out, and that every bridge of any size in the precinct was destroyed except the Easley bridge, and it was partially wrecked. Bridges were gone at Rice's Crossing, Beyersville, Post Oak Island, on Cottonwood Creek and at Cheek's Crossing. A man from Hare walked the fifteen miles to Taylor a few days after the deluge to get his mail. On September 16 John L. Brunner and William E. Thies, postmasters at Taylor and Granger, established an auto-boat service. Mail from Taylor was carried to the river at Circleville by car, crossed the river by boat, and went by car to Granger where the Katy had restored service.[62]

The Opossum Creek bridge at Walburg, and those over Willis Creek at Rudasill and Pope's Spring and the bridge at Friendship were all lost. Precinct 3 Commissioner reported that at least fifty percent of the wooden structures in his district were gone.

Among railraoad damages were the Houston and Texas Central bridge washout at Walker Ranch south of Leander; another bridge damanged between Leander and Liberty Hill; the Missouri-Kansas and Texas bridge washed out over Opossum Creek. The Katy Lake bridge lost numerous pilings and much embankment, and rails were torn and twisted like wire; rail bridges north and south of Georgetown were severely damaged, the bridges over Chandler Branch and Onion Creek washed out, the one at Round Rock damaged, the roof of the depot at Weir blown off, and the bridge at Circleville gone. The other bridges between Taylor and Granger were in bad condition.

Within a week after the county's worst natural disaster of historical times, people were cleaning up, salvaging what they could, planning for the future. Within two weeks, schools were being rebuilt at Circleville, Waterloo and Concord.[63]

The devastation of the 1921 flood was still fresh in the minds of many in the mid-thirties when conservation and reclamation became popular concepts in the minds of the public and in the political philosophy of the time. In September 1936, the Brazos River Conservation and Reclamation District announced surveys would begin on the North and South San Gabriel rivers for proposed dams, and from that day until late in 1972, the subject of dams was much-discussed, much debated and many times Congressional action was postponed. The problem in the thirties and forties was finding funds for dams—there was little opposition to them. When government engineers proposed one for the Laneport area, however, in the heart of rich blackland farms, opposition was heard from those whose past experience indicated that a lake there would be a mud and mosquito flat and that extremely valuable farmland would be wasted forever underneath the lakes. They argued that dams higher up on the San Gabriels would solve the flood problem and that a shallow mud bottom lake would be, like others of its kind already built, unacceptable for recreation. Proponents of the dam location in the vicinity of Laneport included most notably the government engineers who planned it and some landholders who anticipated selling their land to the federal government. One of the landholders was appointed to the board which made administrative decisions in that reclamation district and from that point on the strenuous objections of a majority of those concerned were fruitless. In the decade of the 1960s when the importance of ecological balance first became a matter of serious consideration by laymen, an injunction filed by conservationist James Allison briefly delayed work on the Laneport site on the basis of ecological damage. Late in 1972, however, a Texas court declined further action to prevent building of the dam. Early in 1973 work was progressing on two sites—on the North Gabriel and near Laneport. Whatever the effect of the added weight of the large dams and water reservoirs upon the Balcones Fault near and upon which the new dams will lie, scientists are not certain. It is generally agreed by all sides that recreational facilities created by the lakes will serve many more people than the area could previously, that the lakes will provide valuable reservoirs of water in case there is need for them, that they will help control floods on the San Gabriel and possibly on the Brazos, that several hundred archeological sites of early Indian habitations will be covered by the lakes, along with marvels of natural scenic beauty and wildlife along the upper North Gabriel, and that the building of the dams will boost local economy. A third dam contemplated for the South Fork of the San Gabriel River is also projected.[64]

Much more quietly, and apparently effectively, small dams were built at relatively moderate cost up and down Brushy Creek in the 1960s, furnishing flood control and water for irrigation.

Until the 1960s, most rural areas in the county were dependent upon shallow water wells. To provide a more consistent and safer water source to farmers and rural communities, a number of water districts were formed and systems installed, or were being installed in 1973, to provide water to those communities.[65]

PUBLIC LIFE: THREE GOVERNORS, A PRESIDENT, A PRESIDENTIAL ADVISOR, A MOON EXPLORER, A WOMAN LEADER, OTHERS

In the fields of public service and politics, Williamson County has contributed three governors—Dan Moody and Preston Smith, both born in the county and both governors of Texas, and John Sparks, longtime resident of the county who became governor of Nevada. Not a resident of the county, but longtime public servant representing Williamson and closely associated with it for many years was one of the nation's most active presidents, Lyndon Baines Johnson. Judge Richard Critz of Taylor, a teacher, lawyer, county official and judge, had a long career culminating in his service as justice on the Texas Supreme Court; Judge John Edward Hick-

President and Mrs. Lyndon Baines Johnson.

man of Liberty Hill also taught school, studied law and served in various court posts including Chief Justice Texas Supreme Court from 1948 until 1961. When the Ku Klux Klan trials of 1923 and 1924 took place in Williamson County, the careers of lawyers credited with brilliant work for the prosecution in that case received powerful boosts. They included Dan Moody of Taylor, Harry Graves, Dave W. Wilcox, Will Nunn, and J. F. Taulbee, all of Georgetown, and Richard Critz and E. H. Lawhon of Taylor. All were prominent in law circles for years afterwards. Judge Harry Graves was elected to the House of Representatives in 1929 where he supervised a study on improving Texas government, issued a thirteen-volume Griffenhagen report with recommendations for saving the state fifteen million dollars without curtailing any state services. "Inertia and political expediency" prevented implementation of the project which was generally conceded to have been a brilliant piece of work. Graves served later as justice of the Court of Criminal Appeals beginning in 1937. Judge Dave W. Wilcox was chairman of the Texas State Democratic Executive Committee.[66]

A friend and advisor to several presidents, governors, and other high officials, Colonel Edward Mandell House became best known for his close association with the Woodrow Wilson administration. House was born in Houston in 1858, was educated in the east while his father, a U.S. Senator, operated vast cotton and sugar plantations in Texas. These were inherited from E. M. House's grandfather, who began acquiring land in Williamson County as early as 1867. In 1885 Senator House deeded one-fourth interest in his Williamson County blackland property to his son—a total of 1506½ acres. Edward M. House had moved with his wife to Austin shortly before that time and it was there that his two daughters, Mona—for whom Monadale in Williamson County was named—and Janet, were born. William Malone managed the cotton farm in Williamson County while between 1892 and 1904 House took charge of the successful gubernatorial campaigns of James S. Hogg, Charles A. Culberson (who commissioned House a Colonel on his staff) and S. W. T. Lanham. House also managed the senatorial race of Culberson. When his duties permitted, he visited his Monadale farm. In November 1911, House met Woodrow Wilson and soon after moved to New York as Wilson's advisor in the latter's post as governor of New Jersey. When Wilson campaigned for the presidency, House was a key figure among the candidate's confidants. During and after World War I, House was President Wilson's emissary to Europe on a number of occasions and was his chief consultant in England and France on the proposed peace plans.[67]

Forrest F. Brown of Williamson County met Colonel House in France during World War I. Brown, stationed at American General Headquarters near Paris, went to Chaumont to purchase groceries for his outfit, spotted an American looking around and offered to take him to a hotel. The man introduced himself as Edward M. House, saying he was due at General Pershing's Headquarters. It was raining, so Brown took Colonel House in his wagon to camp to deposit the groceries en route to the General's quarters. "We talked until the bugles called the G. I.'s for an honor guard. Since I was from Williamson County, Colonel House obviously enjoyed a long talk about that familiar place he had not been to see for a long time." House described his land there and commented that he gave ten acres of it to the community for a school. However, the community did not choose to put the school on the donated site, locating it instead close to the gin. "But it was all right. They named the school Monadale for my daughter," House said.[68]

Working long, difficult hours through the war years to assist and relieve President Wilson, House became exhausted and ill in the fall of 1919 after the peace negotiations. He recovered and remained close to politicians, was respected by both Coolidge and Hoover, and had a role in the nomi-

nation of Franklin Delano Roosevelt for president, continuing as an unofficial advisor after his election.[69]

Jessie Daniel Ames, early champion of voting rights for women and

Jessie Daniel Ames, 1920.

of prison reform, founder of a Negro orphans' home and a home for delinquent girls in Texas, resided in Georgetown, was graduated from Southwestern University in 1902. Her husband, Dr. Roger Post Ames, had a
medical career which took him over the entire country as did her career
in the cause of women's rights, but she returned to Georgetown after his
death to live with her mother, Mrs. J. M. Daniel, owner of the local telephone company. When the Texas legislature gave women the right to vote
in the primaries in 1918 but allowed only two weeks for them to register,
Mrs. Ames and others led a massive campaign in Williamson County. As
a result, 3300 women came to the Courthouse by wagon, hack, and on foot
to register. Observers of the phenomenon stated, "There's never been anything like it since." Mrs. Ames was a founder and first president of the
Texas League of Women Voters, was one of the first women delegates to
the state and national Democratic conventions, and held many offices and
positions of responsibility in service and political organizations.

James Shaw of Georgetown served on the State Banking Commission. El-
more Rural "Tiger" Torn, chemurgist, agriculturist, longtime director of the
East Texas Chamber of Commerce, lived for many years in Taylor. He
founded the International Blackeyed Pea Association and publicized that
product over the world as a nutritional food.[70]

The Ku Klux Klan movement which followed the Civil War apparently had few if any adherents in the Williamson County area. It was not until the period after World War I that the organization became a serious factor in central Texas. By the early 1920s county newspapers carried news about the state Klan and commented editorially on its activities. Some writers took cognizance of the Klan's professed social and charitable goals, but most deplored its reputed stand for religious bigotry, racial bias and for violence. Since the Klan was a secret organization it could be blamed for events with which it had no official connection and could deny others sometimes proved in court to have been perpetrated by the organzation or by its members.[71]

At about the same time that the Klan was gaining momentum in Texas, a young Taylor attorney, Dan Moody, was beginning his law practice there. His family was steeped in the traditions of law and of teaching. His father, Dan'l. Moody, as he always wrote his name, moved to Taylor in 1876 where he was claims agent for the I. & G. N. railroad. In his earlier years he had served as a Baptist preacher, then drove cattle between Texas and Missouri. When Taylor was incorporated in 1882, Dan'l. Moody became the town's first mayor. Still later he served as justice of peace, helped establish a building and loan association, and ran an insurance business. Dan Moody's mother was a school teacher, Miss Nancy "Nanny" Elizabeth Robertson, who came with her widowed mother and family to Round Rock in 1883 and, a few months later, moved to the village of Bagdad. Nannie and her brother, William F. Robertson, both taught school at Bagdad, Will leaving his job after two years to study law. He was a member of the first class to graduate from the University of Texas Law School. Two cousins of Nannie and Will Robertson, Lillian and Ruric Wester, also made their homes with the Robertsons at Bagdad. Lillian Wester became a public school teacher, a college professor of French and Spanish languages, and a journalist-teacher in Mexico. Ruric became a businessman in Taylor.[72]

The Robertsons and Westers moved from Bagdad to Taylor in 1886 where Will opened his law office and he and his cousin built a two-story frame family home at 114 West Ninth Street. "Miss Nannie" taught mathematics in Taylor and Lillian Wester taught at Rice's Crossing and also at Taylor. In 1890 Nannie Robertson resigned her teaching position to marry Judge Dan'l. Moody, the ceremony taking place at the Robertson family home. Their son, Dan Moody, was born in that home on June 1, 1893, and there he and his only sister, Mary, were reared. In 1973 "Miss Mary" (Moody) still occupied the family home.[73]

Young Dan Moody's Aunt Lillian Wester was his first teacher in the

Taylor schools. He greatly admired his uncle, Will Robertson, and other members of his mother's family who were lawyers and Dan decided at an early age: "When I am big, I'm going to 'George-town' and be a lawyer." He and his sister were taught to work hard. Dan helped his father in a dairy, sold goods at a premium and, at sixteen while still in high school, began to read law. He was fascinated by electricity and learned a great deal about it. Dan Moody graduated from Taylor High School in 1909. When his father died in 1910, Dan assumed responsibility as the head of the family. After graduation, he worked as a railroad lineman until time to enroll in the University of Texas Law School for the 1910 session. To pay his college expenses, he took jobs as an electrician. Four years later he was admitted to the bar and returned to Taylor where he established a law practice.[74]

Dan Moody interrupted his law practice to serve in the armed forces during World War I. Returning then to Taylor, he began his meteoric political career by running for Williamson County Attorney. At age twenty-six, he was the youngest to be so elected in the county's history. At the end of the term (1920-1922), Governor Pat M. Neff appointed him to fill an unexpired term as District Attorney of Williamson and Travis counties (1922-1924). Again he was the youngest to hold that office. Dan Moody moved on, stumping over the state in a Model T Ford in 1924 seeking the office of Attorney General of Texas, to which he was elected, and continuing his tradition of being the youngest to hold the position. After that term Moody opened his campaign in 1926 for Governor of Texas in his hometown of Taylor. While campaigning for that office he married Miss Mildred Paxton. He was inaugurated governor at the age of thirty-three, the youngest on record, on January 18, 1927.[75]

The administration of the previous governor, Mrs. Miriam A. Ferguson, had been rocked by prison and highway scandals. Governor Moody immediately instituted reforms in the state highway system, recovering large sums of money for the state which had been paid out as kickbacks on highway contracts. He led another movement for penal and banking reforms. A non-drinker, he supported prohibition at a time when that stand was extremely unpopular. As a member of a labor union from his days as an electrician, he espoused labor's causes. During his two terms as governor he also reduced taxes, increased support of public education and worked toward business and industrial expansion in Texas. On the completion of his second term as governor in 1931, he entered private law practice in Austin. He died May 22, 1966.[76]

A clue to Dan Moody's character and determination is revealed in a

news story published shortly after he took his oath of office as district attorney. Soon after the swearing in ceremony which was held in Austin on
a Monday morning, he was due in Georgetown for a session of criminal
district court. Heavy rains had fallen in the Austin area on Sunday afternoon and night and were continuing to fall Monday morning. The new
district attorney, driving his Ford Coupe, picked up Judge James R. Hamilton who was supposed to preside at the court in Georgetown, and they
started in that direction.

> All streams, mudholes and other obstacles were passed in safety until the
> District Attorney and His Honor arrived at Round Rock. There Lake Creek
> refused a crossing and the gentlemen had to back track to the old Round
> Rock-Cockleburr section of the Austin road, thence back toward Round
> Rock to the I. & G. N. railroad crossing near the lime kiln. Here Mr. Moody
> piloted his car onto the railroad track and used it as a highway, successfully
> crossing the bridge across Lake Creek near the depot. An effort was made
> by Mr. Moody to get to Georgetown on the upper Georgetown-Round Rock
> road, but the branch at the Charlie Fulks farm was a little river and they had
> to turn back. At Round Rock again, Mr. Moody and the court impressed
> Constable B. E. Baker to ride with them to Chandler Branch on the new
> highway, having previously telephoned Sheriff Lee O. Allen to meet them
> there. At the Chandler bridge, which has not been completed, the court
> and his attorney successfully waded, walked railroad ties and otherwise
> went forward until they got on the north side of the stream where Sheriff
> Allen was ready with his special bootlegger-catching machine and in a short
> while these vigilant offiicers were at the courthouse, ready for business.
> However, the flood had cut off all but five of the grand jury and the
> gentlemen had to wait until late in the day for other members to arrive.[77]

The young, personable, dashing and efficient young Dan Moody might
well have enjoyed a spectacular career under the most normal of circumstances. As district attorney his prosecution of the Ku Klux Klan in several "notorious flogging cases"[78] unquestionably hurled him into statewide
and national prominence, paving the way for his rapid advancement in
politics. A flogging occurred in Williamson County almost simultaneously
with Moody's taking office as district attorney in April 1923 and, from that
time through the trials of September 1923 and of January-February 1924,
the "red-headed whirlwind" was in the spotlight. The *Williamson County
Sun* of Georgetown endorsed him for the office of state Attorney General
on January 18, 1924, claiming much support for him throughout the state.
Editor John M. Sharpe of the same newspaper endorsed him for the governorship on November 20, 1925.[79]

The story of the Klan trials, which were the culmination of events beginning early in 1923, is revealed in the testimony presented during those

Attorneys Richard Critz, Dan Moody, Harry Graves (top row, left to right); J. F. Taulbee, W. H. Nunn.

trials. A young salesman from Waco, R. W. Burleson, frequently made business trips into Williamson County. One of his boarding places was in the Weir home of Mrs. Fannie Campbell, a young widow of that community. Early in 1923 Reverend A. A. Davis, "a Baptist preacher and anti-Catholic lecturer of the county," delivered a note to Burleson bearing the seal of Georgetown Ku Klux Klan No. 178 and curtly warning Burleson to cease his relationship with Mrs. Campbell. Burleson burned the note but, while calling on customers in Taylor, threatened to kill any Klan members who continued to harass him.[80]

On Easter Sunday, April 1, 1923, Burleson and Mrs. Campbell and two of their friends, Mr. and Mrs. Lee Jones of Weir, drove to Jonah. They started back toward Weir late in the afternoon and, as they approached Mankin's Crossing on the San Gabriel River, they saw two automobiles "with curtains up" and one of them blocking the road. When Burleson stopped his car, eight or ten men wearing robes and hoods emerged from the two parked cars, ordered Burleson to get out, then dragged him out of his car and hit him with a pistol. A pistol was dropped on the ground. Mrs. Campbell immediately picked it up but it was wrenched from her hand and her finger was hurt. Burleson was shoved into one of the curtained cars with his feet left hanging out. The men in the two cars drove Burleson to a pecan grove near Jonah where Burleson was taken from the car. His assailants locked a heavy trace chain around his neck, fastened it to a thorny tree and held it taut so that Burleson's head was tilted back. One man pointed a drawn pistol, threatening Burleson if he cried out. After removing their captive's clothing, the men administered about fifty licks across Burleson's naked back with a heavy leather strap about four feet long, three inches wide. During the whipping, Burleson was questioned, taunted and threatened. He was then loaded into a small pickup truck and driven to the Taylor City Hall and was fastened with the chain to a tree on the lawn. Tar or creosote was poured over his head and body after which the robed men departed.[81]

By this time darkness of evening had fallen. Burleson managed to un-fasten the chain from the tree and, still wearing it around his neck, walked to a nearby building where he saw a light. The light was in the Harber House, a well-known Taylor boarding establishment owned by a widow, Mrs. Amanda Jane Harber. The elderly Mrs. Harber heard a knock at her door about 8:30 that evening, went to the door and there saw Burleson bleeding and covered with tar and wearing a chain. She quickly sum-moned her daughter, Mrs. Lula Ake, and Constable Louis Lowe, longtime Taylor law officer and later sheriff of Williamson County. Lowe testified at the trial that Burleson had many cuts and bruises over his entire body, that his back was raw and that he had creosote or tar in his hair, on his head, ears, face, shoulders and body. He took Burleson to the Taylor City Hall where machinist Arthur Lyons and others cut the chain from Burle-son's neck. Large quantities of oil were required to remove the tar. Mean-while doctors had been summoned to dress the wounds and Burleson was placed on a bed in the fireman's ward until an ambulance arrived to move him to a local hospital. When he was lifted from the bed to be put in the ambulance, blood had run through his bandages and soaked onto the bed. Lowe declared it was the worst beating he ever saw. Burleson was "as raw as a piece of beef from the small of his back to the knees; and in many places the skin had been split and the flesh was gaping open."[82]

Investigations began immediately after the Easter Sunday affair. A special court of inquiry heard a large number of witnesses in a closed ses-sion on April 4, 1923, at Georgetown and the next day five Taylor men were arrested on suspicion of being involved in the beating. They were released on bond. The grand jury met on Wednesday, May 9, to hear evi-dence, and four witnesses who refused to answer questions concerning the case were fined one hundred dollars each. After the hearing, charges were filed against the five men arrested on April 5. The investigation was carried out by County Attorney Albert T. Evans, assistant County Attorney Solon Reinhardt, Sheriff Lee O. Allen, special attorney Harry N. Graves of Georgetown and by constables Louis Lowe and Tom Russell of Taylor. "The Taylor Ku Klux Klan offered a reward to anyone who could prove that the Klan was in any way involved in the beating" and Klan chapters collected funds to retain outstanding legal talent for the defense. Serving as defense attorneys were state Senator A. E. Wood and his brother, D. B. Wood, both of Granger; W. C. Wofford of Taylor, Amos M. Felps of Elgin, Llewellen Duke of Georgetown and W. W. Hair of Temple. Attorneys for the prosecution were led by new Distict Attorney Dan Moody, assisted by attorneys Richard Critz and E. H. Lawhon of Taylor and by Georgetown lawyers Harry N. Graves, Dave W. Wilcox, W. H. Nunn and J. F. Taulbee.[83]

The case of Murray Jackson, charged with assault with prohibited weapons, opened on Monday, September 17, 1923, in Williamson County Criminal District Court, Georgetown, Judge James R. Hamilton presiding. Representatives from local, state and out-of-state newspapers and magazines sent reporters to cover the sensational trial.* "Never in the history of Williamson County have such crowds attended a trial as were present." Much of the testimony was lurid. Although it was called "one of the hardest fought cases tried in Williamson county in years," Judge Hamilton insisted upon and maintained courtroom order and decorum. Attorneys for the defense and for the state were courteous toward each other.[85]

The charge to the jury was presented on Monday night, September 24, a week after the hearing began. More than a hundred witnesses had appeared. The state carefully built an almost irrefutable case against the Klansmen. Final arguments began at eleven o'clock Tuesday morning, each side being allowed four and one-half hours. Dan Moody concluded his two-hour summation at nine-thirty that evening. His sister, Miss Mary Moody of Taylor, recalled that her brother had always frowned on his family's presence when he appeared in court, but on this occasion she drove to Georgetown and sat in the back of the courtroom so that he would not see her. Impressed by his concluding oration, she commented proudly to those nearby about its effectiveness and received, in turn, cold glares. Her neighboring spectators' sentiments were obviously with the defendant. The jury retired at ten o'clock in the evening, returning twenty minutes later with a verdict of guilty and recommending the maximum sentence of five years in state prison. The huge crowd which had been orderly throughout the trial remained so during the closing minutes. Jackson was sentenced as prescribed, was pardoned two years. later by Governor Miriam A. Ferguson.[86]

---

* Texas' Lieutenant Governor T. W. Davidson was quoted by Associated Press on August 18, 1923, as saying, "Kidnapping and flogging of citizens, which has been prevalent in Texas for some weeks, and which has led the Governor to send Rangers to the disturbed district, has spread to three other states—Georgia, Ohio and Oklahoma."[84] The New York *Times* was on strike at the time and ran abbreviated editions during the trial period.

Separate trials in what by then was generally called the "notorious Burleson flogging case" were held early the next year for Olen Gossett and Dewey Ball, both of whom pleaded guilty to the charge of assault with prohibited weapons. Each was sentenced to one year in prison. Charges against one other man were dropped.[87]

The State's case against Reverend A. A. Davis for perjury in testimony to the grand jury regarding the note he delivered to Burleson early in 1923 was tried in February 1924. The defendant was found guilty and sentenced to two years in prison. With that trial the Burleson flogging case was closed. The impressive career of young district attorney Dan Moody had begun, for as the first prosecuting attorney anywhere in the nation to win a legal battle against the Ku Klux Klan, his reputation was firmly established, his political career assured.[88]

During World War II, unusual military assignments were executed by Ross Wildet of Taylor who was on the team which bombed Tokyo toward the end of the war, and by Joe Stiborik of Taylor, crew member of the plane which dropped the first atomic bomb on Hiroshima. Two of Stiborik's sisters, also of Taylor, had unique posts: Mary Stiborik was present at the "little red schoolhouse" in Reims, France on May 7, 1945, when the German surrender was signed, and Cecilia Stiborik, Taylor, was on the staff of General Dwight D. Eisenhower.[89]

Preston Smith, son of Mr. and Mrs. Charlie Smith of the Mount Prospect-Corn Hill community in Williamson County, was born on the Smith farm there. About 1918 or 1919 he attended grade school at Mount

Mount Prospect School was attended by a future governor, Preston Smith.

Prospect, later moved with his family to west Texas. He was Governor of Texas for two terms, from 1969 to 1973.

Alan LaVern Bean, a member of the second team ever to land and walk on the Moon, took his first steps as a toddler in Georgetown where he lived

Alan Bean held by his mother at their Georgetown home, became a moon explorer.

for a year and a half. The family also lived in Taylor for several months. Bean was the son of Mr. and Mrs. Arnold H. Bean who moved to George-town in May 1932 when Alan was about six weeks old. A. H. Bean at that time was with the Texas Agricultural Station at College Station and was engaged in mapping the soil of Williamson County. Astronaut Bean was the fourth man to set foot on the moon's surface, spending about fourteen hours on his moon walk after piloting the landing of their lunar module, the *Intrepid*, on the moon on November 19, 1969. Bean and Charles "Pete" Conrad carried on the exploration while Richard F. Gordon remained in orbit in *Apollo 12*'s *Yankee Clipper*, ready to return the moon walkers to earth. After the suitably impressive words spoken by the first two men to land on the moon in an earlier flight, Bean's folksy exclamation upon this landing made him a popular, unassuming hero. As he and Conrad put the *Intrepid* down exactly on target, Bean exclaimed, "Holy cow, it's beauti-tiful out there." He later reported to NASA headquarters on earth: "Looks great, babe; the crater is right where it is supposed to be." As this history goes to press, Bean was on another second mission in space, this one a fifty-nine day stay on the U. S. Space Lab, July-September 1973. The space-man's mother, Frances Bean, held him for a picture in Georgetown in 1932, a few months after his birth on March 15. His father described the youngster:

> When we lived there, as Alan grew older, even in his buggy when outdoors, if a plane went over he would watch it as far as he could see it. In those days planes flew low over the houses. When Alan got old enough to under-stand flying he always said that was what he was going to do, and in all the years he never changed his mind. And from the time he could crawl around he was always very venturesome and climbed a lot; he never seemed to be afraid. As he grew older he started making model planes, simple ones at first, then on to the harder ones. After filling all the places in his room that he could set them, he started hanging them from the ceiling.

The Bean family visited friends in Georgetown and Liberty Hill for many years after leaving. They moved to Taylor from Georgetown late in 1933, and the next April Mr. Bean took a U. S. government post which moved the family to Louisiana.[90]

EDUCATORS, WRITERS, ARTISTS, OTHERS

Twentieth century education in Williamson County changed from more than a hundred rural schools to relatively few city based schools by 1950. Before the advent of the automobile, the one or two classroom schools to which most of the pupils and teachers walked dotted the landscape, spaced two and three to six miles apart. In most cases, students drank from a common dipper at a well or spring, huddled about a pot bellied stove in cold weather, and school sessions were scheduled so as to free the young people when they were most needed on the farms. As the urbanization of the 1930s and 1940s developed, rural schools almost entirely disappeared. The few survivors of that period were consolidated with larger community schools before 1970.

The only institution of higher learning to survive in the county through the troublesome depression years of the twenties and thirties was South-western University at Georgetown, which experienced extremely difficult times then, but had already outlived possibly a more formidable threat two decades earlier.

Among many outstanding educators and administrators at Southwestern University was Regent Robert S. Hyer, who was gifted in experimental sci-ence and is credited with designing the First Methodist Church in Georgetown.* He experimented with wireless, communicating from the campus to downtown Georgetown with a set, and constructed a workable X-ray machine, the first in the area. Dr. Hyer, along with Southwestern University Board of Trustees chairman Judge M. M. Brooks and several other prominent men, decided that the University should be moved to Dallas. The threat was serious. Dallas "had been assured that if $400,000 in money and a forty acre tract were offered the university would be located in Dallas." A committee of Georgetown citizens including Lee J. Rountree, Mayor R. E. Ward, Dave Wilcox, Colonel W. K. Makemson, J. W. Snyder, W. S. Leake, W. J. Flanagan, C. S. Belford, John D. Hughes, Lee M. Taylor, C. C. Hamilton, M. F. Smith and E. C. Gillett went to Dallas "to protest against the stealing of Southwestern University."[91] The controversy became a statewide affair, much talked about, written about and argued. The Board of Trustees of Southwestern met in a long session in mid-June 1910, voting 21-13 to keep the school in Georgetown. Voting against the resolution were Judge M. M. Brooks, President R. S. Hyer, N. P. Doak, and a long list of ministers, Reverends James Kilgore, W. F. Bryan, O. S. Thomas, James Campbell, C. M. Harless, T. F. Sessions, Ellis Smith, J. M. Peterson, Nathan Powell and A. J. Weeks. The debate simmered and occasionally erupted for a year or more afterwards.[92]

J. Frank Dobie's role in the explosive argument, as a student at Southwestern University, was prophetic of his later career as an outspoken educator-writer. Dobie's pen always moved with sure, incisive, colorful strokes across issues facing Texas, and just so did he defend keeping Southwestern in a small, unsophisticated town instead of moving to a sprawling city.[93]

The twentieth century educators important to Williamson County, and directly or indirectly to the state and nation, are too numerous to name. Many administrators of the county's colleges contributed great quantities of devotion, wisdom and energy to higher education, and hundreds upon hundreds of grade school teachers were equally giving. A very incomplete list includes Dean C. C. Cody,** "the Grand Old Man of Southwestern University, who carried a little black book that contained the name of every student, his grades, and what he owed the institution," whose writings provide much material on the history of Southwestern University; Dr. John H. McLean, Southwestern University Regent from 1891 to 1897, who also recorded much of the school's early history; Dr. George C.

---

* The sanctuary is shaped in the form of a cross, a somewhat unusual but functional plan.
** His son, Dr. Claude Cody, an ear, eye and throat specialist, is credited with a considerable role in the University's survival of its financial crises in the 1930s.[94]

Hester, a mid-twentieth century professor at the University whose teaching was matched by other accomplishments—representative to the state legislature elected in 1932, a consultant in Washington, D. C. for a number of years, frequently called on for advice from politicians and leaders during his years as a professor and after, author of textbooks and other writings. Hester declined the presidency of A. & I. College at Kingsville to remain at Southwestern.[95] During World War II, Southwestern University housed a Naval Training Unit, working closely with the then Congressman Lyndon B. Johnson and others on the program.

In the years when funds were often scanty for the Negro public schools of the county, a number of Negro educators performed unusual feats of skilled administration, good public relations with the white community and at the same time set the incredibly difficult goal of giving the Negro children sound education. O. L. Price of Taylor, for whom the Negro school there was named, was one of these men who gave years of service as principal at the school prior to the middle of the century. Miss Mary Smith of Georgetown, born about 1890, held two degrees from Huston-Tillotson, taught in Negro schools Yarbrough, Bruton (at Jonah), Corn Hill and Jarrell. She married Bud Bailey whose family founded the Bailey community east of Georgetown. In 1953 Mrs. Bailey saw the need for a day care center in Georgetown for three, four and five year-old Negro children so that their mothers could work half a day, years before President Lyndon B. Johnson's administration of the 1960s undertook such a system over the nation. Mrs. Bailey organized and ran the center, at first in a local church. Very gradually the community recognized her valuable service and began supplying some assistance in the funding and operation of the school. It was named the Mary Bailey Day Care Center in her honor and Mrs. Bailey remained active in its work until her death in February 1973. Dr. Norman T. Miller, a professor at Huston-Tillotson College in Austin, was named an outstanding educator in America in 1971. He is descended from the Miller family who lived west of Liberty Hill and figured prominently in the history of a community known as Miller.[96]

In addition to the very early private schools, operated before public school education was available in the county, several parochial schools have been established in the county, all except one still functioning in 1973: Zion Lutheran School at Walburg, Sts. Cyril and Methodius Catholic School at Granger, Holy Trinity Catholic School at Theon (suspended in the 1960s and not yet reopened), and St. Mary's Catholic School at Taylor.

Churches have always been plentiful in the county, appearing simultaneously with schools in the early communities. Where there was one small school, there might be from one to five churches, but they often shared the same building for many years. As rural schools disappeared so did rural churches throughout most of the county, although a few remained quite active and healthy in 1973. For the most part, however, congregations joined with those of larger communities or towns. The presence of a church-oriented University in the county for the past hundred years has provided its own special kind of higher education to many hundreds of Williamson County students.

Numerous distinguished ministers and church officials were born in the county, were educated there or served there during their careers. Among the most prominent were two brothers who became bishops in the Methodist Church. The Marrs family of the Gravis-Corn Hill-Georgetown areas included among its members Miss Mary Elizabeth Marrs. While she and William Angie Smith were students at Southwestern University, their romance flowered and they were married at Georgetown. Their sons, Angie Frank Smith and William Angie Smith, were appointed bishops in 1930 and in 1944, respectively.[97]

Among writers of Williamson County should be named two who gathered extensive materials about the history of the county, Dr. Walton Hinds of Thorndale who wrote a thesis on county history, and Dr. William L. Mann, a surgeon and Admiral in the U. S. Navy, whose hobby was history. Admiral Mann wrote a number of articles for publications and through letter writing and interviews recorded the reminiscences of many county pioneers. His papers are in the University of Texas Archives. Mann was considered, as was W. K. Makemson mentioned previously, the county's foremost historian of his time. Miss Harriet Smither, niece of Captain and Mrs. F. T. Roche of Georgetown, was an author, state archivist and was at one time associated with the editorial staff of the *Williamson County Sun.* One of the most distinguished writers in Texas, James Frank Dobie, published some of his first writings in the *Williamson County Sun,* beginning in 1908 while he was a student at Southwestern University. He was a regular columnist for the paper and at the end of his first year, the *Sun* commented, "Mr. J. Frank Dobie . . . leaves tonight for Chicago. He is a bright young man and makes a good record wherever he goes." When in 1910 the controversy between Georgetown and larger cities raged over possible relocation of Southwestern University, Dobie ably represented the cause of Georgetown and the county:

> The money powers of two cities are bidding on old Southwestern. Probably within another week another bidder's voice will be heard, and, if this noble

old institution is to be auctioned off like the gilded brass of some wandering peddler, Georgetown, it would seem, with its few thousands will stand little show of retaining the prize. And after all what is a University for? To teach a youth to be brazen; to imbue him with the rush and heartlessness and money madness of the great city; to make him oblivious of all that is quiet, and sweet and thoughtful; to cram into his world dizzened brain the dogmas of cold political economists and the precepts of the belles of the upper four hundred—are these the functions that the University, the church college is to perform? God forbid. It would seem that in these days, when the dollar is all too powerful, when man does not have time to think, that the University above all other powers should act as an antidote to these things. It would seem that, to allow its students to spend four years in "plain living and high thinking" would be the *summmum bonum* of the University's aim. Poets and preachers and statesmen, not peddlers and puppets and clowns are the true product of the University. To make room for these and time for thought, sweet songs of birds, pure breaths of air, contact with nature in all her simple grandeur, association with a pure and noble people—these gratifications are necessary. What city has them?[98]

Dr. George C. Hester of Georgetown and Dr. W. Curtis Nunn, formerly of that place and now a history professor at Texas Christian University, have both authored state textbooks, numerous articles and other publications. Henry B. Fox, a native of Granger, attended Southwestern University, worked on daily newspapers, and published his own weekly paper for fifteen years during which time he was named the best weekly writer in the United States. He has published in the late *Colliers, Saturday Evening Post* and *Country Gentleman*, and in *Harper's, Reader's Digest, Farm Journal, Farm Quarterly* and *Progressive Farmer.* His syndicated column, The San Gabriel Philosopher, appears in more than fifty weekly newspapers in Texas including the *Williamson County Sun* in his native county, and in papers in ten other states.[99]

Among artists native to Williamson County have been several teacher-painters. Harriet "Hattie" W. Kritser, daughter of John S. Kritser, a cattleman of Taylor, studied art at the University of Oklahoma where she later taught for many years. Her pen and ink sketches are particularly pleasing and she worked in oils, painting primarily scenes in Mexico and at Fort Davis. Many of her works are in the county. Mrs. Eva Woodall taught in Taylor after having studied in New York and Europe, died in 1915. One of her pupils, Margaret Barnett, later Mrs. W. F. Neubauer, studied with Mrs. Woodall, later in Chicago, and under Alma West Parker at Clarendon College. Mrs. Neubauer sold many canvases to private collectors. Mrs. Ella Koepke Mewhinney, who lived in Bartlett beginning in 1900, studied at Texas Presbyterian College and taught both in Bartlett and Granger. She painted mostly in oils, held numerous exhibits. Alma West of Granger studied art at Southwestern University, taught art at Canyon, married Hardy Parker and lived in San Antonio until he was killed in a train accident, then returned to Granger where she taught for fifty years. She specialized in bluebonnet scenes, but often did other rural landscapes of central Texas, including views of the San Gabriel River. A tapestry of hers hangs over the baptistry in First Baptist Church of Granger. Mrs. Parker painted until she was ninety years old, died at the age of ninety-two in 1972. She signed her works A. W. P. Hundreds of her oils are in homes all over the central Texas area. Fay Bryson Richardson (Mrs. Marshall) of the pioneer Bryson family of Liberty Hill paints in oils, being particularly known for works of historic sites in the area. She frequently exhibits in Central Texas shows, still lives in Liberty Hill.[100] Another artist with pioneer county connections, Sally Gee Pettus, specializes in pen and ink sketches of landmarks in the area, resides in Georgetown.

Frank Callcott, artist and historian, received degrees from Southwestern University and Columbia University, served in World War I, taught from 1923 to 1956 in the Spanish and Portuguese School of General Studies at Columbia and simultaneously studied painting at the Art Students League. His works are many and varied, among them oils and the Texas Centennial Series of eight lithographs and two etchings of famous Texas landmarks which have been exhibited in more than two hundred showings. The series is limited to twenty complete sets, one of which is in the Print Collection of the Metropolitan Museum of New York, one in the Dallas Museum of Fine Arts and a third at Southwestern University. Twelve sets are in private collections. He has held one man exhibitions in New York and Texas and participated in numerous annual national exhibits. Besides landscapes and historic landmarks, he does character studies, portraits and altar pieces. Dr. Callcott has also published several books and articles in the field of Spanish history.[101]

An internationally recognized portraitist, Miss Marie Cronin, lived and painted for many years in Bartlett. She was the daughter of Mr. and Mrs. Thomas Cronin, was born in Missouri but came with her parents to Palestine, Texas, as a small girl. Cronin was a well-to-do railroad executive. Young Marie studied painting, making several trips to Europe as a young lady where she studied about five years under Claudio Castelucho in Paris. Castelucho painted a portrait of her which was exhibited in London, Berlin and Vienna, then later presented to her father. In 1900 she made a pilgrimage to Rome where she was received at the Vatican by the Pope.

While in Paris, World War I broke out, but she remained there to work until the German army was within twenty miles of the city, leaving then only at the insistence and intercession of her father. Four of her oils were exhibited in Salon de Nationale, Paris: "The Dance," "The Lady in Green," "The Lady in Gray," and "The Spanish Woman." They are owned in 1973 by Miss Martha Schrock of Bartlett, Mrs. Tom Foley, Mrs. Virginia Lawson and Edward Clinton Cronin, all of Houston. She was commissioned to do a number of paintings for the State Capitol: portraits of Governors O. B. Colquit and James E. Ferguson hang in the rotunda, her oil likeness of John H. Reagan hangs at the side of the rostrum in the Senate Chamber, and her delicate portrait of Joanna Troutman, the Georgia girl who designed the Texas flag, also is exhibited in the Senate Chamber. Miss Cronin's painting of Governor Tom M. Campbell was not hung, for political reasons it is said, and her portrait of Colonel Alonzo Steele, "The Last Survivor of the Battle of San Jacinto," has also hung in the Capitol. In Bartlett, Miss Cronin's studio was upstairs in her father's railroad offices, and she had studios and worked in Palestine, San Antonio, Austin and New York. She painted numerous works of children, with Bartlett youngsters serving as models, and produced a number of flower panels and landscapes. A number of her paintings won prizes in exhibitions throughout the states.[102]

Miss Cronin interrupted her brilliant career as an artist to act as president of the Bartlett Western Railroad (see) when her father died in 1926, held that position until the line closed in October 1935. She planned to return to Paris to resume painting, but failing eyesight and poor health hindered her. She was able to paint for a while at her studio in Bartlett, but not for long, and she lived out her life somewhat in loneliness there. She died July 24, 1951, was buried in the Cronin crypt of Holy Cross Catholic Cemetery, Houston.[103]

Among architects from Williamson County, John M. Rowlett of Georgetown has designed numerous schools and other public buildings over the state.[104]

The musically minded county had active singing groups, singing conventions, community orchestras and bands and several performers who received statewide or national acclaim. May Thompson Peterson of Taylor was recognized as an operatic performer around the turn of the century; Anita Storrs of Granger was an accomplished violinist; Madame Margarita Agreneva-Slaviansky, whose father directed the Slaviansky Russian Chorus in Russia, came to Southwestern University in 1936 where she taught voice and conducted the choir on tours throughout the United States. Miss Phoebe F. Garver was a longtime piano teacher in Taylor, having studied in Europe, with American composer Edward MacDowell, and elsewhere. As a close personal friend of the MacDowells, Miss Garver brought Mrs. MacDowell (Marian Nevins), a competent musician in her own right, to Taylor for a concert. Miss Garver contributed to the musical culture of the county and even after her death in the 1930s, her influence is still felt.[105]

Distinguished artists and other professional people have come to Williamson County, many of them to make their homes for long years, including particularly outstanding professors and teachers at Southwestern University.

ENTERTAINMENT, SPORTS

For entertainment and social activities after 1900, the people of Williamson County continued to hold fairs in all the larger towns and camp meetings under pleasant groves of trees where often a tabernacle had been erected. There religious fervor and the enjoyment of social gatherings were combined. Veterans' groups such as the Old Settlers Association held annual reunions. The latter was the offshoot of an 1899 Civil War veterans' picnic at Jonah, when that group pledged $130 to build a tabernacle. In 1900 about six hundred attended the meeting of the same group and a similar organization met at Leander about the same time. Sentiment for a county-wide organization led to the formation of the Old Settlers Association of Williamson County on Saturday, August 27, 1904, when a barbecue dinner was served on the Courthouse lawn at Georgetown. The Association approved the printing of two county histories, one by W. K. Makemson of Georgetown and another by John Griffith of Taylor, and enthusiastically made plans for an annual reunion. The organization purchased a collection of early photographs of landmarks in the county and of pioneer residents from D. P. Wilcox. The 1905 reunion was held on the Fairgrounds at Georgetown, later called San Gabriel Park, with about three thousand in attendance. Gradually the affair expanded into an eight-day program, always well attended, featuring distinguished speakers, contests, varied entertainment, the showing of memorabilia of pioneer days, and the undertaking of various projects. Families brought camping equipment and often spent the entire week. Many a romance began in that setting along the riverbank where less than a century earlier an Indian village stood. The unprecedented September 1921 flood destroyed the Old

Settlers facilities in the park and in 1922 the meeting was held on the South San Gabriel west of Liberty Hill. The following year and for several more years the OAS met in Nelson Park at Round Rock. In 1931 T. M. Harrell and Luke Robertson donated tracts of land just west of Round Rock for a permanent Old Settlers Association park, also called Harrell Park. The site was still in use in 1973, with a log cabin headquarters appropriately located there.[106]

Willow Hole on the San Gabriel at Jonah was a popular picnic, boating and fishing place. Lions Head on the North Gabriel, just west of Georgetown on the Shell place, was also the scene of many a fishing-hunting-picnicking affair. When the railroad crossed the San Gabriel between Granger and Georgetown in 1904, Katy Lake was commercially developed as a resort, offering pavilions, boat docks and concessions, and advertised as a delightful spot for outings, picnics, meetings and conventions, with boat rides, fishing, dancing, music, speech making and refreshments among the attractions. Free excursions were offered in July 1904 to the lake by the railroad. For several years the place was much-visited by tourists from long distances away as well as by county groups. Camp meetings, reunions, parties and other gatherings were held there. After it was partially destroyed by a flood in 1908, Professor R. F. Young and his partner, Mr. Moore, owners of the Gann's Mill (old Berry's Mill) property, cleaned and enlarged their old mill pond to make it into "a beautiful little lake of clear, crystal water surrounded by forest trees." They bought five boats from Katy Lake to hire to boating parties, constructed a bath house, and provided refreshments.[107]

Concerts, plays and other theatrical productions were presented by traveling performers in the opera houses of Taylor, Granger and Georgetown. The Taylor Fair Association, which had been organized about 1880, after the turn of the century was responsible for introducing the rodeo performer, Will Pickett, to the public for the first time. Not long after 1900, the purchaser of a "Victor" phonograph was a momentous occasion in the family circle. One diarist recorded in 1906, "Party here tonight to hear the 'Victor' talk and sing."[108] Radio began offering home entertainment in the 1920s.

Precursors to the movies were the magic slides offered before the turn of the century, and Georgetown had an Airdrome about 1900—a building without a roof, with eight-foot walls of sheet iron, and plank seats. It was located north of the Square. Admission was five and ten cents, and the audience watched shaky moving pictures with several minutes' wait between rolls, operated by Dave Goodlett and his son, Sebe.

"The Perils of Pauline," "The Great Train Robbery" and "Ghost of the Hacienda" were among the offerings.[109]

Volunteer fire departments served the towns of the county and nearly all of them sponsored elaborate social activities, including annual parades, barbecues, contests and the crowning of the Fire Queen.

In Georgetown the presence of Southwestern University provided additional social or theatrical activities as well as spectator sports. Even Dr. John R. Allen's much-protected young ladies of the Ladies Annex at the University gave pleasure to spectators, and particularly the young men students, as the girls marched in caps and gowns to church services or to other places. They were not allowed to speak to the male students, but furtive glances and sometimes a lovelorn note could be passed as the girls walked up or down University Avenue. Dr. Allen provided a little amusement of his own. This forgetful gentleman, accustomed to walking frequently with his protégées, sometimes hitched his horse, Betsy, to his buggy and drove to town, fastening the horse in front of the Courthouse. When he had finished his business, he absent-mindedly walked back to the Annex, then excitedly reported to authorities that his horse had been stolen.[110]

Stories abound of extra-curricular entertainment related to prohibition in the early decades of the century. College students at Southwestern University—in a dry town since 1893—occasionally made visits to Taylor, Jonah or other places for supplies of liquor not obtainable in Georgetown, or to Walburg for beer. Former U. S. Ambassador Ed Clark recalls one cooperative doctor who furnished students of his day with prescriptions for medicinal quantities of liquor. Possibly the most circumspect of these somewhat surreptitious trips were those of some stone cutters who were employed about 1900 in construction of Southwestern's new Main Building. They journeyed to Taylor for liquor and one other item, paying $1.25 for a bundle of oats in which they discreetly concealed their other wares when they returned to their job.[111] An order for some whiskey once led to the dismissal of a servant woman employed in the household of Attorney and Mrs. H. E. Mantor of Taylor. Mrs. Mantor, a well-educated, cultured and dignified lady, noticed that the servant had strange and sudden changes of mood—at times happy, cheerful and cooperative, at others snappish, sullen and not very useful. Her employer could find no explanation for the behavior. One day a letter arrived from Georgetown for the woman and since she could not read she asked Mrs. Mantor to read it to her. In all innocence, Mrs. Mantor began: "Dear Sister-in-Christ, for God's sake send me some whiskey. . . ." Mrs. Mantor read no further.[112]

After the turn of the century, spirits which were contraband in George-town were shipped to fictitious recipients there via railway express and held for "John Hancock" until the semi-prudent citizen arrived in town early on "First Monday" to claim his wares. The spirits helped make that monthly trades day a gala and sometimes disastrous affair for the celebrant.[113]

In the first two or three decades of the twentieth century, several pro-fessional baseballers of Williamson County gained prominence on regional or national teams, among them Charley Hulda Mather of Liberty Hill, great grandson of pioneer Samuel Mather; C. M. "Lefty" Edens who played about 1919, later coached at Southwestern University, and was a colorful sportsman; "Dandy" Dave Danforth, southpaw pitcher from Granger who pitched for St. Louis in 1924; and Henry Tate of Taylor, another pitcher.[114]

Interest was high in football in Taylor in 1915 when Carroll Hyde and others met at the City Hall to start a Taylor team. Its personnel included Lynn Talley, coach; Willis Maxson, assistant coach; Jason Forwood, man-ager; Hyde, assistant manager. Players for the Athletic Club were Lynn Talley, a star at Sewannee University; Willis Maxson who held several high school track records for Texas and played football at the University of Virginia; Harry Dolan, Harris Melasky, Jim Baine and Crawford Booth, all of whom played at University of Texas; Roy Darrell and Pet Brown, champion wrestlers; Henry Tucker of Blinn; Mat Mathis of Daniel Baker; Eugene Bergstrom of Wesleyan; and local players Neal McKay, Dan Hallan, Jimmy Hallan, Ernie Womack, Van Coupland, Will Fair-child, Jinks Goff, Doak Phythian, Harry Jones, Joe Michalek, _____ Lehmberg and Dan Walker.[115]

L. (Lycurgus) Nelson, nicknamed "Curg" Nelson by some and "Race Horse" Nelson by others, had a handsome Victorian-style home in north-west Taylor and on the estate a race track where he practiced his trotter horses. His champion was "Stroller," winner of a number of awards dur-ing the decades of this century.[116]

About the turn of the century, a member of the Juvenal family who lived in the vicinity of Hutto took the professional name of Billy Ryan in boxing competition. He became the light heavy weight champion. About 1920 or 1921, "he made a talk to [Muskogee Central High School, Okla-home], on physical fitness. He was an old man then but a fine physical specimen and well preserved, attributing his condition to 'clean' living."[117]

Roy Darrell of Taylor, a champion lightweight wrestler of Texas early in the century. also played on a Taylor city football team organized in

1915 by athletes of the town, which included world champion wrestler
Pet Brown.[118]

Elmer "Pet" Brown, a native of Williamson County, became middleweight wrestling champion of the world in 1914. The son of William T.
and Lula McLaren Brown, pioneer families, "Pet" was born September
12, 1888, at the Brown homestead five miles south of Taylor on Battleground Creek where his father operated Brown's Gin as well as a gin at
Coupland. Three active, husky brothers provided good competition for
young Pet, and all four boys were especially skilled in some field of athletics. Frank Brown was a champion at roping and bulldogging at the
Taylor fairs; Bill Brown specialized in foot racing; Ned Brown was a ball
player. Pet Brown was keenly interested in wrestling from early youth
and became well known in central Texas before he met professionals. He
was courageous morally and physically and was considered an authority
on athletics in general, was said to be modest and temperate, and was
extremely popular. As he grew in agility and strength, he met more and
more formidable opponents. When he wrestled, large numbers of his
Williamson County friends rode the train with him to witness his out-of-
town matches. In May 1914 in the Taylor City Hall auditorium, he met
and defeated Mike Yokel of Salt Lake City for the world middleweight
championship, earning the diamond studded championship belt. Spectators filled every available "nook and corner" of the hall.[119]

Investing money from his wrestling bouts in road building equipment,
Pet Brown gradually built a contracting business and at the same time
gradually withdrew from wrestling. In 1919 he moved to Cisco from
Taylor and by 1922 had entirely retired from wrestling, devoting full
time to construction. The automobile age which burst upon the state about
that time created a great demand for new roads and Brown became one
of the large building and paving contractors of the state. He employed
big crews of men and used about 180 or 190 mules on a job. Brown was
shot at close range and killed instantly in May 1923 by a constable
of Cisco. Brown had left his construction camp near Cisco one weekend
to take a Negro employee to town for medical attention and in his absence the constable arrived and arrested a group of Negro crapshooters.
He was preparing to take them back to town when Mr. and Mrs. Brown,
the Negro patient, and the Brown's friends, Mr. and Mrs. B. Statham, returned to camp. Brown spoke to the constable, requesting that he be allowed to pay the fines and keep the men in camp since they had disturbed
no one. Constable Starkey replied by ordering the men into his car. Brown,
unarmed, pressed his request. The constable turned and shot Brown

through the heart in the presence of his wife and friends. The body was returned to Taylor for burial, where he was mourned by hosts of old friends and admirers from across the nation.[120]

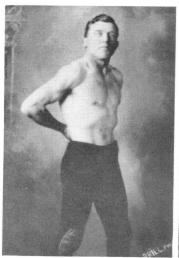 

Taylor champions, wrestler "Pet" Brown and bulldogger Bill Pickett.

The originator of the special art of bulldogging or steer wrestling was a Negro cowman from Williamson County, Willie (Will) "Bill" Pickett. Billed as the Dusky Demon from Texas, Pickett attained worldwide recognition performing internationally in rodeos during the first quarter of the twentieth century. Will Pickett's father, Tom, married a Cherokee Indian girl, moved to Williamson County when there was still a settlement of Indians nearby. Of the five boys and eight girls born to the couple, Will was the second eldest son, born about 1860. Tom Pickett and his boys worked on ranches in the Taylor area, particularly the large John Sparks Ranch south of Noack, managed by Greenup M. Kuykendall. It was on this ranch that young Will Pickett learned how to handle cattle. His youngest brother recalled, "Will got to bulldogging down there in the pasture at night. Moonlight nights he would go out there and get on a horse and bulldog. [His parents] caught him at it and made him bring those cattle [nearer the house] to practice bulldogging so the younger children could see it." The Pickett family also worked at jobs near Round Rock, Georgetown and Taylor, and Will accompanied his father to Mexico on numerous trips to bring back as many as a dozen wild horses. Relatives of this family lived in the Liberty Hill area.[121]

Eventually, Will Pickett developed a unique style of bulldogging inspired at a critical moment when the horse he was riding, Chico, was in danger of being gored by an angry cow. When the cow charged toward Chico, Will grabbed her horns, holding fast as the cow pulled him from his saddle. Chico trotted away to safety. "I just had to keep that old cow from running her horns into my little horse Chico," Will told a fellow rodeo performer named Milt Hinkle. Although Chico was safe, Will knew he still must wrestle the cow to the ground, so he twisted her neck until she went down. Will was angered because the cow had tried to hurt his horse. "I grabbed her by the lips with my teeth and started biting her" and continued to hold on. Meanwhile the ranch boss saw Chico return to the herd riderless, and went to Will's aid. Will still had the horns, for he could not run fast enough to get out of the cow's way if he let go. When his boss saw him holding the cow with his teeth, he said Will looked like a bullfrog holding onto its captive. The ranch boss helped free him from his dilemma. As Will walked back toward the herd and Chico, he mused about a new idea—jumping from his horse, holding the steer's head and horns with his hands and teeth "like the bulldogs did, as it would not cut up the stock as much as the dogs did." Just so "bulldogging a steer" was born.[122]

Word got around about Will Pickett's feat and the Picketts were invited to perform at the Taylor rodeo on the fairgrounds.* There Tom and Will Pickett gave their first exhibition of Will's unconventional style. The same rodeo also featured the Barker boys, local cattlemen, who were star ropers and bronc riders. At the time of his Taylor debut, Will Pickett worked for Lee Moore of Rockdale, who began taking Will to perform at various shows in Texas and the midwest as "Bill" Pickett, the Dusky Demon from Texas. The five foot nine inch performer weighed about 165 pounds. He signed on with Booger Red's Wild West Show, then joined the Pawnee Bill Show. Once at a Madison Square Garden (New York) appearance, Bill Pickett broke his arm during the performance. He was due to ride in a Chicago show a few days later. Refusing to cancel out, he fulfilled the engagement on time, broken arm and all. It was there that the 101 Ranch Show learned of his spectacular abilities and in 1905 the famed ranch hired him to travel with their 101 Wild West Show during rodeo season and to live and work on the ranch near Ponca City, Oklahoma, the remainder of the year. This arrangement suited Pickett for it permitted his

* The Taylor Fairgrounds were established in 1880 on a hill south of town known as Washington Heights (present site of Country Club), were moved about the turn of the century to the prairie north of town. Pickett performed in both arenas.

wife and children to live with him on the ranch. Their eight daughters grew up there. Bill Pickett, the Dusky Demon, performed in the states, Canada, Mexico and Europe. In a Mexico City bull ring he was a spectacular favorite when he bulldogged a Spanish fighting bull.[123] Still active on the ranch as he neared seventy-two years, in 1932 Pickett was kicked in the head by an unbroken horse he was roping. When he roped the animal and approached to slip on a halter, the sorrel reared, plunged and "chop[ped] at Bill's hat brim with his forefeet. Bill was not as quick as he was in years gone by. He did dodge back but one of the hoofs grazed the side of his head, knocking him to the ground. The horse then jumped on old Bill and stomped his brains into the dust."[124] Eleven days later on April 2, 1932, Pickett died. He was buried in the 101 Ranch Cemetery. His wife and daughters continued to make their home in Oklahoma.[125]

The National Cowboy Hall of Fame in 1972 honored Bill Pickett with membership. He was recognized as the "First Bulldogger, First Negro in the Cowboy Hall of Fame," and was the first 101 Ranch showman and the first Ponca City resident to be so honored. The eulogy of his employer, Colonel Zack Miller, when Pickett died, was repeated during the 1972 ceremonies: "Like many men in the old-time West, on any job he did his best. He left a blank that's hard to fill, for there'll never be another Bill." [126]

XII

The Passing Glance*

No one recognized the middle-aged man when he alighted from the I. & G.N. passenger train in Taylor that early afternoon in July 1914. He carried a heavy brown bag and trudged alone in the sweltering heat from the depot up Main Street to the City Hall.

An hour later he walked back to the depot but this time five hundred excited men escorted him and several vied for the honor of carrying his suitcase. Jim Ferguson was on his way! This bit of Taylor history was told to me by a great gentleman, T. H. "Tony" Brunner, who with his partner M. E. "Red" Williams, ran a drug store in Taylor for many years. It is used to begin this chapter because I remember Fergusonism and the battle waged against it by Dan Moody, the first real, live politician I can recall.

Moody was billed to speak at Rockdale, which was a hotbed of Fergusonism and things were a little tense. But the speaking started without incident and Moody, encouraged by cries of "Pour it on Dan!" was going strong when the grandstand fell down, spilling the dignitaries from their seats. It took just a moment, however, for Moody to regain his feet and he finished his campaign talk without further interruptions. Many years later I recalled the incident to Moody and he recited, step by step in minute detail, the circumstances that led to his talk that night, his train ride to Milano Junction from Dallas, his buggy ride to Rockdale, and so on. It was

* *The Passing Glance*, the name of a weekly column written by Scarbrough in *The Taylor Times* 1940 to 1949 and since then in *The Williamson County Sun*, Georgetown.

boring, but astounding. Even at seventy years of age Moody had almost total recall.

Dan Moody, of course, was Williamson County's most illustrious political son. He was tall, erect, red-headed and colorful. He practiced law in Austin many years after serving two terms as governor and visited his friends in this county on numerous occasions. His last public act in the county was to give the dedicatory speech for the opening of the Taylor Public Library.

Lyndon B. Johnson arrived on the county scene when he sought to replace Congressman James Buchanan in a special election in 1936. Judge Sam Stone of Georgetown opposed him and carried this county but the big Austin vote easily won the job for LBJ. The writer remembers Johnson running for reelection in 1938 and being in Taylor to address the Kiwanis Club. Following his talk and the conclusion of the meeting, Johnson stayed in the room and discussed politics with a large number of the members. He was tall and, at that time, skinny. He spun a chair around, put his booted foot on the chair's bottom and deliberately looked us over. "Tell me," he demanded, "how can I be the best congressman in the United States?" Obviously, none of those present knew the answer, so he continued to tell us how he would be just that. He concluded his remarks by saying that he sought no greater honor than to be our congressman, that when he had vanished into the western horizon he hoped we would be able to say, "He made us a good hand!" Johnson, with his top aides John Connally and Jake Pickle, were familiar figures around the county during his congressional years. Connally became one of the great governors of Texas and Pickle a very popular congressman, succeeding Congressman Homer Thornberry who followed Johnson.

Lyndon Johnson was, of course, an outstanding congressman, famed for "delivering the goods" to his constituency. There was a period during World War II when many towns in our district were getting government projects while Taylor continually drew a blank. I remember that someone came up with the idea of a military hospital and everyone agreed that it was something Lyndon could deliver, so virtually every businessman there fired off letters to LBJ, urging him to get one for us. A short time later word went out from the Chamber of Commerce that Lyndon had sent us an important letter on the matter and would we all come to the office and learn the news. Within thirty minutes a huge, excited, expectant crowd had collected at the City Hall and our Chamber manager ripped open the letter. Lyndon told us in that first paragraph that he was proud of Taylor.

This was a magnificent thought, an exemplary project, one we could all take pride in. He was proud of us! Then he began the second paragraph: "*However*" . . . and when this word was spoken, Ray P. Lewis, insuranceman, leaped to his feet. "I move this letter be burned and the meeting adjourned!" Congressman Johnson fared better for Georgetown with an airport that continues to serve the western area of Williamson County in 1973. He also helped Southwestern University secure a Navy and Marine training program that began in 1943 and continued several years after the war ended. About four hundred military officers were enrolled in each class and Southwestern enjoyed an era of prosperity. Southwestern also gained nationwide publicity during this period by becoming a football power and in one season, 1944, defeated the University of Texas, other Southwest Conference teams, and won over New Mexico in the Sun Bowl.

"Tony" Brunner was a great story-teller. He relished the celebrated Badger Fight yarn and also embellished it. "Dr. A. W. Gould," as Tony recalled, "yelled at his wife to open the door to let him in as he ran past his home, kicking mud twenty feet into the air and had to circle the house three times before he could slow up enough to duck into the kitchen door!"

A. W. wasn't the only Gould who could run. I roomed with his son, Albert, now an Austin banker, at Southwestern University and joined him one night to do some net fishing in the San Gabriel park which was off limits to netters. Albert had a canoe which we slipped into the water just above the park and stealthily paddled about halfway up the lake, where we stopped, slipped into the warm river and started putting out the net. Even before we got it fastened the fish were hitting and we knew we were going to get several tubs of good, edible fish. We were paddling back toward the dam when we heard voices and saw a couple of flashlights being played along the bank and then heard yelling as the men discovered the net and came charging down the river to cut us off. Al and I plied the oars with all our strength, hit the water's edge at the dam and ran up that steep bank with the canoe over our heads like a couple of squirrels. We easily got the canoe on the car and raced back to Mood Hall, where we changed from Al's car to my 1926 Dodge Business Man's Coupe and drove down to reconnoiter our net. We casually drove by and saw that a couple of men were sitting near the net, letting it fill with the hapless fish. We made our plans, picked up Mary Jo "Baby Jo" Davidson, a wonderful girl who had pure grit, and drove back to the scene of the crime. I dropped Al at the dam and parked the Dodge almost even with where the net was staked. Then Mary Jo and I strolled down to the water's edge, staying away from the men, who were city officers. Al, in the meantime was noisily making his way up from the dam, shining his flash on the water, When he got about fifty yards from the men at the net he called out, presumably to someone behind him, "I can't find the net," and with this the two men set out after him, in full cry. Al ran down river, Mary Jo and I waited a minute, cranked up the Dodge and drove to a point below the road crossing where Al, who had out run and then lost his pursuers, leaped from behind a big tree stump and joined us in the car. We raced back to the net, frantically jerked it out of the water and into the trunk of the Dodge. We could hear the disappointed yells as we drove away. The next night Al and I had Robert "Bob" Gaines cook the fish there in the park. We fed them to about a hundred Georgetown people, including members of the police department. They knew the score but good naturedly complimented us on providing some of the best squirrel and jackrabbit meat they had had in umpteen years. But, back to the original point, I don't believe Albert's dad ran any faster after the Badger Pull than Al ran down the river that warm, spring evening.

Hard times were upon the county as I grew up. The national depression began in 1929 but it started in Williamson County three years earlier when drouth and boll weevils destroyed the cotton crops. In those days farmers, businessmen and everyone else lived from fall to fall and if the cotton failed or if the price slid downward, as it often did, sometimes going as low as five cents per pound, everyone suffered. Actually it seemed to me that Taylor suffered less under the national depression than it had under drouth a few years earlier. A short-lived oil boom put pep into the Taylor area economy in 1930. Some beneficial effects lingered on several more years and by that time the nation was gearing up to take on Hitler and money was beginning to circulate.

Louis Lowe was the first sheriff the writer remembers, a huge man said to be utterly fearless, even in his later years. He had a great, booming voice and a single campaign speech. He would rise to the podium and declare: "I have seen bigger crowds but never more distinguished people." Lowe was succeeded by Bob Davis, Bernie McLaughlin, "Red" Allen and Henry Matysek, who holds the office now.

In the spring of 1938 I was still attending Southwestern University. I drove to the Texaco station across from the post office then vigorously operated by Abner and Albert Munson. They were in a state of great excitement and agitation. "Guess who's going to run for governor?" Abner demanded of me. "Gosh, I don't know. Who?" I responded. "W. Lee D'Daniel!" he exploded in glee. I was befuddled. "Who's W. Lee O'Daniel?" I asked. "You'll find out, you'll find out!" Munson retorted and the truth was never better spoken. I took a job campaigning for Bill· McGraw and "Pappy" buried him so deep he never crawled out.

The railroad strike of 1921 was one of the saddest episodes in Taylor history, a complete failure ending with a large number of men losing their jobs, and Taylor its railroad shops which had been a strong economic booster in years past. Taylor kids scrapped a lot as I grew up; sometimes it seemed I had to fight my way to school and then fight my way home. For some years after the railroad strike the kids would square off with one of them telling the other, "Go ahead and strike and you'll strike like the striking shopmen!" which meant the striker would come out second best, and sorry for having struck.

Right after the first World War the flapper and sheik craze descended upon the county. Naturally I remember the flappers a lot more vividly than the sheiks and some of the pre-teens bedeviled the girls by calling them "flip-flap-flappers." Just down the street from my home in Taylor lived Judge Richard Critz, who became one of the State Supreme Court judges. His daughter, Genevieve, now Mrs. J. Thatcher Atkin of Georgetown, was the perfect prototype flapper and we kids stood in awe. I tried in vain to master the Charleston. The flapper costume featured a short skirt, which came back into style in the mid-sixties.

Just before the national depression was the great era of the automobile, handcrafted and more expensive than any time before or after. There were the frontwheel drive Cord, Stutz Bearcat, Duesenberg that would run 160-miles per hour, Pierce Arrow, Packard, and numerous other fine machines that in some ways were more advanced than anything seen on the highways even through 1973. Some of the automobiles were selling for as much as twenty thousand dollars and the 1929 crash brought an end to that. Most of the cars went to the junk heap but some were saved and restored to become priceless antiques.

Robert Pfeil of Taylor got the flying bug right after World War I and bought a surplus war plane which he flew around Taylor until he suffered a minor mishap with it and, on demand of his parents, put it in the barn. Many years later the U. S. Air Force heard about it and paid him handsomely for the trophy, by then almost unique.

Top athletic event in the county has always been the Taylor-Georgetown football game, for many years played in the afternoon on November

11, when it often rained. First game I can remember was between the two teams. I climbed the fence in the third quarter with the Ducks seemingly safely ahead and then saw "Chatter" Allen run for touchdowns in the final quarter that gave the Eagles a win. But most of the time the Ducks won and it was my good fortune to be closely associated, as sports writer, with several of these fine Duck teams and also with the coach, T. H. Johnson, who was an outstanding person and a thorough gentleman who had the respect of all people he dealt with. Johnson became superintendent of Taylor public schools and after a long period in that job retired to his ranch on the Colorado, near Plum. And there he lives in 1973, a squire!

The county had some fine athletes and a few really great ones. Among the latter would be, of course, "Pet" Brown, Lester "Pete" Peterson of Taylor who played professional football a number of years, and Dickie Moegle, another Duck footballer who made all-American at Rice Institute in 1954 and played professional several seasons. He became a national figure via television when he was carrying the ball toward the Alabama goal line and was tackled by an excited opposition player from the bench. Among the outstanding athletes was Louie Long who played end for S.M.U., later lost an arm in a car mishap and continued to shoot near bogey golf with one hand. First Southwest Conference game I saw was between Texas and S.M.U. with Long at one end for the Mustangs and Peterson at an end for the Longhorns. The Mustangs had just played the socks off Notre Dame, scorning a cinch tie and losing in a victory gamble. Everyone expected them to beat the Longhorns but the contest was one-sided in favor of the Austin boys. After the game Peterson was walking off the field when he was booted in the rear by one of the Mustangs, a good-natured kick, with feeling, by his old Duckmate, Long.

W. C. "Heinie" Weir was one of the Georgetown great ones, ending his career as halfback and captain of the Aggie team that won the Southwest Conference and then defeated the Praying Colonels of Centre College in a postseason game at Dallas in 1921. It was in this game that the famed Aggie "Twelfth Man" tradition began and in it Weir had a role. In the second half he was carried from the field with a broken leg and the last A.&M. substitute halfback took his place. An A.&M. student sports writer was called out of the press box and given Weir's uniform. Perhaps fortunately he didn't have to go in. Winning that game over the Colonels, who had defeated mighty Harvard during the regular season, gave the Southwest Conference a great boost and didn't hurt the coaching fortunes of the young Aggie mentor, Dana X. Bible.

Notre Dame was believed to be invincible in 1934 when Jack Chevigny, the U.T. coach, took his Longhorns to South Bend. On this Texas team were two Georgetown men, Marshall Pennington and W. W. "Woodie" Weir. When the game was over the Texans had stunned the football world and Georgetown had reason to feel it had made a great contribution to the 7-6 victory.

Southwestern University quit intercollegiate football in 1951 after pioneering the sport in this state. At one time they were within one victory of being named the Number One team of the nation (1944) but local attendance was too low to support the steadily mounting costs of fielding a strong team and the sport was dropped. Probably the most colorful coach in Pirate history was C. M. "Lefty" Edens, a great, hulking, broken-nosed fellow with a ready wit and a tender heart. His former players still get together and laugh at the things "Lefty" said or did. Once, watching them eat steaks after they had lost a lop-sided game, he commented, "They play like Pflugerville High School and eat like Notre Dame!" (Note—in those days Pflugerville wasn't playing championship ball as it has in the past decade.) Edens was drowned on a fishing trip in 1940. He was succeeded by R. M. Medley and he by "Spot" Collins.

Williamson County has sustained a steady growth in the fifteen years prior to this publication. Its population is now believed to be in excess of 40,000, up from 35,000 in 1960. The once sparsely settled west end of the county has grown rapidly in the past five years, especially since Westinghouse opened a manfacturing plant between Georgetown and Round Rock in 1972. In fact, it seems that virtually all of western Williamson County is being subdivided with farms selling for more than a thousand dollars an acre. One major insurance company has projected the City of Georgetown at 35,000 by 1985 although others see a much slower development. Dams above Georgetown and south of Granger (Laneport) are in the immediate offing and promise a new stimulant to business and residential construction.

Not many years ago the county was divided at Georgetown with cotton on the east and cattle on the west, but no longer. Cotton is still being grown around Taylor and Granger but cattle are rapidly coming to the fore. It won't be long, some say, before the west end of the county will be one big residential subdvision while the east part of the county will be a hallmark producer of fine cattle.

Citizens of the county, long relaxed and serene, are just beginning to realize that adjustments lie ahead, some feel that the quality of their living is even now diminished, others are rejoicing their way to the bank with substantial deposits and all know that the old ways are rapidly changing. Landmarks are disappearing and so are memories, the compelling reason why my good wife, Clara, used thousands of hours of her time and much of her strength to make a permanent record of Williamson County, still one of the most interesting and beautiful places in the Lone Star State.

XIII

Thoughts of A County Expatriate

by Linda Scarbrough

The river binds Williamson County together. From the cotton fields and pecan orchards of the eastern blacklands to the mesquite-cedar spotted cattle mesa of the west, the San Gabriel meanders, connects, and forms a distinct soul.

Soon, that river will be no more. Surely, it will remain in part, but once a river has been harvested and contained into large ponds, its character is lost. One of the prime resources of Williamson County—its country naturalness—will have slipped away forever.

To be sure, all will not be lost. Instead of the unmarked boundary known as the Balcones Fault, which splits east and west Williamson County as well a good part of Texas, the county will be signposted by three large lakes. City people from Austin and Waco will ride down in their convertibles and jeeps and think they have found the wilderness.

But for the people of Williamson County, the wilderness will be lost, and more and more changes in the name of progress will occur. Georgetown will be unable to stem the tide and finally bow to pressure to legalize beer-drinking; the county will opt for liquor-by-the-drink, and the appetite for booze will become acceptable, if not much enlarged. Huge housing developments around the lakes will wipe out cedar and scrub oak stands in the western end of the county—something the ranchers could never

* Expatriate Linda Scarbrough is a free lance writer, former weekly newspaper editor and science-feature writer for the New York *Daily News*, is married to Hiram Knott.

manage. Roads will become congested, they will be widened, then more and more cars will flood the county. Growth will occur, money will be made, but there will be a certain loss of innocence.

Much of this rural-to-urban change would have happened anyway, even without the dams. Much has already happened, although to date change merely crept into Williamson County with its head laid low. Soon there will be a building boom centered around the three dams, and development will come out of its shell and hit the county full-force.

As a little girl in Taylor, I remember star-filled nights on the old country road from Georgetown to Taylor. The gentle woods and pecan groves outside the window were jungles in my mind; rich and scary. That road hasn't changed much in twenty years, but with the construction of the dam at Laneport, the pecan and fruit orchards will vanish. Instead, circling the dam from Granger to Circleville to Laneport will be little fishing bait places, beer joints, boat docks and summer homes.

Not much has changed in the western end of the county, either. After a recent airplane flight over Williamson County to photograph pockets of pollution, my sister Donna was overwhelmed at the vast wildness in our own back yard.

"I had no idea how wild and beautiful it is," she told me. "There is a huge, jutting mesa between the two forks (of the San Gabriel) where there is nothing but wilderness. No roads, no houses, no nothing. But it is incredibly beautiful country."

That rugged land will be buried under tons of water when the river's forks are dammed practically to Georgetown's doorsteps. Again, resort development will occur, and probably most of the county's new homes will be built here. Upon a pristine wilderness will come suburbia.

The interstate highway between Georgetown and Austin has already become a focus of booming growth, apparent to all. As a teenager, about a dozen years ago, I commuted from Georgetown to Austin almost every day for ballet lessons. I remember the halting construction just a bit out of Austin, but mostly old highway 81 between the two cities. There were few signs, almost no motels and no restaurants until you hit the Airport Boulevard exchange in Austin.

On those endless trips, I came to especially appreciate Texas springtime. My vista from the Greyhound bus window took in miles of bluebonnets, lavender verbenas, spritely yellow butterweed in drifts, and blood-red Indian paintbrush. Now, of course, the view has changed. The flowers are still there, but one is distracted by housing developments, trailer camps, junk car heaps, motels, auto dealerships and mostly, huge blinking signs almost solid from Austin to Round Rock. Georgetown may be next to follow.

If I sound bitter about the change in the county, I want to correct the impression. I am not. But nostalgia for the flower lined byways; the fine feeling of wilderness, is strong. Williamson County will grow, its schools will improve, its citizens will have better jobs and more comfortable lives—and all will not change when the dams come. Only history, and a feeling.

Notes on the Places of Williamson County*

Abbott Oil Field, near Thrall and Beaukiss (see).

Adkins, rural school between Florence-Jarrell, about 1903-1925.

Ake, large rural school, also used as voting box and for church services, named for William Ake, Sr., who came to county by 1850, moved to Willis Creek about 1861. School, located on Ake's Creek, near village of Small, had enrollment of 66 in 1892, 83 in 1902. Only relic in 1973 was water well, now in a field, near where school stood.[1]

Alligator, rural school and village store near Alligator Creek by 1892, the school said to be two or three hundred yards across the line in Bell County, but listed in Williamson County district; consolidated with Bartlett Schools in 1948. Church services were held in school. Alligator store was between towns of San Gabriel and Lilac.[2]

Allison community on Willis Creek, settled by Elihu Crosswell Allison in 1847. First post office was in the name of Conel, with James F. Allison, postmaster (1878-1880); office was discontinued until 1892 when Calvin G. Allison, then Charles S. Williamson (1893) were postmasters at the same place, now called Allison; mail transferred to Granger in 1894. Allison school was built about 1873 near the creek, was later called "Old Friendship" school, southwest of the later town of Friendship; building was enlarged in 1902 by Woodmen of the World who used the second floor for lodge meetings. Sam Allison ran a store north of the Allison home, Bill Linder a gin nearby, and a tabernacle was built near the school. Allison, Young and other families had large cattle interests there.[3]

---

* See more complete histories of major communities in preceding chapters. In addition to sources cited for this section, general references have been consulted when applicable, including postal, school, city, county, church and community records, and the personal files of the author which contain more detailed information about many places in the county.

Althea, rural village with store, gin, blacksmith shop, and school, the latter consolidating with Bartlett, 1948; located less than a mile over boundary in Bell County and the same distance west of the Milam County line, although the school was in the Williamson County school district.[4]

Andice, originally called Stapp, later Berry's Creek. Joshua Stapp built a log school-church near a spring on his place in 1857, where Cumberland Presbyterians, Methodists and Baptists held union services. In 1876 Andrew "Buck" Jackson operated a small store near there on upper Berry's Creek, was appointed postmaster of Berry's Creek post office, October 30, 1876, succeeded by Benjamin W. Stapp, July 17, 1879; A. Jackson, November 13, 1879; office discontinued December 1, 1879. Reverend William Isaac Newton and his wife, both of whom attended Liberty Normal & Business College at Liberty Hill, were living in soon-to-be Andice community in the 1890s. Newton was pastor of Union Hall Church east of Liberty Hill. Their son, Audice, was born January 5, 1899, and soon after this event Newton applied for a post office, requesting that it be named "Audice." Postal officials misread the name, approved the office as "Andice," November 28, 1899, with Newton as postmaster. Other postmasters were Evans Atwood (1901), John M. Rutledge (1904), Willie D. Davidson (1924), Mrs. Maude Davidson (1929), Mrs. Mary E. Dollahon (1943). White House School, south of Andice, built by 1877, served Andice until about 1925. Andice School consolidated with Florence in 1967. In 1973 Andice had Dollahon Grocery, Gus and Ben T. Jacob's grocery-meat market and slaughterhouse, Andice Baptist Church, Santa Rosa of Lima Catholic Church.[5]

Armfield Store-school district, at Rice's Crossing (see) about 1878.

Avery, early settlement-school-gin, on Brushy Creek, named for Willis Avery, San Jacinto veteran, Indian fighter, cattleman, who came there by 1850. Also settled by Daniel Kimbro who signed petition to form county in 1848. Tom Avery's gin burned in 1878. Early school was also called Kimbro, later Walnut Springs, the latter consolidating with Hutto in 1949. Community name changed to Norman's Crossing (see).

Bagdad, early and thriving town, surveyed in 1854, one mile west of Leander, which replaced it when railroad bypassed Bagdad. Bagdad postmasters were Thomas Huddleston (1855), John F. Heinatz (1858), Mrs. Emilie Heinatz (1866), John D. Mason (1867), John F. Heinatz (1876); post office transferred to Leander, October 6, 1882.

Bailey, rural Negro school east of Georgetown by 1892, named for Harry Bailey, who traded a horse and saddle for acreage near Mankin's Crossing. After the Civil War, Bailey helped other Negro families without places to live to acquire land and settle there, gave land for a school, in which church services were held.[6]

Baker, rural school named for Obed. Baker family, built on bank of North Gabriel 1905, washed away by flood, and when rebuilt was called Jim Hogg School.[7]

Bald Knob, elevation in northwestern county near head of Berry's Creek.

Barker, rural school on Boggy Creek south of Taylor, also used as church, built west of State Highway 95 about 1915, demolished in a storm, was rebuilt east of highway, near Brown Gin (see); named for J. T. Barker, descendant of early settler, E. B. Barker. Barker School consolidated with Coupland and Taylor in 1949.[8]

Bartlett, established 1882 when railroad built there, named for John T. Bartlett, early settler. Postmasters have been Thomas McKnight (1882), James Jeptha Talley (1887), John C. Johnston (1889), Thomas W. Reeves (1890), Charley L. Fowler (1891), Lucas Rowntree (1893); Edward G. Armstrong (1898), Jefferson D. Bell (1905), the office transferred to Bell County on February 8, 1910.

Beaukiss, established 1880 by Samuel M. "Uncle Sammy" Slaughter, a full-blooded Indian, said to have chosen the name for the post office, the reason explained by several contradictory stories. Postmasters were Samuel M. Slaughter (1880), Dan M. Cunningham (1882), Thomas C. Lemaster (1883), Silas A. Abbott (1884), Jesse S. Arnold (1890), Virgil F. Eubank 1890), Edmund H. Guentzel (1894), Silas A. Abbott (1896), Charles K. Ryan (1919), Charles G. Jordan (1931). Beaukiss Union Church was built 1891; Drs. Austin and Wm. M. Houghton practiced there; by 1916, town had two drug stores, three general stores, blacksmith shop, gin, Post Oak Island Masonic Lodge, Woodman of the World, Odd Fellows, a school, Joe Simmons and his String Band. Oil, discovered nearby at Abbott Field in 1930, brought much activity. The well blew in on Saturday, January 18, on the farm of County Commissioner J. C. Abbott. The weather had been unusually cold since before Christmas, reaching four to six degrees below zero. On January 15 there was snow and sleet followed by another norther. In spite of the bitter cold and the ice, sleet and snow which covered the roads, three thousand or more people visited the well on Saturday and Sunday. Most out-of-county visitors were housed in hotels in Taylor. Beaukiss School closed by order of the County Board of Trustees August 12, 1947.[9] Also see Thrall.

Behrnville, named for pioneer settler H. T. Behrens, had a post office from March 9, 1901 to April 9, 1906, with Gottlieb Kalmbach as postmaster. In 1906 the mail was sent through Corn Hill. The community was also called Leubner, or Theon (see). Also spelled Behrenville.

Bell, community named for Calvin Bell who came there in 1852. Legend is that he arrived with only a pair of secondhand boots and a quart of whiskey and asked to spend the night with a settler, who traded the farm to Bell for his boots and liquor. Bell built his home on a hill overlooking the large farm and put up a gin. Henry Lundblad donated land for first Bell School. After Robertson, Union Hill, Chandler Branch, Caldwell Heights schools consolidated with Bell, a larger Bell School was erected, closing in 1949, with pupils being transferred to Hutto, Georgetown and Round Rock. Swedish settlers of community organized Evangelical Free Church at 1884 meeting, later erected church.[10]

Bennett's Mill, early mill in eastern section of county, possibly on James Bennett place.[11]

Berry Grove, another name for Matsler (see).

Berry's Creek, early name for Andice (see), also called Stapp community.

Berry's Creek, also called Johnsonville, north of Georgetown, with school known as Berry's Creek or Boatright school; had store-stagecoach stop-tavern, blacksmith shop, gin and mill. James C. Damron operated the store-tavern after about 1869 and was shot in the back while tending it by two men who came in to buy shells for their gun. A broken tombstone marker for _____ Damron is dated November 19, 1872, believed to be the victim's marker. He lived long enough after the shooting to tell what had happened, but died shortly after at his home near the store. He is believed to have been buried in Berry's Creek Cemetery beside Henrietta Damron. Late in the century a number of Swedish families came to the community and about 1915 erected a small chapel of the Free Mission Evangelical Church. Berry's Creek School consolidated with Georgetown in 1949.[12]

Berry's Mill, erected by John Berry, pioneer settler, patriot, soldier, blacksmith, gunmaker, knife maker, who once repaired a rifle for David Crockett. Mill was built late in 1846 near an especially large spring with a "great fountain of water boiling up out of the earth, just as pure and cold as taste could admire." Berry's springs on Berry's Creek were a watering place for wild mustangs and had been Indian encampment sites. Indians continued to visit the place after Berry moved there and often brought their corn to grind in his mill. John Berry's third wife, Hannah, saw Indians making rattan baskets and other articles from the rattan forest along the creek. The Berry home served as a community church for many years. Berry and his large family were pioneers, have many descendants living in the area. In later years, the mill was called Moore's Mill and Gann's Mill by subsequent owners.[13]

Beyersville, community near Dacus Crossing and Dacus School. Dacus Crossing was mentioned in records soon after Civil War, the school by 1889, where church services were also held. Gustav (Gus) Beyer settled there in 1886, established several businesses; post office at Beyersville was established April 15, 1893, Gustav Beyer, postmaster, succeeded by William Rummel (1898), changed to Wilhelm Rummel a month later; Robert Stumhofer (1906); office closed January 31, 1909. Businesses included stores of Beyer, Rummel, Albert Frerichs, Stumhofer, J. T. Simcik's molasses mill, 1908-1935; blacksmith shops of Albert Becker and Walter Sipple; gins owned by Leopold Bachmayer, Charlie Bachmayer, Ben Thonig; Albert Frerichs garage; Wagon Wheel tavern; Sons of Hermann Lodge Hall used for dances and community activities. Name of school was changed from Dacus to Beyersville at least by 1897. A small oil field was developed on the Charlie Preusse farm about 1940. School consolidated with Taylor in 1950.[14]

Block House, another name for Tumlinson Fort (see) and Block House Springs. Block House had a voting box, school and church.

Blue Hill, so-called for the blue shale bank at the crossing later known as Rice's Crossing; land granted to Jesse Barker by Stephen F. Austin; area settled by E. B. Barker, Willis Avery and William McCutcheon in 1845.

Blue Hill was granted the second post office in the county November 12, 1849, with James O. Rice as postmaster, discontinued April 10, 1857, possibly when Rice was away on one of his many military assignments. When the office was reactivated in 1872, the name was changed to Rice's Crossing (see).

Boggy, rural school, later called Brushy School, nicknamed "Butcher Knife," near Beyersville on Little Brushy Creek. Mentioned 1922-25.[15]

Bone Hollow, location of common grave of Dr. Thomas Kenney, Henry Castleberry and John Courtney, massacred by Indians in April 1844. The site is near a small unnamed branch of Salado Creek almost on the northern county boundary, north of Jarrell.

Booty's Crossing, about four miles northwest of the Courthouse on North Gabriel River. A favorite picnic, fishing and outing area in scenic, canyon-like terrain.

Box Crossing, the third major crossing up the North Gabriel from Georgetown, named for the Box family who settled there.

Brizendine Mills, on the North Gabriel (see Gabriel Mills), so-named for W. L. Brizendine, cabinet-maker, carpenter, miller, ginner, merchant, who came to Gabriel Mills in 1865.

Brooksville, the early name for Florence (see).

Brown, a rural school named briefly for William "Bill" Brown who gave land for school site northeast of Georgetown. Brown anglicized his name; his brother, Gustav "Gus" Braun did not, and built Braun's store in the same community. The place was also called Sommerville for a short time. By 1892 the school was called Ranger Branch, for the stream near which it was located. Texas Rangers were said to have encamped there. Charlie Miller ran an early blacksmith shop, built by Gus Braun. Ranger Branch School was functioning in 1925.[16]

Brown's Gin, on Battleground Creek south of Taylor, owned by William T. Brown, who also had a gin at Coupland. The Brown sons were sports minded, all becoming good athletes. See Pete Brown.

Brueggerhoff, the second name for Running Brushy where a post office was established in 1874, changed to Brueggerhoff in 1882 when the railroad came through, changed to Cedar Park in 1887. See Cedar Park.

Brushy, the first name for Georgetown, where a post office was established November 2, 1847, while still a part of Milam County. The post office is believed to have been near Smith Branch about at the present Southwestern University golf course on the place belonging then to Richard Tankersley, the first postmaster. Name was changed to Georgetown when the county seat was established in 1848. Brushy was the first post office in the territory to become Williamson County.

Brushy, another name for a Swedish Methodist Church at Union Hill south of Georgetown. The church later moved to Georgetown.

Brushy Creek, early name for the community of Round Rock. Brushy Creek post office was established May 27, 1851, with Thomas C. Oatts as postmaster. The name was changed to Round Rock (see) August 24, 1854.

Brushy School, also Boggy School, or "Butcher Knife," near Beyersville; consolidated with Thrall in 1945.

Brushy Valley, a large farming area surrounding present Palm Valley; also Brushy Valley school and church, located near present Palm Valley, as early in 1887, probably earlier.[17]

Buck Cemetery, an early cemetery south of Gabriel Peak and east of the North Gabriel.

Buffalo Springs, see Townsville.

Burkland, flag station on Missouri Pacific railroad east of Round Rock, named for T. A. Burkland.

Burnap, rural school by 1892 in Hutto area, possibly over the Travis County line, named for the Burnap family who lived near.

Busby Crossing, a short distance downstream from Towns Mill Crossing, for James M. Busby who lived there.

Buttercup, village on Buttercup Creek south of Cedar Park, also called Dodd-ville and Dodd's Store, on the old road from Bagdad to Austin, presently slightly west of Highway 183, the site now covered by a water reservoir. Buttercup was a thriving village in the 1870s and 1880s, boasting Dodd's Store, a church and school built in 1878; Drs. Turney and McRall; B. F. Johnson, "a practical and experienced engineer and miller" who had a mill and gin in 1878. Jim Washington, a Negro farmer, brought in the first two bales of cotton that year. The neighborhood reported camp meetings and occasional "social" dances. No school records have been found in the names of Buttercup or Doddville, but apparently Cypress School was near there. Postmasters were Lillie L. Dodd (1880), B. T. Crumley (1881), Frank S. Clark (November 7, 1881 to January 20, 1882 when the office was discontinued). The office was reestablished December 21, 1883 with B. J. Oliver, postmaster, and closed January 12, 1894. Postmaster Crumley was also a medical doctor of Cherokee Indian ancestry.[18]

Caldwell Heights, "a self contained operation of T. J. Caldwell" with three houses, a cotton gin, and Caldwell Heights School, built by slave labor 1850-1860. William S. Palm married Miss Mary Caldwell in 1870 and purchased the place. Main home was restored and in fine condition in 1973. School consolidated with Georgetown and Round Rock in 1941.[19]

Camp Cazneau, Cazneau, an early campsite and assembly point for the Santa Fe Expedition (see).

Camp Spring, or Campground Springs, an early Indian campsite on the north bank of San Gabriel River one and a quarter miles west of Circleville, where the ground was "level as a floor shaded by beautiful elm trees," popular for camp meetings, picnics. On the bank to the south was D. H. McFadin's and C. C. Gillett's Star Mill built in 1857. On the north bank, an early gin was erected. Around the turn of the century, the Redard brothers, Swiss immigrants, operated a truck garden on the place. Auburn C. Stearns planted a pecan orchard beginning 1917. Near the river bank was an Indian sign tree, growing horizontally, until cut by mistake in 1960.

Cedar Grove, sometimes called Cedar Point, a rural school northeast of Liberty Hill and east of Rock House, operating by 1886, burned about

1910 or 1911. Little Hope Primitive Baptist Church founded 1877 in T. S. Whiteley home, reorganized as Center Grove Church.[20]

Cedar Park, town on Southern Pacific railroad, earlier called Running Brushy, then Brueggerhoff, and changed to Cedar Park in 1887. Narrow gauge railroad built through there in 1882, later changed to standard gauge. Large Indian mound on the George Cluck place near a large spring indicated a very early campground. Unfortunately the mound was bulldozed and materials sold at a World's Fair by a transient promoter.[21] The postmasters have been: Running Brushy—Joel Sutton (February 1874), Mrs. Harriet Cluck (December 1874); Brueggerhoff—Lanford I. Crumley (1882), Wesley C. Isaacs (1884); Cedar Park—Wesley C. Isaacs (1887), William B. McKeown (1889), Emmett Cluck (1892), Ora V. Cluck (1929), David A. Cluck (1939), Mrs. Lena Mae Henry (1940), Roscoe H. Faubion (1942), Lena Mae Henry (1944), Roscoe H. Faubion (1945), Ida B. Webster (1957). The community underwent a rapid period of growth in the early 1970s, still underway as this book goes to press, and voted on February 24, 1973, to incorporate the City of Cedar Park.

Cedar Valley, a rural school nicknamed "Seed Tick" for the wild carrot plant growing as prolifically as cedar in the area; school as early as 1884, located between Round Rock and Cedar Park. The old road passing the school followed closely along Brushy Creek and for several miles was actually in the creek bed, passing enormous boulders the size of a room, steep cliffs, and rock ledges. At an early day, an itinerant religious man scaled the bluff and painted a number of scriptural warnings in red paint along the bank.[22]

Centerville, rural school 1902 to 1922, northeast of Granger.[23]

Centre Point had a rural school by 1892, an early gin owned by William Anderson Wilson and sons, a small store and the Centre Point Baptist Church. The congregation frequently met about a mile downstream from the village for baptismal services, near a dam built in 1883 in conjunction with a mining project. Land on the Darby ranch was leased by promoters of a gold mill on the creek. The project was a failure.[24]

Chalk Ridge, nicknamed Terrapin Ridge, an early rural school on Smalley Branch near Mullens Hill on the Georgetown-Florence road. The school was later called Tanglewood. Records of Chalk Ridge date back to 1884. Chalk was a prominent early family in the county; name also was descriptive of soil in that community. Chalk Ridge Cemetery has early burials.[25]

Chandler, or Chandler Branch, a rural school south of Georgetown, west of Caldwell Heights, in use as early as 1857, located on Chandler's Branch, earlier called Ladd's Creek.[26]

Chapel Hill, Negro school near Leander as early as 1887, generally known in the community as Miller School and church, the latter called Liberty Chapel. See Miller.[27]

Chapman City or Chapman Field, oil field (1930) on the J. C. Abbott property east of Lawrence Chapel. Named for the driller.[28] See Beaukiss and Thrall.

Choctaw Corners, thought to refer to the campsite of an Indian who peddled peach trees to early settlers up and down Brushy Creek; who later moved near Kerrville where his trees started many fine peach orchards.[29]

Circleville, near D. H. McFadin-Josiah Dyches place settled 1846. Circleville proper was settled, 1853, by three Eubank brothers who built their homes in semicircle near the south bank of San Gabriel River. Postmasters were James Eubank (1857), J. B. Eubank (1862), E. J. Brown (1867), Seneca D. Brown (1870), I. A. McFadin (1873), James A. Simons (1874), James W. Wayman (1876), Joseph E. Butts (1884), Edward V. Stearns (1888), Harvey T. Stearns (1891), William T. Shields (1894), Hiram K. Gilliam (1898), John V. Rowlett (1904), Daniel D. Nowlin (1906), John P. Teburg (1910), John J. Meeks (1911); discontinued to Taylor, September 4, 1918. Town had early mill, gin, molasses press, tin shop, pewter and carding factories, stores. School consolidated with Jonah in 1949.

Clark, rural school near eastern boundary by 1892, named for Walter H. Clark, who organized it; consolidated with San Gabriel by 1902; San Gabriel School was built of rock from old San Xavier Missions.[30]

Clear Creek, rural school near Mount Nebo in 1857, in western part of county.[31]

Cocklebur, a tavern between Austin and Round Rock on old road, frequented by early day west Williamson countians, named for burs horses picked up en route there.

Columbia, rural school established after 1900 southeast of Taylor, near Helwig and Long Branch schools.

Comanche Peak, a bluff on the San Gabriel east of Circleville on the early D. H. McFadin (present Kirby Vance) place where Indians were said to run buffalo over the bank. Comanche or McFadin Cemetery is located on the same bank south of the river.

Conaway, rural school-community, nicknamed "Plough Handle," on land given by Alex Conaway, in the Wesley Chapel area southeast of Andice. School probably active by 1888; an early gin was built nearby.[32] See Matsler.

Concord, rural school near Bear Creek settlement in western county by 1888, successor to earlier Clear Creek School. Members of the church-minded community helped organize a number of churches over the county. School consolidated with Liberty Hill in 1947.[33]

Concordia, an early name for Walburg. Zion Lutheran Church was organized "at Concordia, Williamson County, Texas" in 1882.[34]

Condron, rural school in 1892 southeast of Coupland where the pioneer village of Post Oak Island stood, named for Frank and Harvey Condron.[35]

Conel, post office 1878, the name soon changed to Allison (see). Near Granger.

Connell, community in western Williamson County.

Conoley, rural school on eastern boundary line, changed to Milam County school district 1919, consolidated with Thorndale 1946.

Cooke Settlement, community at Mankin's Crossing east of Georgetown where David S. Cooke and family lived.

Corn Hill, named for Judge John E. King for his fine corn crops; a thriving town north of Georgetown until bypassed by the Bartlett Western Railroad 1909-1911. Postmasters at Corn Hill were John E. King (1855), Hiram Wood (1867), Tilman H. Lea (1871), Andrew L. Pearce (1875), Tilman H. Lea (1876), William J. Donnell (1876), W. K. Grayson (1877), Otto Felthouse (1878), Montgomery L. Hair (1879), Mrs. Roberta Hair (1882), Montgomery L. Hair (1882), George W. Weatherford (1886), William N. Shaver (1891), Columbus J. Jackson (1892), Johnnie Jackson (1892), Thomas N. Dunn (1894), Rufus C. Brown (1902), William D. Foster (1903), James W. Smith (1904), Thomas B. Thoma (1906), discontinued to Jarrell March 8, 1912.

Coupland, named for Theodore Van Buren Coupland, town in south Williamson County created when the railroad built from Taylor to Boggy Tank in 1887. Postmasters were John Goetz, December 28, 1889; William Goetz, 1906; Duncan M. Broach, 1907; John Goetz, Jr., 1909; Harvey L. Copeland [sic] 1911; Oscar P. Spiegelhauer, 1928; William F. Schwenke, 1950.

Cow Crossing, an early crossing on the San Gabriel between Hoxie and Laneport.

Crockett Gardens, see Knight's Springs.

Crosby, rural school south of Structure in southeastern county, existed two years only, 1902-1904.[36]

Cross Roads, later Lawrence Chapel. Cross Roads had a post office November 1, 1858, with Edmond Laurence (son of Adam Lawrence who changed the spelling of his name from "u" to "w") as postmaster; office was discontinued January 23, 1867.

Cross Roads, or Wyatt's Ville, later called Gravis, (see) north of Georgetown.

Cummings, flag station on railroad between Rattan and Rutledge, southwestern county, had section house.[37]

Dacus Crossing, early community and crossing on Brushy Creek named for J. B. Dacus. See Beyersville.[38]

Damascus, Negro school at Circleville by 1892, near depot south of San Gabriel River; enrollment, 32 in 1892.[39]

Dare Buzzard, also written Dar' Buzzard, extremely early village, familiar in 1856 when *Georgetown Independent* urged a new mail route between Georgetown and Cameron for residents "upon Williamson's or Willey's creek going by Mumfords, Garners, Dare Buzzard &c., to Georgetown. . . . We hope those, who come from ten to 15 miles to our Post office, & who go quite as far to Bryant's Station,* will see the necessity of this route." Legend is that a half-witted boy who saw a buzzard fly overhead, pointed, saying "Dar' [there] Buzzard;" or, that the name was for a tavern or "grog shop" considered by some to be so rough that even buzzards would not dare stay there. Saloon was about 150 yards west of the confluence of Opossum Creek and Yankee Branch, southwest of Granger, south of

---

* Bryant's Station was located on Little River where it intersects the present Buckholts-Davilla road.

the Lump Hill home and not far from Pope's Springs where camp meetings were often held in the Hill woods near the creek.[40]

Davisville, established about 1908, consisted of small store west of Jarrell, moved a short distance to the rail line of the Bartlett and Western when it was built; near Flat Rock School and the station stop of St. Luke. "Doc" Davis and Hill "Peg Leg" Casey ran the store. Dr. Silas McCarty lived near the store in brushy area, was once kidnapped to tend to a wounded outlaw.[41].

Densonville, spread-out community, west of Granger, settled early by Denson brothers, Dr. Tom C. Denson, Jesse Denson, Dr. J. A. Denson; their families provided businessmen, doctors and office holders over the county. Three different Denson schools were located in the community which also had a gin, a small store, the Denson family cemetery.[42] School consolidated with Granger in 1948.

Doddville, Dodd's Store; see Buttercup.

Draco, a Tawakoni (Tuacano) Indian word meaning "favorite place" or "preferred camp," an early Tawakoni Indian village; later was a white settlement also known as Rock House on the North Gabriel. Draco was assigned a post office April 11, 1890, with Olia O. Perry as postmaster; mail was discontinued to Liberty Hill August 25, 1892. The village continued to exist well into the twentieth century and was generally called Rock House. (see).[43]

Dunlop Store, see Mout Nebo.

Easley, rural school on Sam Easley farm west of Circleville, known to be in operation by 1892, probably earlier. David McCurdy Sloan and family brought forty slaves from South Carolina in 1853 by wagon train; at the same time, Sam A. Easley also came from South Carolina, both families settling on the San Gabriel River between Circleville and Water Valley (Jonah). The two Easley brothers, Robert and Sam, married Sloan girls, and David Sloan was married to Mary Elizabeth Easley, creating a close family enclave. Descendants lived on the two family farms more than a century later, the home built in 1854 still standing and in excellent condition in 1973, with most of the original furnishings, many handmade pieces, early tools, and implements making the place a veritable museum. When the families came there, marauding Indians were still about, and a careful watch was kept for several years. Buffalo and deer meat were plentiful in the area. J. P. Smith and family settled just east of the Easley-Sloan farms after the Civil War. Charles G. Wilcox, a relation of the Easleys, purchased land north of the Easley place in 1858. Among the Negro families accompanying the Sloans to Texas were the Craytons, descendants of whom were prominent in the Circleville area for many years. Easley School was abolished in 1916.[44]

East View, an early school on a high elevation with a spectacular view north of Highway 29, four miles east of Georgetown, from where communities or lights of Walburg, Theon, Weir, Jonah, Granger, Circleville and Taylor can be seen. A rock crushing machine stood near the school at one time to pulverize rocks for gravel roads; rock given by the Dan Ahlberg family nearby (and picked up off their farmland) was used to gravel the Georgetown to Taylor road, one of the first in the county to be so treated.[45]

Eckman, rural school, in eastern county, south of cross roads at Shiloh, east of Lawrence Chapel; named for Eckman family there; in operation by 1892; in 1949 consolidated with Thrall.[46]

Elm Grove, also Grove Ranch, community on south bank of San Gabriel east of Circleville, once an Indian campsite. "I have heard that Elm Grove was one of the last Indian strongholds, and troops were finally called to drive them out. When I was a child, Papa showed me several old trees that had had their tops shot off by cannonball."[47] Joseph Rubarth and family settled near there in 1844. Elm Grove was a part of the huge Hoxie (see) Ranch and a Hoxie daughter married into the Williams family who came there. On August 17, 1887, Grove Ranch was assigned a post office with Marion M. Williams, postmaster. The office closed January 6, 1888. M. M. Williams later moved to Taylor, was well-known and affable; his unusual handlebar moustache, half black and half white, gave him the nickname of "Polecat Williams."[48]

Elm Grove, another name for Matsler community (see).

Enterprise, rural school nicknamed Cocklebur, east of Friendship, established about 1900, nicknamed because of the heavy growth of cockleburs nearby. Consolidated with Friendship in 1922.[49]

Everett, station stop near present Thorndale cemetery, located on I. & G.-N. railroad when it was built in 1876. Everett is believed to have been in Williamson County, although present Thorndale is just east of the county line. When Thorndale's first post office opened April 18, 1878, it was listed in Williamson County, but transferred to Milam County in June, 1880.

Fairview, rural school about three miles northeast of the Courthouse, Georgetown, mentioned in records of 1920s, stood north of present FM road between Georgetown and Weir.[50]

Fair View, a rural school near Williamson's eastern boundary in Milam County, consolidated with Thorndale in 1946.[51]

Fisher, rural school by 1883 located about six miles up the North Gabriel [from Georgetown] near cliffs or mountains." Named for Tom Fisher who lived near the school, it was 1.7 miles west of Jenkins Crossing (second Booty's) on the North Gabriel.[52]

Flag Springs, located just east of present State Highway 79 east of Taylor, on the old Allison place; site of Allison Lake; the springs were also called Cowman's Camp during cattle drive days.

Flat Rock, a school also called Buttermilk, or Frog Hollow, at Davisville northwest of Jarrell. Rocky terrain and abundance of frogs on a branch near the school provided names. William Conlee, Selman Cook and Abner Nichols lived in area. Davis Store was near school.[53]

Florence, earlier called Brooksville. Postmasters were John W. Atkinson (1857), J. C. Smith (1858), John W. Atkinson (1859), P. H. Adams (1864), Smith Brown (1866), Miss Nancy Adams (1868), Ozias Benedict (1868), Philip H. Adams (1870), Wesley Surginer (1871), James P.

Moore (1872), Robert B. Caskey (1873), Stephen K. P. Jackson (1882), Sam'l. B. McClain (1885), Madelein Surginer (1890), Mattie A. Surginer (1894), Samuel F. Perry (1895), Joel Preslar (1897), Bessie Cannon (1901), James F. Atkinson (1918), Alton Mullen (1940), W. Henry Taylor 1940), Ernest A. Mullen (1954), James D. Lewis (1966), Oran T. Gray (1967), Cecil Jenkins (1972), Joe Earl Massey (1972).

Frame Switch, small community and railroad flag stop west of Taylor named for David Frame, early settler and cattleman. Solomon George Yakey came there in 1882, started a sheep ranch, in 1884 went to Ohio where he married Miss Mattie Frame; persuaded her parents and family to join him in sheep ranching in Williamson County. Carl Hansen brought a number of Danish immigrants to the area. Frame gave two acres of land on which Yakey erected the Yakey School in 1890. Early cotton gin was operated by Sol Yakey, Auburn Stearns.[54]

Friendship, farming community in eastern county, closely tied to earlier Allison community, fertile farmlands attracting many Czech and other settlers the latter part of the nineteenth century. Early school, church and gin at Allison were succeeded by new ones a short way down stream and when 1921 flood destroyed Allison (also referred to as "Old Friendship"), new school was built on higher ground at Friendship, near juncture of Sore Finger and Willis creeks. Friendship Grange Cooperative Association was active in 1883; outdoor tabernacle, church, stores and gin were added. Store was run by Mr. Winningham until 1920, Dick Williams and "Pappy" Moreland succeeding him. Frank and Joe Cuba built a gin about 1917, and I. J. Mazoch put one up in 1924. After 1950 the expected construction of Laneport Dam on the San Gabriel necessitated farmers' sale of their land and homesites; the early Friendship Cemetery was dismantled.[55] The school consolidated with Granger in 1958.

Gabriel Mills, once-thriving community on the North Gabriel, site of early mill known variously as Mather Mills, Gabriel Mills or Brizendine Mills. Englishman Samuel E. Mather settled there, 1849, built water powered grist mill near present low water bridge. An early customer was Chief Yellow Wolf of the Comanches. Mather also did blacksmithing and the Chief brought him some silver ore to be made into ornaments, offered to lead him to the ore "three suns to the west," which Mather declined.[56] John T. Stewart and family left Tennessee for Texas in 1851, had their horses stolen by Indians in Houston, finally reached Gabriel Mills on March 5, 1852. The Stewart women took their muskets when they did the family wash in San Gabriel River. When serious threats of Indian attack were rumored, the women and children were moved to Fort Black twenty-five miles up the North Gabriel until danger was over. William Williams built a log room with stone fireplace in 1852 between Gabriel Mills and Loafer's Glory, later added another room and eight-foot dog run between, lean-to on the back, loft room above and a front porch; building was restored and bore Texas Historical marker in 1973. In September 1853, Samuel Mather, William P. Rich, Isaac M. Brown, C. A. Russell, Winslow Turner, Robert G. Rice and M. S. Skaggs applied for a

Masonic Lodge, chartered early the next year as Mount Horeb No. 137 at Gabriel Mills (moved in 1915 to Mahomet, Burnet County). In July 1854 "a heavy freshet" washed away the mill "with Lodge Room," after which meetings were held in a log church-schoolhouse built in 1854. "The floor was of black dirt, the seats were made of logs split open in the center, the rough splinters being hewn off with a broad-axe, the roof was of oak boards, split with froe and mallet."[57]

Sam Mather rebuilt his mill, this time equipped to produce flour as well as cornmeal. "People came seventy to one hundred miles to have their wheat ground into flour. At times the mill house was piled from top to bottom with wheat with scarcely room to get around, and sometimes it took several weeks for a person to get his grinding done." John Dunlop, Jonathan Bittick, W. L. Brizendine and N. L. Davis also owned or operated the mill. The Mount Horeb Lodge in 1856 built a two story frame structure to be used by Mount Horeb School, Mount Horeb Church and for lodge meetings. Since the town was near Comanche tribes, guards were stationed outside the Lodge to keep horses from being stolen, and meetings were on Saturday nights before each full moon so that those living long distances away could see well on their return trip home. During the 1850s, members came from as far as sixty miles. M. S. Skaggs was killed and scalped by Indians in 1859.

The Stewart family put up a log store; other Gabriel Mills stores were run by Daniel V. Grant (1858), B. T. Dennis, W. L. and John R. Brizendine. "Grandma" Brizendine owned a fine hack which for many years she made available to anyone in the community needing it for a funeral service. Postmasters at Gabriel Mills were Samuel Mather (1858), Edmund Crim (1863), H. T. Norton (1864), John R. Brizendine (1870 to 1905, when the office was closed). William Scheyli, a fine young German craftsman, lived in the community, designed and built the Mount Horeb Methodist Church in an oak grove on a bluff of the river in 1860. Scheyli built his own distinctive home on a hill overlooking the village, with basement, large rooms on the ground floor, an attic, and a steeple on top. What impressed the community most, however, was a well *inside* the house where water was drawn up by rope and bucket. Cabinetmaker Brizendine, who came in 1865, ran the mill, added an early cotton gin and wool and cotton carding machines, had an active role in the business ventures of the village. In 1893 a bridge across the North Gabriel was dedicated with festive program, oratory by politician "Cyclone" Davis, and a barbecue dinner. By 1911 Jasper William "Will" Asher ran a blacksmith shop near the gin and his wife ran a telephone exchange in their home. Tom Seldon Reed taught school at Connell; his three sons, Dave, Malcolm and Tom became successful businessmen, starting in cotton and cedar businesses. Dr. C. L. Simmons practiced medicine there. Physician Charlie Root, teachers Paul Root and Harold Asher, and professional baseball player Charley "Hulda" Mather, great grandson of Samuel Mather, were among successful professional people.[58] One of Gabriel Mills' best-known citizens was Andrew "Andy" Mather, son of pioneer Samuel Mather.

Andy was born there in 1851, grew to a six foot four inch height, had the "carriage of a man of the range [and was] nowhere more at home than on the back of a good horse." After some years as an Indian fighter, in 1875 he joined the Texas Rangers under Captain Jeff Maltby. Andy Mather was rarely seen without his spurs on. He wore a large, wide-brimmed hat, the best he could buy; his hair usually hung to his shoulders, and his trousers were tucked into his boots. A few years prior to the death of William F. "Buffalo Bill" Cody, who died in 1917, "the old scout was on a visit to Georgetown and he and [Andy Mather] talked long of their experiences" as they sat together in front of the Courthouse. "They looked very much alike, Mr. Mather being considerably the larger of the two but their eyes, form of dress and flowing hair made a very striking resemblance. A friend noticing them talking remarked "There's something between those old boys, isn't there?"[59] Gabriel Mills remained a thriving town for a decade or more in the twentieth century, but when a fire destroyed the Lodge and schools were consolidated, the rural population began moving away. The entire village disappeared within a few decades. Even the old bridge, damaged beyond repair by a flood in 1957, had to be torn down. Now several sizeable cemeteries are the only landmarks remaining of a pioneer village which had risen on the site on Indian mounds.

Gabriel Peak, sometimes called Gabriel Mountain, 1208 foot elevation southwest of Andice, more familiarly known by area residents as Pilot Knob (see).

Gann's Mill, later name for Berry's Mill (see).

Gano, small rural village in southeastern county, settled by Joseph Watson and family and J. R. Wilder and family in 1890s. Jim and David Watson and Bill Wilder ran stores, Reverend C. S. Watson and Andrew A. Wilder preached, J. R. Wilder built a gin, mill and blacksmith shop. Town had a church for Baptist and Christian denominations, and a school, at first known as Gentry, which eventually consolidated and moved to Fair View (see). Postmasters were James C. Watson (1891), Charles S. Watson (1894), John R. Wilder (1895), David A. Watson (1896), Andrew A. Wilder (1900), John R. Wilder (1905); office closed April 30, 1907. Later store managers were J. E. Thompson, W. H. Talley, Gwenn McGinnis and Albert Sheppard; Scott Brown was a druggist, and Drs. Henson and H. Feaster the local physicians. Gano, pronounced Ga-noh', was named for Confederate General R. M. Gano, who organized the Christian Church in Taylor in 1877.[60]

Gattis, a boundary line school south of Palm Valley listed about 1902 to 1939 when it consolidated with Round Rock. Gattis was a family name well known in the county.

Gentry, rural school near Gano (see), predating Gano, as records of the school date to 1878. William Gentry was an early settler there and Gentry's Well was a favorite spot for early picnics and gatherings, including a speech by Judge R. M. "Three Legged Willie" Williamson, and an Independence Day celebration where "accolades [were] directed to old survivors of the Mexican War" Sampson Connell, Adam Lawrence, Cal

Gage and Andrew Berry. W. N. Gentry served on the county grand jury in 1869, captured six wolves in 1886 near his home.[61]

Georgetown, county seat, established 1848 near the county's first post office, Brushy, probably at postmaster Richard Tankersley's home near Smith Branch. The town was incorporated in 1866. Postmasters of Georgetown were Richard Tankersley, appointed November 2, 1847 at Brushy; the name was changed to Georgetown July 27, 1848, at which time the second postmaster was Francis M. Nash; successors were Andrew J. Mackay (1849), Josiah Taylor (1850), Evan Williams (1855), Andrew Marschalk, Jr., (1856), Elias W. Talbot (1857), A. Hart (1861), Moses Steele (1862), Stephen Strickland (1863), Joseph M. Page (1865), Edward H. Napier (1866), George T. Harris (1868), A. W. Morrow (1871), John B. Napier (1871), William K. Foster (1872), Francis L. Price (1873), Ada Talbot (1882), Ada T. Whittle (1884), Daniel S. Chessher (1886), Belle P. Chreitzberg (1888), James Knight (1890), Charles W. Brooks (1894), John L. Brooks (1896), Philemon A. Schaefer (1899), William P. Fleming (1902), F. T. Roche (1914), Lavinia B. Henderson (1916), Josephine W. Roche (1916), Simon J. Enochs (1922), John M. Sharpe (1934), Felix B. Secrest (1944), Lenard R. McLaughlin (1952), Perry Hobson Martin (1954), Charles A. Forbes (1967), J. D. Thomas, Jr., 1967), V. L. Williams (1972).

Gower, community north of Hutto on Cottonwood Creek, with school, post office, store and gin, named for Bennet A. Gower, first postmaster appointed June 8, 1893, who served until the office closed October 26, 1896, after which mail was handled through Hutto. Robert Towns moved a gin from Towns Mill to Gower in the late 1880s.[62]

Granger, named for local Grange lodge, or for John R. Granger, a Civil War veteran; Czech protestant church organized there 1880; railroad built there 1882. Postmasters were Colonel M. Jones (April 15, 1884), John M. Strayhorn (1886), Malcolm H. Addison (1889), John Brazelton (1889), J. T. Spilman (1890), Wilford W. McDaniel (1890), William C. Erwin (1893), Andrew J. Reeder (1897), J. C. Council (1909), William E. Thies (1914), Joseph C. Council (1923), John C. Duffy (1928), Cullen E. Wayman (1929), Anton C. Mussil (1935), August A. Spacek (1947), Emil J. Bartosh (1949).

Gravel Hill, rural school by 1888, about five miles east of Florence on bank of North Salado Creek. When Armstrong family settled there in 1900, land was unfenced and uncleared. School consolidated with Florence in 1946.[63]

Gravis, village which was at first called Wyatt's Ville or Cross Roads. John A. Gravis' name appears in original grant. Village store, blacksmith shop, post office and school. The first postmaster, Collin Dennis Wyatt, requested that the place be named Wyatt's Ville, was turned down by postal officials, after which Cross Roads was suggested and refused. The name Gravis was accepted and the office opened February 7, 1895. Wyatt, saddle and harness maker, maintained a shop for many years. He sold his store to Matthew "Matt" Long Marrs, his brother-in-law, a blacksmith, who ran the store and his blacksmith shop next door. Matthew L. Marrs was postmaster from November 3, 1896 until January 30, 1904 when the Gravis post office was closed. (Pronounced Gra'vis.)

Grover, a flag station on what was first the Austin and Northwestern Railroad line through western section of county, later the Texas-New Orleans, now the Southern Pacific line.

Grove Ranch (see Elm Grove) in eastern section of county.

Guentzel, rural school in southeastern section, named for family there.

Hare community with rural school first built on bank of Pecan Creek in 1888, Guy McFadin the first teacher. Will Gossett put up blacksmith shop in 1889 and about that time a Firm Foundation Church was built; a second school built in 1892 was located nearer the remainder of the village. Early settlers included John McKinney, Billie Burden, the Garner, Payne, Lewis, Bostic and Martin families. William Caesar came to Texas about 1885 from England at the age of twenty. Disobeying his father's admonition not to fight with his brothers, he did so and broke the brother's nose. Because he was afraid of being punished, he ran off, worked aboard a ship for passage to the states. After punching cattle for Henry Pumphrey and Garrett King near Taylor, he and Joe Littleton bought land at Hare. Caesar said Hare was named for the many cottontail rabbits of the community, the locality also sometimes being nicknamed "Fuzzy." Other sources say the town was named for an army officer. As late as 1926 rabbits were abundant there. When the community applied for a post office, the name Prairie Lea was requested but turned down; Hare was judged acceptable. Postmasters were Charles W. McKinney (1900), Noah Sears (1901), Dr. Franklin H. White (1903); office was discontinued February 29, 1904. The general store at Hare had an upper floor where Woodmen of the World met. Other businessmen were J. W. Jones, Bud Scallon and Fred A. Caesar, blacksmiths; Clyde Stearns, Jake R. Lewis, Bob Bostic, Robert Jenkins, ginners; Claude Pierce, E. S. Marcus, John Bostic, T. K. Estes, Clarence A. "Speck" Forbes, Edwin Widmer, Alex Leschber, Ben Leshikar, Reuben Lange, stores; Dr. C. D. Johnson and Dr. F. H. White, medical practice, and Dr. White a drug store; C. A. Forbes slaughterhouse and grain company; Miss Lou Ella Miller of Laneport, publisher of *Laneport and Hare News,* issued for two years about 1923; Miss Emma Moore of San Gabriel, music teacher. The school consolidated with Thrall in 1957.[64]

Helwig, rural school built 1922 near Noack, named for pioneer Julius Helwig, consolidated with Thrall in 1950.

Hochkirk, a Wendish settlement about 1870, later called Noack (see).

Hopewell, very early settlement in southwestern part of county, first called Burleson's Springs (in Rebecca Burleson Survey), plagued by raids of Comanches during early decades of Hopewell's existence. Preachers kept guns beside their Bibles on the pulpit during services; men of congregations kept theirs handy. The 1863 massacre of the Wofford Johnson family took place near Hopewell and their remains were buried in Hopewell Cemetery. Church services were held in 1855 under a brush arbor adjacent to cemetery. By 1869, Cumberland Presbyterians erected a tall one-story church, and school was held there by 1878. A general store stood near the church, and a saloon sold drinks by the dipper. Mountain Masonic Lodge No. 277 was organized August 3, 1863, by J. Dial, W. H. Westfall, W. O. Spencer, B. S. Renick, Robert Renick, D. C. Reed, B. F. Ahren, M. C. Smith, N. W. Johnson, Thomas Osborn, W. Barton and J. N. Stewart. C. C. Black was Hopewell's only postmaster from June 26, 1882 to September 11, 1882. School consolidated with Liberty Hill in 1945.[65]

Hoxie, village north of Taylor which developed after railroad magnate John R. Hoxie purchased nine thousand acres of ranchland along the San Gabriel bottoms and on the prairies in 1878 and erected an elaborate residence and numerous ranch buildings there. The village proper was located near Pecan Creek a short distance south of Hoxie House. Hoxie community included Hoxie School, a gin, a general store, a blacksmith shop set up to tend to Hoxie's stable of fine horses, and a saddlery run by Julius Steinberg, also primarily occupied with Hoxie ranch business. By 1900 the population of Hoxie was 322. Mortimer R. Hoxie was Hoxie's only postmaster, serving from January 2, 1900 until February 15, 1905, when the mail was sent to Taylor for rural delivery. H. M. Hoxie of Palestine, another relative, also bought and sold land in the vicinity soon after the railroad was built to Taylor. John R. Hoxie, capitalist, president of the International and Great Northern Railroad and a former mayor of Chicago, was first associated with Williamson County in 1876 when the I. & G. N. built through Thrall, Taylor, Hutto and Round Rock. In 1878 Hoxie purchased land in the Taylor area, including the huge ranch previously mentioned which extended from Flag Springs east of Taylor north to the San Gabriel River. John R. Hoxie's financial interests elsewhere precluded his living in the county, but his brother, Mortimer R. Hoxie, general superintendent of I. & G. N., did live at Taylor. John R. Hoxie told the brother that "if he would put that land in cultivation out on the river he could have what he made off of it."[66] M. R. and John R. Hoxie began elaborate developments on the place. Several springs near the present Hoxie community furnished sufficient water for irrigation and fed several artificial.lakes, one a man-made island with a boat, and all stocked with black bass, other native fish, California salmon and German carp. When stables and corrals were completed, Hoxie imported many fine horses which provided work for a local blacksmith and saddle maker. Importing and experimenting with several breeds of cattle, Hoxie studied medical treatment for diseases which attacked livestock and determined which breeds were most adaptable to Williamson County. W. W. Mumford, a cousin of the Hoxie brothers, was employed to run the ranch. Mumford's home was at Flag Springs east of Taylor and near the present Taylor City Cemetery, his residence in later years known as the Allison home. The enormous Hoxie House was completed in 1882 after the railroad came through Granger, Circleville and Taylor. Much of the material for the five story structure (including basement, three main floors, an ornamental lookout-type top floor) was shipped by rail from Chicago to Circleville, where it was unloaded and hauled the short distance to the building site. Especially made hand carved mantels, wide stairway, wood trim and fine wood flooring were used. The house was unique in the area, dominating the flat prairie and visible because of its height and massiveness a long distance away. When folding doors were opened wide, already large rooms became larger, supplementing the enormous ballroom for gay and lavish parties which were frequently held there. John R. Hoxie and his family occasionally came down, bringing many guests from Chicago, and a whirl of social events ensued. Guests at the affairs included farmers and ranchers of the surrounding areas as well as townspeople from Taylorsville and other communities throughout the county. For at least two decades Hoxie House was a fabulous place. Mortimer R. Hoxie moved to Electra after the turn of the century; John R. Hoxie died and the place was inherited by his two sons, Gilbert Hoxie, who ran it for a while; the other son came for visits in a private railroad car which he kept on the tracks at Circleville. But the land was mortgaged and Gilbert Hoxie arranged in 1910 with Francis Allison and Fred Welch of Taylor to sell it. Allison and Welsh received several thousand acres of the land for taking care of the transaction. The remainder was cut up into small farms, the Hoxie House was used either by tenants or occupied by a community beef club which tended and stored meat in the basement, or was left unoccupied. It burned to the ground about 1934. Hoxie School first consolidated with Waterloo, then both became a part of the Thrall system in 1949.[67]

Huddleston, a rural school near Huddleston Branch, named for a family by that name who settled near Hutto. Harris Messervy Edens settled in the Huddleston community south of Mankin's Crossing in 1882 and the Clark, Fine, Mankin, Parrish and Parsons families lived in the area. Huddleston School may have been a successor to the earlier Mankin School in that vicinity.[68]

Hudson, a large rural school formed about 1912 when other area schools consolidated, located southwest of Jarrell; consolidated with Jarrell in 1946.[69]

Hunt, a crossing over the North Gabriel and a rural school, named for Hayden Hunt and several brothers who came there in the 1850s, built a log cabin near the river crossing, the fourth up the river from Georgetown. Mart Hunt ran a gin and corn mill on the north bluff of the river and Hayden Hunt added to and covered over the original log cabin to take care of a growing family. An Indian who worked for Hunt and who later obtained a job with a railroad crew was killed during a fracas among the crew and was buried in the Hunt family cemetery. A headstone with the man's name was erected but torn down by vandals, and the Indian's name has thus been lost. Others early in the area were Giles Anderson, John Singleton, Silas Vickers and the Hamilton families. In 1887 the county superintendent of schools described Hunt School as seven or eight miles up the North Gabriel from Georgetown "in pleasant surroundings."[70]

Hutto, town established when the I. & G.-N. railroad came through there in 1876. Hutto was built north of the much earlier settlement of Shiloh. Postmasters at Hutto were J. E. Hutto (June 27, 1877), John A. Blanton (1879), Thomas M. Metcalfe (1883), William H. McCormick (1890), Victor M. McCormick (1891), Thomas H. Flinn (1893), Joseph B. Ross (1897), J. R. Davis (1909), Lillie Wilson (1911), Willis D. Holman (1916), John C. Ray (1924), Ward O. Miller (1933), Walter L. Bergstrom (1934), Oscar Humphrey (1938), Carl Stern (1952), Hugh S. Davenport (1953).

Hyland, rural school south of Round Rock just over the Travis County line, consolidated with Round Rock in 1895.

Jackson, Negro school listed in 1888 as five or six miles east of Corn Hill; in 1925, it was near Bartlett; consolidated with Bartlett July 15, 1948.[71]

Jarrell, Williamson County's youngest town, founded when Bartlett Western Railroad built there. Postmasters were Thomas B. Thoma (March 8, 1912), William E. Votaw (1914), Maynard C. Watkins (1950), James H. Jones (1962).

Jenkins Crossing, earlier called Russell Crossing, where Frank Russell built a rock home in 1868, and where later Richard Jenkins settled. The crossing in recent years has been called "Second Booty's," meaning the second crossing above Georgetown on the North Gabriel River. In the early years, someone from the community operated a kind of postal substation there, picking up mail in saddlebags to be distributed to area residents. The early rock home was removed in March 1973 because the lake formed by the dam soon to be constructed would cover it.[72]

Jenks Branch, a small stream and community in western Williamson County, named for John Jenks in whose survey the stream lies, where many large camp meetings were held after about 1870. Milas, Richard and Nelson Miller, three Negro brothers, purchased land in the area soon after the Civil War and helped other Negro families to settle there. Thus the community was also called Miller community. Milas Miller established a school consisting at first of a brush arbor, put up a building where both school and church services were held. Later, the Liberty Chapel, A. M. E., was erected of rock a short distance west of the original structure. Cemeteries were established near the first church and later on land given by Joe McClain and William David Miller south of the new church. The Independent American Knights of Liberty put up a lodge hall about half a mile east of the Chapel, where community socials, box suppers, church meetings, Bible School were held. When the young people wanted dances, often square dances, they furnished their own music on piano, fiddle and guitar. The Negro community had active baseball teams which played Florence, Llano and Lampasas. The lodge building was torn down about 1913. Others in Miller settlement included the Mason, Barton, Faubion, Schooley, Parks, Thomas, Huddleston, Hollingsworth, Pickett, Gant families, and Tom and Lila Inman, a freed slave and his wife who bought land almost on the Williamson-Travis County line and built a home with a spectacular view of the rugged but beautiful scenery.[73] Miller school consolidated with Liberty Hill in 1949. On another portion of Jenks Branch, James Branch and his family and a bachelor brother, Nicholas, settled about 1846, established a large ranch, and it was near the Branch home that the early camp meetings were held. The last camp meeting held there was in 1883.[74]

Jim Hogg School, built about 1915 north of the North San Gabriel River after a flood washed away Baker School, which had stood near there. The 1921 flood destroyed Jim Hogg School which was replaced by a larger one of the same name; consolidated with Georgetown in 1949.[75]

Johnson, rural school built about 1914 near Thrall for grades one through five. Building torn down in 1933.[76]

Johnsonville, another name for Berry's Creek community north of Georgetown, for a family by that name.

Jollyville, village founded 1866 and named for pioneer John Grey Jolly, a blacksmith who had settled at Fiskville near Austin in 1852. By 1867, both Jolly and the Dodd brothers had stores at Jollyville along with Jolly's blacksmith shop. The Dodds moved to a place called Doddville (see) or Buttercup. Jolly gave land for an early school, also used as a church, and for a cemetery. A new school was built in 1878. Other merchants were Mate Walton, J. M. Forbes, N. N. Turner (saddlery), "Uncle Mack" Hays. Drs. Harrell and Webber were often called from Round Rock for serious medical problems, but a local phrenologist, "Old Doč" Cunningham, an Englishman who rode a donkey-drawn gig, often substituted for the village doctor. Other families who came there early were John Paisley Glenn, James N. Hamilton, W. C. Reager, A. J. Thorp, Byron Jenkins, J. C. Auglin, Elizabeth Shannon and J. H. Crawsin. Because of their proximity to old Pond Springs and the moving of the Pond Springs School to the south, Jollyville and Pond Springs are sometimes thought to be the same community. They were not in the nineteenth century, but had separate identities. Both are located in the area known as Live Oak Prairie.[77]

Jonah, first called Water Valley. When James P. Warnock and Joseph T. Mileham built a mill for wheat and corn in 1857 on the San Gabriel River, a community gradually developed near it. The mill was later operated by J. R. Roberts, who added a horse-powered gin about 1877; by Will Davidson, Captain Thomas Bruce, J. Brack Salyer and J. S. Hays. The name Eureka Mills designated this important industry and occasionally the community. When the community applied for a post office, "Water Valley," then "Parks" were submitted as names, but postal authorities rejected both. Finally in exasperation, someqne remarked that the place had turned into a "Jonah" so far as selecting a name was concerned. "Why not try Jonah?" someone else asked. The applicants did, and Jonah was approved. Postmasters were John E. Walker (1884), G. W. Grammar (1886), Miss Sallie E. Davidson (1886), Abraham M. Bogart (1890), William G. McDonald (1895), John V. Rowlett (1909), William H. Percy (1916), Fine L. Gattis (1951); the office closed September 30, 1971. Early area families included James Madison Burris, John Whitley, Dedrick

Yoes, H. McFarland, James M. Busby, David S. Cooke, J. M. Campbell, Jesse Cyrus, John Hard, William Hard, David McFarland, Elias Queen, Joseph Robbins, Samuel Robbins, Harvey Stearns, Luther Stearns, and Richard Talbot and the Reed, Gattis, Burns and Cole families. Water Valley School was active in 1883 and church services were held there as well as at Live Oak Church at nearby Mankin's Crossing. Jonah had a Methodist Church (1890), Baptist and Church of Christ soon after. In 1921 when a severe flood hit Jonah, the Christian Church, which was west of Mileham Creek just north of present Highway 29, washed across the creek to the east side, was set down without serious damage. To avoid moving it back to the original site, the church bought a strip of land on the east bank and left it in its new location. Drs. Will Orgain, Cook, Bethel Nowlin, W. L. Helms and J. N. Reeves practiced medicine there; Nowlin and Helms also ran drug stores, as did Emmitt Bucy, Ralph Harris and W. H. Percy. The store owners were usually the postmaster. Willow Hole on the San Gabriel at Jonah was a popular picnic spot in the early 1900s, with fishing, picture-taking, boating and "frolicking" among the attractions. A bridge was erected across the Gabriel and proudly dedicated July 2, 1904. But it posed some problems. "The Jonah people want to know if there is not some way to prevent fast riding and driving across the new bridge. Men run their horses on it, and loaded wagons are driven in a trot across it. Unless the practice is stopped, the bridge will soon be ruined for travel." It stood, however, until the 1921 flood destroyed it. Jonah School consolidated in 1971, students being sent to Granger, Taylor, Hutto and Georgetown.[78]

Jones, Negro School in the vicinity of Georgetown in 1892.

Keliehor, a rural community named for Joe Keliehor and family who operated the Keliehor Ranch. The village name has been also written Keliehorville, Keeler, Keelar, or Kellarville. Keliehor is correctly pronounced Kee'-lee-or. The village had a store run by Mr. Vogel and Will Coffield; two gins, the second one built in 1915 by J. C. Poppelz, Sr., on the banks of Yankee Branch; a post office with Freidrich Zahn, postmaster between May 4, 1895, and December 23, 1897, when the mail was transferred to Jonah. Camp meetings were held on the banks of Yankee Branch. Keliehor School succeeded Willis Creek School, located a short distance to the east.[79]

Kennedy, rural school built on the M. Ranken Kennedy Ranch in the eastern section, established about 1915. Kennedy came through central Texas with cattle in the 1880s, returned later to settle permanently.[80]

Kenney Fort, erected 1838 by Dr. Thomas Kenney on Brushy Creek east of present Round Rock.

Kimbro, early school on Brushy Creek. See Avery.

Knight's Springs, also Crockett Gardens, near the North Gabriel River a short distance south of the Russell-Jenkins (Second Booty's) Crossing, a part of the large Joseph Fish tract, sold by Joseph and Nancy Fish to Benjamin Gooch and John W. Owen who built a mill there by 1855. James Knight, son of pioneer Dr. William Knight, bodyguard for Governor A. J. Hamilton after the Civil War, purchased the mill site January 23, 1879, and put in a truck garden where he "raised the first strawberries in the county." During these early years, an unofficial rural mail route predating the federal government's rural system was established between Old Liberty Hill and Georgetown via stations at Rock House and Knight's Garden. Mail was delivered in saddlebags by horseback. The entire route along the North Gabriel encompasses stunning scenery. Knight's Springs has abundant spring water, a spectacular waterfall, high banks with ferns and water plants, facilities for irrigation. The moist, seeping springs are surrounded by hills, giving the area an unusual humidity. From the truck gardens operated by James Knight, later by R. M. Crockett and family, and by the Redard brothers, vegetables were trucked to Austin and sold. Henry C. Bouffard came from Switzerland in 1892, settling at Bouffard Hollow near Knight's Springs.[81]

Laneport, on the San Gabriel River in eastern section, named because of its location on the river and for the Lane family who lived there. An early tabernacle was built on the north bank of the river, but most of the businesses and later, the Church of Christ, were south of the river. Laneport's proximity to Hare permitted both communities to share the services of merchants and professional men, as well as schools and churches. Laneport post office opened in the store January 20, 1891, with Walter J. Lane, postmaster. His successors were Jerry C. Hollomon, Jr. (1892), John T. McCarty (1895), George W. Reeder (1898), Walter L. Johnson (1904), Seaborn B. Maddox (1907, which appointment he declined), James M. Jarrell (1907). The office was closed April 30, 1907. George W. Reeder's store sold general merchandise and coffins; other merchants were James M. Jarrell, Mr. Church, George Conn, John Jackson, Will H. Parker, Richard L. Carlow, Mr. Wendland, Tom E. Starnes, Edgar Werchan and H. E. Wilke. T. D. Griffin ran a grocery store for a short time. Possibly the first blacksmith was a one-legged man, the father of Cleve Allen, who also sold some groceries; Amory Landrum was the blacksmith about 1900 and Johnny Bytell about 1910. Clyde N. Stearns ran a gin there before 1900, later sold to A. K. McNeil. Doctors were C. D. Johnson of Hare, Dr. Green, and B. A. Kirkpatrick. The *Laneport and Hare News* was published in the early 1920s by Miss Lou Ella Miller.[82]

Lawler, rural school and church northeast of Florence, school formed by consolidation of Oak, Stevenson and Centre Point schools. After Lawler School merged with Florence in 1946, the old building continued to be used as Lawler Baptist Church. A school north of Lawler across the Bell County line was popularly known as Hog Mountain School. When a teacher there was asked the name of his school, he replied with cool dignity, "Swine Plateau."[83]

Lawrence Chapel, first called Cross Roads (see). The community had an early store put up by James Olive and a school taught in 1858 by Frederick "Fell" S. Wade, who later wrote of the community and of Adam "Ad" Lawrence who founded it. The store-post office stood east of the school, along with a blacksmith shop nearby. Edmund Lawrence, Adam's eldest son, ran the store along with members of the Olive family. Silas Abbott put up a store and gin south of Lawrence Chapel on the road to Beaukiss about the 1870s. Another gin was run by Jim Laurence (no relation to Ad Lawrence) between Lawrence Chapel and Shiloh, later run by Mr. Arnold, to which was added steam power and a wheat and corn mill. Prior to that time, Ad Lawrence sent his corn and wheat to the Star Mill at Circleville. Other settlers included Henry Inlo Layne (1853), Greenup Kuykendall, and the Slaughter family. The community saw new life in 1930 when the Abbott Oil Field was brought in. The first well blew in January 16, 1930, produced heavily about a year, after which production was low. Pumpers still operated in 1970. The historic Methodist Church at Lawrence Chapel remains in use adjacant to the early community cemetery. The log home built of enormous hand-hewn timbers by Ad Lawrence was standing in 1973, covered over and used as a barn on the place of G. Carl Lawrence, a descendant. The school consolidated with Thrall in 1950.[84]

Leander, town established in 1882 one mile east of Bagdad, when the Austin and Northwestern railroad built there. The line became the Houston and Texas Central, later the Southern Pacific. The new town was the namesake of Leander "Catfish" Brown, a railroad official. Along with a number of businesses from Bagdad, the post office was transferred from there to Leander in 1882, John F. Heinatz continuing to hold the postmastership. His successsors were his son, Charles F. Heinatz (1891), Charles C. Mason (1894), George A. Cloud (1898 who declined the appointment), Archibald J. Rowland (1898), Oliver H. Speegle (1902), Archibald J. Rowland (1903), Eunice E. Craven (1911), Robert M. Hazelwood (1922), Newton L. Craven (1927), J. O. McBride (1943), Rex H. Mason (1949), Mrs. Jo Anne Giddens (1949), J. Smith Cluck (1950), Mary N. Bentley (1956), Darrell R. Sherman (1957), Mrs. Emogene M. Kirkpatrick (1960), Arthur W. Faubion (1963). At the turn of the century, the farmers near Leander raised cotton; Wesley Craven and John Sampley operated gins, later consolidating into Leander Gin Company; ranching and poultry raising were important along with the cedar post business, posts being sold at Leander and many more shipped out by rail. George Allen operated a small limestone quarry in the early 1900s, hauling rock by tractor to the railroad. In the 1930s an Indiana firm bought land and established a large quarrying operation and lime kiln, since which quarrying has been a major industry. The wool and mohair business has increased since about 1940. Residential and business development was rapid in the 1960s and 1970s.[85]

Leubner, village north of Georgetown named for William Leubner and family, also known as Theon and Behrnville. (See Behrnville, Theon.)
Liberty Chapel, see Jenks Branch.
Liberty Hill, early settlement. The town developed many years before a railroad came. Postmasters were W. O. Spencer (1853), George W. Logan (1855), William O. Spencer (1856), George W. Barnes (1860), Squire S. Jackson (1861), Mrs. L. Jackson (1866), Samuel Ellington (1867),

Wilson R. Bratton (1870), Robert N. Renick (1875), James H. Booty (1879), James G. Ward (1880), James K. Lane (1887), G. W. Hewitt (1890), J. M. Pool (1890, declined), Julia Lane (1891), Joseph B. Hutchison (1892), Lulu Grant (1893), James W. Connell (1895), Henry H. Thorpe (1899), John W. Thorpe (1902), Wilson B. Russell (1915), Jim H. McFarlin (1924), Carl A. Shipp (1934), Clyde W. Barrington (1964). Liberty Hill Masonic Lodge was chartered in 1875; the town had a number of active churches, some of them surviving for a century; also the Liberty Normal and Business College, newspapers, numerous small businesses, quarries, gins, a Grange store, a Farmers Union organization, an eight-piece community orchestra after World War I. About 1920 ingenious Arnold Evansted improvised a camera from a five gallon lard can and took many pictures in the community with it. He was handy with tools, had run a mill at Georgetown. When the 1921 flood demolished the Old Settlers Association grounds in San Gabriel Park at Georgetown, Liberty Hill hosted the Association in July 1922.[86]

Live Oak Prairie, region on Brushy Creek near Jollyville, Pond Springs and east.

Loafer's Glory, a rural Apostolic Church near which was a small school located about a mile south of Gabriel Peak (Pilot Knob). The name was used by people of the vicinity not members of the church to describe the unusual enthusiasm of the members. People called the school by that name, too, although it does not appear on official records, was probably the school known as Concord which existed on several different sites (see).[87]

Lodon, rural school in Taylor area by 1892, exact location not determined, but in district with Rice's Crossing, Coupland and Kimbro Valley.

Logan Crossing, San Gabriel River Crossing a short distance east of the Star Mill at Circleville, located on the G. W. Logan place.

Lone Elm, rural school southeast of Granger listed 1892; consolidated with Friendship in 1916.[88]

Lone Star, one room rural school north of Bartlett and Schwertner road, active by 1892.[89]

Long Branch, rural school near Thrall listed 1889 to 1932, when consolidated with Helwig.[90]

Long Grove, rural school and Baptist Church; school consolidated in 1925 with Prairie Lea to form Sanders School.[91]

Macedonia, an early farm community west of present Granger, with school, church, gin, small store. Masonic Lodge was petitioned for in 1874 by J. W. McHorse, S. B. Kendall, Elias M. Queen, J. M. Anderson, J. A. Denson, James Wright, M. T. Hawkins and Daniel Hogan. The Macedonia Lodge No. 443 was later moved to Granger. An early church on Opossum Creek was organized in 1855, probably near Macedonia, members at that early date being the Thomas Gardner, Isaac Wilson, David Staunton, Beauford Bybee, Robbins, Guthrie, Rucker, Willis, Everette, Hughs, Parsons, Dilano and Jesse Brookshire families. In the 1870s, a number of German families moved to the community. Macedonia Baptist and Methodist churches were organized at least by the 1880s. Camp meetings were held on the banks of Opossum Creek west of the church and cemetery. Louis Taylor built a gin there about 1885, later owned by Harvey Denson; Mr. Lyda and Mr. Vitek were also associated with it. A Grange association was formed by Macedonia farmers to handle their produce, with Jess Denson as president, J. M. and Harvey Denson, associates, and Jim Barnett, manager. As Granger developed, Macedonia churches, school and gin disappeared. School consolidated with Palacky in 1949. Today only a large cemetery marks the location of the village. Reverend J. W. Mc-Horse, one of the founders of the Masonic Lodge at Macedonia, was a veteran of the Battle of San Jacinto.[92]

Machu, or Moravia, named for Paul Machu, the first Czech who came with his family to this place north of the San Gabriel and Hoxie Crossing. Machu gave land for a school and a community cemetery. The school was called Moravia, and its one room held as many as seventy-five pupils. It consolidated with Granger July 6, 1949. Machu ran a syrup press at his home, processing sugar cane from about 1900 to 1925. The communtiy had a beef club which met on the Frank Cervenka place; a platform was built where Czech families met for social events including picnics, band concerts, beer parties and dances, some of them sponsored by a mutual insurance group.[93]

Mager, small rural school south of Beyersville in the twentieth century, which consolidated with Coupland in 1945.

Mankin's Branch, early school, listed by 1886, near Mankin's Crossing, believed to have been replaced by Huddleston School.

Mankin's Crossing, San Gabriel River Crossing east of Georgetown near Cooke Settlement, with early Live Oak Church, brush arbor. In 1892 Harvey T. Stearns built a gin on the west bank near the water's edge. It was run by Glenn Stearns who moved it to Weir in 1909. The crossing is on the Georgetown-Taylor road. When wagon travelers forded the river, they had a rough ride where water had cut channels in the rock bottom of the creek. Wagons crossing the channels at right angles must hit them head on; otherwise if a wheel turned parallel into a crack it was usually caught and twisted off the wagon. At the north edge of the old gin site, the first low water bridge was put up at the crossing about 1913, amounting to a wall of concrete on each side and the center filled with gravel. The first time the river rose, the gravel washed away. The county filled in with cement instead of gravel and the bridge is still intact in 1973, a favorite place for picnickers, fishermen and swimmers. When the C. J. Brady family lived near there in 1881, they rode a boat down the river to church services in Jonah and occasionally saw alligators in the water.[94]

Marrs, school at Gravis named for Matthew "Matt" Long Marrs, as early as 1878. (See Gravis.)

Mather Mills, see Gabriel Mills.

Matsler, Matsler Heights, Oak Grove, Elm Grove, Berry Grove, Wesley Chapel, Conaway (school) nicknamed "Plough Handle"—various names for the same locality south of Florence. George and Rebecca Matsler moved there in 1852, Mrs. Matsler starting a Sunday School class under a large shade tree at her home. Church services were held that year by Reverend Rennick and in 1858 Reverend Lewis Gordon Tucker and his wife came there. Tucker called his farm Oak Grove or Berry's Grove and preached in the Matsler and other homes of the community. Reverend Collin Forbes formally founded the Elm Grove Cumberland Presbyterian Church on October 14, 1865. The congregation is still active in 1973. The first church building also served as Matsler School until another was built. The school through the years was in several different locations and was known as Matsler until 1888 when it apparently was changed to Conaway and built on land given by the Alex Conaway family on his farm called Wesley Chapel. Conaway was nicknamed "Plough Handle" School. Wesley Chapel was the site of another church and cemetery. Before the rural school was closed in 1949, it was again called Matsler. It consolidated with Florence. Four miles south of the heart of Florence beginning at Highway 195 is a seven-mile stretch of straight county road leading west, known as Sunset Lane. It was built in the late 1880s at a time when such a *long*, straight road was unique. When Bill and "Snap" Ratliff laid it out and graded it with county equipment drawn by eight oxen, they stopped at the Lee Suttles home nearby and asked Mrs. Suttles to name the road. "Call it Sunset Lane because it will take 'til sunset to reach the end of it," she said. And so the road has been called since that time.[95]

Matthews, community south of present Seward Junction established 1870, when John G. and Leonora Carothers Matthews moved their family and stock from Austin to their newly-purchased farm on the South Gabriel. They lived for a time in a one-room log house with shed which stood on the farm on a hill overlooking the river, near a good spring. The room had one door and one window. Matthews built a stone home which the family occupied in the spring of 1872, although the plank floor to replace the dirt one and glass windows were installed later. "A cook stove soon took the place of the fireplace." The old log house was then converted into a private school for the Matthews and neighborhood children. "It was customary in those days for the patrons to subscribe so many pupils. I remember my father saying that he subscribed 3½ pupils. I am still wondering if they didn't count me as the half pupil," J. N. Matthews wrote. A free school opened in 1874, replacing the private one. John G. Matthews had served in the Mexican War and was a Texas Ranger. A son, Frank W., also followed a career with the Rangers, and another son, Joseph Neely Matthews, was educated at Liberty Normal and Business College, was a teacher at Bagdad and Concord and superintendent at Hutto, Jonah, Florence, Leander and Liberty Hill. He published a newspaper at Liberty Hill.[96]

Midway, name of a school at Weir about 1915.

Miller, a Negro school south of Liberty Hill (see Jenks Branch), consolidated with Liberty Hill on July 6, 1949.

Monadale/Monodale, originally called Springtown (and occasionally written Stringtown), a farming community on Mustang Creek west of Taylor, named for Mona House, daughter of Colonel Edward Mandell House, close friend and political advisor to President Woodrow Wilson. Colonel House had a large farm and ranch at Monadale, as the name was intended to be spelled, although the Monodale form is more frequently used today. Colonel House's grandfather, a planter, began acquiring land in Williamson County in 1867. A son, a United States Senator, inherited it, deeding one fourth of his interest in the Monadale property to his son, Edward M. House in 1885. The 1500-acre farm was developed under the management of William Malone. Colonel House never lived at his farm but came there whenever he was in Texas, donated land for a school site. In 1899 a cooperative gin was built there, operated at one time by Mr. Hudson, in 1906 by H. T. Stearns. The Hugh Burns and Weiss families also lived in the community. The school consolidated with Hutto in 1949.[97]

Moravia, rural school near Granger. See Machu. School closed in 1949.

Moss's Springs, Moss's Well, two miles west of present Old Round Rock. Mark Moss and several others established the first school in the county at that place, which was also a stopping place for the few travelers who passed through the county in the 1840s.

Mount Horeb, see Gabriel Mills.

Mount Nebo, also Dunlop's Store, a tiny community in western section. Store was built around 1900 and operated about twelve years.[98]

Mount Prospect, a rural school north of Georgetown, established at least by 1888, possibly six or eight years earlier, by Thomas Alexander Wierman. Wierman lived in the community, taught Wierman school about a year before it became a county school and was called Mount Prospect. After Wierman built his home, he worked at Towns Mill about five and a half miles to the east. Riding his horse across the countryside to work, he left home very early in the morning, took his direction from the morning star, and returned home after dark each day. Since wild game, including prairie chickens, ducks, geese, quail and wild sheep abounded in the region, he often brought home fresh meat for the family table. Others early in that region were the Ilse and Farmer families. About 1918 or 1919 one of the pupils at Mount Prospect School was named Preston Smith, son of Mr. and Mrs. Charlie Smith, who was to be Governor of Texas from 1969 to 1973. School consolidated with Jarrell in 1949.[99]

Mozo, a small community which developed after the M. K. & T. railroad was built from Granger to Georgetown, said to be named by railroad officials, possibly an adaptation of the family name, Mazoch (pronounced May'-zahk), for Anton Mazoch and for three sons, Steve, Frank and I. J. Mazoch, who built a gin there about 1909. The railroad provided loading platforms alongside the track near the gin. Frank Kaderka had a general store, and a filling station was built there. A community center and a house for gin hands to live in completed the village. August Wolbrueck settled on a farm south of Mozo in 1890, breaking the prairie with two oxen and a wooden share. Mrs. Wolbrueck walked behind her husband's plow, dropping corn or cotton into the furrows by hand. Dan Doerfler settled there in 1895.[100]

Mustang Springs, see Wilson Springs.

Naizerville, earlier called Neusser, village named for Johann Neusser, early settler who purchased land there in 1881. Deed records indicate that the German name gave some difficulty, for it was spelled half a dozen ways. Located southwest of Granger and a short distance west of Mozo on the M. K. & T. railroad, the community had a dance hall, Yankee School nearby, and an early store which was later moved to Walburg and then to Theon. The store contained a post office called Neusser for nearly two years, opening December 30, 1892, with Edward Aschen, postmaster. Two other postmasters were Joseph Klimicek (1893) and August F. Zahn (1894), the office closing May 21, 1894. In 1915, Johann Neusser "and his brothers approached the courts officially to adopt the name Naizer as the American pronunciation of Neusser." Thus Johann Neusser became John Naizer.[101]

Needs More, a village store by that name located a short way east of Block House.[102]

Neusser, see Naizerville.

New Bern, a village settled by Swiss-German and Swiss-French immigrants in the late 1880s and 1890s and named for Bern, Switzerland. Hyman Schoener, one of the first to come, bought land at twelve dollars an acre. St. Paul Lutheran Church was built in 1893 by Ludwig Fuessel, was used as a school with German classes held in the mornings, English in the afternoons. Fritz Stauffer gave land for a cemetery, put up a blacksmith shop run by Conrad Ochsner about 1897, later run by Rudy Bachman. About 1907 a store was established, but closed in a short time. A separate public school was established after 1900, especially remembered for its girls' basketball team, which walked to Turkey Creek School for games. The round trip walk and contest took the entire day. In 1912 New Bern erected a new church, with Gottfried Krieg, Fritz Stauffer and his sons, Fritz Caninenberg, Rudolph Bachman, Gottlieb Krieg and John Krieg doing much of the work. Still another Lutheran Church had been organized at Wuthrich Hill and in 1948 the two merged, moving the building from New Bern to Wuthrich Hill, renamed Prince of Peace Lutheran Church and still active in 1973. New Bern Helvetia Lodge Hall was built about 1908 by families of the community, including Willie Schroeder, the Stauffers and Frank Zimmacker. May fetes, dances, picnics and other social gatherings were held there, with John Schroeder's band often furnishing the music. The Ischy, Bouffard and Redard families went briefly to New Bern, but found land west of Georgetown along the North Gabriel to be more like their native Switzerland, and moved there. Other families associated with New Bern were Charles Contesse, Fritz Walther, Samuel and Charlie Stauffer, the Kautz, Weise, Merkord, Galler, Werchan, Meyer and Widmer families. New Bern School consolidated with Thrall in 1949.[103]

New Corn Hill, a misleading name for a village which its promoters hoped would succeed the much earlier Corn Hill. New Corn Hill was adjacent to or a part of Theon (also Behrnville and Leubner). See Theon.

New Hope, a school and church located a short way west of Block House, the school active by 1874.

Noack, a Wendish settlement first called Hochkirk established when Peter Zieschang moved there in 1870. Visiting pastors served the community until 1891 when Christ Lutheran Church was organized and built. Helwig School was named for settler Julius Helwig. It consolidated with Thrall in 1950. The community took its present name officially when the local merchant, John Ernest Noack, became postmaster on July 12, 1902. Noack post office was open from that time until April 29, 1905, when the mail was handled out of Taylor. A storm blew down the original church in 1916, but it was rebuilt. Green Kuykendall, a Negro man living at Noack, prepared pit barbecue to serve at the church dedication, was much in demand for his barbecue on other special occasions and cooked it for the Noack Store for seventeen years. In 1933 the local ginner, J. A. Zieschang, built a tavern with huge bar, expanded in the 1960s into Noack Bar and Cafe. When the cafe burned in 1969, Martin Schroeder, a carpenter of Taylor, hand crafted a new bar—a duplicate of the earlier one—which he recreated by following photographs. Noack Oil field, a small producer, was developed in 1933 by Fritz Fuchs of Thrall on the Raymond and Victor Sladek farm.[104]

Norman's Crossing, sometimes called Norman, a village and early crossing on Brushy Creek where the Avery-Kimbro-Walnut Springs School was located. M. B. "Mart" Norman came by rail to New Orleans, by boat to Galveston and by rail and wagon to the county, arriving in February 1873. About 1880, he bought a farm south of Brushy Creek, which he plowed, walking barefooted, because he had no money to buy shoes. His father had died, leaving him with his mother and three sisters to support. Gradually increasing his holdings, Norman and M. R. Kennedy of Taylor built a gin at Norman' Crossing, the first of several businesses there. Norman built a two story home, now occupied by his daughter-in-law, Mrs. Isaac Norman, erected a general store, and his son, Isaac, added a garage and machine shop in 1914. Mr. and Mrs. Charles Kuhn and Mr. and Mrs. Marvin operated the store. The old school is now used as a community center. John P. Burns, born in 1850 near Norman's Crossing, was a cattleman-farmer of the community and ran herds into Indian and Oklahoma territory in the 1870s and 1880s. Robinson's Chapel, a Methodist Church, is on the north bank of Brushy Creek, named for John and B. Robinson. Swenson Grove, a Negro school, stood west of the village. (See Avery.)[105]

North Gabriel, a name sometimes used for Gabriel Mills (see). Mount Horeb School there was referred to in some records as North Gabriel School.

Northtown, an early section of Georgetown which developed north of the North Gabriel River before the turn of the century, where there was a Northtown School, a number of businesses, and east of which were the fairgrounds now known as San Gabriel Park.

Nyman, rural school east of Coupland, from about 1915 to 1932.

Oak, rural school north northeast of Florence about 1902. It consolidated with Centre Point to form Lawler School.

Oak Grove, see Matsler.

Old Round Rock, the terminology for the original community of Round Rock, somewhat abandoned after the I. & G. N. railroad was built southeast of "Old Town," creating what was for some years called New Round Rock. Both places had post offices for about twelve years. Postmasters at Old Round Rock were Livingston M. Mays (June 3, 1879), Dora Aten (1889), Miss Alice Mays (1891); the office was transferred to the Round Rock office on December 16, 1891. In 1973 Old Town was being diligently restored, particularly many lovely old stone buildings. The low water bridge marked the place where earlier creek crossings were made, and deep ruts cut in the stone on the north bank east of the low bridge attested to heavy wagon traffic there.

Opossum, an early church on Opossum Creek established in 1855 near Macedonia; also an early school located at Walburg, with fifty-five students in 1892.[106]

Owens, a rural school also called Glasscock Valley School in Glasscock Valley about 1886, two miles west of Corn Hill, named for Samuel David "Jay" Owens who came there in 1879 with cattle, was associated with the Cobb Ranch. The school later became Gravis. Owens often held horse races on his place. Others coming early were Alex and Nancy Ann Brewer Frymire and Daniel Koontz.[107]

Palacky, a rural school established in 1910 west of Granger in the region of Salyer, Macedonia and Ake schools, closed after 1953-54 session, located on Opossum Creek. Named in honor of Frantisek (Frank) Palacky (1798-1876), a national hero to freedom-loving Czechs. Palacky, pronounced Pah-laht'-skee, was renowned in Czechoslovakia as a politician, historian, editor and writer. He was a liberal democrat who desired Czech autonomy and believed it should be accomplished through education rather than revolution.[108]

Palm Valley, school, church, and the center of a large Swedish settlement. Palm Valley Lutheran Church, founded in 1870, is still active in 1973.

Pear Valley, rural school east of Coupland at least by 1892, still in operation in 1924.[109]

Peyton, village between Jarrell and Florence named for Peyton family,* with general store and post office, a half-mile straight away race track nearby; located on Salado Creek. William Anderson Wilson purchased land there, built his home and the store on the creek bank, and operated gins at Florence and Centre Point. The first postmaster was William P. Wells, January 13, 1885; H. D. Newman was appointed December 8, 1885, and the office was discontinued and mail sent through Corn Hill July 13, 1886. Jay Owens raised and trained horses on his nearby ranch (see Owens); his young son rode as a jockey. People of the vicinity often came to see the workouts or to watch races arranged with other area

---

* W. R. Peyton's wife was buried at Corn Hill Cemetery in 1892.

horsemen. Peyton was plagued with floods, and the Wilson home had to be moved to higher ground. Other buildings along the bank were moved or abandoned. One of the Wilson sons, James Vernon "Pinky" Wilson interrupted his college education at Texas A.&M. to serve in France during World War I. While on the Rhine River at Coblenz, he wrote the lyrics for what became the official "Aggie War Hymn."[110]

Philadelphia, a rural school about four miles northeast of the Courthouse at Georgetown, located on the place owned by Aaron Williams in 1868. Richard Critz, later a Texas Supreme Court judge, taught there. The school was in existence by 1883 and until after 1900.[111]

Pilot Knob, local name for Gabriel Mountain or Peak, 1208 foot elevation in northwestern part of county where Webster party was said to have turned back. Mapmakers prefer "Gabriel" since Pilot Knob is name of several other elevations in central Texas.

Pleasant Hill, early settlement on the Bagdad to Old Round Rock road. John Ray Bowmer and his family came there in 1852 from Missouri in a covered wagon, with two mares hitched to it. When Bowmer reached Pleasant Hill, he traded one mare for ten cows and calves. He became one of the county's first teachers; other members of the family farmed and ranched. A small log school was built in the 1850s, and on February 14, 1857, an Old School Presbyterian Church was founded there by Reverend R. M. Overstreet of Georgetown. The seven charter members were Samuel D. and Harriet Carothers, Mary J. Mason, Margaret Carothers, Sarah C. Carothers, Mary E. Faires and Mrs. Sibbi Hanna. The next year, Mrs. Sarah J. Walker transferred her membership, and in 1859, Hester, "a servant girl" of the Carothers, transferred from her church in South Carolina, an early instance of integration. Numerous camp meetings were held near the church. The school was one of the largest in the county before the turn of the century.[112]

Polanka, a rural school south of Taylor and a short distance west of Brown's Gin, established in 1907 and named for Polanka, Czechoslovakia, the town John Pavlik and his wife had left in Europe several years before. Pavlik provided the land for the school, was given an opportunity to name it. Instead of naming it for himself, he chose to commemorate his native home. The one-classroom building opened for the first time November 1, 1908, and continued until in 1949. The name is pronounced Poh-lahn'-kah.[113]

Pollack, see Granger.

Pond Spring, Pond Springs or Old Rutledge, an early community on Live Oak Prairie near a spring which formed a pond. The name took the singular form at first, but long since the place has been called Pond Springs. Pond Spring referred to a log school originally located near the pond, later moved about a mile to the south. Adding to confusion over the names, people living in the area often called the community Rutledge for a large family living there, including Thomas S., William P., H. M., John R., Jim, Manie, Arthur, Clyde, and Neely Rutledge. The Rutledge family built and ran a store-post office and a blacksmith shop across the road from the log schoolhouse. Thomas S. Rutledge became the first post-master at Pond Spring on March 16, 1854. Since the Austin to Lampasas road and stage line went through Jollyville, Pond Spring, Buttercup, Bagdad and Liberty Hill, it passed the Rutledge Store. For a mile and a half to the south of Pond Spring on his property, Rutledge built a rock fence on each side of the road, giving an elegant appearance as the stage approached and passed between the store-post office and blacksmith shop on the west, and the log school on the east. Remnants of the fence remained in 1973. Other postmasters were Elisha Rhodes (1857), Thomas Strode (1857), W. P. Rutledge (1862), Mrs. Ettie C. Rutledge (1866); the office was discontinued July 29, 1880. When the Austin and Northwestern railroad was built in 1882, it bypassed Pond Spring, creating a new village to the northeast called New Rutledge or Rutledge. Old Pond Spring soon disappeared as a village. Sometime after 1887, the small log school was lifted onto logs and moved by pushing it along on them from its place by the pond to the village of Jollyville, about a mile to the south. It continued to be called Pond Spring(s) School. New Rutledge (see) was little more than a mile from old Pond Spring; about halfway between them James A. "Uncle Jim" Walden built a gin about 1888 or 1890. C. Klein and D. F. Waddell were cattlemen near Pond Spring. Although the Pond Springs school system was consolidated with Round Rock in 1969, the school continued in operation in 1973.[114]

Ponton, post office in the Samuel D. Carothers home in 1860, near and east of the crossroads point now kown as Seward Junction. Carothers brought his large family to settle in Williamson County on November 14, 1856. He rode ten miles to Bagdad and back for his mail, in 1860 requested a post office called "Tucumcary," according to W. O. Spencer's history of Liberty Hill. The name Ponton was approved, however, on August 17, 1860, with Carothers as postmaster. Miss M. J. Faires was postmistress from December 3, 1866, until the office was closed April 27, 1867.[115]

Pope Springs, a few hundred yards above the confluence of Willis Creek and Yankee Branch.

Posey Crossing, on Willis Creek a short distance above Granger. Fannie E. Posey, James P. Posey, Rhoda E. Posey and E. F. McMurry were buried in the family cemetery near there.

Post Oak Island, named by pioneers who saw a grove of post oak trees clustered in the center of a grassy, open prairie, located in the southeastern part of the county between the headwaters of Dry Brushy and Middle Yegua creeks. Post Oak Island, the onetime village of Indians, was on an extremely early mail route from Huntsville to Austin and Nashville-on-the Brazos during the 1840s, was well known before Williamson County was formed, and was one of only two or three towns shown on early maps of the county. "The party of Indians that killed Mrs. Robert Coleman on February 18, 1839, at Coleman Fort near Austin were followed to Post Oak Island and attacked February 19. Captain Joe Burleson was killed but the Indians were repulsed." Adolphus Sterne of Nacogdoches camped overnight at Post Oak Island December 6, 1840. He spoke of a Jones family fifteen miles west of Nashville, and said that from there the next seventy-five miles to Austin was Indian country without a house. Mail went through Post Oak Island during the Republic of Texas years. Postmaster General John Rice Jones wrote that he must change the mail route to the south through Bastrop instead of through Post Oak Island as "the carrier was a poor man and his family couldn't get along minus his support if Indians killed him."[116] As the south part of the county was settled in the early 1850s, so was Post Oak Island. The community was assigned a post office August 1, 1855, with I. J. Kidd, postmaster. Others holding that office were Webb Kidd, Jr. (1859), Samuel Porter (1860), Windsor Fort (1862), A. J. Kidd (1862), Mrs. Mollie W. Gage (1876); office was discontinued September 30, 1880. The village had a store which also served as a stagecoach stop, and a blacksmith shop. Post Oak Island Masonic Lodge No. 181 was organized in September 1855, chartered the following year. Petitioners for the charter were R. A. Middleton, Marmaduke Gardner, George G. Rucker, Thomas H. Gattlin, A. S. Harper, T. J. Kidd, C. W. Brooks, J. E. Hutto, and Nathan Willett. Samuel Mather of Gabriel Mills was serving as Grand Master of the Texas Lodge at that time. The Masons built a Lodge Hall which was later moved to Beaukiss where the Lodge is still active. Ed Fielder ran the Post Oak Island store and built a gin there about 1904. The community had one of the earliest schools in the county and by 1878 was building a new one. In 1892 Condron school replaced it, was built just across the road from the business section of Post Oak Island. Post Oak Island completely disappeared between 1915 and 1930; the road was changed and the site is now a plowed field. On the Yegua in the region of Post Oak Island, "the heaviest, thickest timber ever seen" was remembered by old-timers. "It was so dense and so interlaced with grape vines that one had to chop down several trees near each other to get any to fall." It was in this region that the Georgetown Chair Factory in the 1890s sent to get material for chairs.[117]

Prairie Lea, a rural school by 1888, in the northwestern part of the county near the headwaters of South Salado Creek. In 1892 it had two classrooms with seventy-eight pupils; in 1902, eighty-one; in 1923, thirty-four. It consolidated with Long Grove to form Sanders School in 1925.[118]

Prairie Point, school and church on the western boundary of the county near Bear Creek, the school believed to have been just over the line in Burnet County and the church just inside Williamson.[119]

Prairie Springs, see Townsville.

Primrose, a rural school north of Donahoe Creek with a comic nickname, "Lick Skillet." E. M. and Sara White settled there, about five miles east of Corn Hill, in 1875. An early school was established there and by 1892 enrolled ninety-six pupils. The school stood about one hundred yards west of the White home (still standing in 1973 and occupied by grandson, Fred White and his wife) "on the middle of a prairie—not near natural water. We had a lot of trouble getting water," Mrs. Glenn Stearns, formerly Miss Addie Bowmer, a teacher recalled. She boarded with the

White family while teaching there. Primrose consolidated with Jarrell School in 1916.[120]

Puryear, a rural school in the Taylor area by 1892, its exact location not determined.

Ranger Branch, rural school on Ranger Branch east of Georgetown where Texas Rangers were said to have camped, thus naming the branch. The school was a successor to Brown School (see). It consolidated in 1949 with Georgetown.

Ratliff, community southeast of Florence for family of that name, near another settlement called Rocky Point. Bill and "Snap" Ratliff laid out the seven-mile road called Sunset Lane. (See Matsler).

Rattan, flag stop on Austin and Northwestern Railroad 1882, located on Rattan Creek, named for the prolific, hardy vines growing wild in the area, sometimes used to make baskets or furniture. Children ate the black berries the vines bore and got into trouble because the juice stained their teeth. The train went through Austin and Duval in Travis County, then Rattan, Cummings, Rutledge, near Buttercup, through Cedar Park and Leander. Rattan had a post office nearly two years, with postmasters Daniel R. Munn (February 5, 1887); John J. Arnot (March 3, 1887), Erastus W. Kerr (January 14, 1888); the office was discontinued December 7, 1888. An early train wreck was reported in a Merrelltown newspaper when the bridge over Rattan Creek collapsed as the train went over it. The engineer had sufficient warning to jump clear of the train but broke his neck in the leap.[121]

Rice's Crossing, known when the county was formed as Blue Hill (see), named for James O. Rice, postmaster at Blue Hill November 12, 1849, the second post office designated in the county. Rice settled there in 1846, calling it Blue Hill for the blue shale bank at the Brushy Creek crossing there. Austin Mail Route No. 6288 went from Austin through Blue Hill to San Gabriel and Cameron. Rice was one of the best known of the county's pioneers, having come to Texas before 1836. He served with Tumlinson's Rangers who built Tumlinson Fort in the county, was with the Edward Burleson Ranger Company 1838-39, participated in the attack which caught Manuel Flores with key documents and thereby eliminated a large scale treasonable plot against the Republic of Texas, was an occupant of Kenney Fort from about 1838-40, repelled an Indian attack there in 1840, was in the Somervell and Mier Expeditions, was wounded and captured in the latter, but escaped. Rice joined the Snively Expedition in 1842. After moving to Blue Hill, he signed the petition to form the county, was one of the legislative-appointed commissioners to organize Williamson County, and was involved in the first civil case in the county, M. C. Hamilton vs. James O. Rice "for trespass to try title." In the 1850 census, he was listed as age thirty-five, married to Nancy D. Rice, age twenty-five, was a farmer with $15,000 worth of taxable property, much of it land he received for his military service to Texas; his daughter Elizabeth was two. Shortly before 1860, his wife died and he arranged for a guardian for Elizabeth, then rejoined the Texas Rangers. He re-

turned to the county about 1864 and operated a tanyard between the two
forks of the San Gabriel about where the present Georgetown Country
Club is located. Wilbarger said Rice was among the most "experienced
frontiersmen" of the state. Mann said he had wit, humor and never ran
from a fight. B. E. Burns came to Williamson County in 1850; his son,
J. P. Burns farmed at Rice's Crossing, drove cattle to market and bred
fine horses.[122] The Christopher Tompkins dry goods store was in business
at Rice's Crossing by 1866 on the north side of the creek. In 1879 Thomas
B. Hyde, Madison "Mat" L. Armfield, J. R. Hargis and a Mr. Young were
merchants, one store being located at the crossroads. Armfield School
is also mentioned about this time. The community was thickly enough
settled in 1879 to hold an election to determine whether hogs or swine
would be permitted to run at large. Other early residents included Dr.
R. H. Eanes (1881), V. R. C. Avery, Professor Andrews (1882), William McCutcheon and sons John "Jack" and Jesse A., engaged in the
cattle business; Joe T. McCutcheon (1873), Judge Thomas J. Lawhon who
came there with his parents in 1876; Miss Lillian Wester, teacher in 1892,
later a professor of romance languages at the University of Texas and a
relative of Governor-to-be Dan Moody. The Blue Hill post office had been
closed since James O. Rice left the community (1857), but reopened in
the name of Rice's Crossing on May 2, 1872, with Christopher Tompkins,
postmaster. Succeeding him were M. W. Izard (1874), William A. Hargis
(1874), Madison L. Armfield (1877), Thomas B. Hyde (1879), Joseph
B. Hutchison (1883), James S. Patterson (1885), Robert C. Crozier
(1903); mail was transferred to Taylor December 14, 1907. Rice's Crossing
School consolidated with Coupland and Taylor June 20, 1950.

Robbins, a rural school two miles east of Walburg near Opossum Creek,
where two brothers, Richard and Aaron Robbins, settled about 1848.
Aaron Robbins' son, Jim Robbins, owned land a short distance west of the
Double File Trail (which crossed Richard Robbins' place) and near a
small branch leading to Opossum Creek. On Jim Robbins' property the
Robbins school was erected, at least by 1886.[123]

Robertson, a rural school by 1886, located on Robertson Hill south of
Georgetown, more familiarly known as Union Hill (see).

Rock House, a community on the North Gabriel River, one time a Tuacano
Indian village called Draco meaning "favorite place" or "preferred camp."
The name Draco was retained by Anglo-American settlers into the late
nineteeth century when a post office was assigned to Draco from 1890
until 1892. Of all the hundreds of Indian villages which once dotted the
spring-fed streams of the county, Draco was the only town name to
survive well into the Anglo-American period of settlement. The community got its name, Rock House, when the rock Baptist Tabernacle was
built sometime before 1878, for from that year onward Rock House frequently was mentioned in county news. The Rock House School was
designated that year as a tax collection point for the area. The school was
a frame building near the rock Tabernacle and "Rock Schoolhouse" was

so frequently referred to, many incorrectly believed it to have been built of rock. The school was the meeting place in 1878 for a political organization which declared "if we live we will be at the polls." The group asked for the support of people from Circleville, Brushy (Round Rock) and Post Oak Island, three of the oldest communities in the county. Officers of the political group were U. H. Anderson, J. H. Williams, D. C. DeWitt and Benjamin Perry. Pioneer Giles Anderson lived just east of Rock House village. In 1881 S. P. Stubblefield of Liberty Hill moved to a farm west of Rock House and put up a small horse-run gin across the river. It later was converted to steam furnished by wood-fed furnace. Bert Duckett said it processed at most four bales a day, working from daylight until dark. The village store is believed to have been built by the time the post office was assigned to Draco in 1890, with Olia O. Perry, postmaster. The widow Forbes ran the store, married Charlie Booth and the two continued to operate it for many years. Charlie Cole, the local blacksmith, married a Booth daughter and, after the Booths retired, Cole ran the store and a filling station. Around 1900, a Rock House string band performed in community programs; the Farmers' Union was active there in 1908. Seventy-four students were enrolled in a new two classroom Rock House School in 1922. It consolidated in 1947 with Liberty Hill.[124]

Rocky Hollow, early settlement, schools, store and church south of Matsler on Cowan Creek, usually pronounced by residents "Rocky Holler." The Rocky Hollow School, nicknamed "Stump Toe" presumably for the rocky terrain, was for Negro children and was also used as a church. The Yarborough School (spelled Yarbrough after about 1900) was for white students. Although the schools were segregated, a community cemetery near the church was integrated, with people of white and black races buried there. The schools were in operation by 1880. A small store at the top of the hill from the "hollow" was also a stage coach stop and was operated by Ellison Collins from about 1900 until 1915.[125]

Round Rock, originally called Brushy Creek. The name was changed in 1854 at the request of postal authorities when Thomas C. Oatts, the first postmaster of Brushy Creek (1851) was asked to submit another name. Recalling his pleasant hours of fishing with Jacob M. Harrell on the large roundish (anvil-shaped) rock in Brushy Creek south of the village, he suggested Round Rock. Postal records show that "late 'Brushy Creek' " was changed to Round Rock on August 24, 1854, Thomas C. Oatts, postmaster. His successors were Robert J. Hill (1860), George W. Davis (1860), Miss Jordena A. Davis (1865), W. Davis (1866), John Rowland (1867), Finas A. Stone (1874), August B. Palm (1876), Holman T. Ham (1877), August B. Palm (1877). At this point, "new" Round Rock developed with the coming of the railroad. A post office was established there for "Round Rock" and the old office was continued under the name "Old Round Rock" from 1879 until 1891. Postmasters in "new" town succeeding August B. Palm were Joseph J. Boone (1880), John T. Haynes (1881), Mrs. Kate F. Martin (1885), Edward E. Diggs (1889), Joseph H.

Holt (1893), Robert R. Hyland (1897), John A. Hyland (1911), Steve B. Wright (1916), Merrell M. Jester (1919), Frank L. Aten (1922), John W. Ledbetter (1932), Robert E. Johnson (1943), Martin E. Parker (1965). Postmasters at Old Round Rock were Livingston M. Mays (1879), Dora Aten (1889) and Miss Alice Mays (1891). The office was transferred to Round Rock's newer office on December 16, 1891.

Rowe, early school mentioned in county records, apparently in Travis County, probably for Elmer Rowe who lived south of Brushy Creek.[126]

Running Brushy, also Brueggerhoff and Cedar Park (see).

Rutledge, a new village which developed when the Austin and Northwestern railroad bypassed Pond Spring or "Old" Rutledge in 1882. It was named for the Rutledge family of the Pond Spring area. Orginally the narrow gauge rails at Rutledge ran about one hundred yards back of a house which still stood in 1970, but when the railroad converted to standard gauge, the tracks were laid a short way in front of the home. The community had a general store, a section house for railroad crews, a blacksmith shop, a stone quarry and a cedar yard. Rutledge post office opened January 28, 1895, with Otto Stolley, postmaster. Others appointed to the office were George F. Wideman (1897), Edward L. Sorelle (1899), Melvin D. Reynolds (1900), Clara Petri (1900). The office closed September 3, 1908 and mail was sent through Round Rock. Postmistress Petri was the wife of the German settler who established a store at Rutledge. In the twentieth century when Mansfield Dam was being built on the Colorado River, a spur of the railroad was built from Rutledge to the dam to transport construction materials.[127]

Saint John, Saint Luke, Saint Mark and Saint Matthew: "the Four Gospels" station stops on the Bartlett Western Railway (see).

Saint Paul, a Negro school listed in Georgetown in 1892.

Salyer, rural school which stood "like a lone sentinel on the prairie about eight or nine miles down the Granger road and about one hundred yards off the road" (from Georgetown), wrote county superintendent D. H. LeSueur in January 1888. In the community between Queen Branch and Opossum Creek, the school was named for Brack, Henry and Alex Salyer family.[128]

Sam Houston, a Negro school at Weir established in 1922 and dissolved in 1926. In the autumn of 1922, the school participated in the Harvest Festival.[129]

Sam Smith Springs, see Siloam.

Sanders, rural school named for longtime teacher Miss Mary Shipp Sanders, established in 1925 with the consolidation of Long Grove and Prairie Lea; located about halfway between the sites of the two schools it replaced. It consolidated with Florence in 1949.[130]

Sandoval, a village near Turkey Creek in east Williamson County, settled by Carl Streich in 1882. About twelve years later, a large enough settlement developed to apply for a post office. Carl Streich suggested Carlville or Streichville for the town's name but postal authorities did not accept them. Sandoval* was then approved. Herman Pasemann was another early resident, along with others of German, Austrian or French origins. Postmasters were C. W. Obermiller (May 1, 1894), Gustav Zeplin (July 7, 1894), Henry Dabelgott (May 4, 1896), Paul Streich (October 22, 1896), August A. Young (August 5, 1898) and the office was discontinued February 29, 1904. About 1895, Carl Streich built a saloon and bowling alley in which Paul Pasemann was pin boy. Young boys of the neighborhood who were sent to the tavern for a bucket of beer or tobacco were required to stand outside while their orders were filled. August A. Young had a blacksmith shop from about 1898 until the mid-twentieth century, with Conrad Ochsner running it for him a part of the time. Ginners at Sandoval were Clyde Stearns, Carl Streich and sons, Paul and Adolph, Mr. Evans and George Obermiller. Paul Streich and W. E. Bratton ran the saloon for a time. Sandoval Zion Lutheran Church was organized about 1893 and also served as a school. A new school was built about 1920, a new church in 1932. Soon after 1900, Otto Schlickeisen built a general store which Jacob "Jake" S. Melasky bought from him about 1909 and continued to run until 1924. The store was said to handle "everything from wagons to groceries." Hans Benad, Fritz Schier, Edmond Schroeder and Mr. and Mrs. Frank Ovesny were later owners. After the Sandoval Dance Hall was built in the early 1900s, the Hermann Sons Lodge met there and a German recreational club sponsored rifle contests, dances, picnics and May fetes. A Sandoval string band often furnished the music. Werner Fuessel, the community barber, had his shop in the general store. About 1907, Paul Schlickeisen, the deputy sheriff, ran a butcher shop. Approximately twenty years later his sons roped off a rodeo arena where they presented a number of rodeos. The school consolidated with Thrall in 1949.[131] Other families in the community were Boeckmann, Galler, Jechow, Kroeger, Lehmann, Lemmer, Miller, Nolte, Schoener, Schulz, Walther, Wendland and Zenkner.[132]

San Gabriel, town east of Laneport, listed in early records as in Williamson County and assigned the third post office in the county August 13, 1850, with Thomas J. Allen, postmaster, succeeded by John G. Gordon (1853) and Andrew Gordon (1856). On February 21, 1856, postal records were marked "changed to Milam Co." Peter and Jesse Mercer built a crude log cabin on the river at an early age and were attacked by Indians, Peter Mercer being killed. He was the first person buried in the old Locklin Cemetery. Rock from the old San Xavier missions was used to build the San Gabriel School.[133]

San Gabriel Peak (Mountain), see Gabriel Peak.

Saul's Mill, an early mill on Brushy Creek a short distance west of Rice's Crossing, for the Saul family who settled there.

Schwertner, settled in 1877 by Bernard Schwertner and family, a village in

* Manuel de Sandoval was Governor of Texas, appointed by Spanish authorities in 1734. No connection has been established with the town in Williamson County, although the name is undoubtedly of Spanish origin.

rich farming country already established when Bartlett and Western built through it. Postmasters were Gustav A. Matejowsky (August 30, 1912), Earl R. Wallace (1914), Mary L. Duncan (1916), Judson M. Roebuck (1919), William O. Matejowsky (1920), Joseph Tomecek (1926), Mildred I. Tomecek (1957). The school consolidated with Bartlett in 1954.

Seward Junction, so named for the W. R. Seward family who lived at the present crossroads of State Highway 29 and State Highway 183 east of Liberty Hill. Several small stores, service stations, and residences developed there.

Seymour, a rural school two miles east of Gabriel Mills, which looked out on Bald Knob to the north and to the elongated Gabriel Mountain (locally called Pilot Knob) about two miles to the southwest. Seymour, organized in 1892, was named for the Seymour family of that vicinity.

Shiloh, a very early crossroads community a short distance south of present Hutto, on the banks of Brushy Creek. In 1848 Nelson Morey and, a short time later the same year, Josiah Taylor opened small stores at Shiloh. Morey's was on the north bank of Brushy Creek south of the William Juvenal home; Taylor put his up near the Shiloh school house. The stores are believed to have been in dwellings, with a very few supplies, more like commissaries than stores—sulphur matches, axle grease (most likely from bear fat) and a barrel of whiskey. The creek crossing at Shiloh was called Wilbarger Crossing for a pioneer family there, and was later known as Shiloh or Rogan's Crossing. During cattle drives of the several decades after the Civil War, Shiloh Crossing was on one of the primary routes across the county. Josiah and Melissa Kuykendall settled there in 1844 just east of the old Shiloh Cemetery, along with Mark Kuykendall, a brother who lived nearby. Josiah's son, Wyatt, was a year old when they moved; another son, Greenup, was born in 1850. In 1853 a traveler spent the night at the Kuykendall home and as a result, Josiah contracted smallpox and died, becoming the second person to be buried in Shiloh Cemetery. The first was a woman who died as their wagon train passed through. Josiah's brother Mark came to assist him during his illness, developed smallpox and he, too, died and was buried at Shiloh. Mark's son, Jim, and daughter, Mittie, survived him, Jim living at Rice's Crossing. The Kuykendall boys were cattlemen, Wyatt driving many herds to market. He also served as a Texas Ranger. Another family settling near Shiloh were Zara and Mary Smalley Stearns, Zara's sister, Cynthia Ann Stearns (married Reverend James K. Smalley in 1854), and Zara's nephew, Harvey Trueman Stearns. They came late in 1847 from Vermilion County, Illinois, purchased 320 acres of land south of Brushy Creek from Morgan C. Hamilton for $580 on February 26, 1849. A part of the Zara Stearns place belonged to Dr. J. J. Johns of Taylor in 1973. William McCutcheon arrived near Shiloh in the fall of 1846. So many of that family lived there that Shiloh Cemetery is also called McCutcheon Cemetery. James Juvenal settled there in 1848. Just west of the high knoll of the cemetery is the site of the early community school (at least by 1884) and church, the latter built by the Cumberland Presbyterians but utilized as a union church. In a wooded area west of the church (now an open field), camp meetings were held. After Hutto was established, an annual Fourth of July picnic and celebration was held at the camp meeting site by Hutto and Shiloh. "No announcement was made of the event—everyone knew it would be held and everyone came." Several other cemeteries now cluster where Shiloh community was located—Hutto Cemetery, Lutheran Cemetery, a Negro cemetery and a Mexican-American cemetery.[134] Another community in southeastern Williamson County was also called Shiloh (see below).

Shiloh, a small town at the crossroads of FM Road 112 and FM Road 486 in southeastern Williamson County. An early church and store, both of which changed locations, formed the beginnings of the town. Shiloh Baptist Church was founded November 2, 1854, and was located south of the present town at the site of the later Eckman School. Eighteen charter members of the church were Samuel and Clarissa Carr, H. A. and Sarah Sample, W. R. and Elise Hobbs, Pl., Addline, and Naveissa Lawrence, H. and Amanda Waldrop, James B. and Margaret Williams, S. M. Burrough, Dorcus Grouch, Nancy Jordan, Addaline Ralph and Elizabeth Foster. It was moved in 1908 to its site at present Shiloh community. When Lemuel Egger Laurence* came to the community in 1878 he married Louanna Pauline Sample and in later years, although a member of the Christian Church, assisted in building the new Baptist Church. Longtime deacons and trustees at the church were S. M. Slaughter, G. W. Lawrence and Daniel Eckman. The original church probably served as the school, but later when a separate building was erected, also south of present Shiloh, it was known as Eckman School for a family in the area. Eckman School records have been found between 1892 and 1949. The small store was last run by Hobson Simmons and it was closed in the late 1960s.[135]

Silent Grove, pioneer church and school near the home of Reverend W. O. Spencer (west of present Liberty Hill) who held church services in his home in 1854, later in a tiny school built a short distance north of his home. The brush arbor adjoining the school-church became known as Silent Grove. When hot weather made it uncomfortable indoors, services were held under the arbor. Ministers of the church before 1867 included Reverends Talley, Bacon, Grammar, Forbes and H. M. Burroughs. The church constitution listed male and female members separately: John Russell, T. P. Poole, B. F. Johnson, T. K. and W. D. Wood, J. M. Spencer, Pleasant Queen, D. W. Thornton, W. W. Queen; Nancy Russell, M. C. Spencer, Biddie C. Dycus, Elvina Ray, Ann E. Spencer, W. H. Thornton, Martha and Elizabeth Queen, Judith M. Bryson, Mollie J. Thomas, M. E. Chamberlain, L. Myrack, Elizabeth Johnson and Nannie E. Wood. The congregation completed a "large rock building" for a school and church in 1870 or 1871 with all labor donated (except that of one

---

* No relation to the Adam Lawrence family, the latter changing the spelling from "u" to "w" to avoid confusion with L. E. Laurence.

stone mason) and construction was under the direction of John Russell, F. M. Barton and T. P. Poole. Annual camp meetings were held at Silent Grove until 1882 when the services were moved to Liberty Hill brush arbor. A new church was organized at that time and erected in town. The aforementioned custom of segregating the sexes was perpetuated when a new church in the newer Liberty Hill was built with two front entrances, one for men, one for women.

Siloam, a tiny community north of Sam Smith Springs, later Lawhon Springs, in the southeastern section where Marmaduke Gardner came in 1854. He organized a church known as Siloam with six whites and one Negro slave as members. Gardner organized other churches in the area and ordained three ministers, John C. and Joseph Lawhon and J. S. Dunbar. The Negro slave was referred to in Gardner's records as his "prized slave." Gardner had a large family, the slave, and enough equipment "to start all over again" when he arrived at the Siloam site December 1, 1854, bringing his wife there for her health. "Father Gardner" had varied talents. During the Civil War he made boots for Confederate troops; he was a blacksmith, hunter, farmer and one of the early Universalist preachers in Texas. In 1907 Dr. Q. H. Shinn held a convention of Universalists at the Siloam church. The first church building was erected in an elm grove on the bank of a creek near an old schoolhouse about two hundred yards from where the school stood in 1938. When that church burned, a new one was built "at the springs," then was moved to the town of Siloam and reorganized in 1910. David Ervin Lawhon, called the Texas Revolutionary printer, a relative of the Gardners, moved to his farm near Sam Smith (Lawhon) Springs in 1876 where he remained until his death in 1884. He is buried in Sam Smith-Lawhon Springs Cemetery, which has a Texas State Historical Marker. The Siloam school was also organized at an early date; in 1892 it had sixty-two students. It was called Lawhon Springs School when it consolidated with Thrall in 1951.[136]

Small, a tiny village on the banks of Williamson Creek, as the stream is often shown on maps prior to its convergence with the Opossum, after which they become Willis Creek. Residents of the Small community called the upper creek Willis. George Washington Irvin settled there about 1869, farming and rearing his large family there. In the early 1890s Irvin hired "Old Man Talley" and his mules to haul a house to the Irvin place, setting it up on the north bank of Willis Creek east of their residence for a little store. Irvin's youngest son, Ruff, was about four years old. "That store was 'Small.' It was only there for a few years. I remember I was impressed by a few things. Once three Indians came in the store when Mother and I were alone. They asked to buy a mutton. Mother told them it would cost two dollars. They paid it and she told them to go out in the field and select the one they wanted, which they did." G. W. Irvin's son, James F. "Jim" Irvin, was postmaster when the post office opened on June 29, 1894. He was succeeded by Shadrach D. Irvin (1895), believed to be a brother of the elder Irvin, who moved west after a short time at Small. Frank T. Smith was appointed postmaster March 31, 1896, and the office closed February 4, 1898. James "Jim" Mitchell Smith came to Small community in 1877 and built a gin; postmaster Frank Smith was his brother. Ake School (see) half a mile west of Small served as the village school, church and meeting place, was a voting box for many years.[137]

Smart, a school three miles west of Florence on the southwest bank of Berry's Creek, named for Bryce M. Smart and family, pioneers in that area, later consolidated with Sanders.[138]

Smith, rural school east of Gravis and near Corn Hill, at least since 1902. It consolidated with Gravis to form Hudson School.[139]

Somerset, a very early school east of Circleville about half a mile south of the old Hoxie Crossing on the San Gabriel. In 1887 the school had a new debating society ·and preaching was held in the schoolhouse once a month.[140]

Sommerville, see Brown School.

South Gabriel, small town on the south fork of the San Gabriel River near the western county line. The town disappeared when the railroad bypassed it in 1882, most of the businesses moving to the new town of Bertram a short distance away. Both towns were in Burnet County after that county was formed in 1852, but early records listed South Gabriel in Williamson County, including the post office granted that town September 29, 1871, with Thomas Lewiston, postmaster. Postal records show transferral to Burnet County soon afterwards. In 1888 Williamson County School Superintendent D. H. LeSueur had South Gabriel School on his itinerary of visits and the school remained on the Williamson County lists through 1892. It then disappeared briefly. In 1916 a school at the same location reappeared in the county records under the name Wil-Bur School, combining a portion of both county names.[141]

Springtown, see Monadale.

Stapp, pioneer school named for Joshua, Benjamin W. and R. Stapp, south of Florence in the 1850s. See White House.

Stauffer, small rural school southeast of Noack, operated in the 1920s, named for a family of that community including Samuel, Fritz and Charlie Stauffer.[142]

Stevenson, rural school in northwestern section of county near Centre Point and Oak, consolidating with them to form Lawler.[143]

Stiles, or Stiles Switch—see Thrall.

Stony Point, a rural school established by 1892 or earlier, active until 1941 when it consolidated, dividing its students between Hutto and Round Rock. It had absorbed the Palm Valley School in 1924.[144]

Strickland, Strickland Grove, an early school and church "up the Georgetown and Glasscock Valley Road" on Dry Berry's Creek, at least by 1888, probably much earlier. The Strickland Grove Church of Christ met for some years in the schoolhouse. The school had a new building in 1922, painted blue with white trim, and in order to have an eight month school term, each student brought a load of wood for winter fuel, chopped by men of the community. The money saved by not buying wood permitted them to lengthen the school year. The school consolidated with Jarrell in 1949.[145]

Stringtown, see Monadale.

Structure, small business community northwest of Beaukiss which developed in the 1920s when Charles Ryan moved a building there and operated a store. The town also included a gin, two residences, a filling station and possibly one or two other businesses. Clint Lawhon later ran the store. By 1969 the village had disappeared.[146]

Sunset Lane, see Matsler.

Swenson, Swenson Grove, a Negro school on the west side of Norman's Crossing (see).

Sycamore, Sycamore Grove, Sycamore Springs, names for a school and church on the creek of the same name almost on the western county line, in operation at least by 1880 and through 1923.[147]

Tanglewood, school earlier called Chalk Ridge (see) and nicknamed "Terrapin Ridge."

Taylorsville, Taylor (see other references). Although almost unanimously referred to in county records of the 1870s as Taylorsville, the first entry in the U. S. Post Office Department listed the town as Taylorville. The post office there opened August 9, 1876, with J. B. Loper, postmaster, about the time the rails were completed through town. Subsequent postmasters were James B. Simons (1877); listed for Taylorsville: J. O. Frink (1880), John H. Hutchinson (1890). Beginning December 20, 1892, the postal entry is changed to Taylor with the appointment of Edward A. Robertson. His successors were John Lloyd (1894), James A. Simons (1895), Carrie E. Hoke (1898), Frank S. Way (1912), John L. Brunner (1915), Alex P. Hicks (1924), Paula Hicks (1930), John L. Brunner (1933), Mrs. Nell H. Brunner (1948), Daniel M. Hannan (1950), J. B. Dabbs (1973).

Tennill, rural school near Brown's Gin south of Taylor, listed in the early twentieth century, consolidating with Taylor July 6, 1949.

Theon, community north of Georgetown, which was known earlier as Behrnville for pioneer H. T. Behrens; also called Leubner for William Leubner, another early settler and merchant. All three names were assigned at different times to the village for a post office. "New Corn Hill" was the result of an attempt to establish a business community adjacent to Theon to replace the once-thriving Corn Hill after the Bartlett Western Railway caused its disappearance. Large numbers of settlers from Germany, Austria, Moravia, Bohemia and Silesia came to the area in the 1880s and 1890s seeking its fine farmland. In 1889 they founded the Holy Trinity Catholic Church, erecting a modest building on the prominent hill where the present church stands. The site of the first church is marked in the cemetery by a life-sized figure of Christ on the Cross. The present twin-spired brick church was erected in 1913 and a parochial school was operated next door until 1968. German protestant families of the community generally attended one of the Lutheran churches at nearby Walburg. As the community grew, a post office was requested in July 1890 in the name "Bernville," apparently misspelled in the postal records, but that name was not accepted. The application was changed to Theon, a Greek word meaning "to God," possibly suggested by the local priest who knew Greek and by the proximity of the church up the hill from the village. Theon was approved and on September 12, 1890, Fritz Krauss became postmaster. Problems are said to have arisen regarding the post office and it was discontinued July 5, 1892. About that time William Leubner moved his family and store from near Walburg to Theon, to operate a general merchandise and grocery store. On October 27, 1894, Fridrick W. Leubner was appointed postmaster of the community, this time called Leubner instead of Theon. The mail boxes were arranged on the porch of the store and for a brief time a bar was provided inside. Since government regulations forbade this dual arrangement, Leubner built a saloon next door, elegantly furnished and decorated in the Victorian style popular at that time. Toward the end of the decade, the Leubner family moved to Granger and Dallas and the post office called Leubner was closed April 20, 1898. Another merchant, August Kalmbach, bought the Theon Mercantile Store in 1900, operating it for many years and was succeeded by his son, William Kalmbach who ran it in the 1970s with his daughter, Ruby Atwood. A third time applications were made for a post office, and on March 9, 1901, Behrnville was approved with Gottlieb (August) Kalmbach, postmaster. It closed for the last time April 30, 1906. Thom Mrazek operated a gin at Theon about 1884, selling it to Ernst Miersch in January 1891. When farmers brought their cotton to the two-stand gin, it was weighed on a platform wagon scale, was unloaded on the upper floor, and was carried in a wire basket to the stands where it was fed in by hand. Cotton seed fell to the floor as they were separated from the lint, then were stored for seed, feed or fertilizer. Lint dropped on the floor behind each stand where it was gathered by hand into a basket and carried to the press box. When the box was full, a steam engine pressed the cotton, repeating the packing procedure four times for every bale, then tying and bagging the bale. Miersch accepted about one hundred pounds of seed cotton in exchange for ginning a bale. When coal was not available as fuel for the steam furnace, young Paul Miersch cut cord wood to feed it. Miersch had a corn mill at the gin where he accepted one-fifth of the corn as a toll for milling. Emil E. Jungmichel of Walburg bought the gin in 1906; Joe Sladecek's mother and later Alphonse Kott owned it. About 1892 Theon farmers organized a beef club, put up a building in the heart of the village and furnished meat for members until about 1948. Thirty or forty families formed Behrnville Rifle Club about 1888, built a platform a mile north of the present Moravia Hall, where large dances, rifle contests and other social gatherings were held. The Farmers' Inn was built later in the same place. It and a small Hermann and Sons Lodge for a few years provided places for music and recreation. About 1938 the present Moravia Hall was erected a mile south of Farmers' Inn, which was then torn down. In 1973 Theon had an active Holy Trinity Catholic Church, the old western style store front on the general store, a tavern, gas station and cotton gin, possibly

resembling the village of eighty years before more than any other place
in Williamson County. "New Corn Hill" existed briefly around 1910 after
the Bartlett Western Railway bypassed Corn Hill. Believing that a successor to Corn Hill (at this time moving to the new railroad town of
Jarrell) could be established about two miles east of the disappearing
Corn Hill, promoters established a grocery store, blacksmith shop and
saloon atop the hill near the Holy Trinity Church. John Schultz's residence was near them on the hill. The recreation hall, previously mentioned, was put up at that time. Since the business section of Theon was
only about a mile down the hill, the New Corn Hill venture failed within
a short time.[148] Among families who registered baptisms at the Holy
Trinity Church prior to 1899 were John Janosec, Bartholomew Zurovec,
Joseph Valenta, John Pavlasek, Francis Kolar, Anton Hajek, Joseph
Schlesinger, Martin Vrabel, Francis Skrhak, Martin Kopecky, Adolph
Schwertner, Joseph Palousek, Joseph Knapek, Paul Skurka, Ygnasio Kubacak, John Marac, Josef Schwertner, Albert Zrubek, Edward Schwertner,
Jan Kurecka and George Havelka.[149] Theon public school consolidated
with Jarrell in 1949.

Thorndale, now in Milam County; at one time a portion of the community
apparently was in Williamson, first called Everett (see). Three postmasters were assigned to Thorndale when the town was listed by postal
authorities in Williamson County: Miscipsia A. O. Moore (April 18,
1878), J. B. James (1879), James K. Quinn (1879); Thorndale was listed
"now in Milam Co." with the appointment of L. W. Caruthers on June
14, 1880.

Thrall, earlier Stiles Switch, established 1876 when the I. & G. N. railroad
built west from Rockdale, named Thrall in 1901, at the request of the
Stiles family who admired minister-historian Homer S. Thrall, prominent
in Texas at that time. Stiles School was organized there in the 1880s. A
decade later Will Martin and Steve F. Evans put up a gin. Raleigh Riley
opened a general store in 1899 where the post office was established two
years later, R. M. Riley postmaster. Subsequent postmasters were James
C. Douglass (1908), Martha B. Waters (1915), Martha Waters Howard
(1921), Mrs. Burna H. Cain (1922), Millard Arrington (1934), John
Krieg (1935),. William G. Fuchs (1938), Mrs. Burna H. Cain (1956),
Mrs. Doris June Johnson (1970). In 1908 a larger school was built in
Thrall to succeed Stiles School, although several other rural schools continued to operate in the vicinity until the 1920s and 1930s. Until 1915
farming and cattle were the economic mainstays of Thrall. Farmers had
suffered a drouth in 1914 so when an oil well was brought in early the
next year, it markedly changed the life of the tiny village and all the
surrounding area. Population of Thrall jumped from fifteen hundred
people to three thousand within a short time. Farmers, hard pressed for
cash, were able to lease their land for cash. The well, drilled on the Fritz
Fuchs farm about a mile south of town, blew in February 22, 1915, "the
first well ever drilled in the Serpentine formation." An oil boom ensued.
The first hundred wells drilled were described as gushers. Distinguished

officials visiting the field included Alf Landon, Republican candidate for president, Harry J. Sinclair who later established the Sinclair Petroleum Corporation, and J. L. Lattimer, later president of Magnolia Petroleum Company. All told, about two hundred wells were drilled in the area. New oil companies were formed and for several years the activity was hectic, but by 1920 had levelled off. Population of Thrall was 272 that year. The magic of the industrial age was described about this time in a special story from Thrall reporting that "a steel car, especially equipped by the I-G N railroad to burn green weeds, passed here Friday, making about four miles an hour, not leaving a sprig of grass or weed. A car follows with a sprinkler; also this is followed by the section gang with mops to see that all fire is out." Another surge of excitement developed near Thrall in 1930 when a well on the J. C. Abbott property east of Lawrence Chapel was drilled by a man named Chapman, the place being sometimes called Chapman City. (Also see Beaukiss.) A "gusher" was brought in at a depth of 1834 feet on January 18, 1930, about two o'clock in the morning. Production came from the Pecan Gap formation and was estimated at five hundred barrels. Thrall realized increased activity, but the day of the automobile had arrived by this time and much of the bustle was concentrated in Taylor. "The Blazilmar Hotel in Taylor was much like headquarters of a state convention." Crowds there doubled and more than fifteen hundred leases were signed in less than three days. The field proved to be a shallow one and most of the wells failed by 1940, although a few were producing modest amounts in 1973. The Stiles Farm Foundation was established in 1961 by Hadley Alva Stiles of Taylor in honor of his father, James E. Stiles. More than five hundred acres of land and the family homestead at Thrall were set aside for the foundation, all to be preserved, maintained, and operated by the Agricultural & Mechanical College of Texas for agricultural research. The Stiles family main house on the property was demolished by the Trustees soon after they took possession. Another home was constructed and the model farm is still under the jurisdiction of the present A. & M. University.[150]

Tidwell, a farm community and railroad switch near Granger, named for the Tidwell family who lived there.[151]

Tompkins Store, see Rice's Crossing.

Towns Mill, Townsville, named for James "Jim" Francis Towns and family. (See Weir.) Towns Mill, also called Excelsior Mill, was built on the east bank of the San Gabriel River, just above the Double File Crossing and an early Ranger campsite, soon after Towns settled there in 1870. About the same time, Jack Berry shot a seven-foot alligator at the mouth of Berry's Creek nearby; a three-foot one was killed there in 1883. Robert W. Towns, a brother to James, became a partner in the large milling business which expanded its operations over the county and in neighboring counties. About half a mile east of the dam and a mile south of present Weir the Buffalo Spring Baptist Church was founded in 1875 and a Union Sunday School was organized in 1879 near springs which had been watering places for buffalo. A resident wrote in 1890, "The good people of this

vicinity were preparing for the Baptist camp-meeting, and in cleaning
out a spring near the camp-ground they found (as I have been told) a
buffalo's horn in the spring at considerable depth. Hence the name." That
same communication reported that the Baptists would soon erect a church
there. The congregation had been meeting in the Prairie Springs School
since 1875. In connection with the mill, the Towns family operated a gin
and a blacksmith shop. James F. Towns became postmaster at Townsville
on May 6, 1895, after applications for such an office had been made first
in the name of "Midway." The Towns sons became known as mechanical
geniuses who could build and run many kinds of machinery and were
involved in the milling, ginning, automobile and similar businesses. By
the end of the century, Lucy Weir ran a small store at Townsville. When
the Georgetown and Granger railroad was projected in 1890 (completed
between Granger and Austin in 1904), Townsville ceased to develop
further as a village, but Excelsior mill continued to operate until 1913.
After 1904, railroad officials and others promoted a resort at Katy Lake,
which was formed by Towns Mill dam. This enterprise thrived until a
1913 flood devastated many of the facilities. It continues to be a favorite
fishing place in the 1970s.[152]

Tumlinson Block House, Tumlinson Fort (see.) Named for John J. Tumlinson, captain of one of the three first Texas Ranger forces organized late
in 1835 by the Texas Provisional Government. Tumlinson block house-
fort was built early in 1836.

Turkey Creek, a rural school named for the creek near which it stood, down
the hill to the south of Wuthrich Hill, established 1893 on land provided
by Mr. and Mrs. Henry Henkes. Until 1910 school terms lasted three or
four months and one teacher taught all eight grades until 1919. The girls'
basketball team often played against New Bern, about seven miles to the
north, the teams walking to and from the other school for the competitions—an entire day's affair. Trustees before 1900 were H. Priesmeyer,
G. W. Heselmeyer, A. Braker, H. Schwenker, F. Meiske, C. W. Remmert.
The school consolidated with Thrall in May 1950. Turkey Creek got its
name from the abundance of wild turkeys pioneers found in that region
when they moved there.[153]

Tyler, a rural school established south of Taylor near the home of George
W. Tyler who built his residence there in 1872 and soon after gave land
for the school. Records of the school have been found in 1889 and it
was active until it consolidated with Taylor in 1950. The school building
was a short distance south of Battleground Creek.[154]

Type, a rural school southeast of Coupland, apparently established after
1900, and a crossroads community about a mile north of the school,
settled in the early 1900s by a number of Swedish families who organized
a Swedish Evangelical Church there in 1908. Charter members were Peter
Nygaard, Mr. and Mrs. Victor Carlson, Mr. and Mrs. Alfred Jacobson,
Mr. and Mrs. Louis Nelson, Mr. and Mrs. John Sunvison, Mr. and Mrs.
Oscar Jacobson and Mr. and Mrs. August Nyman. School consolidated
with Coupland, 1945.[155]

Union Chapel, school and church located south of present state Highway 29 halfway between Seward Junction and Georgetown. Union Chapel School was mentioned in 1887 when it was destroyed by fire. Union Chapel Baptist Church was nearby. After the fire, the school was either rebuilt or shared the church building; it was consolidated with Georgetown and Liberty Hill schools in 1950.[156]

Union Hall, early community about four miles east of Liberty Hill, settled prior to the Civil War by Billy Johnson, Ben Johnson, John Schooley, E. Walker and Greenleaf Fisk. "These homes all joined and were the only ones in the valley except that of R. Bullington on the Gabriel about two miles east of Liberty Hill," and formed a kind of triangle with the South San Gabriel on the south and west sides. Fisk came from Bastrop there in 1846, built a log residence. Immigration during the Civil War and for a few years after "was at a standstill." Between 1866 and 1873 new settlers in this same triangle were Billy Wilson, Mr. Justice, Mr. Gee, Wig Jennings, A. M. Leatherwood, J. G. Matthews, J. B. Fisk, Gus Hornburg, H. S. Whitehead, L. G. Ford, W. R. Seward and J. H. Hodges. Children attended Matthews School (see) in 1873 and the next year another log school was built a few yards from the first one, this being a free school known as Union Hall. It consolidated with Leander and Liberty Hill in 1949. Various denominations held church in the Union Hall School, and a Missionary Baptist Church was founded about 1888. Founders were T. E. and Susie (Schooley) Martin, R. E. and Addie (Matthews) Allen, A. M. Leatherwood and wife, J. R. Williamson and wife, Virginia Bainbridge and son, C. A. Bainbridge. About 1890 the congregation built a church a mile east of the log house, the new church serving as a new school and community center. Union Hall Missionary Baptist Church continues in 1973 to utilize the sound portion of the old church for its present house of worship. The three mile long battle of Texas Rangers with Manuel Flores and his men in 1839 took place near the Union Hall community, both the Flores party and the Rangers stopping at the spring where Billy Johnson later built his home on the South Gabriel.[157]

Union Hill, also called Cross Roads, south of Georgetown, had a school referred to by area residents as Union Hill, but officially called Robertson School, possibly to avoid confusion with Union Hall near Liberty Hill. The Joseph Robertson family lived just north of the school and a short way west of Bell School in the neighborhood of Calvin Bell and John K. Shelgren. After numerous Swedish families settled near Union Hill, Lutheran church services were held in the schoolhouse, near which a cemetery was established. Music-loving residents formed a community brass band which rehearsed at the school and could be heard a long distance away. When Bell community Mission Lutheran Church and the Palm Valley Lutheran Church were established, Lutherans of Union Hill attended those places of worship. Swedish Methodists attended services in the S. M. Johnson, Christianson, Lundblad and C. J. Monson* homes

---

* In early records the name was spelled Monson, later anglicized to Munson.

between 1871 and 1880, when they began preparing to build a church. They purchased three acres of land for $40, formally organized the Swedish Methodist-Episcopal Brushy Church (Svenska Metodist-episkopalforsamlingens), built it in 1882 northwest of the crossroads of Rabbit Hill Road and Old Round Rock Road. It stood near two old cedar trees which still grow in the cemetery established in the churchyard. Earliest members were August and Anna Johnson, C. J. Munson, Andrew and Ida Swenson, William and Hedda Sandberg, John A. and Anna C. Sandberg, Swen and Charlotte Johnson, Oscar Forsvall, John and Christina Bergstrom, Mrs. Helene Gahagan, and Mrs. Rebecca Lundblad. Annual ten-day meetings were held at Katy Lake until the 1913 flood destroyed shade trees, buried the springs, and washed away "all our possessions." The church moved to Georgetown in 1902, erected a stone church there now known as St. Johns Methodist.[158]

Union House, early church-school at Circleville where various denominations held services beginning in 1855.

Wade, rural school located near a small branch leading to Salado Creek, north of the eastern end of Sunset Lane, named for local family. School records date back to 1888. In 1902, Wade had thirty-five pupils.[159]

Wadkins Crossing, early crossing named for pioneer Sam Wadkins, located on Brushy Creek at the junction of Brushy and Chandler Branch.

Walburg, thriving German-Wendish settlement northeast of Georgetown where early Opossum School stood, the village known briefly as Concordia. The Zion Lutheran Church was organized in 1882 "at Concordia, Williamson County, Texas." Charter members were John Neitsch, John Schultz, Carl Streich, August Doehre, Albert Ramm, Albert Krause, Andreas Schneider, Wilhelm Andres and Jacob Schoemberg. Henry Doering, immigrant from Walburg, Germany, moved to Concordia in 1881 after farming for a year on Berry's Creek. He suffered a heat stroke, was advised to quit farming, so moved to the little church community and established a number of businesses, including a general store in 1882. When Doering applied for a post office, the name Walburg was submitted honoring his birthplace in Germany, was approved July 10, 1886, with Doering as postmaster. "A devastating storm swept through the community damaging the homes of the people, and the accompanying hail destroyed the crops. The church, too, was moved from its foundation by the destructive winds" on June 19, 1886, when the little church building was only four years old. A thirteen-month drouth followed the tornado, severely straining finances and the church had no pastor from 1888 to 1890. About this time, another Lutheran group affiliated with the Texas Synod became active, considered joining the Zion Church (Missouri Synod) congregation, but two points regarding a parochial school and a lodge could not be agreed upon. On March 21, 1880, St. Peter Lutheran Church was organized at Walburg with W. H. Homeyer, C. Jungmichel, A. C. Braun, F. Bredthauer, Theo Granzin, John Granzin, H. T. Behrens, Carl Mueller, T. Kraus, Emil Vogler, officers and building committee. The church was built about half a mile from the Zion Church and both congregations have remained active to the present time. Zion Lutheran parochial school adjacent to the church established in 1882, has a longtime history, with W. G. Bleeke teaching there from 1930 almost until his death in 1968. Businesses and professional people at Walburg have included Henry Doering general store (run by descendants in 1973) and post office; John Schwausch blacksmith shop from 1884 to 1930 and Henry Jacob blacksmith shop opened in 1901, descendants of Schwausch and Jacob still running a smithy business; Adolph C. Braun (who moved to the area with his wife, Annie Mueller Braun and family in 1877), an early hardware store; Gus Braun store later enlarged by Gerhardt Cassens, also owned in later years by Carl Liese and A. C. A. Braun; Miss Frieda Schwausch, millinery shop; gins operated by E. E. Jungmichel, Sam Reynolds, J. C. Poppelz, Sr., F. E. Edrington, Gus Doering, C. G. Doering, J. W. McCann, John Kasperik, H. C. Doering, Martin R. Teinert and Carl J. Doering; Drs. White, Masterson, E. M. Thomas, August Kuhn, Hague, Randolph, J. H. Whigham and W. C. Wedemeyer. Soon after the turn of the century a beef club was organized; Hermann Sons Lodge sponsored dances, and today the community has a large recreational building where social, political and other gatherings are held. C. A. Peters put in a drug store in the early 1890s, succeeded in turn by the elder Mr. Jungmichel, Albert and Walter Werner and I. G. "Mac" McGinnis, an Irishman, popular among many Germans. John Schwausch ran a woodworking shop, repairing wagon wheels and other wooden articles along with his blacksmithing duties. The first postmaster, Henry Doering, held that post until 1900, succeeded by Adolf C. A. Braun (1900), Selma A. Kuehne (1911), John Kasperik (1912), Albert C. Werner (1914), Walter A. Werner (1924), Isaac G. McGinnis (1930), Carroll C. Wedemeyer (1948), Gilbert C. Kurio (1949). Walburg State Bank opened October 1, 1913, with Henry Doering president. It is still active. Garages have been run by Paul Andres, Bennie Draeger and Walter Domel.[160] Walburg Public School was declared consolidated with Georgetown by the County Board of Trustees on May 16, 1950, after an election in which there was no voting box provided in Walburg—the first time the community did not have its own election box, according to County Auditor Ben Kurio.[161]

Wales, a rural school named for an early family in the area, located about two miles east of Andice on the south bank of Berry's Creek.

Walker, a Negro school listed in 1892, apparently in the Jonah-Weir-Georgetown area, but definite site not established.

Walkerton, flag station on the Austin and Northwestern Railroad Company built in 1882, half a mile south of Tumlinson Block House site and south of former home of Judge Alexander Stuart Walker. Several generations of the A. S. Walkers were attorneys and judges, living on the Walker ranch or in Austin. Among prominent personages who visited the Walker family at Block House were William Jennings Bryan and Mrs. Bryan who spent Monday, December 7, 1908, on the ranch. The two families lunched together and the men spent several hours shooting quail. That evening the Bryans rode to Georgetown in one of the early automobiles of the county and he spoke before an audience at Southwestern University.[162] Shipments of the Walker Ranch cattle were loaded at Walkerton.

Walnut Springs, rural school (see Avery, Norman's Crossing). Walnut Springs School consolidated with Hutto in 1949.

Waterloo, rural village of the late nineteenth century on the prairies east of Circleville, near Wuthrich Hill community. Pioneers in the area included Jacob Thornton Bernard who came in 1878, Christian Gottfried Wuthrich (1888) and Josiah W. Rainwater who arrived in December 1890 and built a grocery store. A church and school in the area was known as Somerset, so when the village applied for a post office the name Somerset was requested. The name had already been granted another place, so Rainwater suggested Waterloo, the name of his old home in Kentucky. (Austin, Texas was briefly called Waterloo before it was chosen as state capital.) Waterloo post office was approved May 12, 1893, with Patrick G. Tartar, postmaster. His successors were Patsie J. Gate (1894), Ranza L. Luttrell (1895), Josiah W. Rainwater (1897), John D. R. Cooper (1899), Robert A. Skeen (1899), Josiah W. Rainwater (1901), and Gusta Tindel (1903). The office was discontinued September 15, 1904. The store was run by Floyd Tindel, by the Bernard family and others; a drug store was combined with it at one time. E. M. Aderholt, a ginner in Alabama, heard that this fine cotton-growing community had no gin, so moved to Waterloo in 1891 and had a gin in operation there that fall. Dr. Charles Land moved there about the same time and had a small drug store in his residence. Hamp Gillis came to Waterloo and put up a blacksmith shop in the 1890s. Other settlers were Tom Gossett and R. Compton, better known as "Uncle Razz," who tamed wild mustangs to pull his sulky plow. A telephone exchange was established about 1900. An early church in the area served both as school and church and German families moving into the community generally attended Lutheran services in Taylor prior to about 1894. A Methodist Church was built between Waterloo and the San Gabriel River about 1896, which was shared alternate Sundays with Baptist, Christian and Presbyterian preachers. A Lutheran church was built at Wuthrich Hill (see). Later businessmen at Waterloo were Henry Hejl (groceries and gin about 1915), Mr. and Mrs. J. W. Faykus (store and gin about 1930) with Jerry Drozda managing the store, and later the Faykus sons, Alvin and Ernest, operating both businesses with their mother. Jim Matyastik, Mrs. Ruth Wolett and Herbert Boehm also ran the store. John and Anna Maresh came to Waterloo in 1913 and Maresh ran a horse powered syrup press. Waterloo and Hoxie School annexed to Thrall in 1949.[163]

Water Valley, see Jonah.

Weir, see also Midway and Townsville. Weir was established after the Granger-Georgetown railroad was built and named at the suggestion of Horace M. Weir, first postmaster there, for his father, Calvin Weir, a settler who had lived in the area since 1856. Once during the many decades that the prohibitionist question raged over the nation, Calvin Weir placed a notice in the county newspaper in 1887 stating that "the report in circulation that I am an anti-prohibitionist is absolutely untrue." Weir and his descendants were active in the community for many years. The post office at Weir was under the postmastership of Horace M. Weir (May 3, 1900), Lucy A. Weir (1903), Charlie E. Collins (1905), Anna C. Burnap (1919), Allie Norma Hausenfluke (1957), Hattie M. Burran (1972).. Churches, schools and businesses quickly built up in the railroad town. Businesses were mercantile stores owned or run by Gus Braun, W. C. Gilliam, Mr. Collins, Mr. Magee, Carl Liese, Otto Liese, H. B. Peters, Mr. and Mrs. Carl Hausenfluke; W. E. Boyd Grocery; Harry Percy and W. H. Percy Drug Store; Isom Lister Bank, Weir Union Telephone Company operated by Mrs. Blanche Cash Millholin; Independent Telephone Company operated by Mrs. I. N. (Miss Effie) Daniels; Glenn Stearns gin (1909); J. W. Dowda blacksmith shop; George Messer's Hotel later owned by Mrs. D. A. King; Belford Lumber Company run by Oran Faubion and John C. Sherman, Sr. and Mr. Ridings; H. P. Allcorn confectionery and drug store; A. G. Braun automobile agency; Weir Grain and Elevator Company built in 1957 by Victor Knauth; Martin Buchhorn Fertilizers; Macon Jones, Magnolia agency. The town also had early millinery and barber shops, livery stable, the Airdrome for entertainment, and a small newspaper, believed to have been called the *Weir Reporter*, published about 1910 or 1911; a meat market and a movie house. Arthur Foster of Weir was a distinguished flyer in World War I for whom Foster Field at Victoria, Texas, was named. In 1930 when the United States commercial airlines were being developed, an emergency landing field was erected near Weir by the federal government with a beacon and searchlight for airmen flying between Mexico City and Chicago. The searchlight was said to be visible for thirty miles from the air. During his undergraduate student days at the University of Texas, young Bill Moyers served as student pastor at the Weir Baptist Church. Moyers was on the staff of President Lyndon Baines Johnson, serving as advisor and press secretary during the Johnson administration. Moyers later published *Newsday*, a Long Island newspaper; a book, *Listening to America*, and produced a television series released in 1972 called "Bill Moyers' Journal."[164] Weir School was annexed to Jonah on March 18, 1950.

Wesley Chapel, see Matsler.

White House, a large rural school south of Andice. Originally, the school at this place was called Stapp for a pioneer family in the community. The name White House reflected the school's uniqueness in that vicinity—it was one of the first to be painted white. In 1877 White House teacher R. O. Kerr was offering music along with other courses. In 1892 Miss Lina Hickman taught 73 students. Enrollment reached 131 in 1922, after Seymour consolidated with White House. White House burned and in 1925 a new Andice school replaced it.[165]

White Stone, crossroads community at State Highway 183 and FM Road 1431, so-named for the cluster of quarries and the color of the stone found there. Several businesses operated in the downtown section in the mid-twentieth century and the town had an Assembly of God Church.

White Stone School built of white rock was erected in 1923. "Old Cedar Park" and "Old New Hope" schools had consolidated to form the new White Stone School. It consolidated with Leander in 1954. (Sometimes written Whitestone.)[166]

Whittle & Harrel, a school listed in 1892, its location not determined. Miss Mattie Chapman taught forty-eight students there in that year. Moses Harrel and his wife lived in Georgetown, operated a boarding house there known as Harrel House in the early decades of the twentieth century. Their surname was spelled differently from most of the Harrell families prominent in county history.[167]

Willow Tank Road ran from Structure northeast toward Lawrence Chapel and FM Road 112.

Wilson Springs, earlier called Mustang Springs, located on Mustang Creek north of Taylor, first settled in 1849 when John Gooch built a grist water-powered mill at the springs which he called Mill Hollow. Early travelers and trail drivers often camped or rested at the springs. Gooch transferred the mill property to Ben Gooch, Jr., in 1851, and John S. Wilson bought it in 1854. The name of the place gradually changed to Wilson Springs for the Wilson family, including Robert Wiggington Wilson, Charles B. Wilson who came there in 1856, and James Wilson, who was killed in the Civil War. Charles Wilson went to Galveston for telegraph wire which he used to fence in his sheep long before barbed wire was in use. He was said to be the first in Williamson County to use wire fence. In 1860 Robert Wiggington Wilson built a rock house which stood in 1973. The original structure had slits in the heavy rock walls for protection from Indians. John Speegle erected a gin at Wilson Springs in 1879 or 1880. A school was built and operated there until consolidation in 1949 with Hutto and Taylor.[168]

Woodrow, a rural school built about 1913 a short distance from Post Oak Island, named for President Woodrow Wilson. Woodrow contained two classrooms and replaced the old Condron School at Post Oak Island. Woodrow was annexed to Thrall and Coupland July 6, 1949.[169]

Wuthrich Hill, named for Christian Gottfried Wuthrich, 1872 Swiss immigrant to Texas, and for his father, Mathias, who did not live in William County but gave the land on which the community church was established. C. G. Wuthrich came to the area in 1888, bought cattle for Hoxie Ranch, paying fifty cents a head. He also bought a farm for himself which he broke and planted. He and other German and Swiss settlers attended church in Taylor until 1894, when a Lutheran association was formed at Wuthrich Hill by Henry Priesmeyer, Sr., C. G. Wuthrich, J. Stoll and A. Stoll. Later in the year the association members joined with W. Meyer, Henry Schwenker, Fritz Meiske, August Bracker and H. Heselmeyer to organize the Evangelical Lutheran St. James Congregation of Wuthrich Hill. Until a church was completed and dedicated May 31, 1895, the congregation met in Turkey Creek School. In 1948 St. James and the New Bern church consolidated, moving the New Bern building to Wuthrich Hill and renaming it Prince of Peace Lutheran Church. A cemetery lies adjacent to the church and the Turkey Creek School was a short distance away. When the Wuthrich family came there the land was open prairie and only after about 1890 was it being divided into smaller tracts and offered for sale. The Wuthrich sisters could remember the frightening sound of wolves howling at night, six or eight of them in a pack. "They were very hard on the young cattle. They hid in the mesquite which covered the prairie before it was cultivated. We had to watch for them all the time." The same prairieland was covered with hog wallows, but cultivation has almost eliminated them. Two or three small areas with wallows remained in the Wuthrich Hill vicinity in 1970.[170]

Yakey, school at Frame Switch (see) named for Solomon George Yakey who came there in 1884. The school was active until annexed to Taylor and Hutto districts on July 6, 1949.[171]

Yankee Branch, name of stream and of a rural school near it, west of Granger. Legend says that Union soldiers or "Yankees" camped near the stream during the Civil War or that some of the early families settling there came from northern states, thus supplying the name. Yankee Branch School was active by 1892 and through at least 1902.[172]

Yarborough or Yarbrough, rural school at least by 1888, spelled with the extra "o" in earlier records, in the shortened form in later years. Yarbrough still functioned through 1935. It was in the Rocky Hollow (see) community, eventully consolidated with Matsler.

Youngsport, an early community across the northwestern county line in Bell County. Youngsport Road led there from Georgetown.[173]

Youngstown, a Negro school located near Friendship in 1922, apparently active only during the early twentieth century.

Notes

Full titles of works cited may be found in the Bibliography.

CHAPTER I

1. Arbingast, 9.
2. Udden, 147-148.
3. Interview Snead.
4. Sellards, II, 242-243.
5. Caskey, 31-32.
6. Sellards, II, 400-401.
7. Sellards, I, 328, 331; II, 63, 221, 270, 420; *Leverett.*
8. Dumble, *Geological Survey 1889*, 125.
9. *Ibid.*, 128, 137-138.
10. *Granger News*, May 8, 1969; Lundelius, 16, 24, 26-27, 117.
11. Lundelius, 141.
12. Reddell and Finch.
13. Interview Merideth; Lundelius, 142; Reddell.
14. Lundelius, 161-162.
15. *Ibid.*, 163-164; interview Edwards.
16. Sellards, II, 57; Udden, 18.
17. D. B. Wood Ranch, Joseph Fish Survery, west of Georgetown.
18. *Leverett.*
19. Roemer, 183.
20. Dodge, 27-28.
21. Interview Steelman; *Megaphone*, Oct. 13, 1972.
22. *Williamson County Sun*, Jul. 6, 1972.
23. National Geographic, 51.
24. Dumble, *Second Annual Report*, xlvi.
25. Roemer, 192, 199-200, 207.
26. Dodge, 119.
27. *Ibid.*
28. *Ibid.*, 119-120.
29. Letter, Texas Parks; interviews Wood.
30. *Sun*, Jun. 15, 1972.
31. Morfi, 65.
32. Dodge, 109-110, 234, 239.
33. *Taylor Daily Press*, Feb. 13, 1970.
34. *Georgetown Independent*, Oct. 29, 1856.
35. Morfi, 65.
36. Roemer, 139.
37. *Ibid.*, 139-141.
38. *Ibid.*, 155; Templin; Arbingast, 11; *Handbook*, II, 917.
39. Sanchez, 259.
40. Dodge, 32.
41. Roemer, 3, 10, 287.
42. *Mann Papers.*
43. Besides sources cited on plants and their uses, the author has relied on Irwin's *Roadside Flowers of Texas*, *Encyclopedia Britannica*, information gathered from pioneers.
44. Interview Stallings.
45. Irwin, 127.
46. Roemer, 155.
47. Interview Stallings.
48. Geiser, 148, 161, 165.
49. *Ibid.*, 55, 181, 184, 186-187, 225-239.
50. *Handbook*, II, 159-160.
51. Geiser, 211; *passim.*

CHAPTER II
1. Farb, 192-200, 202, 225-226; *Enc. Brit.*, XII, 62-78.
2. Newcomb, 14.
3. Sorrow, 44.
4. Shafer, 7, 34, 117; Schuetz, 135-168.
5. Suhm, "Excavations," 189-207.
6. Josephy, 100; *Enc. Brit.*, XII, 62-78, 196.
7. Farb, 113, 206.
8. Sorrow, 44-45, 51, 55-60.
9. *Ibid.*, 11-12, 39, 50-51.
10. Shafer, Figs. 2, 4, 5.
11. Campbell, 7-35.
12. Schuetz, 135-168.
13. Jackson, *Fall Creek Sites*, 104.
14. Letter, Smithsonian Institution.
15. Schuetz, 135-168.
16. *Ibid.*
17. *Ibid.*
18. *Ibid.*
19. *Ibid.*
20. Texas Archeological and Paleontology, *Bulletin* XIII, 18, 21.
21. *Ibid.*, 98, 104, 109.
22. Texas Archeological, *Bulletin* XXV, 386, 388.
23. Jackson, *Picture-Writing*, 304, 329, 354, 360.
24. Interview Stallings.
25. Swanton, 309-11; *Enc. Brit.*, V. 22, 76, 186-187; Kenney, 28, 132.
26. Josephy, 217-218; *Enc. Brit.*, I, 754.
27. Farb, 197.
28. Newcomb, 92-94.
29. *Enc. Brit.*, XVII, 1151.
30. Farb, 202.
31. De Vaca, *Journey*, 93.
32. Dodge, 29.
33. De Mézières; National Geographic, 98.
34. National Geographic, 69.
35. Hodge, 779; Newcomb, 136.
36. Josephy, 120.
37. *Ibid.*, 12; Farb, 188.
38. Newcomb, 139.
39. Atkinson, 215.
40. Berlandier, 8-9, 42.
41. Sanchez, 269.
42. Josephy, 121.
43. Newcomb, 139.
44. *Kuykendall*, I, letter, Sept. 1829.
45. Kenney, 27, 31-32.
46. Berlandier, 51.
47. Interview Stallings.
48. Smithwick, 13.
49. Berlandier, 46.
50. Letter, Institute of Texan Cultures, quoting Stallings.
51. Berlandier, 51, 147, 158, Plate 5.
52. De Vaca, *Journey*, 74.
53. Gard, 4.
54. Newcomb, 87; *Enc. Brit.*, XII, 73; XVII, 1151-1152.
55. Cox, 223.
56. Newcomb, 87.
57. Berlandier, 100, f. 111; Joutel, 87.
58. Joutel, 87.
59. Le Clercq, 229.
60. Hackett, 169, 519-520.
61. Hodge, 779.
62. Bolton, *Athanase*, I, 56.
63. Newcomb, 140-141.
64. Atkinson, 211.
65. Hodge, 781.
66. Smithwick, 220-221.
67. Hodge, 781.
68. Farb, 118.
69. *Enc. Brit.*, XXII, 76.
70. Kenney, 30.
71. Interview Stallings.
72. Kenney, 30.
73. *Ibid.*
74. Newcomb, 141-142.
75. Newcomb, 142.
76. Kenney, 29.
77. Newcomb, 143-144.
78. Kenney, 30.
79. Newcomb, 144.
80. Atkinson, 218.
81. Newcomb, 138.
82. Atkinson, 213.
83. Interview Stallings.
84. Berlandier, 89, 94.
85. Interview Stallings; Berlandier, f. 78; Spell, 289-293.
86. Newcomb, 149.
87. Atkinson, 218.
88. Spell, 289-293; Berlandier, 62.
89. Kenney, 32.
90. Newcomb, 148-149.
91. Interview Stallings; Atkinson, 213-214.
92. Interview Stallings.
93. Spell, 289-293.
94. Interview Stallings.
95. Berlandier, 65, f. 62.
96. Hodge, 778.
97. Newcomb, 134.
98. Berlandier, 100.
99. Interview Stallings.
100. *Enc. Brit.*, I, 727; Spell, 289-293.
101. Hodge, 779; Bolton, *Athanase*, 289; Berlandier, 100, f. 111; Newcomb,

134; Mayhall, 20; *Handbook*, II, 783-788.
102. Berlandier, 146, f. 225; Hodge, 782; 782; Bolton, *18th Century*, 432.
103. Berlandier, 100, f. 111; Newcomb, 134.
104. Hodge, 779; Newcomb, 134; *Enc. Brit.*, XXII, 76; *Handbook*, II, 164.
105. Hodge, 778-783; Margery H. Krieger and F. W. Hodge in *Handbook*, I and 11, *passim*.
106. *Enc. Brit.*, XXII, 76.
107. Hodge, 782.
108. Interview Stallings.
109. Berlandier, 146, f. 225.
110. Interview Stallings.
111. Berlandier, 146, f. 225.
112. Newcomb, 353-355.
113. Hodge, 782; Berlandier, 146, f. 225.
114. Berlandier, *ibid.*; Wright, 25; Berta Nance, 87-95.
115. Interview Stallings.
116. Berta Nance, 87-95.
117. Wright, 250.
118. *Enc. Brit.*, XXII, 76.
119. Morfi, I, 84; II, 422.
120. *Handbook* I, 878.
121. Winfrey, *Indian Tribes*, 153-154.
122. Winfrey, *Texas Indian Papers*, I, 28.
123. *Handbook*, I, 879.
124. Winfrey, *Texas Indian Papers*, I, 151, 158-164; interview Stallings: Thrall, 423.
125. Interview Stallings.
126. Webb, *Rangers*, 4-7; Newcomb, 134.
127. Kenney, 27.
128. Newcomb, 99, 107-108, 116.
129. Berlandier, 132-133 and f. 189; Newcomb, 99, 107-108, 114, 130-131.
130. Newcomb, 105, 110; Berlandier, 32, 51, 128-129.
131. Josephy, 119; Newcomb, 125; *Enc. Brit.*, II, 102; XII, 62-78, 196.
132. Gilmore, 134.
133. Berlandier, 42; f. 16.
134. *Handbook*, I, 308, 605.
135. Olmsted, 293; Jenkins, *Recollections*, 171.
136. *Enc. Brit.*, VI, 118; XII, 62-78, 196; Farb, 16; Webb, *Rangers*, 11-15.
137. Winfrey, *Indian Tribes*, 45.
138. Berlandier, 57 and f. 49.
139. Dodge, xxv, 401; Roemer, 274; Berlandier, 122.
140. Dodge, xxv.
141. Goodwyn, 62; Berlandier, 32, f. 17; 34.
142. Berlandier, 44.

143. Roemer, 275; *Enc. Brit.*, XVII, 1152.
144. Morfi, 88; *Enc. Brit.*, VI, 118.
145. Sanchez, 262-263; Wilbarger, 42, 44-45.
146. *Rodriges Letter*.
147. Dodge, 407; Berlandier, 35-37, 44.
148. Smithwick, 186-187.
149. Goodwyn, 62.
150. *Austin Papers*, "Mapa . . . por el Estavan Austin."
151. Smithwick, 177.
152. Ibid., 172-173; interview Stallings.
153. Smithwick, 188.
154. *Ibid.*, 189.
155. Newcomb, 156-157; Winfrey, *Indian Tribes*, 45-50.
156. Interview Stallings.
157. Bolton, *18th Century*, 91, 233; Newcomb, 248-250; Morfi I, 51.
158. Newcomb, 268.
159. Smithwick, 187-188; Makemson, 5; Newcomb 268.
160. Sanchez, 265-266; Newcomb, 273-274.
161. Interview Stallings.
162. U. S. Post Office.
163. Interview Stallings.
164. *Ibid.*
165. Webb, *Rangers*, 11-15.
166. Farb, 118.
167. Bishop, 124-126.
168. Bills of lading, McNeil Depot.
169. Bishop, 148.
170. Josephy, 118.
171. *Enc. Brit.*, XII, 62-78, 196.
172. Farb, 244.
173. Jenkins, *Recollections*, 77, 87, 204; Berta Nance, 87-95; Wright, 250; Newcomb, 248-250, 347, 352-355; interview Stallings.
174. Newcomb, 25.
175. Webb, *Rangers*, 11.
176. *Handbook*, II, 610.
177. Webb, *Rangers*, 4-7.
178. *Williamson County Sun*, May 5, 1892.
179. *Ibid.*, Apr. 27, 1923.
180. Interview Wood; trip to site.

CHAPTER III
1. *Austin Papers*, "Mapa orginal, 1829."
2. De Vaca, *Journey*, 1.
3. Bishop, 10.
4. Interview R. E. McDonald.
5. *Ibid.*; de Vaca, *Relación*; Shepherd, map 190-191.
6. Hackett, 519-520.
7. LeClercq, II, 229, 231, 249, 251-253.
8. Gard, 5.
9. Manzanet, 287.

10. Morfi, 48.
11. Castañeda, I, 362; Bancroft, XV, 391; Gard, 5.
12. Shelby, 23.
13. Hodge, I, 958.
14. Castañeda, II, 42.
15. *Ibid.*, 51.
16. Bolton, *18th Century*, 141; Castañeda, II, 51.
17. Castañeda, II. 52.
18. *Ibid.*; Bolton, *18th Century*, 144.
19. Hackett, 474.
20. Castañeda, II, 131, 137.
21. Hackett, 489-490, 514.
22. Buckley, 39; Hackett *ibid.*; Morfi, I, 53-55, 71.
23. Morfi, I, 199-200; *Austin Papers*, "Mapa original, 1829."
24. Bolton, *18th Century*, 144.
25. Morfi, I, 221-223; Bolton, *Wider Horizons*, 17-18.
26. Bolton, *18th Century*, 27-28.
27. Hackett, 492.
28. Bolton, *18th Cenutry*, 141.
29. *Ibid.*, 30.
30. *Ibid.*, 141.
31. *Ibid.*, 150-151, 153-156; Gilmore, 143; interview Curik.
32. Bolton, *ibid.*, 45, 160, 166, 185.
33. *Ibid.*, 157, 186.
34. *Ibid.*, 173.
35. *Ibid.*, 187-188.
36. *Ibid.*, 197-200.
37. *Ibid.*, 53, 199, 225-227, 234.
38. Donna Scarbrough, trans., William E. Dunn transcript, *Santa Cruz.*, 33-34.
39. Bolton, *18th Century*, 234-237; Gilmore, 19.
40. Gilmore, 31-32, 58, 141-143.
41. Gilmore, 12; Bolton, *18th Century*, 201, 230.
42. Bolton, *ibid.*, 53, 247, 252, 260, 263.
43. *Ibid.*, 266.
44. Morfi, 269.
45. Bolton, *18th Century*, 266; Castañeda, III, maps; Gilmore, 137; *Williamson County Sun*, by Herbert Bolton, Mar. 21, 28, 1907.
46. Gilmore, 137; Bolton and Castañeda, *ibid.*
47. Castañeda, IV, 153-154.
48. Morfi, 54.
49. Bolton, *Athanase*, I, 54-55.
50. *Old Comanche Trail*, map.
51. Yoakum, I, 96.
52. De Cordova, 6.
53. Webb, *Rangers*, 9-11.

54. Kennedy, 231.
55. Webb, *Rangers*, 7-9; Bolton, *Wider Horizons*, 9.
56. Bolton, *ibid.*, 10-11, 107-129.
57. *Ibid.*, 130, 148.
58. *Ibid.*, 38.
59. Bishop, 12.
60. *Sun* clipping, n. d., by W. L. Mann.
61. *Handbook* I, 310.
62. Bolton, *Wider Horizons*, 99.
63. *Texas Almanac*, 1857; James Frank Dobie works.
64. *Handbook*, I, 137.
65. Interview Stallings.
66. Bollaert, 236.
67. McCaleb, 15.
68. Yoakum, I, 44.
69. Gilmore, 137.
70. Hodge, II, 463; *Austin Papers*, "S. F. Austin map, 1829"; Bancroft, I, 623; West, 46.
71. U. S. Post Office; *Austin Papers*, maps 1822, 1826, 1829; *Handbook* II, 532; Bolton, *18th Century*, 8.
72. Yoakum, II, 238; Kennedy, 403.
73. *Cassell's Dictionary*; *Webster's Dictionary*.
74. *Ibid.*

CHAPTER IV
1. Webb, *Rangers*, 9-11.
2. De Cordova, 6-8; Yoakum, I, 213, 229.
3. Hogan, 191.
4. Wm. Co., *Deeds*, II, 353, 355; VII, 156, 256; X, 79.
5. Census, 1850.
6. Bishop, 68; Yoakum, II, 197.
7. Yoakum, *ibid.*
8. *Handbook*, II, 768.
9. Bolton, *Wider Horizons*, 41-42; Barker, *Life*, 90-91.
10. Barker, *ibid.*, 90-91, 521-524; Yoakum, I, 212; *Austin Papers*, II, 271.
11. Stiff; Yoakum, II, 437; Hogan, 81; Smithwick, 9.
12. Barker, *Life*, 143; Yoakum, I, 231; Johnson, II, 748.
13. *Williamson County Sun*, Apr. 27, 1923.
14. *Ibid.*
15. *Ibid.*; Makemson, 8-11.
16. Barker, "A Glimpse," 279-282.
17. Batte, 33; Brown, *Annals*, Appendix I, 73.
18. Raines, *Yearbook 1901*, 82, 84.
19. Barker, *Life*, 329-330, 361.
20. *Frontier Times*, March 1924, 12.

21. Smithwick, 213; Jenkins, *Personal.*, 87.
22. Yoakum, II, 265-267.
23. *Handbook*, II, 690.
24. Brown, *Annals*, I, 85.
25. Wilbarger, 247.
26. De Shields, 90-93; Wilbarger, 190; Brown, *Annals*, Appendix I, 91.
27. Wilbarger, 190-192; De Shields, 90-93.
28. Interview with Mrs. A. S. Walker, Jr., visit to site.
29. Interview *ibid.*; *Kingdom*, 9.
30. Webb, *Rangers*, 20-25, 60.
31. Makemson, 1.
32. Smithwick, 123, 208.
33. *Ibid.*, 123; Webb, *Rangers*, 38-39.
34. Smithwick, 124.
35. *Ibid.*, 177.
36. *Ibid.*, 207.
37. Jenkins, *Recollections*, 241.
38. Johnson, II, 748.
39. Makemson, 2, 3.
40. Wm. Co. *Deeds*, V. 264; XIII, 294.
41. Kemp, *Honor Roll*; *Mann Papers*.
42. Kemp, *ibid.*; *Texas Almanac, 1857-1873*, cond. 637-638; *Sun*, Jul. 7, 1881, Oct. 5, 1950; interview Harrison; Hinds, 132-137 (with spellings and listings as verified by Kemp); *Lone Star*, Huddle's painting and identification.
43. *Mann Papers*.
44. Kennedy, 713; Hogan, 10.
45. Hogan, 81; Bishop, 68; *Round Rock Leader* clipping, n. d.
46. De Cordova, 6-8.
47. Smithwick, 193-195; Webb, *Rangers*, 29.
48. Wilbarger, 222.
49. Winfrey, *Texas Indian*, I, 28.
50. Jenkins, *Recollections*, 94.
51. Yoakum, II, 280.
52. Webb, *Rangers*, 29.
53. Yoakum, II, 283-285.
54. *Sun*, Aug. 7, 1922; *Leader*, by William Lawson, clipping, n. d.
55. Makemson, 2; *Texas: a Guide*, 572.
56. Makemson, 2-3; *Sun*, Jul. 7, 1922, Apr. 27, 1923; *Leader*, Jul. 21, 1905; *Austin City Gazette*, Oct. 30, 1839, Vol. I, No. 1.
57. Makemson, 8-9; Jenkins, *Personal*, 87; Jenkins, *Recollections*, 92.
58. *Kemp Collection*, letter from Blanch Stark Summers, great granddaughter of Dr. Thomas Kenney.
59. Johnson, II, 803.

60. Makemson, 9; Summers letter, *Kemp Col.*
61. Wilbarger, 261.
62. *Round Rock Leader*, n. d.
63. Wilbarger, 277.
64. Makemson, 3-4; *Leader*, July 21, 1905.
65. *Hornsby Papers*.
66. Makemson, 3-4; *Sun*, Aug. 7, 1922; Summers in *Kemp*.
67. Interview Lawrence; letter Eloise Laurence.
68. De Shields, 90-93; *Elgin Courier*, 1917, series.
69. *Houston Chronicle Magazine*, Nov. 18, 1956; Baker, 342, 557.
70. Letter, manuscript, Breeding. Mrs. Breeding is great granddaughter of George W. Glasscock, Sr.
71. Smithwick, 215-224; Yoakum, II, 261; Wilbarger, 144.
72. Yoakum, II, 261.
73. Webb, *Rangers*, 41; Smithwick, 215-224; Jenkins, *Recollections*, 58-60; Wilbarger, 146; Yoakum, II, 262.
74. *Lone Star*, 634; Wilbarger, 148-150; Makemson, 11; letter Burleson.
75. Wilbarger, 148-150.
76. Yoakum 11, 262; Jenkins, *Personal*, 87.
77. Wilbarger, 148-150.
78. *Sun*, Dec. 23, 1921.
79. Jenkins, *Recollections*, f. 58.
80. Smithwick, 224.
81. Nance, *After San Jacinto*, 131, 136; Yoakum II, 259; Webb, *Rangers*, 48.
82. Wilbarger, 158.
83. Yoakum, II, 257; Wilbarger, 156.
84. Wilbarger, 153; Nance, *After San Jacinto*, 123; *Billingsley Papers*.
85. Yoakum II, 259-260; Wilbarger, 157-160; Nance, *ibid.*, 131-132.
86. Wilbarger, *ibid.*; *Sun*, Feb. 20, 1925, by James H. Faubion; Webb, *Rangers*, 48, 50; Brown, *Indian Wars*, 62-66; Senate Executive Document 14.
87. Wilbarger, *ibid.*; Nance, *After San Jacinto*, 136-140, footnotes 78, 137.
88. Wilbarger, 166-167, Dobie, *Coronado's*, 121-124; *Sun*, Feb. 20, 1925, Sept. 28, 1950.
89. Simmons; *Sun*, Jul. 3, 1936; Griffith, *Early History*, 5.
90. Simmons.
91. *Ibid.*
92. *Ibid.*; Wilbarger, 19-22; *Sun*, Feb. 20, 1925; Jenkins, *Personal*, 87.
93. Jenkins, *ibid.*; Simmons.

94. Simmons.
95. *Ibid.*
96. *Ibid.*
97. *Ibid.*; interview Bryson.
98. Simmons; Jenkins, *Recollections,* footnote, 82; Griffith, 5; Austin Public Library, *Austin File, Chronological*; *Austin City Gazette,* Oct. 30, 1839, Vol. I, No. 1. The fact that the *Austin City Gazette* issue was the first ever published explains the apparent tardiness in reporting the massacre. The same issue contained an account of events at Kenney Fort in 1838.
99. Bollaert, 191.
100. Kennedy, 150-151.
101. Hogan, 14.
102. *Route of Military Road*; Brown, *Annals,* Appendix I, 70, 118; *Texas Almanac,* 1966, 15.
103. Yoakum, II, 282.
104. Kendall, I, footnote 74; pp. 89-90.
105. Kendall, I, footnote 74; Carroll, 35.
106. Wilbarger, 374; *Sun,* Apr. 27, 1923.
107. Wilbarger, 268; Smithwick, 260; Jenkins, *Recollections,* 89.
108. *Ibid.*
109. *House Committee Report,* 1845; *Galveston Daily News,* May 28, 1911; *Sun,* Apr. 27, 1923, Jan. 17, 1936; Makemson, 6.
110. Carroll, 2.
111. Webb, *Rangers,* 71.
112. Smithwick, 271.
113. Webb, *Rangers,* 72, quoting Andrew Jackson to Sam Houston.
114. Loomis, ix, 3, quoting *Austin City Gazette,* Apr. 28, 1841; Yoakum, II, 321.
115. *Enc. Brit.,* XVI, 367.
116. Loomis, 10, 17, 18; "Special Order No. 7."
117. Kendall, I, 78-82.
118. *Handbook,* I, 512.
119. Kendall, 78-82.
120. *Ibid.,* 84-85; Makemson, 6; Yoakum, II, 324; *Sun,* Apr. 27, 1923.
121. Kendall, xvii, 83-85, 88; Yoakum, II, 324; *Austin City Gazette,* Jun. 23, 1841.
122. Makemson, 6; Loomis, 25.
123. Kendall, 89-90.
124. *Ibid.,* 90-91.
125. *Ibid.,* 95; *Handbook,* I, 512.
126. Yoakum, II, 323, 328-329; Loomis, 135, 161, 164.
127. Loomis, 168, 185-186.
128. Makemson, 8.
129. Wilbarger, 276.
130. Jenkins, *Recollections,* 85.
131. Wilbarger, 661.
132. Makemson, 9; Smithwick, 141.
133. *Welsh Letter.*
134. Yoakum, II, 366, 380.
135. *Houston Papers,* "Report."
136. *Ibid.,* Houston address.
137. *Ibid.*; *Handbook,* I, 64-65.
138. *Houston Papers,* Houston address; Makemson, 6, 7; *Kemp Collection*; Dobie, *Archives War,* 2.
139. *Matthews Papers.*
140. *Sun,* Mar. 29, 1951.
141. Makemson, 9; *Sun,* Jan. 17, 1936.
142. *Handbook,* II, 791.
143. Mann, "James O. Rice," 30-42.
144. Wilbarger, 279-281.
145. *Ibid.,* 282.
146. Mann, *The Andersons,* 2, 4-6, 10.
147. McCown, 5-6. Mrs. McCown came to Milam County in 1840.
148. Brown, *Annals,* XI, 7-8.
149. Winfrey, *Texas Indian,* II, 41, 61, 81, 160-161, 423.
150. *Ibid.,* 114, 217-218, 385, 391.
151. *Ibid.,* 396.
152. Winfrey and Day, *Indian Papers,* V, 20, 22-24.
153. *Sun,* Apr. 27, 1923.
154. Yoakum, II, 437, 443.
155. Brown, *Annals,* 20-21.
156. Hogan, 16.
157. Jenkins, *Recollections,* 152.
158. Roemer, 224.
159. Makemson, 10-11; *Sun,* Apr. 27, 1923.
160. Ford, 439, 443.
161. Bryson, 216-235.
162. Makemson, 9-10; *Taylor Daily Press,* Jun. 30, 1938.
163. *Mann Papers.*
164. Makemson, 13; *Mann Papers*; *Sun,* Jun. 16, Sept. 28, Oct. 5, 1950.
165. Makemson, 4; Smithwick, 187-188.
166. *Ibid.*
167. Makemson, 4-5; Smithwick, 187-188.
168. Wilbarger, 279.
169. Matthews, *Family Records,* 51; *New Orleans Weekly Picayune,* May 27, 1844; *Telegraph and Texas Register,* May 29, 1844, Jul. 3, 1844; *Clarksville Northern Standard,* May 29, 1844; *La Grange Intelligencer,* Jun. 27, 1884; *Sun,* Dec. 23, 1921.
170. Makemson, 7-8; Summers in *Kemp.*
171. *Round Rock Leader* clipping, n. d.

172. Makemson, 18-19.
173. Stearns, *Family Records*; *Census 1850*; Makemson. The ten-year old Harvey T. Stearns who came in 1847 became the grandfather of the author; he and sons were ginners throughout the county. Dr. Wm. Knight and his son, James, were prominent in Round Rock and Georgetown as professional and political figures. W. K. Makemson was an early county historian, attorney, was the Republican party's candidate for governor of Texas.
174. Stearns, *ibid*.
175. *Lone Star State*, 505.
176. Stearns, *Family Records*.
177. *Lone Star State*, 505.
178. *Ibid*., 251; Wilbarger, 481; Smithwick, 60; *Handbook*, I, 915; Jenkins, *Recollections*, 58 and f.; Hinds, 136; *Round Rock Leader* clipping, n. d.; *Mann Papers*.

CHAPTER V
1. Makemson, 18-19.
2. Makemson, 19; *Williamson County Sun*, Jul. 20, 1921, by Lee M. Taylor, son of early store owner, Josiah Taylor.
3. *Sun, ibid*.
4. Makemson, 19.
5. Memorials and Petitions: *Citizens ask*.
6. *Mann Papers*, Fannie Taliaferro Taylor letter to Mrs. N. Sams, Taylor, Texas, Feb. 12, 1935.
7. Burleson, "History of Robert Hay Taliaferro"; Morrell.
8. Makemson, 18.
9. Memorials and Petitions: *Citizens ask*; Hinds, 67.
10. Memorials, *ibid*.
11. Johnson, II, 806; Raines, *Laws*, II, 76-77.
12. *Georgetown Watchman*, Jun. 25, 1870.
13. Raines, *Laws*, II, 76-77.
14. Robinson, 23, 26, 46, 63, 94, 96-97, 102-103, 123.
15. Yoakum, I, 337; Makemson, 1-2; Smithwick, 62, 64; Robinson, 8, 129, 151, 165, 215.
16. *Georgetown Independent*, Oct. 29, 1856.
17. Makemson, 14-15.
18. Mann, *The Andersons*, 8.
19. *Huling Papers*, letter Nov. 25, 1847; Wm. Co. *Deeds*, I, 224, 400.
20. Makemson, 15.

21. *Lone Star State*, 209.
22. Makemson, 15.
23. U.S. Post Office, *Appointments*, XIX, 90; *Sun* clipping, n. d.; *Houston Chronicle* clipping, n. d.
24. Makemson, 15-16.
25. *Lone Star State*, 818.
26. Wm. Co. *Police Court* P, 69 and ff.; records, framed photographs hanging in County Auditor's Office, 1973.
27. *Sun* clipping, n. d., quoting Thomas P. Hughes, Jr., son of Judge T. P. Hughes, in Georgetown early in 1851 when wagon was utilized; *Brady Scrapbook*.
28. Letters Breeding, *Glasscock Genealogy*.
29. *Ibid*.; *Huling Papers*; Wm. Co. *Deeds*, I, 224, 400.
30. Letters Breeding.
31. *Ibid*.
32. Roemer, 26-29; 60.
33. Smithwick, 14.
34. *Sun*. Sept. 29, 1922, J. R. Dean letter.
35. *Mann Papers*.
36. Hogan, 5-11, 25-27; Yoakum, I, 229.
37. Roemer, 60.
38. Makemson, 13.
39. Webb, *Rangers*, 83.
40. Smithwick, 239.
41. McCown, 5.
42. Roemer, 6, 8-9, 26-28.
43. Smithwick, 236-237.
44. Brown, *Annals*, Appendix I, 83.
45. Smithwick, 237-238.
46. *Ibid*., 17.
47. Brown, *Annals*, 81-83.
48. Roemer, 6, 8-9, 26-28.
49. *Mann Papers*; letters, Breeding.
50. Yoakum, I, 229; Hogan, 46; Griffith, *Frontier Times*, May 1936.
51. Yoakum, I, 229.
52. Smithwick, 247.
53. *Ibid*., 15.
54. Hogan, 226, 228, 231.
55. *Mann Papers*.
56. Roemer, 13-14, 29, 48.
57. Smithwick, 17.
58. *Mann Papers*, "Baptist Historians's Report," letter Taliaferro to Sams.
59. *Ibid*.; Morrell, 258; Makemson, 19-20.
60. Makemson, 18.
61. Brown, *Annals*, Appendix, I, 81-83.
62. Hogan, 147-148.
63. Roemer, 161.

64. Hogan, 197-199.
65. Margaret Tegge Stearns.
66. Hogan, 185, 198, 206, 210-212.
67. Jenkins, *Recollections,* 204.
68. *Ibid.,* 200-204.
69. Dobie, *Tales,* 128.
70. Roemer, 49, 56-57, 71, 75, 87.
71. *Ibid.*
72. *Ibid.,* 66, 185, 190.
73. *Ibid.,* 191, 222.
74. *Ibid.,* 113-116, 195-196.
75. *Ibid.,* 207.
76. *Ibid.,* 207-208.

CHAPTER VI
1. *Census 1850; Lone Star State,* 567; *Texas Almanac,* 1857, 70; Johnson, II, 806; Paddock, 678; Brown, *Annals,* XIV, 9.
2. *Texas Almanac,* 1859, 210.
3. Winfrey, *Texas Indian,* III, 183-185; *ibid.,* V, 66; Brown, *Annals,* XIV, 9; *Texas State Gazette,* Jun. 1, 1850.
4. *Kuykendall,* II.
5. MS. Letter 1857, in hands of author.
6. Wm. Co. *Police Court, P,* IV; *Deeds,* X, 322; Makemson, 16.
7. *Police Court,* P, 140-144.
8. *Ibid.,* 330.
9. *Texas Almanac,* 1859, 183.
10. Grand Masonic Records; De Cordova, 326.
11. Grand Masonic Records.
12. Frances Stearns, *Record Book.*
13. U. S. Post Office; Brown, *Annals,* XV, 47; *Texas Almanac,* 1859, 132; *Mann Papers.*
14. Post Office; *Mann Papers.*
15. Post Office.
16. *Bryson Family* records; *Mann Papers; Texas Almanac* 1859; Brown, *Annals,* XV, 47.
17. *Police Court,* P, 186, 353, 418; *Wm. Co. Index,* 41.
18. *Index to Probate Cases,* Map; Raines, *Laws of Texas,* III, 76, 501, 927, 1337.
19. Rister, 41; Babcock, 186.
20. Presler, map 1851; *Land Office Map 1856;* Colton, *Map 1857.*
21. *Williamson County Sun,* Jan. 12, 1967, reprint from *Georgetown Commercial,* June 7, 1907.
22. *Ibid.*
23. *Police Court,* P, 72; *Texas Almanac* 1968-1969, 457; Milestone, Jim Adkins' farm.
24. *Police Court, ibid.*

25. *Ibid.,* 11
26. *Ibid.,* 11-13.
27. *Ibid.,* 13-14.
28. *Ibid.,* 14.
29. *Ibid.,* 15.
30. *Ibid.,* 120.
31. *Ibid.,* 69.
32. *Ibid.,* 16-21.
33. *Ibid.,* 31, 32, 38, 67; Makemson, 17.
34. Griffith, 10.
35. *Police Court,* P. 63.
36. *Ibid.,* 69, 87-89, 101.
37. *Ibid.,* 17, 137, 140, 149, 156, 186, 192, 194, 197, 199, 208, 262-263, 289.
38. *Ibid.,* 293, 298.
39. *Ibid.,* 330.
40. *Ibid.,* 396-397; Vol. IV, 28, 68.
41. *Ibid.,* P, 216.
42. *Ibid.,* 100, 276, 328, 406, 425; Vol. IV, 18.
43. *Ibid.,* P, 66, 70, 73, 125.
44. *Census 1850.*
45. Webb, *Great Frontier,* 55, 73, 248.
46. *Matthews Papers; Texas Almanac,* 1859, 183; de Cordova, 57; Johnson, II, 806.
47. Hughes; Richardson. Exact spelling found in original manuscript is followed.
48. *Matthews Papers.* Exact spelling and punctuation of original manuscripts are followed in quoted passages in these and succeeding letters.
49. *Ibid.*
50. *Ibid.*
51. *Ibid.; Lone Star State,* 196.
52. *Matthews.*
53. *Ibid.*
54. *Ibid.*
55. *Carothers Papers,* S. D. to John Carothers, Dec. 21, 1859.
56. *Ibid.,* Sept. 15, 1860; *Matthews Papers,* S. D. to John Carothers.
57. *Easley Family History; Eubank-Stearns Family History.* James Eubank was great grandfather of the author.
58. Hayslip letter.
59. *Ibid.*
60. *Ibid.*
61. *Ibid.*
62. *Ibid.*
63. *Matthews Papers.*
64. *Mann Papers;* interview Robertson.
65. *Mann Papers.*
66. *Deeds,* V, 535.
67. *Huling Papers,* Glasscock letter Jul. 14, 1850; Texas State *Gazette,* Nov. 2, 1850. An earlier date has been

cited for this mill, but Glasscock letters and contemporary news accounts appear to corroborate this as the correct date.
68. *Mt. Horeb History,* author's collection.
69. *Census 1850; Deeds,* V, 288.
70. *Deeds,* IV, 179; VI, 102.
71. *Ibid.,* VII, 170; XXXII, 431; XCIV, 95.
72. *Ibid.,* II, 90; VII, 92.
73. *Matthews Papers;* Auburn Clare Stearns, whose father, Harvey T. Stearns, freighted to Circleville.
74. *Georgetown Independent.*
75. *Census 1850.*
76. Red, 98, 102; *Lone Star State,* 567, 723.
77. *Census 1850.*
78. *Ibid.*
79. *Sun,* Feb. 8, 1973; *Texas State Gazette,* Jun. 1, 1850.
80. *Lone Star State,* 818; *Wm. Co. Centennial 1848-1948, passim.*
81. *Sun,* Aug. 5, 1921; author's Files, various.
82. *Ibid.;* Grand Masonic Lodge; *Lone Star State,* 565, 812.
83. *Centennial,* 17-18; *Sun,* Apr. 24, 1936.
84. Kittrell, 230-231.
85. *Centennial,* 17-18.
86. *Sun,* Feb. 7, 1936.
87. *Ibid.,* Oct. 26, 1936; *Mann Papers,* letter Harry F. Byrd to Wm. L. Mann; *Austin State Gazette,* Sept. 17, 1859; *Byrd-Rivers Genealogy,* 17.
88. Red, 333-334; *Lone Star State,* 543, 812, 818; *Sun,* May 19, 1881; *Round Rock Leader,* Aug. 20, 1928.
89. *Palm Family History; Dyer Papers; Nelson Family Papers;* Behrens, *History; Lone Star State,* 751; *People,* November-Dec. 1971, 2; *Brady Scrapbook.*
90. *Georgetown Watchman,* Jun. 22, 1867.
91. Behrens, *History; People,* November-December, 1971, 2, 6; *Leader* clipping, n. d.
92. Widén, 7.
93. *Swenson-Palm Letterbooks.*
94. Severin, I; *Sun,* July. 14, 1966.
95. Interview Gaines.
96. *Police Court,* P, 186.
97. Smithwick, 14, 64, 86, 99, 118-119, 188, 229, 289, 291-292, 294; *Deeds,* VII, 560; Raines, *Yearbook,* 423.
98. Wilbarger, preface.

99. Raines, *Bibliography,* 219; Wilbarger, 7-14.
100. England, 47-59.
101. *Ibid.*
102. *Sun,* Apr. 27, 1923, reprinting 1907 article.
103. *Census 1850.*
104. Letter Mayes.

CHAPTER VII
1. *Wm. Co. Deeds,* I, 55, 95; VI, 286; IX, 8.
2. Interview Harris.
3. *Ibid.;* interviews Millholin, Scoggins, Ellyson.
4. *Deeds,* I, 93, 201, 362, 373-374; II, 76, 84-85, 122-123, 127.
5. *Mann Papers,* Mrs. Robert A. John, Sam Houston's granddaughter, to W. L. Mann.
6. Interviews Scoggins, Ellyson; England, 39.
7. Barker, *Texas History,* 471.
8. *Texas Almanac 1857-1873,* 494; Winkler, 407, 439; James, 335-371.
9. Terrell, 135.
10. James, 335-371; Terrell, *ibid.*
11. Interview Coffee; Flanagan, 182.
12. Rister, 163; *Lone Star State,* 812; Raines, *Year Book 1901,* 89-90; James, 334-335.
13. *Police Court,* IV, 82, 86, 92, 118-119.
14. Interview Gusman, quoting Mrs. Argie Kirk, Seminole, Mrs. Queenelle Flache, Brownfield, family records.
15. Interview Gusman; Bandera County Court, *Book A,* 123; Hunter, *100 Years,* 63-64; *Williamson County Sun,* Oct. 21, 1971; *San Antonio Express and Evening News,* Feb. 14, 1965, Dec. 22, 1968; *A Civil War Tragedy,* 88; *Real West Magazine,* May 1967.
16. *Ibid.,* all sources above.
17. *Ibid.*
18. Bandera County Court, A., 123.
19. Trip to site, Oct. 17, 1971.
20. *Genealogy, Charles and Nathanial Stearns,* II, 244.
21. Frances Stearns, *Record Book,* 139, 142; spelling follows that in letter quoted.
22. Makemson, 11-12; Maltby, 20, 23-24, 26-27, 150-152, 204; *Florence Vidette,* Apr. 3, 1924; *Sun,* Jun. 28, 1973.
23. *Police Court,* IV, 134, 137, 168, 182, 184.
24. Frances Stearns, *Record,* 164; Raines,

Memoirs, 369, 473; Raines, *Laws of Texas*, V, 649; Nunn, *Family Records*; Brown, *Annals*, XXII, 35; *Texas Almanac*, 1863, 31; *Sun*, Nov. 21, 1963, Jun. 10, 1965.

25. *Carothers Papers*.
26. *Matthews Family Records*.
27. Frances Stearns, 168.
28. Interviews Norman, Elmer and Marshall Miller, Mrs. D. W. White, Mrs. Prude; Wm. Co. School Records.
29. Interview Bailey.
30. Interview F. F. Brown; letter Lena Rude King.
31. *Police Court*, IV, 188.
32. Letters Hollingsworth; Institute Texan Cultures.
33. *Georgetown Watchman*, Mar. 23, 1867.
34. Letters Hollingsworth; *Sun*, Jun. 27, Jul. 4, 1878.
35. *Sun*, Jan. 23, Mar. 20, 1879, May 19, 1881; *Georgetown Watchman*, Jan. 19, 1874.
36. Interviews Millholin, Scoggins, Loventhal.
37. Interview Bertie McDaniel.

CHAPTER VIII

1. Dobie, *Mustangs*, 271.
2. *Ibid.*, 97-98; Dobie, *Longhorns*, 7; Hackett, II, 525-526.
3. Dobie, *Longhorns*, 8.
4. Hackett, II, 106; Bolton, *Athanase*, II, 281.
5. Dobie, *Mustangs*, 67, 71, 74, f. 94-95, 144-145.
6. Smithwick, 289-291.
7. Dobie, *Mustangs*, 71; *Longhorns*, 7, 37, 39, 49-50, 84-85.
8. *Mann Papers*.
9. *Ibid.*, interview Hester; Hunter, *Trail*, 109, 340, 657.
10. Handbook, I, 341; Bishrop, 148; *Williamson County Sun*, quoting Cecil Howes, *Kansas City Star*, Nov. 23, 1966.
11. *New Map of Texas* (cattle trails 1866-1895).
12. Dobie, *Longhorns*, 216.
13. *Georgetown Watchman*, Apr. 23, Jun. 18, 1870.
14. Interview Melasky.
15. *Sun*, Oct. 14, 1909.
16. Webb, *Great Frontier*, 189; Dobie, *Longhorns*, 222.
17. *Sun*, May 1, 1879.

18. Webb, *Great Frontier*, 190; *Taylor Daily Press*, Nov. 23, 1956; interview A. C. Stearns.
19. *Granger News*, May 1, 1952.
20. *Mayes Notebooks*.
21. *Texas Almanac*, 1972-1973, 384.
22. *Handbook*, I, 110; Gard, 257-259.
23. *Mann Papers*; interview Draper.
24. *Lone Star State*, 247, 807, 822; *Mann Papers*.
25. Interview Draper.
26. U. S. Post Office; Wm. Co. Deed Records.
27. Maltby, 152; Fletcher, 24, 51.
28. Hendrix, 68.
29. *Mann Papers*.
30. Hunter, *Trail*, 1029, quoting D. H. Snyder.
31. Hunter, *ibid.*, 769.
32. *Mann Papers*.
33. *Ibid.*, Dallas *Morning News* clipping, n. d.
34. *Taylor Press*, n. d., quoting Will Lannen.
35. *Deeds*, XV, 261-263.
36. *Handbook*, II, 923; *Mann Papers*.
37. Hunter, *Trail*, 248.
38. *Sun*, Feb. 14, 1936; *Press*, n. d.
39. *Mann Papers*.
40. Gard, 185.
41. *Ibid.*, 155; Taylor, "The Stork Rides"; interview Friedsam.
42. Hunter, *Trail*, 518.
43. Gard, 58, 185; *San Antonio Herald*, May 17, 1867.
44. Hunter, *Trail*, 612.
45. *Ibid.*, 739; Gard, 190.
46. *Palm Family History*; *Georgetown Watchman*, May 22, 1869, Apr. 23, 1870; *Round Rock Leader*, n. d.
47. *Lone Star State*, 692; Hunter, *Trail*, 28.
48. *Ibid.*
49. Hunter, *Trail*, 374-376.
50. *Granger News*, Jul. 14, 1921.
51. Gabriel Mills history, author's MS.; Dobie, *Coronado's*, 20-21.
52. Hunter, *Trail*, 756; Gard, 211.
53. *Sun*, Apr. 11, 1878.
54. Hunter, *Trail*, 649.
55. Fletcher, 62.
56. *Sun*, Apr. 24, 1925.
57. *Ibid.*, Jun 7, 1888, quoting *Taylor Texan*.
58. Paddock, *passim*.
59. Hunter, *Trail*, 391.
60. *Ibid.*, 162.
61. *Ibid.*, 884.

62. Hendrix, 125-127.
63. *Georgetown Watchman*, May 22, 1869, Apr. 23, 1870; *Round Rock Sentinel*, Jan. 19, 1871.
64. Hunter, *Trail*, 368-372.
65. *Ibid.*, 236-237; Gard, 241.
66. Hunter, *Trail*, 326, 431, 607, 626.
67. Chrisman, 31, 38, 78, f. 4 on 373, 376; Sandoz, 69.
68. Hunter, *Trail*, 721-729; Fletcher, xiv, xv; *Snyder Family*; *Sun*, Sept. 16, 1921.
69. Fletcher, xv.
70. *Ibid.*, xvi; *Sun*, Sept. 16, 1921.
71. Hunter, *Trail*, 724-725, 1029-1030; *Snyder Family*; Gard, 87.
72. Hunter, *Trail*, 727, 1030; Dobie, *Longhorns*, 81; interview Whitcomb.
73. Fletcher, 9-10, 21, 24, 56, 61-62.
74. Dobie, *Longhorns*, 81.
75. *Snyder Family*; Hunter, *Trail*, 1031.
76. Hunter, *Trail*, 725, quoting John H. Sharpe; interview, Meyer.
77. Interview, Landrum.
78. Hunter, *Trail*, 727.
79. Letter University of Wyoming; Fletcher, xiv.
80. Hendrix, 40; *Sun*, Sept. 16, 1921.
81. *Sun*, Feb. 11, 1909.
82. Hunter, *Trail*, 728-729, 1031; *Snyder Family*; *Sun*, Sept. 16, 1921.
83. *Sun, ibid.*; interview Whitcomb, family records.
84. Fletcher, xvii.
85. *Dudley Hale [sic] Snyder*, (Oatts), I, 1-2, 12.
86. *Ibid.*, II, 8-10.
87. *Ibid.*, 12-13, 30.
88. *Scoggins Scrapbook*, Sparks Genealogy.
89. Interviews Harris, Ellyson; *Mann Papers*; *Sun*, May 15, 1879, Dec. 24, 1885.
90. Interviews, *ibid.*; *Georgetown Watchman*, May 24, 1879; *Scoggins Scrapbook*, Sparks Genealogy.
91. *Hunter, Trail*, 505; interview Dellinger (taped).
92. Interviews Landrum, Scoggins.
93. Wm. Co. *Probate Records*, No. 235; *Georgetown Commercial*, Nov. 7, 1902.
94. Interviews Harris, Landrum, Scoggins.
95. Interviews Millholin, Stone, Scoggins; *Guide to Georgetown*; letter Arrington; Nevada Historical Society; *Wm. Co. Hist. Survey Com. Scrapbook*, 112-115; (Mrs. Scoggins attended Governor Sparks' party in Georgetown as a small girl.)

CHAPTER IX

1. Johnson, 806-809; *Texas Almanac*, 1871, 229, and 1966-1967; *Williamson County Sun*, May 8, 1879.
2. Wm. Co. *Com. Min.*, 1884, 1893, VIII, 228, 242; *Sun*, Mar. 28, 1878, Mar. 27, 1884, Jun. 8, 1893, ff.
3. *Sun*, Aug. 22, Sept. 12 and 26, 1878.
4. *Sun.*, Jan. 21, 1891.
5. *Sun*, Oct. 21, 1880, Aug. 11, 1886, Oct. 30, 1890; Wm. Co. *Index*, 307, 309; postal, school recs.
6. Interviews Carlson, Crone, Lax, Fredrickson; church histories.
7. *Czech Texans*, 20-21, 25; *Texas, A Guide*, 442.
8. Letter Bergquist.
9. *Sun*, Jun. 7, 1883; community histories; interviews Melasky, Streich, Jechow; letter Baker.
10. Raines, *Bibliography*, 163.
11. Lee M. Taylor, 58-59.
12. Baptist Church history; *Sun*, Oct. 20, 1966.
13. *Handbook*, I, 602 and II, 127, 181, 407, 777; *Texas Almanac* 1867, 1871, 159; *Taylor Press*, Nov. 23, 1956; church histories.
14. *Sun.*, Dec. 8 and 15, 1881.
15. Grand Masonic Lodge.
16. *Police Court*, IV, 226; V (1873, 1876, ff).
17. *Ibid.*, P, 101; V, 383, 386 ff.; *Index*, 17-18, 35.
18. *Police*, IV, 154, 167, 193; V, 204; interview Lohmann; Wm. Co. Auditor.
19. *Police*, IV, 218-219, 241, 244, 257, 288, 294, 296, 341, 350; V, 300-306, 346, 354, 389, 396; Makemson, 17.
20. *Police*, V, 138, 203; *Sun*, Mar. 3, 1881; *Index*, 44, 46.
21. *Police*, P, 219, 349, 397, 403; IV, 212; V, 82, 87; *Com. Court*, VII, 176, 318, 527, 615, 629; VIII, 176, 318; *Index*, 45, 47, 58, 102, 124-125; *Sun.* Nov. 10, 1887, others.
22. *Com.* VII, 424, 443, 454, 458-459, 534; *Index*, 68; *Sun*, Jan. 5, Apr. 12, 19, Jun. 7, 1888, Jan. 14, Jun. 10, 1965; Makemson, 17; interview Millholin.
23. *Sun*, Jun. 10, 1965; Makemson, 17.
24. *Police*, V, 392.

25. Interviews, Auburn Stearns; Northtown history.
26. *Index*, 17.
27. *Ibid*.
28. *Ibid*., 117; *Sun*, Jun. 5, 1890.
29. *Blackland Reporter*, Jan. 22, 1948; *Sun*, Sept. 27, 1877.
30. Barker, *Texas History*, 622; Raines, *Yearbook 1901*, 74-75, 77.
31. Barker, *ibid*., 628-629; Raines, *Laws*, X, 890; *Sun*, May 1, 8, Sept. 11, 1884, Oct. 28, 1886.
32. *Handbook* I, 11, 142, 409.
33. Caskey; *Lone Star*, 751, 822; *interview* Love; *Palm* and *Nelson Family* records.
34. *Stone Papers*; interview Labaj; *Liberty Hill Leader*, Jan. 1, 1937; community histories.
35. Interview Hall, photo Round Rock lime plant, "established 1870"; *Round Rock Leader*, Jul. 20, 1928; *Sun*, Oct. 28, Nov. 25, 1886, Dec. 15, 1887, Jan. 12, 1888; *Lone Star*, 560.
36. Georgetown history; *Sun*, Jun. 19, Jul. 31, Nov. 27, 1890.
37. *Sun*, Nov. 24, 1887, May 17, 1888, ff., Dec. 31, 1908, Sept. 2, 1971; *Mann Papers*.
38. Griffith, 12; *Taylor Press*, Jun. 18, 1967; *Sun*, Dec. 25, 1890, Jan. 29, 1891.
39. Interviews Atkin, Millholin; *Sun*, Oct. 10, 1878, Jan. 9, 1879.
40. School records; *Sun*, Sept. 3, 1883.
41. School records; *Teachers Manual*, 30; *Com*., VII, 416, 510; VIII, 202; IX, 125.
42. *Georgetown Independent*, Sept. 6, 1856; *Police Court*, P, IV; *Deeds*, X, 322-323; Raines, *Laws of Texas*, V, 1519.
43. *Police* and *Deeds*, *ibid*.
44. *Deeds*, XII, 237, 305.
45. *Sun*, Jan. 26, 1923.
46. Knox; Willbern, 84; *Georgetown Watchman*, Apr. 23, May 14, 21, 1870; *Sun*, Jan. 19, 26, 1923, by C. C. Cody.
47. *Sun*., Jan. 26, 1923.
48. *Ibid*.
49. Knox; Raines, *Year Book* 1901, 377.
50. Cody, 293, 313; *Sun*, Jan. 26, 1923, Jun. 7, 1888 quoting Sanders; Knox, Hester, *Megaphone*; Willbern, 51-80; Ralph Jones, 80-81.
51. Cody, 313, 315; R. Jones, 81; *Georgetown Watchman*, May 14, 21, 1870.
52. Letter Croom; Jones, 105, 253, quoting F. A. Mood *Autobiography*.
53. Letter Croom; interview Meyer.
54. Cody, 315; R. Jones, 102.
55. Raines, *Yearbook* 1901, 377-379.
56. R. Jones, 323.
57. Willbern, 101; Cody, 321.
58. *Sun*, Apr. 28, Jun. 9, Nov. 10, 1881; Hamilton Wright in *Sun*; R. Jones, 320; Southwestern University *Magazine*, 1923.
59. Mood and Cody.
60. R. Jones, 312, quoting Mood article Jan. 10, 1882.
61. Willbern, 105; R. Jones, 345.
62. Hester, *Megaphone*; Willbern, 102-103.
63. Willbern, 104.
64. Willbern, 107.
65. R. Jones, 347-348.
66. *Williamson County Sun* files 1888; Cody.
67. R. Jones, 123; Ray Hyer Brown, 45-46; interview Draper.
68. Southwestern University, *Trustee Minutes* 1896-1900, 43, 45-50, 88-90, 109, 119; interview Draper.
69. S. U. history; interviews Landrum, Harris, Wright.
70. *Ibid*.
71. Raines, *Yearbook* 1901, 378; R. Jones, 418-419.
72. R. Jones, 147-174.
73. Neas.
74. *Sun*, Jan. 9, 1925.
75. Grand Masonic; *History Round Rock Lodge*; *Round Rock USA*, 4; *Deeds*, X, 113-115.
76. *Brady Scrapbook*, clipping from *Sun*, n. d.
77. Grand Masonic; *History Round Rock Lodge*; *Brady Scrapbook*; *Mann Papers*; *Sun*, Jul. 21, Oct. 27, 1881; *Round Rock Leader*, Aug. 20, 1928.
78. *Sun*, Jul. 25, Aug. 22, 1878.
79. *Sun*, Sept. 12, 1878, May 15, 1879.
80. Interview Harrison; *Austin American*, Mar. 16, 1961.
81. *Memorials and Petitions*, File Box 118.
82. *Ibid*.; *Twentieth Annual Catalogue*.
83. *Catalogue*, 39, 41; *Matthews Family*, 96-97; *Liberty Hill Observer*, Aug. 27, 1886; *Sun*, Aug. 12, 19, 26, Nov. 18, 1886.
84. *Sun*, Jan. 12, and 19, 1888.
85. Ledlow; *Handbook*, II, 55; *Twentieth Annual Catalogue*.

86. Interviews Matthews, Barrington; *Handbook*, I, 179, 519; *Sun*, May 20, 1909, April 28, May 19, 1910.
87. Caskey, 25; interview W. L. Wilson.
88. *Ibid.*
89. *Ibid.*; *Sun*, Aug. 7, 1969.
90. Round Rock history, author's files.
91. *Ibid.*
92. *Ibid.*
93. *Ibid.*
94. Interview Harris; *Sun*, Jan. 19, 1882.
95. Batte, 104; *Sun*, Jul. 12, 1883.
96. Nixon, 8-9, 18.
97. *Police Court*, V, 129.
98. Nixon, 134, 146, 234; *Williamson County Record*, Jan. 19, 1874.
99. *Georgetown Watchman*, Jan. 19, 1874; *Sun*, Jan. 23, Mar. 20, 1879.
100. Letters Crumley and Sims.
101. *Sun*, Apr. 10, 1879.
102. *Kingdom*, 22.
103. Letters Crumley and Sims; U. S. Post Office.
104. Circleville history, author's files.
105. *Sun*, Jun. 10, 1965, quoting J. F. Taulbee.
106. Letter University of Texas Law Library; *Handbook*, II, 792; *Sun* Feb. 23, 1888.
107. *Sun*, Apr. 10, 1879.
108. *Texas Almanac*, 1966-1967, 573.
109. Files of newspapers named in sections on communications; *Texas Almanac*, 1872; microfilm *Williamson County Sun* 1877-1973 and stockholder records of the firm; Fred Millholin, Georgetown, *History of Williamson County Sun*, Feb. 7, 1970; Lad H. Maresh, Granger, *History of Nasinec*, 1973; Taylor City Charter; Don Scarbrough, *History of Taylor Times*, March 1973; interviews Vera Allen, R. N. Watson, Harris Melasky, Mrs. Fred Buchanan; histories of communities; letter Downey. *Handbook*, I, 871; files of old newspapers in University of Texas Newspaper Archives, Barker Collection.
110. *Deeds*, XVII, 564; Wallace, 51; Shuffler; *Sun*, Jun. 20, 1878; interview Taylor.
111. *Sun*, Aug. 8, 15, 1878, May 29, 1969.
112. Interview Millholin; *Sun*, Jun. 13, 1878, Dec. 3, 1883, Mar. 11, 1886.
113. Interview Fay Richardson; *Sun*, Aug. 20, 1903.
114. Interview Forrest F. Brown.
115. *Sun*, Aug. 14, 1890.
116. *Sun*, Dec. 24, 1885.
117. Margaret Tegge Stearns, *Reminiscences.*
118. *Ibid.*
119. *Ibid.*
120. *Ibid.*
121. *Ibid.*
122. Interview Bailey.
123. Stearns, *Reminiscences.*
124. *Ibid.*
125. *Ibid.*
126. *Ibid.*; interview Albert E. Jones.
127. *Commissioners*, VII, 29; VIII, Feb. 23, 1895; *Handbook*, I, 73; *Sun*, Jun. 20, Aug. 10, Oct. 9, 1884; community histories.
128. Ray Hyer'Brown, 88.
129. *Millholin Papers.*
130. *Handbook*, I, 430.
131. *Sun*, Jan. 13, 1973, by Hamilton Wright.
132. Carson, 56, 58-59.
133. Stearns, *Reminiscences*; *Handbook*, II, 770.
134. *Sun*, Jul. 30, 1903.
135. *Sun*, Jun. 15, Jul. 25, Aug. 8, 15, Nov. 21, 1878.
136. *Deeds*, XLVII, 236.
137. Wm. Co. *Probate Records*, No. 502.
138. *Nelson Farm Papers*, "Texas Chautauqua Assembly Pamphlet 1891"; interviews Gaines, Harris; *Lone Star State*, 217; *Sun*, Aug. 27, 1885, Aug. 12, 1886, May 1, 29, Jul. 10, Nov. 27, 1890, summer issues 1892, Jul. 5, 12, 1894, May 26, 1966.
139. *Ibid.*
140. *Ibid.*
141. *Handbook*, II, 252; Spell, 289-293.
142. Interview Suttles.
143. *Sun*, Feb. 9, 16, 1899; *Texas Almanac* 1966-1967, 111; *Sun*, Nov. 24, 1970, by Hamilton Wright.
144. Interview Gaines.
145. *Sun* files 1878, incl. Jul. 25, Sept. 5.
146. *Sun*, May 23, Jul. 25, Aug. 15, Sept. 12, Oct. 17, 31, 1878; Jan. 23, Mar. 20, Apr. 24, May 15, 1879; Mar. 9, 1882.
147. *Police Court*, P, 216, 269-273, 362, 404, 434; IV, 24, 37, 55, 79, 138, 154, 160, 178, 201, 205, 224, 239, 245, 260, 271, 302, 389, 419; *Williamson County Record*, Jan. 19, 1874.
148. *Sun*, Dec. 20, 1877.
149. *Sun*, Nov. 23, 1956.
150. *Commissioners*, VIII, 228, 242; *Sun*, May-June 1893.

151. *Sun,* Jul. 16, 1903, May 5, 1966.
152. *Lone Star State,* 751.
153. *Georgetown Watchman,* Jun. 19, 1869.
154. *Sun,* Apr. 19, 1894
155. *Sun,* Oct. 14, 1897.
156. *Sun,* Sept. 4, 1890.
157. Interviews Asher, Harris.
158. *Sun,* Sept. 16, 1886; *Austin-American Statesman,* Jul. 26, 1970, Sec. II, 11.
159. *Sun,* Nov. 18, 1880, Mar. 8, 1888; interview Dellinger.
160. *Taylor Press,* Nov. 23, 1956, quoting *Taylor Texan.*
161. *Ibid.,* interview Dellinger.
162. *Sun,* Apr. 5, 1906.
163. Sonnichsen, 260; *Sun,* May 14, 1970.
164. *Sun,* Jul. 19, Aug. 30, Sept. 6, 1877.
165. *Hardin Papers,* V., letters.
166. *The West Magazine,* Feb. 1965, 116.
167. *Ibid.*
168. *Ibid.;* Preece, 146-147.
169. Sandoz, 49, 140; Chrisman, 82-87, 93-97, 102, 380.
170. *Ibid.*
171. *Ibid.; Georgetown Watchman,* Apr. 23, 30, 1870.
172. Sandoz, 140; Chrisman, 10, 84, 113-115, 120, 122, 125-126, 131, 132.
173. Chrisman, 136, 139-140, 142.
174. *Ibid.,* 145-147 151, 180, 381; Dobie, *Longhorns,* 222, 224; Sandoz, 72, 140.
175. *Sun,* Jan. 16, 1879; Sandoz, 140-141; Chrisman, 152-160, 170, 172, 174, 181-182, 234-238.
176. Chrisman, 183-184, 186-188, 197.
177. Sandoz, 142-145; Chrisman, 24, 272, 345-356, 362; *Taylorsville Times,* Feb. 10, 1879; *Snyder Family.*
178. Webb, *Rangers,* 371-391; Fletcher, 111-113; *Sun,* Jul. 25, 1878.
179. *Sun,* Jul. 25, 1878.
180. *Ibid.*
181. *Ibid.*
182. *Ibid.*
183. *Ibid.*
184. *Ibid.;* Sandberg, 422-424; Gard, 245-246.
185. Webb, *Rangers,* 388, 390.
186. *Sun,* Aug. 8, 1878.
187. Webb, *Rangers,* 390.
188. Bishop, 293; *Austin American,* Nov. 20, 1955.
189. Sandberg, 423.
190. *Sun,* July 25, 1878.
191. *Sun,* Jan. 20, 1972; *World Book,* XI, 22; *Enc. Brit.,* III, 80; *Millholin Papers.*

192. *Sun,* Jun. 11, 18, 1970.

CHAPTER X

1. *Millholin Papers;* Barker, *Texas History,* 531, 566; Potts, 476, *Handbook,* II, 412.
2. *Lone Star State,* 351, 383; letter, Eloise Laurence; *Map of Railroads 1876.*
3. *Taylor Press,* Nov. 23, 1956; *Williamson County Sun,* Jul. 20, 1921.
4. *Deeds,* XVII, 334, 337, 414, 441, 479, 544, 634, 637, 690-691; XVIII, 614, 877.
5. *Taylor Weekly Texan,* Nov. 29, 1893.
6. *Austin Statesman,* Jun. 6, 1926, by Irma Brown; Griffith.
7. *Ibid.; Sun,* Aug. 5, 1921, by Lee M. Taylor; *Sun,* May 19, 26, Jul. 19, Sept. 13, Oct. 25, Dec. 12, 1877; *Taylor Press,* Nov. 23, 1956, quoting A. J. McCarty.
8. *Ibid.; Lone Star State,* 332; *Taylor Weekly Texan,* Nov. 29, 1893.
9. U. S. Post Office; *Sun,* 1877 and ff.; *Taylor Press,* n. d.
10. *Sun,* Jun. 6, Oct. 31, 1878; *Taylor Press,* n. d., quoting *Bradstreet Book of 1878.*
11. *Sun,* Jun. 27, 1878.
12. *Sun,* Mar. 6, 1879.
13. *Ibid.*
14. *Taylor Weekly Texan,* Nov. 29, 1893.
15. Interviews Davenport, Payne, O'Rear, Towns; *Lone Star State,* 430; Fletcher, 22; *Map of Railroads 1876.*
16. History of Hutto, author's files; interview Engdahl.
17. *Ibid.*
18. *Map 1876.*
19. *Snyder Family; Mann Papers;* U. S. Post Office; *Round Rock Leader,* Aug. 20, 1920.
20. *Police Court,* IV, 205, 245; *Georgetown Watchman,* Jun. 19, 1869; *Round Rock Sentinel,* Jan. 19, 1871.
21. *Round Rock Sentinel,* Jan. 19, Sept. 21, 1871; *Sun,* Aug. 5, 1921, Apr. 15, 1971; *Georgetown Sentinel,* Oct. 17, 1872; *Round Rock, U. S. A.,* 46; *Lone Star State,* 744-745; *Mann Papers; Police Court* IV, 76; *Georgetown Watchman,* Jun. 19, 1869, Apr. 30, 1870; interviews Robertson, Mae Brady.
22. *Deeds,* V, 196; Morrell, 258, 341, 347, 385; *Mann Papers.*
23. U. S. Post Office.

24. Interviews Robertson, Mae Brady, Scoggins; *Sun*, May 23, 1968; Hinds, 106.

25. *Sun*, May 5, 1966, quoting J. E. Cooper.

26. *Handbook*, II, 487; letter Breeding; *Sun*, May 26, Aug. 2, Oct. 11, 1877.

27. *Brady Scrapbook*; Deed Records.

28. *Leader*, Sept. 26, 1963.

29. *Austin American-Statesman*, Jul. 26, 1970, I, 15, quoting 1878 *Texas New Yorker*; *Sun* Oct. 3, 1878, Jan. 9, 1879; *Round Rock, U. S. A.*, 12.

30. Entire section on 1876 cites Caudle, 76; Reed, 316, 319, 320; Johnson, II, 806-809; Thrall, 777; letter Hammer, and "Brief History" enclosed, 1-3; *Mann Papers*; Batte, 87.

31. Reed, 322-323; *Handbook*, I, 682; *Sun* 1878-1879, Aug. 1, 1968, Jan. 13, 1972; *Mann Papers*.

32. *Georgetown Watchman*, Jan. 19, 1874; *Sun*, Jan. 23, Mar. 20, 1879, Jun. 3, 1886, Jun. 7, 1888, Apr. 10, 1936, Jun. 10, 1965; *Brady Scrapbook*.

33. *Sun*, Jan. 23, Feb. 13, Apr. 24, 1879, Sept. 2, 1880, Feb. 17, Mar. 3, Apr. 28, 1881; interview Harris.

34. *Sun*, Sept. 3, 1970, by Hamilton Wright; interviews McDaniel, Harris.

35. *Ibid.*; *Millholin Papers*.

36. Potts, 50; Bryson, 19.

37. Interviews, Glenn, Dearing, Cordova; U. S. Post Office.

38. *Ibid.*

39. *Ibid.*; *Kingdom*, 23; *Handbook*, II, 522.

40. T. U. Taylor 51-55; *Kingdom*, 14; U. S. Post Office.

41. Lynch, 354-355; interview Mrs. A. S. Walker; *Lone Star State*, 853.

42. Interview Williamson; Bryson, 51; U. S. Post Office; *Sun*, Jun. 13, 27, Sept. 5, 19, Oct. 10, 17, Dec. 5, 19, 1878, Jan. 9, 23, Mar. 6, 20, 27, May 8, 1879, Jul. 8, Aug. 26, 1880; *Leader*, Aug. 20, 1928; Hinds, 109, 186; *Mann Papers*.

43. *Ibid.*

44. *Sun*, Aug. 5, 1921, Apr. 7, 1966; *Leader, ibid.*; *Handbook*, II, 42; Bryson, 21, 23; *Mann Papers*.

45. Interview Wells.

46. *Census 1850*; *Handbook*, II, 55; Jenkins, *Recollections*, 94, 267; Pennybacker, 329-330; U. S. Post Office; Barton, 18; interviews Fay Richardson, Rowlett, Humphries; *Lone Star State*, 576, 740, 748, 762; Bryson, 35; *Georgetown Sentinel*, Oct. 17, 1872; *Sun*, Feb. 14, Oct. 10, 1878, Nov. 17, 1922, Apr. 21, 1966, Nov. 12, 1970.

47. Bryson, *ibid.*

48. Interview Wells.

49. *Austin American-Statesman*, Jul. 26, 1970, II, 1; Andrus, 30, 32, 36; *Sun*, Jul. 22, 1971, by Hamilton Wright.

50. Potts, 50; Reed, 213; Poor, 33-34; letter Carnahan.

51. Potts, 62; Masterson, 223; Reed, 381; Rand McNalley map 1882, showing Pollack.

52. *Deeds*, XXIV, 431 and ff.; *Lone Star State*, 265; interview Knight; *Sun*, Aug. 11, Dec. 8, 1887, Jul. 20, 1921, Dec. 11, 1936; *Taylor Times Centennial*, 1948; *Taylor Press*, Jun. 30, 1938; *Handbook*, I, 117; *Mann Papers*.

53. *Sun*, Aug. 19, Sept. 2, 30, 1886, Mar. 29, Dec. 8, 1887.

54. History Macedonia, author's files; *Georgetown Independent*, Oct. 29, 1856; *Lone Star State*, 264, 270, 395, 562, 797.

55. *Granger News*, Jan. 4, 1973, by W. C. Reinhardt; *Bartlett Tribune*, Aug. 16, 1940; *Sun*, Mar. 27, 1884, Aug. 5, 1886, Dec. 1, 1887, Mar. 1, Jun. 14, 1888, Aug. 5, 1921.

56. *Sun*, Jan. 5, 1885; *News, ibid.*

57. *Sun*, Jul. 18, 1878.

58. Stearns, *Record*; U. S. Post Office; *Texas Almanac* 1857, 102; *Georgetown Watchman*, Mar. 23, 1867, Apr. 23, 1870; *Lone Star State*, 332; *Sun*, Dec. 19, 1878, Aug. 5, 1921; *Police Court*, IV, 419; *Taylor Press*, Jul. 29, 1951; *Round Rock Sentinel*, Aug. 3, 1871.

59. *Lone Star State*, 462; *Sun*, Dec. 19, 1878, Nov. 3, 1887; Eubanks and Stearns *Family Records*.

60. Reed, 213.

61. Interview Auburn Stearns, Aug. 16, 1968.

62. *Taylor Press*, Jun. 30, 1938, Nov. 23, 1956.

63. *Ibid.*; Griffith, 7-10, 13; *Sun*, Nov. 3, 1887; *Austin American-Statesman*, Jun. 6, 1926, by Irma Brown.

64. Reed, 381; *Lone Star State*, 339; *Sun*, Aug. 5, 1921; Coupland Map.

65. Interviews Goetz, Albers, Speckles,

Polzin; U. S. Post Office; History of
Coupland, author's files.
66. Reed, 385; Masterson, 268; Potts, 64;
letter Whittle.
67. Foster; interview Starnes; *Sun*, Jul.
12, 1883, Oct. 5, 1950.
68. U. S. Post Office; *Sun*, Oct. 28, 1938;
interviews Millholin, Liese family,
Bergstrom, Starnes.
69. Interviews Mrs. Carl Liese, Millholin;
Sun, Jun. 18, 1903.
70. Reed, 445-446; Fisk, 140; Hohes,
558-561; Texas State Railroad Commission, Library Records.
71. *Schwertner Family*; U. S. Post Office;
Interview Schwertner; *Sun*, May 5,
1966.
72. Interviews Eva Harrison, Fred Harrison, Ethel Houston, Rosa Jones, Beulah Foster, Buchanan; Grand Masonic; U. S. Post Office; *Granger
News*, Jul. 17, 1969; *Austin American*, Mar. 16, 1961; *Temple Daily
Telegram*, Feb. 9, 1936; *Marrs Records*; letters Downey, Miersch; *Mann
Papers*; *Lone Star*, 254, 450; 533,
746, 758; *Sun*, Dec. 12, 1877, Jun.
6, Aug. 15, 22, 1878, Jun. 17, 1880,
Jan. 28, 1881, Jul. 5, 12, Aug. 16,
1883, Mar. 6, 1884, Aug. 26, Sept.
30, 1886, Jun. 7, 1888, Jan. 22, Feb.
5, 1891, Apr. 16, 1908, Aug. 5, 1921,
Jun. 13, 1924.
73. Interview Harvill, Houston, Rosa
Jones.
74. Family Records.
75. Railroad Commission records; letter
Downey; *Sun*, Apr. 14, 1910; *Deeds*
1909, 1910.
76. Letter Downey; interview Keeling.
77. Interview Fred White.
78. Interviews, Lonnie Wilson, Watson,
Black, Tipton, G. L. Young; Railroad
Commission Mileage Circular 9-H,
Feb. 23, 1932; Odell Charles for
Railroad Commission, letter June 24,
1969.
79. Caskey; *Lone Star State*, 389; Mann
Papers; *Deeds*, VI, 587; *Dallas News*,
Jan. 12, 1936.
80. Caskey; *Mann Papers*.
81. Caskey; interview Haynes.
82. Interviews Suttles, Love; *Lone Star
State*, 546, 743; *Georgetown Watchman*, May 22, 1869, May 21, 1870;
Round Rock Sentinel, Aug. 3, 1871;
Sun, Nov. 21, 1878, Jun. 7, 1888,
Sept. 5, 1969, Nov. 19, 1970.
83. *Ibid.*; Caskey, 14, 39; interviews
Suttles, Crawford.
84. Interviews Watson, L. Wilson, Suttles, Love, E. Daniell; *Florence Vidette*, Aug. 6, 1898; Caskey; *Sun*,
Jun. 24, 1965, Aug. 7, 1969.
85. Interviews *ibid.*, G. L. Young; *Sun*,
Apr. 27, 1972, by Mrs. R. S. Caskey.
86. Interviews Scoggins, G. L. Young.
87. Railroad Commission Records, XXI,
Report of June 30, 1918, 3-6.
88. Interviews Schrock, G. L. Young;
Bartlett Tribune, May 21, 1926, Jul.
6, 27, 1951.
89. *Ibid.*; Railroad Commission, Interstate Circular No. 10, 915; Hohes,
558-561; Fisk, 140.
90. Letter George Brown.

CHAPTER XI
1. U. S. Census Reports; *Texas Almanac*.
2. *Ibid.*; Paddock, II, 678; *Bradstreet
Book 1878*, quoted Taylor Press
clipping, n. d.; population estimates,
rural communities, *Texas Almanac*.
3. Commissioners Court Minutes *Index*,
312; postal records; *Williamson
County Sun*, Feb. 6, 1908, Mar. 21,
1930, Dec. 15, 1939; Precinct List,
Democratic Executive Committee,
March 1966.
4. *Sun*, Oct. 7, 1909, Jan. 26, 1923.
5. *Sun*, Oct. 15, 1908, Apr. 17, 1936,
May 5, 1939.
6. *Sun*, Sept. 10, 17, 1908, Nov. 21,
1924, Sept. 8, 1936.
7. *Sun* files 1890s.
8. *Sun*, Sept. 24, 1908, Aug. 24, 31,
1972; Clara Jones, 9; Texas Highway
Department, *History*, 2-3.
9. *Sun*, Dec. 10, 1908.
10. *Sun*, Aug. 24, 1972, by Millholin;
City of Georgetown, *Revised Civil
Ordinances*, 32.
11. Interviews Bergstrom, Millholin; *Sun*,
Mar. 9, 1972, by Wright.
12. *Sun*, Jun. 9, 17, Jul. 15, 1909;
Granger News, Feb. 8, Sept. 5, 1912;
Taylor Press, Nov. 23, 1956; *Texas
Almanac* 1966-67, 483-484.
13. *Sun*, 1918 clipping, n. d.
14. *Sun*, Aug. 31, 1972, by Millholin.
15. *Sun*, Apr. 7, Jul. 21, 1922, Sept. 18,
25, 1969, Jan. 7, 1970.
16. *Sun*, Aug. 5, 1921, Jun. 13, 1924,
Jan. 7, 1970; Tax Records.
17. *Sun*, Jun. 27, Jul. 11, 1924, Apr. 3,
1925, Nov. 14, Dec. 5, 1930, Jul.

1931, Nov. 25, 1938, Jun. 16, 1939, Jan. 7, 1970.

18. *Sun*, Dec. 1, 1889; *Press*, Nov. 23, 1956.

19. Interview Conoley; *Sun*, Mar. 4, 1965, Sept. 10, 1970.

20. *Texas Almanac* 1966-67; *Sun*, Nov. 21, 1930.

21. *Sun*, Oct. 7, 1909; *Texas Almanac* 1904.

22. *Sun*, Apr. 17, 1925; *Taylor, Texas*, 5.

23. *Sun*, Sept. 25, 1969; *Texas Almanac* 1972-73, 385; *Handbook* I, 183.

24. *Handbook* I, 11; *Sun*, Feb. 1, Jul. 25, 1930, Oct. 9, Sept. 25, 1931, Feb. 26, 1932, Apr. 10, May 8, Jul. 10, 1936, 1938 various issues, May 3, 1940.

25. Bird, 217-218, 220.

26. *Ibid.*

27. *Sun*, Oct. 30, 1931, Jul. 24, 1936.

28. *Sun*, May 17, 22, 1931, Mar. 4, 1932, Mar. 5, Apr. 16, Sept. 17, 1937; Raines, *Yearbook* 1901, 71.

29. *Granger News*, Jan. 27, 1910, quoting *Taylor Democrat*; Bryson, 9, 10; Raines, *Yearbook* 1901, 180.

30. *Texas Almanac* 1925; *Handbook* II, 403; *Sun*, Nov. 21, 1930, Jul. 31, 1931.

31. Interview Auburn Stearns, O'Rear; *Handbook* II, 353; *Taylor and Its Opportunities*.

32. *Sun*, Sept. 11, 1931, various issues 1938, Aug. 16, 1940, Feb. 27, 1964, Dec. 30, 1965, Shuler Museum.

33. Arbingast, 88-89.

34. Frances Stearns *Diary*; *Granger News*, Mar. 16, 1911; *Sun*, Dec. 28, 1972.

35. Interviews Ploeger, W. R. Scarbrough; *Sun*, Jul. 21, 1922; *Austin American*, Nov. 7, 1971, Oct. 22, 1972.

36. Letter Lindquist; *Sun*, Mar. 29, 1951, Jul. 30, 1970; *Austin American*, Nov. 15, 1968.

37. Letters George R. Brown; Southwestern University Publicity Office, biographical material; *Sun*, Jul. 11, 1924, Oct. 1, Nov. 19, 1970.

38. *Sun*, Jan. 3, 1930; interview McCook.

39. *Commissioners Minutes*, X, 201, 210, 223, 256; *Sun*, Dec. 23, 1909, May 5, 1910, Mar. 4, Aug. 18, 1965.

40. Interviews Don Scarbrough, Lancaster.

41. *Sun*, May 22, 1931, reminiscences Dr. Wm. Gibson Pettus, 1877-1931.

42. Letters Dr. Johns; State Medical Association records; interview Dr. Shepherd.

43. Johns *ibid.*; interview Barrington; *Press*, Aug. 9, 1968; *Lone Star State*, 263; *Taylor, Texas*, 17-19.

44. *Sunday Review*, Nov. 30, 1941, published by *Taylor Times*; *Taylor Press* clipping, n. d.

45. Interview Barrington.

46. Interviews Munson, Beaver; letter King's Daughters; *Deeds* CLXXXIV, 56.

47. Interviews Benold, Gaddy; *Sun*, Aug. 28, 1922, May 11, 1923.

48. Interview Whitlow.

49. Interview Harris; Georgetown City Council minutes; *Sun*, Nov. 12, 1908; *Granger News*, Feb. 1, 1912, quoting *Georgetown Commercial*.

50. *Sun*, Oct. 15, Nov. 19, Dec. 3, 1908, Sept. 23, Oct. 14, 1909, Aug. 11, 25, 1910, Dec. 26, 1931.

51. Hayes, 64-65, quoting Ed Gooch, who changed places with Foster and survived the accident; *Taylor Press*, May 21, 1971.

52. *Ibid.*

53. *Texas Almanac* 1966-67, 111-112; *Sun*, Sept. 16, 1921; *Press*, Nov. 22, 1936.

54. *Sun*, ibid.

55. *Ibid.*

56. *Ibid.*

57. *Ibid.*

58. *Ibid.*; interview Brown.

59. Personal recollections of author; interviews with author's parents, Auburn Clare and Margaret Tegge Stearns.

60. Interview Labaj.

61. *Sun*, Sept. 16, 1921.

62. *Ibid.*; postal records; *Press*, Nov. 22, 1936.

63. *Sun, ibid.*

64. *Granger News*, Nov. 16, 1972; *Sun*, Sept. 18, Oct. 2, 1936, Feb. 5, 1937.

65. *Sun*, April 3, 1969.

66. Heinsohn, 140-141, 248; histories of Theon, Macedonia, Walburg, by author; *Sun*, May 8, 1936, Sept. 17, Nov. 5, 1937, Aug. 26, 1938, Jun. 16, 1939, Mar. 23, 1972.

67. *Deeds*, X, 320; XXV, 419, 421, 501; XXXVI, 497; Smyer, 10-11, 15, 20, 82; A. D. H. Smith, 52.

68. Interview Brown.

69. Smyer, 20.

70. *Sun*, Jun. 10, 1932, Apr. 30, 1937,

Feb. 24, 1972; *Dallas News*, May 1, 1971.
71. *Sun*, Jul. 21, 1922, and others.
72. *Handbook* II, 717; *Dallas News* clipping, n. d.; Wester, 10-12, 20; *Lone Star State*, 547; Griffith; *Texas Bar Journal*; Dan Moody *Papers*; *Pioneer Women*, 15.
73. *Ibid.*
74. *Ibid.*; *Moody-Robertson.*
75. *Ibid.*; *Sun*, Jan. 9, 1925; *Press*, Mar. 15, 1968.
76. *Ibid.*
77. *Sun*, Apr. 23, 1923.
78. *Texas Bar Journal.*
79. *Moody Papers.*
80. Scott, Garry, 2-5; *Sun*, May 11, Sept. 21 and 28, 1923, Jan. 4 and 19, Feb. 8, 1924.
81. *Ibid.*
82. *Sun*, Sept. 21, 28, 1923; interview Anita Smith.
83. *Sun*, May 18, Sept. 21, 28, 1923.
84. *New York Times*, Associated Press story, Aug. 18, 1923.
85. *Sun*, Sept. 21, 28, 1923, quoting Lt. Gov. T. W. Davidson.
86. *Ibid.*; G. Scott.
87. G. Scott; *Sun* Jan. 18, Feb. 8, 1924.
88. Fitzgerald, 56.
89. Personal knowledge of author.
90. Alan Scott, "He's Our Man," 32; letters Arnold H. Bean, Mrs. Frances Bean.
91. *Sun*, Jun. 2, 1910.
92. *Ibid.*, Jun. 16, Aug. 25, 1910 and subsequent issues.
93. See more on Dobie later in this chapter.
94. Heinsohn, 136, 138.
95. Heinsohn, 136, 138-139; *Sun*, Jun. 10, 1932.
96. *Austin American*, Oct. 3, 1971.
97. Marrs-Smith.
98. *Sun*, "S. U. Notes," Apr. 28, 1910, Jan. 24, 1936, Jul. 23, 1937.
99. Letter Fox; *Austin American-Statesman*, Dec. 24, 1972.
100. Letter Fox; *Press*, Nov. 23, 1956; Interview Mashburn; Fisk, 139-140.
101. *Sun*, Nov. 30, 1972.
102. Letter, Lawson; interview Schrock; Fisk, 140; Hohes, 558-561; trip by author to State Capitol to view Cronin paintings, 1973.
103. *Bartlett Tribune*, Jul. 27, 1951.
104. *Sun*, May 5, 1939; First Methodist Church (Georgetown) records.

105. *Austin American*, Dec. 1, 1936; *Sun*, Mar. 27, 1936; Fisk, 139; letter to author from Mrs. Edward MacDowell.
106. England, 3-4, 8-10, 12-13, 16, 32-33; *Sun*, Jun. 28, 1900, Aug. 18, Sept. 1, 1904, Aug. 1906, Sept. 5, 1907, Aug. 13, 1908.
107. *Sun*, Jan. 2, Apr. 23, 1908, May 27, Aug. 5, 1909; England, 3-4.
108. Stearns *Diary*, Aug. 22, 1906; *Sun*, Dec. 31, 1908.
109. *Millholin Papers.*
110. *Ibid.*; *Sun* issues, various.
111. Interviews Landrum and Clark.
112. Interview Mantor.
113. Interview Millholin.
114. Interview Asher; *Granger News*, Oct. 17, 1912; *Sun*, Jul. 4, 1924.
115. *Press*, Nov. 23, 1956.
116. Interview Mantor.
117. Letters Mayes.
118. *Press*, Nov. 23, 1956.
119. *World Almanac* 1914; interview Dellinger; *Press* clipping, n. d.; *Sun*, May 11, 1923.
120. *Ibid.*
121. Interviews Pickett, Dellinger; Hinkle, 30; letter Muchmore.
122. Hinkle, 30.
123. Hendrix, 162.
124. Hinkle, 56.
125. Interview Pickett; letter Muchmore.
126. National Cowboy Hall of Fame.

NOTES ON THE PLACES OF WILLIAMSON COUNTY

(In addition to sources cited below, the following references have been researched in instances where applicable: U. S. and Confederate postal records; church and community records and histories, county school records, Commissioners Court records; census records.)

1. *Georgetown Watchman*, May 22, 1869; interview Irvin; *Williamson County Sun*, June 27, 1878, Feb. 26, 1970; letter Bolding.
2. Letter J. E. Moore; interviews Fowler, Mona Johnson.
3. Letter Whatley; interviews A. E. Jones, Bessie Williams, Ulmer Young, Leshikar; *Broadcaster*, Nov. 16, Dec. 23, 1925.
4. Interviews Fowler, Grumbles.
5. Interviews Gus Jacob, Asher, Whitten, Stapp, Howland; letter Newton; *Sun* Oct. 21, 1971, Oct. 19, 1972; *Deeds* VII, 118; Union Hall history.

6. Interviews Brown, Bailey; letter Lena King.
7. *Commissioners Minutes*, X, 65; Mrs. W. A. Baker family records.
8. Interview Mrs. Victor Johnson; *Deeds* I, 196.
9. Interviews Houghton, Hobbs; *Sun*, Jan. 15, 1891, Jan. 24, 1930; Masonic Records.
10. *Lone Star State*, 538; interviews Brown, Lax; *Sun*, Jun. 9, 1966.
11. *Deeds*, XIII, 148; *Police Court*, IV, 389; *Lone Star State*, 538; interviews Lax, Brown; *Sun*, June 9, 1966; *Mann Papers*.
12. Interviews Sudduth, Snowden, Gunn, Mrs. Lee Travis, Brogren, Landrum; *Deeds* XI, 307, 574, 600; XXXV, 621.
13. Interview Brogren; *Sun*, Jun. 16, Sept. 28, Oct. 5, 1950, Apr. 29, 1951, Jun. 9, 1966; *Austin American*, Jan. 7, 1965. •
14. Letters Bachmayer; interview Frerichs, Kreidel; *Deeds*, XX, 434.
15. Interview Guentzel.
16. *Sun*, May 8, Dec. 4, 1890, Jan. 15, 1970; interviews Mary R. Birkelbach, Mrs. Otto Liese, Mueller; *Broadcaster*, Jan. 1923.
17. *Sun*, Dec. 8, 1887.
18. *Sun*, Nov. 8, 1877, May 16, Jun. 6 and 20, Sept. 26, Aug. 22, 1878.
19. Interview Nash; *Sun*, Jul. 14, 1966.
20. W. A. Baker records; *Sun*, Aug. 19, 1886.
21. Witte Museum Papers.
22. Interviews McCormack, Simpson, Cahill, Addie Stearns; Irwin, 168.
23. Interviews Cocke, A. E. Jones; *Broadcaster*, Dec. 1923.
24. Interviews W. L. Wilson, Hewitt; letter Gage; *Sun* .Jun. 5, 1969; *Taylor Press*, May 22, 1958.
25. Interviews Wayne and Charlie Adams, W. L. Wilson; letter Drennan; *Broadcaster*, Oct. 10, 1922, Jan. 1923.
26. Interview Suttles.
27. *Sun*, Dec. 1, 1887.
28. *Press*, Sept. 1970; *Handbook*, I, 330; *Texas: A Guide*, 571.
29. Letters, Ramsey; interview Stallings.
30. Letter Clark.
31. Interview Asher.
32. Interview Suttles.
33. Interview Asher; *Broadcaster*, Mar. 1923.
34. Interview Cassens; church history.

35. Interviews Dannelley, Gage, Houghton; letters Ramsey.
36. Interview Houghton.
37. Interviews Dearing, Cordova.
38. *Deeds*, XVII, 449.
39. Interview Margaret Stearns.
40. Interviews Ellyson, Lindsey; *Georgetown Independent*, Oct. 29, 1856.
41. Interviews Conlee, Blackman, Whitfield, Fred Harrison; *Sun*, Jan. 9, 1908.
42. Interviews Mary F. Denson, Beulah Denson, Rister, Moore, Lindsey; *Broadcaster*, Nov. 1923.
43. Interviews W. E. Griffiths, Stallings, Humphries, Mathison; *Sun*, Jun. 6, Sept. 12, 1878, Feb. 18, 1909.
44. Interviews Addie Stearns, Mary Sloan and sisters; *Lone Star* State, 269, 393, 479; *News-Monitor* (Johnston, S. C.), Jul. 12, 1911.
45. Letters Lena King, L. M. Millholin; interviews Brown, Edens, Dimmitt, Ahlberg, Bergstrom; *Sun*, Feb. 18, 1909, Mar. 12, 1915, Feb. 5, 1970; *Granger News*, Jan. 29, 1970.
46. Interview Hobbs; *Broadcaster*, Jan. 1924.
47. Letter, Virginia Lawrence.
48. *Ibid*; interview Ulmer Young; *Sun*, Jun. 14, 1888, Jul. 15, 1909.
49. Interviews Ulmer Young, Liska; *Broadcaster*, Dec. 1923.
50. *Broadcaster*, Jan. 1923.
51. Interview Simmons.
52. Interview Baker; *Sun*, Aug. 19, 1886; Mar. 29, 1888.
53. Interviews Caswell, Blackman, Conlee, Fred Harrison.
54. Interview Auburn Stearns; *Handbook* I, 639; *Broadcaster*, Oct. 10, 1922.
55. Interviews Labaj, A. E. Jones, Williams; Batte, 93; *Broadcaster*, Dec. 1923; *Granger News*, Apr. 23, 1970; *Handbook* I, 649.
56. *Sun*, Mar. 13, 1936; Dobie, *Coronado's Children*, 20-21.
57. Stewart, *History Pioneer Lodge*; interview Asher; Cordova, 326; Bryson, 254, 262; *Sun*, May 9, 1968.
58. Bryson, 26, 264; Stewart, *ibid.*; letter Ramsey; *Sun*, Oct. 4, 1877, Mar. 13, 1936.
59. *Austin American Statesman Magazine*, Jan. 17, 1926, by John M. Sharpe; Maltby, 772, 785; Bryson, 101-102; interview Asher.
60. Raines, *Bibliography*, 49; *Taylor*

Press, Nov. 23, 1956; letter Simmons; interview Lawrence.

61. Chrisman, 40-41; *Police Court*, IV, 317; *Sun*, Jun. 3, 1886; interview Cain.

62. Interviews Millholin, Rosenblad, Mary Starnes; *Sun*, Oct. 28, 1938.

63. Interview Claude Wilson; *Sun*, March 29, 1888.

64. Interviews Mona Johnson, Jenkins, Caesar, Forbes; *Broadcaster*, Dec. 1922; Baptist Church Records.

65. Masonic Lodge Records; *Sun*, Jan. 12, 1888; interviews Fulkes, Fay Richardson, Renick.

66. Interview Dellinger.

67. *Ibid.*; interview Ulmer Young; letters Wuthrich, Whatley; *Texas Almanac*, 1904, 25; *Austin Statesman*, Jun. 6, 1926; *Broadcaster*, Dec. 1922; *Taylor Press*, Jun. 30, 1938, Nov. 23, 1956, Jul. 2, 1971; *Sun*, May 30, 1878; *Granger News*, Jan. 27, 1910.

68. Letter Lena King; interviews Edens, Bergstrom; *Sun*, May 8, 1890.

69. Interviews Claude Wilson, Grumbles.

70. Interviews Mathison, Hunt; *Lone Star State*, 609; *Sun*, Nov. 24, 1887.

71. Letter Douglas; *Sun*, Apr. 12, 1888.

72. Interview Hunt.

73. Interviews Miller Bros., Hollingsworth, Prude, Mrs. D. W. White.

74. *Ibid.*; Bryson, 222-228, 267; Fletcher, 89-95; *Sun*, Nov. 5, 1903; interview Upchurch.

75. Interview Hunt.

76. *Broadcaster*, Dec. 1922; letter Nolte.

77. *Mann Papers*; Interviews Glenn, Dearing; Broadcaster, *ibid.*; *Sun*, Jun. 20, 1878, Jan. 9, 23, 1879.

78. Interviews Percy, Brown, Addie Stearns, Thomas McDonald; *Handbook*, I, 921; *Deeds*, VII, 92, 115; LVI, 619; deeds April 1 and 4, 1890, Jan. 23-30, 1895, Feb. 2-4, 1904 concerning mill; *Police Court Minutes*, May 1858, 343; *Broadcaster*, Apr. 1923; *Sun*, Dec. 1, 1881, Sept. 3, 1883, Jan. 5, 1888, May 27, 1909, Aug. 11, 1910, Oct. 5, 1950, Sept. 30, 1971.

79. Interviews Scott, Margaret Stearns, Poppelz (and letter), Tschoerner; *Sun*, Jun. 2, 1904.

80. Interview Kennedy; *Broadcaster*, Dec. 1922.

81. Interviews Fay Richardson, Treuhardt, Wood; *Matthews* Papers; *Deed*

May 23, 1890, Knight to Crockett; *Deeds*, IV, 179; VI, 102; *Lone Star State*, 818; *Sun*, Oct. 16, 1969.

82. Interviews Forbes, J. H. McDonald, Liska, Matysek, Annie Stearns; clipping unnamed San Antonio newspaper c. Apr. 27, 1902.

83. *Broadcaster*, Oct. 10, 1922; interviews Hickman-Baker, McLeod, T. O. Lindsey; interview Watson.

84. Landers; *Sun*, Dec. 18, 1936; interview Lawrence.

85. *Handbook*, II, 42; interview Faubion; *Sun*, Jan. 14, Jun. 24, 1909; Apr. 17, 1925, Aug. 12, 1971.

86. Masonic Records; interviews Matthews, Fay Richardson, Humphries, Parks; *Sun*, Jun. 23, Jul. 7, Aug. 4, 1922; Jul. 1, 1971.

87. Interviews Asher, Humphries.

88. Interview Mrs. Beulah Denson.

89. Interview Bartlett.

90. *Broadcaster*, Nov. 16, 1925.

91. Interview Asher; *Broadcaster*, Nov. 16, 1925.

92. Interviews Margaret Stearns, Gilstrap, Pope, Lindsey, Leggett, Mr. and Mrs. Fred Denson Sr.; letters Zannie Moore, Luther Dorrell; Fanny Eubank Stearns history of Opossum Church; Masonic Records.

93. *Broadcaster*, Nov. 1923; interview Labaj.

94 Interviews Auburn Stearns, Brown, Crone, Harris, Bergstrom; *Police Court Minutes*, May 1858, 342-343; *Deeds*, XVI, 32; *Sun*, Jun. 20, 1878, Feb. 5, 1970.

95. Interviews Suttles, Love; Caskey, 7; *Broadcaster*, Feb. 1923 and Jan. 1924; *Austin American*, Dec. 1, 1960; issues of *Sun* for 1870s.

96. Interview Matthews; *Matthews-Carothers Family Record*, 92-93; *Autobiography of Joseph Neely Matthews*.

97. *Handbook*, II, 223; Frances Stearns *Diary*.

98. Interview Asher.

99. Interview Willie Brady; *Sun*, Apr. 12, 1888, Feb. 26, 1891.

100. Interviews Wolbrueck, Doerfler, Poppelz; *Granger News*, Feb. 26, 1970.

101. Letter, Naizer; *Deeds*, XXVI, 635; XXXIV, 221, 608; XXXIX, 21; XL, 353; XLII, 187; interviews Wolbrueck.

102. Interview Simpson.

103. Interviews Stauffer, Schroeder, A. J.

Priesmeyer, Lehman, Wood; *Handbook*, II, 271.
104. Engerrand, 123-124; *Press*, Jan. 23, Sept. 22, 1970 and clipping, n. d.; letter Bachmayer.
105. Letter Norman; *Handbook*, II, 284; *Lone Star State*, 359; interview Payne; *Sun*, Jul. 22, 1921, Apr. 24, 1925.
106. Interview Margaret Stearns.
107. Interviews Hewitt, Whitfield, Conlee; *Lone Star State*, 461.
108. Interviews Zrubek, Mrs. Bernard Birkelbach, Luksa, Margaret Stearns; *Broadcaster*, Nov. 1923; *Sun*, May 19, 1910.
109. Interview Kreidel; *Broadcaster*, Mar. 1924.
110. Letter Gage; interviews Claude and Lonnie Wilson.
111. Interview Marinda Williams.
112. School and church histories.
113. *Press*, Jan. 24, 1967, by Frances Barton.
114. Interviews Dearing, Glenn; *Lone Star State*, 546; *Georgetown Watchman*, May 22, 1869.
115. Matthews and Carothers family records.
116. Letters Ramsey.
117. *Ibid;* interviews Houghton, Gage, Dannelley; *Broadcaster*, Oct. 10, 1922, Jan. 1923; Masonic Records.
118. Interview Asher; *Broadcaster*, Nov. 16, 1925.
119. Interview Asher.
120. Interview Addie Stearns, Fred White, Caswell.
121. Interviews Cordova, Dearing, Glenn; letter Dearing.
122. Mann, "James O. Rice," July 1951, 30-42; *Handbook*, II, 469; Makemson, 2, 18, 42; Census Records; Wilbarger, 54; Brown, *Annals*, V, 26; Wm. Co. *Probate Court Files* R-1, R-2; *Lone Star State*, 736; interview Hairston.
123. Interviews Robbins family; trip to site; *Sun*, Aug. 1886.
124. Interviews Stallings, Griffiths, Mrs. Humphries, Mathison; *Lone Star State*, 762; *Sun*, Sept. 12, 1878, Feb. 2, 1908, Feb. 18, 1909.
125. Interviews Wayne Adams, Haynes, Aubrey Daniell, Whitfield.
126. Interview Lannen.
127. Interviews Dearing, Glenn, Cordova; *Handbook*, II, 522; *Kingdom*, 23.
128. *Sun*, Jan. 5, 1888.

129. *Broadcaster*, Dec. 1922.
130. *Ibid.*, Nov. 16, 1925; Asher.
131. Bancroft, I, 619; interviews Pasemann, Streich, Jechow, Lehman, Ovesny; letter Baker.
132. Trip to cemetery April 11, 1970.
133. Interview Bohlen; DeShields, 147.
134. *Deeds* I, 113; *Sun*, Nov. 18, 1880, Dec. 25, 1890; Lee M. Taylor, grandson of Josiah Taylor, in *Sun* July 20, 1921; interviews Lannen, Hairston, Payne; letter Johns; Stearns genealogy; trip to site.
135. Texas State Historical Survey Committee, *History of Shiloh Baptist Church*; Scoggins *Scrapbook*; interviews Simmons, Hobbs; letter E. Laurence; *Broadcaster*, Jan. 1924; *Deeds* XLVII, 147.
136. Interview Taylor; Taylor *Press* clipping, n. d.; Texas Historical Survey Committee, material for historical marker; *Deeds*, XVII, 564; interviews Hobbs, J. M. Barnett; *Lawhon Family Papers*.
137. Interview Ruff, Irvin, born at Small 1890; Nina Grimes, daughter of J. M. Smith; *Sun*, Feb. 19, 1970.
138. Interview Watson.
139. Interview Grumbles, Buchanan.
140. Frances Stearns Records; *Sun*, April 28, 1887.
141. Interviews Barrington, Bryson, Griffiths; letter Griffiths; *Handbook*, I, 151; *Sun*, Jan. 12, 1888; 1892.
142. Interview Mrs. A. J. Priesmeyer; *Broadcaster*, Feb. 1923.
143. Interview McLeod.
144. Interviews Deison, Hoyt; *Broadcaster*, Oct. 10, 1922.
145. *Broadcaster*, Oct. 10, 1922; *Sun*, April 12, 1888.
146. *Handbook*, II, 681; interviews Hobbs, Mrs. Simmons; *Sun*, Oct. 23, 1931.
147. *Broadcaster*, Dec. 1922; Bryson, 16-17; *Sun*, Sept. 9, 1880; Mar. 29, 1888.
148. Letters Miersch, Leubner sisters; interviews Danek, Kalmbach, Atwood, Cassens, Father Hughes, Holy Trinity Church Records; *Sun*, Oct. 20, 1960.
149. Holy Trinity Church Baptismal Records.
150. *Lone Star State*, 351, 383; *Deeds*, XVII, 704; letter E. Laurence; *Henderson Papers; Texas: A Guide*, 571; *Handbook*, II, 777; *Sun*, Nov. 5, 1885, Oct. 13, 1887, Mar. 16, 1923, Jul. 25, 1924; *Probate Minutes*,

XIXC, 391-393, 401; Taylor *Press* clipping, n. d., Sept. 22, 1970.

151. *Handbook*, II, 780.
152. Interviews Knauth, Otto Liese, Mrs. Carl Liese, Martinka, Bergstrom, Mary Starnes, daughter of J. F. Towns; Foster, *History of Weir*; *Millholin Papers*; letter Lena King; *Sun*, Feb. 13, 1879, Jul. 12, 1883, Jul. 4, 1887, Jan. 5, 1888, Aug. 28, 1890, Apr. 2, 1892, Oct. 28, 1938, Oct. 5, 1950.
153. *Broadcaster*, Dec. 1922; interviews with Mrs. A. J. Priesmeyer, Wuthrich.
154. *Broadcaster*, Jan. 1924.
155. Severin, 119.
156. Interview Humphries; letters Patrick, Griffiths; *Broadcaster* Nov. 1923; *Sun*, Dec. 1, 1887.
157. *Liberty Hill Leader*, Jan. 1, 1937; *Carothers Papers*; interview Mrs. D. W. White; letters Roberts, Griffiths, Whitted.
158. Interviews Fredrickson, Lawson, Lundelius, Anderson; *St. John's* Church, 1957; *Suvenir Svenska*, 1908; *Sun*, Jul. 10, 1890, Oct. 7, 1971.
159. *Sun*, April 12, 1888.
160. Bewie, 50; *Zion Lutheran Church 1882-1942*; *Seventy-Fifth Anniversary Zion Church*; *The 75th Anniversary, St. Peter Church*; *Deeds*, XVI, 637; interviews Ben Kurio, Jr., Homeyer, Mueller, Cassens, Olga Liese, Marinda Williams, Doering, Wedemeyer, Mrs. Walter Jacob, Mrs. Ben Kurio, Sr. ("Aunt Mattie" or Grandmother Kurio, nee Martha Doering, daughter

of Henry Doering), Braun; Carl Liese Memoirs; *Bartlett Tribune*, Jun. 4, 1926; *Granger News*, May 21, 1970; *Sun*, Aug. 28, 1890, Apr. 10, 1936, May 7, 1970, Jun. 8, 1972.
161. Interview Ben Kurio, Jr., Mar. 26, 1973.
162. Lynch, 354-355; *Sun*, Dec. 10, 1908.
163. Interviews Mollie Aderholt, daughter, J. W. Rainwater; Estelle Young, daughter J. T. Bernard; Faykus, Maresh; *Broadcaster*, Dec. 1922; letter Alma Wuthrich, daughter C. G. Wuthrich.
164. Interviews Millholin, Mrs. Carl Liese, Mrs. Otto Liese, Bergstrom; Foster, *History of Weir*; *Austin American*, Nov. 12, 1972; *Sun*, Jan. 7, 1909, Nov. 21, 1930, Apr. 28, 1966; *Broadcaster*, Dec. 1922.
165. Interviews Suttles, Love; *Sun*, Feb. 9, 1888; *Broadcaster*, Nov. 16, 1925.
166. *Broadcaster*, Feb. 1924.
167. *Sun*, Apr. 3, 1931.
168. *Deeds*, V, 535; XV, 261-262; *Mann Papers*; *Taylor Press* clip, n. d., quoting Will Lannen whose father came to Taylor 1877; *Broadcaster*, Nov. 1922; *Handbook*, II, 923; *Austin Statesman*, Jun. 6, 1926.
169. Interviews Houghton, Gage, Dannelley; *Broadcaster*, Oct. 10, 1922, Jan. 1923.
170. Letter Wuthrich.
171. *Broadcaster*, Oct. 10, 1922.
172. Interview Margaret Stearns.
173. Interview Irvine.

Bibliography

INTERVIEWS

ADAMS, CHARLIE, Georgetown, July 19, 1969.

ADAMS, WAYNE, Georgetown, July 19, 1969.

ADERHOLT, MOLLIE (MRS. CHARLES), Taylor, April 24, 1970; daughter of J. W. Rainwater.

AHLBERG, DAN, Georgetown, January 16, 1970.

ALBERS, CLARA HUNZIKER (MRS. ALFRED), Coupland, July 6, 1973.

ANDERSON, LAWRENCE, Georgetown, September 21, 1971.

ASHER, MR. and MRS. HAROLD, Gabriel Mills, June 25, 1969, and following; also quoting Asher's interviews of Claude Stewart, great grandson of John T. Stewart.

ATKIN, J. THATCHER, Georgetown, 1973.

ATWOOD, MRS. RUBY, Theon, March 19, 1970.

BAILEY, MRS. MARY SMITH, Georgetown, January 10, 1970 and August 15, 1971.

BAKER, MRS. W. A., Georgetown, February 3, 1970.

BARNETT, J. M., Beaukiss, July 18, 1969.

BARRINGTON, MRS. EMMA VAUGHAN, Liberty Hill, February 1970; Georgetown, January 25, 1972, March 12, 1973.

BARTLETT, MISS DAN, Bartlett, July 19, 1969.

BEAVER, ELIZABETH "YANKEE" PLATT (MRS. CHARLES O.), Georgetown, March 27, 1973.

BENOLD, DR. DOUGLAS, Georgetown, April 3, 1973.

BERGSTROM, MARTIN, Georgetown (Weir), January 16 and 19, 1970.

BIRKELBACH, MRS. BERNARD, Georgetown, January 8, 1973.

BIRKELBACH, MISS MARY RUTH, Georgetown, May 15, 1970.

BLACK, J. D., Georgetown, June 26, 1969.

BLACKMAN, MISS DORA, Jarrell, July 25, 1969.

BOHLEN, GEORGE, Laneport (San Gabriel), March 17, 1970.

BRADY, MAE THORNTON (MRS. O. L.), Round Rock, August 1969, niece and ward of T. W. Royston, president Round Rock College Board of Trustees, 1881.

BRADY, WILLIE ROGERS (MRS. PAT), Georgetown, (Mount Prospect), July 24, 1969.

BRAUN, MRS. ARTHUR G., Georgetown, July 1970.

BROGREN, E. E. Georgetown, May 18, 1970.

BROWN, FORREST F., Jonah, September 23, 1969, April 1, 1970.

BRYSON, ESTELLE ASHER (MRS. BILL), Bertram, February 1970.

BUCHANAN, MRS. FRED, Jarrell, June 30, 1969.

CAESAR, FRED A., Route 1, Thorndale (Hare), March 17, April 11, 1970.

CAHILL, MRS. TOM, Leander, June 1969.

CAIN, MRS. W. L., Thrall, April 22, 1970.

CARLSON, PHILIP, Georgetown, June 1969.

CASSENS, WESS A., Georgetown (Walburg-Theon), July 11, September 3, 1969; April 23, 1970.

CASWELL, EDITH (MRS. HOMER), Georgeotwn, June 26, 30, 1969.

CLARK, AMBASSADOR EDWARD, Austin, October 1970.

COCKE, ELIZABETH (MRS. J. S)., Route 2, Georgetown, October 15, 1969.

COFFEE, MRS. JIM, Georgetown, April 21, 1966.

CONLEE, MR. and MRS. WILLIAM H., Jarrell, July 28, 1969.

CONOLEY, GILLIS, Taylor, March 21, 1973.

COOKE, MRS. E. M., SR., Georgetown, 1969.

CORDOVA, GEORGE, McNeil (stationmaster McNeil), June 17, 1969.

CRAWFORD, MRS. ANNIE WYATT, Georgetown, June 11, 1969.

CRONE, ALMA (MRS. SWEN), Georgetown (Union Hill), June 1970.

CURIK, IRIS STEARNS (MRS. JOE) and JIM CURIK, Rockdale, August 10, 1970. Jim Curik assisted at archeological digs, San Xavier missions.

DANEK, JOHN, Jarrell, March 20, 1970.

DANIELL, AUBREY, Andice (Matsler), July 3, 1969.

DANIELL, EVANGELINE JACOB (MRS. AUBREY), Andice (Matsler), January 4, 1972.

DANNELLEY, MARY ALICE CONDRON (MRS. R. A.), Elgin, October 21, 1969.

DAVENPORT, MISS MARY, Hutto, March 11, 1973.

DAVENPORT, MRS. PHILIP, Hutto, October 1969.

DEARING, MR. and MRS. HARRY, Leander (Pond Spring), May 7, 1970. Their home was on site of old Pond Spring store-post office, near first school.

DEISON, MRS. VELMA, Round Rock, May 1970.

DELLINGER, JIM, Taylor, (longtime resident and police chief of Taylor), August 19, 1968, taped interview.

DENSON, MRS. BEULAH, Granger, September 3, 1969.

DENSON, MARY FRANCES (MRS. FRED P., JR.), Austin 21, 1970.

DIMMITT, LILBURN, Georgetown (East View), January 1970.

DOAK, DR. EDMOND DOAK, Taylor, July 1969.

DOERFLER, WALTER, Route 4, Georgetown, February 3, 1970.

DOERING, C. G., Georgetown, March 7, 1970.

DRAPER, JAMES ELIAS, Richmond, California (Queen's Hill), October 16, 1972.

EDENS, MISS LETTIE, Georgetown, June 16, 1969.

EDWARDS, JEWEL and MARVIN, Florence, January 3, 1973.

ELLYSON, JOHN N., Georgetown, March 29, 1969.

ENGDAHL, CARRIE HANSEN (MRS. CARL), Taylor (Hutto), October 7, 1969, daughter of Carl Hansen.

FAUBION, C. P., Georgetown (Bagdad-Leander), February 15, 1972.

FAYKUS, MRS. J. W., Taylor (Waterloo), April 10, 1970.

FORBES, MYRTLE BOSTIC (MRS. C. A.), Thorndale (Hare-Laneport), April 14, 1970.

FOSTER, MRS. BETHEL, Georgetown, June 1972. Furnished *History of Weir*, written March 9, 1903.

FOSTER, MRS. BEULAH, Georgetown (Corn-Hill-Granger), June 1969.

FOWLER, MRS. MINNIE, Granger (Althea-Alligator), January 28, 1970.

FREDRICKSON, MRS. JOHN, Georgetown (Union Hill), January 27, 1970.

FRERICHS, MRS. ALBERT, Taylor (Beyersville), March 17, 1970.

FRIEDSAM, MRS. JULIA, Austin, February 5, August 21, 1973; youngest daughter of George and Harriet Cluck, alert and able to recall times dating to the 1870s.

FULKES, MRS. MAE MITCHELL, Liberty Hill, March 6, 1970.

GADDY, DR. HAL, Georgetown, April 3, 1973.

GAGE, MR. AND MRS. WILBURN, Elgin (Condron, Post Oak Island), October 21, 1969.

GAINES, ROBERT "BOB," Georgetown, February 22, 1973, interview by Don Scarbrough.

GILSTRAP, ANNIE (MRS. C. F.), Austin, April 21, 1970. Furnished Macedonia church records.

GLENN, MR. and MRS. JASPER, Austin, May 7, 1970.

GOETZ, GERTRUDE (MRS. ALBERT), Coupland, August 4, 1973.

GRIFFITHS, WALTER ELMER, Georgetown (Rock House), February 7 and 9, 1972.

GRIMES, NINA SMITH (MRS.), Taylor (Small), May 19, 1970.

GRUMBLES, MAMIE SEXTON (MRS. OTTO), Georgetown (Gravis), January 28, 1970.

GUENTZEL, MRS. IDA MAE, Coupland, c. 1970.

GUNN, MRS. BEULAH, Georgetown (Berry's Creek), June 10, 1969.

GUSMAN, MRS. L. F. SR., Bandera, Texas, October 17, 1971, on whose ranch eight Williamson County men were buried who were hanged during Civil War. Mrs. Gusman allowed access to her *Scrapbook* on the event.

HAIRSTON, CHARLES, Rice's Crossing, March 4, 1972.

HALL, ALMA (MRS. MARSHALL BRYANT), October 4, 1968, quoting her late husband.

HARRIS, FANNY "FAN" BRADY (MRS. SAM), Georgetown, August 5, October 1, 1968; January 11, 1973.

HARRISON, EVA LEE JACKSON (MRS. FRED), Jarrell, August 5, 1969.

HARRISON, FRED, Jarrell, August 5, 1969.

HARVILL, R. S., Georgetown (Corn Hill), June 1969.

HAYNES, ALLA BEA, Georgetown (Rocky Hollow-Florence-Jarrell), June 1970 to January 1973; granddaughter of Jim Haynes; employee of author during preparation of this book.

HEINATZ, EMILIE, Bagdad, 1969.

HESTER, GEORGE C., Georgetown, former professor of history, Southwestern University, 1970-1973.

HEWITT, MRS. MARVIN, Georgetown, July 15, 1969.

HICKMAN, A. BROWN, and daughter, MRS. THELMA BAKER, Georgetown, October 20, 1969.

HOBBS, RAY, Beaukiss, Route 1, Thrall, July 18, 1969.

HODGES, MRS. MARVIN C., Georgetown, 1970.

HOLLINGSWORTH, MRS. ELLIS, Liberty Hill (Miller-Jenks Branch community), June 11, 1969.

HOMEYER, ANNA LIESE (MRS. ALEX), Georgetown (Walburg), February 10, 1970.

HOUGHTON, MR. AND MRS. IRA L., Beaukiss, July 18, 1969.

HOUSTON, MRS. ETHEL JONES, Georgetown (Corn Hill), July 11, and 17, 1969; trip to site.

HOWELL, MRS. IRENE, Georgetown, July 18, 1972.

HOWLAND, WADE, Andice, July 3, 1969.

HOYT, MRS. A. W., JR., Georgetown (Stony Point), July 1970.

HUGHES, FATHER ROYCE, Theon, pastor Holy Trinity Catholic Church, March 19, 1970.

HUMPHRIES, MRS. J. E., Liberty Hill, June 25, 1969; granddaughter of Adam Miller.

HUNT, W. L. "PETE," Georgetown (Hunt community), May 21, 1969.

IRVIN, RUFF, Bartlett (Small community), February 4, 1970; son of George Washington Irvin.

IRVINE, MR. AND MRS. DONALD P., Georgetown, July 1970.

JACOB, MR. AND MRS. GUS, Andice, 1969- 1970.

JACOB, MRS. WALTER, Walburg, June 1970.

JECHOW, ALFRED, Route 1, Thorndale, March 17, 1970.

JENKINS, MR. AND MRS. ROBERT, Route 3, Taylor, April 11, 1970.

JOHNSON, MRS. MONA, Taylor (Laneport-San Gabriel), July 7, 1969.

JOHNSON, MRS. VICTOR J., Taylor (Barker-Brown Gin), September 12, 1969.

JONES, MR. AND MRS. ALBERT E., Granger, March 3, 1970.

JONES, MRS. ROSA, Georgetown (Corn Hill), August 5, 1969.

KALMBACH, WILLIAM, and daughter, MRS. RUBY ATWOOD, Theon, March, 19, 1970.

KEELING, S. A., Georgetown (Corn Hill-Jarrell), February 3, 1970.

KENNEDY, M. RANKEN, JR., Taylor (Kennedy community-Thrall), July 30, 1969.

KNAUTH, VICTOR, Weir (Towns Mill), June 30, 1969.

KNIGHT, MRS. NELL BARTLETT, Bartlett, April 16, 1972.

KREIDEL, ALVIN, Coupland, September 12, October 28, 1969.

KURIO, BEN, JR., Walburg, April 23, 1970; March 26, 1973.

KURIO, MARTHA "AUNT MATTIE" or "GRANDMOTHER" DOERING (MRS. BEN, SR.), Walburg, daughter of Henry Doering, 1970.

LABAJ, MRS. STACY, Granger, quoting interviews with Miss Elizabeth Ederington, Granger, June 1963, and Mr. and Mrs. Henry Rozacky, Sr., Granger, December 6, 1968.

LANCASTER, ROBERT L., Georgetown, 1973.

LANDRUM, NEELY, Georgetown and Dallas (Berry's Creek), taped interview, May 9, 1968; interview February 22, 1970.

LANNEN, MRS. WILL, Taylor, February 6, 1970.

LAWRENCE, G. CARL, Lawrence Chapel, February 11, 1970.

LAWSON, MRS. BEN, Georgetown (Union Hill), August 1970.

LAX, MRS. ERIC, Georgetown (Union Hill), January 27, 1970.

LEGGETT, FRANCES SPIARS (MRS. GENE), Jonah (Macedonia), June 1970.

LEHMAN, HERMAN, Taylor (Sandoval), March 11 and 17, 1970.

LESHIKAR, MR. AND MRS. JERRY, Granger, January 28, 1970.

LIESE, OLGA GRANZIN (MRS. CARL), Georgetown (Walburg), February 2, April 2, 1970; also *Carl Liese Memoirs*, June 1961.

LIESE, MR. AND MRS. OTTO, Georgetown (Walburg), January 18, 1970, February 10, 1971.

LINDSEY, H. E. "DICK," AND MARY ELLEN CAVANAUGH LINDSEY, (Macedonia-Dare Buzzard-Granger), June 1971.

LISKA, W. J., Laneport, March 17, 1970.

LOHMANN, MARIE MAY (MRS. C. A. "DOC" MAY), Georgetown, August 17, 1971; her first husband, "Doc" May, was born in second "courthouse" after it was moved to Jonah and after a log room was added to the frame house.

LOVE, JOSEPH HUTCHISON "HUTCH," Florence, September 5, 1969.

LOVE, RALPH DIXON, Florence, June 1968.

LOVENTHAL, MISS MATTIE, Georgetown, February 20, 1972.

LUKSA, DR. FRANK, Georgetown, March 5, 1973.

LUNDELIUS, ARTHUR "PAT," Georgetown, September 21, 1971.
MANTOR, MISS RUTH, Taylor, April 4, 1973.
MARESH, MR. AND MRS. JOHN, Waterloo, April 10, 1970.
MARTINKA, JOHN D., Taylor, July 7, 1969.
MASHBURN, CLAIRE EASLEY (MRS. GORDON), Georgetown, January 18, 1973.
MATHISON, VIRGINIA HUNT (MRS. OLLIE), Georgetown (Hunt community), May 22, 1969.
MATTHEWS, MISS MYRETA, Liberty Hill, 1970-1973; furnished many family records to author.
MATYSEK, MR. AND MRS. JOE, Hare, March 17, 1970.
McCOOK, ISAAC JOEL, SR., Georgetown, 1972-1973.
McCORMACK, MRS. MAUDE ALLEN, Leander, September 4, 1969.
McDANIEL, BERTIE FOWLER (MRS. GEORGE N.), Georgetown (Bagdad), August 19, 1968; June 10, 1969.
McDONALD, MR. AND MRS. JAMES HARLEY, Hare, April 11, 1970.
McDONALD, R. E., Route 1, Leander, September 10, 1969. Furnished McDonald's translation of de Vaca's original Old Spanish *Relación*, the journal of the explorer's party as it crossed Texas. McDonald concluded the party crossed Brushy Creek and San Gabriel River in February 1535. McDonald was an entymologist of the State of Texas, 1971; had also worked for the federal government on cotton insect control.
McDONALD, THOMAS, Taylor (Jonah), April 16, 1970.
McLEOD, MISS EFFIE, Florence, October 20, 1969.
MELASKY, HARRIS A., Taylor, May 9, 1972, son of Taylor merchant, Joseph "Jack" Melasky.
MERIDETH, DAVID, Florence, February 22, 1973, student of Williamson County caves.
MEYER, MRS. HENRY E., Georgetown, June 1971.
MIERSCH, MR. AND MRS. PAUL, Route 1, Jarrell (Theon), March 5, 1970; helped author obtain other materials about Theon and area.
MILLER, ELMER, MARSHALL, AND NORMAN, three brothers, Austin, June 17, 1971; (Jenks Branch, Miller communities).
MILLHOLIN, FRED W., Georgetown, February 29, 1972, and many others 1970-1973. He also made many personal papers and notes available to the author.
MOORE, LES, Bartlett and Georgetown, September 1969.
MUELLER, MRS. ALFRED, Georgetown, March 18, 1970.
MUNSON, ALBERT, Georgetown, March 27, 1973.
NASH, MRS. JOHN H., Georgetown (Caldwell Heights), October 13, 1969.
O'REAR, MRS. TENA, Hutto, August 4, 1973.
OVESNY, FRANK, Sandoval, March 17, 1970.
PARKS, WILSON, Liberty Hill, June 24, 1969.
PASEMANN, MR. AND MRS. PAUL, Route 3, Taylor, March 17, 1970.
PATRICK, MRS. WOODIE, Georgetown, June 1972.
PAYNE, NANNIE WOMACK (MRS. R. B.), Hutto, October 16, 1969.
PERCY, MRS. W. H., Jonah, 1969-1973.
PESCHEL, ADOLPH, Walburg, June 1970.
PICKETT, BENNIE, Taylor, August 19, 1968, youngest brother of famed bulldogger Bill Pickett.
PLOEGER, CLARENCE, SR., Taylor, interviewed by W. R. Scarbrough, Taylor, March 1973.
POLZIN, MRS. ERVIN, Coupland, November 10, 1972.
POPE, HATTIE TEGGE (MRS. GROVER C.), Granger, June 1970.
POPPELZ, WALTER, JR., Route 2, Granger (Keliehor), January 25, 1970.

PRIESMEYER, ANDREW J., Taylor, April 16, 1970.

PRIESMEYER, MRS. ARTHUR J., Noack, July 7, 1969.

PRUDE, AGNES (MRS. ANDREW), Georgetown, June 11, 1969.

REDARD, MRS. BERTHA, Route 5, Georgetown, 1969.

RENICK, MRS. FAY, Llano (Hopewell), February 5, 1972.

RICHARDSON, FAY BRYSON (MRS. MARSHALL), and MARSHALL RICHARDSON, Liberty Hill, June 25, 1969.

RISTER, M. A., Granger, January 28, 1970.

ROBBINS FAMILY: DAVE D. ROBBINS, EFFIE ROBBINS WALTON (MRS. ELMER), LETITIA ROBBINS HONEYCUTT (MRS. R. H.), JOSEPHINE ROBBINS JENKINS (MRS. ALBERT), Georgetown, January 18, 26, 28, 1970; trip to site of Robbins homestead and school.

ROBERTSON, LUKE, Round Rock, August 29, 1969; March 6, 1970.

ROSENBLAD, MRS. BEN, JR., Georgetown, July 1970.

ROWLETT, MRS. ORA MILES, Georgetown (Liberty Hill), March 18, 1972, step granddaughter of Thornton Poole.

SCARBROUGH, DONALD (DON) LEE, Georgetown, publisher county newspapers, husband of author.

SCARBROUGH, WALTON RAINES, Taylor, February 5, 1973.

SCHROCK, MISS MARTHA, Bartlett, October 27, 1972, close friend of Miss Marie Cronin.

SCHROEDER, MRS. THEODORE, Route 3, Taylor, April 15, 1970.

SCHWERTNER, HERMAN W., SR., Austin (Schwertner), August 8, 1969.

SCOGGINS, MRS. ESTHA HOLE, Georgetown, July 21, 1969; November 2, 1971; neighbor of Nannie Elizabeth Houston Morrow.

SCOTT, MRS. CHARLIE, Bartlett, January 25, 1970.

SHEPHERD, DR. JAMES L., Georgetown, April 1973, secretary Williamson County Medical Society, 1973.

SHIRLEY, G. L., Temple, June 1969.

SIMMONS, MRS. HOBSON, Route 1, Thrall (Shiloh), July 18, 1969.

SIMPSON, MR. AND MRS. EWELL, Leander, June 1, 1969.

SLOAN FAMILY: MISS MARY SLOAN, ANNIE "TUMP" SLOAN MOODY (MRS. HER-MAN), CATHERINE "PUNCH" SLOAN FUCHS (MRS. HERBERT), Jonah (Easley community), May 10, 1968, and taped interview.

SMITH, ANITA AKE (MRS. JAY), Austin (Taylor), February 15, 1973.

SNEAD, NED, Georgetown, January 5, 1973.

SNOWDEN, MRS. MARIAN GUNN, Georgetown, May 8, 1972.

SPECKLES, E. J., Coupland, November 10, 1972.

STALLINGS, ROGER "ROCKY," Tonkawan Indian consultant, Institute of Texan Cultures, San Antonio, June 5, 1971.

STAPP, OSWALD, Andice, June 16, 1969.

STARNES, MARY TOWNS (MRS. ROY W.), Austin (Towns Hill-Townsville), March 22, 1971.

STAUFFER, MR. AND MRS. ERNEST, New Bern, April 14, 1970.

STEARNS, ADDIE BOWMER (MRS. GLENN), Round Rock (Pleasant Hill-Leander), April 1969; January 1, April 1, 1970.

STEARNS, ANNIE FURLOW (MRS. CLYDE N.), Hutto and Taylor (Laneport), March 21, 1970.

STEARNS, AUBURN CLARE, (Circleville, Mankin's Crossing, Frame Switch, Hare), many interviews; author's father, born at Circleville 1878, living in Taylor in 1973.

STEARNS, MARGARET TEGGE (MRS. AUBURN CLARE), Taylor (Macedonia-Granger-

Yankee Branch-Keliehor-Salyer-Circleville areas), author's mother, born at Macedonia.
STEELMAN, DR. E. H., Georgetown, December 27, 1972; archeologist.
STONE, JUDGE SAM V., Georgetown, June 1970, March 16, 1973.
STREICH, ADOLPH, Thrall-Thorndale, April 16, 1970.
SUDDUTH, MRS. JACK, Georgetown, May 8, 1972.
SUTTLES, MRS. DELL TUCKER, Florence (Matsler), October 8, 1968; subsequent telephone interviews.
TAYLOR, MRS. R. B., Taylor, July 1969; furnished *Lawhon Family Papers.*
TIPTON, DR. AND MRS. VAN (ANN), Georgetown (Bartlett), June-September 1969.
TOWNS, MRS. ALBERT, Georgetown (Towns Mill-Townsville), June 25, 1969.
TRAVIS, MRS. LEE, Georgetown (Berry's Creek), May 18, 1970; June 18, 1972.
TREUHARDT, MRS. JOHN L., Georgetown (Jenkins Crossing), July 19, 1969.
TSCHOERNER, MRS. LOUIS, Granger, January 25, 1970.
UPCHURCH, MRS. LILLIE MAE, Georgetown (Leander), July 21, 1969, granddaughter of James Branch.
WALKER, MRS. ALEXANDER STUART, JR., Leander (Block House-Walkerton), September 10, 1969.
WALKER, ROY C., Georgetown, July 17, 1972.
WATSON, RUSSELL NATHANIEL, Florence, August 1 and 5, 1969, former editor *Florence Vidette,* who made those files available.
WEDEMEYER, MRS. W. C., Georgetown (Walburg), March 18, June 27, 1970.
WELLS, ANNIE JENNINGS (MRS. H. J.), Georgetown (Leander), July 1969.
WHITCOMB, GLADYS SNYDER (MRS. J. D.), Georgetown, October 4, 1972, November 1972; youngest daughter of cattleman John W. Snyder.
WHITE, MRS. D. W., Austin (Leander-Jenks Branch), March 16, 1970.
WHITE, MR. AND MRS. FRED, Jarrell (Primrose), June 30, 1969.
WHITFIELD, GEORGE, Georgetown (Jarrell-Bone Hollow), July 15, 1969; February 23, 1970.
WHITLOW, NORMAN, Round Rock, April 5, 1973.
WHITTEN, MRS. LOIS STAPP, Andice, June 18, 1969.
WILLIAMS, BESSIE BRYAN (MRS. FRANK), Granger, March 3, 1970.
WILLIAMS, MARINDA GILLMORE (MRS. LOUIS A.), Austin-Georgetown (Philadelphia School), July 30, 1969.
WILLIAMSON, MISS LEONA, Leander, June 1969.
WILSON, CLAUDE, Georgetown (Peyton, Gravel Hill, Centre Point), May 22, 1969.
WILSON, W. LONNIE, Florence, June 9, August 1, 1969; former supervisor Little River-San Gabriel Soil Conservation District.
WOLBRUECK, ALBERT and OTTO, Georgetown, February 4, 1970, son and grandson of August W. Wolbrueck.
WOOD, JUDGE D. B., Georgetown, May 6, 1970; February 16, 1971.
WUTHRICH, SOPHIE BRAUN (MRS. ERNEST), Bartlett, March 12, 1973, history of Turkey Creek School.
YOUNG, MRS. ESTELLE BERNARD, Taylor, April 24, 1970.
YOUNG, GROVER L., Florence, June 1969, August 1, 1969.
YOUNG, MR. AND MRS. ULMER DOWNEY, Taylor, September 12, 1969.
ZRUBEK, EMIL, Route 2, Granger, January 8, 1973.

LETTERS

Ames, Lulu, Austin, daughter Jessie Daniel Ames; August 21, 1973.
Arrington, Gladys Sparks (Mrs. Ray), Taylor, 1968; niece of John Sparks.

Bachmayer, Mr. and Mrs. Otto, Taylor, April 15, 1970; February 12, 1973.

Baker, Rosalie Melasky (Mrs. Howard O.), Taylor, January 22, 1972.

Bean, Arnold H., 3100 Bellaire Drive West, Ft. Worth, March 14, 1970; father of astronaut Alan Bean.

Bean, Frances (Mrs. Arnold H.), Ft. Worth, April 7, 1970; mother of astronaut Alan Bean.

Bergquist, Carl, Austin, March 2, 1973; architectural design.

Bolding, James T., Temple, c. January 1970.

Breeding, Mr. and Mrs. Seth D., Austin, Glasscock and Hart genealogies, May 1, 1968; January 22, 1972; August 17, 1973.

Brown, George R., Houston, March 1, October 31, 1972; Chairman of the Board, Brown & Root, Inc.

Bryson, Estelle Asher (Mrs. Bill), Route 1, Bertram, December 12, 1970.

Burleson, Roger, Leander, November 11, 1971.

Carnahan, Arthur L., Austin, July 19, 1950, cited in Texas State Railroad Commission records.

Chapman, Mrs. Chatty, Florence, 1969.

Clark, Harry W., Bryan, January 5, 1973.

Croom, Fletcher Metcalfe (Mrs. P. B.), 4054 Grennoch, Houston, quoting her mother, Fletcher McKennon Metcalfe (Mrs. Hunter O.), granddaughter of Francis Asbury Mood, who related a story told to her by Mrs. Metcalfe's mother, Margaret Mood McKennon. Letter dater October 24, 1972.

Crumley, J. M., Lampasas, March 1972; Crumley family records, including war records from National Archives.

Dearing, Mrs. Harry, Leander, September 16, 1969.

Dorrell, Mr. and Mrs. Luther H., Port Aransas, July 27, 1970.

Douglas, W. H., Bartlett, October 22, 1969.

Downey, Robert E., Smiley, Texas, October 18, 1969; April 18, 1973; former publisher *Jarrell View.*

Drennan, Mrs. Nora Cox, Route 2, Winnsboro, Texas, 1969.

Fischer, Ernest G., 5666 Rosemary Place, New Orleans, June 1969.

Fox, Henry B., Taylor (Circleville), December 13, 1972.

Freeman, Mrs. Margaret Bell, Bartlett, September, 1968.

Gage, Mrs. Ollie, Elgin, January 1970.

Griffiths, Mr. and Mrs. Steve P., California, February 4, 1970.

Hammer, Harry E., Missouri Pacific Public Relations Office, "Brief History of International-Great Northern Railroad," October 14, 1969.

Hollingsworth, J. R., Box 148, Amarillo, September 19, 1969; September 16, 1971.

Institute of Texan Cultures, San Antonio, by Bill Field, research associate, quoting Roger Stallings, March 21, 1973.

Johns, Dr. Jay J., Taylor, April 8, 1970; February 19, March 10, 1973.

King, Mrs. Lena Rude, Weir, December 1969.

King's Daughters Hospital, Temple, December 28, 1972.

Laurence, Miss Eloise, Thorndale, 1968, 1970.

Lawrence, Virginia Forwood (Mrs. Lee R.), Taylor, July 10, 1969.

Lawson, Virginia (Mrs. Frank), Houston,'November 18, 1972.

Leschber, Mrs. Alex, Hare, April 11, 1970.

Leubner sisters, Selma Leubner Dodson (Mrs. B. F.), Clara Leubner Clark (Mrs. N. G.), Ella Leubner Short (Mrs. B.), 3717 McKinney Ave., Dallas, March 10, 1970.

Lindquist, J. Benton, Dallas, March 7, 1973.

Lindsey, Tom O., Florence, November 1969.

MacDowell, Mrs. Edward, Peterborough, New Hampshire, March 22, 1945, close friend and colleague of Taylor music teacher Phoebe F. Garver; Mrs. MacDowell played a concert in Taylor.

Mayes, Charles Vale, Edinburg, Texas, September 5, October 28, 1968.

Miersch, Paul, Route 1, Jarrell, 1969.

Millholin, Leslie M., California, February 4, 1970.

Moore, John E., Jr., Taylor, January 21, 1970.

Moore, Zannie Easom, San Antonio, c. 1970.

Muchmore, Gareth, Ponca City, Oklahoma, March 1973; editor *Ponca City News*.

Naizer, Henry L., Austin, March 16, 1970; grandson of Johann Neusser-Naizer.

Nevada State Historical Society, Box 1129, Reno, Nevada, August 12, 1972.

Newton, Audice, C., 1019 La Monte Drive, Brownwood, May 23 and June 21, 1972.

Nolte, Eunice (Mrs. Lonnie), Thrall, April 22, 1970.

Norman, Mrs. Isaac W., Norman's Crossing, October 23, 1969; March 13, 1970.

Nunn, Dr. Curtis, Fort Worth, Professor of History, Texas Christian University, loan of historical materials.

Peeler, Eileen (Mrs. George B.), Taylor, March 14, 1973.

Ramsey, Grover C., 8332 Fredericksburg Rd., San Antonio, June 18, July 6, September 5, 1971.

Richey, Mrs. H. W., Georgetown; loaned original manuscript of letter dated January 18, 1879.

Roberts, E. D., Liberty Hill (Union Hall), August 26, 1969.

Schuetz, Mardeth K., San Antonio, March 4, 1971; archeologist who has studied Williamson County artifacts.

Simmons, Mrs. Nona Wilder, Thorndale, April 23, August 2, 1971.

Sims, Whalecia (Mrs. George), Box 121, Santa Rosa, New Mexico, July 27, 1972.

Smithsonian Institution, National Museum of Natural History, Washington, D. C., by George E. Phebus, supervisor Processing Laboratory, Department of Anthropology, November 11, 1971.

Stearns, Margaret Tegge (Mrs. A. C.), Taylor, June 11, 1970.

Sterling, U. T., Killeen, letter to T. E. Lee, Georgetown, quoted in *Williamson County Sun*, January 26, 1923.

Texas Parks and Wildlife Commission, Austin, by Jack K. Parsons, June 23, 1972.

Trigg, Bess Whittle, Tucumcari, New Mexico, December 2, 1963.

University of Texas Law Library, Austin, with enclosure from *Alcalde*, May 1914, sent January 19, 1972.

University of Wyoming, Western History Research Center, by Gene M. Gressley, n. d.

Watson, R. N., Florence, August 13, 1969.

Whatley, Mrs. Agnes, Taylor, July 10, 1969, granddaughter of Elihu C. Allison.

Whitted, Lyda (Mrs. W.), Route 2, Liberty Hill, February 11, 1972.

Whittle, George D., Berkeley, California, to Don Scarbrough, December 2, 1963.

Winterrowd, Margaret (Mrs. W. A.), Rt. 1, Thorndale, April 11, 1970.

Wright, Hamilton Will, 1934 Sycamore, Abilene, March 15, 1973.

Wuthrich, Miss Alma, and sister, Tillie, Route 3, Taylor (Wuthrich Hill), April 15, 1970; daughters of C. G. Wuthrich.

ARCHIVAL and PUBLISHED SOURCES

Andrus, M. Walter. *Behind This Cornerstone.* Austin: Chapman Printing Co., 1956.

ARBINGAST, STANLEY A., KENNAMER, LORRIN G., and BONINE, MICHAEL E. *Atlas of Texas*. Austin: University of Texas Press, 1967.

ARMBRUSTER, HENRY C. *The Torreys of Texas*. Buda, Texas: The Citizens Press, 1968.

ATKINSON, MARY JOURDAN. *Indians of the Southwest*. San Antonio: The Naylor Company, 1935.

Austin File, Chronological, 1839. Texas Writers Project: Works Projects Administration, District 9. Austin Public Library. n.d.

Austin Papers. "Mapa del pais de los Comanches por el Estevan Austin p. esplican el plan a campana conton dhos Indios, 1827." Texas State Library Archives.

———. "Mapa Geografico de la Provincia de Texas par Don Estevan Austin," 1822. Texas State Library Archives.

———. "Mapa original de Texas por El Ciudadano Estevan F. Austin, 1829." Texas State Library Archives.

———. "Spanish Map of Texas, 1826." Texas State Library Archives.

———. "Stephen F. Austin Map, 1829." Texas State Library Archives.

BABCOCK, JAMES E. "The Story of Bagdad Prairie from 1851 to 1870," quoted by Hinds (see), [circa 1912].

BAKER, D. W. C. *A Texas Scrap-Book*. New York: A. S. Barnes & Company, 1875.

BALCONES RESEARCH CENTER, UNIVERSITY OF TEXAS, Austin, Archeological Division. *Historical Sites*, comp. William Field. MS, 1965.

BANCROFT, HUBERT HOWE. *History of the North Mexican States and Texas*, I. San Francisco: A. L. Bancroft & Company, 1884.

BANDERA COUNTY COURT RECORDS, Book A.

BARKER, EUGENE C. "A Glimpse of the Texas Fur Trade in 1832," *Southwestern Historical Quarterly*, XIX.

———. *The Life of Stephen F. Austin*. Nashville: Cokesbury Press, 1925.

BARKER, EUGENE C., ed. *The Austin Papers*, 3 vols. Vols. I, II, Washington, 1924 and 1928; Vol. III, Austin, 1927.

———. *Texas History for High Schools and Colleges*. Dallas: Turner Company, 1929.

BARNETT, LINCOLN. *The Treasure of Our Tongue*. New York: Alfred A. Knopf, Inc., 1965.

BARTON, LELAH. *History of the Liberty Hill Baptist Church*. The church, 1948.

BATTE, LELIA M. *History of Milam County, Texas*. San Antonio: Naylor Company, 1956.

BATTEY, THOMAS C. *Life and Adventures of a Quaker Among the Indians*. Boston, 1876.

BEHRENS, TEDDY. *History of the Palm Valley Lutheran Church*, MS, n.d.

BERLANDIER, JEAN LOUIS. *The Indians of Texas in 1830*, ed. John C. Ewers; trans. Patricia Reading Leclercq. Washington, D. C.: Smithsonian Institution Press, 1969.

BEWIE, W. H. *Missouri Lutheran Synod in Texas*. Austin: Steck Company, 1952.

Billingsley Papers, Jesse. University of Texas, Austin, Archives, MSS.

Bills of Lading, McNeil, Texas, depot.

BIRD, CAROLINE. *The Invisible Scar*. New York: Pocket Books, 1967.

BISHOP, CURTIS AND GRACE, and MARTIN, CLYDE INEZ. *Trails to Texas*. Austin: W. S. Benson and Company, 1965.

BOLLAERT, WILLIAM. *William Bollaert's Texas*. ed. W. Eugene Hollon and Ruth Lapham Butler. Norman: University of Oklahoma Press, 1956.

BOLTON, HERBERT EUGENE. *Athanase de Mézières and the Louisiana-Frontier 1768-1789*, 2 vols. Cleveland: Arthur H. Clark Company, 1914.

————. *Texas in the Middle Eighteenth Century*. New York: Russell & Russell, Inc., 1962.

————. *Wider Horizons of American History*. New York: D. Appleton-Century Company, 1939.

Bowers Papers, M. H. 1835-1874. University of Texas, Austin, Archives, MSS.

Brady, Mae Thornton Scrapbook. Mae Thornton Brady (Mrs. O. L.), Round Rock, n.d.

BRAUN, ADOLPH C. *Family History.*

The Broadcaster, Williamson County Public School monthly, County School Superintendent's Files, October 1922-November 1925.

BROWN, FRANK. *Annals of Travis County and of the City of Austin*. Austin, 1903. Austin Public Library Archives. Typed copy.

BROWN, JOHN HENRY. *Indian Wars and Pioneers of Texas*. Austin: L. E. Daniell, 189_?

BROWN, RAY HYER. *Robert Stewart Hyer, the Man I Knew*. Salado: The Anson Jones Press, 1957.

BRYSON, J. GORDON. *Shin Oak Ridge*. Austin: Firm Foundation Publishers, 1964.

BUCKLEY, ELEANOR CLAIRE. "The Aguayo Expedition into Texas and Louisiana, 1719-1722." *Quarterly Texas State Historical Association*, July 1911.

BURLESON, RUFUS C. "History of Robert Hay Taliaferro." *The Guardian*, Waco, Texas, 1899.

"Byrd-Rivers Genealogy." *Williamson County Historical Survey Committee Scrapbook*, comp. Estha Scoggins. Georgetown Public Library.

CAMPBELL, T. N. "The Merrell Site: Archeological Remains Associated with Alluvial Terrace Deposits in Central Texas," *Bulletin of the Texas Archeological Society*, No. 19, 1948; No. 13, 1941.

Carothers Papers, S. D. University of Texas, Austin, Archives. MSS.

CARROLL, HORACE BAILEY. "The Route of the Texan Santa Fe Expedition." Unpublished thesis. University of Texas, 1935.

CARSON, GERALD. "The Piano in the Parlor," *American Heritage*, December 1965.

CASKEY, MRS. R. S. *One Hundred and Twenty Years in Florence, Texas, 1851-1970.* 2d ed. Georgetown: Heritage Printing Co., 1970.

Cassell's Spanish Dictionary. New York: Funk & Wagnalls, 1968.

CASTANEDA, CARLOS E. *Our Catholic Heritage in Texas*, 5 vols. Austin: Von Boeckmann-Jones, 1936.

CAUDLE, ROBERT S. *History of the International-Great Northern Railroad.* (Mimeographed copy.) Missouri-Kansas-Texas Public Relations Office.

Census 1850, et al. U. S. Bureau of the Census.

CHRISMAN, HARRY E. *The Ladder of Rivers*. Denver: Sage Books, 1962.

City of Georgetown. *Revised Civil and Criminal Ordinances of the City of Georgetown, Texas*. Georgetown: Commercial Print, 1906.

"Civil War Tragedy, A." Clipping, page 88, unknown publication. *Gusman Scrapbook* (see interviews).

CODY, C. C. *The Life and Labors of Francis Asbury Mood*. Chicago: F. H. Revell, 1886.

COLLINS, HENRY HILL, JR. *Complete Field Guide to American Wildlife: East, Central and North*. New York: Harper & Row. 1959.

COLTON, J. H. *Map of Texas, 1857*. General Land Office, State of Texas.

COX, ISAAC JOSLIN, ed. *The Journeys of Réné Robert Cavelier, Sieur de la Salle*, I. New York, 1905.

Czech Texans. San Antonio: Institute of Texan Cultures, 1972.

DE CORDOVA, J. *Texas: Her Resources and Her Public Men*. Philadelphia: J. B. Lippincott & Company, 1858.

DE MEZIERES, ATHANASE. *Report on the Texas Indians*. University of Texas, Austin, Archives. MS.

DESHIELDS, JAMES T. *Border Wars of Texas*. Tioga, Texas: Herald Company, 1912.

DE VACA, CABEZA. *The Journey of Alvar Nuñez Cabeza de Vaca and His Companions from Florida to the Pacific 1528-1536*, trans. Fanny Bandelier. New York: A. S. Barnes & Company, 1905.

———. *Relación*, trans. R. E. McDonald, Route 1, Leander, MS.

DOBIE, JAMES FRANK. *The Archives Wars of Texas*. University of Texas, Austin, Archives. MS.

———. *Coronado's Children*. Dallas: Southern Methodist University Press, 1930.

———. *Guide to Life and Literature of the Southwest*. Dallas: Southern Methodist University Press, 1952.

———. *The Longhorns*. Boston: Little, Brown and Company, 1941.

———. *The Mustangs*. Boston: Little, Brown and Company, 1934.

———. *Tales of Old Time Texas*. Boston: Little, Brown and Company, 1928.

DODGE, RICHARD IRVING. *The Plains of the Great West and Their Inhabitants*. New York: Archer House, 1959.

DRAGO, HARRY SINCLAIR. *Great American Cattle Drives*. New York: Dodd, Mead & Company, 1965.

DUMBLE, E. T. *Geological Survey of Texas 1889*. Austin: State Printing Office, 1890.

———. *Second Annual Report Geological Survey of Texas 1890*. Austin: State Printing Office.

DUNN, WILLIAM E. *Transcripts from Santa Cruz de Queretero 1716-1749*, No. 768, "Testimonio de diligencias, Executadas sobre los dos Rios de S^n Fra.^{co} Xavier y San Andres, y demas que dellas Conste, prozesadas por mi D^n Jph. Joaquinde Ecay Muzquiz, por Comision del Exmo Senor Virrey de esta nueba espana. Comprenden a la Provincia de Texas," June-August, 1750. University of Texas, Austin, Archives. trans. from the Spanish by Donna Scarbrough, Georgetown, 1972.

Dyer Papers, W. T. & C. C., 1800-1869. University of Texas, Austin, Archives. MSS.

Easley Family History. Miss Mary Sloan, Easley community.

Elgin Courier, Series on Adam Lawrence by F. S. Wade, "Tales of Early Days in Texas," 1917.

ENGERRAND, GEORGE C. *The So-Called Wends of Germany and Their Colonies in Texas and in Australia*. Austin: University of Texas, Bulletin No. 3417, 1934.

ENGLAND, KEN W. *Old Settlers Association of Williamson County, Texas*. 1966.

Eubank-Stearns Family History. (Photocopy, author's collection.)

FALCONER, THOMAS. *Letters and Notes on the Texan Santa Fe Expedition*. New York: Dauber and Pine Bookshops, Inc., 1930.

FARB, PETER. *Man's Rise to Civilization as Shown by the Indians of North America from Primeval Times to the Coming of the Industrial State*. New York: E. P. Dutton & Company, Inc., 1968.

FISK, FRANCES BATTAILE. *A History of Texas Artists and Sculptors*. Abilene: the author, 1928.

FITZGERALD, HUGH NUGENT. *Governors I Have Known*. Austin, 1927.

FLANAGAN, SUE. *Sam Houston's Texas*. University of Texas Press, 1964.

FLETCHER, BAYLIS JOHN. *The Trail to Wyoming 1879*. University of Texas, Austin, Archives. MS.

FLETCHER, BAYLIS JOHN. *Up the Trail in '79*. ed. Wayne Gard. Norman, Oklahoma: University of Oklahoma Press, 1968.

FORD, JOHN SALMON. *Rip Ford's Texas.* ed. Stephen B. Oates, Austin: University of Texas Press, 1963.

FOSTER, MRS. BETHEL. *History of Weir.* March 9, 1903. MS.

GALLAGHER, PETER. *Diary of the Santa Fe Expedition.* University of Texas, Austin, Archives. MS.

Gammel's Laws of Texas. See Raines, C. W.

GARD, WAYNE. *The Chisholm Trail.* Norman, Oklahoma: University of Oklahoma Press, 1954.

GARRISON, GEORGE P., ed. *Diplomatic Correspondence of the Republic of Texas,* II. Washington, 1911.

GEISER, SAMUEL WOOD. *Naturalists of the Frontier.* 2d ed. rev. Dallas: Southern Methodist University Press, 1948.

Genealogy and Memoirs of Charles and Nathaniel Stearns, and Their Descendants, comp. Mrs. Avis Stearns Van Wagenen. Syracuse, New York: Courier Printing Company, 1901.

GILMORE, KATHLEEN KIRK. *The San Xavier Missions: A Study in Historical Site Identification.* Austin: Archeological Program, State Building Commission, Report No. 16, 1969.

GOODWYN, LAWRENCE. *The South Central States.* New York: Time, Inc., 1967.

GRAND MASONIC LODGE OF TEXAS LIBRARY, Waco, Texas. Organizational Records. (Photocopies.)

GRIFFITH, JOHN H. "Early History of Texas"; "Early History of Williamson County"; "The Webster Massacre"; "Williamson County Court House Sketches"; "Sketches of Early Days in Taylor." Taylor, Texas: City National Bank, n. d. Also in *Frontier Times,* May 1936.

Guide to Georgetown. ed. Clara Stearns Scarbrough. Georgetown: Sun Publishing Company, 1968.

Guide to the Lone Star State, A. n.p., 1940.

HACKETT, CHARLES WILSON, trans. *Pichardo's Treatise on the Limits of Louisiana and Texas,* I. Austin: University of Texas Press, 1931.

Handbook of Texas, The, 2 vols. ed. Walter Prescott Webb. Austin: Texas State Historical Association, 1952.

Hardin, John Wesley, Papers, University of Texas, Austin, Archives. MSS.

HAYES, ROBERT M. *It Really Happened in East Texas.* Ft. Worth: Branch-Smith, Inc., 1971.

HAYSLIP, ANN LEE EUBANK. Letter dated May 31, 1855, from Circleville. Typed copy of MS furnished by Mrs. J. E. Page, 224 Harriman Place, San Antonio, 1959.

HEINSOHN, EDMUND. *Fifty Years—Courtroom, Pulpit.* Austin: San Felipe Press, 1972.

Henderson, Thomas Stalworth Papers, 1915. University of Texas, Austin, Archives. MSS.

HENDRIX, JOHN. *If I Can Do It Horseback.* Austin: University of Texas Press, 1964.

HESTER, GEORGE C. *Southwestern University Megaphone.* March 1, 1967.

HINDS, WALTON. "History of Williamson County 1716-1870." Unpublished thesis. Southwestern University, Georgetown, Texas, 1928.

HINKLE, MILT. "The Dusky Demon," *True West Magazine,* July-August, 1961.

History of Coupland, "Texas Community Improvement Program." Coupland Chamber of Commerce, 1972.

History of Round Rock Lodge No. 227 [Masonic]. June 1959. (Mimeographed.)

HODGE, FREDERICK WEBB., ed. *Handbook of American Indians.* Smithsonian Institution Bureau of American Ethnology, Bulletin No. 30, Part 2, 1912.

HOGAN, WILLIAM RANSOM. *The Texas Republic: A Social and Economic History.* Norman, Oklahoma: University of Oklahoma Press, 1946.

HOHES, PAULINE BUCK. *A Centennial History of Anderson County, Texas.* San Antonio: The Naylor Company, 1936.

Holy Trinity Catholic Church Records, in church, Theon.

Hornsby Papers, Reuben, 1837-1862. University of Texas, Austin, Archives. MSS.

House Committee Report for Republic of Texas, Washington, Texas. 1845. Texas State Library Archives.

Houston Papers (Price Daniel/Andrew Jackson Houston), Nos. 12, 14, File Box 29. "Report of the Select Committee, Mr. Jones chm."; "Message, of His Excellency, The President, in Relation to The Removal of the Archives," January 4, 1843, and January 14, 1843. Texas State Library Archives. MSS.

HUGHES, THOMAS, Memphis, Tennessee. Photocopy of MS, letter written by Thomas P. Hughes, Sr., to his mother, March 31, 1851.

Huling Papers, Thomas Byers, 1836-1856. University of Texas, Austin, Archives. MSS.

HUMBLE OIL AND REFINING COMPANY. *Texas Through 250 Million Years.* rev. ed. Austin: Texas Memorial Museum, 1955.

HUNTER, J. MARVIN. *100 Years in Bandera 1853-1953.* n.p.

HUNTER, MARVIN, ed. *The Trail Drivers of Texas,* 2 vols. 2d ed. rev. Nashville: Cokesbury Press, 1925.

Index to Probate Cases Filed in Texas. No. 246, Williamson County. Works Progress Administration. San Antonio: Statewide Records Project, July 1941.

IRWIN, HOWARD S. *Roadside Flowers of Texas.* Austin: University of Texas Press, 1961.

JACKSON, A. T. *The Fall Creek Sites.* Austin: University of Texas Archaeological Research No. 3802 and Annual Report of the W. P. A., 1938.

————. *Picture-Writing of Texas Indians.* Austin: University of Texas No. 3809, 1938.

JAMES, MARQUIS. *The Raven: A Biography of Sam Houston.* New York: Bobbs-Merrill Company, Inc. (paperback ed.), 1962.

JENKINS, JOHN H., SR. *Personal Reminiscences of Texas History Relating to Bastrop County 1828-1847.* University of Texas, Austin, Archives. (Typed copy.)

JENKINS, JOHN HOLMES III, ed. *Recollections of Early Texas, the Memoirs of John Holland Jenkins.* Austin: University of Texas Press, 1958.

JOHNSON, FRANK W. *A History of Texas and Texans,* 2 vols. ed. Eugene C. Barker. Chicago: The American Historical Society, 1914.

JONES, CLARA. *History of the First Christian Church, Taylor, Texas.* Self published, 1963.

————. *Pillars of Faith.* Taylor: First Christian Church, 1964.

JONES, RALPH WOOD. "A History of Southwestern University 1873-1949." Unpublished dissertation. University of Texas, 1960.

JOSEPHY, ALVIN M., JR. *The Indian Heritage of America.* New York: Alfred A. Knopf, 1970.

JOUTEL, HENRI. *Joutel's Journal of La Salle's Last Voyage,* II. Chicago: The Caxton Club, 1896.

Kemp Collection, Louis W. "Kenney's Fort." University of Texas, Austin, Archives. (Typed copy.)

KEMP, L. W. *The Honor Roll of the Battle: The Complete List of Participants & Personnel on Detached Service* (at San Jacinto). rev. San Jacinto Monument: San Jacinto Museum of History Association, 1965.

KENDALL, GEORGE WILKINS. *Narrative of the Texan Santa Fe Expedition.* 2 vols. New York: Harper and Brothers, 1844.

KENNEDY, WILLIAM. *Texas.* 2 vols. London: 1841.

KENNEY, M. M. "Tribal Society Among Texas Indians," *Quarterly of the Texas State Historical Association,* July 1897.

Kingdom in the Hills Cook Book. 2d ed. Volente, Texas: Anderson Mill Gardeners, Inc., 1962.

KITTRELL, NORMAN G. *Governors Who Have Been and Other Public Men of Texas.* Houston: Dealy-Adey-Elgin Company, 1921.

KNOX, HOWARD. *History of Southwestern University.* Williamson County Historical Survey Committee Scrapbook. (Typed copy.) Georgetown Public Library.

Kuykendall Collection, J. H. Books I, II. University of Texas, Austin, Archives. MSS.

Land Office Map of Texas, January 8, 1856. General Land Office, State of Texas.

LANDERS, JOHN P. *A Brief History of Washington Bower, the Home of Henry Inlo Layne, Lawrence Chapel, Williamson County, Texas.* Prepared for Texas State Historical Marker, January 21, 1971.

Lawhon Family Papers. University of Texas, Austin, Archives.

LE CLERCQ, CHRISTIAN. *First Establishment of the Faith in New France,* II. trans. John Gilmary Shea. New York: John G. Shea, 1881.

LEDLOW, W. F. "History of Protestant Education in Texas." Unpublished dissertation. University of Texas, Austin.

LEHMANN, HERMAN. *Nine Years with the Indians 1870-1879.* University of Texas, Austin, Archives. MS.

Leverett Notebooks, S. Note Book No. 2, "Geological Survey of Texas, 1891." University of Texas, Austin, Archives. MSS.

LEVERETT, S. *The Cretaceous Area North of the Colorado River.* Map 1891. University of Texas, Austin, Archives.

Lone Star State: History of Texas Together with a Biographical History of Milam, Williamson, Bastrop, Travis, Lee and Burleson Counties. Chicago: Lewis Publishing Company, 1893.

LOOMIS, NOEL M. *The Texan-Santa Fe Pioneers.* Norman, Oklahoma: University of Oklahoma Press, 1958.

LUNDELIUS, ERNEST L. and SLAUGHTER, BOB H., eds., *Natural History of Texas Caves.* Dallas: Gulf Natural History. n.d.

LYNCH, JAMES D. *The Bench and Bar of Texas.* St. Louis: Nixon-Jones Printing Company, 1885.

MAKEMSON, W. K. *Historical Sketch of First Settlement and Organization of Williamson County.* Georgetown, Texas: Sun Print, 1904.

MALTBY, W. J. *Captain Jeff or Frontier Life in Texas with the Texas Rangers.* Colorado City, Texas: Whipkey Printing Company, 1906.

MANN, WILLIAM L. *The Andersons: A Father and Two Sons with General Sam Houston's Army.* rev. Georgetown, Texas, 1946. (Mimeographed.) Author's copy.

————. "James O. Rice, Hero of the Battle on the San Gabriels." *The Southwestern Historical Quarterly,* LV, July 1951.

Mann Papers, W. L. University of Texas, Austin, Archives. MSS.

MANZANET, DON DAMIAN. "Carta de Don Damian Manzanet a Don Carlos de Següenza sobre el descubrimiento de la Bahía del Espíritu Santo," *Quarterly, Texas State Historical Association,* II, April 1899.

Map of Railroads 1876. Texas State Land Office.

Marrs and Smith Family Records.

MASTERSON, V. V. *The Katy Railroad and the Last Frontier.* Norman, Oklahoma: University of Oklahoma Press, 1952.

Matthews Papers. In private hands of Miss Myreta Matthews, Liberty Hill, 1973, including *Joseph Neely Matthews Papers, History of Liberty Hill* by W. O. Spencer, *Matthews-Carothers Family Records.* MSS.

Mayes, Ben C. Notebooks. University of Texas, Austin, Archives. MSS.

MAYHALL, MILDRED P. *The Kiowas.* Norman, Oklahoma: University of Oklahoma Press, 1962.

McCALEB, WALTER F. *The Spanish Missions of Texas.* San Antonio: The Naylor Company, 1954.

McCOWN, MRS. SUSAN TURNHAM. "Reminiscences." (Typed copy.)

McLEAN, JOHN H. *Reminiscences.* Southwestern University Archives, Georgetown. MS.

MEMORIALS AND PETITIONS. *Citizens of Western portion of Milam Co. ask for a new county to be called "Clear Water."* Memorial No. 241, File Box 65, Letter M, 2-9/124. Texas State Library Archives.

Memorials and Petitions for the Establisment of a State Normal School at Liberty Hill, File Box 118. Texas State Library Archives.

Milestone, excavated on Jim Adkins farm, northwest of Georgetown.

MILLHOLIN, FRED W. *Personal Papers.* Georgetown, Texas.

MISSOURI-KANSAS-TEXAS RAILROAD COMPANY. *The International-Great Northern Railroad Company,* 1970.

————. *The Opening of the Great Southwest 1870-1970,* 1970. (Mimeographed.)

MOOD, FRANCIS ASBURY. *Autobiography.* Southwestern University Archives, Georgetown. MS.

————. *Narrative of the Facts Relating to the Founding & Progress of Southwestern University 1840-1882.* Southwestern University Archives, Georgetown. MS.

Moody Papers, Dan. University of Texas, Austin, Archives. MSS.

Moody-Robertson Family History. Miss Mary Moody, Taylor, Texas.

MORFI, JUAN AGUSTIN. *History of Texas 1673-1779.* 2 vols. trans. Carlos Eduardo Castañeda. Albuquerque: The Quivira Society, 1935.

MORRELL, Z. N. *Flowers and Fruits in the Wilderness.* St. Louis: Commercial Printing Company, 1872.

Mt. Horeb History. Author's mimeographed copy.

NANCE, BERTA HART. "D. A. Nance and the Tonkawa Indians," *West Texas Historical Association Yearbook,* XXVIII, 1952.

NANCE, JOSEPH MILTON. *After San Jacinto, the Texas-Mexican Frontier, 1836-1841.* Austin: University of Texas Press, 1963.

————. *Attack and Counter Attack: The Texas-Mexican Frontier, 1842.* Austin: University of Texas Press, 1964.

NATIONAL COWBOY HALL OF FAME, leaflet about Bill Pickett. Ponca City, Oklahoma: Ponca City Chamber of Commerce, March 27, 1973.

NATIONAL GEOGRAPHIC SOCIETY. *Wild Animals of North America.* 4th ed. Washington, D. C., 1967.

NEAS, PEARL A. Article quoting C. C. Cody about Southwestern University. n.d.

Nelson Family Papers. University of Texas Archives, Austin. MSS.

Nelson, T. E. Farm Papers. University of Texas Archives, Austin. MSS.

NEWCOMB, WILLIAM WILMON. *The Indians of Texas.* Austin: University of Texas Press, 1961.

New Map of Texas (Johnson). Cattle Trails, 1866-1895. University of Texas, Austin, Archives.

Newspaper Files:

Florence Vidette. Vidette office, Florence. 1914-1948.

Georgetown Commercial. Williamson County Sun, Georgetown. partial files 1900-1918.

Granger News. News office, Granger. partial files 1904 to present.

Taylor Daily Press. Press office, Taylor. 1913-1973.

Taylor Times. Williamson County Sun office, Georgetown, and *Taylor Press* office, Taylor. 1940 to present.

Williamson County Sun. Sun office, Georgetown. 1877 to present.

Miscellaneous other newspapers, as cited in footnotes.

NIXON, PAT IRELAND. *A History of the Texas Medical Association 1853-1953*. Austin: University of Texas Press, 1953.

NUNN, MRS. MATTIE EUBANK, Georgetown. *Family Records*. Mrs. Nunn was granddaughter of Joseph Eubank.

OATES, STEPHEN B., ed. *The Republic of Texas*. Palo Alto: American West Publishing Company, 1968.

Old Comanche Trail, 1835, map. Texas State Library Archives.

OLMSTED, FREDRICK LAW. *A Journey Through Texas: Saddletrip on the Southwestern Frontier*. New York, 1860.

PADDOCK, B. B., ed. *A History of Central and Western Texas*. 2 vols. Chicago: Lewis Publishing Company, 1911.

Palm Family History. University of Texas Archives, Austin. MSS.

Panoramic History of Sam Houston, 1972. Institute of Texan Cultures, San Antonio.

PEARL, RICHARD M. *Geology*. New York: Barnes & Noble, Inc., 1960.

PENNYBACKER, ANNA J. HARDWICKE. *A History of Texas For Schools*, rev. Austin: Mrs. Percy V. Pennybacker, 1908.

People. "Industry and Integrity Are Swedish Texan Characteristics." Newsletter, Institute of Texan Cultures, San Antonio, November-December, 1971.

Pioneer Women Teachers of Texas. Delta Kappa Gamma, n. d.

Poor's Manual of Railroads, 1891.

POTTS, CHARLES S. *Railroad Transportation in Texas*. Bulletin No. 119. Austin: University of Texas Press, 1909.

PREECE, HAROLD. *Lone Star Man, Ira Aten. Last of the Old Texas Rangers*. New York: Hastings House, 1960.

PRESLAR, R. W., and VOLKER, W. *Land Office Map of Texas*, 1851. General Land Office, State of Texas.

RAINES, CADWELL WALTON. *A Bibliography of Texas*. Austin: Gammel Book Company, 1896.

————, ed. *The Laws of Texas 1822-1897*. comp. H. P. N. Gammel, II. Austin: Gammel Book Company, 1898.

————, ed. *Six Decades in Texas or Memoirs of Francis Richard Lubbock*. Austin: Ben C. Jones & Company, 1900.

————. Year Book for Texas, 1901. Austin: Gammel Book Company, 1902.

RAMSEY, GROVER C. *Confederate Postmasters in Texas 1861-1865*. Waco: W. M. Morrison, 1963.

RAND MCNALLY & CO. *Official Map of the State of Texas*. Chicago, 1882.

Ranger Rolls. Texas State Library Archives.

RATLIFF, WALTER B. "Biographical Sketch," *Dudley Hiram Snyder Family Collection*. University of Texas, Austin, Archives. MS.

RED, GEORGE PLUNKETT. *The Medicine Man in Texas*. Houston: Standard Printing & Lithographing Company, 1930.

REDDELL, J. R. and FINCH, RICHARD, eds. *The Caves of Williamson County*. Texas Speleological Survey, II, No. 1, 1963.

REED, ST. CLAIR GRIFFIN. *A History of The Texas Railroads*. Houston: The St. Clair Publishing Company, 1941.

RICHARDSON, WILL MANN, Box 2020, Tyler, Texas, June 5, 1973. Typed copy, letter from Thomas P. Hughes, Sr., to his mother, March 31, 1851.

RISTER, CARL COKE. *Robert E. Lee in Texas*. Norman: University of Oklahoma Press, 1946.

Robertson Papers, Sterling Clack. University of Texas, Austin, Archives. MSS.

ROBINSON, DUNCAN W. *Judge Robert McAlpin Williamson, Texas' Three-Legged Willie*. Austin: Texas State Historical Association, 1948.

Rodriges Letter, Rosita. Written January 15, 1846, from Trading House Post No. 2. University of Texas, Austin, Archives. MS.

ROEMER, FERDINAND. *Texas*. trans. Oswald Mueller. San Antonio: Standard Printing Company, 1935.

ROUND ROCK KIWANIS CLUB. *Round Rock, Texas, U. S. A.* Austin: Sweet Publishing Company, 1972.

Route of the Military Road from Red River to Austin, 1840, map. Texas State Library Archives.

SANCHEZ, JOSE MARIA. "A Trip to Texas in 1828," *Southwest Historical Quarterly*, XXIX, April 1926.

SANDBERG, CARL. *The American Songbag*. New York: Harcourt, Brace & Co., 1927.

SANDOZ, MARI. "Tyrant of the Plains," *The Saturday Evening Post*, June 7, 1958.

SCARBROUGH, CLARA STEARNS, ed. *125 Years of Williamson County, 1848-1973*. Georgetown: Sun Publishing Company, 1973.

SCARBROUGH, DONNA MARIAN MARGARET. Translation of "William E. Dunn Transcript No. 768," *Santa Cruz de Queretero 1716–1750*, June 1972.

SCHUETZ, MARDITH K. "A Report of Williamson County Mound Material," *Bulletin Texas Archeological Society*, No. 28, 1957.

Schwertner, Bernard, Family History, Mr. and Mrs. Herman W. Schwertner, Austin, 1969.

Scoggins Scrapbook. See Williamson County Historical Survey Committee.

SCOTT, ALAN. "He's Our Man on the Moon," *Alcalde*. Austin: The University of Texas, January, 1970.

SCOTT, GARRY. "Dan Moody and the Ku Klux Klan," *Southwestern Magazine*, (Southwestern University, Georgetown), May 1965.

SELLARDS, E. H., ADKINS, W. S., and PLUMMER, F. B. *The Geology of Texas. I.* Austin, University of Texas Press, 1932.

SELLARDS, E. H., and BAKER, C. L. *The Geology of Texas. II.* Austin: University of Texas Press, 1934.

Senate Executive Document 14, Thirty-Second Congress, second session, serial # 660, report of Secretary of State correspondence. Texas State Library Archives.

Seventy-Fifth Anniversary 1882-1957 Zion Lutheran Church, Walburg, Texas.

The 75th Anniversary, St. Peter American Lutheran Church, March 31, 1889—April 5, 1964, Walburg, Texas.

SEVERIN, ERNEST, ALF. L. SCOTT, T. J. WESTERBERG, J. M. OJERHOLM, eds. *Svenskarne I Texas, Ord Och Bild 1838-1918*. Ernest Severin, 1919.

SHAFER, HARRY and CORBIN, JAMES E. *An Appraisal of the Archeological Resources of North Fork, South Fork and Laneport Reservoirs, Williamson County, Texas*. Austin: Texas Archeological Salvage Project, 1965.

SHANNON, TED. "Ira Aten and the Disappearing Killer," *The West Magazine*, February 1965.

SHELBY, CHARMION CLAIR. "St. Denis's Second Expedition from Louisiana to the

Rio Grande, 1716-1719, with Illustrative Documents." Unpublished thesis. University of Texas, 1925.

SHEPHERD, WILLIAM R. *Historical Atlas.* 9th ed. New York: Barnes & Noble, Inc., 1964.

Shiloh Baptist Church History, Texas State Historical Survey Committee, November 27, 1968.

SHUFFLER, R. HENDERSON. "Fighting Frontier Printer," *Texas Magazine,* June 5, 1966.

SHULER MUSEUM, SOUTHERN METHODIST UNIVERSITY, DALLAS MUSEUM OF NATURAL HISTORY, material on caves.

SIMMONS, MARTHA VIRGINIA WEBSTER. *The Webster Massacre.* University of Texas, Austin, Archives. (Typed copy.)

SMITH, A. D. H. *The Real Colonel House.* New York: George H. Doran Company, 1918.

SMITHWICK, NOAH. *The Evolution of a State.* Austin: Gammel Book Company, 1900.

SMYER, JOE PATE. *A Real Texan: Edward M. House.* University of Texas, Austin, Archives. May 23, 1950, typed copy.

Snyder, Dudley Hale [sic] Collection. "Cattle Dairy" [sic] written by T. C. Oatts (1871-1883). University of Texas, Austin, Archives. MS.

Snyder Family Collection, Dudley Hiram. University of Texas, Austin, Archives. MSS.

SONNICHSEN, C. L. *I'll Die Before I'll Run.* New York: Harper & Brothers, 1951.

SORROW, WILLIAM M. *Archeological Investigations at the John Ischy Site: A Burnt Rock Midden in Williamson County, Texas.* Austin: Texas Archeological Salvage Project, No. 18, 1969.

SOUTHWESTERN UNIVERSITY BUSINESS OFFICE. *Board of Curators Minutes, Board of Trustees Minutes,* Southwestern University.

SOUTHWESTERN UNIVERSITY PUBLICITY OFFICE. Biographical material on ex-students George and Herman Brown.

"Special Order No. 7" from Bt. Brg. General Hugh McLeod, Camp Cazneau, June 19, 1841. Texas State Library Archives.

SPARKS, JARED. *The Library of American Biography,* XI. New Orleans: Alston Mygatt, 1848.

SPELL, LOTA M. "The First Text Book Used in Texas," *Southwestern Historical Quarterly,* XXIX.

STEARNS, FRANCES HELEN (EUBANK). *Diary.* MS in hands of author.

————. *Record Book, Circleville, Williamson County, Texas, 1855-1895.* MS. in hands of son, Auburn Clare Stearns, Taylor, 1973.

STEARNS, MARGARET M. TEGGE (MRS. AUBURN CLARE). *Personal Reminiscences;* Family Records and Papers. Taylor, Texas. MSS.

STIFF, EDWARD. *The Texan Emigrant.* George Conclin, 1840.

St. John's Methodist Church Seventy-Fifth Anniversary Book, Georgetown, 1957.

STONE, SAM V., *Papers.* Georgetown Area Public Library Archives.

SUHM, DEE ANN. "Excavations at the Collins Site, Travis County, Texas," *Bulletin Texas Archeological Society,* No. 26, 1955.

SUHM, DEE ANN, KRIEGER, ALEX D., and JELKS, EDWARD B. "An Introductory Handbook of Texas Archeology," *Bulletin of Texas Archeological Society, No. 25.*

Suvenir Svenska Metodist-Episkopalforsamlingens I Georgetown, Texas, Tjugufem-Ars Fest, Hallen den 28 Okt.-1 Nov. 1908. Georgetown: Sun Print, 1908.

SWANTON, JOHN R. *The Indian Tribes of North America.* Bureau of American Ethnology, Bulletin 145, Washington, D. C., 1952.

Swenson-Palm Letterbooks, Translation of Swedish Letters. University of Texas, Austin, Archives.

Taff Notebooks, J. A. No. 4. University of Texas, Austin, Archives.

Taylor and Its Opportunties. Taylor: Taylor Chamber of Commerce, n. d.

TAYLOR, LEE M. *The Texan.* n. p., 1908.

Taylor, Texas, City of Opportunity. Austin: E. L. Steck. c. 1915.

TAYLOR, T. U. "The Stork Rides the Chisholm Trail." *Frontier Times,* November 1936.

Teachers Manual 1902-03, Williamson County Schools. County School Superintendent Office files.

Tegge-Allen Family. comp. Clara Stearns Scarbrough. Georgetown, Sun Publishers, 1967.

TEMPLIN, E. H. *Soil Survey of Williamson County, Texas.* No. 10. Washington, D. C.: U. S. Department of Agriculture Bureau of Chemistry and Soils, 1934.

TERRELL, A. W. "Recollections of General Sam Houston," *Southwestern Historical Quarterly,* October, 1912.

Texas: A Guide to the Lone Star State. n. p., 1940.

Texas Almanac 1857-1873, condensed. ed. James M. Day. Waco: Texian Press, 1967.

Texas Almanac, The. 1857, 1858, 1859, 1860, 1862, 1863, 1867, 1868, 1869, 1871, 1872, 1873, 1904, 1910, 1925, 1966-1967, 1972-1973.

TEXAS ARCHEOLOGICAL AND PALEONTOLOGY SOCIETY, *Bulletin* XIII, 1941.

TEXAS ARCHEOLOGICAL SOCIETY, *Bulletins* XXIV, XXV.

Texas Bar Journal, XXIX, No. 8, September 22, 1966.

TEXAS HIGHWAY DEPARTMENT. *The History of Texas License Plates 1907-1972.* Austin, 1972.

TEXAS STATE RAILROAD COMMISSION. Files of Papers, Office of Odell Charles. Austin, June 24, 1969: "Circular Letter, 1924, Stations of Bartlett and Western Railway"; Letter to Texas State Library June 8, 1956, "Rate Mileage Circular" of February 23, 1932; letter to same on November 3, 1954, on bankruptcy of Bartlett and Western; letter from statistician January 16, 1961 on organization of Bartlett and Western; *Accounting Report* of Bartlett and Western as of June 30, 1918; *Annual Report 1930; Official Record,* vols. XX, XXI, 1911-1912; Letter from Chief Accountant, July 19, 1950, about Austin and Northwestern Railroad Company; *Texas Railroad Commission Reports* for 1892, 1893, 1894.

THRALL, HOMER S. *A Pictorial History of Texas from the Earliest Visits of European Adventurers, to A. D. 1879.* 2d ed. rev. St. Louis: N. D. Thompson & Company, 1879.

Time, February 9, 1970.

True West Magazine, May 1967.

TURNER, MARTHA ANNE. *Sam Houston and His Twelve Women.* Austin: Pemberton Press, 1966.

Twentieth Annual Catalogue of Liberty Normal and Business College, Session 1902-1903. Liberty Hill: Index Print, 1902.

UDDEN, J. A. and BOSE, EMIL. *Review of the Geology of Texas.* Bulletin No. 44. Austin: University of Texas Press, 1916.

U. S. DEPARTMENT OF THE INTERIOR. Geological Survey maps.

U. S. POSTAL DEPARTMENT, Washington, D. C., various typed and photocopied records requested by author about Williamson County post offices.

U. S. Post Office Records, Williamson County, Texas, Miscellaneous File (unbound). National Archives, Washington, D. C.

U. S. Post Office Records of Appointments of Postmasters, Williamson County,

Texas. Vol. XXIX, 1846-1855 and subsequent vols. National Archives, Washington, D. C. Author's personal search, September 1968.

WALLACE, JOHN MELTON. *Gaceta to Gazette.* Austin: University of Texas Press, 1966.

WEBB, WALTER PRESCOTT. *The Great Frontier.* Austin: University of Texas Press, 1951.

———. *The Texas Rangers: A Century of Frontier Defense.* 2d ed. Austin: University of Texas Press, 1965.

Webster's New International Dictionary, 2nd ed. unabridged, 1934.

Welsh Letter, John. Letter dated 1842, 7 January. Texas State Library Archives. MS.

WEST, ELIZABETH HOWARD, trans. "Bonilla's Brief Compendium of the History of Texas, 1772." *Quarterly Texas State Historical Association,* VIII, July 1904.

WESTER, LILLIAN. *Memories of Mine.* Austin, 1952.

WHITE, GIFFORD, ed. *The 1840 Census of the Republic of Texas.* Austin: The Pemberton Press, 1966.

WHITEHOUSE, EULA. *Texas Flowers in Natural Colors.* Austin: privately published, 1936.

WIDEN, CARL T., trans. "A Journey from Sweden to Texas in 1867" by Johannes Swenson. *The Southwestern Historical Quarterly,* LXII, July 1958.

WILBARGER, JOHN WESLEY. *Indian Depredations in Texas.* Austin: Hutchings Printing House, 1889.

WILLBERN, GLEN DEWITT. "A History of Southwestern University." Unpublished thesis. University of Texas, 1928.

Williamson County Centennial 1848-1948. Georgetown: 1948.

WILLIAMSON COUNTY COURT HOUSE RECORDS.
  Auditor's Office Records.
  Cattle Brand Books.
  City Plats.
  Civil, Criminal Court Minutes.
  Commissioners Court Minutes. Vol. A (VI) appears to be missing.
  Deed Records.
  Index, Commissioners Court Minutes. 1848-1898.
  Marriage License Records.
  Police Court Minutes Vol. P, 1849-1859.
  Police Court Minutes Vol. IV, 1860-1871.
  Police Court Minutes Vol. V, 1871-1876.
  Probate Records.
  School Records.

Williamson County Index to Probate Cases Filed in Texas, No. 246. comp. Works Projects Administration. San Antonio, July 1941.

Williamson County Historical Survey Committee Scrapbook. comp. Estha Hole (Mrs. Harold G.) Scoggins. Georgetown Public Library. n.d.

WILLIAMSON COUNTY SCHOOL SUPERINTENDENT'S OFFICE, Georgetown. *Teachers Manual,* 1903.

WINFREY, DORMAN H., DAY, JAMES M., eds. *The Indian Papers of Texas and the Southwest 1825-1916.* Austin: The Pemberton Press, 1966.

WINFREY, DORMAN H., and others, eds. *Indian Tribes of Texas.* Waco: Texian Press, 1971.

WINFREY, DORMAN H., ed. *Texas Indian Papers.* 3 vols. Austin: Texas State Library, 1959, 1960.

WINFREY, DORMAN H. and DAY, JAMES M., eds. *Texas Indian Papers,* vol. IV. Austin: Texas State Library, 1961.

WINKLER, ERNEST WILLIAM, ed. *Journal of the Secession Convention of Texas 1861*. Austin: Texas Library and Historical Commission.

Witte Museum Papers. Witte Museum, San Antonio.

World Book, 20 vols. 1965.

World Book Yearbook, 1965.

WRIGHT, MURIEL H. *A Guide to the Indian Tribes of Oklahoma*. Norman, 1951.

YOAKUM, HENDERSON K. *History of Texas*, 2 vols. New York: Redfield, 1855, 1856.

Zion Lutheran Church 1882-1942, Sixtieth Anniversary (Walburg). Georgetown: Sun Print, 1942.

Index

Abbott Oil Field, 414, 416, 436, 458-59
Accidents, 318, 324, 329, 342, 355, 369-70, 447
Adkins, 414
Agriculture, 19, 29, 41, 45, 67, 72, 81, 155-61, 220, 222, 233-34, 237, 326, 328, 351, 355-61, 440, 442
Aguayo, Marqués de, 55
Ake, 217, 346, 414, 454-55
Alliances, 33, 37, 39, 40, 42, 47, 82, 107-08
Alligators, 14, 30, 100, 134, 283, 333, 414, 459
Allison, 218-19, 346, 414
Althea, 415
Ames, Jessie Daniel, 379
Andice, 6, 219, 345, 347, 415
Anglo-American colonization, immigration, 47, 71-112, 219
Animals: see Wildlife
Ánimas, Arroyo de las, 32, 56-57, 66. See also: Brushy Creek.
Apache Pass, 42, 61
Archaeology, xi, 21-26, 49
Architecture: see Dwellings
Archives War, 101-03
Armfield, 214, 415
Art, artists; arts and crafts, 19, 22, 24-25, 27, 31, 39, 41-42, 44, 49, 79, 80-81, 165, 343-44, 392-94
Athletes, athletics, 8, 43, 49, 398-400, 407-09, 443
Attorneys: see Professions
Austin, Stephen F., 29, 39, 42, 44, 47, 71-72, 78
Austrian immigrants, 220, 347, 451, 456

Automobiles, 269, 348-54, 369-70, 407, 463
Avery, 415
Aviation, 355, 407, 465

Bagdad, 91, 146, 149, 197, 217-18, 224, 226, 318-24, 415
Bailey, 192, 390, 415
Baker, 346, 415
Balcones, 3, 6, 8, 25, 69
Bald Knob, 415
Barker, 15, 415
Bartlett, 14, 219-20, 226, 265, 324-25, 334-46, 416
Bass, Sam, 294-99
Bastrop, Bastrop County, 53, 79, 83, 87, 97, 101, 108, 126, 129, 150, 269, 461
Bean, Alan L., 387-88
Bears: bear meat and fat, 13, 30, 45, 84-85
Beaukiss, 219, 268, 346, 416, 446, 459
Bees, honey, 30, 136-37, 272, 361
Behrnville, 345-46, 416, 456
Bell, 219, 416, 461
Bell County, 73, 139, 148, 324-26, 333, 415-16, 435, 467
Bennett's Mill, 217, 416
Berry Grove, 416
Berry's Creek (post office—Andice), 417
Berry's Creek (Johnsonville), 217-19, 346-47, 417, 459
Berry's Creek (stream), 56, 109-10
Berry's Mill, 161, 235, 417
Beyersville, 219-20, 235, 346, 417
Bicycles, 348-49
Blacksmiths, 113, 160, 164, 236-37, 306-07, 309, 312, 315, 328, 331, 336, 340, 426,

428-30, 435, 441, 444, 446, 451, 458, 460, 462
Block House Fort: see Tumlinson Block House
Blue Hill: see Rice's Crossing
Blue northers, 282
Boggy, 89, 418
Bone Hollow, 45, 106-07, 418
Booty's Crossing, 418
Box Crossing, 418
Bridges, 231-33, 280-81, 311, 353, 426, 434, 438, 443
British, 31
Brizendine Mills, 219, 418
Brooksville: see Florence
Brown, 418, 447
Brown, Elmer "Pet," 399-400
Brown & Root, 344, 353, 363-64
Brown's Gin, 399, 418
Brueggerhoff, 219, 318-24, 418
Brushy, Battle of, 42, 87-89
Brushy (Georgetown), see Georgetown
Brushy Church, 418
Brushy Creek (Round Rock), see Round Rock
Brushy Creek (stream), 4, 16, 19, 46, 53-54, 56-57, 59, 61, 83-85, 139, 141, 169-70, 308, 310, 331, 447
Brushy School, 419
Brushy Valley, 419
Bryan, William Jennings, 350, 463
Buck, 419
Buffalo, 3, 8, 10, 12-13, 26-28, 33, 41, 43-45, 47, 54, 60, 65, 79, 82, 98, 100-01, 105, 112, 125, 129-30, 136, 139, 283, 333, 459
Buffalo Springs, 12, 333, 419, 459
"Bullfrog Line," 343-44
Burkland, 419
Burnap, 419
Burnet County, 11, 93-95, 123, 145-46, 148, 171, 322-24, 366, 455
Busby Crossing, 419
Buttercup (Dodd's Store, Doddville), 219, 234, 261, 419
Buttermilk: see Flat Rock

Caldwell Heights, 171, 219
Camp Cazneau, 98-99, 108, 419
Campgrounds, mineral springs, resorts, 238, 278, 334, 396, 434
Camp meetings, 135, 279, 326, 341, 395, 434, 437, 459-60, 462
Camp Springs, Campground Springs, 9, 234, 419
Cassidy, Butch, and gang, 289
Cazneau: see Camp Cazneau
Cattle, cattlemen, cattle drives, ranching, 12.

43-44, 47, 65, 67, 71, 130, 159, 195-216, 229, 234, 239-41, 284, 304, 329-30, 341-42, 359-60, 400-01, 409, 430, 434, 436, 452, 466
Caves, 6-8, 10-12, 361
Cedar Grove, Cedar Point, 219, 419
Cedar Park, 23-24, 171, 261, 318-24, 346, 420
Cedar Valley (Seed Tick), 219, 420
Centerville, 420
Centre Point, 420
Chalk Ridge, 219, 420, 456
Chandler, Chandler's Branch, 337, 419
Chapel Hill, 419
Chapman City, 419, 459
Cherokee Indians, 260-61, 419
Choctaw Corners, 46, 421
Churches: see Religions
Circleville, 5, 8-9, 21, 55, 65-66, 110, 133, 146, 162-63, 191-92, 199, 217-18, 223, 233-35, 276, 283, 324, 327-29, 346, 421
Circuit riders, 136
Civil War, secession, reconstruction, 159, 183-92, 207
Clark, 421
Clear Creek, 421
Clothing, 31, 33, 35, 41-42, 44, 48, 131, 190-91, 261, 274, 343-44, 407
Cobb Cavern, 7, 24, 361
Cocklebur: see Enterprise
Cocklebur Tavern, 245, 421
Cody, "Buffalo Bill," 427
Colleges and universities, 242-59
Colonization, 58-64, 71-73, 76
Columbia, 421
Comanche Indians, 8, 19, 28, 33, 35, 39, 41-45ff., 58, 65-66, 76, 79, 87-88, 92-97, 101, 107, 133, 141, 171, 189, 425, 429
Comanche Peak, 8, 25-26, 421
Conaway, 421
Concord, 421, 437
Concordia, 421, 462
Condron, 421, 446
Conel, 219, 421
Connell, 421, 426
Conoley, 421
Conservation, 13, 26-27, 358, 411-13
Cooke Settlement, 224, 279, 421, 438
Corn, 41, 60-62, 84, 104, 129-30, 139, 146, 158, 160, 326
Corn Hill, 146-47, 184, 217-18, 220, 226, 253-54, 267, 269, 335-39, 346, 422
Corn Hill Academy, College, 253-54
Cotton, cotton gins, compresses, ix, 6, 130, 159, 163, 191, 233, 237-38, 259, 305-06, 311, 321, 326, 329, 335, 341, 344, 350, 355-59, 409, 431, 433, 436, 438,

440, 443, 445-46, 449, 457-58, 460, 464
Coupland, 268, 330-32, 346, 422
Cow Crossing, 422
Crafts, craftsmen, 17-19, 21, 44, 160, 164, 172, 237, 304, 315, 320, 328, 341, 421, 426, 430, 442, 454, 459-60, 463. Also see specific crafts
Crime, violence, 186-87, 230-31, 283-300, 311, 383-86, 399-400
Crockett, David, 417
Crockett Gardens, 162, 422
Crosby, 422
Cross Roads, 422, 428, 461
Cultural contributions by Indians, 48-50; by Spanish, 66-70
Cummings, 318, 422
Czechoslovakian immigrants, 220, 226, 266, 328, 337, 339, 347, 425, 438, 443-44, 456

Dacus Crossing, 219, 422
Dairying, 358
Damascus, 422
Dams, 375-76, 409, 411-13
Danish immigration, 220, 309, 347, 425
Dare Buzzard, 14, 327, 422-23
Davisville, 423
Deer, deerskins, 13, 27-28, 31, 43, 132, 156
Denis, Juchereau de St., 54-55
Denson, Densonville, 423
Depressions, 276, 344, 406-07
DeVaca: see Nuñez Cabeza de Vaca, Alvar
"Dinky," The, 343-44
Disease: see Illness
Dobie, James Frank, 217, 234, 260, 389, 391-92, 423
Dodd Store, Doddville: See Buttercup
Donahoe Creek, 99, 100, 326, 335, 446
Double File Trail, Crossing, 14, 73-75, 96, 99, 100, 109, 149, 333, 459
Draco (Rock House), x, 46, 219, 423, 448
Dunlop Store, 423
Dwellings, other buildings, architecture
County buildings, 125-26, 151-55, 227-31, 364-65
Homes, furnishings, buildings, 48, 67-68, 127-29, 158, 160-61, 163, 171, 215, 221-23, 235-36, 239-40, 243, 250, 252, 254-55, 257-58, 270-71, 276-77, 280-81, 305, 308-10, 313, 317, 321, 325-28, 332, 334, 342, 347, 350, 356-57, 364-65, 386, 394, 426, 430-31, 439
Indian, 28, 33-34, 41, 44, 69
Log cabins, tents, 86, 111, 113, 125-28, 160, 163, 166, 223, 319, 322
Missions, 58-64

Easley, 423
East View, xi, 423
Eckman, 424, 453
Economy, 3-8, 46-47, 67, 71, 81-82, 87, 129, 155-56, 190-92, 195ff., 233-41, 276, 301-44, 355-65
Elm Grove (Grove Ranch), 424
English, Irish, Scotch, Welsh immigration, 173-81, 248, 347, 349, 433
Enterprise (Cocklebur), 424
Entertainment, 238-41, 374-82, 317-18, 332, 334, 395-402, 441, 451, 453, 457, 465
Eureka Mills, 163, 433
Evans, 329
Everett, 424, 458
Excelsior Mill, 234, 333, 459
Explorers, scientists, 8, 19-20, 51-59, 64-66, 387-88

Fairs, 238, 279, 395-96, 401
Fairview, 424
Fair View, 424
Family names: see Surnames
Fences, 145, 163, 216, 271, 284, 436, 445, 466
Financiers, 363-64
Fires, fire departments, 305-07, 369, 397
First Monday, 239-41, 398
Fisher, 219, 424
Flag, county, 365
Flag Springs, 424, 430
Flat Rock (Buttermilk, Frog Hollow), 14, 346, 424
Floods, 370-75, 396, 425-27
Florence (Brooksville), 5, 8, 146, 149, 162, 198, 217-18, 224, 226, 234, 257-58, 266, 269, 334-44, 346, 418, 424-25
Florence College, 257-58
Flores-Córdova plot, battle, 89-92, 173, 461
Folklore, 8, 19, 92, 397, 405
Food, 11-14, 16-18, 26-30, 33, 41, 43, 48, 59-63, 129-31, 134, 137-38, 191, 271-73, 275, 438, 442, 447, 457, 464
Forts, trading posts, 47, 75, 82-85, 93, 104, 148-50, 460
Fossils, 5-7, 10-12, 100
Four Gospels Railroad, 334-44
Frame Switch, 220, 425
Freighting, 137, 163, 329, 341
French immigration, 220, 347, 451
French trade, exploration, 31-32, 43, 52-53, 65-66
Friendship, 220, 347, 414, 425
Frog Hollow: see Flat Rock

Gabriel Mills, 44, 69, 146, 162, 198, 218, 223, 346, 425-27

Gabriel Peak, 5-6, 427
Gann's Mill (Berry's Mill), 110, 162, 235, 396, 417, 427
Gano, 346, 427
Gardens, gardening, 29, 41, 45, 67, 234, 434-35
Gattis, 427
Gentry, 217, 360, 427
Georgetown (Brushy), 5-8, 16, 49, 52, 133, 145-46, 149, 156-57, 165-68, 184-85, 193-94, 197, 207-11, 223-25, 233, 236-41, 259-64, 269, 275-76, 278-83, 285-86, 289, 298, 315-18, 332-33, 346-47, 418, 428, 466
Georgetown College: see Southwestern University
German immigration, customs, 220, 267, 276, 309, 328, 331, 337, 339, 347, 437-41, 451, 456, 462, 464
Government, 26, 33-34, 38, 41, 43, 67, 75, 81, 358-59, 361, 363-65, 377
Governors, 213-16, 271, 279-80, 300, 337, 360, 363, 376, 380-87, 400, 440
Gower, 219, 428
Grange, 234, 327, 425, 428, 437-38
Granger, 200, 219-20, 226, 233-34, 261, 265-66, 269, 276-77, 324, 326-28, 332-33, 346-47, 357, 428
Granite, 3, 323-24
Gravel Hill, 428
Gravis, 219, 346, 428
Greenwood Masonic Institute, 251, 289, 312
Grove Ranch, 219, 429
Grover, 318, 324, 429
Guentzel, 429

Hardin, John Wesley, 289
Hare, 14, 268, 346, 429
Helwig, 442
Herbal medicine, 16-18, 30, 133, 260-61, 419
Hochkirk, 429, 441
Hog wallows, 8-10, 138, 467
Hopewell, 45, 189-90, 218, 279, 346, 359, 429-30
Horses, mustangs, 10, 28, 31-33, 41, 43-44, 46-47, 54, 65, 67, 86, 269-70, 336, 349, 397-98, 430, 434-35, 438, 443-44, 448
Hospitals: see Medicine
House, Edward Mandell, 363, 377, 439-40
Housing, low cost, 364-65. Also see: Dwellings
Houston, Sam, 39, 47, 75, 79, 81, 101-02, 159, 184-85, 193
Hoxie, Hoxie Crossing, 61, 65-66, 219, 346, 360, 430-31, 455, 466

Huddleston, 431
Hudson, 431
Hunt, Hunt Crossing, 431
Hunting, 26-28, 31, 33, 41, 43-45, 96-97, 105, 136. Also see: Wildlife
Hutto, 5, 218-20, 226, 268-69, 301, 308-09, 346-47, 351, 361, 432
Hyland, 432

Ice, ice houses, 236-37
Illness, disease: 33, 38-39, 47-48, 60, 84-85, 100, 109, 132, 167, 259-61, 369, 452
Indians, vi, x, 8, 13, 16, 18, 21-50, 72, 78, 96, 104, 106-09, 129, 138-39, 141, 260, 340, 419, 425-26, 431, 445-46, 448, 451, 454
Indian leaders, 29, 39-40, 42-45, 73, 82, 87, 93, 107, 159
Prehistoric Indians, 21-26, 420
Tribes, 21-50, 32, 38, 46, 73, 260-61, 421. Also see specific tribes
Industrial revolution: see Agriculture, Automobiles, Aviation, Cotton, Cotton Gins, Industry, Manufacturing, Railroads
Industry, Manufacturing, 67, 131-32, 191, 237-38, 303, 311, 314, 341, 355, 358, 361, 409, 446. See also Crafts, Craftsmen
Inner Space Cavern, 7, 12, 361
Inns, 149, 165-66
Integration, Segregation, 312, 347-48, 444, 449, 453-54.
Irrigation, 61

Jackson, 432
Jarrell, 6-8, 24, 268, 335, 337-44, 346-47, 432
Jenkins (Russell) Crossing, 432
Jenks Branch, 279, 432-33
Jim Hogg School, 433
Johnson, 433
Johnson, Lyndon Baines, 225, 359, 362, 376-77, 390, 404-05, 465
Johnsonville, 433
Johnson, Wofford, 45, 189-90, 429
Jollyville, 146, 148, 218, 433, 445
Jonah (Water Valley), 4-5, 111, 163, 184, 219, 300, 346-47, 350, 433-44
Jones, 434

Katy Lake, 334, 396, 460, 462
Keliehor, 219, 327, 434
Kennedy, 434
Kenney, Dr. Thomas, 45, 81, 83-85, 105-07, 133, 173
Kenney Fort, 49, 73, 83-85, 97, 102-04, 173, 434

Kimbro, 434
Knight s Mill, Knight's Springs, 162, 234, 434
Ku Klux Klan, 379-80, 382-86

Labor, 355-57
Lamar, Mirabeau Buonaparte, 47, 82, 98-99
Land: geology, landscape, ownership, ix, xi, 3-10, 28-29, 37, 39, 42, 45, 47-48, 56-57, 96, 109, 137, 142, 149, 170, 301, 321, 411-13, 434
Land claims, land grants, land speculation, 67, 71-73, 81-82, 85, 124-25, 156, 301, 303, 328
Laneport, 23, 55, 219, 268, 346, 435
Languages, names, 6, 11, 14, 25, 27-28, 32-38, 40-43, 48-49, 52-53, 60, 67-70. Also see: Notes on the Places of Williamson County, 414-67
La Salle, Rene Robert Cavelier, sieur de, 31-32, 52-54
Lawhon Springs, 268-69, 454
Lawler, 341, 435
Lawrence Chapel (Cross Roads), 85-87, 146, 218, 287, 290ff., 346, 435, 459
Leander, 219, 226, 267, 318-24, 346, 436
Lee County, 146, 269, 367
Lee, Robert E., 149
León, Alonso de, 27, 32, 53
Leubner, x, 219, 436
Liberty Chapel, 436
Liberty Hill, 16, 46, 76n., 82, 146-49, 207-11, 217-18, 226, 235, 254-57, 265, 269, 285, 318-24, 346, 359-60, 436-37, 454
Liberty Normal and Business College, 254-57, 437
Lick Skillet: see Primrose
Life style, 127, 157, 220-24, 229-31, 239-41, 270-83, 353, 452
Limestone: see Stone
Lipan Apaches, 33, 37, 39, 41-42, 57-60, 66, 76, 87, 104, 107, 138-39
Live Oak Prairie, 110, 433, 437, 444
Loafer's Glory, 425, 437
Lodges, 144, 167, 222, 226, 312, 320, 327, 426, 430, 437, 446, 457, 463
Lodon, 437
Logan Crossing, 163, 437
Lone Elm, 437
Lone Star, 437
Long Branch, 219, 437
Long Grove, 437

Macedonia, 217, 220, 226, 234, 279, 327, 437
Machu, 220, 235, 438
Mager, 346, 438

Mankin's Branch, 219, 438
Mankin's Crossing, 279, 438
Mariano, Father Francisco de los Dolores y Viana, 58-64
Marrs, 217, 438
Mather Mills, 438
Matsler Heights, 438-39
Matthews, 439
Medicine, 16-18, 30, 34, 36, 259-62, 366-70
Mexican immigrants, 71, 224, 348, 371, 374
Mexico, Mexican government, 33, 47, 51, 71-73, 75-81, 89-92, 102-04
Mézières, Athanase de, 39
Midway, 439, 460, 464
Milam County, Milam District (Viesca), 58-64, 75, 79, 81, 105, 114-15, 122, 139, 145, 148, 302, 367, 415, 418, 421, 424
Miller, 192, 390, 439
Mills, millwrights, 21, 71, 110, 129-30, 149, 161-64, 234-35, 310-12, 321, 333, 340, 355, 417, 431, 433, 436
Mining, 8, 236-37, 320, 341
Misión Nuestra Señora de la Candelaria, 60-64
Misión Nuestra Señora de los Dolores del Rio de San Xavier (Misión San Francisco Xavier de Horcasitas), 59-64
Misión San Ildefonso (Yldefonso), 60-64
Missions, 5, 42, 53, 55, 58-64, 67, 451
Mistletoe, 360
Monadale, 220, 270, 378, 439-40
Moody, Dan, 201, 241, 376-77, 380-86, 403-04
Moravia, 440
Moravian immigrants, 220, 456
Moss's Springs, Moss's Well, 113, 440
Mount Horeb, 425-27, 440
Mount Nebo, 440
Mount Prospect, 337, 440
Movies, 396-97
Mozo, 220, 440
Mullens Hill, 420
Music, dance, 35, 37, 45, 49, 123, 276, 278, 306, 394-96, 444, 461
Mustangs: see Horses
Mustang Springs, 441, 466
Músquiz, Jose Joaquin de Ecay, 61

Naizerville (Neusser), 441
National Cowboy Hall of Fame, 402
Needs More, 441
Negroes, 136, 141, 171, 183-84, 192, 219, 286, 332, 337, 347-48, 367, 374, 390, 422-23, 432, 442, 444, 449-50 454, 456, 463, 467
Neusser, x, 219-20, 441
New Bern, 220-21, 346-47, 441, 466

New Corn Hill, 441, 456
New Hope, 219, 442
Newspapers, communications, 123, 163-64, 220, 262-68, 270, 316, 322, 325, 328, 335, 338, 342, 355, 391-92
Noack (Hochkirk), 214, 346-47, 442
Norman's Crossing, 346, 442
North Gabriel, 442
Northtown, 346, 442
Norwegian immigrants, 220, 312
Nuñez Cabeza de Vaca, Alvar, 26-27, 31, 51-52
Nyman, 442, 460

Oak, 443
Oak Grove, 443
Oil, 5, 302, 414, 416-17, 436, 442, 458-59
Old Round Rock: see Round Rock
Opossum, Opossum Creek, School, 11, 96, 100, 443, 462
Owens, 219, 443

Palacky, 443
Palm Valley, 98, 100, 169, 207, 219, 234, 309, 347
Parage de las Ánimas, 59
Parks, 433
Pear Valley, 443
Pecans, 130-31, 234, 360
Peyton, 219, 340, 443
Philadelphia, 444
Pickett, Willie (Will) "Bill," 400-02
Pilot Knob, 444
Pinilla, Fray Miguel, 63
Pita, Brother, 57
Plants, 11, 15, 59, 61, 65, 67, 96, 447
Pleasant Hill, 218, 346, 444
Plough Handle (Conaway), 438
Polanka, 444
Politics, 33, 75, 111, 262, 359, 377, 449
Pollack (Granger), 327, 444
Pond Spring, Pond Springs, 145, 184, 217, 318-24, 346, 444
Ponton, x, 159, 191, 445
Pope Springs, 445
Population, growth, 141-42, 173-82, 217, 345-48, 409, 411-13
Posey Crossing, 326, 445
Postal system, post offices, x, 46, 145-46, 148-49, 159, 166, 211, 261, 269, 307, 309, 312, 318-24, 333, 335, 343, 346, 351, 354, 372, 414-467
Post Oak Island, 146, 149, 218, 346-47, 445-46
Prairie Lea, 346, 446
Prairie Point, 446
Prairies, prairie grass, 3ff., 12-16, 26-29, 41, 57, 59, 61, 65, 96, 138, 269-70, 282, 304, 445, 467

Prairie Springs, 446, 459-60
Prehistoric animals, 7, 10-12
Presidio San Francisco Xavier de Gigedo, 62
Primrose (Lick Skillet), 335, 446
Professions, 133, 156-57, 165, 168, 259-62
Prohibition, drinking, temperance, 8, 217-18, 230, 239, 247, 254, 267, 284-85, 397-98, 430, 464-65
Puryear, 447

Quarrying, See: Stone

Rabbit Hill, 462
Radio, 354, 396
Railroads, 15, 237, 276, 284, 301-44, 361-63, 407, 430.
Ramón, Captain Domingo, 54-55
Ranger Branch (Braun-Brown), 418, 447
Ratliff, 447
Rattan, 219, 318, 447
Reconstruction, 191-92
Religions, rituals, churches, 25, 35-37, 45-46, 55, 58-64, 67, 71, 114, 134-35, 144-45, 162, 170, 213-14, 219-21, 224-26, 248, 251-53, 258-59, 266, 278, 305, 308, 310, 312, 326; 331-32, 341, 390-91, 414, 467
Rice, James O., 81, 85, 90, 104
Rice's Crossing, 55, 66, 97, 145, 149, 198, 218, 346, 415, 417-18, 447-48
Rivers, Robert Jones, 167-68
Roads, trails, trade routes, highways, streets, 12, 26, 30, 48, 73-75, 96, 145-51, 197-99, 231, 239-41, 269-70, 305, 311, 313, 349-54, 399, 412, 445-46
  El Camino de Arriba, 32, 51, 53, 56-57, 96
  El Camino Real, 32, 51, 53, 56-57
Robbins, 448
Robertson, 448, 461
Rockdale, 401, 403, 458
Rock House (Draco), x, 46, 217, 219, 346, 448
Rocky Hollow (Yarborough/Yarbrough), 449, 467
Round Rock (Brushy Creek), 6-8, 20, 112-13, 133-34, 145, 149, 161-62, 194, 197, 207-11, 217-18, 223-24, 236-37, 251-53, 258-59, 264, 269, 279, 285, 289, 294-99, 301, 310-17, 346-47, 370, 418, 443, 449-50
Round Rock Academy-College, 251-53, 312
Rowe, 450
Running Brushy, 146, 218, 318-19, 450
Rusk, Senator Thomas Jefferson, 321-22
Russell Crossing, 432
Rutledge, 219, 318-19, 444-45, 450

St. John (Armstrong), 339-44, 450
St. Luke (Atkinson), 339-44, 450
St. Mark (John Camp), 339-44, 450
St. Matthew (Caffrey), 339-44, 450
St. Paul, 450
Salado, 5, 69, 339-40
Saloons, taverns, inns, 155, 168, 218, 247,
    284, 305-07, 309, 311, 313, 327-28,
    340, 457
Salyer, 450
Sam Houston School, 450
Sam Smith Springs, 268, 450, 454
Sanders, 450
Sandoval, 69, 219-21, 346-47, 450-51
San Gabriel, 16, 148, 451
San Gabriel County, 115
San Gabriel Peak, 451
San Gabriel River, ix, xi, 4, 9, 14, 16, 19,
    21, 53, 56-57, 64-66, 69, 82, 96, 100,
    109-10, 411-13
Santa Fe Expedition, 14, 74, 97-101
Santa María de la Visitación Crossing, 61
Santa Rosa de Viterbo Crossing, 61
San Xavier, 29, 32, 51, 53-64, 67, 69
San Xavier Missions, 60-64
San Ygnacio, 56
Saul's Mill, 451
Schools, education, educators, 102, 113,
    134-35, 143-44, 170, 222, 241-59, 305,
    312, 337, 388-90, 414-67
Schwertner, 220, 335-44, 346-47, 451-52
Seed Tick, 219, 420
Seward Junction, 439, 452
Seymour, 219, 452
Shaw, Jim, 73, 107
Shiloh (south-central), 111, 114, 308, 452-
    53
Shiloh (southeast), 219, 453
Signs, signals, symbols; sign trees, iii, iv, vi,
    30, 43, 48, 84, 419
Silent Grove, 453-54
Siloam, 268, 454
Slaves, Indian, 43
Slaves, Negro, 141, 171, 183-84, 219, 312,
    454
Small, x, 219, 454
Smallpox, 39, 47, 60-61, 100, 132-33, 259,
    369, 452
Smart, 455
Smith, Preston, 337, 376, 386-87, 440
Smith School, 455
Smithwick, Noah, 44-45, 79, 82, 87, 97,
    105-06, 123, 134, 164, 171-72, 300
Soap, 18, 273
Somerset, 219, 455, 464
Sommerville, 455
Sore Finger Creek, 425
South Gabriel, 146, 148, 455

Southwestern University, 135, 242-51, 389
Spain, Spanish exploration and colonization,
    10, 31, 33, 39, 41, 43, 47, 51, 53, 57,
    65-66
Sparks, John, 213-16, 271, 279-80, 360,
    363, 376, 400
Springtown, 455
Stagecoaches, stagecoach routes, 108, 145-
    48, 166, 218, 446
Stapp, 415, 455
Star Mill, 162, 436
Stauffer, 455
Stevenson, 455
Stiles School, Stiles Switch, 219, 301-03,
    346-47, 455, 458-59
Stone, limestone, quarrying, masons, 3-6,
    164, 235-36, 311, 314, 323, 341, 436,
    465
Stony Point, 455
Stores: early village, 114, 166, 218, 452
Street car, mule-drawn, 238-39
Strickland Grove, 455-56
Strikes, 362, 407
Stringtown, 456
Structure, 346, 456
Sunset Lane, 439, 456
Surnames. See also: U.S. Census 1850,
    pages 173-82; County Road Commit-
    tees, pages 150-51

    Abbey, 267
    Abbott, 416, 436, 459
    Adams, 260, 312, 340-41, 424
    Addison, 428
    Aderholt, 464
    Agreneva-Slaviansky, 394
    Ahlberg, 423
    Ahren, 430
    Ake, 141, 165-68, 183-84, 188, 283, 334,
        384, 414
    Albers, 331
    Alden, 259
    Alexander, 153, 164, 166, 184
    Alford, 265, 267
    Allcorn, 465
    Allen, 81, 119, 121, 134, 141, 149, 164-
        65, 183, 249, 263, 265-66, 300, 384,
        397, 406, 408, 435, 451, 461-62
    Allison, 204, 223, 360, 368, 376, 414,
        430-31
    Amato, 303
    Ambrose, 303
    Ames, 379
    Anderson, 80, 82, 105, 110, 112, 114, 119,
        121-22, 124-25, 133, 153, 161, 168-69,
        172, 193, 219 n., 243, 259-60, 300,
        304, 313, 315-16, 333, 431, 449
    Andres, 462-63
    Andrews, 448

Surnames, continued
Angel, 83
Armfield, 448
Armstrong, 164-65, 305, 325, 336, 416, 428
Arnett, 200-01
Arnold, 416, 436
Arnot, 447
Arrington, 458
Aschen, 441
Asher, 110, 119, 172, 426
Aten, 242, 289-90, 300, 443, 450
Athas, 224, 237-38
Atkin, 237, 368, 407
Atkinson, 340-41, 424-25
Atwood, 415, 457
Auglin, 433
Austin, 416
Avent, 327
Averitt, 330
Avery, 80, 110, 184, 202, 216, 415, 417, 448
Babcock, 149, 319
Baca, 266
Bachman, 441
Bachmayer, 417
Bacon, 119, 453
Bailey, 192, 390, 415
Bainbridge, 461
Baine, 398
Baines, 225
Baker, 119, 164, 255, 415
Banta, 125
Barber, 336
Barcus, 250
Barker, 79, 110, 125, 184, 224, 300, 401, 415-17
Barlow, 336
Barnes, 322, 436
Barnett, 438
Barnhart, 74, 83-84, 101
Barr, 368
Barrington, 256, 322, 437
Barron, 263
Bartlett, 325, 416
Barton, 90, 121, 190, 235, 255-56, 430, 432, 454
Bartosh, 266, 428
Bauchman, 320, 341
Beall, 243, 316
Bean, 387-88
Beard, 112, 326, 328
Beardan, 336
Beaver, 333
Beck, 336
Becker, 417
Behrens, 416, 456, 462

Belcher, 327, 330
Belford, 389
Belk, 336
Bell, 197, 416
Benad, 451
Benedict, 341, 424
Bennett, 341, 416
Benold, 368
Bentley, 436
Bently, 218
Bergstrom, 333, 398, 432, 462
Bernard, 464
Berry, 79-80, 104, 110, 119, 122, 125, 161, 164, 300, 333, 417, 428, 459
Beyer, 417
Biles, 335
Bisang, 304, 307
Bishop, 117, 250
Bittick, 426
Black, 269, 285, 311-12, 316, 336, 430
Blackman, 336, 374
Bland, 265, 267, 330
Blankenship, 121
Blanton, 203, 309, 432
Bleeke, 463
Blevins, 341
Blue, 283
Bobo, 341
Boeckmann, 451
Boehm, 464
Boeneman, 331
Bogart, 433
Bohac, 266
Bolding, 203
Bolen, 312
Bomine, 117
Boone, 449
Booth, 306, 330, 349, 398, 449
Booty, 349, 364, 437
Bostic, 429
Boswell, 255
Bouchelle, 149
Bouffard, 435, 441
Bowen, 336
Bower, 267
Bowers, 371
Bowles, 340
Bowmer, 444, 446
Box, 418
Boyce, 144, 203
Boyd, 306, 333, 465
Boylen, 317
Bracker, 466

Bradford, 306-07
Bradley, 306, 330
Brady, 333, 341, 373, 438
Braker, 460
Branagan, 339, 343-44
Branch, 144, 319, 433
Bratton, 134, 322, 437, 451
Braun, 418, 462-63, 465
Brazelton, 428
Bredthauer, 462
Brenecke, 333
Brewster, 341, 354
Bridges, 336
Bright, 164
Bristol, 336
Brite, 205
Brittain, 168, 218
Brizendine, 418, 426
Broach, 422
Broadnax, 306
Brooks, 267, 333, 336, 340, 364, 428, 446
Brookshire, 326, 437
Brother, 106
Brown, 227, 242, 253, 264, 266-67, 305, 326, 328-29, 334, 336, 344, 353, 363-64, 369, 378, 398-400, 408, 418, 421-22, 424-25, 427
Bruce, 202, 300, 433
Brunner, 374, 403, 405, 456
Bryant, 227
Bryson, 147-48, 155, 211, 227, 321, 453
Buchanan, 336
Buchhorn, 465
Buckman, 79
Bucy, 434
Bullington, 461
Bunker, 81
Burden, 143, 429
Burkett, 275, 330
Burkhardt, 237, 278
Burkland, 419
Burleson, 383-86
Burnap, 419, 465
Burns, 204-05, 336, 434, 440, 442, 448
Burran, 465
Burris, 117, 333, 433
Burrough, 453
Burroughs, 453
Busby, 419, 434
Butts, 421
Bybee, 437

Surnames, continued
Bytell, 435
Caesar, 429
Cain, 458
Caldwell, 74, 171, 251, 419
Callcott, 393
Cameron, 263
Cammach, 336
Camp, 327
Campbell, 383, 434
Caninenberg, 441
Cannon, 117, 305, 425
Carlisle, 336
Carlow, 435
Carlson, 460
Carothers, 157-59, 191, 269-70, 319, 444-45
Carstarphen, 306
Carter, 348
Cartledge, 155
Caruthers, 458
Casey, 340, 423
Cashion, 319-20
Caskey, 144, 340-41, 425
Casner, 117, 119
Cassens, 463
Castleberry and var., 83, 90-91, 105-06
Caswell, 349
Cates, 255, 263, 265, 354
Cavanaugh, 188
Cervenka, 438
Chadwick, 117
Chalk, 103-04, 109, 117, 125, 162, 340
Chamberlain, 453
Chandler, 74, 84, 119
Chapman, 263, 320, 340, 466
Charles, 283
Chessher, 219, 428
Childress, 79
Chinneth and var., 80, 83-84, 164
Chreitzberg, 428
Chrietzberg, 228, 245, 279
Christian, 205
Christianson, 461
Christie, 314
Chumley, 237
Church, 435
Clamp, 154, 167, 224
Clark, 307, 325, 368, 397, 419, 421, 431
Clifton, 117, 164
Clopton, 81

Cloud, 436
Cluck, 202, 205, 228, 297, 319, 420, 436
Cobb, 371-72
Cochran, 219
Cody, 242, 248, 279, 389
Coffee, 185, 261
Coffield, 434
Cole, 223, 255, 313, 434
Coleman, 241, 255, 368
Collins, 117, 184, 304, 465
Comer, 338
Compton, 74, 109, 463
Conaway, 421, 439
Condra, 336
Condron, 421
Conlee, 336, 424
Connell, 80, 291, 427, 437
Connor, 107
Conolee, 80
Conoley, 349
Contesse, 441
Cook, 119, 305, 330, 333, 336, 424, 434
Cooke, 265, 312, 372, 421, 434
Coon, 320
Cooper, 237, 241, 263, 304, 313, 464
Copeland, 331, 422
Cosby, 340
Cottingham, 314
Council, 428
Coupland, 331, 398, 422
Courtney, 83, 105-06
Cowan, 117, 122, 125, 166
Cowart, 336
Cox, 144, 322
Craft, 336
Craven, 319, 436
Crawford, 316, 349
Crawsin, 433
Crayton, 423
Crim, 426
Critz, 241, 377, 383, 385, 407, 444
Crockett, 435
Cronin, 338, 343-44, 393-94
Crosby, 79
Crow, 164
Crowley, 349
Crozier, 448
Crum, 203
Crumley, 260-61, 419-20

Cuba, 425
Cunningham, 416, 433
Curtice, 79
Cyrus, 434
Dabbs, 456
Dabelgott, 451
Dacus, 422
Dalrymple, 74, 81, 109, 117, 122, 126, 146, 172, 218, 224, 244, 261, 300
Dalton, 163
Damon, 81
Damron, 417
Danforth, 261, 328, 398
Daniel, 317, 368, 379
Daniels, 465
Darlington, 81, 95
Darrell, 398
Daugherty, 317
Davenport, 432
Davidson, 405, 415, 433
Davis, 107, 251, 309-10, 312, 328, 336, 340, 406, 423, 426, 432, 449
Day, 255
Dean, 335
Delenaugh, 327
Dellinger, 214, 287
Denman, 266, 322
Dennis, 426
Denson, 199, 325-26, 328-29, 423, 437-38
Dewitt, 164
DeWitt, 449
Dial, 430
Dickey, 367
Dickson, 304-05, 331
Diggs, 449
Dilano, 437
Dill, 333
Dilley, 214, 222-23, 314
Dimmitt, 242-43, 315-16
Doak, 219, 238-39, 260, 282, 366
Dobbins, 119
Dobbs, 253
Dobie, 389, 391-92
Dodd, 261, 419, 433
Doehre, 462
Doerfler, 440
Doering, 220, 462-63
Dolan, 398
Dollahon, 415
Domel, 463
Donnell, 422
Donovan, 104

Surnames, continued
Dorsey, 164
Douglass, 458
Dowda, 465
Downey, 267-68, 337-38
Draeger, 463
Drozda, 464
Drum, 336
Duckett, 449
Duffy, 428
Duke, 385
Dunbar, 454
Duncan, 452
Dunlop, 153, 426
Dunn, 279, 336, 422
Durant, 201, 325
Dyches, 110, 117, 133, 160, 183, 326, 421
Dycus, 453
Dyer, 84, 107, 149, 169, 205
Dykes, 227
Eanes, 309, 330, 448
Easley, 160, 184, 241, 330, 423
Echols, 328
Eckman, 424, 453
Edens, 398, 409, 431
Ederington, 326, 463
Edmund, 283
Edmundston, 79
Ellington, 436
Emerson, 333
Emmett, 320
Enochs, 428
Eppstein, 303
Erwin, 428
Estes, 429
Ethridge, 143
Eubank, 144, 155, 160, 168, 188-89, 191, 328-29, 416, 421
Evans, 204, 320, 384, 458
Evansted, 437
Everette, 437
Fain, 238
Fairchild, 398
Faires, 444-45
Farley, 308-09
Farmer, 336
Faubion, 110, 218, 319-20, 327, 420, 432, 436, 465
Faykus, 464
Feaster, 331, 427
Felder, 446
Felps, 385
Felthouse, 422

Felton, 325
Ferguson, 74, 340
Field, 321
Finch, 7, 251
Fine, 431
Fish, 13, 49, 434
Fisher, 229, 261, 327-28, 340, 424
Fisk, 80, 110, 121, 125, 144, 150, 241, 319, 461
Fitzgerald, 154
Flake, 307
Flanagan, 389
Fleager, 234, 341
Fleming, 109, 117, 251, 260, 316, 322, 428
Flinn, 309, 432
Floeckinger, 366
Forbes, 314, 428, 433, 439, 449
Force, 84-85
Ford, 255, 461
Forsvall, 462
Fort, 446
Forwood, 238, 314, 398
Foster, 228, 262-64, 266, 304, 314, 316, 333, 335-36, 370, 422, 428, 453, 465
Fowler, 416
Fox, 265, 267, 392
Frame, 425
Frank, 336
Franklin, 121
Franks, 201
Franze, 331
Freestone, 119
Frerichs, 417
Freund, 306
Fridge, 268
Frink, 304, 306, 456
Frymire, 336, 443
Fuchs, 442, 458
Fuessel, 441
Gaddy, 368
Gage, 80, 428, 446
Gahagan, 462
Gaines, 279, 283, 406
Galler, 441, 451
Galt, 336
Gannaway, 340
Ganns, 235
Gano, 219
Gans, 168
Gant, 432
Gardner, 188, 266, 268, 328, 437, 446, 454

Garner, 143, 204, 326, 423, 429
Garrett, 354
Garry, 237
Garver, 395
Gaston, 331
Gate, 464
Gattis, 427, 433-34
Gattlin, 446
Gee, 461
Gentry, 427-28
German, 165
Giddens, 436
Gilden, 307
Gilleland, 104
Gillespie, 316
Gillett, 143, 162-63, 389, 419
Gilliam, 329, 421
Gillis, 464
Ging, 331
Girvin, 354
Glascock, 105, 114
Glasscock, 87, 124, 126-27, 162, 166, 242
Glenn, 433
Glober, 314
Goetz, 331, 422
Goff, 79, 398
Goldstein, 305, 330
Goldsticker, 303
Gooch, 125-26, 162, 164, 370, 434, 466
Goodlett, 372, 396-97
Gordon, 451
Gossett, 429, 463
Gould, 405
Gower, 428
Graham, 121, 260, 320
Grammar, 433, 453
Grant, 253, 322, 426, 437
Granzin, 462
Graves, 76, 168, 316, 377, 383-85
Gravis, 80, 104, 428
Gray, 125, 334, 425
Grayson, 316, 336, 422
Green, 227, 242, 435
Gregg, 370
Grice, 188
Griffin, 336, 435
Griffith, 216, 330, 395
Griggs, 341
Grimes, 295-96
Gross, 305
Grouch, 453
Grumbles, 336
Guentzel, 416, 429

Surnames, continued
Guthrie, 326, 437
Haeber, 337
Hager, 336
Hague, 463
Hair, 267, 325, 335, 385, 422
Hajek, 458
Haley, 202
Hall, 255
Hallan, 398
Ham, 449
Hamilton, 79, 125, 255, 304, 319-20, 328, 330, 385, 389, 431, 433, 447, 452
Hanna, 112, 201-02, 218, 444
Hannan, 456
Hansen, 309, 425
Haralson, 336
Harber, 384
Hard, 434
Hardeman, 325
Hargis, 330, 448
Harness, 164
Harper, 144, 165, 168, 242, 260, 316, 336, 446
Harrel, 466
Harrell, 84, 104, 110, 113, 119, 122, 125, 130, 134, 164, 310, 312, 359-60, 396, 433, 449
Harris, 119, 168, 264, 288, 311, 313, 428, 434
Harrison, 81, 263, 336
Hart, 117, 298, 314, 428
Hartman, 329
Harvill, 336-37
Hasty, 348
Hausenfluck, 333
Hausenfluke, 465
Havelka, 458
Hawkins, 204, 265, 267, 316, 339, 437
Haygood, 256, 266, 342
Haynes, 341, 449
Haynie, 306-07
Hays, 336, 433
Hayslip, 160, 188, 283, 306, 328
Hazelwood, 436
Heidt, 247
Heinatz, 319-20, 415, 436
Hejl, 464
Helms, 434

Helmuth, 331
Helwig, 429, 442
Hemphill, 243
Henderson, 190, 242, 262, 264, 312, 428
Henkes, 460
Henna, 363, 368
Henry, 420
Herrick, 314
Heselmeyer, 460, 466
Hester, 389-90, 392
Hewitt, 437
Hibbons, 79
Hickman, 255, 377, 465
Hicks, 373, 456
Highsmith, 80, 295, 314
Hill, 330, 423, 449
Hinds, 391
Hobbs, 453
Hodgen, 144
Hodges, 247, 269, 315, 461
Hogan, 306, 335, 437
Hoke, 456
Holder, 257, 342
Hollingsworth, 432
Hollomon, 435
Holman, 306-07, 432
Holmquist, 264
Holt, 450
Homeyer, 462
Hood, 266
Hooper, 330
Hoover, 341
Horn, 250
Hornburg, 461
Hornsby, 79, 85, 90, 104, 110, 119, 125, 319
Hotchkiss, 104
Houghton, 126, 341, 416
House, 363, 377-79, 439
Houston, 184-85, 192-94, 260-61, 313, 316
Howard, 458
Howell, 341
Hoxie, 330, 424, 430
Huddleston, 91, 319, 415, 432
Hudon, 164, 440
Hudson, 241, 255-56, 309, 331
Huggins, 336
Hughes, 117, 156-57, 167, 184, 190, 194, 211, 219, 231, 242-43, 247, 261, 289-90, 300, 315, 340, 389
Hughs, 437

Humble, 320
Humphrey, 432
Hunt, 218, 431
Hunziker, 331
Hurley, 322
Huster, 320
Hutchins, 242
Hutchinson, 456
Hutchison, 437, 448
Hutto, 308-09, 432, 446
Hyde, 398, 448
Hyer, 238, 248ff., 388-89
Hyland, 80, 450·
Ilse, 336
Inman, 432
Irvin, 454
Irvine, 237
Isaacs, 420
Ischy, 109, 171, 237, 441
Israelson, 169, 234
Ivey, 263
Jackson, 204, 218, 325, 336, 338, 340-41, 415, 422, 425, 435-36
Jacob, 415, 463
Jacobson, 460
James, 458
Janosec, 458
Jarrell, 337, 435
Jechow, 451
Jenkins, 112, 136, 263, 300, 425, 429, 432-33
Jennings, 165, 320-21, 461
Jester, 74, 450
John, 162, 340
Johns, 111, 366, 452
Johnson, 74, 81, 91, 112, 164, 172, 188, 219, 234, 335, 349, 351, 408, 419, 429, 435, 450, 458, 460
Johnston, 164, 416
Jolly, 433
Jones, 306-07, 327-29, 337, 383, 428-29, 432, 465
Jordan, 340, 416, 453
Julin, 201
Jungmichel, 457, 462-63
Justice, 461
Juvenal, 111-12, 203-04, 398, 452-53
Kaderka, 440
Kamp, 199, 304-06
Kalmbach, 416, 457
Kasperik, 463
Kautz, 441

Surnames, continued
  Kavanaugh, 264-65
  Keahey, 263
  Keeling, 338
  Keliehor, 327, 330, 434
  Keller, 305
  Kendall, 437
  Kendrick, 144
  Kennedy, 204, 223, 434, 442
  Kenney, 45, 81, 83-85, 105-07, 133, 173, 434
  Kerr, 447, 465
  Key, 218, 261
  Kidd, 446
  Kimbro, 119, 121, 125, 128, 164, 330, 415, 434
  Kimmons, 331
  Kimson, 164
  King, 146-47, 253, 333, 335, 371, 422, 429, 465
  Kirk, 343
  Kirkpatrick, 312, 435-36
  Klein, 445
  Klimicek, 441
  Knauth, 327, 465
  Kneip, 331
  Knight, 110, 114, 121, 133, 172, 204, 233-34, 266, 319, 428, 434-35
  Kolar, 458
  Koontz, 443
  Kopecky, 458
  Koppel, 314
  Kott, 457
  Krause, 462
  Krauss, 457, 462
  Krebs, 331
  Krieg, 441, 458
  Kritser, 205, 392
  Kroeger, 451
  Kroschewsky, 222-23, 305
  Kubacak, 458
  Kuehne, 463
  Kuhn, 442, 463
  Kuler, 325
  Kurecka, 458
  Kurio, 463
  Kuykendall, 142, 201, 205, 214, 250, 300, 312, 330, 400, 436, 442, 452
  Kyle, 187
  Ladd, 74, 84
  Land, 336, 464
  Landrum, 289, 363, 435

Lane, 265, 296-97, 435, 437
Lang, 76
Lange, 429
Lansford, 119
LaRue, 74
Lauck, 320
Laughlin, 201
Laurence, 422, 436, 453
Lawhon, 268-69, 359, 377, 385, 448, 454, 456
Lawler, 218, 340
Lawrence, 81, 85-87, 143, 197, 300, 422, 427, 435-36, 453
Laws, 335-36
Lawson, 84, 169
Laymon, 114
Layne, 436
Lea, 335, 422
Leake, 389
Leatherwood, 255, 461
Leavell, 270
Ledbetter, 113, 312
Lee, 106-07, 164, 169, 188, 224, 253
Lehmann, 451
Lehmberg, 398
Lemaster, 416
Lemmer, 451
Leonard, 307
Leschber, 336, 429
Leshikar, 429
LeSueur, 163, 241, 256, 450, 455
Letting, 328
Leubner, x, 456-57
Lewis, 155, 164, 168, 330-31, 336, 348, 405, 425, 429
Lewiston, 455
Liese, 463
Lindell, 372
Linder, 414
Lindquist, 215, 363
Lindsey, 326
Linehan, 306
Lister, 465
Littleton, 429
Lloyd, 144, 330, 456
Lockett, 263, 265, 268
Logan, 241, 436-37
Long, 305-07, 341, 408
Loper, 456
Lord, 363
Love, 80, 117, 168, 205, 234, 315, 340-41

Lowe, 384, 406
Loyd, 308
Lundblad, 461-62
Lundelius, 358
Luttrell, 464
Lyda, 438
Lydic, 306-07
Lyle, 264
Lynch, 341
Lyons, 384
Machu, 235, 428
Mackay, McKay and var., 117, 164, 166, 398, 428
Maddox, 312, 435
Magill, 80-81, 320
Magruder, 255
Makemson, 110, 114, 121, 125, 168, 172-73, 228, 243, 261-62, 292, 389, 391
Malone, 440
Maltby, 189-90, 200, 427
Mankin, 184, 431
Mann, 124, 303, 333, 391, 448
Mantor, 267, 397
Marac, 458
Marcus, 429
Maresh, 266, 464
Marley, 319
Marquadt, 325
Marrs, 336, 391, 428-29, 438
Marschalk, 164, 262, 428
Marshall, 119, 121, 125
Martin, 326, 368, 428-29, 449, 458, 461
Martinez, 348
Mason, 107, 319-20, 415, 432, 436
Massey, 425
Masterson, 312, 336, 463
Matejowsky, 335, 452
Mather, 153, 162, 204, 300, 372, 398, 425-26, 446
Mathis, 398
Matsler, 166, 342, 438-39
Matthews, 106, 163, 218, 256, 265, 300, 439, 461
Matyastik, 464
Matysek, 406
Mawrey, 256
Max, 303
Maxson, 398
Mays, 80, 113, 205, 251,

Surnames, continued
  269, 311-12, 395, 443,
  450
Mazoch, 425, 440
McBride, 436
McCann, 463
McCarty, 335-36, 423,
  435
McCaskill, 341
McChristian, 144
McClain, 425, 432
McConchie, 354
McCool, 305
McCormick, 432
McCoy, 265
McCutcheon, 110, 417,
  448, 452
McDaniel, 335, 428
McDonald and var., 119,
  285, 300, 311, 336,
  433
McDowell, 341
McFadin, 80, 110, 125,
  160, 162, 183, 200,
  218-19, 233, 306-07,
  329, 419, 421, 429
McFarland, 188, 311, 434
McFarlin, 437
McGaffey, 126, 165-66
McGinnis, 427, 463
McGuire, 233, 235
McHorse, 80, 327, 437-
  38
McKean, 336
McKeown, 420
McKinney, 429
McKnight, 325, 416
McLaren, 330
McLaughlin, 327, 406,
  428
McLean, 80, 263, 389
McLellan/McLennan, 76
McMillan, 183
McMurray, 224, 242
McNeil, 435
McNeill, 227
McNiel, 164
McNutt, 80
McRall, 419
McRea, 336
McSpaddin, 81
Meade, 305, 330
Medley, 409
Meeks, 373, 421
Meiske, 460, 466
Melasky, 199, 224, 304-
  06, 398, 451
Meldrum, 305

Mendel, 330
Mercer, 105, 451
Merkord, 441
Merrell, 74, 84, 98, 104-
  06, 172, 200, 205,
  223, 300
Messer, 465
Metcalfe, 432
Mewhinney, 392
Meyer, 441, 466
Michalek, 398
Middleton, 446
Miersch, 457
Mikeska, 366
Mikulencak, 266, 336
Milbourn, 307
Mileham, 163, 184, 227,
  433
Miles, 255
Miller, 101, 119, 155,
  163, 168, 192, 266,
  268, 314, 322, 330,
  336, 341, 390, 429,
  432, 435, 451
Millholin, 264, 317, 465
Ming, 340
Minor, 305
Moegle, 408
Mohle, 264
Moldenhour, 327
Monday, 308-09
Monger, 336
Monk, 244
Monroe, 227
Montgomery, 183, 243,
  340
Mood, 244ff.
Moody, 201, 219, 241,
  307, 330, 376-77, 380-
  86, 403-04
Moore, 331, 396, 425,
  429, 458
Moreland, 425
Morey, 114, 452
Morgan, 336
Morrell, 335
Morris, 305, 333, 336
Morrow, 168, 192-93,
  203, 227, 243-45, 247,
  313-14, 428
Morse, 269
Moses, 164
Moss, 80, 110, 119, 134,
  325, 440
Moyers, 465
Mrazek, 336, 457
Muir, 266
Mullen, 218, 425

Mumford, 360, 422, 430
Muncill, 283
Munn, 447
Munro, 255, 322
Munson, 406-07, 461-62
Murphy, 275, 330
Murray, 306, 340
Mussil, 428
Myrack, 453
Naizer, 441
Napier, 168, 304, 428
Nash, 74, 166-67, 428
Neal, 109, 316
Neely, 337
Neill, 263
Neitsch, 462
Nelson, 169, 201, 219,
  224, 234, 259, 285,
  330, 358, 398, 460
Nemec, 266
Neubauer, 392
Neusser, 441
Newcomb, 101
Newlin, 169
Newman, 443
Newton, 304, 415
Nichols, 424
Noack, 442
Nolte, 451
Norman, 442
Norton, 426
Nowlin, 333, 421, 434
Nunn, 377, 383, 385, 392
Nygaard, 460
Nyman, 460
Nystrom, 320
Oatts, 164, 211-13, 251,-
  296, 310, 418, 449
Obermiller, 451
Ochsner, 441, 451
O'Conner, 155
Ogle, 165
Olive, 206, 218, 287-88,
  290-94, 303, 435-36
Oliver, 419
Olson, 312
O'Neal, 336
Openheimer, 306
Ore, 119
Orgain, 184, 308, 434
Orr, 105, 305, 330
Osborn, 430
Overstreet, 201, 242, 444
Ovesny, 451
Owen, 133, 142, 162,
  166, 168, 336, 434
Owens, 190, 201, 265,
  443

Surnames, continued
  Oxley, 110, 172
  Pace, 256
  Page, 238, 278, 428
  Paisley, 433
  Palm, 74, 84, 169, 203,
    205, 234, 285, 372,
    449
  Palousek, 458
  Parker, 219, 330, 335,
    392-93, 435, 450
  Parks, 283, 320, 432
  Parma, 266
  Parrish, 431
  Parsons, 431, 437
  Pasemann, 451
  Patrick, 242
  Patterson, 121, 152, 241,
    448
  Pavlasek, 458
  Pavlik, 444
  Payne, 184, 330, 429
  Peace, 333
  Peacock, 265
  Pearce, 368, 422
  Pearson, 268, 306-07
  Peaslee, 238
  Peeler, 267
  Penick, 203
  Penn, 219, 225, 330
  Pennington, 409
  Percy, 300, 309, 433-34,
    465
  Perkins, 119
  Perry, 266, 336, 423, 425,
    449
  Peters, 314, 463
  Peterson, 312, 394, 408
  Petri, 450
  Pettijohn, 112
  Pettus, 316, 393
  Peyton, 443
  Pfluger, 330-31
  Phythian, 398
  Pickett, 214, 396, 400-02,
    432
  Pickle, J. J., 404
  Pierce, 304, 429
  Pietzsch, 325
  Pittman, 252-53
  Platt, 368
  Polzin, 331
  Ponder, 336
  Pool, 437
  Poole, 204, 255, 322, 453-
    54
  Pope, 326, 351, 445

Poppelz, 434, 463
Posey, 243, 261, 326, 328
Porter, 304, 446
Potts, 255, 341
Powell, 306-07
Preslar, 425
Preuss, 331
Preusse, 417
Prewitt, 80
Price, 119, 168, 247, 256,
  261, 390, 428
Priesmeyer, 466
Proctor, 190, 335-36
Puckett, 104, 266
Pumphrey, 203-04, 429
Purl, 237
Putnam, 76
Pyron, 104
Queen, 74, 97, 100, 117,
  200, 333, 434, 437,
  453
Quinn, 458
Rainwater, 464
Ramm, 462
Ramsey, 336
Randolph, 463
Raney, 336
Ratliff, 341, 439, 447
Ray, 432, 453
Reagan, 262
Reager, 104, 433
Reavis, 341
Redard, 234, 419, 441
Redding, 340
Reed, 426, 430, 434
Reeder, 428, 435
Reeves, 416, 434
Reinhardt, 384
Remmert, 460
Renick, 430, 437
Rennick, 439
Reynolds, 245, 450, 463
Rhea, 205
Rhodes, 373, 445
Rice, 81, 85, 104, 114,
  119, 122, 125, 300,
  425, 447-48
Rich, 425
Richardson, 256, 336, 393
Ricks, 311
Ridings, 465
Riley, 458
Robbins, 74, 164, 216,
  243, 434, 437, 448
Roberson, 336
Roberts, 109, 267, 433

Robertson, 218, 241, 314,
  330, 337, 380, 396, 456
Robinson, 143, 314, 442
Roby/Robey, 117, 121,
  205
Roche, 263, 391, 428
Rodgers, 79
Roe, 336
Roebuck, 451
Rogers, 84
Root, 300, 363, 426
Ross, 432
Rountree, 263-64, 389
Rowe, 315, 450
Rowland, 164, 436, 449
Rowlett, 394, 421, 433
Rowntree, 416
Rowsey, 363
Royston, 252
Rubarth, 424
Rucker, 247, 265, 269,
  315, 329, 437, 446
Rudasill, 326, 336
Rummel, 417
Rumsey, 165, 335-36
Russell, 144, 255, 336,
  384, 425, 437, 453-54
Rutledge, 148, 311, 415,
  444-45
Ryan, 398, 416
Salyer, 433, 450
Sample, 453
Sampley, 436
Sandberg, 462
Sanders, 155, 251, 450
Sanon, 164
Sansom, 262-63
Saul, 203, 205, 305, 451
Sawyer, 186-87
Scallon, 429
Scarbrough, 264-65, 267,
  354, 403, 411
Schaefer, 428
Scharnberg, 331
Scheyli, 426
Schier, 451
Schlesinger, 458
Schlickeisen, 451
Schneider, 462
Schoemberg, 462
Schoener, 451
Schooley, 319, 432, 461
Schram, 267
Schramm, 360
Schroeder, 441-42, 451
Schultz, 304-05, 458, 462
Schulz, 451

Surnames, continued
Schwarz-Buehler, 331
Schwausch, 463
Schwenke, 422
Schwenker, 460, 466
Schwertner, 335-36, 451-52, 458
Score, 251
Scott, 267, 306, 309, 326
Scruggs, 133, 165
Sears, 429
Seashore, 259
Seaton, 117
Seay, 164
Sebastian, 305
Secrest, 428
Seward, 452, 461
Seymour, 162, 336, 452
Shaddock, 307
Shaffer, 155, 263, 319
Shanklin, 340
Shannon, 433
Sharp, 263-64
Sharpe, 263, 382, 428
Shaver, 335-36, 339, 422
Shaw, 300, 379
Shell, 164, 166, 238
Shepherd, 368
Sheppard, 205, 252, 310-11, 314, 427
Sherman, 436, 465
Sherrill, 330, 358
Shields, 421
Shipp, 437
Shofner, 341
Shumake, 187
Simcik, 235, 417
Simmons, 255, 327, 416, 426, 453
Simons, 304-06, 329, 330, 421, 456
Sims, 75, 81, 109, 164, 184
Sing, 224
Singleton, 431
Sipple, 417
Skaggs, 144, 425
Skeen, 464
Skrhak, 458
Skurka, 458
Sladecek, 457
Sladek, 442
Slaughter, 218, 416, 436, 453
Sledge, 304, 307
Sloan, 160, 184, 204, 423
Smalley, 74, 104, 110,

112, 121, 172, 312, 452
Smart, 187, 341, 455
Smilser, 319
Smith, 82, 121, 155, 168, 201, 261, 315, 330, 336-37, 341, 376, 386-87, 389-91, 422-24, 430, 440, 454-55
Smither, 391
Smithwick, 44-45, 79, 82, 87, 97, 105-06, 123, 134, 164, 171-72, 300
Smothers, 313
Snyder, 200-01, 205-13, 237, 244, 247-48, 251, 263, 306, 317, 389
Sorelle, 450
Spacek, 428
Sparks, 213-16, 271, 279-80, 300, 360, 363, 376, 400
Speckles, 331
Speegle, 320, 436, 466
Spencer, 191, 255, 322, 430, 436, 453
Spidell, 330
Spiegelhauer, 331
Spilman, 428
Stacy, 264, 266
Stamline, 258
Standefer, 80, 110, 125, 144, 164, 171, 202
Stanton, 326
Stapp, 415, 455
Starnes, 435
Stauffer, 441, 455
Staunton, 437
Stearns, 110-12, 119, 143, 188, 223, 234, 283, 312, 329, 351, 360, 419, 421, 425, 429, 434-35, 438, 440, 451-52, 465
Steele, 168, 214, 243, 263, 279-80, 315, 428
Steinberg, 430
Stephens, 106, 252, 349
Stern, 432
Stevens, 325
Stevenson, 336
Stewart, 341, 425-26, 430
Stiborik, 266, 386
Stiles, 206, 302, 305, 458-59
Stinnett, 205
Stoll, 466

Stolley, 450
Stone, 263, 359, 367, 404, 449
Storey, 341
Storrs, 326, 394
Strayhorn, 327, 341, 428
Streich, 450-51, 462
Strickland, 142, 144, 154, 167-68, 336, 428
Strode, 445
Stromberg, 366-67
Stroud, 117, 340
Stuart, 164, 253
Stubblefield, 126, 190, 243, 322
Stumhofer, 417
Sturgis, 305, 307, 330
Sudduth, 227
Summers, 203
Sunvison, 460
Surginer, 424-25
Suttles, 341-42, 439
Sutton, 420
Swanson, 366
Swenson, 107, 170, 462
Sybert, 336
Talbot, 155, 168, 183, 185, 241, 243, 428, 434
Taliaferro, 114, 225
Talley, 305, 330, 398, 416, 427, 453-54
Tankersley, 121, 125, 200, 340-41, 418, 428
Tanner, 265
Tarkington, 363
Tartar, 464
Tate, 398
Tatsch, 315
Taulbee, 377, 383, 385
Taylor, 114, 154, 164, 219, 234, 243, 256, 269, 315, 333, 389, 425, 428, 438, 452
Teburg, 421
Tegge, 327
Teinert, 463
Telford, 205
Terry, 335
Thames, 330
Thaxton, 74
Thayre, 186-87
Thies, 360, 374, 428
Thoma, 259, 336, 422, 432
Thomas, 316, 367, 428, 432, 453, 463

Surnames, continued
Thomason, 155
Thompson, 105, 162, 282, 305, 310, 427
Thomson, 341
Thonig, 417
Thornberry, 320
Thornton, 453
Thorp, 433
Threadgill, 219, 304, 307, 329, 330
Tidwell, 326, 459
Tindel, 337, 464
Tinnin, 214, 223
Tinsley, 247
Tisdale, 74, 296
Toal, 336
Tobin, 314
Todd, 264
Tomecek, 451
Tomlinson, 304, 341
Torn, 379
Towles, 329
Townes, 261
Towns, 333, 354, 369, 428, 459, 460
Traylor, 336
Triska, 266
Tucker, 164, 267, 282, 287, 296-97, 305, 330, 398, 439
Tumlinson, 44, 77-79, 81, 122, 172, 300, 460
Turner, 153, 230, 425, 433
Turney, 419
Tyler, 460
Ulmer, 330
Upchurch, 8, 94, 319
Utz, 164
Valenta, 458
Vance, 219, 304-05, 329, 421
Vandeveer, 80
Vandever, 336
Van Eyck, 184
Vanicek, 266
Van Winkle, 187
Vaughan, 366-67
Vaughn, 307
Verse, 312
Vickers, 431
Victor, 361
Vitek, 438
Vogel, 434
Vogler, 462
Von Rosenberg, 331

Vontress, 153, 156-57, 167
Votaw, 432
Vrabel, 458
Waddell, 445
Wade, 435, 462
Wadkins, 84, 462
Waggoner, 304
Walden, 445
Waldrop, 453
Wales, 340-41, 463
Walker, 77-78, 142, 154, 168, 173, 205, 260, 303, 319, 333, 350, 398, 433-44, 460, 463
Wallace, 452
Walsh, 236, 314
Walters, 307
Walther, 441, 451
Walton, 433
Ward, 255, 389, 437
Warnock, 163, 433
Washington, 419
Waters, 458
Watkins, 119, 336, 432
Watson, 263, 266, 341, 427
Way, 456
Wayman, 327-28, 421, 428
Weatherby, 263
Weatherford, 305, 335-36, 422
Webb, 252, 368
Webber, 73, 88, 119, 171, 433
Webster, 81, 92-95, 420
Wedemeyer, 366, 463
Weeks, 79, 84, 300
Weir, 201, 266, 333, 460, 464-65, 409
Weise, 441
Weiss, 440
Welch, 330-31, 360, 431
Wells, 80, 94, 164, 205, 290, 319, 336, 443
Wendland, 435, 451
Werchan, 435, 441
Werner, 463
Wernli, 331
West, 392-93
Wester, 241, 380, 448
Westfall, 260, 430
Wheeler, 333
Whigham, 463
Whipkey, 265, 349
White, 191, 255-56, 306-

07, 331, 335, 429, 446, 463
Whitehead, 188, 190, 461
Whiteley, 420
Whitely, 325, 433
Whitmire, 187
Whittenburg, 340
Whittle, 183, 333, 428, 466
Whitton, 336
Wideman, 450
Widmer, 429, 441
Wierman, 440
Wiggins, 242
Wilbarger, 125, 155, 164, 172, 452
Wilcox, 377, 385, 389, 395, 423
Wilder, 386, 427
Wiley, 304
Wilke, 435
Wilkerson, 336
Willett, 446
Williams, 79, 117, 121, 125, 141, 153-54, 184, 227, 300, 330, 357, 403, 424-25, 428, 444, 449, 453
Williamson, 414, 461
Willis, 437
Willson, 267
Wilson, 162, 201, 327, 331, 338, 341, 420, 432, 437, 443-44, 461, 466
Wimberly, 341
Winningham, 425
Wittliff, 331
Wofford, 385
Wolbrueck, 440
Wolett, 464
Wolf, 331
Womack, 305, 307, 398
Wood, 49, 264, 333, 385, 422, 453
Woodall, 392
Woodward, 330, 335-36
Wooldridge, 106
Woolsey, 320
Wright, 282, 317, 326-27, 437, 450
Wuthrich, 464, 466
Wyatt, 341, 428
Yakey, 425, 467
Yeargan, 336
Yearwood, 336
Yoes, 433-34

Surnames, continued
  Young, 237, 336, 372, 374, 396, 414, 448, 451
  Zahn, 434, 441
  Zenkner, 451
  Zeplin, 451
  Zicaro (Ycabo), 303-04
  Zieger, 331
  Zieschang, 442
  Zimmacker, 441
  Zrubek, 458
  Zurovec, 458

Surveying, surveyors, 45, 71-73, 76, 109, 125, 155 163-64, 171
Swedish settlers, 82, 112, 168-71, 219, 309-10, 417, 443, 460-62
Swenson, Swenson Grove, 442, 456
Swiss settlers, 220, 331, 347, 435, 441, 466
Sycamore, Sycamore Grove, Sycamore Springs, 219, 456

Tanglewood, 456
Tawakoni (Tuacano) Indians, 33, 39, 41, 45-46, 65, 96, 106-07, 448
Tanners, 41, 164
Taylor, Taylorsville, ix, 14, 16, 214, 218-20, 223, 226, 233, 237-39, 259, 266-67, 269, 275-77, 281-82, 301, 303-07, 324, 329-30, 346-47, 356, 362, 370ff. 400, 456, 459
Tejas, 33, 53
Telegraph, 269
Telephone, 269, 354
Tennill, 456
Terrapin Ridge, 456
Texaco Inc., 364
Texas Chautauqua Assembly, 214, 248, 279-81
Texas Rangers, 39, 42, 73-74, 77-79, 82, 87-97, 106, 109, 284, 289, 295ff., 300, 426, 459, 460-61
Texas Republic, Annexation, 47, 81, 104, 108, 446
Texas Revolution, 73, 75, 77-81, 268-69
"Texas University," 243
Theon (Leubner, Behrnville), 219-21, 337, 345, 347, 456-58
Thorndale, 302, 458
Thrall, 8, 214, 225, 301-03, 346-47, 370ff., 458-59
Tidwell, 326, 459
Timber, lumber, trees, 5, 15-19, 30-31, 46, 56-57, 61-62, 77-78, 87, 99, 129-31, 234, 360, 446
Tompkins Store, 218, 448, 459
Tonkawa Bluff, 26

Tonkawa Indians, vi, 16, 22, 25-41, 52-53, 56, 58, 60, 66, 76, 96, 101, 132, 165
Tonkawa Springs, 166
Tools, weapons, 17-18, 21, 24, 26-33, 46, 164. See also: Crafts
Towns Mill, Townsville, 73, 100, 109, 149, 219, 234, 283, 333, 440, 459-60
Trade, traders, trades day, merchandising, 46-47, 68, 75, 98, 104, 108, 128, 130-31, 137, 139, 163-64, 229, 239-41, 275, 301-44, 356, 359, 398
Transportation, travel, 26ff., 137, 238-39, 270, 301-44, 348-55, 443
Travis County, 52, 54, 56, 79, 84, 87-88, 90, 97, 101-03, 108, 113, 145-50, 157, 169, 171, 269, 314, 318, 322-24, 367
Travois, 27, 33
Trinity Lutheran College, 258-59
Tuacano: see Tawakoni
Tumlinson Block House, Tumlinson Fort, 44, 77-79, 81, 122, 172, 300, 318-19, 417, 460
Turkey Creek, 5, 14, 450, 460, 466-67
Turkeys, 13, 15, 62, 460
Turners, 164
Tyler, 219, 460
Type, 219, 347, 460
Typhoid fever, 259

Union Chapel, 461
Union Hall, 461
Union Hill, 219, 461-62
Union House, 462

Waco Indians, 33, 37, 39, 41, 96, 133
Wade, 462
Wadkins Crossing, 101, 110, 462
Walburg, 220-21, 337, 346-47, 462-63
Wales, 346, 463
Walker, 463
Walkerton, 318-19, 463
Walnut Springs, 464
War, warfare, raids, massacres, 31-33, 39-41, 43-47, 57-58, 60, 63-64, 76-78, 82-84, 86-97, 100-01, 104-07, 109, 132-33, 141, 159, 340, 451
Waterloo, 219-20, 235, 346, 464
Water, springs, 4-6, 8-10, 14, 16, 25, 28, 61-65, 87, 99, 129, 142, 157
Water systems, water works, 166, 275, 306, 329-31
Water Valley, 4, 433, 464. Also see: Jonah
Weapons: see Tools
Weather, 282, 306, 309, 370-75, 462
Webster Massacre, 24, 92-95, 444
Weir, 268, 333, 346-47, 351, 459, 464
Wendish settlers, 220, 429, 462

Wesley Chapel, 438-39, 465
Wheat, 131, 158, 234, 341
White House, 217, 346-47, 465
White Stone, 318-19, 465
Whittle & Harrel, 466
Wilbarger, John Wesley, 172
Wil-Bur, 455
Wildlife, 7, 10-15, 65, 67, 440, 466. Also
    see: Alligators, Buffalo, Cattle, Horses,
    Timber
Williamson County, 113-26, 143, 151-52,
    154, 217-18, 227-33, 364-65
Williamson, Robert McAlpin, 78, 81, 121-
    23, 167, 172, 300, 427
Willis Creek, 14, 56, 123, 139, 141, 184,
    188, 199, 454
Willow Hole, 434
Willow Tank Road, 466
Wilson, 219

Wilson Springs (Mustang Springs), 162,
    223, 270, 466
Woman's suffrage, 379
Women, 29-31, 43-44, 379
Woodrow, 466
Writers, historians, 171-73, 388-89, 391-92,
    395
Wuthrich Hill, 220-21, 347, 460, 464, 466
Wyatt's Ville, 428

Yakey, 467
Yankee Branch, 467
Yarborough, Yarbrough, 449, 467
Yegua, 69, 268, 445
Yellow fever, 100, 132, 314
Younger, Cole, 467
Youngsport, 467
Youngstown, 467

Zevallos, Juan Joseph, 63